Seeing God Everywhere: Living Your Life as a Prayer

Kevin P. Ryan

DEDICATION

To Mom and Dad, for your constant love and faith-filled modeling.

To my children, who lovingly support their wacky father, each in her/his own way.

To all the students and cross-country runners of Bishop Hartley High School who encouraged my daily prayerful diversions, and most especially those that told me so.

To Matt P., the first to tell me so.

To Joseph O., a fellow writer who never let me quit.

To Thomas V., who has supported this cause more than anyone I know.

To Sharon, who heartens me in ways that I don't even know.

Welcome

While it should be no surprise that prayer is at the heart of this book, essentially, *Life* is what this book is really about. But that opening sentence is rather redundant, for, ideally, life is a prayer, and truly praying is living truly.

I taught at a parochial Catholic high school for twenty-eight years. Somewhere in the last decade or more of that career, the administration made it very clear that they wanted every teacher to begin every class with a prayer. While the mandate added nothing to what I had already been doing, realizing that other classes were now engaging more regularly in prayer, I did stop to wonder about *how* I was going to open my class with prayer. To be sure, I was already not prone to using formulaic, memorized prayers, but assuming that many of my colleagues would now be engaging our student body in more traditional prayer forms, I sought a more natural and personal approach. So, each day before each class began, I would stand before my students, sometimes staring out the window awaiting an "inspiration," or other times seizing an inspired insight that had already come to me since my awakening that day, and I would share what I saw or what I had experienced and then would mold it spontaneously into a prayer. Prayers like these "just happened" for years, and in time, whenever graduates would come back for a visit, the one comment that kept coming back with them was, "You know what I most miss about your class, Mr. Ryan? Your daily reflections and prayers."

For almost as long as I can remember, I have been a "praying person." My parents were both very devout Roman Catholic Christians who raised their family of five children in an environment of prayer; from nighttime bedside prayers, to daily liturgies, from mealtime blessings to nightly Marian month rosaries, our lives were framed with a consistent sense of prayer, and, in general, we all took to it as easily as breathing in and breathing out. But daily prayer doesn't necessarily make one a "spiritual person" anymore than breathing makes one a conscious and a conscientious person. The wedding of a prayer life and a spiritual life needs the vows of commitment and the bands of experience and reflection.

While my childhood was, as noted, shaped by the religious perimeters of my family, like many young boys, I was prone to wander. At thirteen years old, certainly influenced in part by my era, I willfully began exploring the drug scene. I don't remember myself as a victim of peer pressure; I sought, chose, and participated on my own regardless of what others thought or did, although like minds and interests tend to find one another. By the middle of my freshmen year of high school, however, a number of my friends had already been kicked out of our small, parochial school, and, as a member of a "fine, upstanding family in the church and social community," I realized that if I was going to make it out of there without bringing down the "family name," something had to change. Unfortunately, my escape options seemed few and narrow. In the spring of that year, David Wilkerson, an evangelical preacher who had found fame in his suspenseful autobiography, *The Cross and the Switchblade,* brought his "David Wilkerson Crusade" to the local University, and for some, perhaps providential, reason I saw it as a potential window of opportunity out of my apparent dead end lifestyle. While I resisted his "altar call" on the crusade's first night, I returned for a second round and found myself tearfully "accepting Jesus Christ as my personal Lord and Savior" by the night's end. For the next couple of years, my Catholic devotions were complemented by a dedicated involvement in a non-denominational Christian youth group. Ironically, my mother feared that I was being sucked into some type of Christian cult, but our local priest assured her through his observations that "Kevin was still actively participating in the Church" and that "his Saturday night meetings are merely healthy supplements to his spiritual life." I marvel now, with equal parts amusement and horror, at some of my faith-filled proselytizing of those days, but I recognize at the same time that my "youthful baptism in the Spirit," in many ways, saved my life from the crash course I was on. By the summer before my senior year, however, I was growing weary of the limits of my "Jesus Freak" lifestyle, and I soon found myself bargaining with God for a little balance in my life. While it humors me again to think about it, even those bargains operated as lifelines as I slowly drifted back into some of my earlier, less healthful practices. No matter my condition, as I recall the "contract," I would begin and end each day on my knees in prayer; and, indeed, in a variety of "conditions," I did just that.

One of the three central "marks of existence" in the Buddhist tradition is "anicca," which translates loosely as "impermanence." Anicca recognizes the shifting nature of reality, that the only truly permanent thing in our lives is change! To be sure, my next five years after high school embodied this Buddhist insight. By the end of my senior year, I felt that I had a vocation to the religious life, although my interest was not so much in being a priest as it was in being a person of prayer, potentially a cloistered monk. I established some communication with an English Benedictine abbey in Washington D.C. that year, but having no college itself, the abbey encouraged me to get my education first and then check back. Some of my "education," however, was probably not what the abbey had in mind, and within a year I was walking down the church aisle for a different set of vows – marriage! Eventually, through much sacrifice by spouse, child and self, I finished college with an English major and a Theology minor from St. John's University in

Collegeville, Minnesota. Laden with responsibilities and the belief that my diploma would help us to move from our government-subsidized housing and life, my college career was anything but "typical." But through it all, prayer continued to be a constant source of comfort and direction. A few short years after I began teaching, and with a second child now in the fold and a third on the way, I began my graduate work in Theology.

It seems a bit ironic to me now that I would first be introduced to interreligious studies at a Roman Catholic graduate school. Deeply involved in all phases and facets of my traditional Roman Catholic parish church life, I found my spirituality drifting beyond the boundaries of that institutional expression of faith. Sparked by a broader view of God than ever before, I continued my own study into other religious traditions, and frequently joined them in prayer and in dialogue to deepen my understanding of them as well as to foster my own spiritual development. And somewhere in the midst of that evolution, the contemplative side of my spirituality poked its head through the ribs of my skeletal formation and asked, once again, "Hey, what about me?" With the encouragement of my spouse, I took to the "wilderness," venturing into woods and remote landscapes for periodic solo retreats, my version of the ancient "desert fathers." What happened there would shape the better part of the rest of my life.

As my heart had perhaps once known years before, my spirituality is best nurtured away from everything else. In the woods I encountered my deepest insights. In the wilderness I found the presence of the Divine most clear and accessible; and as I became more and more aware of these connections, it occurred to me that a people, indigenous to this land, had once, and in many places still do, come to understand themselves, one another and the Creator, through the gifts of creation. Following the yearnings of my own heart and the whispers of the Divine written in all of the created order, I began to explore further Native American and indigenous traditions. Soon, new doors began opening to me, and through these, my own prayer, social and spiritual lives became more wedded than ever until I realized most acutely that there should be no separation between any of these lives. Life lived well - thoughtfully and reflectively – is a prayer. Once I understood this truth, how I approached everything in my life began to change, and most especially those areas of my life which swallowed the majority of my time: teaching and coaching. In all that I taught and coached, more than anything, I tried to model and to point to the *wonder* of life. Life need not be "wonderful," for it is already "wonder-filled." To see and to understand this truth is to know that all of life is spiritual, that all of life is a prayer.

Alongside my family, my teaching and my coaching careers, backpacking eventually became a very significant outlet for me – a retreat, really. When I first started backpacking as a teenager, I let the "expert," responsible, and experienced adults do all the planning for me. They decided what area of the continent we were going to hike, how we would get there, and what trails we would traverse; they did all of the planning and assembling of necessary supplies, even dictating what would go in my backpack beyond their suggested personal needs. Come trail time, I merely showed up, strapped on my pack and followed their lead. While those hikes were almost always delightful experiences, I realized in time that I was merely "along for the ride." Much later in my life, thinking I knew the process, I dared to explore the landscape on my own. What I most often encountered on these ventures was all that I didn't know, but stumbling upon my ignorance, I grew increasingly more adept and with that confidence, more adventurous. Eventually, welcoming others into "my hikes," I realized that I had become that old "go-to-guy" expert, in charge of choosing the place and the course we would navigate and the provisions by which we would sustain our efforts. These days, I see myself as a "contributor," an experienced source, a helpful guide on journeys where the land itself is the real leader inviting me personally or as a member of a group to come out and discover its amazing offerings. A living and an interested spiritual life follows much the same course of development.

In this book, *Seeing God Everywhere: Living Your Life as a Prayer,* I situate myself as a humble, though helpful guide, offering my experiences and observations for anyone who, like me, desires to travel the fascinating and sometimes frightful trails of a spiritual life. Our longing for love, both to give and to receive it, and the awe-inspiring wonder of the earth and the surrounding universe by which we are often reduced to silence convince me that humans are not simply physical nor accidental beings. There is a spiritual dimension, a Divine Spark, implanted within us all, and connecting us *to all,* that longs to be a part of our every day living and breathing experiences. Religions solicit the discovery and the union of the physical and the spiritual, but then, too often, try to *be* the guide, the signposts, and the trail of an individual's spiritual life journey, sometimes even appearing to usurp the very eyes of the traveler. As with all wondrous adventures, one first needs some essential guidance in the early stages of one's spiritual life, but having achieved some important and challenging hikes led by others, that person may be naturally drawn into deeper and more personal exploration. Even here, some helpful direction is important, but the terrain and the experience of it is one's own. One enters the more personal spiritual quest with the equipment of shared past experiences and the maps offered by accomplished guides, but for the richest experiences, the steps must be one's own. As the sojourner takes those experiential or experienced steps, *Seeing God Everywhere* can, at different times, act as a compass, a trekking pole, a periodic partner, or just some trail mix and a gulp of sustaining water at the rest stop.

Seeing God Everywhere: Living Your Life as a Prayer is quite simply a daily reflection and prayer book, starting with January 1 and ending with December 31. *Seeing God Everywhere* invites the person of faith to explore the dimensions of the spiritual universe that live right inside one's own heart and home, and expand infinitely right outside that person's door. Through these 365 daily reflections and meditations, the reader will be encouraged to listen and to see the Spirit already living within the reader as well as its manifestations throughout the activities of one's daily life and in the grand universe that unfolds and reveals itself everyday. Each reflection begins with a simple observation of life, most often personal in origin, although sometimes more generically identifiable, gleaned from my years as a teacher and a coach, a runner and an outdoor enthusiast, a divorcee and a love-learner. A simple human being just trying to live life to the best of my understanding and ability, I offer the insight that I have gained through my years of study within the literal and figurative classrooms of life. Some of these reflections may stretch people's understanding of God beyond their usual religious perimeters. Along with a variety of familiar Christian references, included here are numerous insights from and "teachings" about Buddhism, Islam, Hinduism and Judaism, along with smaller portions concerning Taoism, Jainism and Sikhism; an ample supply of references to my own spiritual practices within the Native American tradition will also be found tucked within the book's daily reflections. As I once did with my students before each class, each daily entry closes with a simple prayer addressing the Creator/God/the Great Mystery in a variety of visages, with the image and the prayer connected to the content and the lesson of the day's reflection.

For me, the spiritual life – all of Life! - is very much like an ongoing backpacking trip into the wilderness, except in this case, the wilderness is not just "out there," but it is "in here" and "all around" us every moment of our lives. *Seeing God Everywhere: Living Your Life as a Prayer* will provide some helpful, daily companionship for those interested and willing to step into the spiritual wilderness of their everyday lives and potentially to encounter the One they seek in numerous places along the way.

Laying awake in bed on a weekend morning just before the sun came up, my mind drifted slowly about, a slow entry into the day while still contemplating a return to sleep. I opened my eyes letting them add their vote to the question of whether I should arise and start the day or give in to the temptation to drift back to sleep. With the room yet slumbering in its cool darkness, my eyes darted about resting now and then on some shadowy image that would spur a thought that would crack open further my awakening awareness. And then I caught sight of the bright spot on the closet door, a beam of light that had found a fissure in the cocoon of the room. Ah, the sun has snuck up over the horizon, I thought; the morning's sun is no longer an oncoming glow, but is piercing the day and cracking it open with light. I followed the beam across the room and noted the little gap where the blinds did not meet the window frame exactly, and the curtain over the top of the blinds was pulled back just enough that the shaft of light from the emerging day was able to sneak through, throwing a hint of new day joy into the room's darkness. It was time to get up, I decided.

The ability of light to find its way into the dark corners and spaces of our lives is a wonderful metaphor of faith. A well-grounded faith does not come as easily as some might believe. Those of us who have been raised within a culture of religion, where people's affiliation with a church is as natural and expected as going to school, often confuse such "religious involvement" with "faith." But real faith, truly seeing and experiencing the light of the Divine, does not come through simple church attendance, any more than just showing up for class makes one learn. The influences are inevitable, but real learning and real faith need more attentive listening and more thoughtful consideration. Many people live only in the shadows of faith, the glow of predawn light; and many of these, as they get older, tend not to throw open the curtains and blinds, but find ways to seal in the darkness instead. In a world increasingly governed by scientific rationality and economic practicality, faith can become more clouded than ever. The ideas of faith may continue to linger like dust particles in the air, but practically speaking, they might not be rational enough for many people to pursue the light further.

And yet, the light finds its way; it cannot be snuffed out nor utterly ignored. Oh, a person can add room darkening shades and insulated curtains to stamp out the light, but if the window is there, the light will find a way to make its presence known, however humbly subdued it might be. The light of the Divine too has a way of sifting into the darkest places of our lives. Many will deny it, caulk the cracks seeking to avoid it and even board the windows for a more secure closure. But life so often creates fractures in these sealing efforts and through these clefts, Divine light trickles in in questions and through wonder. And there is warmth in the light, and if one will dare to allow the curtains and blinds to be opened, a whole new day of marvelous light can flood the darkness.

God of Penetrating Light, I have dwelled in darkness many times in my life, and even after knowing your light, I have sought to seal it out, denying its warmth and acuity. Sometimes it seems easier to just close my eyes and return to the sleep of unbelief. But gratefully, your piercing light has found its way into my dark complacency and resistance, and I have risen again and again to the light of a more faith-filled day. This day, may I lift the shades and blinds and open the curtains that prevent your light from suffusing my day, my faith – my life.

January 2
Morning Coffee

I have a number of friends, and know many more others, whose day cannot begin without that first cup of coffee. As some people might need a sleeping pill to get them to sleep and to provide a restful night, others need coffee – or some other elixir – to wake them up and to get them going each day. Manufacturers have helped the cause by developing coffee makers with timers so that a person can have everything ready before he goes to bed, and just like the alarm clock that will disrupt his rest in the morning, the coffee maker will start up and offer him a quick cup of solace and a jolt of energy with which to start his day.

As one who has tried to avoid addictions of any kind ("tried" being the key word here) throughout his life, I used to look rather disdainfully at such a mandatory morning movement. In fact, while a fresh pot of brewing coffee in the morning has always had an alluringly delicious scent, I didn't even like the taste of it until I was nearly forty years old! When the scent and the taste became more affectionately acquainted for me, and I did give way to a periodic cup of morning coffee, I pledged that I would always limit myself to just one cup a day, and this of fairly cheap, low grade coffee, so my body would not become physically attached to the morning jolt. Well, as I get down to work this morning with my small pot of coffee beside me, I can see that I have not done so well with *that* promise!

What was true about my mornings in my pre-coffee years, however, still remains pretty much true today. The cup I most look forward to each day, the one that truly gets my day started, is prayer. As with all the different roasts and flavors of coffee, I have tried a variety of prayer forms and times, but a simple morning meditation, a snippet of reflection, and a closing prayer is the perfect spiritual breakfast to jump start my day. The older I get, the more I find breakfast to truly be the most important meal of my day; but long ago, I realized that morning prayer is my real first cup of coffee.

Morning prayer puts my day immediately in perspective. I try to avoid thinking about what I have to do that day, for I want the time to truly be meditative and prayerful, not a scheduled visitation with a daily "to do" list. But sometimes, the weight of the day does press in on this time, and when it does, then I know that the heaviness of it is apparently in need of prayer, and so I will allow it some time too. Ordinarily, however, I want to start my day in mindful gratitude for simply being alive! I got up today! Not everyone will be able to say or to do that. This day gives me another opportunity to encounter and to experience the Divine alive in the world and universe all around me, and I don't want to miss out on that. Morning prayer immediately reminds me of that and calls me into conscious awareness. The working and social parts of my life will have their needs, and I will do my best to address them this day, but they are not why I exist nor are they who I am. Morning prayer also reminds me of that. Yes, some may need coffee to get their day going, and I am becoming more understanding of that need, but to get my day going in the right direction, I need my morning mug of prayer.

God of My Morning Movements, so often I can take my ability to get up each day for granted, assuming that I will rise as surely as the sun with which you greet me. But neither are a given, and most especially my feet planted firmly on the ground. I come to you this morning filled with gratitude for the blessing of life – that I am alive another day! Help me to keep what is most important in perspective today. I have things to do, responsibilities to meet, and people with whom I will be in contact, but before, during and after all of these, there is my relationship with you. May this time with you be the brew to make my day most true.

January 3
First Steps

Her one hand reached up and grabbed hold of the boney arm of the chair while the fingers of the other clasped onto the ribbed rim of the chair's cushion. With chin-up strength, she tugged on the chair while her rubbery legs sprung into action, and then she was standing in an unconscious glow of pride. Without thinking, her hands let go of the chair's stabilization as she swung her body around and faced the room's expansive six feet of open space. The foot seemed to hesitate briefly like one who senses gum under foot, but suddenly it lifted and stepped forward, and almost to her own surprise, the other foot followed suit, as she lunged into her first steps before crumpling to the floor. There are very few more simple and yet amazing joys to witness than watching a child's first steps. So revolutionary is this moment in the child's life, so pivotal in the development of her motor skills that one cannot help but be enthralled by these simple and astonishing movements.

There are a number of stages in the physical development of the human being that we sometimes have the opportunity to witness that can provide wonderful insight into the spiritual realm and the nature of the human person as well. A child's first steps, and the subsequent "first steps" that we take throughout our lives, are a tremendous study in "letting go." One of the key components, a common denominator of each of these first steps is a loosening of the mind's grip. The action is not done thoughtlessly, but it is not "over-thought." In the eyes of the toddler who takes her first step, one can see a sudden joyful awareness of something new being achieved, but there is not the usual obsessive thought-processing going on pre-step that we know all too well in our decision-making as adults. It is almost as if the mind and the body have been circling each other in a dance, and now recognizing each other's step, join hands and move in unison. What is meant *to be* emerges and suddenly it *is*. Years later, I have watched numerous young teens step into the sport of cross-country unknowingly, and quickly become fine, successful runners. But when the next season arrives, and now they "know" what must be done and what is expected, they fail to achieve the

13

same success because the thought of it all weighs down on them so heavily. Sometimes they need to just get out of the way and let their bodies, their minds, and their spirits do what they are capable of doing.

Spiritually, we are drawn naturally to something beyond ourselves. I suspect that science will suggest all kinds of biological reasons for our various emotional responses to given situations, but that we feel as we do in the presence of wondrous and inspirational settings and experiences, suggests much more to me that we are meant to be in communion with the greater universe. There is a natural affinity that we are called to step into, to let go of the obsessive need to understand it all before we move. More often, we need to release our hold from the chair of stability and just make that first gum-shoed step into who we are and what we are capable of being.

God of My First Steps, in giving me life, you blest me with many gifts and with the ability to explore and to discover my potential. Too often I over-process the thoughts of what I can and should do, or allow my doubts and my fears of failure to trip me up before I even take my first step. Be the encouraging parental hands reaching out to me, inspiring me to just let go and to let the gifts of who and what I am step forward confidently, moving assuredly towards you.

January 4
The Pilot Light

In the dark bowels of my basement, surrounded by so much stowed away junk, is a gas water heater. Whether I am home or not, using hot water or not, a small pilot light quietly burns at attention there, ready to alight into a controlled flame should the need arise. When I was a small child, I remember creeping into the darkness of the basement and being comforted by that soft glow that emanated from the water heater's base. I had no understanding or even a concern for what is was or what it did, but it seemed a simple and warm kindness in the cool mustiness of the basement.

In a somewhat similar fashion, in the neglected recesses of our soulful heart, there burns a small pilot light of which we are too often unaware. Within each of us is the kindling spark of the divine ready to blaze into action if only we should turn up the gas of our spiritual life.

There are many other alluring lights all around us: searchlights scan the skies at night; neon lights beckon us to buy; traffic lights determine our starting and stopping. But these are all external lights that persuade my body and my senses; the divine light, deep within me, is what ought to determine if and how I move at all. Like the pilot light at the base of the gas water heater, this divine spark awaits ignition whether we are aware of it or not. Neglected excessively, I not only waste this energy, but worse yet, risk its being snuffed out altogether.

O God of soothing warmth and light, I turn within today to recognize and reverentially creep toward that divine spark that glows within me. You are the comforting source of all of the light that can fill our world with warmth and guidance. Help me to seek the light of your love that burns within me and, having once found it, may I carefully pilot that warm glow to all around me.

January 5
Routines

Most of us probably harbor a gentle aversion to the word "routine," but I suspect that most of us would also admit that without routine in our lives, much of our time could easily slip away in wasted and neglected efforts. After leaving a teaching job of twenty-eight years, mainly because I felt that I could no longer endure the routine of paperwork grading and lesson planning, I found myself working to establish some new routine in my life so that I would not end each day with a sense of spinning my wheels on a mucky surface, the tires sinking deeper into the murk with each day.

Some time ago, my wife took on a new challenge in her teaching career, and with her new job and school district, our morning routine around the house shifted significantly. For years I had established a morning routine so regulated that I could predict to the minute what time it was based on what I was doing at that time. It was comfortable in its predictability: the bathroom visit; the shave and awakening waters; wrapping the body in appropriate clothing; packing the running bag for after school; breakfast of cereal and milk while I perused the morning paper, first the international and national news, a glance at the local news, and a quick look at the previous day's sports scores; well-wishings for the day and a loving send-off as my wife exited; the house now quiet, prayer and meditation time; and, finally, brush the teeth, pop in the contacts, and off I go! Every day was like this for years. And then the schedule of my wife's new job sent all of it out the window. At first I found myself slightly irritated by the shift, and then just frustrated as I tried to figure out how I was going to incorporate all of those movements into a different time frame, and maybe even place. I soon adjusted, and with the adjustment came a new routine that not only grew familiar, but as comfortable as the old one.

Routines can be essential in the proper organization and use of our time; but sometimes these routines can become more important than the needs and details that the routine helps to organize. Occasionally, the apple cart of our routine gets overturned. When it is by choice, as mine was when I left teaching, we might rejoice in the new possibilities. When it is by force, as mine was when my wife got a new job, we might grumble as the apples on our routine-cart go rolling in different directions. But both of these changes are good for us as they move us to reevaluate what it is that we do with our time and why we do it.

Creator God, you have written a routine into all that you have created: the rising and the setting of the sun, the movement of stars and planets, the changing of the seasons - are some of your more obvious "routines." But this same creation is full of changes as well, pregnant with moments that upset the routines. Perhaps today I struggle to adjust to a new routine, or will have my comfortable one upset, or

15

maybe it is simply time for me to reconsider the reasons for my routines. As I establish routines in my life for the sake of efficiency and organization, help me also to remain open to these inevitable shifts and may I see in them an opportunity for a deeper and a better understanding of who I am and what it is that you call me to do and to be.

January 6
Candlelight

Each morning before my daily prayer and meditation begins, I light a candle. The candle serves a number of purposes. Pragmatically, it provides some soft, low light to my dark prayer corner. Symbolically, it is a conscious invitation on my part to welcome God especially into that space and time; accordingly, the flame of the burning candle itself often becomes a kind of focus during my time there, averting my eyes and mind from wandering, and guiding their attention to a symbol of the sacred source. Some days, however, the candle too becomes a bit of a distraction. Seated before the flame, I can become mesmerized by its dance, fascinated by the movements of its lapping.

My prayer space is literally a simple corner in our bedroom, hidden almost behind the bed. A folded blanket given to me as a gift marks the space, upon which are strewn various items sacred to me and, of course, a candle. Tucked in this most remote corner of the room and the house, it is purposefully away from all other distractions. So when the candle is lit to start the prayer, it would seem that its flame would be bright and strong and steady in this quietly concealed environment. But such is not always the case. Obviously, in warmer seasons, if a window is open, the fluctuation of the flame is understandable from the drafts of air; but there are many other times, with no open windows or fans or furnaces running, when the flame skips about the bowl of the candle's mouth, suddenly leaping and then soon huddling low in the candle's pool of melting wax. At such times, I do find that my attention to prayer can be postponed as I begin to marvel at the flame's movement and wonder at its cause. No doubt, the unseen air is moving about more than I realize and is ruffling the illuminating feather, and, perhaps, some chemistry of wax and wick and flame unknown to me is working its magic. One day, however, I realized that the candle itself was offering me a meditation on the art of the spiritual life.

Pursuing a spiritual existence, we all would like the fire of our love, the flame of our existence, to be strong and pure and steady. But how easily we are distracted from our worthy desire. Like the candle set near an open window, sometimes we place ourselves in situations and environments that are unquestionably going to challenge the very root of our resolve. Our flames struggle against the counter flow, sometimes at the risk of even being snuffed out. At other times, encircled by the right "chemistry," we become the image in a Gerard Manley Hopkins' poem, "charged with the grandeur of God" as we "flame out, like shining from shook foil." Yes, I long to be the bright and glowing flame, a source of true light in the world, but how easily I can waver, be dimmed, and succumb to the pressures of distracting life around me.

God of Light, within me burns a divine spark, a light that you wish for the world to see. My flame so often flickers and fights the breezy distractions that threaten to reduce its strength and energy. Keep the flame of my heart directed toward you, the source of all light and comfort; and if the weak wick of my best intentions should bow and curl into its own selfish and melting wax, lift me up to shine brightly, in your image, once again.

January 7
Breaking Into a Training Routine

People who have never been bitten by the "running bug," or who have never been able to slide into the "running groove" are certainly incredulous to a runner's desire to get out for a run every day. Running seems like such lonely, monotonous, and even boring exercise requiring a significantly disciplined stamina; why would one *want* to choose to do that to oneself? Even more difficult for the nonrunner to understand is the choice to run year round, specifically, in the winter. Not only does running appear to be all of the aforementioned trials, but now one throws all of those into below freezing temperatures, and all that might come with those: snow, sleet, ice and bitterly cold winds.

Some people are blessed with a sort of natural stamina for running it seems. These people quickly adapt to the idea of going for a long run, and don't, as most do, have to struggle through the tedious process of developing a stamina stronghold with the ability to run for at least a half hour at a time. Regarding winter running, there is actually a little additional strategy that most experienced runners figure out rather quickly. The key to a more enjoyable winter run is to be aware of and work with the elements, the key one being, the wind. Quite frankly, if one enjoys running, running through a snowfall is a quiet and peaceful delight; but a stiff wind can make a winter run plain miserable. If a person can avoid the wind altogether, of course, this is the ideal, but assuming that the wind is unavoidable, the key is to gauge the run so that one goes out against the wind, and returns with it at one's back. The start of every run always requires a little adjustment period, and in the winter, adjusting to the temperature is paramount. Going out against the wind might seem an unnecessary and brutal tactic, but in the beginning of a run, the body immediately begins to generate heat; and in the winter, of course, this is a very desirable transition. Light layers of clothing are also key here: an inside shirt to absorb the sweat, because, yes, eventually one will sweat, and a quality outer shell that prevents the wind from cutting right through the body. Some of the wind will inevitably get through, but this is why going out against the wind is so important. Before one's body temperature really starts rising due to the exercise and the sweat is only thinking about dropping by to cool the body's temperature, the runner gets the most difficult and cold part of the run out of the way. Then, reaching the "outer limits" of the run, one turns back toward home, all warmed up underneath, and with a wind from the rear to move the runner along. Additionally, if the sweat has started underneath, a cold wind from the back will be far less uncomfortable than the bone-chilling one from the front.

In many ways, developing and disciplining one's spiritual life is a good bit like running, and especially winter running. Quite frankly, like most anything it seems, there is a lot of hard work that must be put forth right up front. For spiritual stamina, discipline is surely necessary, and while the first few spiritual strides we take may feel good, inevitably, a couple of miles done the road, one might begin to wonder, "what am I doing?!" But when one puts the hard work in, right up front, braces herself and runs into the teeth of the wind, a certain amount of confidence develops, and when she turns the corner she will feel the benefits of the hard work, and a little bit of wind at her back. Be aware, sometimes the wind does shift. I can't tell you how often I swear I have run against the wind both ways, and perhaps I did. The spiritual life will do that too. Like running, the spiritual life is always a "work out," but it also always brings varying degrees of satisfaction, comfort, and contentment.

God of Stamina, your love for all creation is far greater than any one could ever imagine, and your endurance of our human shortcomings and failures is well beyond the abilities of my longest run. Help me in my efforts of spiritual training; gently run beside me as I struggle through the early stages of tedium, lack of stamina and flabby discipline. Nurture the heart and lungs of my training so that I too will one day know the warmth and ease of your presence blowing gently at my back.

January 8
Greet the Day

For those of us who have spent some part or all of our lives arising each day to the various, but incessant clamors of the alarm clock, this morning "wake-up call" can undoubtedly affect how we approach the gift of a new day. The bed is warm and comfortable; sleep is soothing and desired - and then the alarm interrupts all of that pleasure and demands that we get up and start our new day. Perhaps we hit the snooze button, but nine minutes later the interruption is renewed, and worse, now we are "running late."

Like many people, I love the morning, but my love for the crispness of a new day dawning does not necessarily make my movement from the luxury of a comfortable bed that much easier. But what a gift each new day is - not just the day itself, but the fact that I am alive and I get to experience it! To encourage and deepen this insight of the gift of a new day, years ago I began the practice of stepping outside as soon as possible after I arise from slumber to greet the new day. In morning darkness or in its emerging light, I lift my head to the sky and admire the fading stars or drink in the soft blue that is flowing out of the night's pallor. I stand on the earth and breath in the scents of the new day, feel its materializing humidity or its comforting coolness, and I speak my first words of gratitude for this gift before me stretching out in every direction.

Sometimes, when I have sucked too much out of the previous day, losing time for necessary sleep, my morning arousal comes with more difficulty and tardiness, and I might fail to "greet the day." But as the sun spills over the morning horizon,

I find its rays reaching out, tapping my shoulder and asking me, "Have you thanked God for the gift of this day yet?"

O God of Beginnings, today you have provided me with another wondrous gift of life. I am alive! - and the beauty and the potential of all that you have created around and within me is here now within my gaze and hands. Help me to see this day as another opportunity to encounter you in sundry ways as I open the gift and explore its possibilities through service, work, play - through truly living!

January 9
Travel Plans

Many people cite "travel" as one of their hobbies when asked to divulge their interests. I suppose that I could add that one to my list of interests as well, but I somehow suspect that most people's idea of "travel" is a good bit different from mine. Interestingly, most people who know me probably think of me as a "traveler," but it has really only been true in my later years of life. I toured many states with my parents and family in the more traditional mode of travel when I was quite young, so that hardly counts for me; and when I was raising my own family, we never had enough money to go anywhere except to where other family members lived. For most people, I suspect, "travel" means going to the beach, preferably ocean, or to the mountains to ski or to famous large cities to explore and take in the cultural offerings and enjoy comfortable hotel accommodations. Traveling to foreign countries is also high on many people's list, but I find that there is so much to see in North America that I am not easily drawn away from it. I have done each of the aforementioned excursions, but they are not the travel for which I hunger.

I love to backpack, probably my true "main hobby," so "travel" to me usually entails going somewhere where I can hike and camp. I have no fears of flying, in fact, I find that every time I do fly I am like a small child on his first flight, still full of awe and wonder; but I do very much enjoy a good "road trip" and can selfishly even favor the solo ones as I get to choose all the music and play it as loud as I want. Of course, I do also enjoy traveling with my wife and know that we always benefit from the good "catching up time" it provides – visits, dream-sharing, reading and just that good energy that comes with being together as we marvel at the varying landscapes of our amazing continent. For better and worse, frugality tends to be a "theme" of all of my travels, and that alone seems to put me at odds with most people's idea of travel.

One of my most important and exotic forms of travel, however, is my "interior journey." This voyage can take place when I am vacation traveling or just staying right here at home, but it truly is the most important and on-going travel that I do. My inner journey is about exploring my spiritual depths, and like traveling to another country, it almost requires a change of language. Trekking through the inner terrain can also be like traveling at night over or through some exotic or amazing landscape; I know that something amazing is "out there" – in this case, "*in* there" – but the glimpses are usually fleeting and shadowed. Patience and perseverance are essential so that the eyes of the heart can adjust to the "darkness" of the unknown, and my normal mode of travel music won't do at all, as this voyage desires quiet to better hear the longings of the soul and the whispers of the Divine gently issuing within. But these are its only costs, unless what I hear and see there should send me back out into the world to share, in whatever fashion is appropriate, what I have discovered on my inner journey.

God of my Outer and Inner Journeys, you are eternally my ultimate destination. Wherever I travel, I am always wide-eyed in search of signs of your presence and directions that will lead me nearer to you. Even though a spark of the Divine resides in me always, I still need to take the time to turn my compass toward you and journey to that most sacred and holy place within so that when I do journey outwardly, my inward communion with you will be my true guide.

January 10
Hearing Aids

The night before my Mother nervously went in to get fitted for her first hearing aids, she asked me to pray for her. With her being given a forty-five day trial period, I asked her, "What's to be feared?" If they work, she hears better; and if they don't, she returns them and nothing is lost. But I also heard in her request an important metaphor about our own "life listening skills."

Mom knew that she didn't hear everything perfectly, but she didn't feel as though her hearing was that bad. She didn't recognize, as her children did, that too often when I asked her a question or offered some information or story, that her response indicated that she had heard something else entirely different, or, occasionally, didn't hear me at all. From my perspective, hearing aids would enhance our conversations making words more clear and less work for her as she unknowingly strained to follow them. Concerts, movies and television viewing would all be enhanced as well and less desirable sounds or ringing tones would potentially be filtered. But, again, from Mom's perspective, she accepted a little loss from age, and figured she was, overall, hearing quite well.

Most of us think that we "hear life" pretty well. We accept that we don't have everything down perfectly, but we feel pretty good about the tone of our lives. I was shocked to realize once when talking with a friend who frequently sings off key, that when he sings, he truly believes he is on key. Sometimes what we think we hear is not what is - and we don't want to hear that either! When I hear my voice on a recording, it often sounds strange to me, and I have asked someone who knows me, "Does that really sound like me to you? Is that really what I sound like?" The answer is always yes, and I find myself cringing just a little bit, thinking that my voice is far more melodious than that. Hearing - and seeing - ourselves for who we really are is not always an easy or pleasant thing. Admitting that I am not perfect, that I do not understand all things, that I do not see or hear everything clearly are important steps in truly recognizing and embracing my real self.

Dear God, you are unfathomable, and yet, often, I like to believe that I hear and see and understand you quite clearly. And if I can so self-assuredly know the Great One so well, surely I can hear and see and know others and myself precisely. Help me to not be afraid to hear the truth about myself, and to accept that quite often, I could use some "hearing aids." Your voice is music to my ears and your visage is a beatific sight; help me to hear and to see you - and all that you have created - more clearly.

January 11
The Gift of Loss

After great joy, anticipation and excitement for over three months, a most hollow and deep sadness entered my family's lives on a cold January night when the three creations of love that we were awaiting months away arrived prematurely into the world outside the womb. I saw each of these miraculous wonders, their perfect little faces, their incredibly tiny little fingers and noses; I touched those precious buds of our dreams, the dear grandchildren to whom I would tell stories and rock their crying voices to sleep, the delicate marvels that would bring my two far-away-daughters home more often to visit their niece and two nephews. But their beauty was quiet and still; the movements that their mother and father had felt and thrilled to perhaps only hours before were now silent. Beyond the waves of tears and dull, stunned movement, the distraught-filled question of why slithered through the hospital room like an uninvited specter. At such a time, no reason or explanation will suffice, if one could possibly even be deciphered.

Life is full of what seem and feel like unexpected "tragedies." The sudden and unanticipated loss of loved ones, the accident or ill-fated doctor's report that catches us unaware – these arrivals are blunt blows to the middle of our lives that leave us sucking for air and gasping for comforting answers, that more often than not, do not truly exist. That they happen to people everyday throughout the world regardless of any defining boundary doesn't soften their tragically defined shape. When they happen to us, to me, they are as unique as they are devastating. All I *know* is that these events are just as surely an integral part of life as are the births, the healings, the victories – all of the successes that we long for and also receive. As we clamor to receive the joyous bounty that life can give and be, we must also be willing to discover that sometimes its basket is empty.

In the Hebrew Scriptures, the wonderful but less than satisfying story of Job stumbles through the ageless question of "why bad things happen to good people." Job, a man, heretofore, with everything "deservedly" going for him is challenged by truly insurmountable losses, but initially responds, "The Lord gave and the Lord has taken away; blessed be the name of the Lord!" (Job 1:21) Job's response is certainly a model of faith, but it is noteworthy that eventually he too will crack and begin demanding answers. The problem is, the question itself is fundamentally flawed in that it posits the goodness and badness of things as something that we apparently earn and deserve. Life itself is a gift. We don't earn or deserve it; it just is – and so are the many things of life that we must sometimes confront, and learn to embrace.

In the Native Tradition, an elder once taught me that in life "there are no good nor bad experiences, only experiences. How we receive and accept the experience will determine how good or bad we make the experience." I know that the bitter grief and the hollow pain I experienced at the loss of those grandbaby triplets is neither a deserved nor an undeserved balance to the great joy and anticipation I knew at the time of and the few months that followed the announcement of their conception. But I do know that to receive the latter, I must willingly embrace the possibility of the former.

O God of a Universe that gives and takes away, hear the hollow echoes of the world's anguish as it struggles to accept, and, forgivably, make sense of its losses. Help me to understand that Life is, pure and simple, a gift upon which I have no ultimate hold. May I embrace the losses, deserved and undeserved, that I may encounter this day just as surely as I wish to receive the gifts.

January 12
Don't Fence Me In – or Out!

Out in the vast plains and mountains of America's western states, I often wonder who and when and how the United States Government laid claim to the land, and then gave or sold it to private owners. Wherever I go out there, I eventually run into fences, demarcations to remind me that "this land is my land, and this land is *not* your land." I understand that many of these fences are necessary lines of resistance to keep grazing herd animals in, but I also recognize by the usual accompanying signs that they intend also to keep people like me out. Throughout Ohio, where far more people are crowded into far less space than the west, one can easily imagine that fences and signs are constant reminders about where you can and cannot be.

I don't advocate breaking rules and laws, but when it comes to some land-signs, I do tend to bend the decrees a bit. On a neighboring *public* golf course, for example, which gratefully *allows* cross-country skiing in the winter, I frequently ignore the roping and its accompanying sign, "Area Closed," that tells me to stay off the back portion of the course. Crossing over a wide creek via three bridges, this hilly and tree-lined section of the course is the most quiet and remote portion of the public land mass. Golfers in their carts and soft-spiked shoes traverse it throughout the other three seasons; now, covered beneath a foot of snow, what harm could any skier possibly wreak on this inviting piece of landscape? So, I gently slide beneath the roping and glide quietly to the back regions of the course leaving nothing but the soft swoosh of my skies to interrupt the quietude and a simple pair of tracks to blend with the nearby deer prints carving trails in the drifts.

In his poem, "Mending Wall," the poet Robert Frost also questions the value of these "separations" as he annually rebuilds the stone walls between him and his neighbor. When the neighbor assures him that "good fences make good neighbors," Frost incredulously reflects, "Why do they make good neighbors?" Dubiously he continues, "Before I built a wall I'd ask to know What I was walling in or walling out, And to whom I was like to give offence. Something there is that doesn't love a wall." Indeed.

When the land locked Europeans came to the Americas and began spreading themselves across the continents, they often tried to deceitfully "buy" the land out from under the Indigenous people who already lived there. A traditional Lakota proverb, paraphrasing one of its greatest warriors, Crazy Horse, says, "The Earth is our mother. One does not sell one's Mother." The famous Chief Joseph, in an address directed towards the U.S. Government adds, "How can you buy or sell the sky? The warmth of the land? The idea is strange to us." Yes, when God created the earth, I suspect that laws of ownership were not part of the original plan. Like the spirit itself, sometimes the body needs to wander; and I am grateful for the expansive wonders of creation in which God has given us to roam.

O God of No Boundaries, in our feeble effort to control all things, we humans seek ownership of the land, even the waters and the sky. You have created all things and have given all things to your beloved creations. While I must respect the legalities of the country in which I live, may I never lose sight of the expansive landscape that opens up within me, the home where my spirit may roam. As I explore the created world, may I even more ceaselessly pursue my inner terrain wherein I will most consistently and certainly find you.

January 13
Pond and Stream

Not far from my home, just a glance away from the Interstate highway running nearby, there is a pond that rests in a quiet depression in the earth, surrounded by trees. On the other side of a little bluff that overlooks the pond, a stream courses its way through wooded and open spaces making its way to a three creek convergence miles away. Having spotted the pond from the highway years ago, I ventured into its quiet recess one winter, when a quick and deep freeze had sealed it shut before the winter's snows had begun, to enjoy a rare outdoor ice skate. Sometime later, during an annual winter romp through the woods, I found myself facing the nearby stream, somewhat swollen in an icy murkiness. Needing to ford it, I searched for the least dangerous crossing, knowing that I would have to step into it at some point or another; a good quarter of a mile downstream, I finally willed myself into the frozen flow and made it across.

Of these two water sources nearly side by side, the pond proved to be an easier and more enjoyable winter fare. But as I reflected on them and what their presence had taught me, I decided that I would much rather be the stream. During my ice skate, the pond offered me enjoyment, a free and easy gift; whilst during my run, the stream had presented me with a discomforting and dangerous challenge. We need both the challenges and the gifts in life, and I accepted both. Beyond these proffers, however, I got to thinking about the water itself. In the summer, the pond is still and murky; its dark waters hardly an open invitation to swim. Yes, its winter vestige had provided me enjoyment, but the pond froze because it was contained, static and even stagnant. The stream, meanwhile, while not deep enough for a true swim, offers a cool respite during the summer's heat. When winter arrives, its open movement resists the freeze and its waters grow even clearer as sudden run-off from rain is held in check by snow flurries. Furthermore, excepting extremely cold temperatures, the stream's frigid flow and quiet gurgle invite the gaze of reflection, if not the challenge to pass through and over it.

I guess that we would all like to be the best of both of these waters, the pond and the stream, but the latter does seem to embody more completely what God intends for us. The pond's calm containment, much like "the easy life," provided me with a lovely winter skate, but its limited borders also make it summer stagnant and winter frozen. As much as I might enjoy an "easy life," the pond reflects the dangers of such a way. Meanwhile, although the stream is something of a constant challenge, open and moving, it dances down its pathway experiencing life's variety, clear and blithesome as it tumbles throughout the year.

O God, like water, the Source of all Life, you not only sustain us with the waters of life, but also use water to teach us about life. Grateful for water's sustenance, I also seek to flow through life as the stream does, a fluid motion that accepts and moves through, in and around all that is in its path. Keep me from becoming stagnant, a murky reflection of your presence in the world. Be the source of my life's flow today, keeping me clear and pure, a gift that challenges and sustains.

January 14
Bargain Bin Spirituality

In my first years of marriage with a child on the way, our young family lived in subsidized government housing in southern Minnesota. Once I completed my schooling and landed a career job in teaching, my income increased, but money continued to be an everyday concern in our household. For most, if not all, of our child-raising years, my family lived "hand-to-mouth;" what little income I made went immediately to the table, roof and other sundry needs of the family, and there were almost always more days left over each month than money. To help stretch dollars, we constantly sought more frugal ways of spending what little we had, shopping at outlets, dollar stores and Big Lots, always in search of some incredible deal.

Gratefully, I don't go to these bargain stores today with quite the same need that I once did, but I have no hesitation to scour their aisles yet when I suspect that they may have what I am looking for. Indeed, I rarely leave a visit to one of these stores without something that I consider to be a "smart buy," a respectable value for my dollar. But while there certainly are some good deals to be found in bargain and outlet stores, if I am searching for some specific utilitarian item, and one that I especially need to last, I try to keep in mind that usually, "you get what you pay for." I mean no disrespect to the plethora of bargain stores that help market a tremendous amount of inexpensive products today, but I have found that economy is of far greater concern in such stores than quality. Sometimes all a "name-brand" item has to offer over a generic substitute is the name and the packaging; but other times, again, you get what you pay for. If it's a quick fix you're looking for, chances are the generic product will serve your need just fine. But if you're in the market for long-lasting furniture, tools, or appliances, you'll likely find yourself shopping again for a replacement sooner than you would like.

When it comes to the spiritual life, there are no bargain centers, for one can't go shopping for a prayer life substitute or purchase a generic ritual to cover one's needs. The effort that one puts into his spiritual life, however, can often be of "bargain bin" quality, for the price of a spiritual life comes on a time-tag, and its bar code tends to measure intention and attention. Like an off-brand purchase at the Dollar Store, something is almost always better than nothing, but if one is truly seeking quality in her relationship with the Divine, a pittance of time will not likely render much depth. Christian churches frequently solicit attendance by quoting Jesus' dismay over his sleeping followers on the night of his arrest, "Could you not keep watch with me for one hour?" (Mt. 26:40). Again, one hour is better than nothing, but if one hour is the best we can do in a week's worth of time, our relationship with the Divine will likely have the strength of a five-dollar watch. Daily prayer and some spiritual reading are more than just fancy packaging, and frequent meditation or attention to the Divine Presence in our lives keeps the spiritual nourishment fresh. Dabble with your spiritual life or invest some real time and energy into it, either way, you'll likely find that you get what you pay for.

Bono, the leader singer of the iconic rock band, U2, once said on a live concert recording as he questioned monies funneled into religious organizations, "Well, the God I believe in isn't short of cash, mister!" Indeed, God has no need for our money, but a quality relationship with the Divine does not come at a bargain rate either. Priceless God, you do not ask much of me, but like any beloved, you simply desire some time and thoughtful attention. My relationship with you is worth more than any grand purchase, and yet you come to me at the mere cost of my purest intention, an extravagant bargain. May I not be so frugal with my timely devotion to you.

January 15
Martin Luther King, Jr. Day

One of our nation's greatest beacons was born on this day in 1929. A simple man from humble beginnings, Martin Luther King, Jr. would rise to international prominence long before the assassin's bullet, a shot heard round the world, tragically ended his life in April of 1968. King is best known for being a champion of the Civil Rights Movement, an effort he entered in 1955 when he led a boycott of the public bus system in Montgomery, Alabama when another early hero of the Movement, Rosa Parks, was arrested for refusing to give up her seat at the front of the "colored section" of a public bus to a white passenger. Throughout his short life, King fought tirelessly on behalf of Civil Rights for African-Americans, enduring over twenty arrests and four assaults. In 1963, *Time* magazine recognized him as their "Man of the Year," and a year later, at the age of thirty-five, he became the youngest man to receive the Nobel Peace Prize;

characteristically, he turned the nearly $55,000 prize money over to the cause of the Civil Rights Movement.

What makes Dr. King's efforts and successes so heroic was that he utterly espoused the principle of non-violence. As an ordained Christian Baptist minister like his father and grandfather before him, early on King wrestled with Jesus' non-violent message of loving one's enemies and "turning the other cheek." He assumed that these words "were only valid when individuals were in conflict with other individuals; when racial groups and nations were in conflict, a more realistic approach seemed necessary." But after reading of Mahatma Gandhi's philosophy and the successes of his actions, King concluded, "I saw how utterly mistaken I was." Despite the arrests and beatings that persisted, like Gandhi, he chose to fight against injustice persevering without ever engaging in any physical violence himself. In a world that seeks to solve so many conflicts through wars and violent revolutions, King and his "spiritual mentor," Gandhi, truly followed the path outlined by Jesus; and despite their assassinations, they succeeded in truly changing the world. Even after their deaths, their model of passionate service continues to be a flame that lights the path for those who dare to make a non-violent stand against injustice.

Although President Ronald Reagan officially made the third Monday of January "Martin Luther King, Jr. Day" in 1986, not all states in the union agreed with the move and many chose to ignore it for years, the last resisting state holding out until 2000. In recent years, a new emphasis has been added to the observance of MLK Day encouraging not simply the recognition of this man's accomplishments on behalf of the Civil Rights Movement, but the participation in the spirit of his non-violent movement. Promoting people to engage in some form of social service on that day -"Make it a day on, not a day off" - Dr. King's famous line, ironically written in his "Letter from Birmingham Jail," continues to inspire: "Injustice anywhere is a threat to justice everywhere."

God of Justice, in honoring Dr. Martin Luther King, Jr., I offer a prayer for all of those today who wear the thin armor of nonviolence in their war against injustice. Like Mahatma Gandhi before him, Dr. King provides me with a legacy of hope, a model of proof that injustice and hostility can be overcome without the weapons of violence. The task in such a battle is daunting and the odds appear bleak and impossible, but given your encouraging strength and the vision of one such as King, perhaps one day we can proclaim with him, "Free at last, free at last, thank God Almighty, we are free at last."

January 16
Training Your Pet

I love animals, but I am not much of a "pet person." I never had a pet growing up. As far as I know, my parents never had one, so I never had one, and so I figured that my own children didn't need one. But in time, they clamored for one, so I started with a hermit crab, a very easy start as crabs are very quiet and need very little attention or care. After some time, however, its complete lack of movement and then smell signaled that perhaps we should have given it at least more care than we had. The next step was guinea pigs. They were long haired English ones, cuter than the average guinea pig, but the weekly need for box cleaning and their penchant for procreation eventually got old, and as the children spent less and less time with them, the guinea pigs were eventually "farmed out." Finally, there was the outcry for a dog. "Over my dead body!" I responded, and then, apparently, while on one of my solo retreats one weekend, I must have died, for when I came home, there he was, a cute little cocker spaniel mutt. The kids named him Bungee, perhaps at least acknowledging that this pet was a huge leap, especially for their father.

Because none of us really knew any better, we never actually trained Bungee; subsequently, although he was an "outdoor pet," his listening skills and response to our "commands" left an awful lot to be desired. When he got outside the backyard fence, getting him back home again was never an easy task! Not surprisingly, I suppose, in the cosmic irony of life, Bungee and I got to be pretty good pals, and, quite frankly, no one took him out for walks and runs more than I did. When he would join me on my predawn runs, I would secretly unleash him and let him explore; he would follow the scent of anything and would try to leave his mark on everything.

Our minds, and more to the point, our spiritual lives, are often like untrained dogs and uncared for pets, wandering around, doing whatever they will, or just neglected altogether. Many people desire a spiritual livelihood, but few take time to nurture it, to train the mind, the body and the spirit to work collaboratively. Hoping to develop some spiritual routine, I open some time in my day for prayer, but when I arrive in that "space of prayer," my mind, like Bungee, goes off whimsically exploring. So I collar my spiritual wanderings with formulaic prayers and readings that keep my mind leashed during my quiet walk, but, in time, when I return, I begin to feel like I have merely been on a tread mill.

Like with pets, a little training is a good and necessary exercise in our spiritual development. Divine Master, I seek a deeper relationship, a true companionship with you, but unleashed from the backyard of my routine prayers, I am too often aimless and unfocused, wandering away from you rather than toward and with you. Help me to seek spiritual training and to employ real spiritual disciplines that will not tether me to your side, but that will find me at your side, willfully and happily, a true companion.

January 17
Music to My Ears

Along with the standard "weather reflection," one of the more common "ice breaker" questions that arises when we first meet people is: "What kind of music do you like/listen to?" For me, this actually is a rather important question for I so love and enjoy music, and I tend to believe that our musical choices do say something about ourselves; so, I often approach my answering of the question with some delicacy.

Quite frankly, I have just never been able to embrace country music; even with the "rock-influenced" version of country music, the twang of the singers just annoys me. I have a fairly low toleration for most rap music as well, although I'll admit my music collection hosts more than one selection of angry "rock-rap;" it's a sound I like to unleash now and then. The instrumentation of bluegrass I find uplifting and engaging, but the vocals make even country music singers' sound tolerable to me. Operatic music - oh, lord no; I just can't do it! Symphonic and orchestral music have their place in my life, but they occupy a very slim slice of my musical preferences. Pop, easy listening and folk music (if one can somehow separate those three definitively) all are very tolerable for me, but they tend not to stir anything significant within me. The only music that truly does that is rock and roll. I am a rocker at heart, and few things can uplift and rejuvenate my spirit more than a good rock concert. Of course, like all the other musical genres, rock has numerous visages. I love hard rock, but don't care much for heavy metal. I like a lot of classic rock, but let *me* define what is "classic." And then there is jazz! Here again, the variety is extensive, and, for me, my rock tastes influence my jazz flavors - the more jazz-rock fusion it is, the better. So, how am I doing so far? What do you make of me based on my musical interests and dislikes?

Sometimes I am rather shocked to learn what type of music other people enjoy or find disdainful. Some of my dearest friends love country; my spouse thoroughly enjoys bluegrass; and some dear colleagues listen only to classical music - you know, the symphony, orchestra and operatic stuff. And I love all of these people - despite their musical tastes! Indeed, judging people simply based on their musical interests is a silly move. But, quite frankly, casting judgment based on *any* one thing is rather silly. And yet, we all do it many times. I don't know what has ultimately spawned my musical interests - or yours; there are certainly a variety of factors, and differing ones at that to be sure. How easy it is to allow our interests and tastes to be the standard by which all others are judged.

I wonder what kind of music God prefers? We think of God as being all-embracing, all-accepting, but I can't help but feel that God can't possibly like *every* musical style; and, then, I have a nagging feeling that God would not necessarily agree with my code of acceptable music. The fact of the matter is that music is simply just one of our many forms of human expression, and while God probably doesn't care all that much about music in general, I suspect God does care tremendously about the "expression." Music does help us express ourselves sometimes, and our musical tastes just might say something about us, but to judge one another based solely on these expressions is a disservice to the variety of people that God has created and the variety of music that these people have created. Music has many expressions, and like music, we human beings are an incredible variety pack. God, help me today to recognize how often I might evaluate - judge - people based on small, trivial indicators. What moves each of us is usually very different, and there is a very good chance that we all could learn much from one another's "movements." Perhaps today I might turn my music down and listen to the sounds of another.

January 18
A Divine Spark

One night I stayed up very late with my son in front of our fireplace enjoying some simple conversation and the deep, mesmerizing quiet that so easily descends in the fire's glow. We stoked the fire continuously for hours adding numerous large and solid dry logs, but eventually the need for restful sleep lured us away from the fire's gaze and we went to bed allowing the fire to privately die away. The next day we drove a couple of hours away to join a friend for an afternoon of football, and upon returning home, I set to work at my dining room table preparing for the week of classes ahead. In the quiet of my workspace, I suddenly heard from around the corner, the sound of a log tumble forward, and then, almost immediately thereafter, the soft lapping of flames. As home and hearth had stood idly by in our absence since the night before, I curiously arose to investigate the sound, and turning the corner into the living room, I was shocked to see some small flames pulsing from an old log. For perhaps eighteen hours, the thick, blackened log had silently held the heart of the fire, an ember of the night before, deep within its core, and now breaking open, it offered its light and warmth. Stirred by its offering, I quickly stoked the fire, adding some kindling and more, and then moved my work space to enjoy it once again.

Sitting before the renewed fire's kind comfort, I was drawn to recall the words of the contemplative Christian mystic and Trappist monk, the late Thomas Merton, who once wrote in his book, *Thomas Merton in Alaska,* that "Deep in our hearts is the most profound meaning of our personality, which is that we say 'yes' to God, and the spark is always there. All we need to do is to turn towards it and let it become a flame." Just the night before, although it could have been decades ago, I sat with my son and was touched by something deeper than the both of us, more sublime than the warmth and light of the fire, and yet those very elements were truly at the heart of the experience. The tender mercy of our God, "the spark that is always there," had been kindled in our night's sharing; we had turned towards it, knowingly or not, and now, sometime later, it broke open once again and had "become a flame."

Indeed, within each of us is a spark of the divine that longs to flare up and out and to provide light and warmth and comfort to the world and all of the inhabitants around us. But this spark does require some tending; it needs to be stoked by the labors of our loving attention given in relationships, service, contemplation, and prayer. If left unattended, the spark will not go out, for its source is the divine within, but buried within the very heart of the log, the ember may simply smolder unsuspectingly awaiting the necessary nurturing.

Dear God, the Flame of Life, you have placed within me your divine spark, an ember of your love. Our world, so often a cold and ashen pit, is in need of your guiding light and comforting warmth. Too often, I ignorantly forget the gift of your loving life that burns within me; break me open, let the spark tumble forth, and hearing, feeling, smelling, and seeing your bright tongue of fire, may I rekindle the flame and help to bring your bright reassurance into the world again and again.

Last night's weather report blabbered on about the impending snowstorm due today. A massive front, shown on the map covering more than half the nation pushed on by a frigid Alberta Clipper, emboldened the forecaster's predictions. But all morning I have been glancing out the window and studying the horizon for the onslaught that so far seems like nothing more than empty words. An hour ago, flakes softly began to descend, but after a few handfuls, this simple tease abated. Birds are rustling about in the bushes outside my window, some cardinals providing a stunning contrast of vibrant red against the cold and austere white backdrop, while squirrels hop about attending to their apparent daily tasks. What do they know of last night's report? Do they sense it in the air and feel the weight of it approaching?

The Weather Channel seems to have become one of our nation's most popular television viewings, and every day the local news gives nearly a third of its half hour of import to weather prognostication. Ah, but we humans love forecasts, as if the meteorologists' predictions will make the climate of our lives "just so." Even the forecaster's on-screen colleagues cheer and chide him about his reports as if he somehow holds the controls of what he predicts; and how often do we throw disparaging curses the weatherman's way when his hope-filled forecast gets rained on or snowed under. Ultimately, what we are all grasping for is a sense of control, the ability to be prepared for and to manage the environment around us. To that end, the forecast is bleak.

As I end this reflection, light snow is finally beginning to descend like flour from a sifter; perhaps last night's forecast will be right – this time. Sure, there are often signs all about us that might help us to predict and prepare for what may be ahead, but ultimately, we have little to no control of "what's to come." The birds and the squirrels outside my window received none of last night's forecast, and I suspect that they will manage this apparent storm just fine. Maybe we should learn a little something from them: let go of the expectations; go about one's daily business; and embrace whatever it is that arrives at our door each day.

O God of the Unforeseeable Future, lead me more fully into this present moment, into this new day of possibilities. Let me not be paralyzed by fear or forewarning of what might be, but to walk confidently and courageously into what is. I may not have the natural sustainability of my fellow creatures of the earth, but through your faithful assistance and love, and my own simple awareness, may I weather whatever shower, storm or sunshine this day will provide.

January 20
Annoying Sounds and Silence

My wife was born and raised in small town Montana, and most everywhere that she had lived or that had been an important setting to her since her birth were also small towns. She had known expansive, wide open spaces all of her life where towering buildings are almost non-existent and even if a freeway is laid nearby, its course is lightly travelled. And then she married me and moved east of the Mississippi where large cities are splattered across the landscape and freeways are twenty-four hour racetracks. One evening in her first year of living in Ohio, as we sat grading papers together at our dining room table, she dropped her pen and with an anguished look on her face said aloud, "Argh! Can't they just stop? Where are all of those people going?!" A bit confused, I asked her of whom she was speaking. "That traffic!" she said in anguish. "Don't you hear that? It's driving me crazy!"

"That traffic" was the faint hum of the interstate highway over a mile away. The windows of our home were shut, but sure enough, one could detect an annoying drone from the freeway that wafted over the neighborhoods, strip malls, and trees and dropped into the quieter corners of our lives. I had to admit that even though I had lived in this home for years, I had never really noticed the incessant noise before, and had certainly never been bothered by it. But coming from a land of expansive quiet, she could hear nothing but the noisy pollution that rattled her concentration and comfort.

Interestingly, I have heard more than once from "city people" who spend a night in the country or camping out in the wilderness that they find it difficult to get to sleep because it is so quiet. Normally, of course, we associate sleep with "peace and quiet," but if one's comfort zone has been developed within the framework of noise, peace and sleep do not necessarily come hand in hand with quiet. Comparing the two experiences, my wife's reaction to the noisy traffic and the city dwellers response to the quiet, provides an interesting awareness of how we are products, sometimes even "victims" of our environments.

We all know, sort of intuitively, that not everyone sees and hears things the same way. However, deep down, perhaps, we might believe that the differences are not actually real, but are simply one or the other person's misconceptions of a given experience. But recognizing my wife's angst over the noise, and hearing of the restlessness of another's blanket of quiet, I realize that we do, in fact, hear things differently; and just as surely as we hear and respond to sounds differently, how simple it is to imagine the different ways that we see and understand other aspects of our lives differently as well. Our inability to accept the different perspectives of others often creates tremendous conflicts in our lives. Again, we can loosely accept that "we are different," but it is far less easy to embrace that some of our differences are real, and are not just misguided and misinformed perspectives. When I sit back and hear with another's ears, I allow myself also to better understand how what she hears can affect her in the way it does, and not simply judge her by the sounds and understandings that I perceive.

God of All Sights and Sounds, like you, our world is a magnificent array of views and resonances. Oftentimes, I too quickly believe that what I perceive, is – and that there is no other "real" way of seeing or hearing something. Open the scope of my vision and broaden the range of my earshot so that I might better understand another's experience, and, in doing so, work towards creating a more thoughtful, harmonious and beautiful environment in which we all may live peacefully.

January 21
Noisy Silence

As much as I really enjoy music and seize every minute I can to fill my private drive-space and many of my daily runs with it, when I am home alone, I relish the quiet. Sometimes I shock myself just a little bit when I suddenly realize that I have not listened to music for days even though I have had the whole house to myself. The fact is I am easily distracted by any noise, but especially music and talking, and when I am home and working on something, I need to have a veil of quiet over me to successfully accomplish whatever my task may be. Music – any noise – thwarts my productive energy and trips my concentration until my effort is demanding double time.

Shortly after my wife made her anguished complaint abut the traffic noise, I found that each time that the wind was blowing in the right direction, I too was struck by the excessive volume of the interstate freeway as it rolled in as consistently and as relentlessly as waves to the shore. Soon, this new noisome annoyance was butting in on my quiet space, and even when I tried to block it out, imagine it wasn't there, it seemed to slip into the house through unseen cracks. My morning prayer time, previously blanketed by the typically subdued activities of the day's start, is the worst. To the incessant roar of the eighteen-wheelers hauling their loads across the country is added the daily rush hour as the bedroom communities funnel toward the city and work. Some mornings, kneeling back on my prayer stool, I find myself fending off disgruntled thoughts, annoyed by my inability to focus in my meditation as my attention gets sucked away by outside distractions. Lately, however, I am beginning to think that maybe these distractions are good and necessary challenges to my meditative practice.

Our world is full of noise pollution and so much of our manufactured environment teases us with sensory distractions. To live out our spiritual lives most effectively, we need to foster an ability to live within them more efficiently. Famously in the past, but with no less fervor today, some people choose to leave society and to abandon material comforts so as to better nurture their spiritual needs. Monastic communities were built in isolated places and provided austere conditions so that the spiritual seeker could be immersed in the nutritive silence of prayer and meditation. Retreat centers today, generally, are located on wooded grounds and countrysides that buffer the noise and confusion of life for the retreatants. Our spiritual life seems to desire and need quiet, but it is not how and where we live our daily lives. Nevertheless, a healthy spiritual life must be lived out daily; thus, our ability to sustain a healthy spiritual existence while living within the noise and confusion becomes almost imperative. And so, amidst the noise and confusion of life, I must kneel or sit down to pray and to meditate.

God of all Sound, my heart seems to hear you best when all is silent, but so rarely is my world engulfed in such quietude. While I seek you out in still places, the ripples of the noisy world often spill into my space and distract my attention directed toward you. Help me to transcend this confusion when I cannot escape it, and perhaps even to hear your voice within the noise and the confusion. I seek peace everywhere, but may I find it first and foremost within my very being.

January 22
Cross-Country Skiing

Like running, cross-country skiing is a uniquely personal and relatively simple form of exercise. Of course, nothing, beyond yoga and tai chi, beats the simplicity of running and its lack of necessary equipment. Beyond a good pair of running shoes, and some might argue that need, all one needs to engage in running as exercise is a little desire; any space will do. Like running, cross-country skiing can be enjoyed alone or with another, although visiting while skiing is far more difficult than while running. Some equipment, of course, is necessary, and the space to engage in it can be highly limited. However, given the right equipment, space and a little practice, there are few exercise forms that can equal its value in output.

Beyond the plentiful physical benefits of cross-country skiing, there are some spiritual benefits that one might enjoy as well. Few activities - like running, swimming, yoga, and cross-country skiing - provide the practitioner with such a fully healthful experience, health of body, mind and spirit. In cross-country skiing, the whole body is physically engaged in the movement of each stroke; the upper body receives as demanding a workout, if not more, than the lower body while the heart and lungs are consistently required to provide the energy necessary to sustain the workout. Once one is able to master the rhythm of skiing, than the mental and spiritual aspects can emerge more easily as well. Like running and swimming, cross-country skiing provides one with a sense of total escape. The cares of the day are released as the rhythmical movement of the sport provides a salve that sinks deeper than the skin and even the muscular structure. As tensions are released, calm can be the balm.

To achieve the full benefit of the sport or exercise of cross-country skiing, an aesthetic appreciation for the environment is also necessary. If one likes the winter season, then skiing will access the spiritual dimension quite naturally; if one is averse to winter, then, perhaps, skiing might help one to better appreciate it as this full bodied activity provides physical, mental and spiritual revitalization. Spiritually, one is called into a relationship with the land, much as one is with the water in swimming. Establishing a synchronistic rhythm with the contours of the earth, the skier seeks balance in each stroke of the flatlands, is challenged by uphill grinds, and is rewarded by downhill glides. The beauty of the skier's "playground," the woods, the stretches of open land, and the hills and mountains that she strives for, are all encased in winter's grand wardrobe, and each view is interrupted only by the soft shush of the skis over the snow and the skier's own rhythmical breathing and heartbeat. When all is in balance, a meditative state naturally enraptures the skier's effort.

Creator of All, the beauty of the earth and the magnificence of the human body, you provide for me so many opportunities and ways to encounter you. Utilizing the gift of my body in private exercise that engages me with so much of the beauty of your creations, I find myself naturally and simply drawn to the heart of all things, to the One whose pulse courses through us all. Help me to seize these opportunities to exercise my gifts and my body, and in so doing, encounter your presence all around me and deep within me.

January 23
A Blanket of Sacred Words

Although the temperature had dropped into the high teens, the morning sun's radiance offered a blanket of reassuring warmth as I joined more than a hundred other runners for a midwinter half marathon. I had not trained particularly well for the event, but my intention at registration time was more about the community experience on a long winter's run. The just over thirteen mile course started at the high school of a small neighboring village and drifted through the countryside on quiet back roads surrounded by wide open farmland lying fallow beneath crusty snow; six and a half miles out, a simple turn around, and then six and half miles back to the finish.

Warmed by the kinship of runners sharing in a rather crazed idea, the first half of the run melted away like a spring thaw. Miles dripped away under the sun's affectionate energy and as I turned the corner to head back, I noted that the shirt beneath my windbreaker was damp with sweat as was the stocking cap on my head meant to keep in the warmth. Within the first half mile of the return route, I realized with some horror that the comfortable ease of the race's front half had been due in significant part to the wind having been at our backs, and now, for the next six miles we would run straight into its biting teeth. As the sun softened to a winter glow and the wind chill hardened its clench, I pulled at the scarf that had been uncomfortably warm around my neck earlier and tightened it around my face, trying to protect my nose and mouth. Soon, however, the condensation of my warm breath wetted the scarf and the wind's chill froze it, and when I gave the scarf a quarter turn to find a warm, dry spot for my face, I felt its frozen fabric resting against my numbing ear already damp from my sweaty cap. With just under five miles to go, I honestly questioned whether or not I could finish the race.

As the icy breath of fear intertwined with the wind chill, my mind desperately sought a warming reprieve both from the external cold and from the internal negativity that were freezing my numbing effort. It was then that my heart felt the soothing whisper of my mantra and I knew immediately how I would make it to the finish line.

A mantra is merely a word or a formulaic group of words that one mindfully repeats in prayer providing, at its simplest level, concentration, and on deeper levels, a kind of spiritual energy. Hinduism is the contextual origin of the "mantra," a Sanskrit word that emerges from the Vedas, a set of sacred Hindu texts. Roughly, the term comes from two Sanskrit words, "manas" referring to the mind, and "trai" meaning to "protect" or "free from"; thus, in essence, the intention of a mantra is to free oneself from the mind, or in times of meditation, to protect one's sacred space from the onslaughts of disruptive thoughts, or in the middle of a midwinter half marathon, to meditatively thaw the fears of frostbite and hypothermia while prayerfully encouraging one's push toward the intended goal. In the rhythm of my stride and breath, I began to repeat my sacred phrase over and over for the last four miles, and wrapped myself in its blanket as I crossed the finish line.

A mantra is an important tool to deepen one's prayer life, and the power of it can be used in any tradition. A sacred name, a favorite scripture passage, or perhaps a phrase from another prayer can all be utilized as mantras. In meditative prayer especially, it provides one with an anchor when the mind wants to drift off into other less prayerful and mundane bays. In times of stress and dis-ease, it is a soothing balm that calms the tension of the moment and invites the tranquility of the Divine presence into the agitated occasion.

Soothing God, sometimes I prayerfully come to you with specific intentions, sometimes with words of thanks and praise, and other times with the need to just be present to your sacred presence. Today I consider for the first time, or will renew my wakefulness to the power of a sacred mantra. Help me to consider how this prayerful tool might enhance the concentration of my prayer life and be a source of comfort during the disquieting moments of my daily life. Is there a special name by which I best know you, or a tender phrase that seals my attention to you? May I find sacred words ever ready in my heart, mind and mouth.

January 24
Feeling Good is No Accident

Most mornings, I feel like I pop out of bed with a grateful vibrancy, appreciative that the curtains of another day are slowly opening and that I am either on the stage for another act or contentedly viewing from a cushioned main floor seat. Either way, I am just happy to have another day in the theater of life. Despite my daily joy in realizing that "I am still alive!" like so many, I suppose, I can easily slip into an underappreciated sense of healthfulness. Despite the challenges I have endured and the abuses I've dished out on my over a half-century-old body, it works quite well, and I count on its willing response daily. My body's response, in fact, is often the source and the vehicle of my daily joy. I mean, if every day I woke up feeling physically or emotionally miserable, I suspect that my grateful vibrancy might start wandering into the theater's lobby and looking for the exit signs. So when my health gets bitten by the latest virus or infection or my body is racked with some injury, or, after pushing myself too far, I find the whole system pulling hard on the brakes, I then reluctantly remind myself just how grand "good health" really is.

The truth is, very few people ever think much about the amazing intricacies of their body. Quite frankly, that we exist at all is absolutely miraculous. As if mirroring the very universe in which we exist, each person's body is an incredible universe of interconnections. Every moment of our lives, our bodies are on the job, busy doing many things that keep us alive. The essential activity of the heart and lungs, constantly and faithfully provide the in-and-out movements that sustain us. The digestive system, receiving our gastronomic fanfare, ceaselessly processes and distributes all that it receives, happily and unhappily, I suspect. Even when we are sleeping, giving the more physical aspects of our body a chance to rest and recover, these internal organs continue to engage in the high demands of their workload; and if any one of these should fail us, a couple or more hiccups in the system, the life that we enjoy, or at least, how we enjoy it could quickly be over.

In our job lives, most of us need a little pat on the back now and then just to be sure that what we do is being noticed and appreciated. When is the last time that I thanked my body for what is does for me – twenty-four hours a day, seven days a week, 365 days a year – with no vacations, no time-off?

God of the Universe, you have created each of us as a microcosm of the expanse of your creation. Just as I so often take all that is around me for granted, so too do I too often take all that is within me for granted. I am a miracle, an amazing creation within the beyond amazing universe. Today, in all of my movements, may I mindfully consider the inner workings of my body – from each breath I take, to the soft murmur of my heart and the blood it pumps, through the nutritive process that sustains me, and on to the entire framework that allows me to move and do anything at all – and considering these, offer words of thanks for their job well-done, and praise to the one who has made it all possible.

January 25
Before the Snow Melts

The forecast for the day was for rising temperatures; the annual January thaw was about to begin the weatherman reported, with highs reaching the 40s. For at least a week straight, I had been clipping my cross country skis to the tips of my boots and heading out for a daily energizing workout against the backdrop of winter's clear and refreshing landscape. A good snow comes so infrequently to my "neighborhood," but for the second year in a row, we – well, those of us who *love* winter – had enjoyed winter storms that provided deep and quality snow for skiing. But the forecast that day was the first tone in the death knell for our snowy base. Hearing that moribund peal, I arose a little earlier that day, when the temperatures were still dangling in the low 20s, hoping to salvage one last ski before the frigid, sparkling, diamond dust melted away. With work spread across my table already and a schedule of events just ahead, my early rise for a morning ski was truly a carpe diem move.

To push the opportunity further, I even shelved my morning meditation, made my simple offering to the blessings of the day, and hurried off to my "cross country playground" figuring that the harmony of body, spirit and nature would be prayer enough for that day. Indeed, with the snow still soft and supple beneath my skis, in the carved tracks of my and other skiers' previous "body and nature communions," I sang quiet hymns of praise with the rhythm of my movements in the grace of the sun's rising rays. An hour later, my skis retired for the day and until the next hoped for snowfall, I stepped back into the rhythm of the workday as the snow quietly and slowly commenced its ebb.

Sometimes we need to set the cares of work and other demands aside and seize the opportunities of playful rejuvenation. Often, such a move will feel irresponsible and careless, and if it is done with frequency and lack of concern, it can be that. But more often than not, such occasions for leisure and renewal are rare blessings, and we would do well to grasp them heartily. Tasks and expectations will be forever before me, but a grace-filled snowfall in my part of the country is a rare invitation to come out and play. Work surrounded me long before the first flake drifted to the ground and will be there still long after the crystal drifts dissolve away; as the melting snow will nourish the earth and prepare it for the new growth of the spring season, so its welcomed and accumulated arrival provide me with a refreshed and energized winter spirit.

God of Simple Graces, thank you for the small and natural wonders with which you bring me restoration. Help me to recognize these gifts and to seize the opportunities that they offer me. Yes, this day has work that must be done, and I will attend to it, but encourage me to see the balance in life into which play and exercise invite me.

January 26
Advanced Placement Spirituality

When I taught high school English, I had the good fortune to be the Advanced Placement instructor for the Literature and Composition course for over fifteen years. Two of the most significant joys of teaching this course in particular were that the students were most often highly motivated and conscientious about their work, and, given the nature of the course, that I, the instructor, had complete autonomy in deciding what was to be read and taught. The exigent aspect, however, of both of these "joys" was that I always felt a tremendous responsibility to choose literature that would be both challenging and entertaining for the students. I issued in each year with a renewed sense of excitement and anxiety.

One of the age-old questions that English teachers sometimes ask and are often asked is "What makes a book 'a classic'?" Why are the works of Thomas Hardy, who few high school students would choose to read, often listed in the "classic" column, but not those of the prolifically successful Stephen King, who would be a much more natural choice of such readers? Additionally, with the College Board also encouraging some modern selections, if one of the criteria of "classic literature" is that it has "withstood the test of time," how is one to know which "modern literature" might eventually be "classic"? Anyway, the point of these questions is that the annual choice of the literature always left me a bit apprehensive. I wanted the choices I made for my students to be worth their time, not just to stimulate them intellectually and to prepare them properly for the A.P.

Exam, but also to encourage their lifelong love of reading. The truth is, in the end, such a selection process was pretty much a "no-win" situation. Though I annually changed up the selections, inevitably, every year some students would love one book, while others would despise it, and what worked one year was likely to flop the next. Kids! What's a teacher to do?!

We all likely have some difficult decisions and questions to face throughout our lives, ones that never seem to have a definitive answer. And yet, day after day, year after year perhaps, we keep plying away thinking that some day we will come up with the magic formula, or discover the fulfilling answer. I often wonder how much thought and time and energy people put into the decisions and questions of their spiritual lives. For many, "religion" is their spirituality, and for many of these, their religion was simply given to them, like me assigning my students a certain novel of *my* choosing. But what holds and stimulates not only our interest, but also our spiritual growth? I am not proposing that people simply take their spirituality like a smorgasbord, picking and choosing only those things that suit their fancy; quite the contrary. Just as some of my choices would not have been my students' choice, they took them on, and after reading, thinking, discussing and then writing about these works, they too discovered a love for the book. How much more should we be doing something similar with our spiritual lives - thinking about, discussing and critically analyzing what, how and why we believe what we do. Such a process ought to make us, as my A.P. course preparation did for me, both anxious and excited. We all need to stimulate our spirituality and encourage its lifelong development.

Classic and Modern God, you are always the same and yet ever new. I could spend my whole life reading others' reflections about you, and meditating on my own ruminations of you, and still only cover one corner of the library of you. My spirituality permeates every aspect of my life; oh, how I need to be better informed and more deeply stimulated so that I might live it out more thoughtfully and more completely. You are *The Classic*, the One that truly withstands the test of time; read me like a book and indelibly write your ways into my heart.

January 27
Spiritual Weightlifting

I dislike weightlifting and have always found it a training regimen for which I put up strong resistance. Although I was blessed with a rather naturally athletic body and skills, my frame has never been particularly muscular by nature. Perhaps my aversion to weight training is a subconscious dislike for the enclosed space of weight rooms. I am admittedly an "outdoor person" and my early memories of weight rooms are of concrete block quarters that are close, musty, and dimly lit – something like a dungeon; but that's a rather weak argument given the bright and spacious design of most modern workout centers. Maybe it is the "intimidation factor." While I consider myself relatively strong with a good sense of balance, the lack of tone in my upper body muscles just makes me feel "wimpy"; and weight rooms always seem to be full of bulging and ripped lifters who might mistake me for one of their light weight barbells. But as I get older, I have begun to realize that if I want to continue to stay as active as I have always been, then I need to add some strengthening routines to my exercise life. Happily, the "science" of the weight room has shifted too, and techniques have broadened from simply lifting weights to a variety of plyometric, core, and isometric drills as well. So, one winter while backing off of my daily running a little bit, I let go of my fragile ego and stepped into the weight room for some strengthening and toning.

The truth be told, within a couple of months of my few-days-a-week-effort I did notice a difference, and I felt good about it. I didn't *look* any stronger, but I felt it and I knew that I *was* stronger. Later that spring while on a solo backpacking trip traversing the Superstition Mountain ridge, I unexpectedly encountered one of the most challenging solo hikes of my life. Requiring some dangerous four-limbed climbing while loaded down with my forty pound pack, the poorly marked trail challenged every part of my body, and I remember numerous times when I was acutely aware of and grateful for the strengthening and conditioning that I had done in the weight room in the previous months.

Working on our spiritual lives is much like my vision of weight training. Daily prayer, reading and meditation are not always something that we are easily drawn to; they require work and discipline, and the results are rarely immediate, and sometimes not even noticeable at all. But suddenly, in a pinch, we realize how our approach has changed. We sense a different source of strength about our movements, and our bodies and spirits are more balanced and controlled. We know a deeper peace and discover a level of comfort unknown before our efforts. I'm reminded of an old childhood joke where three prayerless men are lost at sea in a dingy. In their despair, they begin to ask one another if any one of them knows anything about how to pray. Acknowledging their ignorance, one finally inserts hope by noting that he lived next to a Catholic Church growing up and remembers hearing people in the lower hall of the church every Tuesday night; perhaps he might remember some of the "prayers" he heard back then. So, bowing their heads, the man reached back into his memory and began: "G47; B11; O72; I23…" I don't know if his "intentions" were enough to salvage their safety, but the joke might give one pause to consider: one just never knows when one might need some tactical spiritual assistance, so it might be good to listen up and learn a little bit.

God of Strength, my spiritual life is often in need of a little toning and some good fortifying, but I rarely take the time to do what is required. Help me to make room in my daily life for some spiritual exercise, and to act on it with dedication and perseverance, so that when I find myself climbing a mountain of compunction or lost in a sea of confusion, I'll know I've got the means to endure.

January 28
Sculpting the Self

I've never been gifted much in the visual arts. I think I have a pretty good photographic eye, but my sketchings and paintings leave much to be desired. I can also be pretty crafty, but my work is usually fairly simple and not terribly original. And I remember working with clay and wood back in my teen years, but the one never "fired" me up and the other left me a little "bored." One other medium, which I have never tried, and likely never will although I am greatly fascinated by it, is sculpting. In all other art forms, the artist kind of "builds" the work. With drawing or painting, an image is created via the hand of the artist; a blank page or canvas is given new life through the artist's strokes. While something already exists in woodwork and pottery, the artisan still builds upon what is there, what they have, and errors can be shaved, sanded down or reshaped. In the medium of sculpting, however, while there is a foundational chunk of rock that is manipulated, one does not add to it nor can errors be easily remedied. In fact, the great sculptor, Michelangelo, is credited with saying, "Every block of stone has a statue inside it and it is the task of the sculptor to discover it."

As the sculptor works with a single block of stone and seeks to discover the statue that lives inside it, every blow that he makes must be carefully measured. Once a chunk is severed from the larger whole, it cannot be replaced or erased or recovered. In a sense, each blow of the hammer and each carving of the chisel is a final one. From the largest severed hunks to the delicate etchings of detail, each strike must be carefully measured and precisely stroked. A person may approach the spiritual life in a similar fashion.

Like the block of stone with a statue inside it, each human being is created with the image of the Divine embedded within longing to emerge. Unlike the sculptor, however, working on a separate piece of stone outside of himself, each of us has the opportunity to discover and to uncover the statue of our true self within. But how we go about this carving and shaping is not so unlike the sculptor's task. Words, actions, and even thoughts become the rough as well as the delicate blows that allow our deeper selves to emerge. When we carelessly wield the hammer of actions, or misdirect the focus of our chiseling words, we can do significant damage to the best part of our sacred selves. Accordingly, it is important that we approach the fashioning of our spiritual lives with careful thought and deliberation.

Gratefully, because it is the Divine within me already that I seek to uncover, my errant blows, injurious as they may be, need not be irreparable. Nevertheless, each notch of the pick and each score of the chisel ought to be carefully considered as I give shape to this sacred stone. God of Artistry, you sculpted the universe with magnificent precision and beauty, sealing within all of your creation your indelible print. In each of us, you have placed a spark of the Divine, and then have given us the means by which we can uncover your sacred image, bringing it to the surface of ourselves, polished and holy. Be in my thoughts, words and actions, and guide the strokes of my hammer as I seek to reveal the best part of me – which is you – to the world.

January 29
Sing from the Heart

I have a habit – the jury is still out on whether it is good or bad – of frequently busting out into a line or two of singing whenever someone says something that reminds me of a particular song. Most often the sung line is sprung from a specific word or phrase that corresponds directly to a song, but occasionally it could even be a thematic connection. For those unfamiliar with me, my musical outbursts must initially appear as just an oddity, or a quaint fancy. Many times people don't even seem to register the connection between what was said and what I sing in response, in which case, I'm probably just annoying. But I don't do it for the attention, or to humor or educate; I really just can't help it. Music so bounces around inside me and is so easily jarred out of me, that the simplest word, phrase, scene, occasion – anything! – can send me into song.

My wife often marvels how from the moment I awaken each day, I almost immediately have a song in my head, and am freely singing while she is still working at getting her eyes to stay open. In public, it is no different as I have little pride and no shame in almost absent-mindedly sharing what, for me, feels like "a gift." If a song slips into my head randomly or otherwise, I release its good feelings right out loud, with a little respect to the volume of course. My oldest daughter will sometimes become a bit exasperated with me – "Dad, really?!" – she will say as I inadvertently interrupt another conversation or setting. But when her younger sister suddenly fell into the habit, I began to reflect on its influence a little more.

Turns out, my Father used to embarrass me to no end around my friends when he would do precisely the same thing, only with songs of his era or bad renditions of ones from ours. So, this penchant for song almost appears to be a hereditary thing, now being transferred to my youngest! As much as that is true, I think that if I had to genetically pass something on to my children, well, what finer gifts than music and song. Music helps to create an atmosphere and solicits emotion, and singing personally engages one in that atmosphere and emotion, helping to generate levity and good feelings. Of course, an excess of it can be downright annoying, I suppose, but maybe that's just the price sometimes of being misunderstood. I once heard a minister encouraging his congregation to sing say, "God gave you your voice. If it is beautiful, use it to praise and thank him; if it is awful, now's your chance to get back at him!" Either way, I don't want to cage this bird's songs.

God of My Musical Heart, I thank you for the gift of song. I thank you for how it specifically links me to my father and to my daughter, but more importantly, how song actively engages me in sending out lighthearted cheer into the world. We are all called to bring goodness into the world, and as this is one of my offerings, let me sing proudly aloud. Song can soften the severity of our lives and march us into mirth, and I'll sing to that!

January 30
Full of Yourself

In the somewhat subtle climax of one of the most classic teenage angst movies of all time, *The Breakfast Club*, when the group of five Saturday detainees begin to let go of their separate egos as they challenge each other to step away from theirs, Claire Standish, the socialite princess of the group rails about how difficult it is to be popular, to have so many people looking up to her and watching everything she does. To her honest but egotistical confession, Brian Johnson, the brainy nerd of the Saturday detention crew, laughingly muses, "Claire, you're so conceited. You're so, like, full of yourself." Being "full of oneself" is a rather interesting phrase, for it actually implies that because of the nature of one's fullness, one is actually quite empty.

The word "conceit" is rooted in the word "conceive" whose origins suggest, "to take in and hold." When I think of the word "conceive," I tend towards the procreative sense of it, which, of course, "takes two." But "conceit" evolved from "conceived" in the sense that one takes into the mind and grasps a vain view of oneself. This conception is usually a "party of one." Interestingly, it is also a party without invitations, for if, when one is conceited, he is "full of himself," then there is no room for anyone else. Hence, I conclude, it is a pretty empty party as well.

Years ago, the phrase "looking out for number one" was popularized, with the "number one" being oneself. One could argue that Claire, and others, are not being conceited, they are just taking care of themselves, you know, looking out for number one. But are we all really supposed to see ourselves as "number one"? Is that as deep as our interests and cares go? Obviously not. So much in our society and world would suggest otherwise, however. From feeling good, to looking good, to being in control, our airwaves and advertising sanction our pursuit of being full of ourselves. And if one is not able to muster enough self-confidence in oneself, then one tends at least to invest one's image and confidence in the next appropriate smaller group: from friends or "posse" to school or team, from city or state to national identity. In each of these mirrors, we are to see the bold aplomb of self, either singularly or in the common face of the group.

Our world is so much bigger than you or me or any one group or even any one nation. One of the first great rewards of the space program was the amazing and beautiful image it provided of the blue-green earth suspended in the universe. Looking at that lovely marbled bowling ball floating there in space, one cannot see anything distinctly "me" or "us"; merely, there is the one planet, Earth, which we all can call home, and upon which we all must learn to live together as one family. Whenever I get too full of myself, I am empty of the truth of our shared existence. When I am conceited, I take in and hold onto a misconceived view of our common home. Everyone should be included in the party and no invitations should be necessary.

God of Oneness, sometimes my concerns and view of life are horribly self-centered. Full of myself, I have little to no room for the concerns and views of anyone else, and I am empty of you. All things have their origin and life in you. Draw me more closely to understanding the relatedness of all things and our oneness in you, and help me to empty myself of conceited notions while I fill myself with a love for others and an attention to their needs.

January 31
No Edge Lines

Along highways and county roads that are under construction or repair, a variety of warning signs are often posted. Dressed in the classic orange warning ware, and occasionally in the lime-green neon-like flare, these signs announce warnings about slowing down, watching out for workers, and other necessary safety precautions. On roads that have been newly paved, one sign that has always captivated my attention reads: No Edge Lines. Literally, of course, it is acknowledging the temporary lack of the usual white line that marks the outer edge of a driving lane, where the pavement ends and the gravel berm begins. My captivation, however, concerns another level of meaning which this sign frequently begs from me.

What the sign suggests – No Edge Lines – is that even though one is driving watchfully along a highway and would assumingly be aware of where the road begins and ends, a line demarcating the boundaries of the road is still necessary, as if we need specific indicators of where the road ends and where danger begins. If this is true with my driving, how much more true might it be with nearly everything about my daily life? Off road, the daily stuff of our lives – relationships, jobs, myriad choices – we often travel without "edge lines." Arguably, like the road with no edge lines, we can still "see" where the pavement of safety and good choices ends and the gravel berm of tenuous traction begins, the risk-filled, slippery slope of less than "good decisions." But how do I truly know where the edge line is? What is my internal edge line that assists my daily decisions, and from where does it come? Like a road with no berm at all, some decision-making seems obvious, like appropriate and inappropriate behavior in a relationship or job setting; but perhaps there are relationship-roads with paved berms where it is okay for me to slip over the line, expanding the width of my self and interpersonal awareness.

Spirituality provides a kind of edge line for my life; without it, perhaps, I need the sign "No Edge Lines" to remind me that although I think I know where I am going, I can easily slip over the edge and into more dangerous terrain. Spirituality does not guarantee that my life will be without danger, only that with it, my life has some built in markers - some fading, some newly painted – that will provide me some essential guidance on my drive through life. And when I turn onto new pavement on my journey, when I face new and untraveled experiences, like the state Department of Transportation, my spirituality may post an internal warning sign to me dressed up in orange - No Edge Lines – reminding me to slow down and to be wary of this new environment under construction.

43

God of Safety, you allow us to be behind the wheel of our own lives. I can learn the rules of the road and carefully get through most of my life unscathed, but I will inevitably be faced with some varying road surfaces, maybe even some true off-road experiences. I look to you for a little roadside assistance, internal warning signs and reminders of who I am and what my place is on this intersecting, interchanging network of life's highways and byways. Help me to know where the appropriate edge is in all that I do and say; help me also to willingly and safely slip over and outside that edge if the road I travel becomes too narrow or too dangerous itself.

Due in large part to my Mother's morning routine, I bought into the idea that "breakfast is the most important meal of the day" a long time ago. Mine is rarely a "true meal," but I thoroughly agree that one's body needs some valuable nutritional intake at the beginning of the day to jump-start the system properly. While the digestive system never seems to get a rest, it certainly has time enough to slow down during my night's sleep, and without a little breakfast, it can stall out early and delay some of my day's most important movements. For me, a healthy bowl of cereal is all I need to kick my day into gear.

The number of cereals on the market today is absolutely incredible. The average grocery store has nearly one whole side of an aisle dedicated to various cereal brands and types, and while this plethora of selection may indicate an observance of breakfast's necessity, it also reveals our lack of careful eating habits as many of the selections have very little nutritional value. Choosing any one of the proffered selections may get my metabolism moving, but certain selections will send me on my day in a much more healthful state of body and mind. I certainly don't avoid a little morning sweetness mixed into my cereal, reaching only for a steady diet of bran and whole oats, but sugarcoated calories are not my lucky charms either. I tend to like the mix of my Grandmother's dry shredded wheat now flavored with its various crusty frostings, and the plain old oat and wheat flakes of my childhood now tossed with honey and vanilla flavored nut clusters. These seem to provide me the best of both worlds, a little nutritional medicine with the spoonful of sugar to help it go down.

As cereals do for our morning metabolism and physical well-being, religions can offer our spiritual lives a necessary jump-start and some important nutrition as well. If one has been born and raised in a specific religious tradition, then like my mother's breakfast – and spiritual – influence, good habits have perhaps already been established. But if one is just stepping into a new desire for physical and spiritual well-being, then the choices for religions is perhaps even more overwhelming than the selections of cereals in the grocery store aisle. In both, some careful reading, questions and experience are essential in making one's choices, especially regarding the spiritual. Arguably, the practices, services and rituals of all established religious traditions will provide some measure of nourishment, but the very fact that there are so many choices suggests that, like cereal, one flavor doesn't suit everyone, nor are all choices of equal nutritional value. Unlike choosing one's cereal, selecting a religious tradition that adequately meets one's spiritual needs is not nearly so simple as rendering a product's "Nutrition Facts" and sampling its flavor. As with cereal, however, our spiritual tastes and needs may be quite different, and different faith traditions may touch our hearts and spiritual needs in varying ways; and while most faith traditions will "argue" that their path is the best, through all of my reading, study and experience, I cannot concur that one flavor provides equal savor and zest for all. I would not encourage random samplings, but prayerful, thoughtful and engaging dialogue with those traditions to which one feels most inclined.

Breakfast is said to be the most important meal of our day, and while skipping it may not be disastrous, many studies suggest that its absence will diminish the quality and health of our daily life. To live a healthy spiritual life without the nourishment of any religious faith tradition seems a bit like going without breakfast, or at least some morning cereal. Of course, what we eat is perhaps as important as that we eat, so there is more to this whole plan than *just eating something.* To that end, one part of our spiritual pursuit ought to simply be how we will feed and motivate our spiritual lives.

Nourishing God, as I seek to discover an enlivening path that leads to the heart of you, I consider my need for daily nourishment beyond the yearnings of my own heart. It is easy for my spiritual metabolism to grow lethargic; I need the stimulation and sustenance of good spiritual food. If I look to the nutritional grains of others for assistance, help me to read well the packaging and the ingredients, and to find the source of nourishment that will best serve my spiritual hunger and your divine design.

February 2
Primal Religious Traditions

One of the opening chapters of a textbook that I once used in teaching World Religions was titled "Primal Religious Traditions." The book's intention was to open the discussion of the world's religions by acknowledging, and honoring in some part, the traditions of indigenous peoples across the globe whose spiritual practices might arguably be seen as the real roots of what is called "religion" today. These traditions, interestingly enough, were not really separated from other aspects of the people's lives, but were woven right into the very fabric of everyday life. Because the languages of indigenous people were, essentially, never written down up until two to three hundred years ago, it is difficult to know for sure how their languages evolved, but I have read, and find it very easy to believe that Native Peoples of North America, while very spiritual people, had no word for "religion" in their vocabulary originally. It was only when people from other lands came into the Natives' lives insisting and enforcing upon these original "landholders" a new system of beliefs, that a word developed to refer to the new teachings: religion.

Prior to the arrival of the Europeans, and even today where "traditional Native practices" are honored, spirituality is not a "religion;" it is as way of life. Religion implies a series of beliefs and practices that a group of people adheres to, an important component of defining a people's culture. Religions usually become institutionalized structures, and sometimes the leadership and practice of the religion can run counter with the leadership and practices of the larger society. Standardized services and rituals are conducted, but their weekly routine often separates them from the mainstream flow of their society. People have their "work life" and their "social life," and if they should desire to pursue a "spiritual life," they join a religion with its once a week services and sundry other meetings for service and social projects. While the separation of these "lives" seems obviously absurd – like a mafia family maintaining its strict observance of

46

Catholic ritual while ignoring all of the moral ramifications - for many centuries, and arguably in many locales today, it is quite normative.

The beliefs of indigenous people, however, posited their spirituality right at the heart of their everyday lives. Religion seemed to imply something I *do*; spirituality is who and what I *am*, and this naturally governs what I do. God was to be found and encountered not simply in a specific place – a church or mosque or synagogue – but, well, everywhere, for all is imbued with the spirit of the one who created it. Every movement of everyday is pregnant with the possibility of encountering the Great One, and, therefore, all actions are done with respect to that truth.

The irony of all of this "difference" between religion and spirituality is that, of course, there should be no difference. A religion should foster a deep and personal spirituality in its adherents, where one's religious/spiritual life is not separated from the rest of one's daily existence. In such practice, the goal is focused on nurturing strong, individual, spiritual people, without care for what is best for the institution. And what is best for the individual will also be what is best for the society.

God of All Life, help me to take some time to reevaluate my own spirituality. Upon what is my faith grounded? If my church should crumble, will my faith disintegrate with it? Or is my faith in you bigger than any simple set of guidelines and institutionalized ritual? If I claim to be a "spiritual person," is my spirituality evident in all of the decisions of my life, regardless of the milieu? May I look for you everywhere this day and find you in everything.

February 3
A God by Any Other Name

A rather common question that I have heard voiced and been asked many times in my teaching years regarding the many religions of the world is whether or not believers are ultimately praying to the same God, or put another way, do the different religions each have a different God? On one level, it seems, each "believer" might answer these questions somewhat differently or, at least, have his or her own perspective. But if there is only one God, as my inclination is to believe, then it matters little if one religion and its adherents *believe* that their God is somehow different from the God or gods of other religions; ultimately, if we are praying to *a* God, then it *is* the same God. In this case, the real issue is about how different people and religions *perceive* the one God.

Many non-Muslims believe that the people of Islam pray to a different God because of their use of the name Allah. But "Allah" simply means "God" in Arabic, and thus when a Muslim proclaims "there is no God but Allah," he is simply making a strong monotheistic statement: *There is no God but God*. Interestingly, Muslims honor what are known as the "Ninety-nine Most Beautiful Names of God," and many would admit that the Quran, from whence these most beautiful names are derived, speaks of even more than ninety-nine. Actually, they

47

are not so much *names* as they are *attributes* of God, ways in which God is perceived. In effect, one might add that the *essence* of God can never be revealed, or fully comprehended; thus, we grasp for ways of seeing and understanding the one God. Scrolling through the list, believers of any tradition would not be surprised by most of the "names," but would likely acknowledge that a Muslim's perception of God is no different than their own; still, there are a few titles that might raise a curious eyebrow just as surely as one person's view of God or an entire religion's view of God is often questioned by those outside of it.

English translations of Native American names for God are often rendered as "the Great Mystery," and perhaps this reference might be seen as the final word on these questions of whose God, what God and how many Gods. How presumptuous it is for any religion, let alone any one person, to proclaim or even believe that it or he has this Creator of All Things seen and unseen "figured out" and properly labeled. God is God, and I am not; that is all I know for certain about these "God questions." The creation story of the Hebrew Scriptures says that God created humanity "in his image; in the divine image he created him; male and female he created them" (Genesis 1:27). Ironically, humanity has spent its entire existence it might seem, trying to create God in humanity's image. Perhaps if we all spent less time trying to figure out God, and more time trying to understand ourselves, the God within us all would be more clearly revealed.

Great Mystery, God of All, I cannot fully comprehend the universe of things; how much less can I understand the Creator of that universe? I do not wish to couch my faith in ignorance, but keep me humble in my ways, and let me not approach you in arrogance either. Help me to search my heart and to live respectfully among all of your creations; thereby, may I come to know what I need to know of you. The Quran proclaims, "The most beautiful names belong to Allah: so call on him by them" (7:180); teach me, reveal to me, the name by which I may best know you.

February 4
A Comfortable, Prayerful Fit

Around our home, I often wear an old sweater of my Father's that I "inherited" from him some fifteen to twenty years ago when he let go of it after receiving a new one as a gift. Only one of its five buttons is still intact, while both pockets have their own "pocket," a tear along the top ridge of the fabric. Both sleeves are badly frayed, and one elbow bears a burn hole from a drowsy evening when I sat too close to the fire and caught a smoldering spark. Some days while wearing it, I think, I really need to get rid of this old thing, but it is just so darn soft and comfortable that I can't seem to make the break. I have a couple of hooks in my closet bearing worn out, holey jeans that have similar stories. What is with this inability of mine to let go of old, used clothing?

Actually, it is not just any "old, used clothing;" it's the stuff that keeps on feeling good and comfortable despite the age and condition of its material. The fabric feels so friendly; the pants fit the waist and hips like an accepting partner, and the sweater drapes the shoulders and lingers on the arms as a close companion who doesn't need our best all of the time. We'd put them on everyday if they didn't need an occasional wash and we could always just hang out around the house.

One morning when I joined my Mother for her daily prayer rituals, I noticed her leafing through a series of printed prayers, and discovered that she read these prayers nearly every day. My first thought was to question why she would keep reusing those same, old prayers; surely they must have lost all meaning and intention in their daily repetition. But then I realized that they had become something of a mantra to her, that there was comfort in their "knownness." Like my cozy old sweater and jeans, the words of those prayers daily fit her heart, and she could slip into them, or wrap them around her shoulders with soft ease.

Prayer takes many forms, just one of which is prepared, written drafts, and sometimes the heart needs the easy comfort of these thoughtful formulas. Meditation takes effort, a neat ironing of the prayerful fabric, and personal, intercessory prayer can feel like one is searching for the well-coordinated outfit. But a well-honed, common prayer can be the lounge wear that we need on any given day, words that clothe us with a prayerful state and express our simple inner needs.

God of Simplicity, I don't need to dress up my prayer life everyday. Some days it's best to hang around in my pajamas a while, or to slip into that comfortable sweater and an old pair of jeans, and to fall back on the tried and true prayers of my life. Like a mantra, may the well-worn words of these prayers provide my heart with the comfort and warmth that my daily prayer life seeks. When a prayer fits just right, it's okay to wear it everyday.

February 5
The Mountain of God

I have scaled a variety of mountains and have used an assortment of tools, maps and trail markers to assist me in my climbs. Although none of my adventures have required any significant technical ability, each peak potentially offered an array of approaches with a range of difficulty. Some mountains are so inaccessible that if their peak is to be reached, there may be only one reasonably legitimate method. Although there are a couple of courses, for example, to the summit of Mount Everest, our planet's highest peak, most who have reached it only choose but the one "easiest" route. The spiritual life, seeking union with God, is often likened to climbing a mountain, and it seems especially appropriate when discussing various religious traditions and their common goal of union with God.

There are many who fear ecumenical movement and interreligious conversations. So steeped are they in their singular denominational perspective, they worry that such interaction will distort or even destroy the trail of their particular faithful expression. Indeed, finding common ground on which to stand in interfaith discussions is highly problematic, as each religion tends to uphold a "founder"

49

with a unique "divine message" that often runs counter in at least some respect to that of another religion. But as *all* Christians claim Jesus as their singular guide, fears of ecumenism tend to represent a misunderstanding of its intentions. The adamancy of superiority that once marked the Roman Catholic Church's posture has likely cast a long shadow that stretches into present concerns. The official goal of ecumenism today, however, is not the restoration of a single Church with a single and unified approach – *one* way of doing *all* things. Instead, recognizing and even embracing different approaches, ecumenism seeks "unity in essentials" – the essentials that Christians proclaim in their "Apostles Creed." It is not unimportant that differences exist in prayer styles and worship forms, and in sacramental and ritual practices, but these, one might argue, are not the "essentials." Rather than allowing these differences in particulars to irrevocably separate people, in ecumenical unity, perhaps, they could be sources of growth, different tools, ropes and compasses by which others might be assisted while remaining comfortably on the path of their chosen expedition.

For true respect to develop among different faith traditions, however, each religion must let go of its sense of exclusivity. Regarding interfaith dialogue, I have long appreciated the image of different paths up the single Divine Mountain. While all people of faith essentially believe that God is One and long for unity with the Divine, religions present different maps on how to reach that peak of unity. Although I will not personally argue that one map is superior to another, I can accept that some trails arguably do present "easier" passageways than others. But when religious traditions present their way as the *only* way, they essentially invalidate other traditions and suggest that not only will the other's map not get one to the top of the Divine mountain, but that those who follow another map are on a different mountain altogether.

I find it very difficult to believe that the one who created us all would choose to be impossibly inaccessible, or would limit accessibility to but one path, or, even more, limit accessibility to a select group. Throughout the history of humankind, people of nearly every culture have stood enraptured at the base of the mountain of the Divine, looking at it from a number of different perspectives and studying its contours from their vantage point in search of a way to ascend it. And while the experiences of the different paths up the mountain have clearly been as diverse as the paths themselves, there seems much evidence in the writings and in the stories of these faith-filled adventurers that there is more than one trail to a successful summit.

Awesome God, you are the Summit of all human yearnings. Centuries of generations have looked longingly to your heights not for ways to conquer you, but to commune with you, to stand, sit, kneel and lay before your majesty. I am one of those seekers who is sometimes confused and sometimes enlivened by the various maps which circulate and the guides who offer their direction and assistance in reaching the summit of you. Direct me towards that path which you would choose for me, as I thoughtfully, prayerfully and faithfully step towards you.

February 6
The Coupon of Love

For much of my adult life, my family and I had to live a "hand-to-mouth" existence. Raising a family on a single, parochial school income, I stretched each paycheck to pay the necessary bills and to put food on the table; a savings account was a gaunt and anemic stranger. In such a lifestyle, when we dared to "go out to eat," coupons were the essential guide as to where we would go; what eating establishment was nearest to where we lived, and which would provide the best deal for our dollar were the two most important coupon questions. Eventually, the income source doubled and then each increased, and we were able to venture beyond the nearest location and most economical fare, but I have never entirely let go of my "coupon habit." Just because I have more doesn't mean that I should be less frugal.

What I came to realize in the transition, however, is that shopping for a restaurant with coupons as my guide did not always truly provide me with the most economical night out, and certainly not the most savory. The old saying, "you get what you pay for," became more and more ostensible. I might buy a large pizza and "get one of equal or lesser value free," but the main ingredient of these pizzas tends to be dough. Or, perhaps I am offered five dollars off of my bill, but to receive that discount, I first need to spend twenty-five - "excluding tax, tip and alcoholic beverages." And to "enjoy one complimentary lunch or dinner entree," I first need to purchase another entree, "of equal or greater value," limiting my choices to a page of the menu rather than being free to select more randomly. Sure, there certainly are deals to be had, but often, one will compromise on what one exactly wants.

The same can be said for our spiritual development: you pay for what you get. While there are no spiritual coupons, we do often try to squeeze the most out of our "spiritual dollar," buying into the shortest local service or the least taxing ritual, and thinking that we will come away with a satisfying and fulfilling experience. True, we won't likely leave such a repast empty, but the most savory spiritual food and the most nutritionally valuable spiritual ingestion are usually not in the coupon book of bargain deals. If I truly seek spiritual nourishment, I need to be willing to invest some time and to pay the price of dedication and discipline. I can be fed at lesser tables where I compromise my spiritual needs, but I will only be filled when I patiently sit at God's table and select from God's menu.

Great Master Chef of the Universe, I long to dine at your table, but too often I am unwilling to pay the price of your nourishment. The bargains and flavors of this world look so appealing to me, and I am so easily persuaded to be served less nutritional and less satisfying spiritual food. Your banquet table often seems so austere in comparison to the offerings of the world; tempt me this day with the coupon of your love, and lead me toward the table that you have reserved for me, a spiritual meal where I will taste and know true satisfaction and fulfillment.

February 7
The Medicine Wheel

Hanging directly over the place where my wife and I lay our heads down to rest each night is a simple Medicine Wheel that I made for my wife upon our engagement. In fact, the hoop itself was her "engagement ring" as she was never one to want or wear rings. I fashioned this Medicine Wheel from a single, long braid of sweet grass, one of the four sacred medicines in the Native tradition. Around the hoop, I attached prayer ties in the colors of the four cardinal directions honoring their importance and welcoming their meaningful truth into our relationship. Finally, in the center of the hoop dangles a small, fluff loon feather, the only one I have ever had, as a sign of my desire to give of myself to this relationship.

In my spirituality, the Medicine Wheel is the most sacred design of life; it is a constant reminder to me of how life is and, given that, how I ought to live. All of life is a very sacred circle, and so many of the creations reveal or proclaim this truth. From the round tree trunks, to the nests that birds build, to the holes dug into the earth by animals, to the shapes of eggs and planets and fruits and nuts, so much of the created order reminds me of the truth of the Medicine Wheel. The cycle of the seasons, of course, encompasses each year of our lives and reminds us of our own physical mortality; and our own lives are part of this same cycle. However, each year – each day! – we have the opportunity to receive the gift of life anew and to help shape it toward some good, and the Medicine Wheel teaches me about "goodness" itself.

The four directions remind me of all that life is, that life is all things and that all things are life. We all desire the enjoyable and warm southern breezes of life, those days when the tenderness and the rapture of love are radiant in our lives; these are "good" days. But while most of us would seek to avoid the chilling northerly winds of life, those times when we suffer hardship and loss, these "Alberta Clippers" are a part of life too, part of the circle, and we would do well to embrace them just as we do the more gentle winds from the south; these days of adversity are "good" days too. The sun that rose this morning in the east offers to us not only its warming rays of life but the reminder of the gift that life is; how will I embrace and live this day? Change is inevitable and constant; will I welcome the opportunities that change brings? And when the sun sets this evening in the west, intimating the destiny of all things physical, I am provided another daily opportunity to "look within," to reflect on the direction of my current path in life.

Culturally, we are taught that only comfort and well-being are "good," but the Medicine Wheel teaches that all of life, every facet of experience, is a potential kernel of goodness. How I plant, nurture and harvest each experience in life will determine its "goodness." When I offered my wife that hoop, I was telling her that I willingly embrace all that she is; I am grateful for how she warms my life and for how she challenges it. I opened my heart to the changes that a life together with her will bring as we move through our lives toward our inevitable end.

God of All of the Directions, help me to embrace the sacred hoop of life. Physically, I know that I am mainly drawn towards those things that "feel good," but spiritually, help me to more deeply understand that all things "are good." To recognize your presence in all things and to feel the nudge of life in all experiences, this is how I want to live my day today. May your embrace encircle me, and may my heart be as wide open as the center of your encircling hoop of love.

February 8
Real Knowledge

In the context of a Theology course on "Faith and Belief," I used to engage students in considering two ways in which we can "know" God. The first and most common approach, especially to the average American person of faith, I labeled as "Notional Knowledge." In general, most "Church people," particularly throughout the East Coast and Midwest, are essentially born into an institution of faith which was founded on a scriptural tradition. From this establishment, various doctrines and dogmas of faith, from a local congregation to an international community, developed and were added based on centuries of faith experience and varying degrees of "reason." These sacred writings and teachings are then presented to the people of faith who either passively accept them, or after some careful discernment, embrace them wholly and actively as their own faith. While this approach to belief and faith in God "works," the downside is that given a contentious dark night of the soul, the one-dimensional words, ideas and experiences of others may not be personally adequate.

A second, and I would contend most invaluable, approach to understanding the Divine is through what I labeled, "Real Knowledge." Simply put, Real Knowledge can only be achieved through personal experience. Real Knowledge is not founded on scripture and tradition, although it can clearly be enhanced by these forms of Notional Knowledge. Real Knowledge takes root in our heart, and then is augmented by considerations of the head, although these considerations can sometimes prove more detrimental than valuable. Like love, faith cannot be proven, and sometimes it will necessarily rebel against reason. Such a rebellion, however, does not mean that faith is totally "unreasonable," for reason is the work of Notional Knowledge. But, if one's faith is to truly be vibrant – living, breathing, bleeding, sweating, emoting – than it must touch the Real Knowledge of God, an experience that is known so deeply in the heart and in the guts that no dark night can defeat it.

The irony of Real Knowledge is that it can never be fully "shared." My Real Knowledge experience shared with you essentially becomes, for you, Notional Knowledge; it is simply another person's testimony. Testimonials, of course, can be moving, but ultimately, they are not mine. So how does one encounter Real Knowledge? A relationship with the Divine is a "relationship," and like falling in love, you must first choose to pursue the object of your heart's interest; devote yourself to that relationship and open yourself to the possibilities that the one who

53

is love might have in store for you. And don't let too much reason get in the way of great relationship!

God of Heart and Head, knowledge and understanding of you are not unreasonable, but a true relationship with you cannot be founded solely on reason. I seek a deeper and more meaningful relationship with you, but in a world where everything demands to be proven, I need to let go of absolutes, to open myself to the mystical possibilities enfolded into our existence, and to fall headlong into the heart of you.

February 9
Discovering the Word

The opening pages of James Joyce's famous, semi-autobiographical novel, *A Portrait of the Artist as a Young Man*, often immediately confound the reader if they don't entertain her. With nursery rhyme-like tone and vague stream-of-consciousness imagery, Joyce sought to convey his view of life from his earliest childhood perspective. As the title of the book suggests, the reader is invited into the mind and inner workings of "the artist," but not one that already is, but an artist to be – "as a young man." Importantly, the artist, in this case, is a writer, and as words are the special medium of the writer, the reader sees "the child writer-to-be" immediately fascinated with words. The associations and imagery that words conjure and create in the mind of a child yet learning language are subtly communicated through Joyce's fascinating exploration. His study always reminds me of my own captivation with words, both as a child and even today.

I especially remember the first time I saw the word – or is it a phrase? – "vice versa," read in a "Dennis the Menace" cartoon of all places! Unsure of how to even pronounce it, I clamored for a dictionary to discover its meaning: "conversely; denoting reciprocal relationship or reversal of order." Hmm. That did little to solve my confusion. In the following weeks, almost as if the whole world had just recently discovered or created this word, I began to see it everywhere it seemed. It was only later, in the on-going development of my own vocabulary through the discovery of other and more fascinating words that I slowly began to realize that these "new words" which seemed to suddenly appear everywhere once I learned of them had always been there. The only, but very significant difference, was that now I was *aware* of them!

Our spiritual development works in much the same way. From a position of faith, God, the Great Spirit, the Ultimate – whatever word or phrase one might want to use to identify the Universal Life Force – is always present, existing in an eternal now whether we choose to acknowledge this "Being" or not. I may go for years without ever "reading" its presence, ignorant that the Word even exists; but once I turn in faithful awareness toward this Energy, I begin to recognize its presence everywhere. And, just as words take on different meaning given their context, now the "context" receives new meaning given "the Word." You know, sort of vice versa!

In Revelations, the final book of the Christian scriptures, Jesus, who is viewed as an incarnation of God, is referred to as "the Alpha and the Omega," a reference to the first and last letters of the classical Greek alphabet. God, it is proclaiming, is the first and the last, the beginning and the end, and, I might add, everything in between. Once I become aware of the Creator's presence in the world and in my life, like a new word, I will see the Creator's handwriting and word play everywhere. God of the Beginning and of the End, open my eyes to your presence in everything in between.

February 10
On the Wing of Prayer

In the Native American tradition, which is an integral part of my life, the eagle is one of the most esteemed of all the animals, revered as the carrier of our prayers to God. Certainly, in certain parts of the country, eagles are fairly plentiful. When I visited Kodiak Island, Alaska, I saw bald eagles as commonly as I might see crows in Ohio. But for most of my life, an eagle sighting is a rare and wonderful experience. Indeed, not every encounter of an eagle, for me, necessarily represents a significant spiritual occasion, but there have been times when, clearly, God was "breaking through."

Another important belief in the Native tradition is that nothing should be taken without something being given back. The traditional "gift" that is given when someone takes or harvests or asks for something is tobacco, one of the "four sacred medicines." Thus, when a dear friend of mine had offered to help a dear and old friend of hers take down some dead trees so that he could use them in his woodworking trade, I encouraged her to take along some tobacco as an offering before their harvest. Days later, I inquired if she had done so, and after she admitted failure, I told her that we would return to the site of their harvest soon and "complete the deal."

It was a month or more later when I next visited her home, and almost having forgotten my pledge, I suddenly recalled it late in the day as I was about to leave. Asking her to take me to the site of their harvest, we drove to the outskirts of town, down a long driveway to a farmhouse and then to the small grove of trees beside it. Stepping from the car, we walked almost prayerfully into the stand of trees as I pulled out some tobacco and readied myself for the offering. Clutching a small handful of my belated, proffered gift, I began to pray, honoring first the four directions and the presence of God all around us; then, lifting the tobacco offering into the air, I looked upward to honor Grandfather Sky, God's protective and loving presence always above us – and there he was: an eagle, yes, a manifestation of God's presence. A mere fifteen feet above us, sitting on a limb overlooking the whole prayer was a bald eagle; I immediately fell to my knees, for I knew I was standing on holy ground, and completed the offering, thanking the earth for all that it renders. I suppose the eagle had been there when we entered the grove of trees, although neither my friend nor I ever saw it, and it never left its perch until we had completed our prayer and offering and turned to walk away.

Many times, in their struggling faith, people just want to know that "God is there" and that what they do is okay, even "right." And sometimes, God does, in fact, break though our temporal reality to let us know he is there and that what we do is all right. When that bright sun of his presence breaks through the thick cloudbank, make sure you are not wearing your sunglasses, or worse yet, your blinders.

Immanent God, I thank you for the many times that you have blessed me with your reassuring presence, manifested in countless and often unassuming ways. Help me, help all people of faith, to live with our eyes wide open to your interactive presence in our lives. Too often we blind ourselves with doubt and fail to recognize the very thing that we long for, signs of your wondrous presence among us. May my prayers today and always be carried to you on eagles' wings.

February 11
Why Ask Why

One of the first words that most children seem to latch onto early in their language development is "No!" Not surprisingly, when this word makes it into our short list of common utterances, our physiological and emotional main attraction is ourselves. Early in our lives, each one of us truly "feels" as though he is the center of the universe, a universe, albeit, that doesn't extend much beyond one's grasp and vision. But as our sense of the universe expands and with the expansion, our interest in things beyond ourselves, another word creeps into our lexicon, one that probably brought us no end of annoying attention during our formative toddler years: "Why?" This simple interrogative expression reveals our innate desire to understand things outside of ourselves, and it is also, perhaps, the precursor to our demand for meaning, and the reasons for why we must do what we do right down to why we even exist at all. The questions sparked by "why?" are very important and "reasonable" considerations, but later in life, we likely discover that not only are the answers to our questions not quite so definitive as we would like, but they also appear to change as easily as the seasons.

Most of what distracts and grabs and holds our attention in the world are merely human "creations." Nothing that is political or economic is "natural" to the world, and arguably only a few things cultural might be. So, when we seek reasons as to why things are done, we should be aware that the answers are, like the things themselves, "contrived." In all things political and economic, and in most things cultural, there are no "natural" reasons for what we do, no inherent universal cause; we have created these things, and subsequently, the reasons for them shift with the reigning leadership which often influences and is influenced by the populace opinion. But human beings – all of creation – were not made *for* these things. Human beings made these things to create a certain order among each other and our societies, and sometimes, to create some meaning in our lives.

Long before politics, economics and cultures were created, human beings existed, and one might venture to imagine that before these human creations that now so often answer our questions of "why?" there was a more simple answer to our existence. Interestingly, however, these human institutional creations have become so important that we have forgotten to even consider this most fundamental question of our existence, relying instead on the answers that pertain to what we have created. What moves you more than anything else, and why does it? If your answer is something that is entirely connected to a human concept and invention, then say "no," let go of it, and ask yourself the question again and again until you reach the most "natural response." If you can't get there, then count yourself among the world of people who have been swallowed up by the tidal wave of human fabrication, and start praying that you might find a board to surf your way out of it. This is not to say that the human manifestations are wrong, for they are socially quite valuable; but rather, consider that individually you might be missing a more simple and fundamental guide for your life.

God of All My Questions, Creator of All the Answers, I can go through life half asleep to the powerful question of "why do I exist?" content instead with whatever I am told and whatever society creates for me to believe and to follow. Once upon a time, I awoke to an awareness of something beyond myself and I began to ask "Why?" Encourage me to not lose that sense of inquiry, the urgency to know, for I suspect that beneath all of the humanly created answers, you have an ultimate cause, a real reason, a divine answer waiting to be rediscovered.

February 12
Where is the Soul?

In my Theology courses, I love to challenge faithful students with the question of the soul's whereabouts. In religious and spiritual circles, we so frequently and easily speak of the soul as though it is a common "thing" – everyone has one, we might say - and yet we all know that thorough explorations of the human body have never been able to locate and identify it. No, we conclude, the soul is "metaphysical," which, to put it simply, means that it is beyond the physical. But in a world so driven by scientific evidence and empirical knowledge, such a label can seem drastically inadequate. And yet, in truth, when it gets right down to identifying the whereabouts of the soul, it is about all that we've got.

Indeed, we do live in a very physical world. Our sense of reality is almost exclusively governed by our sense of perception, a perception that is almost exclusively governed by things tangible. But the soul is a faith issue, and like the soul, faith extends well beyond the boundaries of the physical world. My question to students of "*Where* is the soul?" is really a "trick question." It moves them to think of the soul as a "thing" and it challenges them to identify or define the soul in tangible terms. But the real challenge for the person of faith is not to reduce the soul to an empirical explanation, but to willingly move beyond the tangible and to perceive the possibilities of there being a different way of seeing reality, one that transcends the physical.

Belief in the soul is a recognition of the Divine Spark that resides in us all – in all things; and while it does not take up residence in a physical way, nor is it simply "a spirit" that one catches. The soul is the heart of our very essence. If it resides, as Jews, Christians, and Muslims see it, in humans only, then it is our unique link to the Creator and to eternal life; and if it resides in all things, as many Eastern religions perceive it, then it is not simply the heart of my essence, but it is also the unifying strand linking me to the Universe of All Things.

Metaphysical God, in a social environment that is so driven by facts, statistics, and scientific evidence, my intellect as well as my heart can so often struggle to understand and accept spiritual principles and a reality that are supernatural, abstract and incorporeal. I appreciate and even desire those times when your metaphysical presence seems to break into my very physical reality, but help me to not lean on such needs, but to faithfully seek a deeper understanding of your presence and the truth of my very soul existing in a realm that transcends this transitory life.

February 13
Candlelight Love

Striking the match, the sulfurous flame flared up and then quickly receded to a gentle glint as I touched it to the wick of the candle. The energy transferred, the candle warmed to a soft glow as the cold, waxen walls that cupped the flame felt the first sweat of their impending meltdown. The tongue of fire, first leaping in a celebrative dance of new birth, lapped back and forth as if to lick the candle walls, and then momentarily came to attention, its ethereal muscles straining against a waver. Within minutes, a pool of melted wax cascading from the cupped walls began to encircle the flame, and the depth of the wick incrementally submerged. As if a spasm of courage, the bright tongue leaped up again, but as more wax pooled, the flame conceded to a smaller posture and seemed to concentrate on establishing a subtler pose.

This display is a near daily observation of my morning prayer as I call light into the darkness through the simple lighting of a candle. Watching this simple light show, however, has often fostered many other reflections in my meditative ritual, not least of which is its semblance to the way we often experience love.

Love is an energy that, I would like to believe, encircles our world at all times. As love has many visages, we see love manifested in a variety of ways. While it is perhaps the lesser of love's types, romantic love has a very important role in our lives, let alone the propagation of the human species! Occasionally, when the wick of our life comes into close contact with the energy of love, we, like the candle, flame on. Often, protectively cupping ourselves from the emotional traps of love, we, at first, cautiously embrace the soft warm glow that seems to fill us when we find ourselves attracted to another. But as a relationship begins to develop, we dare to let the tongue of love's fire dance and leap more spiritedly, and with the heat of the dance, feel our protective walls begin to soften and even melt. Surrounded and submerging in the pool of love's delight, we likely find, however, that maintaining the ecstatic dance of new love is beyond our capacity. Momentarily, we may resist the need to slow down and to develop a dance of

58

moderation. The flame leaps up again, but eventually concedes, now seeking to steady itself, love on an even keel, a more steady course.

Most people dream about, even long for the flash and brilliancy of romantic love, but looking to the candle, we ought to learn that the initial flare will likely be short-lived, and if the glow of love is to be lasting, a more temperate approach will need to be established. The candle flame that consistently flashes too brightly and boldly will likely be consumed by its own energy, the protective waxen walls melting into a drowning pool.

God of Love, the creative energy of your love once flashed the universe into being. Perhaps the stardust of our ancient selves longs to brush against that great fire again, and in our romantic encounters we feel its heat. Your love, and the energy of that love that sustains the universe, is a glorious light, and I am called to be a part of that light. Help me to live in love carefully, respecting the power of its energy. May I be a source of comfort, light, and warmth to another, but also to the universal need for love, without consuming the gift of this great fire.

February 14
Staying in Touch

Years ago, my wife and I started a tradition of sending out greetings and a letter to our many friends and acquaintances around Valentines Day. As teachers gearing up for exams and incoming research papers, and with my coaching season just a little over a month behind me, the more common Christmas letter just never worked for us. Between work and preparation for the upcoming holidays and the inevitable travel associated with that for us, the last thing we needed was to be creating time to get the letters out. By February, we figured, things would be slowing down a bit, and we might be better organized with our time management; plus, what better time to send our love and affection around to our dear ones than on Valentines Day?

Our mailing always includes a rather lengthy letter outlining the major events of our past year; some people seem to bristle at these "form letters," but we see it as an opportunity to stay in some kind of newsy touch, and it sure beats a simple signature on a card. Still, I will always admit that as well-intentioned as the effort is, I hate to think of how many of my "important relationships" hang on the thread of this annual form letter. It seems a weak ventilator, a hurried C.P.R. on a wheezing relationship.

Nearly every new calendar year, I make a *private* challenge – so that nobody else knows of my failure – to reenter the birthdates of family members and dear friends in my new calendar and to make a point of sending out a simple birthday card on each of their dates. I have yet to follow through with it, however. Good, healthy relationships matter to me, and are even an essential part of my spiritual development, but often there is very little evidence of their value in my life. Essentially, I deal with what is immediately before me each day, and, of course, family and friends are usually not what stand immediately before me each day, and so, too easily, correspondence with them gets shuffled to the side. I do hold each of them close at heart, but I could do much better in holding each of them, from time to time, more close at hand as well.

O God of Deep Companionship, today I pause to remember and pray for specific dear loved ones with whom I have not been in contact for a long stretch of time. Perhaps an activity, or a word, or a special shared song will spark a memory of them, and I will once again receive the blessing of their love and kindness in my life. Today I want to send out the "good vibrations" of my love to them as well. I have allowed my life to be too busy to stay in frequent contact, but may these dear loved ones know, somehow, this day, how loved by me they are.

February 15
Paired Dancing

A very popular television program at the time of this writing, in the era of "reality shows," pits couples against each other in a dance competition entitled, "Dancing with the Stars." As its label suggests, the contestants are not just a bunch of "average citizens," but nor are they true dance partners either. While one of the couplings is a legitimate dancer, the other is craftfully selected from the world of the public eye – a politician, an athlete, a musician or an actor. These two "dancers" must then work out a series of routines to various music and show that they can "move together" better than the others. True partner dancing is not something that people attain easily; it certainly comes with some good, hard work.

Paired dancing can serve as a good metaphor for relationships in general. For friends, lovers and acquaintances to work, live and love successfully, some tough, nitty-gritty work is almost always required. Independently, each person may have a good sense of rhythm and fluidity, but the coordination of the two individuals and the synchronization of their talents is essential if the pair is to dance in step with one another. Ideally, partners recognize each other's strengths and weaknesses, and then choreograph a relationship that does not exploit but enhances. Inevitably, during the "routine" of our relationships, there will be some stumbles.

Confrontations in a relationship also carry a dance "jingle": It takes two to tango. How do we respond to disagreements between friends and loved ones, even among acquaintances where consistent rhythm is not as necessary? If the steps of another offend me or cause me to trip, how do I respond; do I seek to reconcile or to retaliate? My response can either diffuse a tension or can heighten it; the communion or the corruption of the relationship will take two.

God of Partnership, you have called me into the dance of life, sometimes to dance alone, sometimes in a line, and sometimes with a partner. When I step into the paired dance, help me to let go of myself and to let the rhythm of two souls create the choreography. May we work toward balance and shared responsibilities, supporting and challenging one another to be, not necessarily our best individual selves, but our best together. And when we step out onto the dance floor, may the energy and cadence of our movements cause others to want to get up and join in the dance of life as well.

February 16
Who's Behind the Wheel?

Arriving at our destination, be it home or job or errand, we put the transmission of our vehicle into park and turn off the engine. Regardless if we will soon be leaving, such a routine is very practical, a standard operating procedure. I even find that when I am in a stalled out traffic jam, or waiting in a slow moving drive thru, I'll shut down the engine of my car rather than waste the gas. We understand the economy and prudence of such practice regarding mechanical things, but we often don't do the same for our physical and spiritual lives. If there were a "miles per gallon" sticker stuck on the window of ourselves, we would probably find a very poor average.

If we look at our bodies as a motor vehicle, then our minds would logically be the engine that propels the system. But unlike our cars, where the engine only runs when we turn it on, and it only truly compels the vehicle when we push on the accelerator and give it gas, we often leave the engine of ourselves running, even when we pull our vehicle in for the night and are ready to shut down. Yes, it would seem that more often than not, I hand over the key to myself to the engine of my mind who, like a belligerent child, goes racing off in all sorts of directions wasting energy, seeing flashing lights in the rear view mirror, and crashing into things. The truth of the matter is, most of us need some better brakes on our vehicles and, more fundamentally, to reclaim the keys to it.

Too often, my mind is in control of what I do, and I forget that I am the one who can control the mind. Busy with the tasks of my day, I frequently let my mind pester me like a back seat driver with all that I am doing wrong or failing to do. Caught up in media and cultural hype, I allow my mind to issue red alerts of fear about any and all sorts of issues, people, and concerns. I need to push on the brakes. Home from work, my mind nags me about what I need to do tonight and chastises me as lazy for wanting to just relax a bit and be present to my wife and family. I need to put it in park. And when I finally go to bed with the engine still idling, I restlessly think about what didn't get done today and what must be done tomorrow. I need to turn the engine off.

My spiritual life, guided by prayer, needs to slide into the driver's seat. Properly "trained," one's spirituality can provide a far better ride than the unattended mind will do. Through routine daily prayer and spiritual readings, the acuity of one's vision improves and quiets the fear-mongering, restless mind when it wants to rev up its engine and take over the wheel; and if the mind should temporarily seize control, a mantra and other simple prayers can be the brakes to bring the potential danger to a stop before it ever gets going full speed again.

Many young people await their sixteenth birthday when they will have their first legal opportunity to get behind the wheel of a car alone. But everyday of my life,

61

I make the choice of who or what is going to drive me through the day; will it be my mind recklessly absorbed and influenced by societal designs, or will it be my better spiritual self, sparked by the divine design within me? A mantra, daily prayer, and spiritual readings keep this latter driver better informed, more knowledgeable about the use of the accelerator and the brakes, more adept at seeing what is before me and what is in my mirrors. Loving God, I implore you to be my True Trainer, welcoming you through and into my daily prayers so that you might help me to be in better control of the speed, the direction, and the starting and stopping of my daily movements.

February 17
Sweet Harmony

When people listen to music with headphones on, they can often get so engrossed in their own musical dimension that they forget that someone else might be near, watching, talking or listening. What the neighbor is listening to, of course, is not usually the music of the headphone wearer, but the headphone wearer's "version" of that music. With headphones on, lost in the music, we usually don't realize what we sound or look like as we "jam away." Sometimes I have worn headphones and have fully engaged in the sing-along joy they can provide. With a good pair of headphones over my ears, I can become a "true rock star," hitting every note, and nailing every word of the lyrics. Of course, to those who might stumble in on my private little concert, my vocalizations sans instrumentation might be slightly less enjoyable if not downright discordant. I've snuck a listen to my harmonies sometimes when listening to music on headphones. Inside the phones, I am perfectly on key, but as I hold the note and lift the phone from my ear - ooo - not so much.

This kind of "headphone listening" is often how we go through much of our lives. Inside our "own little worlds," within the reason of our own minds, we are certain that all of our values, actions, words and ideas are all quite properly aligned, a wonderful harmony that all the world would delight to hear. But the "sounds" that we emit, quite often, are cacophonous; the lyrics that we sing may not be, in fact, the ones intended - the ones written into our very souls. It's good to sing our own songs, and to walk to the beat of a different drummer, but it's important that we don't get too smug in our own rhythm.

O God of Harmony, help me today to remove the headphones that I sometimes wear that hide the truth of "my sound." I want to send your good music into the universe. As I listen to you more carefully, may the song you have written within me emerge from me more clearly and most harmoniously.

February 18
A Frigid Flow

Whenever I hike along or kayak rivers and streams, I cannot help noticing the evidence of the water's ebb and flow. In Ohio, the banks of nearly any tributary are often tree-lined, but the trees and underbrush that serve to prevent erosion frequently give way to it, and today's shady overhang seems to eventually become tomorrow's unsuspecting snag in the murky waters. Natural and human-made refuse, swept away by fast flowing flood waters, frequently litter river banks and outline the breadth and the depth to which the waters have swelled. On a late summer day, when a river or creek's waters trickle serenely over shallow rocks and pebbles, it is hard to imagine that this tributary was once a raging torrent chewing away at the banks and sweeping away grand old trees, but I have experienced this force, and I know that it is not to be taken lightly.

One winter while on an annual expedition with some friends through a nearby city nature preserve, we came to our usual watery challenge, to ford a wide creek in mid-winter. I had crossed it many times before at this time of year, sometimes with a thin, icy sheath bearing a light dusting of snow, sometimes a quiet, reverential winter flow, and, occasionally a bone-chilling, knee-deep submersion that awakened and heightened all of my senses. But this particular year, we were in the midst of an early winter thaw from a recent ice storm, and the waters were flowing as fast and as furious as I had ever seen them at this time. With some concern, but with more confidence, I took the reins of command and asked my companions to let me ford the way, remembering where the sandbars that would aid the crossing task were, and where the rocks over which one might stumble might be. My first step into the torpid waters was a quick reminder to stay focused and to not become overly alarmed by the frigid flow, but the very next step assured me that this was unlike any crossing in years past. At knee-level, I could feel the dangerous tug of the murky current, and with the waters quickly numbing my submerged senses, the balance I sought in my next step seemed tenuous, at best. One or two more steps further and the waters rose above my waist and lapped at my chest. I wheeled around quickly realizing that crossing this stream today was neither brave nor courageous; it was stupid. My face must have screamed the freezing words of fear that suddenly rippled through me as I could feel the waters grip starting to wrench my feet from under me. One of my partners read my face well: "Are you alright?!" she yelled quickly. Trying to remain calm, my words and expression simply said, "No!" In a flash, she reached in and pulled me from the waters before they swept me away to what would have almost assuredly been an icy, watery grave.

Great God of Ebb and Flow, so often I create an illusory world of control. There are trails I have blazed and rivers I have forded that have given me a confidence that I can handle anything, that I am in charge of my destiny. But the power that you have infused into the created world and the force of life's happenstance-nature tell me otherwise. Sometimes I accept responsibilities or make decisions that can jeopardize my and others' emotional, mental, physical, and even spiritual safety. The waters - cold, deep and fast - rise quickly, and I look for a saving hand. Help me to make wise decisions this day that respect the power and energy of the situations in which I might find myself; and if I should falter, mercifully extend your hand and pull me out before I should drown.

The weekend. It is has such a nice ring to it, doesn't it? In America, it almost seems as though we live for the weekend, with all sorts of advertising and special offers meted out for this unique coupling of days. Even when our weekends are busy and full of other chores and responsibilities, it is still "the weekend," and that seems to at least mean a break from the normal routine and schedules of our daily – weekly – lives. Setting aside the time clocks and the demands of our jobs, ideally, on the weekend we do what we want to do, even if it is something that needs to be done.

I have no intention in engaging in scriptural interpretation here, but what a wonderful stroke of genius it was for the earliest writers of the Hebrew Scriptures to have God rest on the seventh day of creation. They must have already known how wedded we can become to our jobs, how all-consuming work can become for us, and, more insightfully, how much we need to put it all aside on a regular basis and to do something else. In scripting, "God rested on the seventh day from all his work which he had made," those writers validated the necessity of rest that surely every worker then already felt in his bones; and by noting that even God needed to rest, they wrote the goodness of this rest right into the people's hearts.

Of course, in the very next line of this same story, the authors note that God ups the ante of the needfulness and the goodness of this day of rest by adding, "And God blessed the seventh day, and sanctified it" (Gn. 2:2-3). In God's blessing this day and making it holy, our need for a break from work becomes not simply a physical respite, but also an invitation – and later, a Commandment – for spiritual nourishment as well. As God rested, so too should we. And as God designated the seventh day, the Sabbath, as holy, so too should we honor the Creator of all things and this day that he has sanctified.

Contrary to what many Christians believe, technically, the Sabbath, the seventh day, is Saturday, and not Sunday. But given our modern work schedules and demands, I don't much think it matters exactly which day we honor, so long as we honor at least one. The fact that church, synagogue and mosque services are traditionally held on a certain day, and with specific historical reasoning within each tradition, can undoubtedly govern or, at least, influence which day a person chooses, but not everyone today can truly orchestrate that commitment. But it is important that we mindfully make an effort on at least some day through our week to step away from the busyness of our lives and observe a "Sabbath day."

Gratefully, for many of us, "the weekend" is a full two days and not just one day of rest. This fact ought to all the more allow us the ability to observe a Sabbath day in our week. Do something fun and revitalizing, something that allows you to let go of the rest of the week's pressures and work responsibilities; but let there also be time to reflect and to remember who we are and whose we are. Life is a gift to be enjoyed and we dishonor the Creator if we allow it to be an endless drudgery of work. So step back and remember that God rested too, and then honor the One who created you and commands you to enjoy it!

Restful God, too often I allow the demands and the responsibilities of my work to be my master. Help me to rein in this excessive attention to my employment, and to remember the simple and invigorating aspects of life. I need to carve into my week with greater fervor than the demands of my job, time and space to playfully enjoy life, and to reverentially give honor to the one who has created it.

February 20
The Sunrise of You

One of the things that I miss the most since I left teaching is seeing the sunrise each day. I don't miss it because I sleep in each day, although I clearly don't keep the same hours any longer, but I rarely leave home now, and when I do the sun has already made a pretty good climb up the ladder of its course. I face the east each morning as I sit down to write and can see the sky above the trees and bushes that line our backyard, but the horizon is well below the neighborhood houselines and so I miss out on any of the grand fury of the sun's rising.

When I was teaching everyday and the sun rose early on long days, I would have these incredible morning drives. A short stretch of my daily trail cut due south with the eastern horizon quite spread open to my left. So many times the sun was just below the horizon while I drove this stretch and the sky would be a smoldering bank of embers just ready to ignite once again. From this southerly course, I would then turn west, not offering a particularly advantageous view of the sunrise, but the highway behind me often served as a bowling alley for the sun's glowing and rising orb, and as it rose, the rays rolled right up my back and into my rearview mirror, a perfect strike. More than once I darn near ran off the road shooting wondrous glances into my various mirrors, amazed at the flourish creeping up behind me. On shorter days when I arrived at school in the dark, I was still blest with an east facing window, and even though there were homes across the street from me, there was space and sky enough in the school's front yard for me to have wonderful views of the sun's grand entrance. As luck would have it, the sun often rose directly between two homes and straight into my awaiting and astonished gaze.

To be present to any sunrise is good, but on some mornings, one feels especially blessed when she witnesses a magnificently beautiful rise. As if the Creator has crouched down and tossed a large hand full of twigs on the orange, purple and pink glowing embers just below the horizon, suddenly flames spark and then the whole eastern ridge bursts into flames. With the whole of the eastern sky temporarily ablaze in fiery color, the rim of the sun swiftly slips over the horizon and if sight had sound, the fanfare would be deafening as the golden orb ascends in all its flaming grandeur.

Perhaps you will think that I am exaggerating, but when human beings are "on fire" with life, when the life of the Divine burns within them, they too are just like a magnificently beautiful sunrise. When a person meets such a one as these, he can see right away the notable difference of the holy one, and can feel the warming glow. And I do not mean just "Saintly people;" I mean people like you and me. Call it "having a good day" for starters, but it is so much more than that. When a person "gets it," when she truly feels and understands the blessing that each day of life is and she wears it with a gratitude that runs as deep as the blessing is wide, then she literally glows. She is on fire - kindled, stoked and blazing with the love of the Divine. To see and be with such a one is to stare eastward into the glory of the rising sun. So go ahead, let the fire of God burn brightly within you; arise like the sun!

Astonishing Creator, you have blest me so many times with the gift of a magnificent sunrise. You lit my day, stirring the sleeping embers of my heart with the glorious view of the sun's rising splendor. Ignited by these blessings, I too can carry the brilliance of the divine spark within me, its glow and warmth more than my body can contain. Enkindle me and let me be ablaze with your love.

February 21
Spiritual Map Quest

With the onslaught of *MapQuest* and then the more personalized GPS systems, the old traditional map seems to be slipping out of pragmatic existence. Like digital, LED watches spelling the demise of children's ability to read a conventional, number-faced clock, these ready, easy-to-use directional systems appear to make maps obsolete, unnecessary at least. But what so many mapquesters and GPS users don't realize is that the old conventional map offers and, on a variety of levels, represents something more.

Simply put, the reason why *MapQuest* and GPS systems are so "successful" is that they give straightforward and, much more often than not, accurate directions from point A to point B. But during the process of using these aids, many times the person using them, essentially, has no idea of the direction he is going, nor any specific sense of where he presently is; the person is merely following another's directive, confident that he will arrive at the requested destination using the shortest route possible – and usually does. But in following another's directives, the seeker often fails to be observant of other signs and details of the route and is often oblivious to the compass-direction by which he is traveling. Furthermore, alternative routes are rarely pursued, unless, by accident, a wrong turn is made and the system shuffles its deck to renegotiate the next course of action.

When I use a conventional map, however, I see "where I am" in proximity to other things – streets, cities, and states. I see where I *can* go, alternatives that provide different sightseeing opportunities, or longer, but perhaps faster routes. Setting up my own course of action via a map lets me know not just the destination to where I am going, but what is along the way that might offer further interest and enjoyment. And I want this information in my road travels just as surely as I do in my spiritual journey.

Too often, people give their spiritual lives over to a MapQuest religion, or the directives of a charismatic, spiritual-GPS advisor. Such direction finding can be very helpful, but one should never toss away her own ability to read the maps as well. *MapQuest* and GPS systems provide valuable aids in getting us where we want to go, but they do not reflect anything of the personal interests and needs of the seeker. They merely tell her which way to go and where to turn and when, and when followed blindly, the traveler is oblivious to any other possibilities. Maps engage the traveler; help her to see where others have gone, and where she could go. Given this insight, she then might consult the "system" to find out which way is preferably suggested and why. Traveling in the journey of life is too important, too personal, to be given over fully and blindly to another's directions. God has equipped us with so many wonderful tools with which we might find our way; we would do well to utilize all of our tools – maps included.

God of My Direction, it is you that I seek in everything I do and everywhere I go. Just as modern life oftentimes seeks to make things "easy and accessible" for people, I can easily drift into what is easiest and most accessible for my spiritual life as well. Help me not to relinquish control of my spiritual life, but to take an active role in the mapping out of my spiritual journey. The helpful directions and knowledge of others are important sources of guidance along my journey, but encourage me also to willingly and knowingly engage in the directional decisions of my voyage.

February 22
Presidents' Day

As a child, I remember honoring the birthdays of Presidents Washington and Lincoln annually. These extolled dates, both in the month of February, each gave us pause to recall the history and the mythology that surrounds these two important models in American history. Somewhere in the 1980s, however, an evolving movement to combine their dates under one commemorative date known as "Presidents Day" finally came to fruition. Since then, my memory always recalls my childhood reflections on Washington and Lincoln, while I seek to honor the present, and all former presidents for the enormous task they welcome in leading one of the world's greatest countries. From my vantage point, it's a thankless task, and it is beyond me why anyone would covet such a responsibility!

Interestingly, there is some discrepancy even today as to the spelling of this national day of recognition: Presidents, President's, or Presidents'. The middle one, President's, is a singular form and, generally, only refers to Washington when used. The other two forms might be seen as limited to Washington and Lincoln, but I have come to prefer to extend it to all presidents, with a special wish for the insightful light and courage of Washington and Lincoln to guide the present leaders. Both in what this land has to offer as well as in what the people of this land seek to offer the world, the United States truly is an incredible beacon of hope for freedom and justice. Surely, our history is not a pure and innocent one, nor is our present mode of governing and procuring justice for all without blemish. But, by and large, the freedoms and opportunities available to the citizens of the United States are unlike many others across the globe, setting a high bar for us to achieve and for others, perhaps, to aspire. The leaders of such a country need our prayers always. The power to govern is a right offered to all, but the selection to do so should be seen as a privilege, an honor to be of legislative service to the greater good of the entire country; but this power, as so much classic literature has portrayed, can be corruptive, and absolute power can corrupt absolutely.   How many wonderful orators and leaders have fallen to the temptations of their power-filled offices, have forgotten their call to the service of all, while embracing instead a self-serving few. However true or mythological the stories of George Washington and Abraham Lincoln might be today, these two men are the personification of self-sacrificing leadership, and their stories, careers, and lives serve as fine models for all of us, and especially our nation's leaders.

In my thirty-plus years of voting as an American citizen, I have probably been more disgruntled about our elected officials than I have been happy with them. But regardless of what my opinion is about this or that leader's character and policies, I figure that the best way I can serve those who are elected to serve us is to pray for them. May they have the vision to see what is best for our country in the long run, and the courage to strive for this vision in the present.

God of Truth, I pray for the leaders, the elected officials, of our country. A true democracy, where everyone's voice is heard and represented would perhaps be chaotic on the grand, national scale. So in our Republic of representation, bless those who are called and selected to serve the greater good of the country. Give them the insight to see truly and truthfully what is best for our country: its land and resources, its people, and the relationships it forges with all. Make them strong in character, models of justice and goodness for its citizens, and wise in judgment, beacons of hope and peace in a divisive world.

February 23
Measuring a Decision

Like many words, the etymology of the word "meditation" has a number of derivations. One of the most common, from the Latin, is "to think over, consider seriously." A form of this thoughtful consideration, a more poetic view, is captured in, perhaps, an older Indo-European root "to measure." No matter which version one chooses, the notion of "weighing" a decision seems to pervade both.

Connotatively, meditation is usually associated with prayer. If I told someone that I meditate daily, she would not likely think that I was merely sitting down each day to do some "thoughtful decision-making." It is far more likely that the person would assume that I was spending time daily in quiet, prayerful reflection. But when the idea of "decision-making" is added to the thoughtful, reflective equation of meditation, the posture of meditating becomes far more active, and given its prayerful posture, it is also "interactive."

So often, individuals take on enormous amounts of stress when weighing an important decision. Often, we seek advisors, counselors, and confidantes as we process the decision at hand, but in the end, if we are bold enough, we take the full weight upon our shoulders and step forward with a committed choice. People of faith have a ready partner in all decision-making: God. The problem with this "source" of partnership, for most people, is that we don't get easy, ready answers. While most of us would be a bit embarrassed by the public pronouncement, there is still something in all of us that sometimes just wants a clear answer like Dorothy gets in the classic movie *The Wizard of Oz* when the witch writes across the sky: Surrender Dorothy! Hers was not a requested nor a prayerful response, but it was clear and accessible, and that is often far more than what we get when we seek the advice and counsel of others – let alone God!

But meditative prayer is where our decisions should be placed. Meditation provides a calming environment and a quiet posture within which one can more reasonably face the present puzzle. The advice and ideas of others, while often valuable, can too often be just so much noise, interference tangling the airwaves of our adjudication. To place oneself in the stillness of God's presence is to quiet the many voices, and to let the soft whispers of the heart emerge more distinctly. If one has sought outside help, meditative prayer might be the best and last place that the weighing and measuring are done; the suggestions have been laid before the decision-maker, time now to quiet the voices and let God write upon the sky of our heart.

God of Meditative Silence, I did not enter this world alone, nor am I called to face each day and each day's decisions alone. You have gifted me with a mind with which to reason, and friends and family with whom I can confer. But in prayerful meditation, all of the voices and turmoil of measuring a decision can be sifted, quieted, and in this space, the true direction may emerge. Lead me into your quiet fold, burdened as I often am with choices, and let me listen to your voice, the quiet comfort of your whisper.

February 24
Get Out of the Way

While meditation provides a comfortable and comforting forum in which to measure and thoughtfully consider decisions, when we regularly bring such adjudication into our prayer life, we may be only cleaning out a closet and placing its contents in the garage. Another aspect of meditation not captured so well in its etymology is "silence." Now, this prayerful silence is valuable in decision–making, but decision-making is not equally valuable to prayerful silence. In fact, prayerful silence is not simply quietude, but also emptiness.

Arguably, prayer and meditation are not the same thing. Although one might reasonably assume that meditation is a form of prayer, the focus and intention of meditation is most often quite specific, whereas prayer assumes a very broad spectrum. Hence, it might be better to say that I can bring my decision-making into my prayer, but I empty myself of all decisions when I meditate.

Like decision-making, too often when we pray, we come to the table with all sorts of issues, ideas and possibilities, and we present them in prayer to God like one might present a business idea at the conference table. "Here, God, here is what I have researched and discovered my possibilities to be; now would you please make the decision for me." Or, perhaps, I arrive at prayer with my decision already privately made, and I emerge from the prayer imagining that God has given me the stamp of approval or validation through my prayerful posturing. But if we see meditation as more about silence and emptiness, then when I meditate, I come empty handed to the table, no preconceived notions, just an empty vessel seeking God's fulfillment.

Such emptiness is the real hard work of meditation. We humans love to be in control of things, especially decisions that concern our present and future. But if I truly seek God's counsel, then I must truly step back, get out of the way, and allow God to fully inhabit my space. How can I possibly hear God's voice, or receive God's "sign," when my space is so cluttered with the noise of my and others' voices and exhibits.

God of the Emptiness of Silence, still and quiet me. When I come to you in meditative prayer, help me to come empty-handed, not full of myself and my ideas and my desires. Empty, hollow and still, I will await your soft presence and your quiet voice to slowly nestle in beside and within and all around me so that I might more clearly know your will.

February 25
Snow Skiing in Ohio?

It should come as no shock that Ohio is not exactly a "ski destination." With its highest "peak" near the center of the state, a towering 1549 feet, the opportunities to carve some good grooves down the slope are a little slim. Ironically, the state's best ski hills are not near its highest point, and while the Appalachian foothills of southeastern Ohio are the most "mountainous" in appearance, their annual snowfall is quite limited. To its credit, however, I think that Ohio does the best it can to meet the ski needs of its residents making the most of the hills it has and the climate it gets.

To compensate for the erratic and unpredictable climate and the frequent shortage of snow, the local ski hills resort to "making snow." A good cold snap will typically lack precipitation, so the Ohio ski "resorts" will pump their own "snow" from private holding ponds creating a ski base that is often two to three feet deep. Whenever I go for an afternoon or evening of skiing in the late winter, I am always fascinated by this interesting appearance of winter on the slopes, while all around the landscape is brown and snowless. Driving to the ski destination one would think that the day's intentions are futile; but on the slopes, one might believe that winter yet abounds.

This stark contrast is most evident when I ascend the slopes via the lifts, and, standing atop the ski hill, look out over the valley and opposing hillsides. Under my skis and down the slopes immediately before me, I view hillsides dressed in a full wedding gown of snow. But looking out beyond the parking lots to the countryside that spreads out below, I see a landscape that wears pauper's clothes with ne'er a hint of white to be found.

Many times in our lives, our environment or the conditions surrounding it are far less than ideal, and so often we blame this less than ideal reality for preventing us from doing what we want to do or we use it as the excuse for why we don't do what needs to be done. But "ski resorts" in the middle of Ohio are evidence that sometimes, if one wants something bad enough, or if something urgently needs done, a person can often find the ways and means to accomplish his goal. If I want to deepen my spiritual growth and enhance my daily prayer life, what is preventing me? Oh, I've seen a warm westerly wind or an afternoon winter rain quickly wipe out the efforts of days of snow-making; desire and effort are not always enough to achieve one's ends. But the fact that we generally have a season of skiing every year in Ohio is sign enough to me that desirable ends can often be achieved through some energetic effort.

Creative God, who knows how and with what you spun this universe into being, but here it is, made from something or created from nothing. So often I use the lack of perfect conditions or the absence of what I need to excuse my lack of production or my absence of effort. I realize that not everything can be accomplished by simply willing it into being, but I also know that I could likely achieve far greater things with better initiative and greater effort. Help me to utilize the gifts I do have so that I might better reach for the things that we could have.

February 26
Jalapeno Desires

I have a son who takes great pride in being able to eat and "enjoy" very spicy, hot food. For me, the idea of learning or "training" to endure the intense tastes seems incongruent with eating enjoyment; subsequently, I have pretty much avoided excessively spicy foods. One year, however, while I was "single-again," I went shopping with my housemate who snatched up a couple of jalapeno peppers from the produce aisle and tossed them into our cart. Now I had never eaten one of these little guys before, much less had purchased one, so when we later decided to fix up a special tray of nachos, I saw no particular problem with cutting up a couple of these harmless-in-appearance-peppers and spreading them around on the late night snack. After adding a couple of other toppings and then toasting the whole array in the oven, I encountered my first real bite of a jalapeno pepper. I will never forget the experience. That simple slice of pepper on that harmless crispy chip went from, "oo, that's kind of spicy," to a full-blown five alarm fire in my mouth. As I raced from the living room to the kitchen to douse the flames with water, a surge of fear ran through me that my esophagus itself was going to collapse under the intensity, and that my breathing which seemed to create a backdraft would also cease to function. For a time, no cold liquid seemed to adequately turn back the sensation of fear and discomfort.

I love all forms of sweet peppers and enjoy their colorful display in a salad or a wok or any variety of vegetable dishes. People often wrongfully assume that a bright red or orange sweet pepper will certainly be hot, only to find that they truly are absolutely harmless. But I have come to know that a simple, little green jalapeno pepper, no bigger than the size of my pinkie finger can pack a wallop that a person had better be ready to receive. I find that "selfish desires" can sometimes be just like these little jalapenos.

Siddhartha Gautama, the one who is known as "the Buddha," understood that at the heart of all of our human suffering, not simply physical, but more importantly, emotional and spiritual dis-ease, is selfish desire. The second of his Four Noble Truths offers a clarification to the first Truth which proclaimed that all life is suffering; and the cause of that suffering the second Truth unveils is selfish desires. What is not so clearly conveyed in the Buddha's Truths, however, is, like the little jalapeno, how unsuspecting and harmful these desires of ours can be.

Desire is not the evil here. The real question lies more in our desire "for what" and "to what extent." I desire a deeper relationship with God; no harm there. But what desires prevent me from fully pursuing that deeper relationship with the Creator; "ay," Hamlet once said, "there's the rub!" For these little personal desires of ours can sometimes be a dangerous flame that is not so easily put out. The end of Buddha's teaching, "Nirvana," means "to blow out" or "to extinguish." But as I learned from my first unwitting encounter with the "harmless jalapeno," dousing the flames of our selfish desires takes more than a simple sip of sacrifice, more than a cupful of kindness. Extinguishing a "jalapeno desire" can take gallons of thoughtful and careful effort.

God of my Desires, I find my reflections on your Being are both colorful and delicious. But I am so easily drawn toward other things that appear equally bright and similarly delectable. In you, I find true nourishment, in flavors like no others. Teach me to be careful in my selection and pursuit of desires, to know that what appears harmless can sometimes be most dangerous. May the heat of my passionate desire for you prevent me from being burned by the unsuspecting flames of my own selfish desires.

February 27
Electrical Desires

Around every electrical power station, one will find a high chain-linked fence rimmed with barbed wire, or a brick-pillar and metal-rod fortress encompassing the power's boundaries. Such protective structures not only indicate the importance of the energy walled within, but suggest something about its dangerous nature. Even with less enclosed aspects of the electric system, overhead and buried wires, we are given numerous advertisements and signs to "beware the danger" above or below us. Apparently, electricity is a very bad thing.

Electricity, however, is obviously not some evil force in our midst from which we should shy away, or attack and destroy. Quite the contrary, without electricity, for most of us, our lives would be pretty miserable. Providing not only desired light, electricity heats and cools our homes and foods, while we clean, sustain and enjoy just about everything else due to the power of its energy. Certainly, electricity is a very good thing.

The truth is electricity is really neither good nor bad; it just is an important source of energy, like our desires. Desire too can be a much-maligned energy within each of us. Sacred texts speak of desire as being a root of evil, a serpent tempting us to eat from some forbidden tree. But desire is also the energy that we call upon in our service of God and one another. The desires to achieve, to discover, to succeed have all brought wonderful inventions and comforts to our lives, like, say, electricity! Yes, desire and electricity do have much in common. They are both energies that stimulate us, opening doorways of possibilities for us and providing opportunities for broader experience and deeper understanding; but they both can kill us as well. A person who does not recognize and respect the power of electricity and handles it carelessly can easily be bitten by it, even die. Likewise, if we allow our desires to become selfishly driven, and do not respect the power of our desires left unchecked, carelessly pursuing only for our own powerful pleasure, we can be bitten, even die. Even the "proper use" of electricity and our desires can lead to harm. The energy of each is such that if one does not properly respect it, is not carefully aware of its power, even in a "good use" of them, the person can get burned.

Powerful God of all Energies, my desires are neither good nor bad; they are simply "my desires." What makes my desires valuable is how I use them; to what end or purpose are they directed? When my desires are selfishly driven, they are a live electrical line twisting and snapping on the ground, or an unprotected power station left to the whims of vandals and the ignorant. But if I turn my desires toward you, and if I direct my passionate appetite toward the service of others, this powerful energy not only will be less dangerous, but also can be a true source of light and warmth and comfort to many. Thank you for all of the energies that sustain our lives; help me to be a source of energy in helping to sustain all life.

February 28
Suffering through Winter

I love winter and enjoy the different opportunities for exercise, play, prayer and reflection that it can offer. When the snows come, I want them to stay, and so I embrace the crisp and deep freeze of a winter's day, appreciating its companionship with the snow's beauty and offerings. In my "neck of the woods," warming winds on cloudy days can blow through and imperceptibly eat away at the snow pack; on such days, I find myself clinging to the quietly receding cover, worrisome that I have not yet had my fill of winter's gifts. But when the bright day arrives, when the sun sparkles warmly on the winter morning and the temperatures begin to inch and then leap above freezing, I find my affection for winter melting more quickly than the mounds of snow at the end of my shoveled driveway and the icicle swords acquiescing into mere daggers. Sun-splashed mornings with a scent of some distant spring wafting in the air softens my frigid frolicking, and my body begins to remember the joy of soaking up solar energy.

I do not suffer through winter like many people feel they do, but I suppose that I have learned to enjoy winter somewhat like I have learned to embrace suffering. To be sure, in both there is a kind of physical hardship; but in each there is something to be gleaned from the challenges as well. I never long for suffering like I do sometimes long for a good, hardy winter, but I do find that suffering can enhance my experience of and deepen my joy in living. Once suffering descends like a quiet night snowfall or with the gusto of a winter storm, and I drop my resistance to its inevitable and temporary presence in my life, I begin to appreciate the fragility of life and thus honor the joy-filled gifts that also lie beneath the chilling blanket. And when suffering abates, as it always will do, like waking to the sun-splashed day, I see life more brilliantly and more ardently than ever before.

God of Winter and Spring, of Suffering and Rejuvenation, I thank you for the ebb and flow of life. While I do not long for the discomforts of life's wintery challenges, help me to recognize in them the restoration that is so often being carved out in me through their icy flow. Assist me in seeing that suffering is but a winter's season, and that in its melting, I will be called back into the warmth and excitement of spring's renewal, stronger and more desirous in my deepened appreciation for the gift of life.

February 29
A "Leap" Year: The Spirituality of Bread

Having dropped off my son and daughter-in-law at the airport for an early morning vacation-flight, I swung into the parking lot of a local family bakery that had recently opened to pick up a couple of morning sweets for my wife and me. A year and a half out of my full time teaching career, I had begun contemplating what my next career, or at least temporary job, move might be. "Part-Time Help Wanted," the flyer taped to the bakery counter whispered to me, and as I paid my bill, my mind suddenly started clicking off all of the reasons why *this* might be a fun opportunity for me. So I applied, and two weeks later I was on the other side of the counter selling baked goods.

In much less than a year, the life of that bakery, as well as my own, would change dramatically. From a simple satellite store selling fresh goods baked at the parent store, our location, adding an all-wood burning oven, became the sole operation of the family business and my small part-time customer service job morphed into a nearly full-time baker *and* customer service post. Through the rising expectations of my new job, I was acutely aware of some greater leavening force at work in the dough of my life.

When he was demonically tempted in the desert during an extended fast to "command this stone to become bread," Jesus responded by quoting the Hebrew Scriptures, "One does not live by bread alone" (Lk. 4:3-4). Indeed, our bodies need more varied sustenance than simply bread, but bread has long been something of a symbol of "food for the world." And with my own hands now kneading the ingredients of its making, I began to see deeper and more spiritual layers in this essential nourishment. Learning about and partaking in the process of the bread making, from grain to loaf, I realized how this elemental art mirrored so much of our own spiritual journeys. While each loaf of bread has fundamental components - flour, salt, yeast and water – the measurement of each of these along with the addition of any other sundry ingredient can and does radically change the final product; even the weather, the climate and the timing of the process have significant effects on the end result, the loaf of bread.

No two loaves of bread, not even of the same type of bread, are ever "the same," and just as surely are we all different, and not just in appearance, but in the deeper folds of our ever-evolving creation as well. Although we are all created, fashioned by the Master Baker, the ingredients of our spiritual development come from so many different lands and the kneading of these elements are so affected by our various environments. Indeed, our entire lives are something of an ongoing leavening and shaping process, and perhaps the baking itself is never done until we transition into the next life where the fullness of our own bread of life comes to fruition.

God of Sustenance, you provide us with the essentials of life - the flour, salt, and water – and knead into us the vital yeast of the spirit that can spur our growth, our rising. All that is around me also affects my development, augmenting my physical and spiritual expansion or diminishing it. Continue to work your hands into the dough of my life, kneading me when I grow slack or slow; and let me be evermore mindful of the effects that my environment, those given and chosen, have upon all that is within me and whatever might come from me. Shaped in your image and to your likeness, may I be bread for the world.

March 1
Who Needs New Years?

So how are your "New Year's Resolutions" coming - or going? Perhaps two months ago, you were all fired up about how "this year things are going to be different," and so after celebrating the end of another calendar year, you "turned over a new leaf" and spoke of hopeful changes, sealing them with the baptism of your resolutions. But that was then; what is it now?

It is interesting how so many of us need certain important calendar dates to motivate us towards the changes that we need, often, every day of our lives. We look for the perfect timing or some magical alignment of the planets thinking that these external charms will ensure the success of our endeavors. A certain holiday, the beginning or end of a school year, a birthday, or the most common, New Years - all of these dates can serve as the pivotal calendar moment in which we first or repeatedly make our leap towards change. As if I began yesterday, today or tomorrow, the results would be entirely different.

Like New Years Resolutions themselves, there is another famous cliché that, despite my never liking it much for its triteness, I have to still honor it for its simple truth: "Today is the first day of the rest of your life." If something is in need of and worth changing in my life, then what am I waiting for?! Today is the perfect timing that I have been looking for; today, I begin where I am. To wait for a certain, special date is likely just one more piece of my procrastination pie, a dessert I feast on regularly. Instead, I can get up from the table today and begin affecting the changes in my life that I long for; and when I falter, as I inevitably will, tomorrow is the next "first day of the rest of my life," and I can begin again.

O God of Resolve, we mark the highlights of our lives and of history with special dates and titles. But my solitary life, and this world's existence, sometimes can ill-afford the wait that we ask them to carry. Perhaps there is a change that needs to come in me or in our world, and it ought to begin this day. Help me to not fall back on the comfy chair of waiting, with its cushions of dates and perfect timing. Stand me up and push me out the door; let me begin with hope and a prayer to live and to be the changes I hope to see in my life and in the world.

March 2
Supporting a Slump

I am very big ice hockey fan. Having played the sport from the Pee Wee leagues all the way through high school, and then following it closely on and off though my adult years, I was ecstatic when my "home city" of Columbus won a NHL franchise years ago. I jumped aboard their "fan wagon" immediately, and have been a true supporter ever since, despite their many - and continuous – lean and struggling years. At a recent game with the team locked in the jaws of a vicious slump, my affinity with them slipped into another level.

On this particular game night, the team was playing, honestly, about as badly as I had ever seen them, at least in many years. Noticeably frustrated and totally lacking self-confidence, they made glaring errors and gave up "soft goals" as they stumbled into yet another ego-crushing loss. At times, the opposition seemed to be playing "keep away," like two older brothers teasing their kid brother. As the game slipped further and further out of the home team's grasp, and another series of insufficient play was registered, the crowd began to hurl disgruntled rounds of "boos." I, too, was disgusted, to be sure, frustrated by "my team's" inability to find itself and move forward again, but I could not join in on the negative fray.

Professional athletes get paid way more than the true value of the function of their "work," but that issue aside, most of them take what they do very seriously, and just like their fans want from them, they too want to win. "Our team" is very young, peppered with a few seasoned veterans, and I know they are doing everything they can to bring home a victory, but for all their desire and hard work, right now, they simply cannot get through some of the more difficult and intangible mental aspects of the game. I am certain that they are "dying inside." And last night's boos were no consolation.

Not only every religious tradition, but probably in most societies or cultures in general, people are asked to be sympathetic, if not empathetic; we are all well familiar with the cliché to "walk a mile in another's (insert appropriate footwear)." But how well do we really live this "other perspective"? Sure, there are times when others' lack of effort or interest or success needs to be called to task, but many times, our own needs and expectations cause us to rain down so much negative sentiment on the very people who are already buried beneath the dung hill.

God of All Lost Causes, your view of this creation must often be like my view of my struggling, stumbling and losing hockey team. Though you may be disgusted with our efforts and many of our results, I believe that your love for all of your creation continues to breath life into this "franchise," hoping that one day we humans will "get it," will understand our place and role in the oneness of all things and will play up to our ability. Help me to be a more positive and loving supporter of all life as well. Challenges and expectations have their place, to be sure, but let me recognize in the eyes and efforts of others what they need to better succeed, and to offer my support rather than my disdain.

March 3
Quilting a Spiritual Life

My wife is a quilter. She made her first quilt sometime back in high school, and has dabbled with quilting ever since for much of her life. Before I met her, a quilt to me was pretty much just a somewhat fancier bed covering. I had seen quilts many times at department and linen stores, and while they were usually a little pricier than a simple full size comforter, the cost seemed quite reasonable. But when I started visiting quilt stores with my wife, I was initially appalled at the cost of a handmade quilt; they were easily three to ten or more times more expensive than a department store quilt! Why would anyone buy such a covering when he could go to a large department store and get the same thing for so much less. Except, it isn't "the same thing."

Although they are a bedcovering, handmade quilts are more like artwork; and like artwork, the amount of time, energy, thought, and material that goes into the finished product is almost incalculable. The problem is, like so much else in our world, factories and mechanized production reduced the true value of the real handiwork of a quilt. A mill factory can set up a patchwork quilt with machines that sew the pieced top, and then stitch the batting and the backing altogether; within an hour, perhaps, a new quilt.

But when someone makes a handmade quilt, first there is the decision about the design. Once a design is chosen, then there is the selection of fabrics, and the effort to bring variety and color schemes into the overall design. Buy the fabric, and now the quilter will begin to cut and place and pin the pieces together. Usually, this piecework will be done in squares, and once all of the squares are completed, then the quilter will hand stitch the squares together. With the artwork of the pieced top completed, the project is certainly underway, but the job is far from done. Next, the batting, a center layer of material originally used to provide warmth and now also used for quilt-stitching effect, and the backing will be pinned to the patchwork top – and then, the quilting begins! Heretofore, the work has only been "stitching," but the sewing of the three layers together by hand with intricate designs is quilting. From start to finish, such a job, done by careful and thoughtful hands, will take months. So now, put a price on it. And when the quilt is done by your mother or your grandmother, your uncle or your son, all who will inevitably put their loving touch into each stitch, can you see how the cost begins to escalate to a point where it truly is "priceless." Thus, "real quilts" are so often given and never purchased at a cost.

Our spiritual lives are unquestionably very much like quilting. I can go to a variety of stores and get some type of covering for my bed, maybe even an inexpensive quilt. It will look nice and it will serve the purpose of keeping me warm, but it will do no more than that. A handmade quilt comes with "a history." From the chosen fabric, which may even include a loved one's old clothes, and the selected design, which may incorporate an ethnic connection, down to the piece stitching and quilt binding that are done with human hands that we, perhaps, know or have known, hold or have held – this quilt is truly one made of love and devotion. So, what kind of spiritual blanket do I lie under? How much time, how much love and devotion am I willing to give to my spiritual life. To the careless observer, there may be little difference, but when I pull that cover over me each day and night, there will be a world of difference.

Comforting Creator of our patchwork lives, although I long for a warm and meaningful relationship with you, too often I choose to stitch my life to you in inexpensive, time-saving methods. If I truly seek to be a comforter of love in this world, I need your guiding hand to quilt the pieces of my life to the fabric backing of all life and to you, the warm batting that connects and is between us all. My spiritual life ought not be a simple purchase, but a labor and artwork of love, with a living and protective history.

March 4
Illiteracy of Love

I was married for eighteen years before my first marriage officially came to an end through a divorce. Divorce was a deep pit, certainly the lowest point in my life, for during that time, looking back over my marriage, I could easily recall many good memories of romance, happiness, and laughter. What happened to that relationship? How could two people support and love one another for so many years, bring children into the world and raise them together, and then, just lose sight of it all, and, essentially, quit. Neither of us were "bad people." We were respected members of councils, boards, churches, schools, and we had many and various friends. We did not physically abuse one another, nor was there physical infidelity, but somewhere in the midst of all of our involvements and responsibilities, we lost sight of each other, perhaps, ourselves, and certainly our life as a couple.

Some relationships necessarily end because of violence or some too-difficult-to-get-over impropriety, but more often than not, relationships likely end because most of us are so "illiterate" about love. So many of us aspire to be in love and to know love, but really, we receive so little training for it. Unlike all of the rest of our academic subject matter, we generally "learn" love through observation. We grow up watching the interaction of our parents, and because they are *our parents*, we assume that everything that they do is "model." Then, as we become more independent, we witness the relationships of others and make personal evaluations and judgments of these relationships based off of our meager fieldwork so far. Finally, when the hormonal shifts start happening within us and we "feel" something that we want to associate with love, we make further interpretive estimations about this thing we call "love."

Because I taught in a private, parochial high school, I rarely encountered a student who was illiterate; none truly were, but some had obviously been erroneously pushed along or had done a wonderful job of pretending to know and to understand more than they actually did. One student I remember in particular was always quite engaging in class discussions, and his contributions were always thoughtful and, usually, quite well-spoken; but when he had to read or to write something, his system failed him. And so it is for many of us with love - we are a bit illiterate. We've listened and observed enough that we appear to understand and to know what we are talking about. But this understanding only goes so far, and then we start scrambling, too often believing that we really know what we are doing and holding fast to "our way." Feelings and selfish needs corrupt our lexicon of love, and soon, we are merely pretending love, hiding behind a false diploma of love we thought we received when we married, instead of "going back to school" and trying to learn what we apparently missed out on the first time.

O God of Love, I long to discover and to experience love and all of its many facets, for to know love is to know you. But like a restless student, I have not always been attentive to the lessons of love that have been given to me, and sometimes I apparently must have just skipped the schooling altogether. Consumed with the concerns of my own appearance and needs, and nestled behind the facade of what I think I know, I too often stumble blindly through my relationships creating hurt and misunderstanding. Today, I stand ready to learn anew; direct my steps toward your school of love, a school of true higher learning.

March 5
Waiting in Line for Prayer

I must confess: I am one of those lane-shifting drivers that you probably hate. My driving is quite legal; I don't speed or ignore stop signs. I just can't stand traffic, and so I am constantly trying to "get ahead" by shifting over to the lane that appears to have fewer cars. It happens in the grocery store too. I sometimes walk back and forth in front of the checkout lines guessing at which one will move faster before I commit to a certain line; even the cashier is a variable factor that I recognize in the weight of the decision. Once I commit, I still find myself glancing over to the second and third choice lines, now gauging the accuracy and measuring the success of my decision. This line-jumping mentality is a very silly game, I know, but I suspect that I am not its only player.

Our lives are very busy, and most of us abhor any waste of time, seeking to squeeze the last drop out of every moment that we have. Over the years, however, I have begun not so much to question the desire to squeeze more out of my time, but to consider into what is my time being squeezed. When I am line-jumping, either in highway or grocery store traffic, I am likely fully engaged in the rat race of life, moving from one busy intersection to the next. I drain my energy juices overworking one project, and then hurry to the next project wherein I will squeeze what is left of my time and energy. Impatiently frustrated by waiting in lines, I waste additional energy fuming over lost time. How much better would this line-time be spent if I gave it over to refueling my energy instead?

Finding and making time for prayer are the most fundamental challenges of developing a consistent prayer life. Now, certainly they are not ideal, but traffic jams, grocery store lines and all other beyond-your-control-wastes-of time are valuable opportunities for prayer. True, these moments will not provide time for spiritual reading or ritualistic prayer, but they are prayerfully rich on a couple of levels. Fundamentally, I have just "found" some time for prayer, and seizing it, I have brought a little more of the necessary nourishment of prayer into my life. But to make this nourishment possible, another effort will be necessary, through which additional benefits will be rendered; the effort is to let go of "time loss anxiety" and the benefits will be more patience, comfort, and happiness.

If I have to drive at times when heavy traffic is inevitable, then all of my worrying about lost time whilst I shift from lane to lane is out of my control. People have to buy groceries, and if I have to shop when others do, I might as well accept that I will have to wait in a line to get checked out. Accepting these delays as inevitable parts of my daily life, and then turning them into prayerful opportunities make my life more calm and simple, just plain better.

Timeless God, too often I try to squeeze more out of my time and energy for work and other projects, and leave no time for you. You are the creator of first energy and the giver of all life; I need to give more of my time to you so that I might better receive the energy that you have to give me. Help me to let prayer seep into all of the parts of my day, to recognize and then seize the myriad of simple opportunities where I can slow and calm down, and welcome your presence into the ongoing rush around me.

March 6
Love Notes

Throughout my years of teaching high school, the little "love note" passed from one admirer to another in the hallway between classes never seemed to lose its value. Always providing an especially important thrill of affirmation for freshmen and sophomores, these packages of affection, folded and tucked so precisely into their familiar triangle shape would still bring private delight to even juniors and seniors. I suppose text messaging and the like have reduced the volume of the paper note, but there will never be anything quite like receiving and reading words of affection in the scrawled penmanship of an admirer. In fact, even after years of marriage, I find myself still taking great delight in the giving and receiving of little love notes every now and then. The surprise of finding one on a pillow, in a lunch or briefcase, or sneakily tucked inside some luggage while on a trip from home always makes me pause, smile and then sigh at the goodness of love's gentle and simple touch.

A gentle and simple holy teacher of meditation, Eknath Easwaran, wonderfully brought to my attention years ago that God also offers us so many "love notes." I have never forgotten his correlation, and now marvel, almost daily, at the regularity with which God sends them my - our - way. I may be driving to work, still longing for the bed's warmth and comfort, dreading a bit the load of the work day ahead, when suddenly, over my shoulder, color starts to pool in the eastern sky, and then radiant rays reach out and kiss me with the goodness of this new morning and day. I may be straining through the middle miles of a long run through a wooded park when suddenly a deer unsuspectingly emerges from the brush, stands quietly on the trail ahead of me looking me in the eye, and then softly vanishes into the brush again. I may be burdened with a night's worth of paperwork, and needing a stretch and break, I step outside to breathe in some night air and to sip from the night sky when suddenly a shooting star scrawls a signature "I love you!" across the darkened canvas. These, and countless other simple and unexpected gifts, are God's little love notes to us all.

When relationships are going awry and feelings have been hurt, sometimes I've seen students roll their eyes and toss their heads with an air of "I don't care" when the proffered note is slipped into their hand. Perhaps the note offers an apology or attempts to assuage a misunderstanding or seeks to reaffirm the affections that have recently been missing; but if the receiver fails to take hold of the note, open and read it, all of its potential power is lost and then drains away. So too with God's love notes. We must live with our hearts and minds wide open to the presence of God around us, awake to God's frequent design of dropping little love notes across our path. If we don't, we miss the joy and the resiliency with which these love notes infuse our lives.

Loving God, my love note to you this day is a heart full of gratitude for the many ways that you stop me in my tracks, embrace me with the beauty of your creation, and tell me through these sudden glimpses that I am loved. Help me to be mindful of your love always, to walk through life with my eyes wide open, knowing that just around this next corner, your hand my be reaching out to me with a little love note for me to receive.

March 7
Tournament Time

Years ago when my oldest daughter married, she chose a date in October, Columbus Day weekend, thinking that people might have a more accessible three day weekend. Unfortunately, for me it was one of the most important weekends in my annual fall coaching season, the weekend of competition for which, quite frankly, we steered all of our training. I will just say here that I was not particularly happy with her chosen date, and I remember playfully chiding her that this would be the last wedding of hers that I would attend on this particular weekend. It was *my daughter's wedding*, for heaven's sake, so I bucked up, made the necessary arrangements with my assistant and then happily engaged in my daughter's grand day; but I did privately stay in touch with my team's results on the wedding day.

Some years later, our school's head boys' basketball coach, a man whose primary focus at the time was coaching basketball, faced a far-more challenging hurdle. Throughout the season, he carried the weight of his brother's impending death to cancer. Any other year, Coach K, as he is affectionately known, would engage in basketball-talk nonstop throughout his season and the months that surrounded it; he was not obsessed with winning, but like me, he believed in building his teams toward tournament time when winning truly mattered. In district, regional and state tournament races and games, each competition results in the life or death of your current season. But in that particular year, there was a true life or death situation that transcended any one team or season. As fate would have it, Coach K's brother passed away the first week of tournament play and, of course, he was not walking the sidelines or sitting on the bench prodding and encouraging his team's performance as it fumbled its way to an early tournament and season exit. When I talked to him privately sometime later, he admitted that he just needed the season to be over. "When your brother is dying," he said, "it's kind of hard to think that a basketball season matters."

82

Our lives are full of "important" things that we believe deserve and need our absolute attention. But when truly important life transitions come along, we are given an opportunity for some different perspective. It is not that our choices and involvements are all meaningless and trivial; they, too, have an important role in our own and in others' lives; obviously, however, not all are of equal value. God of the Vital and the Trivial, help me not to miss these opportunities to reevaluate where and how I spend my energies. Even more, may I not need these profound life and death reminders to put things in perspective. Life is a precious gift; may I attentively celebrate its richness not from a distant vista, but standing at the heart of its ebb and flow.

March 8
The Divine Respite

Some dear friends of mine have managed to slice the intrusion of television right out of their personal home lives. I often think that I, too, could do without a television, and could truly benefit from a life free of its clamor and time-consumption. But sometimes, it sure is nice to just be a couch potato, to vegetate before the television losing all cares and concerns. Sunday football and evening hockey games are especially comforting to me. I despise the excessive importance and money that we invest in professional and collegiate athletics, but I cannot deny that I frequently enjoy the vicarious experience of sporting events and their cathartic rewards. When my daily life is full to the brim with the pressures of expectations and deadlines, I find it a simple release to allow myself to become absorbed in an athletic competition, or some other TV entertainment; in those hours of viewing, I can forget about the stress and blow off some steam.

For my friends without television, their respite may come in the form of a book or some gardening or any variety of hobbies that allow them to temporarily forget about the larger world that surrounds and weighs upon them, and lose themselves in a simple what-is-only-and-immediately-before-me activity. The key to both the television viewing and the hobby activity is that I lose my "busy-self," the self that stresses over what needs done and what others expect of me, and I relax within a simple, often mindless, framework.

Ideally, our spiritual lives ought to be such a source of comfort and rejuvenation as well. In fact, when I am truly and fully engaged spiritually, even the need for any working respite, be it television or hobby, is lessened. When my life is spiritually grounded, I begin to see the world and my life more accurately. When I recognize myself as a child of God and lose myself in an ever-emerging awareness of what it is that God calls me into and to be, I am able to loosen the intense grip of social and personal expectations. Indeed, work life can become as light as my entertainment and hobby fare.

Loving God, your very beingness seems an endless respite to me. To work, and to rest, within you are a comfort. It is so easy for me to become wrapped up in me, and to make the expectations and demands on my life bigger than life itself. But you are Life itself; you are all that I truly need. All else is little more than a vicarious and cathartic exercise. Yes, I live in a society and a world that solicit numerous demands on my time and person, and frequently I need to step back and to let go of the anxiety and stress that accompany these demands. Help me today to better understand that when I lose myself in you, that I can live more free of these social and personal concerns. Assist me to open the book that is you, to tune into your presence that is all around me, and to cultivate your presence more fully into every part of my daily life.

March 9
Miracles

When I taught courses on the Judeo-Christian scriptures, Christian students would sometimes question the miraculous stories that would occasionally be presented in these documents. Some would even ask why God doesn't provide such wonders today; if God did, they might add, faith and belief would come far more easily to people. In response, besides trying to make a distinction between the "facts" of a story and the "truth" of the story, I would also argue that such miracles and wonders do happen today, but the difference is in how we "see" them. A non-believer might see a certain event as a coincidence or as a unique but natural and explainable phenomenon, whereas a true believer will experience the event through the eyes of faith.

In the Gospel stories of the Christian scriptures, Jesus is often shown bringing sight to the blind, hearing to the deaf, and speech to the mute among many other miraculous deeds. I don't doubt that Jesus did in fact perform some of these healings, but beneath the physical change in the person healed was the more important spiritual shift. I am sure that the truth of Jesus' teachings and the charisma of his very presence changed people's attitudes and actions - their very lives. Some people who could not see, hear or speak were very likely healed of those maladies, but those same people and many more, after hearing and seeing Jesus speak and act, never saw, heard or spoke of life and all of God's creations in quite the same way themselves. They were all miraculously changed.

Many of the scriptural miracles and wonders certainly can be explained scientifically or rationally, but the *why* and the *when* of an event can stretch the experience of it well beyond the simple *what* and *how* of the event. We can offer all kinds of explanations for the wonders of space - the stars, the sun and the moon, and the planets - and we can track the intricate physiology of the human body and its various systems - circulatory, digestive, muscular and nervous - but the very existence of these wonders and the depth of their contingency, through the eyes of faith, enters into a universe of the mysterious and the mystical. In short, they are, indeed, miraculous.

O God of magnificent wonder, bless me this day and always with the eyes of faith. Open my heart to the wonders of your creation. Gifted with a mind, I might see, hear and speak to the nature of how things function; but let me not be so shortsighted as to miss the mystery that pervades all creation. The eyes of understanding can alleviate ignorance; and the eyes of faith can deepen the miracle of our understanding.

March 10
The Natural Cathedral

Many times before or after I travel to some major city of the world, people will ask me whether or not I will or did visit some famous cathedral or church or mosque or temple. Oftentimes, I do, but if the truth be told, I am far more interested in the landscape outside the city than in any structure within it. Yes, I have marveled at the gravity defying architecture of a grand cathedral and have exclaimed over the extraordinarily beautiful artwork within its walls; I am astonished by the geometric symmetry of a mosque and fascinated by the incredible detail in a temple. But, for me, nowhere do I encounter the presence of God more palpably than in the natural world.

Indeed, I recall sitting on a ledge in the belly of the Grand Canyon and simply repeating over and over for half an hour, "Oh my God!" and then turning ninety degrees and starting the mantra all over again. And my words were not simply exclamatory words of awe, but they were truly spiritual utterances as I sat rapt in this visage of God's magnificence. Now, anyone could likely be moved to spiritual wonder in the presence of that colossus, but I need not grasp for the extreme. The quietude of some local woods, the haunting sound of a loon's call, the moon's gentle emergence from beneath a clouded and changing sky, the glassy reflection of the morning spread across a northern lake, the meditative trickle of water over rocks in a small stream, a young spruce sprouting from a fissure in a granite boulder, the incredible carving and deathly silence of a narrow slot canyon - these and so many more have literally and figuratively brought me to my knees. Yes, human made structures of worship are sometimes wondrous and old, but to gaze upon and to listen to the sights and sounds of the ancient created world and universe is to be, most assuredly, in the midst of the wondrous and accessible handiwork of God.

Step out anytime, anywhere and find something of wonder to observe. If you are so lucky, perhaps you can climb to the top of some hill or mountain, or walk through some deep woodland, or sit silently at the feet of the ocean's tumbling tide; but you can also look carefully into the opening bulb of a tulip around your front step, or study the encompassing wrap of the vine on the building next door, or observe the careful flight of any number of birds that inhabit your neighborhood. Each and every one of these is a song of praise, an artistic vision of God's grandeur.

Creator God, give me the gift of wonder, the gift of living with my eyes wide open to all that you have created above, around and below me. I have been born into the cathedral of your magnificent splendor, and awaken each day in the temple of your love; as I gaze today into the cupolas and minarets of your universal mosque, may I stand, kneel and prostrate myself in the presence of your awesome creative power.

85

March 11
The Table of Faith

For many years, I had the privilege to teach students some essentials about many different religious traditions. Hoping that a little knowledge might garner some fundamental understanding and with it, a certain necessary respect for the beliefs of others, I openly encouraged questions and discussions that might also enhance the fervor of their own faith as well. When I was amazed or puzzled by the beliefs of a religious tradition, even my own, I candidly shared that too, believing that all can benefit when we honestly share our faith struggles.

To that end, one of my most painful and ongoing spiritual heartaches is when I read or watch some scrap between two different but long-established religious traditions, each convinced that its approach to God and its placement of primacy in the pantheon of spiritual paths is the correct one. Although the "holier than thou" attitude is a bit distasteful and often makes me wince, I can at least swallow the bitterness of this approach in that while each side may be sure that its way is "better," at least there is some acknowledgment of the other's "value." But when one tradition blatantly discounts the gifts and the presence of the sacred in the other, then I am deeply distressed. That being said, it may sound contradictory when I say "some congregations of faith (and by that label I do not mean any entire religious tradition but smaller groupings potentially within a tradition) have it wrong." The "it" in this case is purposely vague, as "it" could be as specific as an errant attitude towards others or as grand as God him/her/itself! For me, any gathering that does not have love as its true foundation and does not seek the full goodness of all others is "suspect."

While the clash of religious traditions can bring me great consternation, I find that when and where the "truths" of traditions overlap, I receive more than equal amounts of contrasting joy, especially traditions that come from opposite sides of the world and that people often assume have absolutely nothing in common. From a most foundational belief like the "golden rule," the essence of which is found in essentially every religious tradition, to more specific, if not exotic, convictions like shared beliefs in the existence of angels or little people, whenever I encounter such commonalities in vastly different cultures, places and times, it gives me pause. Why and how is it, I wonder, that these different groups of people from such different places could arrive at the same conclusion? Is it not possible that there is a divinity at work here - different people shaped by the same heart?

It is inconceivable to me that a God who created and creates all people would do so discriminately. For the vast majority of people of faith and even those without it, the when and where and to whom of their birth has much more to do with their chosen path of faith or disbelief than anything else, and if there is a buffet of religious traditions from which they might choose, even this display is rather time and culturally seasoned. To think that God prefers the flavor of one established tradition and detests another seems a rather unsavory recipe, a spoiled idea that belongs aside the "divine right of kings." Again, I do not speak indiscriminately here, as if every path of faith is "equally good" and "equally true," but if the love of God, others and self is truly its basis and clearly its focus, I am very confident that God is the primary ingredient of the dish being served.

God of Great Diversity, given the disparate regions and cultures of this wonderful earth, it seems quite natural that you would provide a tremendous spread of refreshments and nourishment on your table of life. Just as I am culturally drawn to one set of flavors over another, so it also seems possible that people across the globe might be favorably drawn toward you through one religious tradition's nourishment over another. Perhaps one tradition truly is more flavorful or nutritional than another, but prevent me from making that judgment of others' tastes. If it truly strengthens them in love and guides them on a path of unifying peace with you and all others, I pray that they might eat heartily and that we might all share in our just desserts.

March 12
Communities of Faith

I was recently invited to pray with a group of School Sisters of Notre Dame de Namur who live in community together on the grounds of Trinity College in Washington D.C. Their order had founded the college for Catholic women in 1897, although it became coed in 1960, and now welcomes students of all faith backgrounds. Today, the convent is occupied by only a small cluster of aging nuns, almost all former professors at the college, yet all very actively engaged in some way or another at the school. The structure of their home, like the nuns' bodies themselves, shows the wear of years, although their and its architecture still reveal the beauty and sturdiness of fine craftsmanship and care. Welcomed, I entered their hallowed hallways and made my way to their simple chapel area, once perhaps a large conference room, now a high-ceilinged holy space embroidered with dark woodwork and windows open to the air and sounds and light of the campus surrounding the building.

Taking a place near the back of the chapel, I added my voice to their songs, joined in chorus to known prayers, and observed quietly all else beyond my grasp. When a scriptural passage was to be proclaimed, or a ritual performed, one of the aged women moved slowly to the front, her once, no doubt, energetic and agile frame a mere shadow of itself now. I wondered then, where would this community be ten or fifteen years from now? A few younger nuns were also there among us, but these were African women visiting or in study, who would eventually return to their homelands to carry the gospel of their spiritual beliefs and religion to their own people. But letting go of my concern for the future of this cloister of nuns, I saw the present truth of their inspiring commitment to their lives of faith. Each of them has served and changed countless lives; each of these old women was once a beacon of hope and encouragement to other young women seeking a better and more holy world; and each of them continues to dedicate herself tirelessly to those same ideals, and will as long as she lives and her body permits her.

Religious orders of Catholic nuns and priests today in North America certainly face significant challenges regarding the decrease in their numbers and the difficulty of financial sustainability. According to some statistics at the time of this writing, the average age of the occupants of so many of these convents and rectories is fifty-five to seventy years old. But these people do not know "retirement" in the secular view; they serve in endless capacities with a timeless zeal. One may argue that the "lifestyle" of such religious communities is dying, but if it is, more tragically, perhaps, the truly dedicated life of faith is as well.

God of Dedication and Community, all people are called into the service of one another. Whether we choose to serve within a religious community or in parenting or through any number of secular organizations that encourage community service, all of us are challenged to be people of daily faith, living and being what our hearts and spirits proclaim. For those who have chosen to dedicate their lives solely to a faith-filled service, I pray for their continued strength and courage to be constant models of faith and commitment. For those whose faith is lived out in the secular environment, help them to realize that they too can be signs of dedication, lives that reflect the promise of God's love.

March 13
A Trace of Light

Some mornings before the day's clouds have assembled beyond the horizons for their daily rally and then disperse in all directions creating their ever-changing artwork across the firmament, the sky is an expansive blue canvas tautly stretched awaiting the cosmic brushstrokes. Often, however, the first strokes are not "cosmic" at all, but sweepingly human. Like chalked fingertips streaking across a clean blackboard, these first strokes upon the day's fresh canvas are "contrails" or "vapor trails," artificial clouds of condensed water vapor created by the exhaust of aircraft engines. Scratching geometric patterns across the canvas, these visible aircraft pathways seem to be a gift of litter. With their criss-crossing oblique lines creating beautiful designs across the clear sky, they seem a lovely invitation to look upward and marvel at the simple randomness of their artwork; and yet, they are also signs of intrusion, careless footprints across the dew-fresh grasses of a virgin field.

Wherever we human beings go, it seems, we leave a trail of our imprint behind. Axioms encourage us to "tread lightly" and to "leave no trace," but no matter how soft our steps might be, our hard efforts always create a wake of some refuse. Given the human size and weight, some evidence of our path is almost inevitable, although it is not simply individual footprints that we carve across an open plain. The pollution of noise, the destruction and waste of our "developments," and the outright garbage of our lifestyle are all forms of our human footprint upon the earth and its atmosphere, but such debris need not be seen as trash alone.

Just as the vapor trails of aircraft sometimes create a network of beautiful designs though they cloud the loveliness of a clear sky, we too can transform the disorder that our efforts often create into more useful designs, a kind of eco-art. Many times the first question is, and should be, should we carve up the land at all? But given that it so often is, the next question should be, could we make the cut a precise incision of the least invasion and avoid a crass slash of disturbing intrusion? And I do not mean this in industrial terms alone, but also with regards to the decisions that you and I make everyday. Where and how do my steps trod, and what kind of trail do I leave behind me through my actions, words and thoughts?

Near the end of The Beatles classic animated movie, *Yellow Submarine,* the character of Jeremy Hilary Boob Ph.D., his heart full of love and kindness, dances across the battlefields of the evil Blue Meanies and beneath each of his steps, flowers spring up. We should be so lucky. Boob's colorful return on his footprint is the stuff of cartoons, but we too, and not just by accident, can truly do a better job of being more carefully respectful with each step we take, physical and otherwise, leaving a more aesthetically beautiful footprint.

Like the vapor trails across the morning sky, "Generations have trod, have trod, have trod; And all is seared with trade; bleared, smeared with toil; And wears man's smudge and shares man's smell," writes the poet Gerard Manley Hopkins, saddened by the imprint humanity leaves upon the earth. But Hopkins also sees God's creative energy rejuvenating the earth, and we should be co-creators in that revitalization. God of the Cosmic Design, you have blessed us with a universe of beauty that we too often mar through our careless efforts, words, and even thoughts. Instill in me a deeper sense of responsibility for what I take and for what I give back to the earth and to your universal spirit that pervades all things.

March 14
Resistance to Training

I remember the day when I finally stepped back into running after a nearly three month hiatus. It was a beautiful early spring day in March when the birds and the buds seem to dance in the delight of the oncoming season, and all the creations send out the cosmic invitation to come out and play. I knew it was time to strap the running shoes on again and to breath in the emerging new year's energy. Prior to my running respite, I would usually run at least five miles an effort, and having done so for years, I knew that my body was wired for an easy five-mile jaunt. So, responding to the cosmic invitation, I chose a five-mile route through my nearby neighborhoods and stepped out into the brilliant day and reintroduced myself to running. The first miles peeled away effortlessly, like entering the doorway of a long awaited homecoming. But somewhere in the third or fourth mile, my body's energy began to wane - and quickly; and as I turned the corner heading into my fifth mile, the finish line of home felt like it was life-threatening miles away.

Much to my surprise, for the next few days after that run I could not get over how sore I was. Sure, I knew I had taken a significant chunk of time off from running, but I had also been running consistently for more years than I could even remember before my intermission. It seemed very unfair that my body should respond so negatively to my renewed intention to run. I took a couple more days off before I ran again, and each time I returned to running, I would also renew my rest period. It was a most rebellious reentry!

Gratefully, reestablishing, or establishing for the first time, a routine in one's prayer life does not bring the same kind of physical travails, but energizing one's prayer life does come with a similar force of resistance. Like physical exercise, even when we know that our spiritual life is stale and flabby, and our spirit is thirsting for some refreshment, making time for a new routine and then sticking with it consistently is often a real tug-of-war between our body and our will. Observing his disciples drifting off to sleep in his hour of prayer-filled need, Jesus nailed the heart of the experience when he said, "The spirit is willing but the flesh is weak."

The older I get, the more easily I seem to lose my "physical edge." To get my body back into shape takes real discipline and a consistent and dedicated effort. Appropriately, perhaps, because the pace of prayer and meditation do not require the physical exertion that is necessary in training the body, I do find that reestablishing a disciplined prayer routine is not quite as taxing, but it certainly does not come easily. Consistency of effort is necessary in both fields.

God of Constancy, I seek to develop a strong relationship with you nurtured through the practice of a dedicated and consistent prayer life. Invigorate my meditative stamina and keep me focused on my long-range finish line, union with you. To paraphrase the words of St. Augustine, my heart is restless until it rests in you.

March 15
Befriending Spirituality

When I first met my best friend, he was a student of an adult education course I was teaching for a Catholic Diocese on ministry. As the story goes, he was initially taken by my long hair and my use of inclusive language during ritual; I was a break from the norm of his spiritual and religious experiences. After he and a partner asked me to work on a prayer service for which they were responsible, we got to know each other on a little more personal basis rather than the previous teacher-student relationship. Our friendship did not take off quickly, however, for there were various and odd interconnections that we would encounter along the way and would have to pass over before the gift of a loving friendship could truly begin to take root.

Oddly enough, when I hold the two of us up, side-by-side, we are far more different than we are alike. I am quite athletic and outdoorsy, and although he does enjoy swimming, he would be more apt to have a cigarette while I go for a run. I enjoy following professional sports, especially football and hockey, and played these sports for years of my early life; he humors me with phone messages talking of recent games and players about which he has gleaned an "informed opinion" from a recent news article or sports-talk show. I love to listen to a variety of rock and jazz music, but easily turn to a driving, hard rock and try to stay abreast of the new music scene; he knows all the words to musical show tunes. My social drink of choice is a beer, preferably dark; he will opt for a Manhattan or a snifter of Scotch, if anything at all. Now, we are not total opposites. We have a variety of things in common, not least of which was the pain and anguish of divorce, but he was already remarrying before I was even separated. Most importantly what we share is our faith and the desire to find and to stay on a spiritual path. Interestingly, this one area of our lives, where the overlay is so distinct, provides the foundation of our friendship from which all other differences are either rendered unimportant and indistinct or come together to shape a complementary whole.

A valuable and deep friendship, like our spirituality, is so essential in our lives, that if and when these two should meet, both the friendship and the spirituality will be deeply enhanced by the other. Independently, a person may nurture his spirituality and arrive at a more conscious understanding of the unity of all things, the contingency that links us all; but, this web of interconnection often seems too amorphous, too transcendent to be fully realized alone. When friendship, however, enters into the dynamics of our spirituality, then some small part of the nebulous nature of the cosmic web becomes more palpable. The hopes and dreams that often bud and spring forth from one's personal spiritual development are no longer isolated in the desert of questions that often sucks dry the necessary nourishment. Instead, one is transplanted into a garden where the blooms and blossoms of another or others reinvigorate one's own growth, a network with irrigation. And so with my friend and me, despite our various differences, the roots of a wonderful relationship have worked their way deep into the soil of our lives as we challenge and support one another on our spiritual journeys.

Immanent God of all creation, the very nature of our existence links us to all that you have created, and yet, so often, we only experience ourselves and the creations in isolated, independent ways. Through friendships, some of the intangible interconnections are made palpable, and the hard questions of doubt are softened through shared reflection and perspectives. I need friendships that engage, challenge and embrace me in my spiritual development. Today, I pray that the roots of those friendships that are already growing around me will deepen, and that the blossoms of these might send seeds into the world fostering an expansive garden of spiritual delight.

March 16
A Fashion Statement

With each new season of the year, advertising fliers sport the latest clothing fashions that will help us "look good" as we slip into the new spring, summer, autumn or winter. Shifts in design - solids, stripes, plaids, or some combination - and color - soft, vibrant, pastel, and various schemes - are marketed, and with them, the belief that to wear otherwise is a social suicide risk.

Years ago, I lived in a neighborhood that was slowly evolving into an Asian immigrant pocket, and I soon noticed among my new elderly neighbors a complete disregard for American fashion "needs." Almost daily I could observe the dear seventy-plus year old Chinese couple who lived next door to our family dressed in their favorite pale print polyester knit slacks, when such fabric had long since slipped from the "acceptable fashion" page, complemented with lovely and vibrant blousy plaid tops. The color schemes were totally unacceptable in, perhaps, any fashion period, and the mismatch of designs were visually cacophonous. Yet, there they were, happily oblivious to their inevitable American social suicide, apparently caring only for what fit and for what was comfortable. Imagine!

What *is* fashionable and who is deciding this status can be, and often is, highly questioned. But one look around in any given season will reveal that most of us do "fall in line," even if a bit reluctantly, eventually. We care about "how we look," and believe that what we wear says something about who and how we are. I often wonder if we are ever concerned about our "spiritual wear."

Regarding spirituality, "fashion expectations" can certainly creep in as well. Christianity first became "fashionable" with Emperor Constantine's Edict of Milan in 313 C.E. Much later during the Reformation in many parts of Europe, Roman Catholicism would become very unfashionable; although in some parts, lack of adherence to its mandates might bring far worse than simple "social suicide." Today, New Age views might appear fashionable to some, but are iconoclastic mismatches to others. Once again, do people care more about "how they look" rather than "who they are"?

O Great One beyond all fashion, I too often spend too much time and energy being concerned about what I wear and whether it is "acceptable" or not. Today, help me to look within and to take some stock of my spiritual wardrobe. What does it say about me, and does it truly reflect my own spiritual awareness or merely represent ideas I neither understand nor truly believe? The physical clothing I wear might be fashionably driven, but may the fit of my spiritual dressing be appropriate, comfortable and true.

March 17
Discovering Ethnicity

Years ago, when I was attending and then leading workshops on prejudice and discrimination awareness, I was often struck by my lack of ethnic identity. Americans of white, European descent all eventually pretty much looked the same. While I can recognize some differences in the features of an Eastern European, and clothing, mannerisms and even some physical features might distinguish a "true Italian" or "true French," most "insert an ethnicity"-white Americans all pretty much look about the same. Racial differences are obviously easy to define, but not many can tell the difference between an Irish-American or a French- or Italian- or an English-American. They are all, pretty much, well, "just white."

In fact, many European immigrants, wanting to be accepted in the "New World" sought to lose their previous national identity, changing their names and discouraging the use of the "old language" even in the home. Subsequently, when I was raised, my ethnic identity was hardly spoken of. Furthermore, once the ethnic labels and identities were dropped and somewhat "lost" through "intermarriages," most white Americans became "ethnic mutts": a half of this and a fourth of this and a fourth of that.

My name and deepest roots run with the Irish, although I do have some significant German in there too. I have always easily identified with the Irish; the spirituality of their ancient people resonates with mine today, and their sense of family and the importance of religious influence have also provided an easy link, but there was little in my childhood which fostered these connections, so, for much of my life I was just a white American. Then, one year I rather whimsically decided to take my two oldest children to watch the annual St. Patrick's Day parade in our city. The celebrated day had always seemed to me to be nothing more than another American party effort, a "good reason" to sell lots of beer in the name of being Irish for a day. The parade itself was nothing much, a few bands and a float or two. But what struck me most as we sat curbside that day was all of the *people* marching in the parade, celebrating, just through their presence, their Irish heritage. Here was a major United States city, in the middle of the day, shutting down significant arteries in the city so that people of Irish descent could walk through the streets with an air of pride that said, "This is who I am." And for the first time, I thought about who I was ethnically and, then, "remembering," I asked myself, "why are you just sitting here; why aren't you out there walking with 'your people'?"

God of the People, so many of us go through our lives too often detached from our heritage and a sense of our roots. These things are not "who we are," but these ethnic, racial and cultural frameworks, in fact, do provide us with a groundwork, a sense of origin – connections to people and to a place. Guide me into that place of connection; join me with people who can celebrate their past and give their present a renewed spirit in the light of that history. I am ultimately bound to the whole of humanity and the universe, but let me not miss these simple family ties that provide me a smaller home in the great circle of things.

March 18
A Blessed Greeting

When visiting a Hindu ashram or temple, one might very well be greeted by a sign or a respectful devotee welcoming the visitor with the kind words of "Om Namah Shivaya." If Christian and/or generally unknowledgeable about these ancient Sanskrit words, the visitor might be confused at least, or alarmed at worst, thinking them some type of prayer to a polytheistic deity not her own. In fact, the phrase *is* a kind of prayer, but given in a greeting it is a welcoming prayer of blessing and remembering.

Sometimes referred to as "the Great Redeeming" or "the Five-Syllable" mantra, Om Namah Shivaya is actually a six-syllable phrase that honors God and the in-dwelling of the Divine in each of us. The opening "Om" is a simple recognition of the sacredness that surrounds us at all times, a sacredness of which we are a part on every level of our consciousness, and in our coming, our being, and our going. The five-syllable part of the phrase then begins with "Namah," which, on the most literal level means "adoration and respect," but is more practically applied as "I bow to," to which one might add "in adoration and respect." The next word, "Shivaya," may be for non-Hindus more problematic, but addressed carefully, the faithful cannot help but notice likely connections to their own traditions. Shivaya is a reference to Lord Shiva, one of the three visages of the Ultimate One. Along with Brahma, the creator, and Vishnu, the preserver, Shiva, often referred to as "the destroyer," is one of the most honored images of God in all of Hinduism. His title as "the destroyer," however, is greatly misunderstood as one who brings ruination as opposed to Vishnu's preservation. What Shiva ultimately destroys is the ego, our false identification of the self through old habits and various attachments. When we die to the self and destroy our egotistical self, what we are left with is the purified version of ourselves, that self so beautifully defined in the Hebrew creation story as "made in the image and likeness of God." Thus, greeting one with "Om Namah Shivaya," the welcomer is saying, "I bow to the God within you," not to some separate deity or to an idolatrous image, but a kind acknowledgment that each person is made in God's image, and to that spark of the Divine within each of us, the welcomer respectfully bows. In this honorable greeting, I am both blessed and reminded that God dwells in me too, and I have a responsibility to work towards being a truer representative of that image and likeness.

So often we greet people out in public with mindless utterances of "Hi," "Hey," or "How are you?" Imagine if we greeted one another regularly with words that both bless us and call us to the task of being who and what we are: God's own. Americans spend millions of dollars each year trying to physically look better, making alterations to their outward design. Om Namah Shivaya calls me to attend to my inner most being, to destroy those things in me that prevent me from being a model for the one who created me and daily gives me life. God of Pure Beauty, strip away from me all that separates me from you, all that keeps me from being a true image of your likeness in the world; and help me to respectfully honor others in a way that both blesses and reminds them of who and how holy they are, as well.

March 19
Barroom Karma

In old classic cowboy movies, there is almost always a saloon scene where all the frivolous banter spilling over the player piano background music whilst a serious game of poker unfolds nearby suddenly comes to a very abrupt halt as a certain notorious character steps through the swinging door entrance. As the unwanted guest's very presence permeates the barroom, a pall drops over the noise of the scene and all eyes turn toward him. Unfortunately, long after the "lawless days of the old west," most of us are probably all too familiar with people whose very presence brings a certain anxiety whenever they walk into the room. Perhaps because of some ugly past experiences, these people don't have to say or do anything; the uneasiness that arrives with them is loosely locked in the fear of what *might* happen now that they are here. Today, we might simply say that these people have "bad karma."

Karma, a Hindu Sanskrit word that is tossed about rather loosely in the modern western world, is most simply translated as "action." But the reason that we associate the term more with the idea of "aura" is that we subconsciously recognize that one's actions do create a certain character profile, and, in time, a kind of aura. With further reference to the idea of action, karma is also sometimes described as "what comes around goes around"; or, "what you sow, so shall you reap." Hence, the person whose actions have been born consistently of anger and violence now carries with him an aura of fear and uneasiness wherever he goes. Happily, the opposite is also true.

I am hopeful that we also know people who, whenever they walk into a room, provide an aura of levity, sometimes even joy. Some might call them "the life of the party," but their presence provides something more important than simple jocularity and good fun. Their arrival is like the sun's rising over the horizon on a bright and clear spring morning or, in less happy times, that beam of sunlight that finds its way through the thick cloud bank on a grey day, reminding us that the sun is still there shining above us. If there is any good to be found in a difficult situation, people of "good karma" will find it and bring it to the display table. No matter how dismal a situation may be, when these people are around, the heaviness of the heart is lightened and hope forever lingers somewhere within reach.

So, what kind of "karma" do I bring to the world around me? When I enter the figurative saloon, does a fearful hush spread across the room, or do people feel inclined to joyfully shout, as in the old "Cheers" episodes, "Norm!" Do I bring uneasiness into the world or comfort?

Our God is pure and loving karma, and as we are made in his image, our actions and our presence ought to reflect that goodness, that warmth. As I move throughout this day, help me, God, to be mindful of my actions and my words, and to realize that they each impact the world around me. There is enough hurt and fear in the world already; how wonderful it would be if my simple presence could provide some hope, some comfort, some joy.

March 20
Miracles Springing Up All Around

It will come so quickly that you'll miss it, but it will come so slowly that you'll never see it happening. Spring blossoming. It is one of the most incredible miracles that unfolds before our very eyes each year, and yet so many people fail to see the mystery, the divinity of it all. For years I fielded questions about why God doesn't reveal God's self like God apparently did back "in the old days." So many young Christians, dazzled by the spectacular stories of the Hebrew Scriptures and mystified by the miracle stories of Jesus would ask why God doesn't provide them with similar signs. The eyes of faith sometimes come with blinders.

Miracles are not so much actions or events that defy natural law, but rather, seeing the mystery within natural actions and events; and few are more magnificent and mysterious than the miracle that we call spring. After the death-defying frigidity of winter, the natural world often emerges from beneath the melting drifts of snow a besmudged remnant, a cast off from a happier and holier time. Then, with the temperatures slowly rising and the sun lingering a little more graciously, suddenly there is the hint of the miraculous in the air. One week, the trees and ground cover are tombstone shadows of a previous life; the next week, there is the almost imperceptible nudge of buds being pushed forth from the apparent moribund vegetation; days later, the buds are pursed lips receiving the kiss of sun and rain; and finally, one day, as if we never saw them coming, blossoms of soft and brilliant hue and scintillating scents leap in a glorious proclamation of life against an ever ripening green background. And there we stand, aware or not, inside a living, breathing miracle of life.

One can scientifically study the hows and whys of the spring season, but such explanations are the blinders we allow to be placed over our best and faith-filled eyes. That things happen for a reason is simply one explanation; that they happen at all, and in such a glorious fashion, goes beyond all explanation. God is alive and well and actively engaged in our modern world just as surely as God was miraculously engaged in the ancient world. If we miss God's latest revelation this spring, we have only our own blinders to blame.

Mysterious God, help me to remove the blinders that prevent me from seeing the mysteries of life springing up all around me. The miraculous movements of your creation are an exultation of your presence, vibrantly alive in our world. What I think and know about this world will always be limited by the blinders of this life; allow me to breath deeply and to see clearly the mysterious wonder of You.

March 21
Carving a Spiritual Trail

Most great monuments and grand cathedrals are built upon a foundation of concrete, and rise up from a pedestal of steps that ascend to the honored and sacred edifice. These steps serve as the pathway to the often protected entrances of these dignified structures. On a recent visit to Washington D.C., a city that is, perhaps, marked by such buildings of distinction more than any other in the United States, I was struck by how the marble and granite steps outside these grandiose structures had developed a kind of trail-like quality about them. In the wilderness, a commonly used path will inevitably be worn bare and a trough will be etched into the earth from the excessive wear, but I wasn't expecting to see such deterioration in the concrete and solid rock of these monuments and cathedrals. What ultimately moved me was the realization that these well-worn furrows in solid rock represented a consistent devotional attention to these sights.

It takes far less wear and tear to create a trail on the earth than it does to carve one into the granite steps of national monuments and holy cathedrals, and it all makes me wonder what kind of path one might find on the spiritual terrain of my life. The steps themselves and the depressions in them created by years of foot traffic ascending to the entry ways of grand buildings provide an obvious directional of where to go; but trail finding across a wilderness like the badlands of the Dakotas can be a bit tenuous as the human pathways can be easily confused with the numerous divergent interchanges created by the wandering bison. So what kinds of trails and trail markers have I created in the development of my spiritual life?

A one day walk into the spiritual wilderness will not leave much if any impression, and if my heart has been hardened, like granite, through years of neglect, I won't likely even leave a footprint. No, if I want to be comfortable in the wilderness and know my way around, and if I want to truly honor the sacred space and places of my life, then I need to "go there" with some regularity. Infrequent and undisciplined steps won't do.

Paths are created and steps are worn when people consistently choose to follow the direction of their hearts, when they dare to venture into the less traveled inner space and desire to ascend the spiritual stairway. God of Grandeur, soften and coax my heart daily to explore the trails and steps that might lead me closer to you. Others have surely gone before me and their strides may provide direction and guidance for me, but I must also walk on these paths or find my own comfortable way, and must do so with consistency so that each walk is not a new and wander-lost amble, but a course that leads me faithfully to you.

March 22
Like a Bag in the Tree

My wife recently happened to meet a former student of mine from many years back, and while visiting, she mentioned to the young woman that I was working on some prayers, like those I had spontaneously shared in the classroom for years. Hearing of this effort, the former student smiled and said, "Has he written about the garbage bag in the tree yet? I remember the first time I visited his classroom while taking a tour of the school," she continued, "as he started his opening prayer for the class that day, he looked out the window, and spotting a plastic garbage bag hung up in some tree branches, he proceeded to make a prayer about it. I'll never forget it," she added. "It was the quirkiest and coolest prayer I have had ever heard." The funniest part of the story is that when my wife pressed her further, the young woman could not remember what the prayer itself was about, only its motivating subject matter. Quite frankly, I don't remember either, as most of my prayers in those classroom days were absolutely spontaneous, but I suspect I developed an analogy to our being blown about through life, and how often times we can get hung up or stuck along the way. Thinking back on it now, I believe the bag stayed there in the tree for a while, and its ensnared presence became a bit of an ongoing prayer for the next several days.

Indeed, sometimes the fits and throes of life can leave us feeling like just so much garbage, abandoned by all, drifting aimlessly in the winds of life's changes and challenges. And like the garbage bag ensnared in the tree, we can get so entangled in our own mess, either stepping into it or creating it ourselves, that we get hung up, believing that we are unable to move or to make a change. At such times, feeling horribly out of control at the merciless whims of the universe, we grasp for any attentive assistance from others who might release us or save us from our collared mess. One word, one heartfelt glance, one outstretched hand – or the absence thereof – can make all the difference in the world.

That young woman, once a visiting student, then a daily student of mine, must have heard countless prayers, noted too many lectures, and taken a wide variety of tests in my classroom, but years later, the one thing she most remembered was a prayer about a bag caught in a tree. Could I possibly have known that day how that prayer would catch in the branches of her life and stay there for so long? So many times we may strive to leave lasting impressions through "great acts," when, in truth, the smallest acts or the simplest words are what may be carried through a person's lifetime. It makes me wonder what other ridiculously simple things I have said or done are also still blowing about the landscape of my former contacts, and to what effect are these things remembered. As a kindness, or an injury?

Captivating Creator, you have created us to be your presence, alive and at work in the world. Most often, I move about my day oblivious to the ways that I may be healing or harming others. Help me to be more mindful of the simple, yet powerful impact that my words and actions may have on others. That I can ensnare or release others from the entangling branches of harm and hurt is an astounding endowment; may my actions and words not be thoughtless or irresponsible winds loosely blowing about the cares and needs of others.

March 23
Seeking Forgiveness

One very important and rather unique aspect of the Roman Catholic Church is its long-standing tradition of the Seven Sacraments. Martin Luther, one of the primary and most influential of the Protestant reformers, accepted some of these sacraments, three to be exact, as did other reformers, while many more rejected them altogether. A Sacrament that was not officially accepted by any of the Reformers, deeming it unnecessary and not useful, is Reconciliation, or more archaically referred to as Confession or Penance. In the Roman Church's canonical tradition, Reconciliation was most formally mandated in the Fourth Lateran Council (1215), but the Church teaches that Jesus himself instituted the gift of forgiveness of sins when he breathed the Holy Spirit upon his apostles and said, "Receive the Holy Spirit. If you forgive the sins of any, they are forgiven; if you retain the sins of any, they are retained" (John 20:23). Since the time of the early Church, public and private confession of sin has had a storied evolution, and the reformers ultimately rejected the practice of confession to a priest or minister as unnecessary with the assumption that it is enough to confess one's sins just to

God. Regardless of how one feels about the Roman Catholic Sacrament of Reconciliation, philosophically, at least, there is some arguably good sense to it.

The three great monotheistic religions – Judaism, Christianity and Islam – are quite close in their understanding of sin. Essentially, it is a failing to live up to the standard of perfection that God calls us toward; it is an action, willfully and conscientiously made, that misses the mark of our best selves. As it is an action, more often than not, it has some "social" ramifications, meaning, other people can be affected by my individual action. Surely, there are private sins known only to ourselves, but most sins do have some kind of communal consequence. Given that my actions do not simply involve just me (and God), one might argue that my reconciliation should also involve more than just me (and God) as well. If I lie or steal from another, is it enough for me to say, "gee, God, that wasn't very nice; I sure am sorry I did that." To be truly reconciled, should I not also seek forgiveness from the one whom I offended? Many times, however, we may not even be aware of the lives we have offended, or have reasonable opportunity to contact them. In this case, the minister becomes like a surrogate victim, and our apology is extended to him. More importantly, perhaps, is the apparent human need to "get things off of our chest." Consider all of the "confessing" that goes on in the world, some at great financial cost: psychologists, counselors, friends, bartenders, and even total strangers. And why do people do this? Because when we do something, or fail to do something that we know was wrong, this "sin" damages us internally as well. We so often carry guilt like an overburdened backpack; it can affect us spiritually, emotionally, and even manifest itself physically. To admit to another that I have failed, that I am weak, that I have let people down, is to own my responsibility for my actions, and when I embrace my culpability, I do, most often, feel better and healing can take place.

I am not now suggesting that we all embrace and adopt a sacramental reconciliation program, but I do think that we need to consider how we seek and find forgiveness for our shortcomings and failures, especially when they bring any kind of harm to others. It is not easy to go to another and to admit our deficiencies, but when we realize and accept this dis-ease, perhaps that too becomes further incentive for us to walk a more holy path every day.

Forgiving God, I am weak and I often fail to live up to the person, the being, that you created me to be – one made in your image and likeness. I come to you seeking forgiveness for the many times I have failed not only you, but often, loved ones as well as people I may never know. With this prayer, encourage me to seek out proper reparation by asking forgiveness from those whom I have knowingly failed, and by choosing to live and to be a better reflection of you.

March 24
The Change of Forgiveness

In one of William Shakespeare's most famous dramas, *Hamlet*, there is an extraordinary scene depicting the real conflict that often ensues in our search for true forgiveness. King Claudius, the uncle and now stepfather to the title character has secretly murdered his brother, Hamlet's father, usurping the throne and then marrying the widow, Hamlet's mother. Through a well-designed ploy, young Hamlet punctures the scab of Claudius' guilt sending the new king back to his chambers where the audience will overhear him divulge his remorse and futilely seek forgiveness.

Admitting to the guilt of his crime, Claudius both desires forgiveness and yet acknowledges his unwillingness to let go of the good fortune that his crime has provided him: "But, O, what form of prayer can serve my turn? May one be pardoned and retain th' offense?" His questions underline a common dilemma known to many where our soul, "struggling to be free, art more engaged!" We may wish for forgiveness from a particular shortcoming, but we may not be as willing to relinquish the shortcoming itself or to embrace the consequences of our deeds, in which case, as Claudius notes, what good is our act of repentance "when one cannot repent?"

So many relationships and good lives are ruined not so much by a single act of evil or failure, but by the individual's inability to truly change, to truly turn away from the damaging shortcoming. Indeed, far less than good actions frequently have favorable results, and it is the feel-good nature of these results that so often make true remorse and genuine sorrow for our failures difficult to embrace. Sincere regret requires change, and change is not something that we humans often take to naturally or easily.

Back in the 1980s, the then First Lady, Nancy Reagan, coined the slogan, "Just Say No!" in her anti-drug campaign. While her intentions were good, what her jingle failed to realize was that drugs make people feel good and help them to mask whatever pain it is that they are running from. "Just say no" is no better than "I'm sorry" without the desire or the design to change one's behavior.

The inability to change what I know is wrong and the repetition of a failure are usually sure signs that something else is lacking in my life. God of Healing and Change, help me to look carefully at the habitual shortcomings of my life, and to recognize the possible sources of my breakdowns. So often I am all too aware of and even remorseful about my imperfections, yet I am equally unwilling to let them go. I may wish to change, but I feel incapable on my own. Be my strength and encouragement as I seek to face the truth of my behavior and to transform those areas of my life that ultimately cause others and myself pain.

March 25
An Appetite for Health

Frequently scrolling through some part of the framework of my email account will be an advertisement for the latest diet. Diet fads have become such a common part of our marketing media that one might logically surmise that a diet plan is something for which most people seek, if not need. From *South Beach* to *Scarsdale*, following *Atkins* or *Jenny Craig*, each plan touts a special path to weight loss satisfaction and a trail to that desired svelte body; even a cereal only diet provides a *Special K* plan.

Perhaps our need for a compatible diet has grown out of another popular modern fixation, food preparation. Like so many women of her time, my mother surely had the *Better Homes and Gardens Cookbook.* Dressed in its familiar picnic tablecloth, red and white pattern, this five-ring binder was the staple of nearly every American household cooking shelf; today, however, it is merely one in a veritable library of cookbooks in our homes. While Julia Child and Graham Kerr, the Galloping Gourmet, perhaps, pioneered cooking on television, they would have to clamor for air space now, fighting off the likes of Emeril Lagasse, Wolfgang Puck and Rachael Ray, amongst the myriad of "cook-off" shows and travelogue shows in search of the world's most exotic delicacies.

With all of this attention to the preparation of food and then its dietary modifications, it is easy for us to forget what, essentially, food is for: nutritional sustenance! Our bodies need food to survive and, in the long run, this need is not for just *any* food, but for healthful, nutritional food. Like using a cheap oil or a bad gasoline in your car, the vehicle will likely operate, but the quality of the ride and then the life of the engine will both be compromised. Similarly, if we are looking to lose some weight and then stop eating entirely - fasting for weight loss - or cut out certain types of food that contain essential nutrients, we may achieve a temporary goal of shedding some pounds, but the loss will not be a healthful, nor likely a lasting one.

O God of Sustenance, like so many of your magnificent creations, we are not made to be entirely self-sufficient. Just as my soul hungers and thirsts for you, so does my body need proper nurturing. I have but this one body to see me through this life. Indeed, human creativity has fashioned a delicious variety with which to satisfy our palates, and the fine delicacies and desserts can be exquisite rewards in our often busy and humdrum lives. But let me not forget how, and for what I have been created. Help me to nurture my body with the food that it needs, just as surely as I come before you daily seeking victuals for the soul.

March 26
A Hunger for God

I am always a little bit surprised when a after a hearty morning breakfast I find myself hungry and ready to eat again just a few hours later. Am I really hungry, I think to myself, or is it just because it is around noon and it is "lunch time"? The routines of our eating can become just that – routines – and we can forget the real importance and the real need for our consumption. I have known many families who eat a structured breakfast, lunch, and dinner and at very specific times every day. There seems a certain value to that, a kind of regulation of one's body, but one also has to wonder if the body needs that kind of control. Food is necessary for the health of our bodies, and the sharing of it with others can also provide a kind of spiritual nourishment alongside the physical; and through the culinary arts, food transcends the usefulness of mere sustenance and becomes a full sensual experience of sight, smell, taste and, sometimes, even sound. But it is precisely because of all of these good things that surround our intake of food and drink that the art of fasting is of equal importance in our spiritual lives.

Fasting, the abstaining from food and often drink for a certain length of time, can be one of the most spiritually invigorating gifts that we can give our body and soul. Food is necessary, but our habitual intake of it skews food's importance and reveals our body's enslavement to it. To put it most simply, as eating satisfies our physical hunger, fasting responds to our spiritual appetite. When I fast, I conscientiously remind myself – and teach my body – that I am more than just the physical, and that my spiritual self needs equal parts nourishment as well. The body and spirit are not in opposition here, as if the deprivation of one is the only way to feed the hunger of the other. There already exists an imbalance where the body usually gets the most attention and is always served first, and fasting is simply an effort to restore some of the balance between the body and the spirit.

How and when and why one chooses to fast is all part of the prayerful movement of this wonderful exercise, and a little practice will help to answer many of the fear-filled questions that people often carry about fasting. Some good literature can provide valuable guidance as to the duration of one's fast and whether or not one will choose to abstain from all fluids as well, but these are the "mechanics" of fasting, and they should not overshadow the heart of the art: one's intention. Fasting is a living, breathing, hungering, thirsting prayer for "more": more attention to the soul, a deeper hunger for the Divine, and an unquenchable thirst for the union of the two. When I fast, I say to my body and all things physical, "Look, I know that you are important, and I enjoy and appreciate you, but I need you to know that there is something even more important to me;" and then the conversation shifts toward God and I can truly say, "Great One, my relationship with you is the most important focus of my life, and on this/these days, I give you my full attention." Instead of eating, I now have more time for prayer, and when the gnawing pangs of hunger and the parched yearning of thirst creep in, I am given countless reminders of who matters most in my life, and who and what I want in control of my life.

Besides the spiritual benefits, there truly are many good physical reasons to fast as well. But if this cessation from the physical seems too demanding or is medically unwise, a person might also consider "fasting" from other habits and addictions in one's life. For me, a simple thing like abstaining from music, a deep love and common part of my day, for a stretch of time can create similar fasting reflections as well as create more quiet space in my life for prayer and reflection.

Insatiable God, for you I truly hunger and thirst; of you I can never have enough. Help me to discover other pathways that can truly feed my desire for you, and give me the strength and the courage to pursue them. My body is a gift with which I have been entrusted, but assist me in teaching it that it is not the lord of my life; I reserve that honor for you. Emptying myself today, I turn towards you and ask for your fulfillment.

March 27
Holding Hands

Whenever I had the infrequent opportunity to visit my Grandmother during her last years, I most enjoyed just sitting before her and holding her hands. By then, her "present mind" had drifted away and she was mainly living in glimpses of the past, but such a perspective only enhanced the soft grasp of our hands. Having held nearly one hundred years of life in those hands, the skin had become like wax paper, soft and translucent. Gently caressing the backs of her hands, I found the blue veins beneath the thin veneer were unlabeled roadmaps of her history. The children, grandchildren and great-grandchildren she had held, and all the toils of diapers, housecleaning, sewing, and cooking that she had lovingly endured were all somehow etched into those hands. Holding them in my own hands was like holding a sacred history, a wisdom not of word or action but of wear.

Nearly twenty years later, while spending time with my own Mother in her last days, these same thoughts came rushing back to me as I found myself gently holding her hand one day. As my thumb softly stroked the delicate relief of the back of her hand, I wondered anew at all that these, my Mother's hands, had known. While reminiscent of her own Mother's hands, they were not her Mother's, however. Although my Mother's hands also conveyed the wisdom of wear, her choices and her experiences, her trials and joys were her own; the network of roads on the map of her hands was surely different.

Physiologically, hands are arguably a human's most important tools of action. Very little of what the fully-abled person does does not involve the use of hands, and so, by metaphoric extension, it is reasonable to see one's hands as a type of expression of one's very life. Subsequently, when we touch or hold hands, we do grasp something at the very heart of another's being. There is a cliché about the depth of one's awareness that says, "I know (whatever the subject might be) like the back of my hand." While this axiom of "knowing our hands" may be a bit of an exaggeration, the adage suggests that we do study and are aware of our own hands, and in "knowing our hands" we know something deeply of ourselves. In the Hebrew Scriptures, at a time when the early Israelite people felt forsaken by God, the prophet Isaiah spoke to the people reassuring them that God held them ever near: "Behold, I have engraved you in the palm of my hands" (Is. 49:16). Carved into the hands of God, the prophet suggests, we are known and are very much at the heart of God's activity. To know our own hands, and to know the hands of a beloved other is to be consciously engaged in our own and in others' inner lives.

Loving God, I seek to be received into your hands, and pray that you will gently hold all of my loved ones – and all of your creation – in your all-encompassing hands. To be engraved into your hands, to be known by you and to be at the heart of your activity are my greatest desires. Take my hand, and lead me in your ways.

March 28
Thy Will Be Done

Many church communities have thoughtfully developed "prayer chains" amongst their willing and interested members. In daily and weekly phone calls or emails, participants are informed of needs within the community and its membership that could use the power and gift of prayer. Even without these systematic prayer chains, I hear myself and others offering the support of our prayers to another as well as sometimes, in our most dire of needs, perhaps, asking for prayers ourselves. If we think of prayer as being a loving and supportive embrace that holds the needs and very life of another in our arms, how wonderful is this gift of prayer for one another.

But sometimes I do think that our approach to prayer can create a kind of double-edged sword. What is it exactly that we are praying for? Are we trying to bargain with God or do we think that God, perhaps, doesn't see things as God should and so we send our prayers as reminders to God, as if to say, "Hey, I got something here for you that needs a little more attention than you seem to be giving it right now." And further, "Here's what *I* would like you to do with it." And if and when things don't work out quite like we would want them to, as we prayed for, do we say that perhaps we haven't prayed hard enough?

The scene of Jesus praying in the Garden of Gethsemene has always impressed me as being a valuable model for prayer. In this scene, Jesus must feel like his world is absolutely caving in on him. Something of a rebellious leader with a holy and good cause, he has had the support and attentive affection of the masses for some months, even years, now; but on this night, near the heart of the political and religious center of his world, he no doubt feels it all slipping away in misunderstanding and confusion. Even his best friends, his most constant companions, in this scene have fallen asleep leaving him, in his prayer, feeling quite alone. In his anguish, he asks God if it might be possible to "let this cup pass from me," admitting his fear of the difficult task that appears like a dark storm brooding before him; but then he adds, "not as I will, but as you will" (Mt. 26:39).

Prayer is an overt recognition both that we know that we cannot do all things on our own, and that we believe that, in fact, we are not all alone. If we stand squarely in the faith that our experience is "shared," the belief that God does care and is "in this" with us, then how much better it would be for us to seek the will of God - "thy will be done" - and to embrace the challenges before us rather than always simply asking for "our way."

Compassionate God, life is not always easy, and the obstacles that I face can sometimes feel overwhelming, even life-threatening. I need your help to make it through many of these challenges, and while I would prefer for you to sometimes just sweep into my troubles and make everything all right, I ask for your will to be done, not mine. Buoy me with the strength and the confidence that I might need to make it through life's struggles, and if the storm clouds should clear, may it be your shining face that greets me.

March 29
Love Your Enemies

The wondrous effects of love are so self-evident. An infant that is cuddled, tenderly spoken to, and playfully tickled with the eyes of love emerges consciously into a world of awareness and sensitivity. Young teens, unsure of themselves and unable to see their own gifts, break from their protective cocoons, spread wings and attempt to fly when the sunlight of love first warms their encasement. Adults, dry and disenchanted by careers and livelihoods that no longer satisfy, suddenly scurry once again like autumn bees collecting the summer's last nectar when they are rejuvenated by new love and friendships. Love is exciting and enlivening!

It is no wonder, then, that essentially all of the spiritual paths throughout history and across the globe have love as a centerpiece in their message. The rallying cry to "love one another!" seems almost an unnecessary reminder given the obvious power of love's effect. But, I have to admit, that sometimes I think that the master teacher, Jesus of Nazareth, took this whole "love thing" a bit too far when he challenged us with his version of love: "But to you who hear I say, love your enemies, do good to those who hate you, bless those who curse you, pray for those who mistreat you" (Lk. 6:27-28). What!? Love my enemies - those who hate, curse and mistreat me!? Surely, you must be kidding, or at least, you mean for us to "just be nice" in return. No, the challenge truly is to "love your enemies." For love is transformational and healing, and imagine what the power of love might do to even the most hardened of hearts.

Nevertheless, I admittedly struggle with this ideal to love my enemies. Political pundits whose only purpose, it seems, is to tear down the best efforts of others while they perpetuate a shrouded selfish agenda of their version of constitutional rights - love them? The insatiably thirsty capitalists who think nothing of raping the land and its resources for their own profit, or who see nothing wrong with abusing the ignorance of others for their own personal gain - love them? The fanatical terrorists who cheer the destruction of innocent lives and are able to sacrifice even their own people for a cause that would ultimately provide no real freedom and respect of others - love them? And the answer keeps coming back, "Yes."

O God who is Love, I am most grateful that I have had the great fortune to be loved into and throughout my life, and through that love I clearly understand its power and grace. But when you ask of me to love *everyone,* even those who seem born of hatred and desire only to perpetuate selfish ideals, I falter miserably. Can I truly love *everyone*? I feel that I am incapable of such a challenge, and yet, born of your love, made in your image and likeness, I do believe that I must push ever forward in an effort to meet that challenge. But I cannot do it alone. Please, help me God, to truly love one another.

Most of us have been guilty at one time or another to the blindness of our own predilections. Whenever I hear someone say, "Well, I'm not prejudiced, but…" I always roll my eyes and think to myself, "Oh, yeah, and you don't breathe either, right?" The way I see it, *everyone* is prejudiced in at least some small way; it is just plain inevitable, a circumstance of our cultural upbringing. Why is it that we favor certain foods over others, particular clothing and hair fashions, and specific teams and alliances? All of these things are heavily influenced by when and where and to whom we are born, and our bodies and minds run a remarkably covert operation to construct strong but nearly invisible fences between what is familiar to us and what is not. And "amazingly" enough, we tend to favor those things most familiar to us, and develop an aversion toward the unfamiliar. Essentially, predilections are shaped by our cultural upbringing and, through time, these preferences subtly morph into prejudices.

When we "proclaim" that we "are not prejudiced," what we really mean to say is that we don't discriminate. Prejudice is nearly impossible to avoid, but acting upon one's prejudice – discrimination – is what a person does have control over. Like stereotypes, one's prejudice is not entirely unfounded. There is usually some "history" that reveals a "general affinity" of one thing over another, and evidenced enough, assumptions emerge. I know many Italians, and most of the Italians I know definitely have a predilection for pasta. Were they born with that penchant for pasta, or did they learn it from the families in which they grew? And since nearly every Italian I know prefers pasta dishes, my stereotype is that all Italians like pasta; the general assumption is true enough, but its particular application to *every* Italian is, of course, not true. Furthermore, entering the realm of "acting on one's prejudice," when I invite an Italian to dinner, do I only serve pasta dishes because, after all, that is all that Italians eat?

For many people, to admit to prejudice seems akin to confessing to discrimination; but the two, while unquestionably related, *are* very different. When I recognize and admit my prejudice, I take the first step towards gaining control over it. Be it towards food, clothing, or more importantly, people, knowing wherein my prejudices lie allows me to more conscientiously address how I act upon those preconceived notions. When I sense my prejudice towards another person or group or country on the rise, I know that I need to step back and evaluate those feelings immediately before I say or do anything else. I can soften and, perhaps, change my prejudice over time, but I can prevent and eliminate my discrimination, my negative "re-action" to my prejudice, right now.

God of Truth and Justice, it is almost impossible for me to go through life without developing and harboring some prejudices. Where these have been wrongfully planted, help me to uproot the vile weeds. Where they have been deposited by the wild winds of experience and enculturation, assist me in identifying these growths that are not indigenous to the better part of my soul, and prevent them from taking over the best of who I am. Aware of my general prejudices, may I set them aside when I deal with specific people in particular situations, pruning away the hurtful thorns of discrimination.

March 31
But the Flesh is Weak

After years of putting in daily runs to keep in shape and to maintain a healthy lifestyle, I decided that my body could use a little rest, so I took about a three month hiatus from running. When I returned, it was with the eagerness of the spirit, but I found that the body was not so cooperative. Shocked at how quickly and thoroughly I had seemingly lost my edge in running, I swallowed the truth and set out to earn back my stamina. A year later with only short spurts of comfortable running strung throughout the calendar, I found my spirit waning as I continually faced an unresponsive body. Questions puffed out of my panting breaths: Was I suffering from some subtle lethargic ailment? Had I aged just enough that my intermission from running had plunged me into an abyss from which I would never fully emerge? Was I being too easy – or too hard – on myself in working to regain my earlier conditioned state?

Such struggles and questions are not unique to the body; the spirit knows them well too. Although I have never had the need to take a three month hiatus or any intentional extended break from my spiritual practices, some times I do find that, like my body, my spirit grows a bit lethargic in its exercises, and my prayers and meditations feel like air-filled balloons drifting on a loose string. Similar to the questions that arise when my physical condition feels flabby and undisciplined, the questions of the soul smolder like a dying coal and the fragrant incense of my efforts resists igniting. When this torpor of body or spirit pitches camp within me, there is certainly the temptation to just leave it alone and tolerate the scoundrel neighbor. But experience has taught me that an eviction notice is the better approach; this is not the time to just give in.

When Jesus' disciples joined him in his darkest hour of doubt, they showed an interest in supporting him, but then fell asleep leaving him quite alone. Observing their weakness, Jesus noted, "The spirit is willing, but the flesh is weak." Indeed, our best intentions for spiritual and physical exercise often come from a very willing spirit, but they too often trip over the body's less than equal vigor, fall, and sometimes go right to sleep. If we are to advance on our spiritual journey and have a body to carry us along the way, we need a disciplined and dedicated body *and* spirit.

Faithful God, I know too well how weak my body can be despite my spirit's encouragement, and how my body's weakness can put a mighty strain on my spirit's willingness. I seek health in body and spirit, and know that one cannot succeed without the other. You have gifted me with this body and encourage me through the spirit; help me to discipline these two comrades to work in balanced synchronicity so that I may run enthusiastically with a light spirit toward you, the source of my and all energy.

April 1
Patient Passion

At the heart of the Easter Triduum, the three celebrated days in Christianity prior to the religion's central event of Easter, is "the Passion of Christ." The first two of these three days honor Jesus' emotionally riveting last supper with his closest companions as well as his arrest, torture and execution; the final day before Easter reveres the quiet and deep sadness that followed his burial. Interestingly, our more common use of the word "passion" today has taken on a somewhat different twist. Along with the word "passionate," we tend to think of passion as something for which we feel strongly, and often these can be very personal choices and beliefs, or, almost conversely, very public heroic acts. Love, too, is quickly associated with things of passion and passionate. Now, in the Christian story, Jesus clearly possesses and professes some very personal beliefs, which inevitably lead him toward personal choices that culminate in his very public heroic act. Furthermore, his personal beliefs and his ultimate sacrificial act of death were, in the Christian tradition, totally done out of a spirit of love. However, much more aligned with the imagery of "the Passion of Christ," at the etymological heart of the word "passion," from the Latin "pati," are "suffering" and "enduring"; and these are arguably the qualities most associated with "the Passion of Christ."

As one might suspect given the Latin root of "pati," the words "patience" and "passion" share the same etymology. While we do think of patience as "enduring," we do not necessarily think of it so much as "suffering." But, perhaps, there is something more for us to learn in the connections of these words, stories, and experiences.

Although we have reduced it to little more than "waiting quietly," patience, we have been told proverbially, is a virtue, and a virtue, in this case, of cardinal quality. Indeed, if patience is not only "enduring" by waiting quietly, but includes "suffering" during that wait, then it logically becomes a virtue of higher quality. Likewise, if we are willing to endure suffering to achieve something for which we are passionate, then the depth of our love and commitment to that passion in fact takes on rather heroic qualities as well. Given these connections, I might conclude that patience should always be at the heart of our passions, and that when we are truly patient we willfully embrace and endure suffering.

The Christian stories of the Passion of Christ and of Easter are extraordinary in their claim that, through Jesus, God steps into our human experience and willfully embraces the suffering of misunderstanding, rejection, fear, and even death, as we know them. To be patient in the face of such pain and to endure it is no easy task, and yet, in the next chapter of the Christian story, we are all called to share in that Passion of Christ, and so enjoy his Easter. Maybe a good dose of patience can help us be more passionately involved with one another and with the one who created us all. Patient and Passionate God, help me to see and to embrace my moments of patience as a sharing in the suffering and the love of your extraordinary passion.

Reinserting the yeasts of enduring and suffering into the mix of passion and patience gives rise to the age-old question of the value of suffering itself. Except for a true pathological masochist, no one really wants or seeks suffering and pain, but it is difficult to ignore the role that suffering has played, perhaps, in all spiritual and religious traditions throughout humanity's history. Indeed, nearly every great spiritual leader and teacher has not only endured great suffering in his lifetime, but has also willingly embraced it. Given this fact, it is hard to not believe that there truly is value in suffering.

Suffering, of course, can have many visages. When my nose, ears, eyes and chest are locked up in what feels like a monumental battle with some head and chest infection, I am suffering. But when I place that temporary condition in the context of other more life-threatening diseases and personal losses, it probably ranks pretty low. Additionally, while it is difficult to pinpoint and rank emotional suffering, it is no less difficult to endure, and sometimes even more life threatening, than physical pain. The point of these considerations is that with regards to the spiritual value of suffering, what the source of pain is and the degree to which one suffers are not quite as important as how one embraces the suffering and to what end one chooses to endure it.

Without question, suffering humbles us, and a little humility is always a necessary ingredient in our spiritual recipe. But much more than simply humbling us, suffering provides us with a perspective of life that we too often and too easily lose when we distance ourselves from it. Self-sufficiency is a good "achievement," but being able to care for all of one's own physical and emotional needs can blind a person to some other essential facts of our existence. People can eat, exercise, sleep and live as healthfully as possible so as to sustain a quality level of well-being, but the proof in the pudding is that, ultimately, we are not in control. Our good health is truly a great gift, and while people should not ignore or neglect their role in its maintenance, we cannot control every factor in our environment. Suffering is a reminder that I am not in control. Related to that lack of total control, while some of us need others in our lives more than others do, we are all social beings, and we all do receive nourishment from the attention, care and help of others. In suffering, that nourishment is conceivably essential, and while I may choose to resist it and claim that it is unnecessary, people will find ways to knead it into the hard dough of my life, and everyone benefits from that exchange whether realized or not.

I have long thought that a rare, few Evangelical Christian churches do their congregations a great disservice when they preach what is sometimes called a "Gospel of Affluence." Their errant message suggests, sometimes even proclaims, that if one accepts Jesus of Nazareth as the Son of God and as personal Lord and Savior, the person will obtain complete health and wealth. The lack of either of those then becomes evidence of a need for greater effort, deeper faith. No, Jesus himself wholly embraced his own suffering and poverty, and reached out especially to those enveloped by it. Yes, suffering makes us more aware of the goodness of life, the giftedness of life; it offers renewed perspectives of who is really in control and what matters most to us in our lives.

Perhaps the fact that suffering is so often an ingredient of our lives whether chosen or not suggests that it is an essential leaven. God of All Suffering, I do not blame you for the travails that so many must endure, and I suspect that like most of us, you empathetically endure the pains of others. I need not rush toward pain, for it will likely find me soon enough, but when I must eat the bread of suffering, help me to chew on it thoughtfully, patiently, and passionately, realizing that it too is food for nourishment.

April 3
Choosing to Suffer

Every year during Ramadan, Muslims go through a month long sacrifice of fasting from food and drink from sunrise to sunset. Likewise, many Christians during the early spring season of Lent willingly choose to relinquish some food, drink, or activity for forty days. And every June, many people who honor and follow Native American traditions gather together in different places across the country for the Sun Dance where they will fast, dance, pray, and often endure some physical pain. Each of these traditional acts of sacrifice is an acknowledgment of the value of suffering. However, these examples are particularly unique in that they do not simply embrace suffering, but appear to even seek it. Because suffering tends to strip us down to the essentials of life, many religions and spiritual practices do, in fact, encourage people to move towards their suffering, even suggesting that one "create" a little bit of it for himself. These willful creations of suffering are, in truth, usually little more than personal discomforts, but they do steer our hearts and minds into the deeper considerations of what most matters to us.

An athlete engaged in serious training willfully endures a certain level of suffering. Research and practice have shown the athlete, that if she wants to improve, fine tune and perfect her skill, then she must be willing to challenge and to stretch the apparent limits of her physical ability. In a similar fashion, spiritual practices that include the acceptance of physical discomfort are sometimes offered as ways to improve and increase one's spiritual resolve. In these cases, the acceptance of discomfort is offered as a deeper spiritual rejection of our rather normative attachment to the physical desire for comfort. The meaningfulness and the benefits of such chosen "suffering," however, go beyond the physical, expressing an intentional belief in things spiritual.

Interestingly, the opening examples are, essentially, sacrifices that are done within a community setting or lived out within a community context. In our shared choice of sacrifice, of suffering together, we create a two-fold solidarity: there is the communion of people sacrificially acting together; and this community action joins them with a larger community on whose behalf they may be sacrificing. This latter act of solidarity is also an acknowledgment of the "sacrificial community's" belief in the power of prayer and action. The word "sacrifice" implies a "sacred action, a doing on behalf of or for the sake of another." One's intention should not be, as it likely was in the ancient past, to manipulate God through sacrifice; however, the person of faith no doubt is offering a more strident voice of prayer through his sacrifice. While he may do all that he physically can for the sake of whatever it is that he prays, choosing "sacrificial suffering" – figuratively stripping oneself down and embracing one's own fragility - is an acknowledgment that he is not in control and he cannot do it all. All I truly have is myself, and while even that is a gift from the Creator, I willingly offer back some part, in sacrifice, to the one who has given me all. In a sense, rather than trying to conquer the universe through one's own intellectual efforts and physical prowess, a person accepts his frailty and inadequacy, enfolds it into the universe of things – into God's hands – and therein discovers a clearer harmony and a deeper solidarity with the universe, with God. Choosing to suffer, not simply embracing the suffering with which we are often faced, should only be done after much prayerful thought and consideration. Like so many things, it too can be of the "ego," whereas its intention should be entirely selfless.

The wounds that the earth and the universe endure at the hands of our irresponsibility and greed suggest to me your willingness, Creator God, to embrace suffering on our behalf. You too must ache at our treatment of one another and of all your creations, and yet you allow us to endure, experiencing both the joys and pains of life. Let my meager acts of self-sacrifice join me in solidarity with you and with the growing pains of the universe, an act of repentance for what we have done, and an act of hope for what we might yet become.

April 4
All Life is Suffering

Buddhism provides an *entirely different* approach to the issue of suffering than what has been considered the last few days. Paradoxically, one might conclude from the Buddhist perspective that "all life is suffering," and that really, "suffering doesn't even exist."

Siddhartha Gautama, the enlightened one – the Buddha, did not leave his luxurious lifestyle at the age of twenty-nine to seek what Westerners might call "salvation," or a heavenly reward. Unconcerned with life after death, he questioned the pangs of this earthly existence. After years of being shrouded from the harsh realities of life, when Siddhartha first encountered disease, old age and death, he felt overwhelmed by the anguish and pain – the suffering – that he saw in these inevitable experiences. To counter this suffering, he sought answers in the religious texts of his culture, the Hindu Upanishads, Vedas and Gitas, and looked for respite through the Brahminic rituals of the Hindu priests. Like so many other great spiritual seekers, he also chose physical deprivation as a way to gain insight, enduring pain and extreme fasts. But while every effort afforded some temporary, insightful glimpse, he always found himself right back where he started, surrounded by the suffering and the imminence of sickness, old age and death. As the legend goes, dissatisfied with all of the traditional outlets, one day Siddhartha finally sat down beneath a Bo tree deciding that he would not leave there until he discovered an answer to his question of "overcoming suffering." Deep within meditation, the young prince confronted the demonic onslaughts of the passions that so often tempt and ensnare us, and through these battles he moved towards his enlightenment: through simple discipline and clarity of the mind one could achieve contentment, the heart of the "salvation" he sought.

Fearing that his new awareness could not be put into words, but driven by a deep compassion for all, Siddhartha, the Awakened One, reluctantly agreed to teach his new-found truth. In his first sermon, he outlined what would become famously known as "The Four Noble Truths." The first of these truths is that "all life is suffering." However, as the Buddha would continue, this suffering is not an unavoidable evil, but rather a creation or a result of our own passions, for the second truth is that "the cause of suffering is selfish desire." What the Buddha had discovered was that our suffering is not so much the result of outside forces, but the consequence of our own clinging self-interests. So enamored to things and people are we that the very thought of losing them, let alone the losses themselves, send us into the "suffering" of fear, anxiety, despair and emptiness. Associating the body and its constant desire for pleasure and comfort with "the self," we suffer when our imagined "self" is denied or fails – gets sick, ages and dies. Proposing a way out of this vicious entrapment (the third truth), the Buddha outlined simple but specific courses of action to separate the body's interests from the "true self" in the Eight-fold Path referred to in his fourth Noble Truth.

In Buddhism, suffering is not so much about physical pain as it is about the mental and emotional anguish of unhappiness and dissatisfaction. The Buddha's plan is not a life of austerity, but one of "detachment," letting go of our selfish desires. God of Enlightenment, you are the focus of my desires, although all too often I am consumed by my own selfish interests and allow them to be my "god for a day." The pleasures of this life are not evil, but they are not lasting either. Help me to enjoy them with detachment, knowing and accepting that they are fleeting. My only real suffering is when I am detached from you. Help me to let go of my selfish interests and, attached to you, find lasting happiness and contentment.

April 5
The Love of Detachment

The first of Buddhism's Four Noble Truths, that "all life is suffering," can make Buddhism sound like a very negative approach to life; similarly, the idea of "detachment" in Buddhism is sometimes easily misunderstood as being disconnected from the cares and concerns of this life. Nothing could be further from the truth, however. In fact, much like the mission and message of Jesus of Nazareth, the Buddha was a man full of compassion, and a follower of his teachings must aspire to nothing less.

First of all, again, in Buddhism "suffering" might be better translated as "unhappiness and discontentment," and none of us would seek or want either of these. In fact, we spend most of our lives pursuing happiness and contentment, and in this pursuit, we continually bump into suffering, for we fail to realize or accept another essential principle within the Buddha's teachings, that "life is impermanent." Further, the desires that are seen as the root of our suffering are not evil in and of themselves; what makes desires problematic are the selfish interests that we attach to them and our belief that not only will we have happiness once we fulfill these desires, but that also somehow we can make these things last, that we can defy the inevitable impermanence of our lives. But aren't these the very things that we seek "in" and "from" love? How can one not be attached to another "in love"?

In Western marriages especially, we tend to think in terms of, sometimes even use, the language of "unity," that the "two shall become one." Indeed, in a healthy marriage, while one should never lose his or her personal identity, the couple must often work together "as one," compassionately concerned for the good of the other and the shared relationship. The Buddha and Jesus would suggest that we need, in fact, to assume that view with everyone. But isn't that being "attached"? To be lovingly committed to another person and to best serve the needs of all life is not an attachment unless I hang my happiness on the hooks of the others' presence and their responses to my proffered love. To be attached to another is to believe that I cannot live without the other, that my happiness is impossible without this person or that thing in my life. These are the attachments that will lead to inevitable suffering for not only are the people and things of our lives impermanent, but so too may be the love I receive from them and the enjoyment and happiness that they may provide. The Buddha's compassion, like Jesus' unconditional love, is truly giving while letting go of the selfish desires for something in return. If I receive love in return, I can be grateful for love's contentment, but if I receive nothing, I can still be content for gratefully knowing and accepting the impermanence of all things.

Loving God, you alone are truly permanent, your love truly eternal. I know something of that love and find great joy in it through the gifts of loving people and the beauty of your creations. But these people and things, like my own life itself, are impermanent. Gladden my heart with these temporary joys; sustain my heart with the awareness of their brevity. Help me to be a compassionate model of your ceaseless love and your eternal presence.

April 6
Don't Drive Thru Life

While a European friend was visiting my wife and me some years ago, she was rather amused by all of our "Drive Thru" conveniences. The pick-it-up-as-you-go expediency of fast food restaurants is so common to Americans that we rather expect it, and the same might be said for the handiness of bank tellers. But when our friend observed pharmacy prescription windows, and then, the last straw, beer and wine drive thrus, she had to utter, "Oh my!" Actually, "amused" might have been her "kind perspective," for she also felt that such conveniences spoke of a subtle laziness in Americans. And, you know, I really couldn't argue against her point.

Perhaps more than just a love affair with convenience, and even deeper than a simple laziness, these drive thrus represent a kind of self-centered attention. Convenience and laziness are ultimately about "me," keeping my life easy and effortless; and when the effort is nothing more than putting my vehicle in park and stepping inside a building as opposed to driving through it, one might easily conclude that we have gotten awfully soft. If it were for time-saving purposes, one might at least have an alternative argument, but most of us have accepted waiting in long vehicle lines in lieu of getting out and stepping up to the empty counter inside for our purchase. We like to be served in comfort with as little hassle as possible, even if the comfort is nothing more than our own vehicle and the hassle is getting out of it.

Don't get me wrong: convenience is not an evil, and few, if any, have we demanded. But the fact that we have so many "luxuries" and conveniences in our lives perhaps speaks to a societal awareness of our softness, and a society which then chooses to feed and fatten it. And when we accept and then expect ease in one part of our lives, it is easy to anticipate it in others. From physical pleasure to spiritual leisure, one way can lead to another. Few things in our lives are inherently evil or wrong; the key, once again, is how we allow or prevent ourselves from being manipulated by our want of ease. One shouldn't feel guilty for using a drive thru, but maybe periodically, it might be worthwhile to think about how often one does use them and why. This simple exercise of mindfulness can help keep one's self-centered softness a little less flabby.

God of Fitness, in creating me, you invite me to be an active participant in life. Gifting me with good health and a body capable of extraordinary movement and dexterity, you bid me to put my faculties to energetic use. Sometimes I just want to drive through life and be served, and sometimes, I can. But help me to remain mindful of my inactivity so as not to grow physically soft and spiritually weak. As I drive through life may I not pass the windows of opportunity to counter my self-centered indulgences.

April 7
Selflessness

All the great religions of the world speak of the importance of selflessness. For some it is a kind of duty for one's acceptance by God and salvation, while others speak of it more altruistically with no regard for reward or recognition. Each of the Ten Commandments of Judaism essentially rejects self-interest, speaking instead to the respect and honor of others. Jesus, the incarnation of God in Christianity, commissions his disciples by saying that "if anyone desires to be my disciple, let him deny himself" (Mt. 16:24), and then willingly sacrifices himself to show just how far he means. Stories abound in Islam of "eethaar," the Muslim expression of altruism. From soldiers who die of thirst after passing up water to give it to others they deem more in need than themselves to the near-starving prophet Muhammad giving his newly acquired flock of sheep to another who desired them, these examples give flesh to the Quran's words that "they give others preference over themselves even though they were themselves in need"

(59:9). The Eastern traditions of Hinduism and Buddhism also are founded on selfless practices and views. Combining the "Margas," or paths, of Karma Yoga and Bhakti Yoga, one is dutifully drawn not only to service in Hinduism, to act on behalf of others, but to do so out of love. Buddhism, perhaps, takes selflessness furthest by essentially "requiring" a denial of the self, recognizing that the source of all of the suffering which prevents us from happiness and contentment is the egotistical self. The role of the bodhisattva, one who postpones his own nirvana, his own enlightenment, until he has guided all his fellow beings to the same source of fulfillment, is nothing less than an embodiment of the altruistic principle. Yet, despite all of the directives from these and from many other religious traditions as well as the cultures themselves, human beings seem to struggle with this principle of selflessness more than any.

To overcome selfishness takes discipline; one does not choose to be selfless and then quickly achieves it. So much within us and so many forces outside of us tempt us "to look out for and take care of number one," the self. Perhaps part of our difficulty is that we try to do too much all at once instead of honoring the strength of the self's pull, like trying to run a marathon before we feel comfortable running two miles, or climbing Mt. McKinley before we have tackled the foothills of the Appalachians. One has to start more simply and work her way up.

Skipping a drive thru, spoken of yesterday, and parking the car instead is a simple practice in self-denial, although it does little if anything for anyone else. But once you accomplish some small steps and realize that you can survive – and happily – then move to the next level, sacrificing on behalf of others; again, keep it simple. Do something with a friend or spouse that he or she absolutely enjoys but that you would otherwise resist because of your lack of interest in it, and do it with love, not out of duty or expectation. Let the other's happiness and joy be the only happiness and joy you seek.

Generous God, you have given me so much in this life, and yet I so often selfishly seek to satisfy myself more and more. My hands can be your hands; the love you have for each of us can be revealed through my simple acts of selflessness, giving time and energy to others without seeking reward or merit. Give me the strength to step outside of my own interests and to serve the needs of others. When there is less me, there will be more you in my life. Help me to make selflessness my greatest need.

April 8
The Spirit is a Movin'

After my elderly Mother was diagnosed with acute myelogenous leukemia and given only a couple of months to live, her children rallied around her taking turns around the clock so that she could remain in the comfort of her home and enjoy their love and support until her end. I will always feel like I got to share her ten last best days. During that time, I would arise each day at 7:30 to join her in her morning prayer and meditation ritual. No matter how tired I might have been from the late night before, it was a reviving joy to turn the corner each morning and see her fragile, dying body waiting patiently for me to join her.

One week after she died, at home again with my emotional and physical exhaustion seemingly assuaged, I awoke one morning eager to return to my own old routine. Planting myself in my prayer corner to open the morning with my daily meditation and prayer, I lit a candle, just as my Mother had done for all of her meditative years, and settled into a prayerful posture. Immediately I was quietly aroused by a curious sound, two gentle taps that seemed to come from one of the drums hanging on the wall beside me. I smiled curiously thinking about my Mother. Five to ten minutes into my meditation, I gently opened my eyes and was quickly fascinated by the movement of two prayer flags within a larger bundle hanging limply before me. Thinking that perhaps it was merely the energy from the heat of the candle some three feet below the flags, I extended my hand to feel the sensation of this curious airflow. I felt nothing, no heat nor breeze, as the house was still shut up in the cool spring morning. Nestling back onto my prayer stool, I watched with prayerful amusement as the yellow flag celebrating new life and the green flag honoring our common Grandmother, the earth, continued to gently dance on the unseen breath of a kindred spirit for the extent of my prayer.

Who knows why exactly those flags moved so softly in the still air of my room, or what harmless settling of the house created those gentle thumps, for me on that morning, I was absolutely sure that my Mother had come to join me in prayer. And why not? For those of us who believe that this earthly life is not only not all that there is, but that there is even a connection linking *what is* to *what will be*, why should one not also harbor the possibility of touching that connection? If we proclaim an eternal life, then we should be willing to live in that eternity, or at least experience it now and then, in this here and now.

Eternal God, today I respectfully remember and honor those spirits who live without end, those loved ones, as well as the many unknowns, who have entered fully into the celestial realm. Just as surely as there is much moving about me right now unknown to my limited human sensibility, your presence and the spiritual presence of my forebears lingers lovingly about me. I need not go looking to capture or to see these manifestations, but help me to be open to their loving presence which, perhaps, longs equally to share some time with me.

April 9
Living In a Fog

While fog is frequently seen as a driver's nightmare, I always welcome it as if it were an ephemeral entrance into the dream world. But unlike nightmares and dreams from which we awaken and discover we have only been peering into our subconscious world, for me, fog makes manifest an imperceptible reality of the very essence of life. Ironically, while we think of fog as closing in and limiting our vision, it is instead an opening to the awareness of the connectedness of all life.

116

In the first creation story in the ancient Hebrew Scriptures, before God created the heavens and the earth, it reads that a mighty *ruah* (wind) swept over the waters. In the second creation story that follows, after God molds man from the clay of the earth, the text reads that God then "blew into his nostrils the *ruah* (breath) of life, and so man became a living being." Finally, this word, *ruah*, is also used in much the same sense as the Greek *pneuma*, which can be translated as "spirit, wind, air and breath." Hence, what is implied is that the Spirit of God, present in the wind at the beginning of creation and in the life-giving breath to the created man, can be experienced, or is made palpable in the very air that surrounds us, in the very breath that sustains us. These things which seem invisible to us in a tangible way then "come to life" in the semblance of a fog. When there is fog, the air around us, the air that unites us all, becomes "visible."

In a similar fashion on the other side of the globe, in the Native American *inipi* or sweat lodge ceremony, inside "the womb" of the sweat lodge, *p'o* (fog) is created when water intermingles with the heated rocks of the earth. This *p'o* is then referred to as the *waniya* (breath) of God surrounding us; engulfed in this presence and breathing it in, the participants are cleansed both physically and spiritually. Thus, when I encounter fog, I see how the whole world around us is like a womb, and as we mindfully dwell in this "universal *inipi*," we are sustained and united to all living things through the *waniya*, the breath of God, moving about us always like a soft breeze.

Life-Giving God, I am surrounded always and everywhere by your life-giving breath. People long to see your face, to experience your presence in their lives, but too often assume that you are ultimately inaccessible and remote. Help me to be mindful of your essence, your Spirit, in the air that surrounds and provides me with life this day. May I not live blindly in a fog unable to see your presence, but may the fog reveal to me more palpably how very present you are everyday.

April 10
Deer God

In my last year of high school and then immediately thereafter, I found myself drawn to a quiet, monastic life. Ironically, my adult life and career have been wrapped up in closely working with people. Somewhere in my early thirties, however, the more ascetic spirit and voice within me called out once again, wanting some attention. I eventually responded by taking semiannual treks "into the wild." In those first years, my wilderness was the forestlands of southeastern Ohio. I would head into the wooded hills, pitch my tent, and spend the next couple of days prayerfully alone.

One of my favorite activities during those reclusive days was to try to catch sight of a deer as I wandered about exploring the landscape. In the early spring, sometimes even before the first whispers of greenery were poking through the forest floor and the woods were not yet overrun with thick brambles and dense undergrowth, I could break from the common trails and follow those created by the four-legs that knew this land as home. Likewise, in the late fall, with the forest opening up as the leaves fell and the lower plants turning within for the winter, these same trails were even more pronounced, and tracking an imagined great buck became a day's effort. Soon, these "hunts" became a metaphor for my search for a deeper understanding of God.

Deer are magnificent animals. Their sheer size displays their power and strength; their majestic stature reveals their beauty; and their movement unveils their agility and speed. These are large animals whose presence and movements, particularly in the spring and fall it would seem, would be very easy to discover. I would move about the woods with soft step, a walking meditation created naturally by my search, stealthily following a deer trail. There would be evident signs of their presence nearby always: prints in soft soil; decaying and fresh piles of scat; antler rubs on trees, marking boundaries or scratching new growth; and sometimes, the fond discovery of a resting place, once beneath the cover of brambles, but now exposed. Like the God I believe in, there were signs everywhere of its presence, but each day wandering endless miles through the woods, I was unable to come face to face with that which I sought - the deer and God. How could something so large move about so quietly through the woods and hide itself so completely in the increasingly exposed landscape? Even my soft step crackled leaves and twigs beneath foot, but rarely, if ever, would I hear such a sound from the deer. I would return to my tent each night, satisfied with the effort of the day, but disappointed by its lack of results.

Then, early one morning as the sun rose over the hillside and started its slide down into the ravine where I was camped, its light my wake-up call, I quietly unzipped my tent door and crawled out of my humble hovel. On my hands and knees, I looked up the slope and there they were, three deer standing quietly above me. I had not sought them out nor followed any signs; I had merely stayed in one place, resting, and they had come to me.

Sacred scriptures often speak of God's grandeur, and those of us who believe, long to see this wondrous beauty that is God. Sometimes I think if I could only get a glimpse of God, how much more easily and deeply I would believe, and I go off in search, hoping for that sacred sighting. But the truth is, God need not be sought in such a fashion. Sit down, be still, and know that God is near. Great One, too frequently, I set off wandering in hopes of discovering you. Help me today to realize that I need not track you down; I merely need to quietly sit still, listening and watching carefully, and know that you are just outside my tent door.

April 11
Submission to God

When I first started teaching about World Religions nearly twenty-five years ago, Islam was recognized as the world's second largest and the fastest growing religion. Today, its numbers are estimated still to trail those of all Christian denominations (Protestant, Roman Catholic, and Eastern Orthodox) combined, while the rate of its growth is no longer clearly estimable and rate rankings and percentages of growth are very difficult to measure given the varying sizes of the many religions of the world. Nevertheless, Islam continues to be a very popular choice amongst people of faith throughout the world. One of the main reasons that Islam is often cited for its increased growth and popularity is the simplicity of its faith tradition.

While all religious traditions encourage one's individual relationship with God, Islam, which literally means "peace and surrender or submission to God," especially acknowledges this simple and private relationship between God and the adherent; if one submits his will to the one God, in this surrender he will know true peace. Priests and ministers, and the ritual practices that are often uniquely theirs, are not important to Islam. Each person is born pure, and through dedicated and sincere worship of God and in kind and compassionate care of God's creations, one can draw ever nearer to the one God, Creator of all. Like all religions, there are certainly more "rules" and structure to Islam than what first meet the eye, but fundamentally, the Five Pillars of Faith encompass the essentials of the faith: 1) There is no God but God, and Muhammad is his prophet; 2) pray five times a day; 3) honor the holy month of Ramadan by observing the daily fast from all food and drink from sunrise to sunset; 4) give alms to the poor; and 5) if physically and financially possible, make a pilgrimage (hajj) to the holy city of Mecca at least once in one's lifetime. In short, honor God, and God alone; pray frequently; sacrifice annually through a one month fast and through almsgiving; and make a pilgrimage to Mecca, the center of the Islamic world, sometime in one's life; these are the essentials of Islam, of submission to God.

Although Muslims (adherents of Islam) hold weekly congregational meetings, usually on Fridays, for prayer and study at a local mosque, all daily prayer whether alone or alongside others is a private conversation between the adherent and God. Along with honoring many of the prophets of Judaism as well as Christianity's Jesus of Nazareth, Islam gives Muhammad preeminence as the "Seal of the Prophets," the one through whom God revealed finally and forever all that is needed; but Muslims are very careful to not deify any of the prophets, rejecting even any representation of them so as to avoid any threat of idolatrous worship of them. In these simple practices, one can see that Islam truly is a very personal faith where the mob scenes of extremism that too often get played out in our media are entirely incongruent.

There are often many discrepancies and misunderstandings even within a religious tradition, let alone between varying religions, and Islam is no exception. Many people in the West are troubled by Islam's apparent aversion to Western culture, alarmed by what they perceive as an oppressive Islamic state. But many Muslims fear the influence of Western culture simply because its values and interests do not ring true with the Sharia, the "way or path" of God's law as revealed through the sacred text of the Qur'an as well as through the sayings and examples set down by the prophet Muhammad in the Sunnah. In fact, a Muslim's disdain for Western culture is really no different than the Christian Right's similar attitude towards it. Capitalism and the "liberties" that Americans "take" are no more aligned with the teachings of Jesus than they are with the Sharia. Like the "Religious Right" in the United States, predominantly Islamic countries want an environment where the ideals of God govern the land, not the individual freedoms of a secular society.

The spiritual path of a Muslim is essentially a deep relationship with God, focused through daily prayer and a healthful lifestyle. What's not to love about that? Allah (a word that simply means "God" in Arabic), you are the One God. So often I make my relationship with you more difficult than it needs to be, creating all kinds of hoops though which I must jump. While rituals may guide me into a closer proximity with you, and congregations may unite me with the family of all believers, may I never neglect to work daily on my most fundamental relationship, the one between you and me.

April 12
Pain in Pennsylvania

A number of years ago over a spring break spent quietly alone, I decided I needed a little "wilderness fix." A bit short of time and cash, I realized that I needed to keep the hike fairly close to home. I had always wanted to explore some part of the Appalachian Trail, but after exploring the map, I realized that the quickest jump into the A.T. was still a very long day's drive away from central Ohio. Searching further, I stumbled upon an area in the Allegheny National Forest just south of Warren, a little town in the northwestern most regions of Pennsylvania, just south of the New York state border. The next morning I packed my car, finding ample space for my loneliness and lost-at-love melancholy, and headed northeast.

Later in the day, somewhere in Pennsylvania, in what appeared to me as some small, God-forsaken town, I stopped for gas. After a quick stretch, I slid my credit card into the pump and commenced the refill, quietly sipping the somber aura that seemed to engulf this dirty, little town. While I was lost in dreamy observation, a young man, perhaps in his late twenties or more, emerged from the gas station's quick stop shop. Dressed in dirty jeans and a soiled blue tank top, he seemed upset about something, and soon that something followed him out the door, a woman attired in the station's uniform smock. I don't recall what words were exchanged, or if there even were words that passed openly between them, but having suffered through the pangs of a broken marriage not long before myself, I felt immediately the emotion of the moment. Words are not necessary at such times; the face and the body's posture speak volumes. The pain and the sense of despair that quietly boil within one, sputter and spit out their mess like a simmering pan of spaghetti sauce left unattended on the stove. The gas tank filled, I grabbed my receipt, got back in the car and continued my drive to my lonely destination; but I have carried those two young lovers with me ever since.

Many, if not all of us, know at some time in our lives, loneliness and the pain of heartache. When we are in that stew, it is all we know, and we often feel quite alone. But we are not alone. What struck me that day as I drove away from that small Pennsylvania town whose name I don't even remember, and whose boundary I will likely never cross again, is that there too, just as in every large city to small village across the globe, people are hurting. All of us desiring attention and love and affection, and rightfully and wrongfully, we explore the desire seeking satisfaction; and often we get hurt, and that hurt feels like the biggest and the loneliest thing in the world.

Our fears and failures, our losses and loneliness are real, but no one of them is the biggest thing in the world, nor are we alone in them. God, help me today to recognize that the discomfort that I might carry within me today does not separate me from others, but actually joins me with them. And if today I am free of such discomfort, keep me mindful that somewhere out there, somebody else's world feels like it is caving in; perhaps I might provide them some air, some relief. Pain and loneliness *feel* big, but love and beauty are far more grand, far more real and lasting.

April 13
Senioritis

Every spring, and sometimes much earlier, in high schools all across the nation, an insidious virus starts to work its way into the hope-filled graduating class. Some students have developed a strong resistance to the viral strain, while others appear highly susceptible to the contagious virus. Ironically, while a virus requires "living cells of an organism," with this particular virus, once it locks in on the nearing graduation teenager, its symptoms make the organism – the student – appear lifeless. The virus is called "senioritis."

Arguably, this sinister virus is not limited to high school seniors, although they seem to be one of the most symptomatic and primary carriers. Older adults nearing retirement and people of all ages who have a job they disdain or a valuable relationship that has lost its flavor can also suffer from senioritis. The symptoms of this malady are usually quite obvious, and because schools have regular evaluative check-ups, for the high school student, there is often more frequent and ready evidence of the virus. The most common symptom is lethargy, or to put it in more colloquial terminology, laziness. Seeing the end of his high school career just ahead, and with all the necessary requirements for his graduation safely locked in, the senior begins to wonder, "What's the point?" If there is a reasonably good answer to that question, however, the student's viral infection pretty much ignores it or obliterates it altogether with other symptomatic responses such as, "Who cares? I've already been accepted to the college of my choice anyway." Indeed, college and university acceptance letters sent out in late winter or very early spring do not help in the fight against this virus, as one of the important incentives for a high school student is thus fulfilled. Assignments are neglected, classroom discussions grow drowsy, test preparation goes into a tailspin, and grades plummet; even extra-curricular involvement can be affected, sometimes dropped altogether.

Indeed, senioritis can infect anyone at any time throughout life. We get bored with what we do, with the way things are, and instead of injecting new life into these environments, we get lazy and do nothing. For the high school senior aspiring to further education who has heretofore been an involved, dedicated and conscientious student, such a shift is disingenuous for it opens the door to new bad habits that will only have to be broken when he returns to school the next fall. Additionally, and this is true for people of all ages, senioritis is selling the gift of life short. On the personal level, one looks his gifts in the eye and then "flips them off"; interpersonally, the virus carrier's attitude and lack of production mocks the values and drive that others have dedicated themselves to, the effort that "gets things done." And worse yet, when senioritis infects a relationship, the carriers spit in the face of love.

We all need breaks from what we do. Vacations are given from work, and summer, winter and spring breaks are built into academic calendars, and lovers who know better may even offer each other periodic solo excursions or outings with "the guys" or "the girls." But laziness and carelessness in anything that we do is a dangerous betrayal of the gifts that we have been given. Our jobs, our schooling, and our relationships are *not* who we are, but they are very important aspects that help to define and refine what and how we are.

God of Life, in breathing your spirit into us, you give us sacred life, inviting and encouraging us to actively engage in and maximize our experience of life. Sometimes I do grow weary and do lose interest in what I do; help me to be mindful of how I respond to this weariness and boredom. Inoculate me from the virus of senioritis, so that I might not misuse or neglect the gifts with which you have blest me, nor be a contagious source of infection to others.

April 14
Penny Thoughts

A number of years ago while moderating the service club at the school in which I taught, a fund raising proposition for the fight against leukemia crossed my desk; the program was called "Pasta for Pennies," wherein the "homeroom" of a school with the top fund raising percentage would receive a gratuitous pasta dinner from a local Italian restaurant sponsor. Between our parochial school's own fund raising efforts and the many other programs that our service club tried to support, I initially leaned toward passing on this particular request; but after conferring with the sodality's acting president, a young gal who had essentially spearheaded the club into existence in the first place, I agreed to accept the challenge. "Sure, we can do that!" she exclaimed, "and whatever it is that we are able to raise will be that much more than the Leukemia Society had in the first place."

In the following weeks, the club organized classroom representatives for the period just after lunch, with the simple proposition that each day for two weeks we would solicit the student's small pocket change – pennies – in potential exchange for a free pasta dinner. For my part, I supported the idea, but I put very little effort into its advertisement; dipping into the same well over and over, I felt, is only going to dry up the source.

After some relative success in the first week of "competition," the classroom representatives amped up their enthusiasm and encouragement, and suddenly it was not just the loose change from the day's lunch that was being dropped into the decorative coffee cans being passed about each day, but students were confiscating their piggy banks and coin jars from home and dumping them into their "team's" coffers. With a poster charting and breaking down the ongoing success, and a daily announcement offering "play-by-play" of the fund raising competition, the involvement, the contributions and the success continued to escalate. When the campaign drew to a close, three classrooms had earned a free dinner, and our relatively small school had raised nearly $15,000 – in change! - on behalf of the Leukemia Society.

Pennies have almost become a "throw away" denomination in our nation's currency, but this little coin, joined to one big effort, created a community of generosity and a substantially helpful donation to a worthy cause. It was a fine example of how "every little bit helps," and when "a lot of 'littles' join together, big things can happen." The penny of one student's willing heart pumped life into my dis-eased blood, and provided the arterial flow of a campaign's success.

O God of Small and Wondrous Miracles, you often use the most unsuspecting people and the most meager means though which to accomplish your grand designs. How many potential successes have I shot down through a negative attitude or an unsupportive voice? How many simple efforts have I ignored that were the seeds of your generous will seeking simple nourishment. Help me to pick up the penny people and possibilities in life, and to join with them in making what may seem a small, but wondrous contribution.

April 15
The Glistening Thread of Faith

Some mornings when the sun is just beginning its crest over the neighborhood rooftops and its rays run like fingers through the long hair of the backyard's vegetation, I catch a glint of an errant spider's thread lifting and falling in the morning's awakening air. The thin stray filament is essentially imperceptible except for these momentary morning shimmers that catch my eye when I glance out a back window. It almost always causes me to pause and to stare into the airy space a bit longer, waiting for a gentle breath of air to lift up the fine strand once more while the sunlight tiptoes across the flaccid fiber. With the momentary glimmer bringing it to light again, my eyes comb the seen and the imagined length of it trying to follow the strand to its origin, often the backyard clothesline or a window ledge. From the glistening thread's high origin, I glide back down the stretch of it and then realize that it is not truly hanging loosely or limp in the air. As a single strand, it appears unfixed and vulnerable, but at the end of its length, I find it attached to the birdbath or the hammock frame or maybe even a single blade of grass far below. And then I ponder the truly amazing leap of faith that is represented in this single thread's glint of light.

With all of the movement and activity that goes on in the backyard throughout the day, it is highly unlikely that the spider who created this marker of faith will get much further with his project; but the single strand that I sometimes catch in the morning light is likely the beginning of a boldly creative effort. Sometime during the night or the very earliest of morning hours, a spider started its long ascent of our home's exterior wall eventually reaching the hooked attachment for the clothesline six feet above the ground – what would that distance be in the spider's eyes? Then, the spider tightropes across the taut clothesline until it finds an agreeable point at which it must believe if the wind is just right, it can leap into and be carried by the air, reaching a designated point of landing, or if missing it, the ground while it leaves its filament trail streaming behind. Then, I suppose, it climbs back up its own strand and starts the process all over again, doing this over and over in the hope of creating an expansive web. Of course, one simple "walk though" by an unsuspecting two-legged, and the whole eight-legged project comes crashing down.

In religious and spiritual circles, the idea of a "leap of faith" is quite common. Essentially, "faith" is a confident belief or trust in something or someone that cannot truly be proven. Because of the "intellectual gap" that usually exists in a matter of faith, there is a necessary "leap," a point at which one freely chooses to let go of the final "unanswerable" questions and leaps steadfastly into the ethereal expanse of faith and belief. The spider's thread drifting in the morning light is such a wonderful glint of this faith leap. Just as in faith, the spider's leap is no doubt done in some form of confidence, although there must have been a highly frightening first time jump. But driven by a grand belief, and understanding, of what could be, the spider leaps and is carried on the winged air of faith to a new spot, not one of resting, but one where he sets forth on the next and even greater tasks. Will all of his faithful designs "succeed"? Absolutely not, and nor will ours, but the landing of the leap from one point to another, and the glistening evidence of what has been breached captured momentarily in the morning sun speak to the beauty and the value of trustfully acting on one's beliefs.

Faithful God, sometimes in the soft silence of the morning light, I catch glimpses of your faithfulness to me, the loyal reassurance of how you have so often caught and held me closely. Cupped in the web of your fingers, I daily choose to leap into the celestial light of my experienced beliefs, confident that though I might miss my mark, you will receive and love me all the same. You are the strong tether to which I am always attached; into that certainty, I faithfully leap.

April 16
Not a Blind Leap

Those who would deny faith, especially faith in a divine, cosmological presence, and who choose to cling only to things rational and empirical, have perhaps never confronted the true relational challenges of faith. Along with "the leap of faith," another common tag is "blind faith." While there is a certain "darkness on the edge of town" about faith, I don't think that it should ever be truly "blind." In all of our most loving and dedicated relationships, there are oftentimes challenges that tug at our roots, rock our foundations, or more simply upset our applecart. But the best of our relationships endure these trials and stumblings, not without fear or question, but in fact *with* and *through* them. A blind relationship is one that smacks too much of ignorance, as in "turning a blind eye" to the destructive behaviors and attitudes that ultimately uproot, undermine, and ruin the relationship altogether.

Religions so often want to make the presence of God so palpably obvious and a relationship with this Divine Presence so easy, that the inevitable struggle that comes with our understanding and choosing any valuable friendship gets watered down. A person's entrance into faith may come through cleansing baptismal waters, but the depth and the strength of one's faith will be best established through baptismal fires. One does not simply "receive" God and then all is well anymore than we might "meet" someone and immediately be "best friends." Faith, a confident relationship with a living God, emerges more purified from the fiery trials that inevitably flare up in our lives; grows stronger as we build from the enduring knowledge of the quakes that shake our core beliefs and understandings; and is enlivened by the confrontational questions that are periodically silenced by answers that animate and breath truth.

Faith is not the conclusion I reach after years of study and experience anymore than my marital relationship is the conclusion of my wedding day. There may be a moment in time when a faith-filled relationship takes root, is founded or is set upright, a chance meeting, a blind date or even a scheduled appointment. But from that moment on, if the bond is to be lasting, it will willingly leap, with eyes wide open, feet-first and headlong into whatever questions and challenges may arise. Faith is not a blind belief in an unknown and unseeable God. It is a relationship of trust that the One that I now only partially know and that I both intuitively and experientially understand will come to greater light through our challenges, establishing our friendship on firmer ground with deeper foundations.

God of All of My Questions, Doubts and Fears, I do not come to you this day in despair of challenges, but with the readiness to embrace them. Through the unknown you come to be more known to me. I want my relationship with you to be lived with my wondering eyes and my questioning heart wide open, confident that in your time, I will see and have answered what I need to know. My Dearest One, walk in faith with me this day.

April 17
To the Morning

Early morning defines stillness. It is perhaps the most sacred time of the day, though holiness is at the heart of every moment. To awaken with the sun's earliest glow and to rise with its magnificent and piercing grand entrance is to be enveloped in the sublime. How shameful it is that I do not start every day receiving this blessed kiss.

Of course, not *every* morning unfolds in such a consecrated veil. Some days arrive under the blanket of a thick cloud cover or a dense fog, while a steady rainfall and threatening skies sometimes dampen the spirit of other mornings. But setting aside these exceptions, the stillness of the morning seems to invite me into prayer more than any other time of the day. The sound of stillness is not empty; there are still morning songbirds in the spring, and echoing crickets chanting their final night vespers in summer months. But these are meditative sounds, not the distractions that overwhelm the stillness as the world's inhabitants emerge from their sleepy lives.

William Wordsworth, the father of the early nineteenth century Romantic Period and a worshipper of all things natural, appears to be conceding to the artistry of human-made structures over nature in his famous poem, "Upon Westminster Bridge." He writes of London from his viaduct perch noting that "Earth has not anything to show more fair." But importantly, the fairness of the city is that it "now doth like a garment wear the beauty of the morning; silent, bare...a calm so deep!" The real majesty of the city is thus revealed through the elegant robes of the dawning morning and the fact that the city's "mighty heart is lying still."

Sleeping in is sometimes a necessary resolve, and not all who arise early pause to sip from morning's sacred cup, but we all would offer our day a great service if we first quietly slipped down morning's hallowed hallway and bowed reverentially to the blessing of the day before putting on the clothing of our responsibilities and the garments of societal demands.

God of the Dawn, my prayer today is a communion with the stillness of the morning. Let these printed words be my last for now; anything more is dross, unnecessary accessories to the daybreak's flowing gown. May the sound of your gentle, still presence envelop me as the soft whispers of the morning carry me through this blessed new day.

April 18
Running Late

Depending on which state a person teaches, most teachers have to renew their licensure every handful of years by attending a certain number of workshops and courses and jumping through the requisite number of hoops to gather the required "Continuing Education Units." One winter some years ago, I discovered that I had procrastinated long enough in gathering my C.E.U.s to have put my teaching recertification in jeopardy. With time running out, I quickly signed up for a spring quarter American Literature course at a local university and became, for the first time in many years, a "classroom student" again.

The class met only one evening a week, so it fit nicely into my own teaching schedule, although the course work itself required some significant reading and writing time outside of class. One particular week I had been crunched for time and had not yet completed my weekly written assignment, but with three hours between my own teaching day and the evening course, I was unconcerned: I made plans to simply stay at my own school and work away at what needed to be done before heading off to the university class. When my own school day ended, I soon got to work. The words flowed easily for me and as I completed the assignment with ample time before class, I decided to push on a little further into the work – make some revisions and perhaps jump a little into the following week's assignment. I felt that I had been keeping a close eye on the clock with my travel time frame well in mind, when suddenly a bit of alarm shot through me as I realized I had better pack up my things and get going so as not to be late.

After bolting out the door and heading to my car for the half hour trip to the university, I realized I was really cutting it close and began to chastise myself for my poor planning. As luck would have it, of course I immediately ran smack into rush hour traffic; I had not considered that in my time-planning, and immediately set into cursing the fates. Bobbing and weaving through the traffic as best as I could, I eventually made it to my exit, only to be greeted by road construction. Humph. I didn't count on that either, and again, my angst rose. Finally, arriving at the university, I found the parking lot full and as I began circling the neighboring blocks looking for a parking spot, I was acutely aware that any remnants of the ease and leisure of my after school time and work had been significantly pulverized.

Hurrying along to class, I tried to regather my composure by putting the last half hour and more behind me. Reviewing the circumstances and the choices that had led me to this "late moment," I realized how the choices that I had made and the circumstances over which I had no control had collectively contributed to my situation, and being upset about them now, or fretting over what I should or could have done differently wasn't going to change one part of my tardiness. Furthermore, I was *here*, safely on my way to class even if I was ten minutes late. Exhaling my tension, I entered the classroom, found a seat and enjoyed another stimulating class.

Too often I allow myself to get all upset, even angry, at things that I have either caused or over which I have little or no control. I make choices everyday; can I live with the choices that I make? If not, then *I* have the choice to change how and what I choose. And sometimes, life *is* a traffic jam; not because of me, not for me, it just is. The world does not revolve around my needs and my time-frame. God of Quiet Repose, help me "to breathe" properly and mindfully through every moment of my life: accepting the choices I make or changing how and what I choose; and embracing the circumstances I am given, knowing that my negative emotion will do nothing to change them.

April 19
Finding a Spiritual Trail

Sometimes when I am hiking a well-worn trail through the woods, I give pause to consider how this trail first came to be. Who or what started the first etching of this path, and why here, and not over there? Was it first a deer trail, four-leggeds carving a course of expedient practicality, or was it a thoughtfully designed network of serviceable function plotted by two-leggeds? Whatever the answer, it is interesting to consider how dense forestland can be broached by the practical development of a trail.

When a person finds herself drawn to the edge of the woods of her spiritual development, she might peer into the dense growth that lies ahead and step back from ever entering for lack of a perceptible trail, as well as the fears of what might lurk unsuspectingly ahead. But walking the treeline of the forest, one will usually find a simple and easy access that invites the explorer to step into the interior of the canopy and to follow the footsteps of previous sojourners. In the greenness of her first steps, she may wonder why the path begins here or to where it will eventually lead, but she should take some comfort in the worn clearing that the path provides each plant of the foot – an invitation to an opening.

Many people seeking deeper spiritual understanding or enlightenment have both timidly and confidently strode out into the dense forests of spiritual discovery. Some have gingerly stepped into the underbrush and have created a simple, lightly treaded path, while others have boldly carved a trail easy for followers to perceive and pursue, some even providing significant markings along the way. Like the comfort of a well-worn trail through the woods, or the attraction of a more subtle footpath, we have been given a variety of courses through which we might begin our journey into the spiritual woodland. We may enter the hike alone, but we are not alone in entering the hike. Many have gone in before us, and many more will follow in our footsteps. If I am unsure as to where to begin my journey, I ought to take much comfort in the worn trails that provide something of an initial map. Along the way, I will likely discover a variety of spur trails, and I might even seek to venture out on my own, but for starters, it's best to follow what has been given.

Mysterious God, the End of which I long for on all spiritual trails, I often comb the edges of the spiritual woodlands looking for a safe and comforting entry. Be with me this day, and every day of my journey once commenced, and help me to choose my trails toward you wisely. May I find comfort in the wear of the trail, with signs of discovery and rest along the way. And if, in time, I should grow more confident in the density of the terrain, perhaps you shall invite me to explore and create a bit of my own gentle path in the network of our communal trails.

April 20
Plant Life

Sometimes after a vacation or some other extended break from work, I find myself wrapped in a lethargic blanket. I have generally always liked my jobs, so it is not the difficult task of throwing back the protective covering of ease and facing the cold air of something undesirable; rather, enfolded within inertia, I am content with the comfort that comes with ease and could just as well roll over and return to dreamland. One spring, amidst the full-bodied enjoyment of all the beauty that was emerging around me, I began to wonder about how all the trees and plants feel each spring when the rising temperatures and celestial shifts signal them to "get back to work," to do what they are called to do. Dormant for months in a restorative slumber, their roots quiet and still, their stalks and limbs and trunks stiff and barren, trees and all vegetation must groan heavily under this beckoning arousal to life. And yet, leaning into them more closely, I realized that very little, if anything, about them speaks of a resistance to stand up and grow again.

No, quite honestly, there seems to be much eagerness in the trees and plants resilient return to work each spring. From the perennial daffodils, tulips and crocuses that impatiently poke their revitalized bodies through the undisturbed soil at the first breaths of a spring, to the flowering bushes and trees that shout alleluias to the sun's warm glow, to the rich shades of green that grow deeper and more full with each spring shower, all of these creations seem to enthusiastically grasp for what is ahead. Or, perhaps, with each cyclical ebb and flow, they have come to know how they will grow and they rush toward this growth with ardor. Indeed, rather than wondering if the trees and plants know my lethargy, maybe I should be looking to them for the inspiration to seize the life coursing within me, to get moving, and to get back to growing!

We all need a break now and then, a vacation from the daily routines of our lives; even the natural world affirms this truth. To float or be carried like seeds on the wind to a new place, or to simply turn reflectively within wherever it is that we are, these are necessary movements in our growth. But growth will ultimately only come when we throw back the covers of our leisure and let the juices of life flow energetically through our veins once again.

God of Rejuvenation and Growth, sometimes I forget who I am, and get buried in my lackadaisical shroud. Help me to feel, as the trees and plants must feel, the life that flows within me, that needs to stretch its limbs and reach towards the nourishment from which I will blossom. I know that I need to rest from time to time, but if I am to fully realize the growth to which you call me, I need also to respond to the awakening urges to stand up and reach toward you.

April 21
Thirst

An Arizona daughter and son-in-law are always quick to remind me to take enough water when I go hiking in the desert. I have always felt a bit like an old camel who can go a long way without needing to constantly hydrate, so I tend to nod in agreement with their suggestion, but then take my minimalist amount anyway. A little water will be enough.

One spring while visiting them, I took off on a two-day hike to the top of and then along the crest of the Superstition Ridge in the mountains just east of Phoenix. It was desert, to be sure, and this was high elevation desert. Arid and unforgiving in its lack of water, even the trails on this hike were difficult to follow, and in some places, each step had to be carefully measured to avoid the "bite" or stab of numerous varieties of cactus. After the first day's challenging ascent, the ridge walk's physical difficulty seemed greatly reduced, and now the task was to simply stay on course and avoid stepping on cactus.

Before hitting the trail the next morning, I surveyed my water situation. With miles of simple ridge walking ahead and then a steep descent, I was very confident that my remaining liter would be more than adequate. Of course, in this high desert, there is literally no shade, and with the terrain a continuous lunar landscape pocked by threatening cacti, trail navigation was the day's endless challenge. Sure enough, late in the day, I made a wrong turn, and while I suspected that I had made the error, I kept pushing on to the next crest, and then another, and then another, thinking it would provide me the exit access I was looking for. When I finally was able to pinpoint my bearing, I was down to less than four ounces of water, with a steep descent ahead followed by three more miles of desert heat.

Eventually, I made it back to the trail head, an hour or more late and water long gone, and met up with my son-in-law who was quick to share the rising fears that had coursed through him in my delay. His words of care were kind, but not nearly so kind as the bottles of cold water he pulled from a cooler.

There is nothing that our bodies need for survival more than water. It is no wonder that water is used and is such an important symbol in nearly every religious tradition. For just as our physical bodies need water to survive, so too do our spiritual selves need a nourishing water of life. I may think that a little water, a little prayer, can get me a long way, but sometimes I find that if I am not careful, my well can run dry. Creator God, the source of all waters, keep me mindful that just as I need water to sustain my physical self, so too do I need you, the Life Spring, to sustain my spiritual life. My spiritual terrain too may be challenging and dangerous, arid and unforgiving, but with you, my water source will never run dry.

April 22
Meditative Healing

I coached track and field or cross-country or both for twenty-eight years. Given that time, one can easily imagine that I had to deal with numerous running injuries, from muscle pulls to strains, from sprained ankles and knees to shin splints and stress fractures. No season went without a customary loss of an athlete to an injury.

With every injury concern, the athlete would immediately be searching for some quick and easy comfort. I got to know the training room mantra of recovery: R.I.C.E. – rest, ice, compression and elevation. Some athletes would follow the trainer's and my advice immediately, not wishing to lose any more time than was necessary for healing. Others would forgo the directives of the treatment and assume that they could "run through the pain" and eventually overcome it, or felt that their own remedies would be better, or, not caring enough to recover quickly, lazily ignored the treatment altogether.

Despite my understanding and experience with injuries, I must admit that as a runner myself I am, perhaps, the worst at accepting and implementing my own "good advice." When chronic aches and pains show up through overuse or abuse, I know that they are signs that I need to slow down and to give my body a rest, institute a little R.I.C.E. But rarely do I. So often, we know what is good for our physical health, but we fail to take the time to implement it. The same might be said for our spiritual lives.

While excessive mileage and improper stretching can cause physical injury, underuse and lack of "stretching" can cause spiritual ailments; but just as each physical injury has necessary methods to restore health, so too do our spiritual infirmities. Prayer is, perhaps, the water of our spiritual well-being, but one form of prayer, meditation, is an essential salve for getting and keeping our spiritual lives in good health. In meditation, we place the cushions of stillness and silence around our aching selves, and easing the volume of our words in prayer, we invite the healing touch of God's energy to enter into this quietude to restore and to rejuvenate our spiritual health. Meditation is the spiritual R.I.C.E.: rest, introspection, comfort, energy.

Healing God, just as I sometimes fail to implement the proper therapy when my physical body requires healing, so too do I ignore the requisites of my spiritual self. Meditation is an antidote through which I allow you, my True Doctor and Personal Trainer, to bring your healing and restorative touch into my life. Help me to heed the signs regarding my spiritual health, and to administer the proper steps through which I may obtain my most vibrant living.

April 23
Decisions, Decisions

For the last half of my high school teaching career, I taught only seniors. Some of my colleagues groaned at the idea of my steady diet of this "I-can't-wait-to-get-out-of-here" group of students, but I felt it was a rare blessing and wouldn't have wanted it any other way. True, there certainly can be a kind of arrogance in their occasional "I don't need this anymore" attitude, but most of the time, I stood before a hungry group of students, a step away from their adulthood, eager to have a more full access to life's buffet. Despite their eagerness to "get out there," most seniors really are not that sure of where they are going, or even where they *want* to go, and these "directional questions" exert a tremendous amount of pressure on them. I did my best to assure them frequently that not having answers right now was okay; they didn't need to know just yet.

As graduation time nears, seniors are often asked what college they plan to attend and in what they hope to major. The former question is reasonable, but the latter always seems a bit silly to me. At seventeen or eighteen years old, how can or should anyone know exactly what he wants to do – much less for the rest of his life!? There is so much to be experienced and learned before such a question can be answered. A year or two later, the tension for them mounts all the more. Once in the college setting, they will soon have to "commit" to a major and structure their curriculum game plan accordingly. Atop the indecision is often a mounting financial debt as well and the escalating student loans only make the decision seem at once all the more imperative and oppressive. At such times, the pressure, the guilt and the fear of indecision can literally seize and freeze the young adult making any decision at all seem impossible.

Although the actual age of the title character of William Shakespeare's classic tragic drama, *Hamlet*, is incongruent with these young adults, the deep throes of indecision that he faces provide an incredibly poignant example of the inner turmoil young people – that we all! – sometimes face today. In Hamlet's story, he must choose, in a sense, between life and death: does he obey the ghost of his father and murder the uncle, now stepfather, who he believes is responsible for his father's death? Is the ghost even for real, and if so, does it speak the truth? And what is his mother's role in all of this; do her apparent weaknesses reflect the weaknesses of all women? These are bizarre circumstances and questions that Hamlet faces, to be sure, but those that youth – and we – sometimes face seem no less bizarre when we are in the midst of them. After fending off the temptation to just bail out entirely, rejecting his suicidal considerations, Hamlet still flounders as he now seeks the "perfect moment" for the "perfect decision." Of course, there rarely if ever is a "perfect moment" and so when he does finally act, the tragedy of his decision-making is in full motion.

The tragedy of our decision-making, and those with which young adults often find themselves strapped, is that we believe that all of our decisions are final and irreversible. Indeed, many decisions do need very careful consideration and should not be taken lightly, but there are many others that weigh upon us too heavily, that take on life-or-death implications when in fact they are of far less significance. Like Hamlet, we too often entrap ourselves through our own unnecessary indecision. There is consolation for Hamlet and insight for us when near the play's end, Hamlet finally realizes that he is unable to control all things and to manipulate a perfect time; he concludes: "The readiness is all" (V, ii).

There have been many and will be many more important decisions that I will have to make in my lifetime. I will, of course, treat these decisions with the respect that they deserve, but I must be careful not to let them control and paralyze my living. Knowing that I am ultimately not in control of the outcomes of my decisions, what I will need more than anything is a willingness, a readiness, to embrace all of the possibilities of my decisions. God of Resolution, I pray today for all of those, including myself, who are faced with difficult decisions in our lives. Grant us the strength to not be overwhelmed by the pressures of our choices, the insight to choose most wisely, and the readiness to accept the joys and the consequences of all of our decisions.

April 24
Vocational Listening

One of the most difficult decisions of our lives is when we are faced with the question of our "vocation." When I was a child, the word "vocation" seemed relegated to only those who chose a life of vowed religious service; the rest of us, I guess, were to go out and "make a living." Indeed, vocation does imply something a little more special than just "a job." The word itself literally comes from the Latin "vocare," which is "to call" and "vox" which is "voice." Nevertheless, gratefully, today I find the use of the term applying to a much broader context, that one's way of life, even if not specifically religious or spiritual, can be "a calling." This better application, however, doesn't make the decision any less difficult; it only widens the playing field.

One of the reasons that makes the decision of our vocation so difficult is, perhaps, locked inside how we understand the source of our vocation. Viewed as "a calling" from a "voice," one's vocation is usually thought to come from outside of one's self. From the former exclusively religious connotation, a vocation was viewed as "a calling" whose "voice" was from God. While such a calling certainly provided one with a sense of a uniquely divine commission, it also raised a variety of questions about how one "heard" this "voice" and placed a tremendous amount of responsibility on how one responded to it. Additionally, the former view seemed to also assume that any other life choice was purely personal, maybe even selfish, and that God was not much in that mix. But if God is to be seen as the Creator of us all, would it not be reasonable to assume that, while we are not predestined to it, there is a kind of "plan," a "better-for-us" intention that might be written into the very heart of our being.

While analogies, sometimes, should only go so far, I look again to the creations for a source of insight into my own vocation. Just as certain trees and certain plants produce certain kinds of fruits, vegetables and blossoms, perhaps each of our lives too is designed, called to a certain vocation wherein each will best produce. Given our ability to think and to choose, we might in fact select other than what is best for us, but what is best for us is not calling from outside of ourselves, but is right here within us; it is how we were made and who we are. The difficulty of recognizing our vocation then is not within us, but is outside of us; it is all the social noise and confusion of others telling us what they think we should do and be, and how we should do and be it. Many times we know "in our heart" or we feel "in our gut" who it is that we are and, perhaps, what it is that we "should" do because the one who made us has "wired" us to hear this inner voice, this vocation. But too often we listen to the "voice of reason," the authority of others, the rationale of economics, and the status quo of society, and we allow these voices to drown out the one voice that most matters, the inner voice of our spirit which is most directly in contact with the source of our being. Can others be helpful in our vocational discernment? Of course they can, but only insofar as they keep calling us back to our own inner voice and do not instead try to lead us down the path of their agenda for us.

Source of my Being, my Living and my Direction, you know preeminently for what I have been best created. My vocation may be sewn into the very fabric of my being, waiting for me to uncover it and wear it proudly and confidently. As a person of this world, I am often easily persuaded by it. Speak your truth into my heart, and may I listen attentively and carefully for your words of direction and guidance. What is it that you want me to be? Who I am. Help me to understand the who and the what of my am.

I was taking a short lunch break from my writing one afternoon, toodling through some social emails as I nibbled when an instant message bubble on my Skype account with my daughter opened up: "Hi Daddio! I'm sure you're busy writing but if you can, call me." Mid-week and midday, I thought to myself; this can't be good, knowing that she should be at work. I skyped her immediately.

For days I had not felt right "in my guts" as a variety of small fires seemed to be constantly burning into my attention making me feel strangely uneasy, the scent of something smoldering. Soon greeting each other through our Skype, I quickly "cut to the chase" sensing at once that another small fire was about to ignite. "I got fired from my job on Friday," she said trying to color the odor with a whiff of optimism and a sniff of "I'm okay" confidence. My heart sank despite her best fabricated perfumes. She had had the job for only a month, and at hiring, had been given a very deep pool of responsibilities. For at least two weeks, she worked at deciphering the business and its needs, and then moved to translate her role in light of those as she slid into the daily expectations of her new job. And then, on a Friday, she was called into an executive assistance's office and told that the man who had hired her and who just two weeks ago had stood before the entire office staff not simply introducing his new employee, my daughter, but confidently stating everything that she was "going to do" for them, was now "letting her go." No particulars given, no "here's-how-you-failed" reasons, just "let go."

As her father, I wanted to rush to her side immediately, like I might have done decades before when she fell off her bicycle on a first two-wheeled attempt. I wanted to kiss the scraped knees and palms, and hold the shaking, fright-filled body close to mine with the assurance that everything would be just fine. But she was 2000 miles away, a young woman making it on her own, and all I could really do was share with her my deep sadness, my great love, and my eternal support of her.

For her part, she assured me that it was "just another bump in the road," the corners of her mouth turning up slightly in a smile of resignation as we both futilely fought back tears. I offered some coach-like encouragement on her next steps, and asked her to be open to the cosmic movements of it all. "Maybe you *are* meant to be doing something else, and avoiding it, Grandfather God just keeps swinging open an invitational door for you to step into your 'true vocation,'" I concluded wryly. But my heart was simply aching for her and I felt helplessly distant even after visually sharing our tears though the magical convenience of Skype. The bump in her road felt lodged in my throat as I stared into her image on my screen. "I will be holding you very close in my prayers and in my thoughts," I told her before we volleyed loving good-byes. It was all I had and all I could do.

God In My Sorrow and Pain, I believe that your cosmic heart aches too when we humans treat each other unjustly, and when the "stuff" of life reduces our self-esteem to sizes too small for our big hearts. Like a parent, you too no doubt know the sorrow of wanting to step in and remove the pain, but also the need of stepping back and allowing the blood of the bruise to heal the soft spot of the wound. When dear ones hurt, oftentimes the least and the best that I have to offer are my prayers, sent to you with the incense of my love curling around them. Please receive them, and if you would, bring the gentle, healing balm of understanding and insight to those wrapped within my loving prayers.

April 26
To Build a Fire

Journeys to the wilderness for me are usually, in some part at least, a spiritual retreat as well. Subsequently, many of the necessary movements of getting to and establishing a campsite have a sort of meditative and prayerful posture about them. Building a fire would be one of the most obvious examples. Certainly one can throw some dry twigs and branches atop wads of newspaper or some other easy fire starter, snap a lighter or match to the base and hope for the best. But more often, I like to thoughtfully and carefully approach the building of a campfire, recognizing that its light and warmth will eventually serve as the heart of my campsite. Prayerfully, I make a simple offering to God and the earth asking for assistance in the gathering of wood and pledging that I will do my best not to misuse or waste the windfall and deadened branches that I might find. Once the wood is collected, broken, cut and separated into relative piles, I work towards creating a spark, then a kindling flame and, eventually, a fire, slowly nurturing each phase so as to create a deep heart within it. Later, before I head off to bed, I try to bank the embers and bury them under the warm ashes hoping that in the morning, with a little stirring and a few delicate, dried twigs, I can simply blow new life back into the heart of the fire and enjoy its warm comfort again.

Now, honestly, my approach to fire starting is not always so tedious, for there are many more simple and easy ways of getting the desired results, and often, with a companion or more, I simply let it go altogether knowing that there is something in all of us that loves to bring a fire to life, and this time it is not my turn. But on my own especially, it is a prayerful labor of love that reminds me of the hard work that is involved in the nurturing of our spiritual lives as well. Like carefully gathering and sorting wood, I need to take some time now and then to reflect on my spiritual needs and development, to organize and plan my next steps. Starting with a spark and nurturing it to a flame, I see that God has blessed me with a "spark of the divine," the gift of life itself, and I need to nurture that spark carefully so as to allow the presence of God in my life to flame on in bright and comforting ways. And once burning, the fire of our spirituality needs constant care, the wisdom of aged branches, the fuel of cured logs, and sometimes a soft but strong breath, like God blowing life into the nostrils of his creation in Genesis. One can take many "shortcuts" in his spiritual development, but when one truly puts his mind to it, thoughtfully and carefully, although the results may appear to be the same, he will know that at the center of his "fire of faith" is a heart with a deeply glowing ember.

O God of Bright and Warm Light, help me this day to carefully build a fire of your love. If I have been lazy and complacent with your gift, stir the ashes of my slumbering heart and guide me to seek the silent embers of your love that need only for me to rekindle them so that they can once again break open and become a flame.

April 27
An Idle Warning

When I was first designing a creative writing course for the high school at which I taught, I affectionately chose many of the philosophical approaches to writing espoused by Ken MacCrorie, a writing instructor who taught at Michigan State University. MacCrorie's lessons challenge students, writers - all of us! - to observe life carefully, and to see within it what he called "fabulous realities." A fabulous reality is a fun concept, but, essentially, it is simply catching the odd juxtapositions of some of the world around us, and thoughtfully learning from the irony of a given situation. Having taught the concept for years, I find myself always on the lookout for fabulous realities, especially when I go on my daily runs. With nothing else in or at hand, my mind and eyes are free to roam the landscape as I run, thoughtfully observing anything within their gaze.

One day while on a run down an old country road besieged by the encroachment of "new developments," I came upon a pick-up truck that was part of the road construction a quarter to a half mile ahead. The workday had already ended, and so there was no worker or crew even in sight; appropriately, the truck was off to the side of the road and locked. But what really caught my attention was that the truck was turned on, lonesomely idling there for the night. Now, I am certain that the truck had not been absentmindedly forgotten there that day, for I quickly surmised that the reason that it was on was to power the flashing warning sign, concerning the road work ahead, that had been mounted in the bed of the vehicle. But here, on this still quiet road, at a time when our country sought greener approaches to life and our economy was forcing significant slashes to state and local jobs and programs, was a state-owned vehicle, quietly idling with lights-a-flashing throughout the night. I was quickly reminded of the clichéd metaphor, "the lights are on, but nobody's home."

As I continued my jaunt down the road, a deeper metaphor began to flash within me. How many times am I just like that truck: locked and idling, a warning flasher blinking its message of "stand back" while I waste energy going nowhere and doing very little. Amidst the outcries of global warming and economic mismanagement, I often pull off to the side of life's road and flash my resentment, my anger, my sorrow, and my worry over others' reconstructive failures, meanwhile offering little to nothing of constructive value. It's easy to be overwhelmed by the challenges of our world, to crumble under the personal injustices I sometimes encounter; but where am I directing my energy and to what end?

Vigorous God, help me today to turn off my wasteful, idling engines of resentment and anger, and to unlock and open the doors that have prevented greener, healthier ideas to enter into my driver's seat. Perhaps there is work to be done on my roadway of life, but idly flashing warning signs with no positive construction in sight is not getting the job done. Rather than laughing or scoffing at the fabulous realities around me, help me to make my reality fabulous.

April 28
The Spiritual Marathon

Some years ago, a new bumper sticker started showing up on American cars that was a kind of quiet and subtle mark of solidarity amongst marathon runners. With simple black numbering on a white egg-shaped background, the sticker softly proclaims: "26.2" – the mileage distance of a standard marathon. The innocent sticker seems to proudly profess, "Yes, I ran that distance!"

Marathoners shape a rather unique community amongst themselves. Only they truly know and can appreciate the effort that each sincere marathoner is dedicating to his or her programmed efforts. The time and miles that it takes to truly prepare for such a race make the mileage of even daily runners such as myself seem small and insignificant. I took pride for years in logging a thousand miles every year; a good friend of mine who has posted some impressive marathon times has lately been putting in one hundred miles a week! At that pace, in less than three months, he is covering what was my very proud annual goal.

Numerous friends of mine have competed in a variety of marathons, from the famous ones in Boston and Chicago, to the Marine Corps Marathon of Washington D.C. and onto the Flying Pig Marathon in Cincinnati, Ohio, and many points further west and south. Of course, nearly all of these friends were not necessarily competing in these races to win overall, but the competition was ultimately within themselves, the challenge of personal improvement, both body and mind. I remember when I ran a few marathons myself years ago. The first seventeen or so miles always had a festival-like feel as we runners shared in the joy of the race day finally arrived, the payday of our months of quiet, arduous effort spilling into giddy conversation and encouraging support as the miles unfolded. But in the last third of the race, all around me seemed to go quiet as each runner turned within himself to face the real work of the chosen challenge.

Living a healthy spiritual life seems a bit like preparing for and running a marathon. In many ways, for realized "success," the whole process becomes "a way of life." Good spiritual development, like satisfactory marathoning, takes much more than a simple daily jaunt. To consistently make a "run at prayer" is valuable, but the training goes beyond these "runs" and must spill into nearly every phase of one's life, how one rests and what one "ingests." The community of faithful runners is important as well, people who understand the hard work and, as one popular book once called it, "the loneliness of the long distance runner." Having others or another to share in the dedicated task of training and the commitment to consistency is always beneficial, both in running and in spiritual living, but there will always come a race time when, no matter how many supportive others are nearby, the adherent knows that it is time to turn within and test the deeper layers alone.

In the spiritual realm, of course, one is never truly alone with oneself, but alone with the Source of Life itself. Like the faithful Muslim on the hajj who arrives in Mecca and is surrounded by a sea of white-clad brothers and sisters all bowing in unisoned prayer to the Creator, the marathoner begins his race amidst a throng of thousands of runners; and just as the Muslim sojourner will, no doubt, turn within to face that Creator one-on-one in his own isolated prayer, so too the marathoner's race will not end before the runner turns within and quietly faces his own gifted and practiced determination.

God of Community and Solitude, this life sometimes feels a bit like an endless marathon, a constant training ground where we seek to improve on our time and commitment. In the very nature of my being, I sense that you call me to go out and to engage in the community of Life, both to seek and to offer support of others on the journey; and, I believe that at times, I must turn within and quietly encounter you one-on-one. Provide for me the partnership that will strengthen and enhance my spirit so that when I must log the hard miles, I know that I will not be utterly alone, but running in stride with the One who gives me life.

April 29
Can You Handle This?

There is a rather popular line in religious circles aimed at comforting us when we feel overwhelmed by life's challenges that says, "God doesn't give you anything you can't handle." Now, maybe I have read into this saying a little too literally, but I have really never liked its sentiment, for a couple of reasons. First of all, some people's lives are just plain miserable. Born into poverty and abuse, abandoned through deaths or lack of love, some people's reality truly is "the worst case scenario." Surely and gratefully, these people's lives may be the rare exception, but such stories are not pure fiction. Additionally, some people become so distraught with their circumstances that they see no way out but to take their own lives. Suicides, essentially, are cases of mental illness, and, arguably, the person who takes his own life is not in his "right mind." But in the light of the not-so-comforting-saying, I wonder, well, did that person get more than he could handle?

Another and more important reason that I don't care for the saying is that I don't care for its "theology," if you will. What the line suggests to me is that somewhere out there a God is manipulatively messing around with our lives, and seeing how we do with his challenges. Personally, I don't think that God "gives" us those kinds of things. When life's challenges seem overwhelming, I don't believe that God is "testing" me; it's just, well, *life!* Life isn't always easy and it is often quite tough. Either through bad choices or rough circumstances or just plain "bad luck," undesirable things happen to people all the time just as surely as unwarranted blessings and lucky things happen to people as well.

Finally, rather than evaluating my ability to "handle" a challenge, I prefer to think of it as my ability to "embrace the challenge." Because I believe in the power of prayer, I do believe that God can and sometimes does intervene and may alter the difficult situations of our lives, but if I bank on divine intervention every time I'm in a fix, I'll likely find myself very disappointed by God's "response" most of the time. Instead, I ask myself if I am willing to embrace what God is willing to allow in my life? From this perspective, the question is not about whether I am physically or spiritually strong enough to endure the challenge, but rather, am I open enough to accept it, knowing that, most often, I cannot accomplish much of anything entirely on my own. Subsequently, I seek the assistance of others, and I fall on my knees and pray.

Loving God, I am certain that you do not desire pain and suffering for me any more than I do for myself. In a world that bleeds and breeds so much violence, hatred, carelessness and misunderstanding, I will inevitably be confronted by the sometimes awful challenges that they will present. Help me to embrace my challenges as opportunities to understand myself better and to acknowledge my need of you and others. Perhaps I will receive something that I cannot handle alone, but, to paraphrase another line, if it doesn't kill me, it will, perhaps, make me stronger!

April 30
Vertigo

When I first heard that one of my older brothers was suffering through a bout of vertigo, a physical malady marked by the sensation of spinning, I jokingly wrote to him that while some people had taken to the somewhat new stationary cycling workout known as spinning, perhaps he had misunderstood the intention of the training method. Later, my not-so-funny-joke became even less humorous when, enduring another round of vertigo, my brother was forced to rule out the possibility of a brain tumor. Gratefully, he did, and then my deflated joke disintegrated altogether as I stepped from bed one morning not feeling well, and as I lay back down, I found my whole world spinning wildly around me.

I had imbibed a little more than usual at a party the night before, so I initially castigated myself for my excess. But as the wild spinning continued throughout the day when my head would move or rest in certain positions, I began to question my original thoughts about the cause. That night, and the next morning, sure enough, whenever I laid my head down, all about me began to whirl, and I felt once again that I was a child spinning wildly on the small roundabout at my neighborhood playground. On the third day of this routine, I finally began investigating my condition and discovered that I too, with no particular rhyme or reason or connection, was suffering from vertigo. As the week wore on, the worst of the spinning sensation receded, but each time I would get up from sitting or laying, my world seemed always a little off-kilter and I adopted tentative steps like those taken shortly after exiting a vicious amusement park ride. Writing to my brother to share our new affinity, I received a quick note back from him: "That's a bummer. I hope it passes quickly and is never heard from again."

As others have no doubt encountered, my physical experience with this miserable and unannounced disorder of vertigo left me somewhat incapacitated for over a week. But such spinning out of control is not limited to the physical, and it often renders us incapacitated for much longer than a week. Sometimes when we give ourselves over to too many responsibilities, excessively volunteering our services, or the demands of family and work bunch up and become overwhelming, we can also find ourselves spinning out of control. Like vertigo, lying or sitting down is unlikely to help the symptoms, and perhaps will only exacerbate them; but unlike vertigo, where the cause and the end of the symptoms can only be rendered to speculation, when we spin out of control emotionally, mentally, and/or spiritually, the cause and the end of our malady are often within our choices.

O God of the Revolving and Evolving Creation, too often I allow myself to sink into dizzying despair by making choices that demand more of my time and energy than I can healthfully give. You are God; I am not. Help me to be mindful of what I can and cannot handle at given times in my life. As the world turns, and with it my involvement in its various movements, help me to offer my hands and time to everyone's best benefit, and if I should choose too much and find myself swirling in inadequacy and despair, help me to reach out and grab hold of the calming hands of support of those who can steady and sustain me.

May 1
May Day Basket

When I was a child, May Day – the first day of May – was always a special day of excitement and anticipation. The historical ethnic customs of May Day are all quite fuzzy, and I am not really sure where or how my neighborhood friends and I were introduced to the celebration of May Day, but anything that provided free candy and a little romance certainly wasn't going to be questioned.

The tradition that circulated in my childhood neighborhood on May Day was a kind of anonymous gift giving. The fun began by weaving simple, small May Day baskets out of strips of colored paper, with a single strip arching over the basket as a handle. Once filled with simple candy items, each basket would be secretively toted to the home of a favored receiver. The May Day basket giver would then place the basket on the doorstep of the receiver, knock on the door, and bolt quickly away. The quickness of the sneak away, however, could be altered somewhat due to a final piece of the May Day tradition. As I recall, if the receiver could get to the door in time to spy the giver, he or she was beholden to chase after the giver and return a kiss of gratitude. So, as one might well imagine, if it was a kiss for which one sought, a slight linger or "trip" might prevent a quick getaway. Overall, however, the fun was in receiving the simple, freely given gift of the May Day basket and its candy contents.

I am often reminded of my childhood May Day fun whenever I step outside for my daily greeting of the day only to find the morning already long awaiting to embrace me warmly. On such mornings, I feel as though God has dropped by and left me a little May Day basket sitting on my front step, and lifting up the basket of the day's holdings, I offer my grateful heart in thanks.

What's not to love about an early spring day where we receive simple baskets of candy and love on our doorstep? And yet, this is what God does for us each day that we are able to rise from the night's rest and greet the candied love of a new day, freely given. Shouldn't we rush out the door looking to return to the giver a simple kiss of thanks?

O God of May Day Basket Memories, I give thanks to you today for the wondrous gift of life you have left upon my doorstep this day. Pardon me if I fail to immediately retrieve its contents, taking for granted too often the day's generous offering of life. May I recognize in this day a basket brimming with the sweet gift of life; and as I have been gifted, so may I go out and drop simple gifts of kindness and love upon the doorsteps of others.

For so many years of my life, the alarm clock, set at the same time each day would go off and my day would start. The routines of each morning would precede the drive into work, my teaching job of twenty-eight years, and the day's lessons, grading, discussions and whatever else might serendipitously arrive would unfold until I would transition into the after school coaching job which would lead me to the end of that "at work" day. Once home, I would often prepare a meal or enjoy the fruits of another's preparation, relax briefly and then hit the nightly paper work of more grading. The eyes weary and the head heavy, eventually, I would succumb to the weariness of the day and go to bed only to start the whole process over again six hours later. Sound familiar? The details need not be the same, but I suspect that most people can relate to the sense of the routine of it all. It was not a bad life, but it was a life marked by the groove of repetition; it is, essentially and inevitably, what happens to most people once they get a job and start their "career."

These days I might sit quietly at a window in our home and watch others rush off to the beat of this work-a-day routine, sometimes wondering just how long it will be before I am sucked back into it. Where is it that we all go, rushing about? Yes, a job, I know, but beyond the pragmatic needs of work in a society, where and why do we go there?

The other day I sat at the window looking out into the backyard at the flurry of spring activity in which the entire natural world seemed engaged. Birds of various colors and sizes scurried about making homes, searching for food, seducing one another or protecting their championed mate. Squirrels raced across the lawn, dashed up trees and leaped from branch to branch; they too seemed engaged in the home, food and procreative drives. A bunny suddenly appeared from beneath some bush or hollow, paused to nibble through its fearfully alert pose and then dashed off with its white tail a bounding ellipsis. And beneath and above and around them all, the greenery of the trees and hedge and grasses and weeds imperceptibly nudged their way forward as well. And I thought to myself, maybe they are not so much unlike us, or, we, perhaps, are not so different from them. Each day, we go about our business of building a home, finding some food, and establishing a relationship with which to share and expand it all.

But surely, for all of us, there is something more at play – and work – going on here. Are the movements of the natural world "all work" to them? The animals and birds seem to pause far more often, and just reflectively sit – like I do when I am watching them. Perhaps we all could use a little more time to just sit back and watch each other, and to look into ourselves as well. What am I doing here, and why am I doing it? The answers do not have to be eye-popping enlightenments, nor entirely definitive, but perhaps if we would just stop, regularly, and observe, we might discover some answers sitting like colorful birds on trees, or swash-tailing squirrels on limbs waiting to reveal themselves.

Observant God, when was the last time I took some time to just sit back and ponder life – mine and the whole of creation. My life needs discernment, periodic examinations of who I am and where I am going and why I am going there. A gentle pause permeates the movements of all living things; is it not likely that you have created me with this same need? Help me to step away from the flow of things today and just observe; perhaps you are waiting for me there right now.

May 3
A Forgetful Fall

Within Christianity, the fall of Adam and Eve, also referred to as "the Original Sin," is an act of defiance against God's directive that the couple could eat whatever they wished within their palatial garden except the fruit from the Tree of Knowledge of good and evil. While the "first couple" was tempted by the Serpent to eat of this forbidden fruit and did not choose it solely on their own, this Christian rendering of the Hebrew Scripture story reveals not only humanity's propensity to choose "evil," but also the catastrophic repercussions of such a choice. Created perfectly and settled in an idyllic land, Adam and Eve chose an ultimate evil, and with their singular selfish choice, so goes the Christian theological perspective, the relationship between God and the whole of creation was altered.

Muslims see this sinful event of Adam and Eve somewhat differently. In Islam, humans are not created of perfect light, nor are they naturally evil or necessarily prone to it. Born with a natural inclination to submit to God, we are yet weak, can become distracted, and "forget" who we are. From this perspective, then, sin is a disobedience to the will of God when we forget who we are, but it does not corrupt the heart and mind of the sinner, nor cause irreparable universal damage.

I find this idea of forgetfulness at the root of sin very appropriate. The Hebrew (Jewish) scriptures, honored by both Christians and Muslims as well although not with equal importance, cite that humanity was created in God's image and likeness: "in the divine image he created him; male and female he created them" (Gn 1:27). The theologian Matthew Fox once recognized this as our "original blessing" – what we are! But oftentimes we forget who we are, and when we do, we go against our best nature, our original blessing, and failing to surrender to the will of God, we sin. Think of a time when you failed "to do the right thing." Were you consumed by evil, or did you forget who you were, losing sight of your innate connection to the Divine and choosing something less than your very best?

Following this line of thought further, to conquer sin one must overcome forgetfulness, and forgetfulness is beaten back by remembering. And what is prayer if not a remembering of the Divine, pauses in my day to reflect on God's presence; or better, a constant state of being where I live within the knowledge that the Divine is all around me and lives within me? When I live in this state of remembering, how can I possibly forget who I am and so choose to not follow the will of God, or be tempted by selfishness to commit an ultimate evil?

143

Too often I succumb to the lure of selfish desires and the opulence of greed, forgetting that all I have and need is already offered to me through God's gracious love. Divine One, be the source and focus of all of my remembering. Help me to never forget that you are the Source of all Life, and that made in your divine image, I have only to remember you and who I am, and I am whole.

May 4
Forgiveness

Some years ago, a girlfriend from my teen age past stumbled upon my name in an Internet listing from my place of employment and sent an email of inquiry, wondering if I was the Kevin Ryan whom she sought, noting hometown and our old school. I can hardly begin to describe the wave of emotion that rolled over me, for I too had often wondered about her over the years, thought about her well-being, quietly sorry for the way things ended between us so many years ago. It was not that ours was a relationship that was "meant to be," or that I had somehow been injuriously cruel toward her, but if we are to understand that our first relationships help to shape us and how we grow into and do relationships in the future, this was one for which I carried a kind of humble and melancholic gratitude. Was I the Kevin Ryan from her past? Yes, I am, but I am hopeful that I am not the same person that I was.

When I received the email, it had been over twenty-five years since I had last spoken with her, and I had carried a guilt around within me ever since. Actually, there had never been anything especially formal between us, but my time spent with her and the words shared certainly indicated that she had captured some part of my heart at the time. She was years younger than me, and I was, perhaps, her "first love," but when I moved away for school and "found somebody new," I let her go as if I didn't care. But I did, and I never forgot how awful it must have been for her to think that she had been cast away so easily, so simply. Human beings should not treat each other so callously, and I had been a poor model.

Having been found, through some brief correspondence, I sought forgiveness from this old friend for my past actions and found that the guilt that I had carried had long since been forgiven. Sometimes we will hurt others, and we may never get the chance to ask forgiveness or give reparation directly to those offended. If we carry some sour taste of guilt within our mouths or guts for some time, perhaps it is the appropriate flavor of a kind of cosmic justice. But we must move on. We must forgive, or, in this case, be forgiven, but not forget; for healing comes through forgiveness, and improvement of our character can come through not forgetting.

Forgiving and Loving God, who knows but you the many people that I have consciously or inadvertently offended throughout my life. If I can receive forgiveness from another, help me to humbly seek it; but from the many of whose hurt I am responsible though, perhaps, unaware, and now unable to seek forgiveness, I look to you for your healing touch. Jesus of Nazareth offered in a prayer that we would be forgiven as we forgive; Francis of Assisi concurred that it is in pardoning that we are pardoned. If I am aware that I have failed in the past, I can humbly seek forgiveness and then learn and grow from my failure, by being better to those in my present life; and, for those times of which I am unaware, may I receive the grace of forgiveness when I willingly and lovingly forgive those who have hurt me.

May 5
The Least of These

"Do you care if I sit in this seat next to you here," he said to me, pausing in the Greyhound Bus aisle awaiting my response. "No, no, certainly! Have a seat," I said and offered a welcoming gesture in return. Dropping into the seat beside me, his cigarette cologne complemented his scruffy month-old beard and his bedraggled mane of white hair that spilled from his ball cap. "Whew, it's been a long, bad day already," he started. "I've been waiting in that Baltimore bus depot for hours. I'm gonna have me a fifth of vodka tonight when I get to Hagerstown to smooth this day out." I understood his angst, for I had just spent nearly three hours in – or near - the Washington D.C. depot after a "bomb threat" had postponed all trips and cleared the station until the nonsense got sorted out; our delay had been the cause of his, but I couldn't quite concur that I would smooth out my day with a fifth of vodka at the end of it.

His age was hard to guess, for his face was weathered and road weary. Mid-fifties to sixty going on eighty, I would guess. His right eye was dead, or glass, and the cheek and socket bones surrounding it appeared to have caved in with the loss, although the maimed appearance was no doubt the cause of the sight loss. His left eye, the one good one, had a soft kindness about it, and with it, his tired and dirty appearance gave me no anxious concerns or fears. As the bus inched away from the depot and headed west, my seat partner commented on how quiet the bus was today. "People must be tired after the long wait," he concluded, and with the rest, he appeared to quickly melt into a weary sleep, although my corner of the eye glances were never sure of that as all I caught sight of was his milky right eye, perennially open. But with the mouth gaping unhinged like the eye above it, I assumed that the left eye was, as the body, at rest. When he would stir or cough through a nicotine congestion, I would venture to engage him in conversation a bit. "Is Hagerstown home?" I asked. Yes, it had been at one time, but he left it years ago after getting busted and then paying his fine for public drunkenness; apparently, he felt he'd take that act elsewhere and had eventually ended up in Baltimore. As we neared his destination, I queried further. "What's waiting for you here?" There was a pause, as if the question had shown up on his doorstep for the first time. "Nothin' really. I don't know anybody here anymore. I guess I'll go have a beer somewhere, and then get me a fifth and head to the park. Do a little people watching." He chuckled softly and then coughed through loose phlegm again. On the far south end of the small, Maryland town, we pulled into the bus stop for Hagerstown, a simple shed of a building tucked behind a gas station and a McDonald's. "I've never been this far out of town before," he noted. "I guess I'll have a bit of a walk before I get to town tonight. Stretch my legs out." I wished him well and then he was gone.

Somewhere in Hagerstown, Maryland tonight, or maybe he has moved on to someplace else by now, my hour-and-a-half-bus-seat-friend is, perhaps, sitting in a park with another fifth of vodka, watching life drift by as if he is a mere spectator. Once upon a time, he was likely some parents' pride and joy; he was a child at play; he was a teen with dreams; perhaps, he had once known love and even had a family of his own. Who knew, and when, that he would end up like this: a destitute drifter, friendless except for the next fifth that will kiss his lips. There are so many lost souls out there in our world, human beings, forgotten and left behind like the refuse blown and stuck against the highway fence lines as we travel cross country. But no less than me, they are human beings made in the image and likeness of God; and that truth always gives me great pause.

O God of the Abandoned, your face has so many different visages; your presence arrives in our lives in so many different shapes and forms. At the height of his charismatic career, much beloved by his followers, Jesus, teaching about care for the poor and the outcast, concluded "whatever you did for one of these least of mine, you did for me." Caught up in our own world of responsibilities, concerns and cares, the homeless and other forsaken lives can easily become invisible to us. I can't take them all in, God, and I can't even feed them all one meal, but I can still care for them, and try not to let them become invisible and worthless to the world. Today, I offer this simple prayer for all the lost souls out there, but help me also to remember to look for and to see you there, present in each of them just as surely as I know you to be present with me right here and now.

May 6
Treat Me like Dirt

In late 2009, a documentary movie entitled *DIRT! The Movie* was released receiving substantial critical acclaim. The film sought to tell, in the words of its advertising releases, "the story of Earth's most valuable and underappreciated source of fertility – from its miraculous beginning to its crippling degradation." Naturally, as a person of the soil and a lover of all of God's grand creation, I saw and enjoyed the movie, its message easily resonating with my own views and beliefs. Interestingly, shortly after viewing the movie, I overheard someone remark rather disparagingly how, in a given disrespectful situation, he had been "treated like dirt." Although the simile is a bit cliché, with the film fresh in my head, I was struck by the poignancy of the comment and, like the film makers' intention, wondered if and how we could reverse the meaning of that phrase.

Fundamentally, I suspect that everyone knows that dirt is essential to our very existence here on this earth; however, how we live out and respect that understanding seems shrouded in ignorance. As the movie's promotional information notes, "in modern industrial pursuits and clamor for both profit and natural resources, our human connection to and respect for the soil has been disrupted." As an important cog in the capitalistic machinery of food production, dirt is too often erroneously viewed as a kind of endless and naturally recyclable commodity. Without sufficient foresight, little care was given to the effects of all that we did and do to this valuable and essential "skin" that covers some of the earth's surface. From the fertilizers injected into it to stimulate plant growth and the pesticides that seep into it to prevent crop damage to the human and nuclear waste that we attempt to hide beneath its surface, all of these actions have had damaging effects on this vital membrane to which we are intimately linked.

Many creation stories portray humanity being born of the earth, emerging from it or being shaped of it. The Hebrew Scriptures convey the famous story of God creating humanity "out of the clay of the ground," and later this first human being given the name "Adam," which etymologically is the masculine form of the Hebrew word "adamah," meaning ground or earth. All of these stories recognize our deep affinity with the earth, with dirt, and yet centuries later, we seem to have forgotten, buried if you will, this essential relationship, treating it instead as if it is some lifeless commodity that can be used and abused thoughtlessly and leading us to say with unfortunate characterization and understanding, "being treated like dirt." Wouldn't it be wonderful if, in remembering who we are and from where we came, this same cliché were to become a compliment, an affirmation of being treated with reverence and respect?

God of All Creation, religious funeral services often remind us that we "are dust and to dust we shall return." How unfortunate it is that we too often only die in this truth, while failing to *live* inside and with it. No human being should be treated as anything less than what he is – a human being, and a human being that is deeply rooted in and to the soil. Help me to remember and to live always with a compassionate connection to all of my human brothers and sisters, and to our shared Mother, the earth that supports, feeds and sustains us.

May 7
Wakiya Oyate

Many people have a natural fascination with thunder and lightning, powerful forces that solicit raw wonder from within us. Naturally, equally as many people have a significant fear of this power as well. Out in the Great Plains of the Dakotas, I have sat high upon a butte, riveted for hours, watching thunderhead storm clouds slowly rolling in from miles and miles away. Lightning ripples across the western horizon, but the thunder's voice is silent, so far away is the storm that the sound dissipates before it can reach my hearing. At home in Ohio, when a storm roils, I often move to my back porch and sit rapt in wonder at the force that crashes and shakes the earth beneath me.

In the Lakota tradition, this amazing force is no mere scientific phenomenon. The *Wakiya Oyate,* or Thunder Beings, are part of the very energy of God. Coming out of the west, the wakiya provide insight into the power of God. When the rumbling thunder and flashing lightning from above first arrive in the spring, the new year, they shake the earth, arousing and beckoning the sleeping plants and animals to awaken; it is time to grow they seem to say. The lightning reaching down from the heavens, from Grandfather Sky, touches the earth, energizing it with renewed life. But these storms are also coming from the west, and the west, among other things, represents the destiny of all living things on earth, death - not an ultimate end but the end of life as we know it here on this Grandmother Earth. Thus, just as storms tend to do to us quite naturally, in the presence of the Wakiya Oyate, we ought to stand in a posture of deep respect of the awesome power of God - the one who gives life, but the one who can also take it away.

We want our relationship with God to be personal, and a well-developed and nurtured spiritual life ought to develop such a relationship. But it is also important to know that God is God, and I am not. God must be respected. He is not my "buddy," but a loving teacher through whose friendship I may grow more acutely aware and more properly aligned with all that he has created. I may come to understand the what and the how of thunder and lightning, either scientifically or spiritually, but I will do well either way to stand at a respectful distance in the presence of its powerful energy.

Omnipotent God, in the experience of your magnificent storms, I encounter some part of your awesome and mysterious power. I long to sit at your feet, like one gazing to the skies as the storm rolls overhead, listening to your teachings, and learning from your instruction. Keep me humble as I approach the sacred spaces and experiences of life that you provide for me each day.

May 8
Soft as a Rock

When we feel very sure about our position on a given topic, or certain about our commitment to a specific relationship, we often characterize our firm posture with the cliché, "solid as a rock." Of course, even though we know that rocks come in a variety of different compositions, the assumption is that, more than generally, rocks are "hard" and not something that we would risk bumping into. Hence, to carry the cliché a little further, sometimes a decision between two topical positions or people can place us "between a rock and a hard place."

On the other hand, when cascading spring waters recede in canyons and creeks, once-submerged rocks often appear revealing the determined carving of the water's persistent flow. The incessant current hews undulating folds and chiseled holes, soft curves in the ancient rocks' apparent solid mass. Such sculpturing leads one both to question the "solidness" of rocks and to consider the power of fluidity. Additionally, in places such as Bryce Canyon, Arches and Canyonlands, one can encounter the wind's effect on rock. In these places, terrain which was, perhaps, once an ocean floor, now reveals exotic hoodoos, bridges and monoliths sculpted by the unseeable but persistent wind. Again, the metaphoric impenetrable rock seems to melt under the touch of a soft hand.

Of course, all of these metaphors betray the time-lapse effect behind the imagery. Rocks are, indeed, hard, and changes do not happen to them rapidly. That being said, one can still make an issue of the fact that rocks are not, well, "rock-solid." They can change – and so can we and our apparent "rock-solid" positions. Probably like rocks, we humans seem rather resistant to change, and it does not move through us easily. Nevertheless, we are being sculpted all of the time by the winds and the waters of change that necessarily move all about us. We may believe that we are solid in our positions and personality, but to deny change in our lives is to ignore the evidence of even the rocks. This moment, willfully or not, you are likely being reshaped; will the waters and winds of change that swirl about you bring softer, more subtle curves to your being, or in your resistance, will the edges be sharpened?

God of Change, you flow in and through me always, and with you, the movements of life can be sculptors upon the shape of who I am and what I am to become. Too often, I resist the inevitable changes that are happening within and around me, and cause myself more pain in doing so. While I should not be loosely blown about by the winds of change, nor swept away by their waters, help me to receive their movements more hopefully and to allow their temperate blows to soften my being and to create the hollows and holes wherein you might move through me more fluidly.

May 9
Moving with the Tao

"Bad things" in life happen to people all the time. Sometimes, I really believe that maybe there is a very specific cosmic reason for these bad things, "a divinity that shapes our ends rough-hew them how we will," as Hamlet once noted insightfully. But other times, I tend to think that these "bad things" are just life itself. There are no "good" reasons; they just happen – it is the way of nature. One philosophical, and, more importantly, spiritual approach that has helped me to better understand and to accept these cosmic shifts in the world as well as in my personal life is Taoism, an ancient Eastern way of approaching life that dates back as far as the 6th century B.C.E.

Taoism, from the word "Tao" (pronounced "dow"), which is simply translated as "way," is not a religion that proclaims itself as a map or a path or a "way" to the divine. Taoism has no personal God like people of the Western world are so used to honoring, but speaks instead to the energy, the force of God if you will, that is both the ultimate source of the universe as well as the principle of order that sustains it. Like trying to fully understand the reasons for all "good and bad" things, the Tao is beyond full human comprehension, but it can be understood to varying degrees through a careful observation of "the Way of nature."

One of the most recognizable, but likely most misunderstood images of Taoism is the symbol of the Yin and the Yang, a simple circle where the dark yin and the light yang gently curl into each other in perfect symmetry. This circle, a symbol for the necessary balance of the universe, suggests that neither the passive yin nor the aggressive yang is superior, but that each plays an important role in the universal balance of things. To further exemplify the need for each and the balance of them, a smaller circle of the opposing color can be found in the heart of each side revealing that there is also always a small part of one within the other. Thus, in Taoism, good and bad events become more relative and more about balance. The "good rain" that farmers need on their fields may also be the "bad

149

rain" of another community's flooding. The "good deep freeze and snow" that the earth and the things of the soil need each winter to rejuvenate the seeds and the nutrients may also be the "horrifying freeze and snow" that takes the lives of stock and other wild animals.

From the Taoist perspective, the excess of our aggressive yang nature, so common to our Western approach (think in terms of our politics, our economics, and even our social lives and athletic pursuits), needs to be complemented with the more passive yin, or we risk throwing the universe of things out of balance. And when "bad things" happen - forceful "yang events" - rather than embracing and moving with them, which would be the yin response, we more often retaliate or confront them aggressively, creating further instability in our environment. Thus, whether there is "a divinity that shapes our ends" or it is "just the way it is," the real "spiritual movement" of our lives is revealed in our response to these events, these challenges. Like a leaf floating in the Tao of the river, when I embrace the possibilities inherent in unsuspecting change, in difficulties, in "bad things," then the universal current, the Way of things, moves me toward where I should be. But if I fight it and resist its flow, I will more likely be hurt by the tension and rigidity of my posture.

I cannot dictate the current or the direction of the cosmic flow – the goodness or the badness of things - but I can choose to dive in and actively, though lithely, float within it through prayerful acceptance. Creator of the Tao, the Cosmic Way, the whole universe of things flows from you and back to you. Sometimes I slip off into unknown tributaries and find myself floundering in stagnant waters, or feel threateningly pulled towards a dangerous waterfall. I want to float safely in your energetic surge, supplely circulating in the river of life. When difficult times arise, help me to receive the possibilities of change with receptive arms. And for those I love, and for all who are swept into this cosmic flow, may my prayers of care for them be a soft buoyancy as they shoot the rapids that inevitably lie up ahead.

May 10
Wu Wei

I have received a few speeding tickets in my driving history, but not one of them was because I was truly speeding. Each one arrived during a moment of ignorance, when I missed the sign for a sudden and significant speed limit drop in a neighborhood or through a school restricted area. On the highway, I am wedded to the "cruise control" and I truly don't speed beyond the "legal" five miles over the limit. I have found my rule to be both an economical and a safe way to travel, and I never have to worry about those sneaky patrolmen with their hidden radars. Somewhat ironically, I suppose, I really dislike getting behind slow drivers, people who stay in the fast lanes on highways but go absolutely no faster than the "real" speed limit, and often slower, or who clog up business thoroughfares with their slow methodical driving. In such instances, I will attest, I can become a rather "aggressive driver" weaving back and forth between lanes just to gain a car or two advantage.

Unfortunately, during these more aggressive stretches, I have often found that I gain very little. Few things in driving are more aggravating to me than when I accelerate and bob and weave through traffic just to get ahead of the annoyingly slow, and in my estimation, subsequently dangerous little, old lady driver only to have her pull up beside me at the next stop light while I am waiting. As much as I hate to admit it, in truth, she is the one who is driving more safely - *and* more economically. In fact, her mode of driving embraces the primary virtue of Taoism, known as *wu wei.*

Although there are numerous ways of defining it, the most simple translation of wu wei is "nonaction;" however, while the slowness of my adversary often seems like no-action, that is not exactly what this virtue implies. A more modern adaptation of wu wei might be "to go with the flow" and not push the pace, and this is exactly what Granny does in her unhurried and disciplined driving. When the light turns green, she slowly accelerates, avoiding the "jack rabbit start," until she safely obtains the speed limit, and proceeds accordingly until the next mandated stop or desired turn. She stays in her lane and moves forward. The impatient ones, such as myself, want to advance more quickly, and we promptly become irritated by people who, as we see it, stymie our progress. But the truth of the matter is, on a normal business street, even one with four lanes, there is no controlling "the flow." On a usual day of commerce, between the steady stream of traffic turning onto and off of the thoroughfare and the intermittent stoplights placed strategically along the way, the chances of one "getting ahead" are very meager. In such a situation, a person is far more likely to get frustrated than he is to get ahead.

Patience, humility, nonaggression and noncompetition are trademarks of wu wei. Embracing the passivity of the yin, the person who practices this high virtue does not step away from life's flow, but merely moves with it patiently. All around us, especially in the cities of our Western world, people are driven by the aggressive yang and the desire to "get ahead." Wu wei is not opposed to getting ahead, but humbly knows that one only truly moves forward in nature's good time. To do otherwise is an uneconomical use of one's energy and potentially creates dangerous confrontations.

God of the Way That It Is, sometimes through my haste I do accomplish things "ahead of time," and so believe that my aggressive behavior is the "winning way." But most often when I try to control the tone and the flow of all things around me, I only achieve frustration and annoyance. Help me to see in the "heavy traffic moments" of my life, opportunities to practice wu wei and its accompanying trademark virtues. When I place my life in your cruise control, I let go of my control and patiently allow you to cruise through me. And at your speed, I will not only avoid tickets, but I will always be right on time.

May 11
Remembering Mother's Love

On the morning of the first Mother's Day after my mother died, I didn't feel any particularly new or deep sadness. I was certainly aware that on this day I would not be calling and visiting with my mother as I had done for at least the thirty previous years since I had moved states away, nor would I be rushing to get a card and gift in the mail so that it would arrive on time. No, the day arrived like so many other days, and I pretty much went about the business of the day, not thinking much about mom, but not feeling as though I was purposely avoiding thoughts of her either.

Later in the evening, realizing I had not taken time for my daily meditation yet, I quietly slipped to the back of the house and into my prayer corner. My wife, who was obviously far more cognizant of the day's dissonance than I was, sometime later stepped back "to check on me." Gently creeping up behind me, she laid her hands on my shoulders and said, "I just came back to see if you were alright." For a brief flash, I wondered upon what her concern would be based, and then it slowly started to hit me. After assuring her that I was fine, my wife retreated, but in her absence, I suddenly felt the presence of my mother slide into the room and settle some place right beside me, or maybe it was moving about beneath my rib cage.

For the next few minutes, words rolled out of me with little thought or intention; it was a simple conversation with my mother, the first that I had since I spoke to her last at her graveside. Warm tears welled up in my eyes, and slowly rolled down the shoreline of my face. There were no waves of grief or deep sadness crashing against the rocks, but I finally recognized the melancholic wave of the seaweed beneath the surface of my waters, the gentle sway of the tide's ebb and flow. We sometimes carry these dear, dear loved ones so closely within us that we hardly notice their presence or their absence; they seem merely a part of our very own existence. But now, peering into these waters, I saw my mother, detached from this life, though never fully gone from it, signs of her everywhere around and within me. I finally wished her a happy Mother's Day that day, and I sensed that somehow she received it with the same love that she had for years previous.

O God, the True Mother of Us All, I know you in large part through the love of others, and especially through the love of my mother. You, who are love, extend to us life and love through the gentle touch, the kind words, and the tender mercies of those who love us, especially through the selflessness of our mothers. Today, I especially honor the love of those who have given me life in so many ways, from the woman who birthed and loved me into life, to the many other people who have nurtured me. Though I may lose track of them during my lifetime, or though I may lose them from this life, may I never forget to keep them gratefully alive through my own acts of gentleness, kindness and tenderness.

May 12
Valuable Stuff

Before my mother died, she asked my sister-in-law, who is a tremendous organizer, to take charge of cleaning out the house when the matriarch "moved on." My sister-in-law took the request to heart, and soon after mother's death she was making arrangements with the family to "inherit" the furniture and goods of the house, as well as a local urgent needs center to accept some new donations. Because of the distance between us, some eight hundred miles, I received phone calls periodically during this transitional period inquiring as to whether or not I wanted this or these particular items. Each time she called, I found myself struggling with the "stuff question." Good furniture was at stake, some of which had come to my parents from their parents, so it carried both nostalgic or heirloom weight as well. But underneath the utilitarian and sentimental values was the very large question of "do I really *need* it?"

My own house was already stretching at the seams with beautiful and memorable stuff. My wife's family heirlooms and collectibles rival the stock of many American pioneer museums. These treasures which offer us a tangible connection to our ancestors seem priceless, and yet, they are just *things*, often of little practical use. And here I was, faced with the question of adding more!

When we see the devastation and poverty of those who have survived some natural disaster in some far off land, or who simply live in a culture of poverty, we can be quickly embarrassed by our wealth of stuff. Most of us have far more "stuff" than we will ever need, from dishes and kitchen needs to our bursting closets of various seasonal clothing to the comforts of our furniture and appliances. The real question is not so much whether or not I *need* all of these things – because I don't – but rather, how *attached* to these things have I become, even to the things that I don't have now, but could have later – like my mother's furniture! Living simply in a nation of excess, as we do in the United States, is a very real challenge. No, I don't need to just give everything away, but, yes, I do need to seek a better balance between what I need and what I want; between what is valuable – and on what level – and what is necessary.

Loving God, you are my greatest "treasure." Ultimately, my greatest wealth is in the richness of my relationship with you, and that relationship is lived out, in some part, in how I relate to other people and to things. Help me to periodically take inventory of my stuff, and to question its true value. If my home and life are cluttered with so much stuff that it is difficult for me to move about, it is very likely that there is even less space for you to move in and reside with me as well.

May 13
A Darkened Vision

Sometimes I don't see very well and it darkens my heart. No, I don't mean that my eyesight and my blood-pumping organ are specifically connected; it's that sometimes my view of an event or of other people gets skewed by my own biases and prejudices, and then my misperception sours the better part of me, making me think or act less than kind.

I have a former colleague friend with whom I honestly share nearly nothing in common, except my previous job. She and her husband are good people who would do anything for me, but I still often struggle over our obvious differences. From politics to religion, from local to international issues, I would bet that we almost always fall on the opposite side of the fence. Knowing this, I consciously avoid any topics that might steer us into an inevitable head-on collision of differences; the couple doesn't seem to see what I do, however.

Some years ago, we all were invited to a wedding in the family of a mutual friend. As the wedding was out of town, shortly before leaving home, my colleague called and volunteered that we carpool. Now, while I am all for energy-saving efforts, I knew that our schedules – theirs, to always be "well on-time" and ours, not-so-much – and potentially our dispositions might not be compatible riders, so I declined the offer. As "history" would have it, my wife and I, typically running late, left for the wedding nearly a half hour after my colleague's proposed departure time. Of course, beyond their penchant for being "on time," there were some other good reasons for their earlier departure. Caring for their physically disabled child who was joining them for the wedding, the wife, the sole wage earner of the household since a recent accident had placed her husband on disability, knew that she would need some additional time if she were to arrive on time and enjoy the wedding. Despite their earlier exit, however, when my wife and I arrived at the church for the wedding, we found ourselves pulling into the parking lot just ahead of our colleague friends. Emerging from their car with complaints of directions, the wife grumbled further about the lack of help they had received when they stopped and sought some guidance at a nearby convenient store, an insinuation that carried a clear ethnic indictment. Privately horrified by her comment, I lost all care for her situation and wondered how it was that we were actually "friends."

Days later and back at school, my colleague dropped in on me to visit about the previous weekend, and in doing so, confided with me about the weight of responsibilities she was carrying, and how the burden of the preparation for and the getting to the wedding had almost crushed her. As she unraveled her story to me, my own careless attention to her needs emerged from the shadows and I began to wonder how it was that she could actually call me "friend." My wife and I were two healthy, able-bodied people going to the same place days before as my colleague who desperately could have used some assistance. But locked in my busy little world, smug in my altruistic vision of myself, I truly missed an opportunity to offer a simple helping hand that would have assisted unwieldy steps, saved directional confusion, and provided a more enjoyable day for my colleague, my "friend." And had I stepped forward, the exasperated comment that was "all I heard" would probably never have been spoken.

Jesus once warned against judging others, commenting: "Why do you notice the splinter in your brother's eye, but do not perceive the wooden beam in your own?" (Lk 6:41). How easy it is for me to see the small shortcomings of others and everything that is wrong with the world, and to miss my obvious opportunities to make a difference. Sometimes I don't see very well and it darkens my heart.

As if carrying a simple flashlight in a dark space, I too often shed light on the inconsistencies and failures of others, while in the darkness all around me sit my glaring errors. God of Vision, open my eyes to the needs of others when I allow myself to be blinded by my own prejudices and judgments of them.

May 14
Confronting Our Truth

There cannot be many people who abhor confrontation more than I do, and I don't say that with even a hint of self-flattery. I have long considered my aversion to confrontations as one of my most glaring flaws, a substantial shortcoming. It is not as though I want to be an aggressively assertive person ready to insert my view whenever I think the world around me needs to hear it; in fact, I most often don't say anything because that is precisely the person I don't want to be. But I do figure that I have sometimes done untold damage to others and myself when I have withheld the urgings of my heart out of a fear of rejection and misunderstanding. There is an important difference between speaking one's opinion and speaking one's truth, and in wanting to avoid the former, I suspect that I too often fail to do the latter.

As emotional beings, we all can be quickly affected by passionately charged stories and situations, and our world is certainly full of such occasions. Abuses and violence of all kinds on the individual level, and political decision-making and economic mismanagement on the social level can all ignite the short fuse of our emotions and have us exploding angrily, the shrapnel of our opinions spraying in uncertain directions. Detonations such as these, rantings that blast from the gut of our emotions, are based primarily on rising opinions, and many of us would do better if we would "think twice and then say nothing" when it comes to such diatribes. But issues that have their roots embedded in our hearts, these need to be spoken, for others' sake sometimes and for ourselves most of the time.

Opinions are usually related in some way to these "heart-truths," but they are only the sucker shoots of the parent plant; they may make the plant look larger, and may even grow as large as the parent plant, but they drain energy from the tap root and ultimately make the fruit of our truth less palatable. The well-pruned truth of our hearts, however, needs, even deserves, to be heard. Flowing from the life spring of who we are, our truth keeps us in touch with what most matters in our lives, and so when we feel the roots of that being injuriously tugged, we need to speak up. And this is not simply self-preservation, although sometimes that will be in the mix; this is standing up for what each of us knows is right. It might mean "calling out" a good friend for his erratic behavior, or speaking up at a public forum on behalf of those who have been denied a voice or whose voices have been silenced. There is definitely risk involved, for not everyone will see it as I do, and they may even resent me for it, but if it comes from the heart, and one "just knows" when it does, then I must speak my truth.

A long time friend of mine with whom I am most surely diametrically opposed on most political and economic issues sparked my fuse just before one election. He had always taken a sort of diabolical pleasure I assumed in trying to instigate arguments between us, and, for my part, I had done all that I could to avoid his land mines. But on this particular day, I stepped right on one, and as I exploded in an uncontrollable retort to his incendiary comment, I knew that I had not only lost control but "face" as well. Without speaking from my truth, I attacked with my opinions and the result was a miserable feeling of carnage for all who were within earshot. After another more recent, but less volatile episode, I sat down to write him a letter days later. When I finished it, I turned it over to my wife, asking her, "You know how sometimes you are supposed to write what you want to say to someone, and then tear it up? Is this that letter?" After reading it carefully, she handed it back to me and said, "No, this is your truth; you need to send it and he needs to hear it."

God of the Heart, so often my truth gets tangled up in the suckers of my opinions and the weeds of my fears, and I either allow them to grow wildly together or I prune them recklessly cutting the voice of all away. Grant me a more prudent approach, and help me to better separate my opinions from my truth. Then, rooted firmly in my truth, give me the courage and the strength to say what sincerely needs to be said, confident that the trunk can endure whatever storms might follow.

May 15
Drawn Into the Beauty

I must confess that I can be easily captivated by the beauty of the human form, and I don't think that I am unique in this appreciation. I believe that most people are naturally enamored by the beauty of a human face as well as the subtle and obvious endowments of the human body. In truth, many relationships begin, especially romantic ones, by one person being drawn to another's appearance, the outer attractiveness calling one to discover the potential inner beauty as well. Further, the inner beauty then, somehow, seems to enhance the outer beauty, for sometimes people seem to become more attractive the more we get to know their inner beauty. Given this seemingly inherent allurement of external beauty and then its accompanying desire to encounter and to know more about the person behind the form, it strikes me that perhaps we ought to be more similarly captivated by the beauty of the creations and want to know more about the "Person" behind their forms as well.

I am most acutely aware of this parallel in the spring of the year when the blossoming trees are in full bloom, and the perennial flowers have stretched their slender necks from a crusty earth to reveal a dazzling and sometimes dizzying display of colors in exotic forms, with a scent that is of their nature, not a masked perfume such as we humans might wear. Beyond the biological and the botanical explanations for their existence run deeper more fundamental questions of the how and why of their existence. From a divine cosmological perspective, what is the reason for such breath-taking and mesmerizing beauty? If a deeper beauty, which we so often seem drawn to lies beneath the external beauty of the human form, what wondrous beauty courses beneath the skin of these natural wonders?

I cannot help but feel that such magnificent springtime displays are part of God's annual flirtation with his beloved creation, of which we humans are an integral part. As bees and birds and other forms are naturally drawn to these blossoming testimonies of God's love, are we too supposed to be sucked into receiving the flavors, the scent, and the vision of God's love for us? Here they are – and here it is, God's love - freely, vibrantly spread out like a grand banquet and an extravagant bouquet.

O God of All Things Beautiful, thank you for the exquisite beauty of your creations, both human and natural. Drawn so to these forms, I wonder at what you might have in store for us in the deeper layers of our lives. Just as I have discovered the inner beauty that enhances the human appearance, may I be drawn more deeply into the depths of your love expressed so marvelously, so freely, in your sublime creations.

May 16
Lawn Care

My wife has been very upset in recent years at the continuous onslaught of "creeping charlie" on our lawn. This quite unwelcome weed has literally taken over our backyard, and it won't be long before its shooting tendrils spread beneath the surface and consume the front and sides as well. At first I didn't much care; in fact, in the spring it provides a rather pretty purple blossom and I just thought it rather nice to have this field of purple in our backyard. But as there is now nearly no grass left and its autumn face is nothing but a tight scraggly beard, I must confess, I am a little closer to my wife's sentiment. This caring so for our lawns in the United States has often been something of a paradox to me though, or perhaps, it is more of reminder to me of our silly fixation with appearances. Every time I start to get upset about the weed infiltration, I find myself asking, "so what?"

A lush, green lawn is certainly a beautiful frame around a nicely kept home. But it is a rather vicious cycle that we have created. People seed or sod the land around their home, and then proceed to fertilize and aerate it regularly; all of these, of course, at a fairly considerable cost. Once they get their lawns growing well, then they must mow them regularly and weed them accordingly. Of course, lawn mowers are not cheap, and these too need periodic maintenance checks, not to mention the fill of gas and oil that goes with every mowing occasion. If the home owner is really into having an enviable lawn, then along with everything above, comes weed trimmers and edgers and borders and who knows what else. Finally, there is the endless concern about what might be happening with the neighbors' lawns: are they caring for them as we are; will their dandelions or creeping charlie make their way into my yard; and, if they do, might we need to have "a talk" about this?! So, when I stop and think about the time, the money and the physical and emotional energy that goes into this lawn, I quickly begin to wonder, what's the real point of it. Ultimately, isn't it all just about some "appearance"?

So much of our lives, it seems, is given over to this excessive and even compulsive behavior for the sake of appearances. From clothes, to hairstyles, to make-up, to cologne and perfume, from cars, to furniture, to dishes and silverware, we spend endless hours working for, seeking and purchasing, and then caring for our many possessions and needs - and, ultimately, all in the name of appearance. I guess one could say that there is nothing wrong with wanting to look nice and have nice things, and taking good care of those things once one has them certainly seems appropriate, but how much time do we spend on taking care of *who we are*?

Wondrously Ethereal God, while we know essentially nothing of your appearance, we claim to know you by who you are, a God of Love. Is just the opposite true for myself: I am well familiar with my appearance but know little about who I am and what you call me to be? Perhaps as I mow the lawn this week, or work in the flowerbeds, I might take off the headphones and just use the time to also do some work on my internal landscape. Help me to weed out the unhealthy aspects of my character and to fertilize my spiritual needs.

May 17
Our Place in the Universe of Things

From my vantage point, a great disservice was caused by the translation and interpretation of a line in the first creation story rendered in the Judeo-Christian scriptures. In the New American Bible version of the story, after God has created the heavens and the earth and all that dwells upon the latter, God fashions humanity; "male and female he created them," and then blessing them, God said, "fill the earth and subdue it. Have dominion over the fish of the sea, the birds of the air, and all the living things that move on the earth" (Gn 1:27b-28). For me, the disservice is created by two words which have maligned the relationship that much of humanity, particularly Western Civilization, has had with the rest of the created order: "subdue" and "dominion."

These two words are, by their nature, adversarial. To subdue something implies an embattled relationship where, in this case, humanity is called to conquer or overcome by force. Once winning the battle, the second word, dominion, encourages humanity to assume supreme power and authority over its conquered foe, in this case, the rest of creation. To think that we human beings are intended to have this combative relationship with nature has provided innumerable justifications for our abusive mistreatment of the earth and the Western European mentality that spilled across the Americas in the form of "Manifest Destiny." Beyond the harm that we have inflicted on so many of the creations is the additional arrogance of our sense of entitlement given in the command to "have dominion." First of all, giving witness to a tsunami, an earthquake or any number of "natural disasters," one would have to conclude that we human beings hardly have supreme power and authority. That we can "conquer" any "wildlife" at all is due only to our disingenuous creation of weaponry, for I would dare to say that in a "grizzly bear versus man" confrontation – mano a mano – the fair-skinned one is not likely to win the dispute.

How much better it would be – and is – when we see our proper place in the universe of things. Were all things really created *just* for humanity, or do we, like all other created things, have a place and a responsibility in maintaining a certain balance in the universe? And if all of creation *does* exist for humanity, perhaps it was so that we might *learn* from it, not "subdue and have dominion" over it. Although humans and all other life forms are certainly created differently, I have discovered that when I observe carefully and watch thoughtfully any and all of these "other life forms," I stand to learn a tremendous amount about the way life is, and I dare to say, the way life *should be.*

Creator God, you have filled the world with so many wondrous creations, vast in number and variety, whose very existence can speak to us of how we are to live. Forgive me and all humans who so often arrogantly see ourselves as the superior life form while failing to receive the lessons that you provide us through the lives of other creations. Help me to live as a careful observer and a caretaker of all that you have created, realizing that as I bring harm to all other living things, I ultimately bring harm to myself as well.

May 18
The Force of Water

Water is the singularly most essential element for almost all life, not least of which are humans. We could go for many days without eating, but without water we would much more quickly perish. And yet, one has only to observe a swelling creek or river, let alone hurricane waters, to know that the force of water can be equally as destructive to life as it can be sustaining. When rain falls incessantly and tributaries deepen, broaden and accelerate, anything in the path of the rushing waters is in peril. I have stood rapt in awe in slot canyons where narrow high desert corridors have been carved through sandstone and rock by the sudden and powerful force of water rushing headlong into an otherwise immovable mass. It is almost unfathomable to imagine that the great mystery that is the Grand Canyon was slowly but relentlessly created over millions of years by the relentless flow of water - and yet, the canyon's central artery, the Colorado River, seems an obvious piece of evidence to the carving force that shaped this colossal laceration on the earth's surface.

Human beings have managed to dam and to redirect waters, but left unattended, all of these human made efforts to control water will eventually crumble under its indomitable force. On warm and rainy summer afternoons as a child, along with neighborhood friends, I would build rock and sand dams in creeks and street gutters, engineers in the making, attempting to constrict the expanding flow. Our efforts were always a source of limited pride, as their demise signaled a deeper truth that the force of nature was far greater than the force of humanity.

159

I have always preferred to believe in the essential goodness of humanity, but I am also keenly aware of our apparent selfish penchants. Created in God's image, we all should naturally flow, it seems, within a river of goodness, the ceaseless movement of love. And yet, one quick look within and outside of myself reveals swelling streams of egoism that frequently threaten to burst over the banks and wipe out whatever is in my way. Anger, self-pity, resentment and selfishness are all currents that can redirect what is best in me and send me out onto destructive courses that violate not only the goodness of others but the gifts of creation as well.

O God, you are the wellspring of all life, the force that can nourish and diminish all created things. Created in your image, I possess an energy that, like water, can be a source of life and a cause of destruction in the world. Often, I believe that I can build the dams and the irrigation ditches that move this energy in ways and to places that are beneficial to life; but, too often, I realize that I am incapable of controlling the emotions and desires that can easily misdirect my good intentions. Help me today, O Sustenance of life, to be a tributary of your nourishing waters, a river of love carving a path toward you.

May 19
Being Sense-able

We don't often consciously think about our senses. Like breathing, we simply expect them to do what they do even though almost our whole life depends on them. The senses are doorways into our interactions and experiences with the world – with life itself! Amongst friends or in a larger group, perhaps you have been challenged before with the ice-breaking question: "If you had to lose one of your five senses, which would you give up?" It's a horrible thought, of course; no one would *choose* such a thing! Along with fueling some discussion, however, the question certainly makes one suddenly aware of just how much and how often we rely on our senses. How could we go without any one of them, and what would be some of the specific deficits of such a loss? And, of course, the question also likely reminds us that some people *do* go without the use of a certain sense or senses, and this awareness almost always solicits a sympathetic reflection on their behalf.

Food is sustenance, and if I were starving, I just might eat *anything,* but imagine if you could not enjoy the tastes of so many delicious fruits, vegetables and food preparations. Ethnic foods and flavors would be absolutely immaterial. And what would entice me to these delectable dishes and delicacies if not for their wonderful smells? And what would steer me clear of some potential danger or unpleasantry if not for the fair warning that sometimes wafts my way? When I have a bad batch of poison ivy, I suppose the loss of the sensation of touch and feeling might be okay, but such a loss would also mean that I would never again feel the warmth of the sun on my body and the gentle, soothing touch of a soft breeze. Romance would be mechanical; holding hands, foreplay, making love – what would these amazing actions become? Many people have gone through their whole lives in darkness, and some have lost their sight later in life, but to either never know the beauty of the creations or to have known the beauty and then to lose it, such a darkness is unfathomable to me. Similarly, the gift of hearing is so much a part of every day of my life; from music to voices to even the sound of silence, I float in a pool of sound awareness always. But to live in a senseless silence, having known or never knowing what is beyond those sound-sealed walls, what could possible be the "music to my ears"?

I dare not offer any answer to the question of "which sense would you lose" for fear that I just might, in fact, lose it. No, instead, let me take some time right now to engage thoughtfully in each of my five senses and recognize what a tremendous gift each of them is; then, let me give the giver of the gifts praise and thanksgiving.

God of All Senses, for humans, life is not simply about existing, but also engaging in our existence. Through the tremendous gifts of the senses, you invite us to explore the universe that surrounds us and to interact with the earth upon which we live. Could I live without one or more of these senses? Yes, I could, for many people have not only endured life without one or more of them, but have thrived despite their loss. But, gratefully, you have given me the ability to live within a fuller awareness of your creations, a deeper intermingling with life itself. Today, and everyday, may I mindfully see the beauty of your creation, hear the sounds of all things, smell the scents of the living and the dead, taste the goodness of sustenance, and feel the sensations of love and life – and, in so doing, give you praise for such a wondrous existence.

May 20
Five Wild Horses

Life is full of so many wonderful pleasures, and our senses have been created in such a way as to lead us into these many pleasures. Arriving home or as a guest in someone else's home, we are greeted by the delicious scents of a cooking meal prepared with hands of care and a heart of love. A warm embrace enfolds us as we step into the home's comfort and we feel the love that touch can offer. In the background, perhaps, music softly extends the harmony we feel with its lilting sound, and looking about, we see love conveyed in the comfort and care of the home and the people that greet us. Welcomed and warmed in this entry, we sit at table and consume the delectable tastes of the food prepared with loving care. Enshrouded in this framework of love, this scene appears as a consummate experience of goodness; but not all scenes of the senses are thus bound.

Indeed, our senses are doorways into many known and unknown pleasures, but as satisfying as these pleasures can be, like over indulging in even the best of meals, one must be careful to not be overwhelmed by the senses. In the beautiful Sanskrit text of ancient India, the *Bhagavad Gita*, Lord Krishna is called upon to teach the troubled Arjuna who is faced with a war in which he must fight against his own relatives. The story itself serves as an allegory for life, and seeks to instruct the reader so that he may establish balance and harmony in life and so live it more wisely and, thereby, more joyfully and fully. In the story, Krishna is

161

driving a chariot in which Arjuna is seated. The chariot represents the physical body, and with that, the individual mind; the five horses that pull the chariot, interestingly enough, are the five senses. But while the five horses may pull the chariot, the driver, in this case, Lord Krishna, holds the reins of discriminative awareness; and so it is the driver who lives in awareness that is ultimately in charge of the direction and the speed of the chariot.

The senses are powerful forces in our lives, and left unchecked can be like runaway horses resisting all efforts of taming and reining in. Imagine being seated in a chariot with no reins and five wild horses running at their whim; it is a dangerous proposition, and yet it is a ride into which many people step with some frequency in their lives. As Lord Krishna teaches Arjuna, so must we sit up and listen to the instruction of the importance of living with a discriminative awareness. The horses can bring us to many sensual pleasures, and these pleasures are not evil or bad in themselves, but it is important that we hold the reins of this chariot we drive and not be pulled about aimlessly by the whims of our senses.

O God of my Deepest Desires, I thank you for the wondrous gifts of the senses, and for the many marvelous pleasures that they provide. But a life fat on pleasure is an existence lean on wisdom and lacking the fullness of my deepest desire, which is you. Help me to seize the reins of awareness and to be mindful of the deeper yearnings of my heart which reside below the simple sensations of the senses. While I may find temporary pleasure in the world of the senses, I will only find true and lasting rapture and bliss in the realm that is you.

May 21
The Three Gatekeepers

Many years ago, for I want to distance this event as far away from my present as I can, I was enjoying lunch with some of my colleagues in the faculty lounge sharing thoughts and stories about the imminent graduation ahead as well as memories of past ones. One of my teaching friends, a woman known by all to be deeply passionate and emotional about all that she does, began to share with us how she had cried throughout her high school graduation, lamenting so the end of such good and desirable years. As she completed her story, I thoughtlessly allowed the sarcastic musings of my mind to spill across the table. "Really?" I said with my best poker face. "You cried? I'm shocked." My colleague, and I dare to say, friend's head slowly lowered as if to contemplate the food before her; but then she rose from the table, gathered her things and quietly walked out of the room.

We have all probably said something for which we later, if not immediately as in my case, deeply regretted. Sometimes our utterance is merely said in ignorance; we harmlessly say something unaware that our words are carrying a stinging nettle. Other times, we might know that our words are barbed, but we think them essentially inoffensive and assume that while they might prick their subject, they certainly won't pierce or puncture. And then, of course, there are the times when we know our words are venomous but thinking that the poison is either necessary or not truly toxic, we say them anyway. Often, in the end, it doesn't matter which of the three types of "foot-in-the-mouth" diseases we contract, the embarrassment, the guilt, or the humiliation we receive in return is much the same.

There is a famously popular Arabic proverb that I have read and heard in a number of different places, but am always grateful for its reminder. "The words of the tongue," it begins, "should have three gatekeepers." That thought alone might be enough, but then it goes on to "name" the gatekeepers. "The first gatekeeper asks, 'Is it true?' The second gatekeeper asks, 'Is it kind?' And the final gatekeeper asks, 'Is it necessary?'" My experience teaches me that if I make it past the first two gatekeepers, every once in awhile I might slip by the third one while he is napping. But the first two sentinels ought to be resolute in their questions and firm in their disallowing passage unless the answers are affirmative. Was my statement to my colleague "true"? Well, arguably yes, but was it "kind"? Definitely, no – and that should have been the end of the story; "necessary" would have simply been another negative strike.

Another important proverb with which I am familiar although I do not know its exact origin states: "Think twice and then say nothing." This line too places guards at the door of our mouths asking us to reconsider the necessity of our words. Of course, if we all followed this one consistently, the world would be a rather quiet place, void of much conversation. If what we have to say is true and kind, then its necessity is not so difficult to justify. A little embarrassment over a compliment is not such a bad thing, and sometimes a small truthful kindness can spark some wonderful conversation. But had I taken the Arabic proverb to heart years ago, I would not have felt the shame and embarrassment that I did when I knocked on my colleague's door after I quickly finished my lunch that day to apologize for my lack of kindness and respect.

Comedians and politicians, it seems, make a living out of ignoring the three gatekeepers. You and I sometimes suck life from the living when we ignore them. God of Kindness and Truth, set before my mouth the three gatekeepers to question and watch over my words. Much of what I say is probably unnecessary, but if it is not true or kind then it is also unwarranted. May I think twice before I speak, if I should speak at all.

May 22
Geese and Gander Don't Always Flock Together

My wife is not exactly a "morning person," so on weekends, if possible, she likes to take advantage of sleeping in a little longer. In the spring, however, with the windows thrown open wide inviting the fresh air of the new year inside, she sometimes has to contend with the annual spring liveliness of the local songbirds as well as some feisty ones migrating through. Although my wife is a gentle soul, she very much enjoys her sleep, and more than once I have heard her mutter in response to the incessant chatter of the birds outside, "Oh, would you *please* shut up!" So, while I might welcome the songs of birds to herald me into the next life, I realize that not everyone would necessarily offer them that same invitation.

The fact is, there are many things in life to which people have very different responses. Even individually, a person may have a range of responses to the same or similar things based solely on the "timing." Again, using the opening example concerning my wife, her response to the morning songs of birds is entirely based on "their timing." In truth, she loves the melodies of birds, and has even posited herself in a North Dakota field just to record for her own nostalgic need the tunes of the western meadowlark. But there is a time and place for everything it seems, and when she wants to sleep in, for her, that is not a time for them to speak up. Sometimes we invite the chatter of others, and other times we want only the music of silence.

Of course, these differing preferences both between people and within people have an easy spiritual correlation as well. As with exercise regimens, there are a variety of ways to strengthen one's spiritual awareness, and no one of these practices is necessarily better than all the others, and no one of these is necessarily going to have the same results all of the time. Personal preferences are absolutely acceptable, and even with these, timing is often very important. God is way bigger than any one spiritual practice, and isn't it wonderful that God has provided us with so many access doors? For some people, religious rituals best open their senses to the presence of the Divine; for others, such events are too distracting and formulated. One person may access her path to the Divine through meditation, while another may be unable to satisfy the required concentration and silence of meditation. One group may discover spiritual fulfillment through chanting or repetitious prayers, but another circle may feel that the songs and words are too empty and impersonal. And yet, rituals, meditation, chanting, and so many other spiritual practices are all historically proven and legitimate avenues towards the seeker's desired fulfillment and communion with the Divine; and, as with all physical exercise, one does not have to limit herself to just one practice. Some days, meditation will best fit your need while other times the heart will yearn for community prayer and ritual. There is an old saying that goes, "What's good for the goose, is good for the gander," suggesting that what is good for one is good for another. But regarding spiritual practices, not even "birds of a feather" necessarily need or want to "flock together." For me, the birds may be prayerfully singing up the sun in the spring, but if they wake up my wife, they may need to be singing some prayers if they want to be around when the sun goes down.

God of Many Feathers, as you have created a multitude of birds, and as we appreciate and enjoy those birds in a variety of ways, so too are there many ways for us to wing our way toward you. Certain songs of the Spirit may call to me in different ways, and I may be called by one song more than another at different times. Thank you for making yourself so accessible to me, for singing your way into my heart with such variety and offering my spiritual development much more than a wing and a prayer.

At The Ohio State University, there is a small arboretum on the west end of the campus, replete with groomed walkways and benches weaving thoughtful trails amongst the varied trees and flowers. Nestled in the middle of this green and gentle nook is a labyrinth, designed after the famous Chartres Cathedral Labyrinth in France, providing visitors an opportunity to meditatively walk into their own inner workings and do a little soulful reflection.

Ironically, the northern and eastern edges of the arboretum are flanked by two of the campus' busiest streets, while the western perimeter spills into the Agricultural Department's spread of buildings with their parking lot closing off the Arboretum's southern border. Escaping these more obtrusive boundaries, one can look to the blue canopy of the sky above where the network of vapor trails will reveal the flight path of the city's International Airport some ten miles away, planes departing and arriving in a steady stream overhead. And yet, despite all of these busy and noisy infiltrators, the Arboretum still rests like a quiet oasis in the midst of the incessant confusion.

An incredible variety of trees, some educationally labeled with small markers, and a random spread of flower gardens, are the real distractions from the noise and busyness from which the visitor looks to escape. This oasis is not unique, of course; many cities have such parks and green provisions that remind us of what once covered all of this land before we "developed" it with buildings and the network of transportation thoroughfares. None, perhaps, could be more famously ironic and iconic than New York City's Central Park. But for all the irony of the placement, these metropolitan oases are important "monuments" to what we know to be true: the human spirit, body and soul need "natural refreshment."

We can fill our time and lives with the business of education, commerce and whatever other human made system we want, but we will always need a quiet place to retire at various times in our day and life. It is a sad individual who has been so consumed by the busyness of life that he fails to even perceive and appreciate any longer this deeper and essential human need. For him, the nourishing waters of the oasis have evaporated.

O God who also Dwells Amidst the Noise and Confusion, let not the busyness of my life drown out the quiet whisper of your creations that urge me to rest, to be still, and to be rejuvenated by their vibrant existence. In a world of so much come and go, buy and sell, help me to stop and to gently receive the proffered gift of these oases nestled unsuspectingly amidst our metropolitan disarray.

May 24
Body Alarms

Back in the 1980s, I was a young coach making a mercurial ascent through the Track and Field coaching ranks of Ohio high schools. The teams I coached were consistently at or near the top at the end of each spring season's State Championship, but with the success came an annual pressure of "what will it be this year?" During that time, I remember that somewhere in the midst of each season I would begin to develop a nagging sore spot, usually on my left side, in my upper back just below the neckline. As I would be driving to a meet, the ache was impossible to ignore, and I would rotate my left arm and apply pressure at the point of the pain with the fingers of my right hand. Since I was not actively or regularly doing any lifting, over time I began to realize that this ache was somehow related to the stress of the season.

Nearly ten years later, while going through a marital separation and an eventual divorce, three times I experienced the most extreme and debilitating physical pain of my life when my sciatica seized up and my back went out. The first time it happened was just a day after I had shoveled my driveway and sidewalks after a heavy and deep snowstorm; given the shift in physical activity, I assumed it was a result of the shoveling. I was laid up for nearly a week, hardly able to move out of bed. Four months later, however, on my May birthday, I was simply standing in my kitchen cutting carrots for an evening dinner at which I was hosting all my children, when suddenly everything seized up again and I dropped to the floor. Now carrots can be a little tough, but I knew right away that this time was not because of some different and difficult physical labor. Too slowly, I was beginning to realize that I had a new "stress point," that the ache near the base of my neck had now dropped down into my lower back, and the stress was not over a Track and Field team's success, but my very life spinning out of control.

So many people compartmentalize their lives thinking that we are one part body, one part mind, and, if they are spiritually minded people, one part spirit or soul. I suspect that I fell right into the middle of that belief back then and easily ignored everything that my body was trying to tell me – in fact, was screaming at me. All of these parts, if they are "parts" at all, are really one thing. For convenience of discussion, I may separate these areas of my life, but my body, mind and spirit are meant to function as a unified whole, and when I fail to honor that relationship, that union, there will be repercussions. Our bodies do a wonderful job of trying to let us know when we are doing too much; and these warnings are not simply with regards to too much physical exertion, but also emotional, mental and spiritual imbalance as well. Stress of all kinds will manifest itself in physically alarming ways, and we would do well to listen to and to honor what our body is telling us by making some changes. Today, any twinge in my lower back, or any soreness just below my neck, to the right or to the left, is an immediate alarm system to me. I stop whatever I am doing and immediately begin to reevaluate how many and what kinds of fronts I am presently occupying in my life. There is some kind of tension going on within, and before the war breaks out, I had better negotiate a treaty.

God of Wholeness, the creation of the human body is magnificent enough, but within that body you have provided us with a wonderful check and balance system. Help me to live with awareness of my whole self, attentive to the signs that my body might be sending me regarding my physical, mental, emotional and spiritual health. To ignore the signs available to me is to disrespect the very gift of life that has been given to me. When I am not well in any way, help me to work collaboratively to bring wholeness and healing and unity back into my life.

May 25
A Load of Worry

Continuing on the theme of listening to one's body, when the tension of stress begins to surface in my body, be it in the lower or upper back, I do spend some time reevaluating my life and all that I might be trying to juggle. The taproot of the problem is usually worry, but this source has numerous runners shooting out from it siphoning energy from many other areas as well. Essentially, we worry about "results." If it's a course I am teaching or a test I am taking, a meet I am coaching or a race I'm running, a party I am hosting or a reunion I am attending – any and all of these can rack my body with the aches of stress. Naturally, we all want things to turn out well, and when we invest a significant amount of time and energy, and maybe even money, into something, we worry about its success. We want our "investment" to have a good return.

The primary runner shooting off from the taproot of worry is "expectations." We do not simply worry about the success of the event, but how it meets our expectations, our definition of success in this case. Expectations are likely to be based on a fairly personal or, at least, individual set of criteria. For me, much of my life was tied up in "what everyone else might think." Part of my conscience in life was the echo of my father's voice whenever I was in or on the brink of trouble: "Remember, what you do is a reflection of the family and affects the family name." With that directive, everything I did for so much of my life, while it already bore a heavy dose of personal expectations, carried the additional burden of how my actions and choices might reflect on, as well as affect others. That we typically visualize burdens as something we carry on our backs, is it any wonder that my back would receive the manifestation of my stress?

While my father perhaps unknowingly strapped me with quite a load for much of my life, he also provided some good shoulder straps and a hip belt for the loaded backpack with another line: "Ninety-five percent of the things we worry about," he would often say, "never happen." While the first line of his weighed me down for many years, this latter one has become something of a mantra for me in more recent years, and quite frankly, it's true! We worry and worry about how some effort of ours will turn out, driven by internal and external expectations and notions of success, and, in the end, most, if not all, of our worry is for naught. Either everything turns out just fine, or even if it doesn't follow the map of our plan, the destination we arrive at is equally good, sometimes even better. I can guarantee that my dad's "ninety five percent" quote was not an invitation to carelessness, for he certainly was one who measured success, but it was a comforting reflection that we need not waste so much energy over worrying. When I worry, important vitality is siphoned off of my energy tanks; imagine how much stronger and vibrant my energy might be with eighty – let alone ninety five - percent less worry!

Supportive God, some days my body literally aches from the burden of worry that I carry. Life is precious and good, and I certainly do not wish to waste or to carry it too lightly; but the worry of my expectations and concern for success only tarnish the gift and make this bearer of the gift ever more weary. Help me to see that the burden I carry is often a pack that I choose to strap to my back, and it is also one that I can choose to remove without stepping away from the task itself. Lighten my load today with the knowledge that ninety-five percent of the things I worry about will never happen.

May 26
No Retirement

I will admit that when my youngest daughter graduated from college, I privately hoped that my parenting duties were now "officially" completed, at least on the financial and directional levels. I knew better, of course, but I suspect that I was not alone in this fantasy of "parental retirement." I mean, I was in no way rejecting or forgetting my children; it was just this errant belief that somehow each of them was now an independent, happy, and on-the-way-to-success individual, and my job now was to lean back and enjoy the beautiful unfolding of their lives. I guess I hadn't been looking in the mirror very much, had I? Obviously, I had failed to recount all that had transpired over the past thirty years of my own life, when I was last my daughter's age, and how often I had teetered on the edge of disaster only to receive a saving hand or shoulder from a dear friend or a sibling or a parent.

The fact is most of us don't enter *any* relationship with the intention of being a life-long counselor or coach or caregiver. I mean, let's face it: we step into and create relationships because it seems like they will be good for us – for *me!* And healthy ones are – but they also carry a certain kind of life-long commitment to the other as well. In marriage, we publically commit to this responsibility, acknowledging from the start that there will be ups and downs and we agree to work through and with them all. With children, our society legally binds us to them, enforcing behavior that, while most would find natural from parent to child, seeks to protect the child's life and safety. And with siblings and friends, well, I guess we just do it to ourselves; the roots of connection run deep and intertwine, and suddenly we find ourselves empathetically aching with the other just as surely as we share in the other's joys and welcome the other's supportive affirmations.

We all probably know someone or some family whose life seems to be "golden," void of the trials and tribulations that we must endure. Chances are we don't know that person or that family very well – or, they keep their "stuff" very well concealed. Financial struggles, marital and other relationship problems, miscarriages, and the various consequences of poor judgment and decision-making litter the playing fields of *all* of our lives. And when our loved ones stumble over this refuse and fall, most of the time, whether they realize it or not, they need our loving assistance. Sometimes it will be in the form of a particular need, money or some other assistance; but most of the time, the need is just for understanding, not money nor advice, just *being there*. And, ironically, this quiet support of love is often the most difficult to provide because we like to believe that "we know" how to fix and care for everything that ails everyone else.

Yes, every valuable relationship, be it spouse, child, sibling or best friend, carries a secret lifetime-commitment-card, and those "lifetimes" are guaranteed to have a share of pains and sorrows. I didn't arrive in this world alone; I didn't bring children into this world alone; and if I choose not to die alone, then neither my sufferings nor those of my beloveds will be experienced alone. Once our hearts commit to working together, there is never a retirement from our relationships.

Relational God, by creating Life you must have committed yourself to sustaining it. Like a good and watchful parent, you must cringe at some of my decisions and actions, but I know that each morning, there you are, ready to love me all over again. Help me to be more like you, a being of unconditional love, willingly embracing not only the joys of my relationships with others, but the missteps and tragedies as well.

May 27
Voluntary Service

When the school at which I taught for nearly thirty years made "service hours" a mandatory requirement of graduation, I must admit that I rather deeply, although privately, questioned the decision. It was not the idea of service that furrowed my brow with misgiving, but the requirement of it. In fact, for many years before the decision, engaging in some kind of service project had been something of a requirement for my senior Social Justice course. After all of our study of the world of injustices, it only seemed appropriate, even necessary, that students would take the book knowledge to task and get out and work for some change through their service. Nevertheless, I knew then that making "service" a "requirement" seemed contradictory to the very term of "service," like getting paid to volunteer. But mine was a "course requirement," and the failure to follow through did not necessarily mean one would fail the course, let alone be prevented from graduating altogether. I felt that service was so important, however, and its experience so valuable and often so "infectious" that I was willing to "force" my students into it, confident that most would willingly choose to do more once they experienced it. So, unlike the graduation requirement criteria that looked too much like coercive service to me, I still offered my students researched and written alternatives to the hands-on service assignment.

Not all service, of course, is "rewarding," and that is why, all the more, one needs to enter into it with a truly voluntary spirit. One year, a group of students went down to serve food at a local homeless shelter for their "project." Arriving on the scene, however, they were instructed instead to clean-out dated and questionable food from an old walk-in freezer. This was not the way they wanted to serve! Other individuals were sometimes shocked by the less than enthusiastic or apparently ungrateful response to their service or for the food that they offered. How could "beggars" be "choosey"? Such attitudes within service totally miss the point. Service is, first and foremost, selfless. It is not about doing what I want or expecting certain results or responses. Service is simply about serving others regardless of the task and without concern for the response. In preparation for and in response to negative experiences in serving, I would simply tell my students, "If someone is ungrateful for your service, serve some more; if someone disrespects your service, serve some more. Just remember, when your service is done, you get to go home to all that you need, want and have; those you serve will return to the streets where they will have little of what they need and even less of what they want."

Most of my students, however, were enamored by their service experience. In writing of what they did and how they felt, many would conclude by saying, "I wish that I had not been required to do this. I felt bad knowing that I hadn't freely chosen what I was now so enjoying. I received so much more than what I gave. I look forward to volunteering again all on my own!" While there were certainly a few disgruntled students, a few years after the "graduation service requirement" was mandated at my school, our student body's charitable service increased manifold; perhaps a little "coercive persuasion" at first is okay. Indeed, when we serve from the heart, most often we receive much more than we ever give.

God of Service, you call us to be God for one another, to manifest the love and care that you have for your creation through our hands of service. For all of those who serve, strengthen and encourage them if and when their efforts seem useless and disrespected. And for my part, help me to not only see the needs of others all around me, but to willfully step forward in response to them, offering my assistance with an ever ready and cheerful heart.

May 28
Memorial Day: All the Living and All the Dead Giving Their All

Every year on the last Monday in May, the United States observes Memorial Day, a date that honors all Americans who have died fighting in any war. The roots of this day, however, can be found planted in the Civil War with many different states and smaller communities honoring their lost loved ones by decorating their graves on a uniform date. General John Logan, the national commander of the Grand Army of the Republic, in 1868 first proclaimed and then observed the commemorative day placing flowers on the graves of Union and Confederate soldiers at Arlington National Cemetery. While it would be years later before the southern states would officially recognize the date, choosing dates of their own to honor their Confederate dead, Memorial Day was first intended as an act of reconciliation, a time for all the living to come together and to honor all the dead who gave their all. More officially, the southern states joined the observance of Memorial Day after World War I when the emphasis of the day was shifted from just the Civil War to, as we know it today, American soldiers who have died in any war.

Admittedly, as I am essentially a pacifist, I struggled for years trying to properly honor Memorial Day. Unable to humanely embrace any phase of war, I felt that if I honored those who died in war I was somehow also validating war itself.

Perhaps through my observational experience of the various "Gulf Wars" where I have done my best to support the soldiers without necessarily agreeing with the wars, I have arrived at a different perspective, one that enables me to observe Memorial Day faithfully without condoning war philosophically.

One of my most fundamental difficulties with wars is that they are ultimately waged by people who were born into them "by chance." Our nation fights on behalf of its ideological views just as surely as our opposition does theirs, but very few soldiers on either side ever truly choose what those views are. We each are born where we are born, and by and large, we take on the views of that larger community. Had I been born in the boundaries of the "enemy's" country, I might just as well be fighting on their behalf, or, as the poet Thomas Hardy once wrote, "Yes; quaint and curious war is! You shoot a fellow down You'd treat if met where any bar is, Or help to half-a-crown." But here I am, an American citizen, born here by chance, enjoying the relative ease and excess that our nation, so I have been told, has achieved through war. I may not agree with all of our nation's ideas or the ways that we came to achieve the freedom we so proudly proclaim, but I would be a fool to say that I do not appreciate the benefits of being an American citizen.

Just as opposing countries often see the world differently, so too is that true between the citizens of any one country. I see things the way I do, and try my best to stand by them, just as surely as other American citizens see things their way and must do their best to uphold them. Some believe war is necessary, and whether I believe their ideology or not, and whether their philosophy is true or not, I arguably enjoy the fruits of their labor, or more appropriately, the triumphs of their loss of blood and life. I do not ask them to go out and fight wars for me, for I choose to have no war with anyone. But as they fight the wars of their causes, and perhaps *are* rightfully responsible for all that I enjoy because of what they do, I absolutely honor them.

Memorial Day was founded in reconciliation of the horrible cleft between the North and the South in the Civil War, but nearly 150 years later, there certainly is some evidence that not only does the scar remain from that war, but that the resentment that surrounded that war is yet an open wound for some. Individuals saw and see things differently, and frequently others are called upon to die for those differences. For those that die on behalf of "truth," I honor their heroic efforts; for those that die on behalf of "what they thought was the truth," I mourn their tragic loss. Both sides equally die for "their truth." May God help us all to discover what the truth really is.

God of Truth, many have died in the name of freedom, fighting for the values that they are certain we all deserve and should uphold. You have given us this tremendous gift of life, and I do not know for certain exactly how far I should go to protect it nor at what cost. I offer an honorable prayer of thanks for all of those who have chosen or who have been called upon to sacrifice their very lives on behalf of their fight for freedom and justice; to that thanksgiving, I add a prayer for all of us today, continually engaged in the battle of understanding the truth, that we may see more clearly what it is that you call us to do and at what cost should we answer that call.

May 29
A Half-Century Celebration

When my oldest brother turned fifty over a decade ago, he actualized plans to gather friends and family at a retreat center in Montreal, of which he was then director, to share in both a celebration of life and a reflection of our mortality. Also taking advantage of the Jazz Festival that the grand Canadian city was hosting at the time, the gathering brought together a wonderfully eclectic group of people to share prayers, meals, meditations, music – Life! One of those in attendance was a mutual friend of ours from Switzerland who a couple of years later tossed out a large invitational net announcing her approaching fiftieth birthday and encouraging all connected loved ones to join her in ascending a particular Swiss alp. She wrote that she had gazed up at L'Pigne d'Arrola for much of her life and had dreamed that one day she would stand atop it; on the week of her fiftieth, two years away at the time, she announced that she would seek to fulfill that dream. "Come to Switzerland," she invited us, "and join me on the journey." And two years later, my wife and I, some siblings, and nearly thirty other of her friends and family did just that, summiting the magnificent peak on a brilliant August morning.

So impressed was I by these wonderful celebrations of life at the midcentury mark that I vowed that I too would seek to arrange and host some sort of special gathering on my fiftieth birthday. I had always longed to visit and to experience the magic of Ireland, and so nearing my half-century birthday, I checked out some options, weighed possibilities and then invited my siblings and their spouses, and our Swiss friend to consider communing in Ireland for a week. Unfortunately, I was not quite so organized as my predecessors, and despite my efforts and good intentions, well, the Emerald Isle is still on my wish list. My fiftieth birthday came and went without a whole lot of fanfare, but such colossal and unique gatherings are not exactly the only point here anyway.

Indeed, a memorable celebration surrounded by loved ones is a wonderful way to honor any year of one's life, and a fiftieth birthday certainly seems to offer an extra-special reason. But beneath the celebration itself is the more important solicitation to take some careful time to reflect upon one's life: where I have been; where I am; and where am I going? Sharing that time with loved ones helps to conjure the stories that have shaped our lives, to honor the role of the loved ones in those stories, and to welcome and to encourage the continued support of those loved ones. But whether loved ones can join us or not, the necessary reflection can still unfold.

We move through life so methodically sometimes that we almost forget that we are "living" – as in changing, growing and moving toward our fruition. Our lives can become so routine, so mundane, that we fail to reflect on why we do what we do and what, after all, "a living" is for. Birthdays, in general, and various decade plateaus, in particular, offer wonderful opportunities for us to do some of this reflection. And, of course, just as the reflection doesn't need to involve large gatherings of people to celebrate it, neither does it need to be limited to one's birthday. But since we are so often drawn into our measurements of time, birthdays can be especially poignant occasions to give pause to the movements - past, present and future – of our lives.

Giver of Life, I did not ask to be born or to be given this life; but called into being either through love or accident, here I am – alive and living! Each day of life is a gift, perhaps requested, but not earned, just goodness waiting to be received and explored. The celebration of one's birth, be it my own or another's, invites me to consider the mystery of this great gift of life, and to evaluate how well I have received and utilized this gift. On "my day," or some other appointed day, or maybe even today, help me to find clarity as I take some time to consider the gift of life that you have given me, and to recommit myself to embracing the gift more fully, more thoughtfully, more soulfully.

May 30
Shooting Life's Rapids

On an incredible sun-splashed day along the rugged cliffs and rapids of the Potomac River, just outside Washington D.C., I ended my bouldering Billy Goat Trail hike at the Great Falls overlook. The Potomac, taking a southeasterly bend at this juncture, is a wild, open mouth, with the teeth of huge boulders creating plunging falls and dangerous rapids around a rocky mid-river island. And there, along the walls of the overlooks on both sides of the fairly expansive river, small crowds had assembled that day to cheer on and take vicarious pleasure in the precarious pursuits of the river kayakers.

Toting their colorful vessels overhead, the kayakers gingerly stepped across the island's boulder field and found a safe entry point back into the raging waters. Then, from around a corner they would appear in mid-paddle, dancing gingerly on the river current as they angled for the V-cut of the rapids between two large boulders, dropping five to eight feet to the river's next tier. Catching the fall's undertow, the kayakers slipped out of the surge and nestled against the base of the large rocks, apparently regathering nerves and breaths before the next big plunge. Once satisfied and prepared, each paddler inched back into the river's flow just below his previous drop, swung his kayak around and steered head on into a twelve to fifteen foot drop. As the collective breath of the onlookers seized in anticipatory fear, the nose of the kayak tilted and then dove perilously into the surging rapids of the waterfall. Sometimes, the colorful vessel would emerge from the waters like a fishing bobber, upright and unscathed, while other times, it would pop to the surface bottom-up, and the paddler would then swing his body around beneath and set the kayak aright to assure the onlookers that all was just fine. A sudden cheer, probably never heard by the paddlers over the sounds of the crashing waters, would erupt in satisfaction from the various overlooks.

I couldn't help thinking about what it was like for each of those kayakers the first time that they took those plunges. Clearly, these efforts were not their first, for there was confidence and surety in all of their movements. Similarly, each of us is faced with countless plunging waterfalls throughout our lives. We may not be accomplished kayakers, but I suspect that most of us have known the heart-stopping fear that those paddlers must have known when they steered their vessels through treacherous and indifferent waters for the first time. And like the kayakers, leaping into our deep and threatening fears, most often, we bob back to the surface pretty wet, but essentially unscathed and looking ahead to the next drop-off. The exhilarating rush of risk never goes away, for each dive unfolds its own mystery, but we gain confidence with each plunge and take some small comfort in the successes of previous endeavors, the small cheers from the overlooks.

O God of All Great Plunges, you do not simply stand by in amusement as I make my way through the tumultuous waters through which my life must sometimes pass. But I do suspect that you are an interested onlooker, concerned for my right choice of passage through the challenging currents, holding your cosmic breath even as I spill over the cascading tiers. Unlike the kayakers, perhaps, I do not necessarily go out in search of the challenge, but I do know that to get further downstream I may very well need to make my way through some precarious challenges. Watch over me, always, and give me the strength and courage and confidence to bob right back up to the surface when I must necessarily leap into the fears and challenges of the cascading river of my daily life.

May 31
A Seed is Planted

Occasionally when I am mowing our lawn, especially in the spring, I will come across a random maple tree sapling, no more than a simply stem with a single leaf, boldly trying to establish itself right in the middle of our yard. Appearing as though it has almost been planted there intentionally, the young maple tree is actually a "survivor," just one of thousands of seeds that got blown about over the year and found fertile soil, space, water and, until my mower comes along and takes it out, time enough to grow. One of the variety of helicopter seed bearers, the maple tree produces potential offspring by the hundreds of thousands as they fall away from the tree in whirlybird fashion, sometimes spinning away quite a distance from their source. Fruit bearing trees can randomly spread due to the digestive process – and placement of it – by the animals that sometimes feed on the trees' produce. The multitude of ways that plants and trees proliferate is a fascinating study in serendipity and determination. Humans ought to be grateful that they do not have to fight for their existence in quite the same way.

Arguably, of course, we are a part of such a struggle for survival in that the union of a single sperm, one of millions seeking such a goal, with a single released ovulating egg is not entirely unlike the random tree or plant seed seeking germination and roots amongst the millions of other seeds with which it must compete. Unconscious of our own conception, however, we are generally ignorant of the astonishing journey each of us must make before we even enter the amazing voyage we call "life" after we are born.   The growth and nurturing necessary throughout our lives are merely additional "layers of incredible" to the series of stratum that exist since our very conception. Modern photography has taken the human eye into places, perhaps it should not go, allowing us much more than mere glimpses of the wonder of conception and early uterine life. Seeing and understanding all that must occur during the gestation period of a human life, one cannot help but marvel that we exist at all!

The process of seed production, fertilization, implantation and the healthy development of a human fetus or a maple sapling may appear radically different on many levels, but they both share in the amazing wonder of conception and life. "How can this be?" is an absolutely natural question, more natural than conception itself it would seem! To the "ways and means" of this "order" I am continually drawn and I can never reach anything but a faithfilled response to it.

For growth – for life – to happen, it seems that nearly all things need a "union" of forces first, and then exceptional nurturing. God of All Creation, how the trees and plants and animals and humans, how *all life* is conceived, is such a miraculous process that I find myself silenced in the awe-inspiring presence of the mystery. There is a certain "struggle" written into the very conception of all things, and yet the panoply of seedling wings and tails and the network of interconnected nurturing that you have created to enable these conceptions and growth speak to your guiding hand, your creative energy. I bow in honor to the sacred mystery of life. Let not my "knowledge" ever reduce the "wonder" of it all.

In each of the Synoptic Gospels of the Christian Scriptures (Matthew, Mark and Luke: those Gospels that "see together"), a version of Jesus' famous "parable of the sower" is recorded, with the Teacher's explanation of the parable following it. On one level, both the imagery of the parable and its accompanying explanation can be seen as fine addendums to yesterday's "seed reflection," but an important difference between the two is that in Jesus' parable, we are not the seeds, but the soil in which the seed is planted. The seed of the Gospels' parable is "the word of God," and this seed, according to the parable, is sown upon all soils, to everyone. However, because there can be such discrepancy over what "the word of God" is, and to whom and how it is received, for our purposes, I would like to offer a slightly different approach, to see "the seed" more as the "soul" or the "Divine Spark" planted within us all.

Unlike the amazing miracle of conception and growth of all living things that seems to have a kind of random quality about its nature, from the faith-filled perspective, when conception and life happen, the soul or Divine Spark is simultaneously and deliberately present. It is not given to a select "some," but to all, and, as it is given to all, all are called towards a unity of things rather than division. And here is where the environmental soil of the parable and of our lives becomes so important.

In Jesus' parable, rugged and rocky soil and soil overrun with weeds and thorns not only fail to nourish the seed, but in fact can kill it. The Divine within us all, however, can never be truly eradicated; one might faithlessly deny its presence, and cover and ignore any sign of it whatsoever, but from a landscape of faith, one's very existence is a sign of the Divine as well. The environment of our soil is, nevertheless, of absolute importance. Will the presence of the Divine within me be acknowledged and nurtured, or will I, refuting its presence, allow it to lie dormant for as much as my entire lifetime? From this perspective of the parable, religions can be seen as types of implements that help churn our soil, and fertilizers for the nutritional sustenance of the soil of our soulful selves. Religions can plough the soil of ourselves, but not so that a seed can then be planted, for the seed is already there. Religions overturn the soil so that the planted seed might be realized and then they provide an aeration service, hopefully giving the seed room and air enough to breath while providing deeper pockets and furrows with which to receive necessary spiritual nutrition. Interestingly, once the seed takes root within us, then we become not only the soil in which it grows, but the gardener of our soil as well. Our task then, as both gardener and soil, is to continually nurture the growth of the seed so that the Divine Spark has the opportunity, as poet Gerard Manley Hopkins wrote in "God's Grandeur," to "flame out, like shining from shook foil."

God of the Seed and the Soil, you have sown within the soil of my soul a sacred, golden seed that when realized and nourished provides roots that connect me to all things, and to the very heart of all things which is you. Like a good and careful gardener, may I tend to my soil with diligence and attentiveness, nurturing the seed of the Divine within me, the shining fruit of your spark.

June 2
Traveling Out and Within

I love to travel and my preferred mode is with a backpack to any destination in the wilderness. In the exploration that comes with travel, we have the opportunity to experience places and people and so many other aspects of life that are likely beyond the domain of our usual daily observations. I count myself most fortunate that I have been physically and financially able to summit mountain peaks, plumb deep canyons, scour narrow crevices, swim in the underworld of ocean waters, and become absorbed in expansive forests that reach up and out and down. But, while these many adventures into landscapes ascend heights and plummet depths and reach in all directions, they are, essentially, only linear; they are one-dimensionally "earthbound." However, my great interest and joy in such travel is that it need not remain limited to this "one dimension."

When I head out into these expansive landscapes, I also find myself being drawn into another, deeper, inner journey as well. While I unquestionably discover things previously unknown to me in my earthbound adventures, so too do I encounter unknown landscapes within me. Some of these encounters provide self-understanding, testing the boundaries of my physical capabilities and facing the fears that limit my ability to move further, deeper, into darker unknown regions. And, more importantly, they provide spiritual insight as well as I stand rapt in awe at the wonders of God's creations and peer into the mystery of my place and role within those creations.

Returning from these backpacking adventures, I often emerge with a photo album's worth of pictures and, surely, with or without the photos, rich memories of the experiences and scenery; but I come back changed within as well. When I explore the recesses of the earth and allow those experiences to move in and through me, my own spiritual landscape is never quite the same.

Creator God, this wondrous earth that you have created, with all of its amazing inhabitants, provides for me tremendous opportunities to discover and to better understand you and myself. Help me to make time, and help to provide me with the means to explore the proffered gift that spreads out around me. Encourage me to journey out to the landscapes of your creation and, in doing so, to delve into the spiritual terrain within me. Through these outward adventures may I make inward discoveries.

June 3
Into the Wild Will

One summer a number of years ago, I watched a special TV report as Tom Brokaw interviewed the extreme hiker, Aron Ralston; at about the same time that I was reading Jon Krakauer's novel, *Into the Wild,* of another extreme hiker, Christopher McCandless. The characters in both of the exposés were real people whose fantastical stories deeply impacted me when they first came to public light.

After graduating from Emory University in 1992, McCandless willingly forsook his rather wealthy family background and future to pursue a life of wild adventure and quiet repose. His ultimate goal, to live in solitude in Alaska ended tragically when, ultimately trapped by the spring flow of the river and his supplies depleted, he mistook a poisonous plant for an edible one. With less spiritual intent, Ralston became accidentally trapped in a remote Utah slot canyon when he ventured off without clear notice of his whereabouts for a weekend hike. Although, unlike McCandless, he survived his experience, he lost a portion of his arm in the process as he literally had to cut it off to escape his pinned captivity beneath a large boulder. When I first heard about each of these stories, I remember thinking to myself, "this guy is nuts, irresponsibly nuts!" But years later, watching and reading their stories, I was struck by how "normal" they each were, and, more importantly, how easily I understood McCandless' spiritual-like desire to experience the creations at their most intimate and raw level, and Ralston's habitual tendency to just take off into the wild with little plan and no real safety back-up in place. While their choices and actions were certainly beyond my usual excursions into the wild, I was awakened to some alarming parallels.

In McCandless and Ralston's reckless behaviors, I saw my own flaws. My most fundamental awareness was that what I *want* to do, even passionately, is not always what is best for me either physically or spiritually. It was not so much that what I desired was wrong or bad, but that, too often, my passionate interests were rash and negligent of other's concerns and my own well-being. I quickly began to reevaluate my trip preparations and the decisions that I would make on solo excursions. No longer would I leave without notice or record of my potential whereabouts, and once out there, longing to climb up that or investigate this, I found myself asking, "Is this where you want to die? Is the intrigue of this desire worth dying for?" I want to live my life to its fullest, and such a desire often means taking some risks; the spiritual life itself is replete with risk-taking. But an adventuresome life does not have to be a reckless and irresponsible one; to that end, a little taming of the will can be quest enough.

I am so grateful for Life and I so want to experience the heights and the depths of the fullness of Life. Thoughtful and Protective God, help me to differentiate between responsible risk-taking and careless exploits. While the question may seem extreme, help me to honestly ask myself in the midst of my desire-charged interests and passions, "Is this worth dying for?" What you offer and teach me through my experiences is of little value if I cannot return to share them with others. Your will is my greatest desire; let not my own desires be my will's only guide.

June 4
A Dry Heat

Where I live in Ohio, any day in the high eighties is a *hot* day. When the thermometer registers ninety and above, look out! Ours is a very humid environment, and while I won't pretend to understand the science of humidity and temperature, I do know that a high former makes for a very uncomfortable latter. My daughters, meanwhile, live in central Arizona, essentially, in the desert. There, one hundred-plus degree temperatures are often normative, but we all know the cliché about the southwest: "It's a *dry heat.*" What this cliché has come to mean to me is that because the air is not so thick and uncomfortable, one doesn't necessarily realize just how hot it is, a bit like the story, perhaps, of the frog who unsuspectingly sits in the slow-to-boil water.

Another important difference is sweat. Hot in Ohio equates to a constant dripping, saturated feeling. Once your clothes get wet from sweat, they are not likely to dry for they are now like the air, heavy with moisture. Even during times of drought, the morning grass is often wet with the nighttime dew. When camping in wooded valleys in Ohio, I have found my tent and the ground around it so wet with dew that one might easily think that it had rained through the night. Now, I still sweat when I am in Arizona, but there, it is almost as though the dry air, thirsting for some wetness, immediately absorbs my perspiration while the sun bakes what escapes the air's thirst right out of my clothing. The fact of the matter is that both environments can be uncomfortably hot, although in very different ways.

I find that stressful times are much like heat and these differences in heat. Stress makes us uncomfortable, makes us sweat. No one *wants* stress; it just happens to be where and how we live. And as we do with heat, we try to avoid it by conditioning the air around us. Altering the temperature to a more comfortable degree, we lock ourselves inside a bubble of security from the oppression of stress' heat. But all around us, outside, it is still miserably hot. Extending the connection further, how we recognize and are affected by the heat of stress is also different. Yes, like a humid Ohio day, sometimes our stress wears on us so that we become lethargic, all energy sapped. Other times, in our "Arizona stress," we are aware of the pressures, but we somehow feel like we are more in control; you know, it's a "dry heat." But humid or dry, the pressure of stress is still hot and uncomfortable, and while we might try to calm ourselves by modifying the air around us, we can't avoid the truth of what's inside.

Unlike the weather which we must learn to deal with in whatever environment we choose to live, we can turn down the heat of stress, and not by simply fabricating the air around us. Rather, by changing the flow of air within us, we can learn to better handle the heat. We can "hydrate" ourselves better through more thoughtful choices and through the calming effects of meditation. Today, God, when I feel the temperature of my stress rising, help me to step back and to reevaluate the choices that I have made and will make, and so prevent my overheating.

June 5
Working for a Vacation

Work governs so much of our modern lives that most adults are never able to fully enjoy the profound gift of being alive, and the multitude of simple gifts that adorn its basket. Because of work, our lives, in many respects, have become ruled by the clock. Our jobs are usually the centerpiece of our schedules, and all social, private, prayerful and restful times are governed and shaped around this focal point. Furthermore, as the demands of our jobs often require so much energy and attention, it seems natural to want to conserve these qualities during our down time, subsequently making much of our non-working time rather lackluster. How often have I said, "no," to an evening's gathering of friends or have felt it necessary to cut it short because "I have to work tomorrow morning"? How many hobbies or satisfying tasks around my home and family are incomplete or never even started because I lack the energy at the end of the workday or sufficient time in the workweek to do them? Yes, a job – work – is necessary, even essential, in our modern world, but I can't help but think about all that we have lost to its monstrous appetite for time and energy.

In Native American tradition, time was not viewed so much as a commodity that could be bought and sold for the burden of work, but more simply as "a presence." To be sure, "time" was measured, but their clock was a cyclical one based on seasonal and natural changes. For some Native peoples, the day itself had four sacred times: sunrise, sun-overhead, sunset, and midnight. But think about how we have lost this sense of "sacred time" and the "sacred presence" of time, of just being. Summer time may be most special, though not necessarily "sacred," to many people because it is the season of vacation – a time away from our all-consuming work. But even when we vacation, we are often driven by our sense of "work time," for we only have so much time off and we must cram as much into it as we can. Many Europeans refer to "vacation time" as "holiday." Perhaps holiday would be a better word for us all in that its roots are a reference to "holy day;" thus, time away from work, or more precisely, the all-consuming nature of work, is holy.

Most of us cannot afford to simply reject work outright; it is essential to our economic survival. Furthermore, work is a valuable tool in creating meaning and purpose in our lives. But our work is not life itself, nor should we pin our identity and our sense of self-worth solely on our jobs. The essence of life is within our very being; to be "fully alive" is to be fully aware of life, to engage fully in life. When my job consumes so much of my time and prevents me from being fully aware of life, it ceases to be enlivening.

Timeless God, from my finite perspective of life, the infinite is nearly absurd to me, and so I organize "my time" into preferential segments trying to make the most of the time I have. But so much of this finite time is given to the task of work, to the commerce of economic survival, and not to the enjoyment of life's simple and profound gifts. Help me to refocus my life, to reconsider how and upon what my time is spent. Life is a sacred gift to be experienced; each day is a holy day. May I work more at realizing and being this truth.

Don't get me wrong; if you live in this modern world and are a member of a human society, work is pretty much unavoidable. A job is necessary and essential. But, that being said, how much of life have you missed because of work? I mean, if I just stick to the most tangible events, for me the tally is rather frightening: one of my best friend's wedding; some nieces' and nephews' graduations; some longed-for concerts; a couple of my children's sporting or artistic events (although these were always a priority for me and I missed very few); the funerals of numerous aunts and uncles, and most especially, my dear Grandmother; and countless visits to and from friends and family. And if I were to include more spontaneous moments – an overdue romantic date with my spouse; late night visits with special ones that want to go all night; seasonal meteor showers or a show of northern lights – the list could be endless! And what about healthful habits that take time to initiate, to develop and finally to become routine: running and exercise; yoga; tai chi; quilting and knitting; woodworking; reading and writing; meditation and prayer? There just never seems to be enough time, except for the regimen of our workweek, and even here we often scratch for more time to get more work done.

Stop and think about how much time you put into your work each day or each week, and include the preparation and commuting times. Then, add your average hours of sleep and meal times. After all of these, if you've got any energy left over, how much time do you have to give to your other needs and interests. Again, these solicitudes are not to make the idea of work more deplorable, but to give us pause in considering how our days are spent and numbered. And the need for our jobs to be satisfying and affirming looms even greater when put into this perspective!

Better yet, after giving all of your time a good shake down, take some time – make some time! – to do more of those things that make life what it should be: enjoyable! Play with your child. Ride your bike. Sit in a hammock and read a good book. Lay beneath the canopy of the sky and watch clouds or marvel at the stars. Just be still, and quietly commune with the wonder of the universe. Pray.

Creator God, when you shaped the universe, was it work for you, or was it the expression of satisfying creative energy? My life is so often dictated by the demands of my job, by the needs of my work, and so rarely do I have or make time for the things that truly – I want to believe – matter the most in my life. I know that I must make some difficult decisions about how and when and where I spend my time, but I invite you into that decision-making process. Help me to better prioritize my time and to seek deeper clarity about what things really matter the most to me and why. Life is so much bigger than my job; it is so much bigger than my needs and interests. I call you into the center of it all! Create in and through me!

A stretch of highway running north and south off of the east-west Interstate 94 in North Dakota is known as "the Enchanted Highway." The advertised "enchantment" is a series of enormous metal sculptures along the road that rolls over the graceful plains of North Dakota for 32 miles, from the Interstate Highway to the town of Regent, thirty-two miles south. The artist that conceived of the project, and who designs and builds these sculptures is a resident of Regent, a former teacher and administrator. Fearing that his quaint town of Regent and its inhabitants and businesses might simply slip out of existence someday with its primary and dwindling economic source of farming, the artist decided to sculpt attention toward his home village. Interstate highway road signs champion the "Enchanted Highway," encouraging travelers to slip off the endless expanse of I94 at exit 72, and take a short, enchanted cross country voyage; rest and refreshment, of course, can then be found in Regent.

The term "enchantment" is normally associated with a magical effect or quality; to this end, I have often felt that the highway's title is a bit of a misnomer. The sculptures, towering above the landscape from fifty to over one hundred feet tall, are ingenious creations made primarily from scrap metal. They are certainly not unattractive, but they seem almost incongruent in their environment; perhaps another denotative entry of "enchantment" better defines them: "to delight to a high degree." If there is magical quality about "The Enchanted Highway," it is to be found in the soft backdrop of North Dakota's rolling farmland and exotic buttes that rise as unsuspectingly as the sculptures do across the expansive landscape. Although cut from a different fabric, the blanket of this land is no less "big sky" than its neighboring Montana. As the eyes grow as wide as the searching land, the traveler's mind, enchanted by the farmland stretches of greens and yellows, drifts back to an earlier time when the prairie grasses no doubt undulated like waves sweeping gently toward a shoreline, lapping at the mystical buttes whose presence defy understanding.

Oftentimes human beings miss the obvious, natural beauty around them, captivated instead by some human-made creation that is also surely pleasing and architecturally wonderful. Homes and villages nestled into a beautiful valley or sculpted into rugged cliffs and hilltops garner our attention whilst we miss the beauty of the landscape that drew the architects and residents to the place. Like the biblical Tower of Babel, we can miss the grandeur of God in our efforts to build our own edifices to the sky. Perhaps, the architect of The Enchanted Highway knows that the enchantment lies in the landscape that no one steps out to see, and so he lures the traveler into the real enchantment through his delightful, though less enchanting, periodic displays.

Enchanting God, each one of your creations, each one of us, is a beautiful creation, an ingenious sculpture of your handiwork. Too often, perhaps, we try to redesign the landscape of ourselves before looking carefully and deeply into your artistry. Help me to first be mindful and attentive to the beauty that is around me and in me before I set out to recreate. Nudge me to seek out the beautiful gifts waiting to be discovered without and within me. May I not miss the signs along my highway that lead me into your enchanting heart.

June 8
On Eagle's Wings

In many Native American circles, the eagle is traditionally held as one of the most sacred and honored creatures in all of the creations. Although it may not be the largest, the strongest nor the most high flying bird in all of the world, in North America there are few if any birds that can match the eagle in all of those categories. Given its majestic, soaring flight, the eagle is often referred to as the "bearer of our prayers;" like the Hebrew scriptures reference to our being borne up "on eagle's wings," the traditional belief is that the eagle carries our prayers to the creator upon his ascending wings. While the sheer size and beauty of an eagle make a viewing of it ever impressive, these spiritual connections have often made my encounters with eagles especially reverential.

Whenever we "brush up" against the sacred, there is a tendency to look too hard or too deeply into things, a desire to find significance and meaning in every occurrence, as if each encounter must inevitably be some kind of "sign." Traveling out to the western states where the sighting of an eagle might be more common, I am admittedly "all eyes" on the lookout for them. On one Montana visit as I was traveling from Livingston to Billings, I remember diligently keeping my eyes peeled for the sight of an eagle, scanning the landscape, looking in all of the "appropriate places." As the netting of my viewing kept coming up empty, it occurred to me that even if I did spot an eagle in the way and places that I was looking, it would only be a kind of "zoo sighting," where the conscious expectation undermines the emotional, and potential spiritual, impact of the encounter. What I wanted was the kind of sighting that leaves me surprised and astonished, captivated by the gift of the sudden sighting; but there could be no "surprise" in the way I was looking. Realizing the error of my intentions, I let the desire take flight, and put my mind to the driving for which I was responsible.

Not long thereafter, as I crested a small pass in the foothill mountains between Big Timber and Billings, I saw up ahead what appeared to be a large stump just off the side of the interstate highway, with ravens hopping all about it in apparent curiosity or ire. Drawing nearer to the scene, I suddenly realized that there was no stump at all, but a massive bald eagle sitting atop a carrion mule deer, and the ravens, like baying dogs, were barking their disdain for the powerful foe who sat astride their desires.

Too often I go about my life looking for signs, injecting "what I want" into the peripheral scope of my vision when "what I need" may be just ahead and right in front of me. I am not going to suggest or even try to interpret meaning into the eagle that "came to me" that day, although a person could probably have a heyday infusing symbolic significance into my roadside "vision." No, the real message for me is just to stop looking *for* things and simply to *be* a more attentive watcher.

With such vision, *what I need* is much more likely to come to me than *what I want*.

God of Vision, help me to live with my eyes wide open and my heart receptive and clear. You know my true needs and see beyond my selfish desires. Receive my prayers today, rising to you on eagles' wings; may I not be a crow selfishly stirring to pounce on my appetites, but the raptor calmly in control, perched atop those lifeless longings.

June 9
My Big Sky

My wife is from Montana, the Big Sky Country, and has relatives in North Dakota, a land whose sky is no less large. Out and up there, the earth sprawls out leisurely beneath a sky that stretches endlessly, an expansive canvas upon an eternal frame. I want my heart to be as open as that beautiful sky.

It is common for people to lay back and observe clouds, playing with their shapes, looking for identifiable forms. But beyond the movements and the paintings of the clouds is the expansive canvas of the sky. We think of the sky as blue, but depending upon the time of day, the temperature, the environment below, the lighting, and any number of things, the sky's tone is not merely a range of blues, but can be many other colors as well. And across this grand canvas float the clouds of many and varied experiences. Again, science has labeled cloud types and origins, but beyond the scientific observations of clouds, we might see in them, and in their sky canvas background, a way of life to model. I want my heart to be as open as that beautiful sky.

The sky, like our lives, appears to be ever changing, and change is one of the first lessons we need to learn about life. On this expansive canvas above, wisps of clouds sometimes drift by aimlessly, while in stark contrast, at other times, thunderous billows flex and toss taunting rumblings. Be they graceful strokes, or subtle wanderings, or imposing formations, these clouds often dominate the terrain of the sky. But these vaporous models are the truly changing things; their backdrop is actually a constant, merely reflecting the changes beneath it. I want my heart to be as open as that beautiful sky.

I cannot stop the many changes that drift in and out of my life every day any more than the sky can stop the presence and the movement of the clouds. Change, as surely as the clouds, will come. Sometimes it will bring beautiful and fun arrangements, while at other times it will appear threatening and fearful. But like the sky, I want to be gracefully open to the changes all around me, to allow them to simply happen, whilst I remain constant above the inevitable and the temporary brushstrokes. I want my heart to be as open as that beautiful sky.

O God, more vast than the infinite sky, I pray that my heart may be as open as the sky-canvas is to the daily brushstrokes of the clouds. Change will happen in my life always, coloring or disfiguring it in various ways, but beyond the colorations and formations, I long to be stretched upon the framework of your constant love. I may appear lost, vanquished by a cloudy cover of change, but as the latest change dissipates as the clouds always do, may I be found wide open, expansive, and beautiful in your light.

June 10
A Good Map is Hard to Find

Whenever I go to the Minneapolis-St. Paul area, where some of my extended family live, I inevitably get lost at some time. I love both of these cities, but I can't help believing that the city planners did a rather lousy job of organizing the extensive freeway system that courses through this expansive metropolis like the human nervous system. Hearing of my latest plight while visiting for a wedding, a niece offered me her GPS system to get me through the rest of my stay. I declined, but when she thrust it into my hands later that night, I conceded, and when I returned it, had to admit that it saved me no end of confusion and time during my visit. A GPS certainly makes finding one's way around much easier, and I suspect that its presence in cars and on cell phones will become more and more common, but I still have a core resistance to its use in the wilderness.

With the absence of a GPS, a good map becomes essential. In road travel, most everyone nowadays googles his destination and follows the GPS-like directions of "Mapquest." But in the wilderness, a good topographical map is necessary. I have used simpler maps before, ones that depict the trail but lack the topo lines that indicate the contours of the earth one is traversing. Without these lines, navigation can become a little more dicey when the wilderness is truly wild.

One time while hiking the Spanish Peaks Wilderness south of Bozeman, Montana, an area that seems well traveled and, subsequently, relatively easy to navigate, I jumped into the mountainous terrain without a good topo map. The hike out was quite simple: start at the trailhead, turn right at the split and ascend the heavily traveled trail to the upper lakes. Encamped in the floral beauty that rimmed a pristine mountain lake, I branched off the next day for an easy day hike before continuing the descent of my intended loop. Perhaps then I should have taken notice of the numerous side trails that branched off in various directions, some the avenue of humans, others of animals. Returning to my campsite, I packed up my things and jumped back on the trail on which I had arrived, intending to continue on the loop back to the split near the trailhead. The hike in had been a rigorous climb the day before, and I was looking forward to an equally steady descent this day. Much to my chagrin, however, for much of the first hour I found myself powering up a stiff ascent again, one that lacked, though it needed, some switchbacks. As I crested the peak of the climb and saw the inevitable descent ahead, I pulled my meager map out again to get a better feel for my direction. Observing my map, which had no topo lines giving me indication of ascent or descent, I felt nervously off course. According to my compass, I was heading

185

south by southeast; looking at my map, and with the assumption that I should have been descending and not climbing, I felt that my direction should have been more definitively eastern. Sensing that I must have missed the main trail somewhere down below my climb, I reluctantly backtracked thinking that, according to the map, the descent immediately in front of me would only end at a no outlet lake to the south. Returning to the bottom of my opening climb of the day, I found no trail signs or indications that I had gone wrong, but still unconvinced, I struck off on another trail around a different lake figuring it might lead me to the trail that surely I must have missed. This trail led to another which led to another which then suddenly gave out as I stumbled upon another interior lake in the wilderness. Twice I circled this small lake, once high, once low, looking for an egress route, but finding nothing other than the same faint path that had led me back there. Pulling out the map again, I determined that I was at one of two unnamed lakes in the middle of nowhere; whichever one I was at, it seemed to me, a northern course would eventually get me back on a trail. Relying solely on my compass and the faith I placed in it, I bushwhacked north down a steep, mountainous ravine. Twenty-five minutes later I came upon the trail on which I had ascended the day before.

Losing your trail on your spiritual journey often seems unlikely as religions and spiritual texts seem to offer so many sign posts along the way. But sometimes the spiritual ascent of the mountain can be so rugged and so challenging that we begin to second guess our path; at such times, lacking a spiritual GPS or a good topo map, we might find ourselves suddenly wandering onto unknown terrain and feeling lost in a spiritual wilderness. Faith becomes the only "sure" guide as we turn inwardly and seek the guidance of the heart.

O God of All Things Wild, I wish for my life journey only and always to be headed in the direction that seeks union with you. Sometimes, through my inadequate maps and my poor decisions, I can lose track of which way I am going and on which course I should be traveling. On a spiritual quest, the journey is as important as the destination, but help me on this trek to read the signs along the way, to be aware of the natural and supernatural guideposts that you might provide. And if I should wander away unwittingly, show me the due north that leads me back, directly to your heart.

June 11
Solo Tripping

I love "road trips," and, I must confess, that I especially like them alone. Driving for hours on end in my private little cubicle of transportation, I can choose whatever music I want to listen to and I can turn it up as loud as I want knowing that I will offend no one and that no one will have to shout over it in conversation. Likewise, maybe I am in need of some quiet, reflective time, and with a simple push of the car stereo dial, I have it. Hungry or not, bathroom need or not, I have full control of where and when I will stop.

Sometimes when I am traveling across the country, either in preparation or in spontaneity, I realize that I am in close proximity to this or that old friend or relative, and, perhaps, I should stop and visit. In such occasions, I begin to weigh the question of whether or not I can "afford" to stop, with both the time and the finance of the diversion being part of the question. I soon reason that stopping will cost me valuable time, and, not to mention, worse yet if they are a little out of the way, the additional mileage and the gas that comes with it.

It all sounds pretty self-centered doesn't it? And it is. But this is not only how I go through many of my solo road trips, it is how I often go through life itself. We love our freedom and our independence; we love to be in charge and to be in control. Like a solo road trip, many of us would like for all of the decisions of our life's journey to be in our hands, that we could govern when and where and why we stop and go. But just like the road trip, in our lives there are many others on the highway, and there are many in need of a ride, and there are some just waiting for a visit. Can I afford to stop and give my time and attention to another? Can I invite another into "my space" and make it "ours" instead, sharing all that might come with it, sometimes compromising my desires?

O God of Communion, it is so easy for me to seek out and find time for my own needs and interests, and while some of this time is necessary for me, I know that you also call me into a communion of human hearts, time, and energy. All creation shares in this sojourn of life, and we all grow through the support, the guidance and the protective care of each other. Help me to more freely give of my time to others, and while I do not give it for this reason, remind me that in my giving, I too receive what it is that I might need. Sure, I enjoy the dip into the solo road trip, but maybe there is a bigger splash ahead for me, for us all, when I dive into the car pool.

June 12
Doing Being

Whenever friends or relatives announce their plans to come visit my wife and me, I find that we quickly move into "planning mode." Ohio is not exactly a "vacation destination," so we don't often get the opportunity to host people for any length of time in our home, or in and around our fair city. Subsequently, when people do come to visit us, I always feel inclined to make the most of their time here and start organizing a schedule of things to do. The downside of this approach is that sometimes in the midst of all of our "doings," we fail to properly and fully "be" together. It's a common malady in my family tree it seems.

An early example I can recall of doing rather than just being was on a weeklong backpacking-canoe trip with my family in the Boundary Waters of Minnesota when I was a young teen. A sister-in-law and my eldest brother, both of whom were avid outdoors people with a vast working knowledge of the North Woods, spearheaded the trip. To this day, my next oldest brother and I still joke about our leaders' need "to push it," always trying to cover the most territory possible in a day. On such excursions, of course, it is natural and necessary to keep moving so as to fulfill the charted course, but my brother and I often felt that the sense of urgency to push on dominated the pleasurable experience of what was already before us. Similarly, reading articles in *Backpacker* magazine about ultra-hikes, I often bristle at these stories because I wonder just how much these hikers truly see of the trail and all that it has to offer. The focus of these tales seems far more about a person just "hauling-ass" and boasting about covering a miraculous stretch of ground rather than about the beauty of the hike and the experiences one encounters along the way. Hiking in this way is, again, a bit like the doing versus being question.

While hiking trips with family and friends today are taken at a far more leisurely pace with a less aggressive and impressive allotment of miles, other immediate family gatherings are still often based on doing things. The Ryans like "to do" things; we swim, ski, bike, hike, boat, run, blade and golf, and then regroup around a shared meal at the day's end. Conversely, annual reunions with my wife's family are really centered around being together; every meal of every day is a "gathering call," and her kin are content with hanging around looking at pictures, visiting, and, well, just *being* together.

Even when I visit my daughters today in Arizona, I find myself having to conscientiously slow down so that I might step more fully into the rhythms of their lives and more deeply enjoy the gifts of their presence. I can "do together" very naturally, but I too often fail to "be together" as well. Doing is good, but it is important that one allows enough time and space to just be so that the words, the looks, the touches, and the silence that need to be shared and experienced have enough time to open up and be present.

God of Infinite Presence, I am grateful for the many opportunities and abilities that you have given me to *do* things, and so experience life; but help me to not miss the gift of simply *being*. In doing, I sometimes avoid another's need, and sometimes even my own need, to just be. When I slow down and step into another's presence, or invite another into my quiet presence, I often discover your presence in our midst as well. We have been created and called to be love for one another. Help me to be mindful that the gift of love is sometimes just a presence.

June 13
Indian Time

One of the greatest difficulties for us "doers" to "just be" is locked within our sometimes excessive desire to use our time efficiently, and "just being" feels like such a waste of time. I have a reputation for being late, but my frequent tardiness is not based on carelessness or maligned clocks; quite the contrary, in most of the occasions when I am late it is because I have been trying to squeeze one more thing into the time I have before I must leave. I hate wasting time, and I frequently seize those loose change minutes to get one more thing done, only, what I choose to do needs more time than what I have, and then I end up being late.

When I visit my daughter and her husband out of state, they often use my visit as their vacation time too. Vacation mode for them includes sleeping in late and doing what they want at their own pace. But after a couple of days of just leisurely "hanging out" and allowing loose plans to be easily shifted or dropped, my fear of wasting time comes around like an unseen mosquito buzzing at my ear, and once again I start to think about what I should be doing.

In Native circles, we often jokingly refer to "Indian Time." Historically, when daily life centered around the simple but essential needs of life, a prudent use of time was often important, but the "time frame" and schedule for what needed done could be very flexible. Things got accomplished when and as they were needed. On many reservations today, with so few job opportunities and so much unemployment, cultural Indian Time wears a similar visage. With so little to do and so much time with which to do it, the urgency of doing slips away further. One does what *needs* to be done right now; the rest will have its time later, when *it* needs to be done.

Interestingly, I adapt to the slower pace of reservation life much more easily than I do to the relaxing pace at my daughter's home; in this easier adaptation, I realize the affect of the environment on my willingness to slow down and to just be. While it is a stereotype, Indian Time is more of a lived reality on the Reservation. Void of the busyness that so often surrounds modern society, the landscape itself seems to invite one into a slower, more reflective pace. But off of the Reservation and back into the hubbub of city life and crowded neighborhoods, my western European way of thinking where "time is money" begins to fret again about my wasting of time.

A healthy spiritual life needs some Indian Time. Yes, we are called to live out our faith in all facets of our lives, but if we do not take or make time to just be, our more active times will be less spiritually inclined. Spiritual nourishment arrives more efficiently and evidently during slower and quieter times. The soft whisper of God's voice and the gentle pull of the spirit can be received anywhere, but our receptivity to them is far greater when we periodically remove ourselves from the busyness and time demands of our lives.

Timeless God, perhaps there is a season for everything, a time for every purpose under the heavens. In my compulsive desire to control my life, I also want to control time and what happens on my watch. My desire to efficiently use my time is not wrong, but help me to avoid becoming obsessive about when something is done. To hear your voice and to receive your nourishment takes time – quiet, slow, and reflective time. May I make time this day and every day for your gentle and unhurried presence.

June 14
Flag Waving

Along the drive from Cincinnati to Columbus, it is hard to miss a particular residence alongside the interstate with very strong Confederate leanings.

Traveling north, one is first met with the site of a large Confederate flag painted on the roof of an old garage up ahead on the right, and in passing the dwelling, a living one snaps rather arrogantly in the wind along the fence line between it and the highway. Whenever I pass this place, I can't help but acknowledge the rancor that seems to froth within me and ooze out the corners of my mouth. I want to "flip off" whoever lives there, or volley some reciprocal derision their way.

Many who honor the Confederate flag would say that they are remembering a southern culture that was driven into the ground by the American Civil War. It is not a political statement or a covert support of anti-abolition; they are merely revering a historically misunderstood ethos. But I have never been able to buy that argument. It is too much like posting a swastika and then arguing for its ancient Chinese symbolism of peace; yes, it is true, but is that *really* what the person intended? I never see people of southern gentility flying the Confederate flag; it only seems to be honored by people who epitomize the "red-neck" stereotype. So what's their agenda, I think to myself; are they saying that we should return to an age of slavery and legislated white dominance?

Right about this time is when I bump my head on the low beam of my own prejudice. First of all, *assuming* that the intentions of the Confederate flag waver – or pick some other divisive symbol of your own – bears an underlying hatred for a particular government or political party or group of people, the more important personal, and spiritual, question for me is: How do I respond to another's hate? When I become angry and resentful over someone else's assumed or real prejudice and hatred, am I offering a healing balm to the wound or am I picking at its scab?

When people rather boastfully flaunt their counter-cultural views, chances are they are not hoping to win over converts to their cause. My guess is they need their voice to be heard, and sometimes, perhaps, they hope that the sound of their voice irritates "the other side" enough that the opposition does something stupid in response and thereby validates some point in their agenda. In truth, they gain "power" by stirring up the malicious coals of my ever-smoldering prejudice. Subsequently, my first "better" response is no response at all; and my next, best response is to send out love and an effort of understanding in return. My argumentative words and legislated silencing of other's opposing, even hateful views, will never change their hearts, and perhaps nothing will. But if there is any chance of softening their views, it will only come through my efforts of love and understanding.

Gentle God, sometimes I think of myself as so "liberated," so educated and cultured by understanding and receptivity, and then I run smack dab into my own prejudices and realize anew how much work there is to be done in my own life. Help me to recognize and to acknowledge my own intolerance; then, clothed in this awareness, may I work at disarming the ire I feel towards those whose views not only don't match mine, but also seem rooted in bigotry and bias. I cannot control the flags that others choose to fly on their poles, but I can prevent theirs from negatively influencing the colors of mine. May I honestly and faithfully string up a banner of peace and justice.

June 15
Listening to the Leaves

Stepping outside today to make my daily morning offering and prayer, I was struck by the whisperings of the trees in the leaves high above me as the wind gently stroked them. There is a grand oak tree surrounded by other smaller trees just across the street from my home, and on summer evenings, particularly when storms may be an hour or two away, I love to sit on the back porch watching and listening to the conversations of the trees. Theirs is not a language, of course, that I understand, but I can't help wondering if there isn't some kind of sharing going on up there amidst the leaves and the branches. In fact, there does seem to be a kind of communication that they are having with us.

This morning's whisperings were the rumors of a gentle day ahead. The sky was predawn steel grey, but the delicate breeze was like the soft, awakening nuzzle of a mother's breath on the child's cheek. The leaves softly rustled in response, slowly throwing back the covers to greet the emerging daylight. During stormy times, the voice of the leaves changes altogether. As the storm watch brews, the scurrying of the leaves anxiously warns of the approaching change; take cover and be prepared, they seem to say as their branches sway back and forth as if stretching for the challenge ahead. When the storm arrives, the trees do not stand rigid, but shout encouraging words back and forth to one another as they sway with the wind's charge; the leaves clamor in a fanfare of support. And in the most fearful and anxious times, the leaves fall gravely silent. Stillness is the voice of concern, a quiet warning in the hush.

What will be the sounds of my life this day? How will I move with the winds of change and challenge that will blow through and around me today? And will my responsive movements be a tight, solitary grip, or will I be able to relax and join with others in celebratory as well as care-filled support? Are the leaves shaken by the wind, or do they dance on it – and what will be my reception of life's changing breath?

Great Spirit of the Winds, your creations often offer a voice and a sign to us of what is and of what is to come. Help me to listen carefully and thoughtfully to your voice in the leaves; while it may be a language or a vocabulary I do not know, perhaps there is a feeling in the sound that I can more easily interpret and understand. And what will be the language of my movement and choices today? May my whispers, shouts and silence be a potential source of comfort and communion with others this day.

June 16
Sharpen the Blade

There must be a very dull spot on my lawn mower blade. I have noticed of late that whenever I mow, after each swath, there is a slim strip of uncut grass. At first I thought I was just doing a poor job of mowing in a straight line. Realizing that wasn't so, I figured that with each pass of the mower, the outer wheels were matting down the grass so that with the next pass the grass was laying down and not getting cut. But after I increased the overlapping of each pass further, I noted that the strip still remained. The only conclusion, it seems, is that there is a very dull spot on the blade, and it is just not getting the job done.

My life seems full of little uncut strips as well, places I mow through and just can't quite seem to keep things even and straight. In some ways, I have gotten so used to those patchy areas that I don't even recognize them any longer; I have simply learned to accept their undulating flow. But occasionally, when I look behind me, I'm a little disappointed by the unevenness of things, and I tell myself, "I can do better than that." But making personal adjustments doesn't always remedy the situation either, does it? Sometimes, the flaw may be in the "tools" we use, or something entirely out of our grasp altogether. Still, I tend to think that the effort to improve the situation is worth it all the same.

O Even God of Unevenness, your love is steady and strong for all of your creations, but we, your creations, do not always participate and communicate with that same consistency. On the one hand, I am not God, and perfection is not necessarily in the order of my being; on the other hand, as a creation of God, made in God's image and likeness, I am called to be as perfect as I can be. Let me not settle for the irregular strips in my life, the patchy places of a dull life. Sharpen my human skills so that I may cut through complacency and sloth, and provide the best image of my Creator that I can – steady, even and true.

June 17
Rancheria Falls

One of my first solo backpacking trips came at an especially deep canyon on the topographical map of my emotional life. My California sister had invited me, even paved the way, to visit her and her family for a couple of weeks one year as my teaching year came to a close. At that time, on the home front, my marriage was going through its latest phase of unraveling, and when I left home, the terrain there was a rocky shoreline with harrowing waves building. Whether I should have left home then or not, I cannot, even now, say, but I packed this sea of confusion and fear into my luggage, and headed west.

While visiting my sister, I openly shared the troubles and stresses of my life, most especially the bleeding wound of my failing marriage. Along with daily ice cream, we shared much laughter and sightseeing as well, but throughout the visit, undeniably, no tasty frozen treat, no bandage of words or emotional support could stop or hide the bleeding. Subtly, depression was the infusion I gave myself in replenishing the "blood loss," and as it coursed through my veins, hopelessness became a jaundiced new symptom.

After the first week of visiting, I made plans to drive south to Yosemite National Park to hike into the backcountry wilderness in its northern regions, the Hetch Hetchy Reservoir. Loaded with the weight of camping needs on my back and of emotional shards in my gut, I hit the trail that courses around the southwestern edge of this beautiful reservoir. On the eastern side, mountainous slabs of granite rose from the glistening depths of the restrained water, while the wooded trail I traversed intersected with bone-chilling waterfalls and streams of melting snow, where switchbacks occasionally gave way to expansive views of earth and sky unions. Later that day, a campsite established alongside Rancheria Falls, I sat drop-jawed, mesmerized, by the incredible force and sound of the river that carved its way down the mountain toward the less natural reservoir below. The threatening waves that I had carried with me from home were consumed by the majesty of creation, were caught up in the overpowering cascade of love that gushes forth from God's gift of the earth. It was here, for the first time, that I consciously saw and understood how small even our greatest concerns are. Not that my concerns did not exist or matter, but rather, in the framework of the larger gift that is life, my suffering paled.

All around us, every day of our lives, are simple, and sometimes magnificent, gifts that God offers us to enjoy. They are salves for wounds, caramel poured over our already delicious ice cream, higher ground from the dangerous crash of waves on our rockier shorelines. When we focus only on our problems, our stresses, our bleeding gashes, we most often miss the very gifts that can save us. The beauty of God not only surrounds us, but also resides within us - and it is far more grand, far more powerful, than any wound we choose to carry. Today, take notice of the beauty that is all around you and the gifts that reside within you; then, let these refreshing and glorious streams of God's love wash over you to cleanse and to heal the wounds that have been bleeding the life out of you for far too long.

June 18
Broken Lives of Communication

The night before I left to visit my sister and her family in California for nearly two weeks, my wife and I had a horrible misunderstanding. Conflicting schedules were keeping us apart for yet another night, and while I prepared for the evening with a sense of "everything was alright" thinking that we had satisfactorily discussed the issue, she unquestionably saw it much differently and told me so just before I hustled off for my engagement. The rest of the night was bitter, and the next day I flew off to California. When I returned, eagerly arriving with a determination to renew and revitalize our relationship, I was greeted with her request for a separation that would end ultimately in our divorce.

The matter of the conflicting schedules that finally toppled our marriage, of course, was not the real issue. The structure of our lives had no doubt been teetering for a long time. For years, my former spouse had felt neglected, relegated to a second-class status while I poured myself into my career, making time for teaching, coaching, parish council, school board, church choir and anything else that I felt commissioned to assist. These were not selfish things, but they did consume "our time" leaving little to spare for the two of us and our family.

Weeks before that ill-fated night, we had stolen away for a weekend together without the children. It was a rare escape, and I remember us playfully and lovingly immersing ourselves in each other. Returning home, however, I quickly slid back into the concerns and pressures that awaited the new workweek, and my shifting of gears seemed to drop the transmission of our relationship right to the pavement, and it never got repaired. Weeks later when I left for that California trip, even though it had been months in the making, for her, I was walking away from a gasping relationship for the last time.

Perhaps that relationship was doomed from the start seventeen years earlier; we will never know the "absolute truth" about it. While I can easily recall many very happy and memorable events and stretches in the life of our marriage, it was often racked not just by conflicting schedules, but also by unshared career goals, fears and questions of emotional infidelity, and more than anything, perhaps, the lack of communication that surrounded its ultimate demise. We had given each other separate space before, and had attended counseling individually and together, but in the end, my feeling so blindsided by her request for a separation only signals that the lines of communication were deeply flawed.

Communication is at the heart of every loving, valuable, and good relationship. From afar, it seems like such a simple and easy skill, but up close, beneath its apparently plain veneer run multi-layered textures and grains. Communication is not "just talking." It requires openness and honesty at all times, and a reciprocal willingness to give and to receive the truth of one another's lives. Communication does not try "to fix" another's view, however skewed it may appear to be; it may offer another important perspective, but the feelings and emotions of one person's experience are what they are, and changeable is not usually one of their characteristics. In the life of a good relationship there is nothing more demanding, more difficult and more essential than good communication.

Loving God, teach me to be a person of good communication. I have failed miserably, one time already to be sure, and many times no doubt without even knowing it, because I was failing to communicate well. In prayer, I often sit quietly in your presence and listen for your still and imperceptible voice, but I come to you each day ready to listen. Do I offer that same readiness to the many dear ones in my life, those who in fact may be communicating your message to me? Because you are God, you know the inner workings of my heart; assist me in daring to reveal to my beloveds what they need to hear of me. For all of us to truly be in communion with one another we must communicate.

June 19
With a Face You Least Expect

When my first wife and I separated, I had no place to go to in initially granting her wish for space and time, but thinking that it would be only months before we reunited, I checked into the nearest and most humble of rental possibilities. We had been struggling to make ends meet in one home, so I had little means with which to establish a second. Finding nothing that I could truly afford or fit what I thought would be a very temporary need, I racked my brains for other outlets. Sure, I had friends that would have willingly taken me in, but they all had families and busy lives, and my own thoughts of a distraught, thirty-seven year old man moving into their homes, coupled with my own deep, narcissistic embarrassment kept me homeless and searching yet. It was still early in the summer, so I next thought that maybe I could pitch a tent on the land of some country-living nuns that I knew, and perhaps by fall, the storm clouds of our marriage would dissipate, and I would return home. But before I made a move on that idea, another thought dawned as I recalled a colleague who I knew to be single and I thought lived alone in his own home. So I bandaged my wounded pride, and gave him a call.

Although we were exactly the same age, he had only entered the teaching profession a few years earlier and had been teaching at our school for one or two years, having followed other jobs and more adventure out west for a decade. I suppose I would have called him a friend then, but we were really little more than acquaintances at the time. I had a family, a daughter already in high school, and I had been building a teaching career in support of them for nearly fifteen years already. Though recently engaged, he was still single, and from my rather sheltered perspective, lived his singleness in ways that I never really had, having married so young. I had joined him at a bar one time for a beer and a game of darts, and I knew from that brief excursion that we had little in common. And when he accepted my proposal of renting a room and some space in his house while my wife and I patched up our marriage, I discovered that we had *very* little in common.

As it turned out, my marriage only unraveled further, and with it so did my emotional state of being. The space that I thought would be but a few months of rent evolved into my "new home," and along every step of the transition, this peculiar friendship was taking shape. My colleague had offered me a most reasonable monthly rental fee, no contracts or leases to sign, and when I couldn't quite make the bill, he always waited patiently for when I could. I had been used to not having money, but now I truly didn't, and when the two of us went out for the night, he always managed to pay the bill without embarrassing me or holding it over my head later.

For my part, I brought life to a quiet residence stripped to the bare essentials of living. The house had been my colleague's childhood residence, an inheritance now that his parents had moved to a family farm in their retirement. I cooked meals on a dormant stove, invited my children into the shuttered living space, relit fires beside the hearth that had been cold for years, and brought a Christmas tree and decorations in for the first time in perhaps a decade. Just before New Years, my friend's father died very unexpectedly. An only child, my housemate was at his fiancé's home when I received the news by phone, and I was quickly thrust into the heart of his family as I stepped with him toward the tumult of his father's death. By this time, our friendship had truly been sealed.

Even today, over fifteen years later, our personalities could hardly be more dissimilar, and our interests and perspectives tend to look off in very different directions. Yet, this "colleague" is truly my friend. Two very different men going through what would be, for each of them and for very different reasons, one of the most difficult years of their lives were brought together that year. Neither of us would have chosen the other beforehand to see him through the anguish of those days, and yet, I am certain today that we each got the exact person that our lives needed at that time. God of Friendships, I know that somehow you were right there in the midst of that amity. You knew and know me better than I know myself, and offered me a most unsuspecting hand, and allowed me to return the favor. We are all called to be God for one another, but sometimes we will be very shocked to discover just how different God can be; what shapes and faces he will assume. May I keep my heart and eyes ever open for our next surprising encounter.

June 20
The Mechanics of Ritual

In the Lakota tradition, *hanblechia* is one of many important ceremonies. The word is most often translated as "a vision quest" or "crying for a vision," but such labels tend to romanticize the experience too much. I like to think of it more simply as "fasting with intention." Yes, in the "old days," when a man went hanblechia, he was, perhaps, more truly "crying for a vision," seeking direction and clarity in his life. Today, I too seek clarity and direction through fasting, but I don't go out with the expectation of receiving a vision. If God has something to reveal to me, and I come to God with openness and receptivity, perhaps I will receive some sign, but most often, a sense of cleansing and clarity are direction enough for me.

Like rituals in most all traditions, to go hanblechia comes with some fairly specific guidelines, although the particulars of these will certainly vary from one region to another. Too often, guidelines morph into some kind of "magic formula;" if these and those items are specially prepared, and this and that action is performed, then the desired link between the Creator and the practitioner occurs and visions and all sorts of other mystical events are realized. The guidelines *are* important, but perhaps not so much to conjure up the spiritual world, as to transport one's intentions more properly to and into the spiritual realm. For example, cherry saplings are often required for hanblechia, but what if I search as ardently as I can to locate some but am unsuccessful. Perhaps I live in an area deplete of them, what then? Should I assume that this ceremony just isn't meant for me, at least not now? That's a worthwhile consideration, but there may be another answer or reason as well.

What I find most important about "the mechanics" of any ritual is that as I attempt to satisfy the "requirement," I discover what is at the heart of my intentions. To faithfully pursue certain "requirements" and to follow through various "required steps" force me to conscientiously ask myself why I do what I do. Having just the right colors and just the right tree for a given ceremony are not half as important as the prayer-filled effort I put into trying to have just the right colors and tree. The tree and the colors are not magic in themselves, but the effort and intentions I put into them reveal the depth of my intentions, and that is where the mystical experience begins – with one's intentions.

O God of My Desires, I fast and hunger for you, for a deeper relationship and understanding of you. When I seek special direction and clarity in my life, or when I sacrifice some part of my time, energy and resources for the prayerful intentions of others, help me to always come to you with a sincere heart. Let me not get too caught up in the trappings of ritual, or in my expectations for results. I come before you humbly and respectfully; you are God and I am not. Look into my heart and know that my intentions are true, humbly revealed through my hearty efforts to do things "just right."

June 21
God in the Dark

Each time I head out "into the wild" for my periodic retreats, I am quickly stimulated by the thought of my special time alone in some "sacred space" with God. In my head, I begin to imagine, loosely rehearse, scenes of our time together: prayerful routines, meditative settings, ritual possibilities. With the excitement of a first date, all the steps of the "courtship dance" are played out in my mind with much anticipation. But in all of this preparation, I almost always forget that a relationship is a two-way street, and that I am not fully, if at all, in charge.

One year, when I was exploring the idea of "fear," especially our fear of the darkness, I decided to wait until after sunset before I started my trek into the woods. I wanted to venture back into my campsite without light, feeling my way towards my goal while thoughtfully monitoring my fears along the way. Biding my daylight time, I took off on a short hike without my pack or any supplies, to watch the sun set and, perhaps, the moon rise over a quiet lake a mile or two into the woods. It was a trail I had never been on before, so I gulped down the beauty of the sights as I ventured towards the lake. A stand of ancient trees gave way to the scented beauty of a large pine grove, and I remember thinking that these pines had to have been planted after a clear cut, for they stood in incredibly straight, geometric lines. Eventually, older trees and thick underbrush appeared again, as the land gracefully slid into the cup that held a resting lake. The sun was already behind the trees on the opposite side of the lake as I nestled into a comfortable spot along the shoreline to watch the darkness descend.

I had not checked the status of the moon ahead of time that night, and once the sun set, I discovered that the moon too was already low in the southwestern sky. As the temperature began to drop with the darkness, the moon sinking with them, I decided it was time for me to head back to my car, gather my belongings, and there commence my first nighttime journey to a campsite. In the waning moon's glow, I made my way back up the slope that had descended to the lake, but once into the pine grove, I suddenly found that the trail was, essentially, imperceptible. The bed of pine needles that covered the forest floor and tamped out most of the undergrowth made each footfall the same as the previous one, with no feel of a trail. With no flashlight along, and the moon's glow fading while lost in the forest's dense growth, I looked up for a sense of direction only to find that the linear rows of pines extending in all four directions created a grid of mirrors. Before I realized it, I was descending to the lake again, embarrassingly having walked only in a circle. I found my way back to my lakefront starting point, and started over; but, once again, reaching the pine grove, I was unsure of my direction and next steps. Back to the lake, where I could fathom direction, I decided to hug the shoreline to its southernmost tip and then strike out from there, but my dark steps soon found their way into swamp land, and I was forced to turn back again. Wandering aimlessly into the woods, I began to realize that my nighttime journey had begun earlier than I had planned, and in a different location than I had intended; I might not get to my desired destination tonight, and I might be without my packed belongings.

God of the Light and the Darkness, so often I thrill to meet with you, but too often I want it to be on my terms. I know that you long to meet with me as well, but in *our* relationship. Help me today to open my eyes and to look toward you, but also help me to open my heart to what you want me to see, which may or may not be what I envision. In my darkness, provide me with your light.

June 22
Magical Moments

It was in the season and the Land of the Midnight Sun; although nearly eleven o'clock at night, the sky was frozen in a perpetual shade of dusk. The herring baited hooks of our fishing lines had been suspended above the sea floor for only fifteen minutes or so, dancing about enticingly I imagined in the one hundred foot depth, hopefully luring an unsuspecting halibut. Since moving to a new spot in the widening mouth of Larsen Bay, a deep inlet off the southwest corner of Kodiak Island, a small jewel that must have tumbled off the mainland of Alaska millions of years ago, we hadn't had a hit, and my mind and eyes began to drift, looking out further towards the opening expanse where bay becomes ocean. And then I saw the spray rise from the water in the distance, and with more excitement than any halibut landing would ever provide, I turned to the skipper of our sea skiff, a longtime childhood friend and now host and fishing companion. "Mark! Is that spray out there possibly from whales?" I clamored. Shifting his position in the boat, he too now saw my wonderment, and after we quickly reeled in our lines, he pulled the motor to its gurgling and water churning life and we stealthily began our pursuit of the gentle, watery giants.

For over an hour we gave a quiet chase. Each time we would near the small school of whales, seeing their arching backs break the surface and their blowholes send a fountain of spray into the air, they no doubt sensed our presence and escaped further out until at last we could follow them no more. Directing the skiff back around, Mark headed towards a rocky outcropping that rose from the water like a petrified iceberg between this corner of Kodiak Island and another small island, an additional chip from the bag of jewels that had spilled from the mainland. Like jimmie cake decorations, cormorants and other various sea birds dotted the imposing structure, a safe haven perhaps during a watery flight, and just as we were drifting by it, we had a rare spotting of a puffin in flight just over our heads. A couple of hundred yards further as we made our way to a small inlet on the diminutive neighboring island, we crossed paths with a pacific loon, a first-sighting ever for me, and then lighted to an arctic fox prancing across the shoreline beach just ahead. Thinking we might slip onto the shore of the little island and have a look around, we next spied a pair of grizzly cubs tumbling about playfully on the beach, their mother's head popping up now and then out of the tall beachhead grasses in which she was apparently grazing to check on her brood. As Mark snapped off the sputtering motor and we softly landed, the cubs now racing up the beach and into the grasses in search of their mother's safety, he said to me with amazement, "Kevin, are you magical or what? I have lived in Alaska for twenty-five years, and I've never experienced so many amazing encounters all within an hour!"

Isn't it amazing when sometimes all the personal planets of our lives seem to align and we find ourselves magically transported to the center of wonder? Sure, some remote region of Alaska, no doubt, offers such an opportunity more than others, but still, the alignment can happen almost anywhere and can be manifested in many shapes, from the relationships with those around us, to a fortuitous confluence of events, to a wondrous convergence of natural things such as Mark and I experienced that midnight sun summer night. And such communions cannot be created or recreated; they just seem to happen spontaneously, serendipitously, providentially – yes, divinely. When a special package such as these arrives at my doorstep with no return address, I know exactly from whom it originated.

Lavish Lord of All Creation, today I pause to remember just some of the unwarranted and incredible gifts with which you have so often filled my life. It is too easy for me to latch onto unforeseen troubled times and forget the astonishing moments in my life when I have been gifted beyond reason. If (and they will) difficult circumstances arise in my path like an imposing offshore crag, help me to decorate them with the joyful memories of your magnificent past and present gifts.

June 23
Indian Head Nickel

Years ago, an artist friend of mine was commissioned to do a painting with a Native American theme. I don't recall if she was directed to go a specific route with it, or if the entire piece was her own inspiration; but I do remember the end result of her work being both a beautiful "portrait" of a Native as well as a stark statement of America.

The animus and imagery of the artist's work was the old United States "Indian head nickel," minted between 1913 and 1938. On the front of the nickel was a profile of a Native American man. With his hair braided and two feathers falling from the back of his head, his visage is mainly that of a Plains Indian. Appropriate to the region of his appearance, the backside image of the nickel is of an American Bison, often erroneously referred to as a buffalo. This animal has always been revered amongst Plains tribes as a special gift from God, appearing to the people in a desperate time and providing them with not only food, but the means by which to make tools, clothing, blankets and sundry other useful items. With the exception of the eagle, no other animal is perhaps so honored and respected by the Plains Natives than the bison, a fact that makes the ruthless and senseless near-annihilation of it by the early frontiersmen all the more disdainful. In the painting, the artist blended these two images, with the standing bison appearing as both a shadow behind and part of the structure of the Native's profiled face. The nickel's circle, however, became the rim of a ceremonial shield upon which the bison's image appears and beyond that hoop is yet another shield from which stream sacred eagle feathers. Unlike the coin, the Native appears to be wearing a colorful blanket around his shoulders, the blanket being one of the most traditional Native gifts even today, a most simple and essential representation of home and protection. Everything in the painting speaks to the symbiotic pride and respect of the two "relatives."

Finally, as if to acknowledge the "inspiration" of the images, scrawled in bold, imprint-like lettering across the bottom of the painting are the words "FIVE CENTS." A culture, an ethnic nation, a revered and sacred animal – all reduced to five cents. Native Americans were "sold out" by broken treaties and lies, their lands and lifestyle bartered away by a money-hungry way of life they knew nothing about. And for their loss, they got represented on a nickel for twenty-five years in American history. Now, like the Indians themselves, these nickels are lost and out of circulation.

The way that white, western Europeans treated the Native American people when the former came to this continent is not uniquely despicable; it was not the first time that indigenous people were treated disrespectfully nor was it the last. Our world's "nations" have been carved out of countless wars that are ultimately based on greed and power; the carnage rages on even today.

God of All Peoples, greed and power have so blinded humanity throughout history, and their ravenous designs continue to etch their gluttonous visage across our world today. I offer a prayer this day for all indigenous people whose cultures and lives have all but been annihilated by the conquests of others. And as I pray for them, may I stand for them as well and be a voice that questions, challenges and denies any further violations to any and all of God's people.

June 24
A Foundation of Sand

Along the eastern shoreline of the great Lake Michigan are numerous stretches of towering sand dunes. The first time I visited one of these areas, at the southern most tip of the lake at the Indiana Dunes National Lakeshore, I was absolutely amazed by this seemingly out of place movement of nature. I always associated sand dunes with the ocean or austere places like the Saharan Desert, and while each of the Great Lakes has an ocean-like appearance from its shoreline, each is still a lake, a freshwater body of water enclosed in the middle of our continent. Years later I spent a number of nights on these dunes much further north at Sleeping Bear Dunes National Lakeshore in Michigan. At this site, there are dunes that tower nearly two hundred feet high, and dive with a dangerously steep grade to the beautiful waters lapping below.

Hiking through the woods of the Warren Dune State Park in Michigan, I found myself mired in the wonder as much as the deep sand when, right in the middle of a forest of mixed deciduous trees, I encountered a dune, perhaps only fifteen feet across, that rose over one hundred feet from the gentle woodland trail below. Muscling my way to the crest of the dune, each step a sink and slide struggle, I marveled at its very presence there. Dunes are very much a living force, each year their slow encroachment swallows another chunk of the forest or whatever land abuts them; their presence gives real depth of meaning to the phrase "sands of time." What was its shape a century or two or three ago?

Sand dunes are a great example of the force and power of the natural world. We all know that over time, things change, but dunes provide ample and palpable evidence of that truth; and it doesn't really matter how long nature's way takes: what will be, will be. Nature speaks to the surety of life – and death; although we may stymie nature, like the imperceptible movement of my life toward my inevitable death, it will not be stopped.

In the wonderful, even if tragic, story of Job in the Hebrew scriptures, as the story's namesake has one after another blessing in his life stripped away before he ultimately crumbles under the weight of his losses, he openly and gently lets go of them with his prayer of acceptance: "The Lord gave and the Lord has taken away; blessed be the name of the Lord!" Indeed, nature seems an appropriate image of the Creator Lord, giving and taking away without distinction. Dunes reveal that all that we hold, like the very sand that embodies this amazing moving force, can and likely will slip away through our grasping hands.

God of Immutable Change, astonished by the powerful force of nature, I realize that we have little power over the energy that you have written into the creations. We humans build monuments to our successful endeavors and heroes, as if such memorials will forever seal the achievements. But nothing that we hold in this life, indeed, not even our very lives, is immune from the changes of time. Keep me mindful of life's frailty, and of the temporal nature of our achievements. Perhaps you are pleased with our efforts and accomplishments, and encourage us to continue; but you also give us ample signs to know that the foundation of everything in this life is merely sand.

June 25
Obstructed Growth

Whenever you take your next walk or run or hike through woodlands, be especially observant of the ways that trees grow. When we think of trees, we most likely think of them as tall, straight and strong structures, but not all are, of course. Many trees grow slowly beneath a thick canopy of branches and leafy foliage overhead. If you look carefully at the forest floor, you will observe that the thriving saplings are in areas most conducive to the sunlight and the moisture. Other trees are forced to grow around things, a fence post or line, or another fallen tree which, sometimes having caught some part of the sapling as the larger tree fell, now bows the younger tree for the extent of its life.

I was taught once, or read somewhere, that some of the trees with a particularly interesting hook, like an upraised arm with the elbow pointing downward or outward, were strapped at a certain angle in their early life by Native people so that as the trees grew they would provide a literal, directional sign for others walking that trail. But trees grow much faster than we realize, and so today, that explanation is rather unlikely given the human habitational shift of the land. Such a bow or hook in the trees' shape could be the result of just about any obstruction in the trees' early life; and these "deformities" are precisely the point of my encouraging you to observe carefully the growth of trees.

Most of us have already had or will have some very challenging "obstruction" in our lives, and these obstructions will often shift the direction of our growth. The trees teach us about adaptation, however, and about learning to grow around the obstructions of our lives, to grow in spite of the obstructions. When life comes crashing down on us, or someone tries to bend and shape us into a certain form, we are inevitably going to be affected. But enduring the obstruction, we can turn heavenward again, straighten ourselves and reach for the light and the air and the nourishing rain that continues to fall all about us.

Once we are able to see and embrace the deformities in our own lives, perhaps then we can help others to see and embrace and grow through the obstructions in their lives as well. We are too often quick to judge the deformities in others rather than carefully observing the pain of injury and heartache that is likely in the history of the impairment. Many times I have stopped to remove a fallen tree or release a young sapling burdened by the weight of another, to free its growth once again. Do I see and do that for other humans as well?

God of Growth, I long to grow tall and straight and strong, but often times I am disfigured by the unforeseeable and heavy limbs of change, and the miscalculated and visible efforts of others who wrongfully try to shape me. These obstructions can bend and even break my spirit. Observing the trees, however, can bring me confidence that the obstruction need not stop or destroy my growth; it is an impediment from which and around which I may still grow. Help me, Great One, to bend, but not break, and to reach toward the heavenly light once again.

June 26
Caught in the Trail's Web

While I like to think that every time I go for a run there is an element of prayer involved, a conscientious exercising of the gift of my body, some runs are clearly more prayerful than others. For quiet reflection, an early morning run is the perfect matins, the body and the day awakening together, warm breath meeting cool air, a profound "Yes!" to life. Trail running also provides another particularly exhilarating and prayerful run. With my love of the creations and the way that they open me to God's presence, it is like running through a Cathedral. While the terrain inevitably forces a somewhat slower pace, it also creates a prayerfully attentive run, and in this "temple" I often find much valuable insight.

Along with keeping one's eyes carefully affixed on the changing topography of the run, on wooded trails one has to be especially watchful of spider webs. On infrequently travelled trails, spiders often weave webs across paths fastening their tapestries on a tree or bush from one side to the other. A wooded trail run will almost always include some web-swathing and render at least one face or chest web-swaddling. Now, I realize that most people would find such "obstacles" reason enough not to run trails at all, but for me, I find these web-encounters along a challenging trail as just part of the insight.

Years ago, I developed a kind of "relationship" with spiders. Many people fear these rather extraordinary eight-legged creatures, but for me they have often been a source of insight, frequently making an appearance at pivotal, and often prayerful, moments in my life. So, to be greeted by a spider and its handiwork doesn't particularly bother me. Most fundamentally, a web across a trail always reminds me to "live with awareness." Like so many inconveniences and challenges in life, a spider web across the face or chest is not going to cause me any particular harm, but I try to avoid them all the same. Too often, however, in my daily life I fail to live with awareness, and I keep bumping into and creating simple problems for myself. The ups and downs, and the twist and turns of trail running coupled with the possibility of a web-encounter are a wonderful reminder to me of living with attentive awareness.

The webs themselves, of course, bridging one side of the trail to the other are also an easy reminder of the interconnectedness of life. Assembled overnight or through a series of days, this "past" construction can snap me to attention on my "present" run into the "future," reminding me of the interlacing of all of my life movements. And our choices on life's various trails unquestionably have an impact on the web of life, respectfully honoring and contributing to it or ignorantly and irreverently crashing through it. Furthermore, the web's placement across the trail is not to catch unsuspecting humans; it is simply part of the spider's sustenance and livelihood. I want people to honor my efforts to these ends; how well do I do the same for others?

Although many people are afraid of spiders, truly, they are generally very docile, non-aggressive little creatures weaving amazing designs. To see a web across a trail in the morning light gently beaded with dew is a special gift. A spider's delicate body speaks of its inherent gentleness, but it moves through life with a necessary strength creating beauty even in its efforts of sustainability. We too by our nature are rather unassuming creatures doing our best to weave a web of beautiful design in the midst of efforts of "survival." Again, a "web encounter" draws me to look within and ask myself what kind of design am I creating and for what purpose and intention.

When I was a child plying lies to escape my indiscretions, my father used to chide me with the old axiom, "Oh what a tangled web we weave when first we practice to deceive." Not all of our life-weavings are good or are done with the right intention. A morning trail run down a path with periodic spider webs becomes a moving meditation on the fabric of my life. Creator of the Web of Life, you give me the most simple and unsuspecting opportunities to look within and to do a little self-evaluation of my life. As I make my way down life's trail today, may I be attentively aware of my words and actions and the kind of web I weave with each stride. Will I add to the beautiful design of life today, or will I thoughtlessly disrupt the pattern leaving broken, sticky strands hanging in my wake?

June 27
Daring to Travel Makoshika

Some years ago as my wife and I were making our fairly common trek across the vast expanse of eastern Montana on the way to North Dakota, we decided to slip off Interstate 94 at Glendive for some gas and lunch. We had seen signs for Makoshika State Park many times before, but as the park was always a diversion from our course in the midst of a fairly long day trip, we had always ignored them. However, after picking up some sandwiches, we decided to swing by it, have lunch there and take a little look around.

The name "Makoshika" comes from a Native American Lakota phrase referring to a "land of bad spirits." Similar in terrain to the "badlands" of North and South Dakota, indeed, the landscape is very unyielding in terms of supporting life; in this respect, its title is appropriate. But "badlands" have an austerity that transcends the severity of their conditions and ascends to a level of unique and stark beauty; in this sense the only "bad spirit" would be the one who cannot recognize the magnificence of such a place. To my wife's and my surprise, Makoshika was an incredibly beautiful nugget lodged unsuspectingly in the oft-forgotten plains of eastern Montana. What was intended to be a "picnic stop" turned into a three-hour excursion.

Even more than the Dakota badlands, Makoshika's terrain is deeply weathered, exposing ancient rock layers that emerge in curious and fascinating formations, as well as an impressive history of dinosaur fossil exposure. After a quick stop at the visitors' center, our spirits were continuously drawn into the heart of the park. The park roads, little more than wide, eroded trails, were only fit for a high axle, four-wheel drive vehicle, but unable to resist the allurement, I kept dangerously inching my low-slung compact car further and further into the captivating landscape. Wherever we could, we exited the car and followed trails out to stunning overlooks and enticing pinnacles as the plains' winds buffeted us and challenged our safety atop various precipices. As we reluctantly peeled ourselves away and continued our trip back on the interstate, we knew that we had stumbled upon a special gift that day.

Oftentimes, some of our most special rewards in life come from "happy accidents" or following through on whimsical ideas. Common sense tells us not to go down those untrodden paths for fear of what we might encounter; but my spiritual sense sometimes tells me to go down those trails out of the excitement of what I might encounter. That day in Makoshika, my wife and I challenged the rational advice of "sticking with your plan" and followed instead the spiritual tug of "follow your heart." We lost some travel time on our trip, and I probably strained the sensible limits of my car's undercarriage, but in a territory once known for "bad spirits," our spirits were uplifted by the wind and the terrain and we received the good blessing of the land.

Audacious God, religiously, people are often taught to follow "the straight and narrow path," but they can easily confuse this path with "the wide and paved highway." Sometimes I need to get off the well-traveled, "safe" road and dare to venture down and up the narrow, unknown one. Yes, danger may be found there, but if I approach such trails with a good and seeking heart, I am confident that you will not only protect me as you see fit, but you may also show me new wonders that will draw me ever closer to you.

June 28
A Helping Ranch Hand

As I approached my decision to leave my teaching career, I often occupied my "wondering time" with thoughts of what I would do next. After years of being in a classroom with the challenges of "showtime!" every time the bell rang, and the demands of endless paperwork when the bells fell silent each day, I longed for a new job that would be outdoors, that would require less human contact and that would end each day when the job's "last bell" sounded. Perhaps it is romantic nonsense, but I still dream of being a "ranch hand."

Some years ago I had my first chance to sip from the cup of this "dream job" when my wife's North Dakotan, cattle raising uncle needed a little extra help with his herds in the early summer. On a spread of land already close to my heart, I joined Uncle Jim and his crew rounding up cattle and pushing them through a series of corrals for their annual insemination process. His ranch, nestled into the hills, river valleys and ravines of both green and rugged pastureland, was the absolute antidote for my outdoor employment desire. With a crew of just four to six people, sometimes fewer, human interaction was considerably less than what I was used to every teaching day, and more of what I wanted. Work needs and plans would be laid out each day and would continue to unfold spontaneously with the day, but beyond the necessary words of work, we shared only otherwise jocular comments and observations. When the work of the day was done, or the day ran out of light, we shared food and refreshment while we reviewed the day's accomplishments and spoke loosely of tomorrow's needs. There was a simple and quiet comfort in the soothing darkness of each falling night, and the shared acknowledgement of tired and aching bodies was salve enough to urge their recovery. When the sun rose, we would saddle the new day and ride it again through the necessary chores and needs of the ranch; the pace, a controlled canter, had direction, purpose and an end as sure as the cup of coffee that opened the day and the bottle of beer that would close it. Unfortunately, the need for my help was very limited, a special task force at a certain time of the year, a helping, family hand more than a real "ranch hand."

I have returned my lips and body to the cup of this temporary ranch life each year since my first sip. For me, physically taxing though it is, I find it something of a "spiritual retreat." It is not mindless work, but the mind can slow down while the body, fully engaged, exercises its gifts. Outdoors and on the land, there is nothing artificial about the day's tasks; the job is about raising cattle, cattle that will provide sustenance, and food is an essential need of life. If it is hot, I sweat; if it rains, I get wet, but always I am wholly connected to the creations, embracing whatever *is*. Such plodding movement is what the daily spiritual life is all about. There is purpose; there is nurturing and nourishment; and there is a connectedness to all of the essentials of life. The spiritual life is not easy, but it does not require an advanced degree either. One simply must engage himself in the life of it – in life itself.

God of the Land and of Hard Work, the evolving life of your created universe reveals struggle, friction, energy, and accomplishment. As a member of this wondrous universe, I choose to engage in the movements of its life, to be a contributing member to the sustenance of all things, not just a receiver. Grateful for my mental and emotional abilities to think and to feel, I also add my physical exertion to the carving of a universe in motion, a melding of the corporeal and the spiritual. May I always have time and places enough to step away from what I always do, to work a little bit more on just being what I always am.

June 29
Needing to Be

On the ranch, there are always a few things that *need* to be done, a couple of things that *should* be done, and one or two more that *could* be done. The "needs" usually get addressed first, but after that, the worker's wants take over, and the "shoulda's" and "coulda's" go in the order of the worker's desires. Once during my summer-helping-ranch-hand years, we had taken care of the "needs" of the day and were now looking to squeeze one more "oulda" out of the day. The sun had already begun to melt like a slab of butter in a heated old cast iron fry pan, thinning and slipping to the edge of the day, leaving a warm glaze across the darkening sky in its trail; but as if in an act of universal balance, a full moon was just beyond the lip of the eastern horizon offering a soft glow in response to the impending darkness.

With the horses still saddled, Uncle Jim mentioned that "we should probably check the heifers out in the pasture to see which ones are in heat. Then, we'll get those first thing in the morning." I mounted that "shoulda" as quickly as the horse I was about to ride out to the pasture. The task was simple: with pen and paper in hand or pocket, I would ride up the rise to the pasture where the ovulating heifers were herding, and watching for signs of their readiness, I would scribble down the tag number of the "ready cow." By the time I reached the circling herd, their ovulating energy making them very communal, darkness was falling fast giving the job a rising sense of urgency. Imagining myself a far better horse rider than I am, I moved as quickly and as stealthfully as I could through the agitated herd looking for the activities and signs of their apparent "readiness" and scrawling down the appropriate number from the heifer's ear tag or brand. I was not long at the task before the darkness made my feeble efforts futile, but it seemed as if the entire universe was reining me in to stay awhile longer. With the sun's light resignedly melted, the moon was now fully aglow well above the east ridge while the stars on the west rim and directly overhead offered a glittering reply to the darkness's entrance. Calm descended with the impending night, and even the cattle's restlessness slipped away with the light. Leaving my unfinished task behind, I slowly rode my horse back to the crest of the hill, where, with my head dropped back and my mouth open in reverential awe, I suddenly felt as if I were the Grand Marshall of a Universal Parade emerging all around me. Just before my horse heard the whinny of its friends back at the corral and made his unsolicited bolt for home, I remember whispering aloud to the grandeur of the moment a prayer of wonder: "Can you believe that you are seeing, doing and being *this* right now?!"

God of the Moment, there are many things in my life that need to be done, that are simply essential to the daily flow of life. And there are many things in my life that, perhaps, I should do because they provide further goodness in the world; and, of course, there are many more things I could do for they might be of some value in the universe of things. But sometimes the best doing is just being – being present to all that already is. At such moments, all shoulda's and coulda's need to melt away like the setting sun, and allow being to rise like a full moon on a summer's night.

June 30
Sharing Life's Road

I suppose that every state has its cadre of living roadside dangers, fowl and fauna whose landscape has been interrupted by humanity's arteries of pavement and construction. Most of the time and in most places, their sudden appearance is primarily nocturnal, but while the nighttime lowers the number of vehicles on the road, it also limits the visibility of their drivers. Subsequently, mornings too often reveal the carnage of last night's unsuccessful road crossings. In Ohio, the rotting carcasses of raccoons, opossums, skunk, and deer are common sights along back roads and highways, while the evidence of a belligerent goose ineffectively wandering from a holding pond or a golf course is becoming a more frequent sight in residential areas. I have seen armadillos in the Southeast, and javelinas and roadrunners in the Southwest, and more than once I have had to pause to let bison lumber by in western National Parks.

Through all of my travels and roadside observations of living and dead animals and birds, I have found that the state of North Dakota has a unique claim to a high population of ring-neck pheasants. Oh sure, I have seen them in many other states as well, but nowhere are they more common than in the wide open spaces of grain fields and wetland pockets and the butte dappled landscape of North Dakota, so perfectly suited for the pheasants' habitat needs. There is really only one major interstate highway that runs straight through the middle of the state from east to west; beyond that, everything else is "a back road." Like most birds, pheasants are generally not nocturnal, so as a person drives about North Dakota during the day, he is sure to encounter more than one rooster pheasant racing along or across the road, or see a hen and its brood making their way dangerously close through a ditch, or eye the colorful remnants of those that got too close and lost in their tangle with oncoming traffic. A rooster's brilliant flare of colors is always a beautiful surprise when it suddenly rises from the low grasses beside the road, and a hen with its clutch of chicks all in single file behind her is a startling and humorous hazard. Because the population of humans, and subsequently the traffic, is so low in North Dakota, the pheasants seem to almost forget about the dangers of these large masses of steel that come roaring down the back roads periodically, inevitably ending their lives if they should not move quickly enough. And so it becomes the driver's greater responsibility to be more thoughtfully aware of their presence, and to do his best to avoid being the pheasants' grim reaper.

Driving a vehicle on the roadways anywhere is full enough of dangerous surprises, and these various animals and birds only contribute to the peril. But whenever I hear people get upset about the presence of some critter on the road, I cringe a bit and wish that they would remember who or what was there first. When we step or drive into any situation, it is important that we consider where we are and respectfully act according to our environment. We don't have to avoid such places or cease being who we are, but we can be more observant and more careful about where and how we trod. This is not just defensive driving, but respectful living.

Reverential God, you have filled your creation with countless inhabitants, things rooted and things constantly on the move. No one of us is sole proprietor of this creation; you have given it to all and ask that we seek a balance between all. Help me to live evermore respectfully with all of the creations, aware that humanity's ever-expanding needs and desires often infringe on the very existence of others. Observant on my road in life, may I thrill to the sudden appearance of other creatures and not bring harm or death to them as we cross one another's trails.

July 1
I Scream for Ice Cream!

I love ice cream! In our freezer at home, one can almost always find at least two flavors of ice cream awaiting an after meal dessert or ready to be embraced as a late night snack. Sometimes my ice cream eating will go in spurts. I might have zero urges to dig into it for a week or more, but later find myself incapable of rejecting its daily urge for a long stretch. There have been numerous nights where, just before heading to bed, I decide that I must satisfy my desire for that creamy succulence; a friend of mine even helped me to rationalize the desire further by observing that with mint chocolate chip, my personal favorite, the aftertaste is so refreshing that I might not need to even brush my teeth!

The truth of the matter is, that after wolfing down a mug of my favorite ice cream, or lapping away at a smaller proportioned cone, oftentimes I will find that I am not truly satisfied and that this last hit of caloric intake was quite unnecessary. Like the temptation of a buffet spread even when we are satiated, our desires look for more. There is a big difference between *need* and *desire*, and our wills are frequently enslaved by the latter rather than honoring the former.

Ice cream is delicious, and, of itself, is pretty harmless. But when I am unable to recognize it as a desire and not a need, I show signs of having a bigger problem than just wanting to consume ice cream in excess. My love of ice cream also provides me a wonderful opportunity to discipline my will. Each of us probably has some, or any number of tempting desires. The desires themselves are not bad, but how we respond to them might be. Certainly with regards to eating, and likely in most areas of our lives, the answer to the question of "can there be too much of a good thing?" is "Yes!" I do not need to throw out all of my desires, but I do need to better discern the difference between those things that I truly need and those things that I simply want.

O God of my deepest desires, help me daily to make the distinction between what I truly need and what I want. Too often, I allow the line that separates these two to become blurred, throwing another log onto the fire of my desires rather than dampening it with a simple bit of water. May my hunger for you be my most insatiable desire as it is my need; and when I have adequately trained my will, perhaps then, I will treat it to a little ice cream.

July 2
A Hat to Remember

A favorite hiking hat of mine, dressed in my typically favored earthen tones with a little boot print on its brim, simply reads, "Hike Alaska." Beneath the lettering is a small oval frame of mountains, no doubt a silhouette of Denali, the anglicized Mount McKinley. Returning from a recent backpacking trip into the desert where this hat had been a source of daily protection, I was amused to note a series of almost parallel salty sweat lines that cut a jagged line around the hat and across its brim, forming a mountainous profile that appropriately rose over the wording of the hat's simple command. As interesting as the shadowy shape was, it was also a reminder to me of the effort that had been involved over the rugged desert landscape.

I found a hike in the less traveled terrain of the Superstition Mountain Wilderness outside of Phoenix, Arizona to be one of my most challenging journeys. The earth there is more than parched; it is baked hard and dry, and, subsequently, a trail is often not very well defined unless it receives very heavy foot travel. In the more remote regions, the flourishing cacti adorn the trail with their exotic shapes and sizes, but the variety and density of the needled flora often make the trails potently dangerous; each step must be carefully chosen. And if the spiny trees and prickly cactus don't puncture the hiker's awareness, the rugged volcanic rock will. Rocks everywhere are "hard," but many times they are "softened" by the elements of time, smoothed and rounded by winds, water and sand. In the Superstition Wilderness, however, they are dry land corral reef, treacherously jagged and sharp, tearing at the soles of one's boots and scratching the skin if one simply grazes the perilous rock. Add to all of these conditions, a fairly relentless dry heat from the unshaded and penetrating sun. Armed with a less than adequate water supply and clothing protection, this wilderness will reduce the pleasure of one's hike quickly and substantially.

Each hike has its own adventure, but these desert hikes always seem to provide a special notch in the feeling of accomplishment. Having successfully navigated, and not without error, one of the more remote backcountry trails of the Superstitions, I was now impressed by the residual reminder written in salt around my cap of what I had endured. The scrapes and scratches scrawled randomly on my arms and legs would soon heal and disappear, but these salt lines seemed more permanent in their memorial etching.

We ought not dwell on the difficult trails that our lives have endured at times, but perhaps it is valuable to recall them now and then and to allow their memory to bolster our self-confidence in what we can overcome. A privately concealed scar, a simple photograph of the landscape, or trivial uneven salt lines edging a hat can be simple reminders to the bearer that I can go into the deserts of life and still come back alive. I don't need to boast of my accomplishments, nor challenge myself to them regularly, but it is good for me to know that if I should stumble into rough terrain again, I can endure.

God of the Deserts, so many great spiritual leaders and mystics went out into the desert seeking clarity in their vision of and vocation in life. Desert experiences, real and metaphoric, can challenge us to the core of our survival instincts, teaching and revealing to us our vulnerabilities and our need for life-sustaining qualities. When I emerge from any desert experience in my life, help me to be strengthened and encouraged by what I have sustained, and to avoid the arrogance of a conqueror's victory. Let me wear my salt-edged hiking hat not as a badge of accomplishment, but as a reminder to what I, assisted by your emboldening presence, can endure.

July 3
An Angel of Light and Air

When my first wife told me that she wanted a separation, I ran into a dark hollow. Recovering from the blow of her words, breathless and stunned, I staggered to the door, got in my car and drove away into my own oblivion. I returned home again in the darkness of the night, and I would remain in its shadow for at least two years.

Separation and divorce had just never been words that I permitted in my vocabulary. It was not as though I didn't use those words, for surely they must have come up in many anguished conversations before the demise of that marriage, but I just never dreamed that they could actually ever really apply to me. And when they did, I went under deeply. No other experience in my life darkened my world so, and without my realizing it, everything in my life reflected that darkness. I allowed the house that would become my new home to remain austere, stripped to essentials. The color schemes and decorations inside were atrociously not mine nor me, and yet I settled for them and allowed them to paint me. Running, appropriately, became my constant outlet, and along with its release, I dropped twenty pounds from an already fairly fit body. Of course, people offered a variety of help, but in my self-inflicted darkness, I could not see that I even needed it.

A year into this clouded existence, I received a grant for five weeks of summer study in Minnesota with fifteen others from across the nation. I knew enough that I needed to get away from the wretched subsistence to which I had confined myself, but after excitedly grasping this special blessing, I assumed a similar posture during much of the educational venture, living alone and pouring myself into the course work with little time for socializing. Just before the five weeks ended, however, something must have awakened me, and I allowed myself the luxuries of company, laughter, conversation and even dance. I had absolutely no romantic interests or desires at the time, but through my one week of socializing, one woman in particular showed especially kind interest in my life, and a year later as she was traveling through Ohio, I invited her to stay a night or two at my home.

I will never forget the first morning of her stay when, after she had risen for the day, I walked down the hallway to the room in which I had put her up, my room, the only room in the house that I thought reflected some warmth and revealed something of my personality, and found it flooded with light and air. A person of light and air, she had awakened that day and had done what she would have always done, but what I had never done in my two years there: she pulled back the drapes, lifted the blinds and threw open the window. Life was streaming into that room and wending its way right down the hallway, spilling into every dark corner of the house, and in its light, for the first time, I truly saw the gloom with which I had enshrouded myself. Sometime after her visit, I began to renovate that home, and more importantly, my life.

211

When the anguish of our lives becomes more than we think we can bear, rather than seeking the loving assistance of others, we too often slip away from the very help that we need and bury ourselves in some darkened corner of self-disdain. This is not the existence God wants for us, and despite our worst intentions, sometimes God will find a way, or a person, to crash through even our bleakest moments. God of Airy and Spacious Light, you long to come into our lives and fill us with bright hope and loving possibilities, but you most often wait for an invitation. Thank you for sometimes overlooking my inhospitable ignorance, and for stepping into places into which I should have bid you to come. And thank you for sending that angel of light and air into my home to unknowingly open it, and me, to the goodness of life just outside my window. And thank you for allowing, in time, that angel to descend into my life, and for my room to eventually become our room.

July 4

Independence Day

On nearly every Fourth of July for the last decade I have risen early to join a "throng" of about one hundred runners for the annual West River Health Services Fun Run in Hettinger, North Dakota. Preceded by a one-mile children's run, the race starts alongside the village's still active railroad tracks and grain elevators, and then loops around the murky, though pleasantly serene Mirror Lake which frames the south border of the town. After the awards, the most important of which is always which local family had the most participants, I join others of our clan at the local firehouse for an all-you-can-eat pancake breakfast. By the time we emerge from breakfast, the townsfolk are setting up their folding chairs and grabbing their favorite parade space. The community Pioneer Band, with our evening's hostess on flute, marshals the entourage, but along with a couple of well-intended floats, the parade is mainly old fire trucks, new diesel rigs, horses and farm implements, each with a plentiful supply of candy to be tossed to the eagerly awaiting children. As noon approaches, the crowds meander back down to the lakeside community park where a free lunch of roast beef or chicken salad sandwiches, a handful of potato chips and a ladle of cold baked beans right out of the two pound can is served up by local organizations. After our free-range feeding, our clan tends to disperse to golf games, a museum visit and laughter around photo albums; many of us regroup at the home of our evening hostess to help ready the yard, set up tables and spin the last homemade ice cream for the night's picnic. The picnic brings together the layers of three interconnecting families, with ninety year old elders to one year old toddlers and slices of every generation in between; a variant group of seventy will encircle the yard, lifting up songs and prayer to initiate the festive gathering, with held hands connecting us all. Awaiting the ice cream dessert after the meal, instruments emerge and solos, duets and sing-a-longs create a spontaneous concert that will take us up to dusk, when the family pilgrimage commences to the top of "shelf-rock," a historical pasture-butte of sandstone and shale just beyond our gathering place, to watch the fireworks display staged back down at the lake.

Many times throughout the festivities of this small town Fourth of July celebration, I feel as though I am living within a Norman Rockwell painting. But it is all very real, and it is what truly provides for me the sense of Independence Day. It probably comes as no surprise, but I am not a "blind patriot;" there is much about America that saddens and even disturbs me. But for every one of those "spoilers," there is a handful of reasons why I love my country, and the reunion of a loving, extended family clan each year in the safe comfort and surrounding beauty of Hettinger, North Dakota is one of them. The United States is a wonderful country in which to live, with opportunities unlike, perhaps, anywhere else in the world. Although ours is not a perfect country, we are a great nation that offers much to the rest of the world. On this special day of our nation's independence, let us be very thankful for all that we have, and prayerful for all that we could become.

God of Freedom and Justice, for generations the United States of America has been a beacon of hope and a source of aid to so many people throughout the world. I thank you for the many gifts that we enjoy in this country, from the beauty of the landscapes to the multitude of resources and opportunities. Help this country and all of its citizens to better recognize that the prosperity we enjoy is a gift, not a private right, and to willingly extend the joys and benefits of our gifts to the lands and people beyond our borders.

July 5
Playing with a Short Fuse

Buying fireworks and shooting them off around our home was never an option for me when I was growing up. Beyond the safety issues, my parents were frugal people, and fireworks were just a noisy waste of money, not to mention that at the time they were locally illegal. Such restrictions, however, certainly didn't keep a young boy like myself away from them entirely. There were always those kids in the neighborhood whose families didn't see the fireworks issue quite like my parents did, and I would always latch onto these companions and their explosive fun and games when the Fourth of July rolled around. As is often true with those things that one can't have, I always desired to have my own firecrackers, and so after all the raucous exploding and firing away was over, I would usually scour the area looking for the fireworks that for one reason or another had not gone off. Firecrackers without fuses could be folded in half, and the silvery powder, exposed and spilling out of the crack, could be lit sending out a wild and spinning fizzle of sparks. Often times, however, I would land on a real coup, a firecracker whose wick had, for whatever reason, gone out preventing the explosive outburst. With such a find in hand, I would gently tug on the wick in the hope of lengthening it a bit more, and then, succeeding or failing, engage in my own firework excitement.

Most of the time these forsaken fireworks had dangerously short wicks, and after igniting them, I had little time to step out of harm's way. Many times my ears were left ringing for hours from the close proximity of the explosion. Insanely, as was frequently done with full-wick firecrackers, I would hold one in my hand while it was being lit and then quickly toss it so that it would explode in the air. Fortunately I never had one explode fully in hand, but more than once, it was near enough that I felt the numbing effects from the near tragic mishandling. Apparently I wasn't a very quick learner!

From my present vantage point, I figure that my parents had it right all along and, quite frankly, I pretty much followed the same route that they did regarding fireworks with my own children. Of course, fireworks aren't the only explosive things that can be expensive and harmful. People can be too. We all probably know someone who has what we call, appropriately, "a short fuse." Short-tempered people can be very volatile, and because their fuse is so short, one can never be sure when and what might set them off. As with the dangerous fireworks that I played with as a child, we would do well to simply avoid the short-tempered person, but people are not like firework refuse lying around to be discovered. They are often our co-workers, our neighbors, and even family members, so learning how to handle them properly is more the task. And maybe the dangerous explosive is me, a more hazardous circumstance, to be sure, but one in which I have a greater potential to control and to diffuse the risk.

God of Safety, life itself is quite unpredictable and occasionally I find myself in dangerous or threatening situations brought on by explosive, short-fused people. Stress and other tensions can often shorten my own fuse and make me a less than patient and understanding person, and sometimes the heat of another can spark the worst in me as well. I cannot usually control others, but I can control how I react to them and how I respond to my own short-fused emotions. When I encounter dangerous explosives, help me to just let them lie or, better yet, diffuse them altogether.

July 6
The Music of Memory

My nearest sibling in age is a brother three years older than me. As I was growing up, he was a tremendous influence in my life; although he rues the type of influence he might have been sometimes, I count his presence throughout my early life as invaluable and the bond that was forged in those years has provided us a strong connection. The paths of our careers and other later life choices certainly have had a thinning effect on our relationship at different times in our lives, but whenever we get together, we can almost effortlessly slip into the ease of our younger-years-relationship. One area that has especially kept us connected is music.

Years ago, I suspect that our political and spiritual views would have been essentially inseparable from one another, a fact of childhood influence, perhaps, more than a careful and thoughtful brotherly orchestration. Today, I think it is safe to say, we wander in different woods. Our musical interests too have changed a good bit over the years, but in this area of our lives, we are always able to meet each other on the edge of our groves and to invite the other into some new and special grotto. However, there is an old stand of trees in the open space between our two groves that represents our foundational music; deeply rooted and thick-trunked, these trees, with our initials carved so deeply into them, provide us a meeting place where, coursing our fingers through the bark and carved grooves, we can stand on solid, common ground. Every time we reunite, and it happens but once or twice a year, one can bet there will be a sharing of music. Old tunes will drift like falling leaves from the branches above, and the space that has pooled between us will fill with our unfolding smiles. Then, stooping to collect a particularly colorful leaf, we will break into singing, our stiff and unrehearsed voices straining to find the harmony that once bound us like ivy to the tree. Comfortable again in what we know, we dare to lead each other into our more private space, our own groves, where we can stretch one another's boundaries, just a little bit, once again.

Music is such a wonderful medium through which we humans are able to relate to one another, and, of course, there are others to be sure. But to have something that clears the dank air that collects between our loved ones and ourselves during long absences is a special gift. Yes, many relationships can simply "pick up where they left off," but many times we need some kind of common ground meeting place to remember who we were before we can lead a companion into who we are.

Familial God, today I lift up in prayer a dearly loved family member and/or friend, and offer my thanks for his or her presence in my life. Perhaps our lives have taken many different turns, and now head in very different directions, but let my thoughtful prayer for them today fall like fresh autumn leaves, colorful and vibrant, older versions of our greener selves, nutrients for the ground upon which we walk today. And like a song floating on the air, may the drifting leaf of my memory-filled prayer move something in my dearly remembered ones this day, and may they know in the drifting of time, that they are very much loved and appreciated.

July 7
Loved Ones with Mirrors

Allow me to explore my relationship with my brother and our musical-memory foundation a step further. One autumn evening, totally unannounced – as correspondence between us most often is – I received a phone call from my brother who was just exiting a local pub in his home city. With hardly an opening greeting, he quickly seized the matter of the moment, and in a voice of mandate emphatically said, "Drop whatever you are doing right now; go to your local music store and buy the Damian Dempsey CD; you will not be disappointed." Catching me at home busy with my work, his bidding merely made me laugh. My brother continued to explain that he had happened upon this artist that evening performing at the pub, and he was so taken with his music and knew beyond question that it would touch me as well. Now, I trust my brother's judgment in these cases most of the time, but knowing that our present musical tastes have swerved down different channels, I just didn't feel it necessary to rush out and buy into his suggestion right then. The dereliction is, I never pursued it at all.

Nearly two years later during one of our infrequent reunions, he popped the aforementioned CD into his car stereo as we were travelling. In an almost forgiving manner, he reintroduced his previous assertive suggestion by dropping a couple of sample songs on my ears. As I was caught up in an ongoing conversation, however, the new music moved over my skin without sinking into its pores. Perhaps he recognized its ineffective reach, so when we parted, he snatched up the CD and handed it to me. "Here," he said, "I've listened to this enough. I want you to hear it now."

Driving away alone, I figured that I had neglected his recommendation long enough and so I slid the recording into my disc box and tuned it in. Dempsey's thick Irish brogue and idioms brought me immediate warmth, but as the lines of one song caught my heart like a briar, I fought through his accent to better follow his words in the ensuing tunes. Who knows how the "simple twist of fate" works, but all I can tell you is that before the next song ended, from the thorn of a single briar I became entangled in the thick brush, and cathartic tears began to flush out a delicious melancholy. And I must now add, though I rather despise cell phones and especially their use while driving, I immediately called my brother and left him a very grateful and tearful message.

Sometimes loved ones know us better than we think they do, sometimes even better than we know ourselves. I couldn't help thinking that these songs to which he had called me so emphatically years before actually reached more deeply into who I am than they did into who he is; and knowing that, he insisted on my listening to them. Isn't it wonderful to be given the gift of loved ones with mirrors?

God of My Longing, of My Deep Inner Self, you long for me to know myself, and when that self is true and good, you validate my knowing through the kind words, gestures, and presence of loved ones who hold mirrors. Today, I give you thanks for the gentle and sometimes more forcible ways that you help me to come to know myself. In gratitude, may I too be a willing and helpful mirror to others who also seek and need self-understanding.

July 8
An Oasis

The idea of an oasis always rather fascinated me when I was a child. I remember dreamily imagining the early Israelites, lost in the desert for so many years, wandering about in search of the next desert oasis. Cartoons and children stories like *Sinbad* would create for me an image not of a desert island, but of an island in the desert. All around would stretch the endless sand and rugged desert terrain, and then suddenly, like a green jewel fallen from the heavens, an oasis would appear amidst the desolation. Towering palm trees were the visual marking of an oasis, like modern day neon signs, that flashed hope of refreshment and shade. Clusters of Bedouins would take up temporary residence encircling the oasis, and this sanctuary of replenishment would be a constant "rest area" on the desert highway. In an apparently barren and uninhabitable land, the oasis was naturally the sign and source of life.

Decades later, I remember the first time I encountered an oasis. With rather arcane directions, my son-in-law exited an Arizona highway and started across the desert on a rough-and-tumble road. At some point, we veered into a southwestern wadi, and continued our seemingly directionless advancement. Stubby canyon walls grew up alongside the dry riverbed and then, suddenly, he stopped and said, "I think this is it." We got out of the jeep, climbed over some rocks and, sure enough, there it was, a small pool of water from a desert spring surrounded by canyon walls, scrub trees and brush. Miles away, a desert highway inched its way through the barren terrain oblivious to this simple wayside rest hidden beneath the desert's austerity.

A couple of years later, I would have my first personal and accidental encounter of an oasis. Backpacking with my daughter in the Four Peaks desert wilderness northeast of Phoenix, we had spent our day hiking a dry river bed and then up to the jagged ridge top that encircled a portion of the desert. Cactus of all varieties dotted the landscape of the rugged and mountainous desert, but there was no water to be found anywhere. Descending from the ridge, we made our way into a canyon where suddenly there were trees - no, not palm trees – but cottonwoods, and thick, taut underbrush. Pushing through the tight, low growth, we suddenly came upon a small stream that was the source of all of this new and green growth, this desert oasis. Tucked deep in one of the folds of the desert's rugged terrain, this little refuge was nearly imperceptible until one was almost entirely on and in it. We took comfort there, enjoying the cool and refreshing water and relaxing in the shade of the low-slung boughs.

If you live in or near woodlands, as I do in the northeastern United States, an oasis is something of a magical place. The extremes of desert life and the lack of water are hard images to hold in these parts. But you might likely know what emotional and spiritual aridity are like. Those of us who have been on a spiritual journey for much of our lives know how lonely and disconsolate meandering through a "spiritual desert" can be. The landscape appears desolate, and only the cacti of questions and doubts are able to take root here. In such times, we hope for, even need the unsuspecting oasis.

God of the Oasis, many times my spiritual journey towards you will slip off course and I will find myself wandering, like the early Israelites, in a spiritual desert. Lost in questions and doubts, despairing over a broken relationship or a failed job, I can drift dangerously into a parched wasteland of confusion. Provide for me a spiritual oasis, a place of comforting retreat where I might replenish my low supplies and, once again refreshed, find my way back to the path that leads to you.

July 9
Light and Night Vision

My fascination with the human fear of darkness began years ago, and at a certain point I decided that I would try to conscientiously confront it. For some years then, during my regular solo retreats into the wilderness, I would always include a "night walk." These excursions into the darkness were not done with total blind abandon. Most often I would familiarize myself enough with an area or a trail during the daylight hours so that I was not taking some overly dangerous risk like walking along a cliff's edge or falling into some cavernous hole. However, once the cover of night had been fully pulled over my whereabouts, I would venture out into the wooded or open space without aid of any light, as acutely attentive to my thoughts and emotions as I was to my limited vision.

Lacking light and, subsequently, clear eyesight, one's mind becomes intensely perceptive of sounds and profoundly sensitive to the feel of the earth beneath one's feet. I quickly realized that our fear of the darkness is nothing more than our fear of the unknown; because we cannot see fully in the dark and we do not know for certain what is around us, we are afraid. Additionally, we project our fears; fearful in our lack of perception, we imagine that something is "out there," even when there is little evidence or reason to assume that there is. What is there before us in the darkness rarely is any different than what is before us in the daylight; thus, if I am unafraid in the light, then my fear in the dark is, essentially, imagined. One time I remember this point being brought home to me with special clarity and light.

I had successfully navigated a long stretch of a trail through rather dense woods one night reading the sensitive map of my footfalls. The next morning, in the clear light of the day, I went for a run along this very same trail, sightfully attentive to the path, as one must be when trail running. Somewhere down the trail, I suddenly sprang into the air with great alarm and fear when I perceived a rather large snake on the path. Leaping over the frightening creature, I turned back around to get a closer look at it only to find that it was merely a twisted branch. While laughing at my mistake and myself, it occurred to me how this same harmless branch had likely been on my trail last night, and in the darkness had caused me no alarm, no fear. And yet, here, in the light of day, I had misconstrued a simple branch for a terrifying snake. Interestingly I realized that while in the darkness we might fear a projection of something that is not truly there, in the light we are sometimes alarmed by our misperception of something that is there but that is not truly harmful. Thus, in the darkness, if we extinguish and cease our unwarranted projections and, without light, are not prone to misconceptions, the darkness can become a "safer" place than the light.

Okay, maybe that is a bit of a stretch, but the point is, we all could be far better attuned to our surroundings. There is just too much fear in the world, and so many want us to live and to be governed by fear. What wrongful projections do we make about people and places that we do not know – the darkness? And what misconceptions do we create about people and places that we think we know – the light?

God of Clear Vision, you see to the very heart of things, and know the truth of what truly is and what is simply imagined. I often dwell in the darkness of unknown fears created by me or through others, and sometimes I live in the light of misperceptions, believing that what I see is when it is not. Help us all to live in the light of honesty and truth, and to dispel the dark fears of misconceptions and falsehood.

July 10
White-Knuckled Journey

When my wife and I married, we chose to transport all of her life's belongings from Montana to Ohio in a large rental truck with a flatbed trailer attached, loaded down with her additionally packed car. The truck space was jam-packed with essentially no space for another item. With friends' aid, we had filled every bit of the hull like a three-dimensional jigsaw puzzle, ignorantly unconcerned about the weight distribution. Smug in our economical usage of all the packing space, we headed off on our journey.

No more than fifteen minutes into our journey, the highway descended a small hill to a bridge crossing the Yellowstone River. Traveling slightly under the speed limit, when the truck bumped over the highway-bridge abutment, the attached trailer began to sway slightly back and forth. The weight of the trailer and the force of its sway then caused the truck to simultaneously rock as well. I don't know what this unanticipated movement looked like from outside of our vehicle, but I can assure you, at that moment, my wife and I truly felt like we were going to die. I immediately took my foot off the accelerator and lightly pressed the brake while my hands squeezed the steering wheel in a death grip as I tried to ease the undulating truck and trailer back to an even pitch. The fact that I am telling this story is evidence that I succeeded, but the rest of the thirteen hundred mile trip would be pockmarked with numerous occasions of the same frightening episode. Today it is known as our "white-knuckled trip."

We frequently overload our lives with expectations, responsibilities, and commitments that have us driving through each day on a white-knuckled trip. Gripping our steering wheels with a fearful clench, we wonder not only how we will make it, but sometimes even, if we will make it through the challenges of a given day. And because we believe that we are the ones who packed the load, or, at least, accepted the role of driving it, we muscle up and deal with it even at the cost of our physical, mental and emotional well-being.

Perhaps you've seen the bumper sticker, "God is my co-pilot." I've often ridiculed those claims thinking, wouldn't it be better if God was my pilot? The former is more true though, I suppose, for we do need to accept the loads that we choose, and not irresponsibly turn over all of our overloads to God, or anyone else. But we don't need to go it alone either. God is not going to literally slide into the driver's seat of our cross-country move and help get us home safely, but when we find ourselves overly burdened by our good and bad choices, by the circumstances with which life presents us, I believe that our God is willing to slide into the seat beside us and offer some comforting assurance that through faithful prayer, and even some nervous sweat, we can arrive at our destination safely.

Supportive God, the journeys of our lives often do become overly burdensome, due either to our own choices or the simple circumstances of our existence. Gifted with life, I believe that you do not wish to see us suffer or to go through life rigid and white-knuckled by fear. I seek your protection, above, below and all around me as I make my way through this day. Help me to learn from my mistakes, to pack my load with more balance; but mercifully, do not allow me to continuously live my journey in fear.

July 11
No Problem!

Years before my wife and I were married and she was impressing me with her willingness to backpack and hike in the wilderness, we had an experience that has provided us with something of a humorous "rally cry" ever since. During a cross country trip one summer, we ventured into the North Unit of the Theodore Roosevelt National Park in northwestern North Dakota to spend a couple of days hiking. The Park, a beautiful though little known national jewel quietly nestled near the center of North America, is characterized by "badlands" with an overlay of green. In this park, expansive prairies suddenly give way to the rugged terrain that Roosevelt himself described as "so fantastically broken in form and so bizarre in color as to seem hardly properly to belong to this earth."

On an afternoon hike when our goal was to reach Achenbach Spring, we quickly lost the trail after crossing the Little Missouri River. Bison, "in rut" at the time, had apparently knocked down the trail sign post we were looking for, and the criss-cross of their numerous meandering trails created a maze that led us into a desolate canyon corridor. Perusing the meager map I had along, I boldly announced that, by my estimation, if we could merely scale the cliff-like rise immediately in front of us, we would find ourselves on the plateau where we could then wend our way to the spring. Staring up at the rugged wall before us, my wife, with absolute confidence in her voice, responded, "No problem!" Perhaps we laughed a little bit, but we were newly in love and probably figured that the strength and courage of our love alone would probably boost us to the top of the ridge in no time.

Scaling the wall was a full four-limb feat, but the early stages of the climb came easily and our confidence rose with each step and pull. Just short of the top, however, the grade of the wall literally became straight up and down, and as I clung to the sharp and sometimes crumbling dried clay-rich rock wondering what to do and where to go next, I realized that there was no turning back. Thirty feet in the air, I was scared, but aware of our dilemma, I knew that I had to muster my best courage and pull myself up to the edge and hurl my legs over the top. Removing my daypack from my back, I threw it up on the ledge above, and then quietly grabbed the best that was in me and muscled my way to the top. Relieved, I turned around to find my partner now at the same physical and mental precipice from which I had just ascended. "I don't think I can do it," she said, all of her earlier confidence drained, and as the wave of realization crashed over her, her body began to shake as she clung to the cliff face with fear-filled paralysis. There was no way I was going to let her fall, and my voice and body told her so with a courage even I didn't know that I had. Laying belly down, I extended my arm toward her. "You're going to have to trust me on this one. Give me your hand; I won't let you go!" And reaching up, her hand clasped mine and I pulled her body up with everything I had in me. Safely on the top, exhausted by fear as much as by effort, she broke into tears and we collapsed into a seated embrace, holding each other's fragility.

Ever since that moment, whenever my wife and I are staring into the face of a very difficult task, we laughingly and lovingly offer each other the supportive rally cry: "No problem!" While the simple phrase may sound like an energetic vote of confidence, it now represents for us a deep awareness of ourselves. Courage and confidence are wonderful qualities, but taken in excessive doses, they can make us arrogant about our abilities, and ignorant about our weaknesses.

God of Insight, so often I want to appear and to be stronger and more confident than I truly am. I do not wish to shrink from challenges, but I do need to more honestly evaluate them and my ability to face them. You are my ultimate source of strength and courage; help me to know my potential and my limitations more truthfully. In that knowledge, may I embolden myself to the tasks at hand, and take comfort that I might find your trustworthy hand reaching out to never let me go.

July 12
Facing the Challenge

Having researched a little bit about the landscape before another solo hike into the Theodore Roosevelt National Park badlands, I knew enough to think to myself how treacherous it might be in rainy conditions to get out of the river valley I was descending into. On a blistering hot summer day, the trail I traversed was a crumbling uneven surface as hard as concrete, pock-marked by bison hooves; I knew, however, that when the rains came this bentonite clay quickly became a slippery soup almost impossible to walk through, let alone to climb up. But the heat of the day soaked up any real concerns I carried and the rest dripped off me like the sweat that was soaking into my backpack. Later that night though, while I thrilled to the magnificent lightning show from the confines of my tent, the concerns poured back over me as heavily as the rain that accompanied the storm.

Sure enough, after crossing the valley floor the next morning and reaching the steep canyon-like hillside that I had descended earlier, I met up with the greasy surface that I had feared. Thinking the best of it rather than assuming the worst, I took but three oozing steps, and even with a trekking pole in hand, my left leg shot out from under me and I could feel my groin groan under the sudden stress. Trying to save my fall, I lunged my weight onto the pole in my right hand only to feel my right shoulder muscles strain against a potential tear as I slipped to my knees and onto my palms. Pulling myself up, now covered by the slick goo and with a shoulder and a groin aching, I knew at once that a simple half hour hike to the top was going to be neither a half hour nor simple.

Years ago, I used to teach a "coming of age" story by Doris Lessing from our sophomore literature book entitled, "Through the Tunnel." In the story, a young, only-child boy who has lost his father challenges himself to swim through a dangerous underwater tunnel that he spies local boys, native to the island he is visiting, deftly achieving. After days of preparation and practice, the young boy finds himself feeling already physically broken and half spent, but on the eve of his departure from the island, he realizes he has no alternatives. Standing firm in his commitment he dives in despite the weaknesses.

Frequently, when I am faced with a difficult task, it seems that the whole universe pauses to observe my effort and to hurl derision and doubt my way. Of course, the pressure and the stress of the situation squeeze some of the very energy that I need to succeed, and my body responds with white flags of insecurity. Sleep is less restful, and my health plummets like a badlands cliff as I feebly gaze at the ridge I must obtain. These are "coming of age" moments for me. They are not archetypal transitions from a weak boy to a man, but they do represent the challenge of truly embracing who I am. In these experiences, it doesn't matter if one gets to the top of the ridge or through the tunnel, or not. What matters is how one chooses to face the challenge, to discover a different trail or to dive into the waters despite the weaknesses. If I succeed, I will be stronger and wiser; and if I fail but live, I will be stronger and wiser; and if I die, I do so fully embracing my humanity, who I am.

In a letter to the people of Corinth, St. Paul once wrote that, "For when I am weak, then I am strong" (2 Cor. 12:10). What he meant, and it is more than worth noting, is that for a person of faith, these challenging experiences also call us into a closer union with the one who created us. Paul is stronger in his weakness because in it, he leans entirely on God. As I found my way to the top of that "badland," be assured, it was not upon my strength alone that I relied.

God of Challenges, I do not see difficulties in my life as "tests" but as opportunities. I believe that you take no interest in testing me or the will and faith of people. Instead, the life you have given me, and the paths that I choose, often present me with the opportunity to face my humanness, its strengths and its weaknesses, and in embracing those, to faithfully join hands with you in reaching for the best of who I am. When I am faced with challenges, be the breath in my lungs, the trekking pole in my hand, and the sure footing beneath my feet.

July 13
Portaging Life

On the northernmost border of Minnesota, where United States woodlands and waters dissolve into Canadian landscape, is the BWCAW, the Boundary Waters Canoe Area Wilderness. The Canadian side of this wilderness is known as

Quetico Provincial Park. When I was first backpacking and canoeing this northern wilderness in my teens, the BWCAW was known for being slightly more forgiving in its assistance to the adventurer. Portages, land trails that lead from one waterway to another often circumnavigating impassable rapids or swamp lands or just large landmasses, were marked by signposts identifying one's geographic position as well as the portage length. Quetico thought these markers too unnatural and obtrusive to the wilderness experience and did without them; eventually, perhaps not to be "outdone" by the Canadians in wilderness machismo, the BWCAW removed theirs as well. Another significant amenity that the BWCAW used to offer on overly long and arduous portages was a "canoe rest," a simple structure of two standing wooden poles with a cross beam between them on which the portaging canoe carrier could, as the name describes, rest a canoe.

Quite frankly, the carrier is the one who needs the rest, not the canoe. Portaging a canoe, sometimes with a pack on one's back as well, means flipping the canoe (weighing anywhere from 45 light Kevlar pounds to the older aluminum or canvas models weighing in just under or over 100 pounds) overhead, resting the padded gunnels on one's shoulders, and marching down and up and over trails that can include fallen trees, protruding rocks, swampy terrain, thick underbrush and constant root exposure. Portages are measured by "rods," roughly the length of a standard canoe, about eighteen feet. An "easy" portage will be less than fifty rods, the more challenging ones stretching out over 150 rods, at least a half mile or more, although the topography of the portage can make all the difference regardless of length. So, in the past, the BWCAW provided canoe rests on lengthy portages, an almost insignificant opening along the forest trail where one could angle the canoe onto the cross beam of the rest, slip out from under its weight, and relax one's aching and tense shoulders. But no more.

Without canoe rests, the adventurer now has to be a little more creative and inventive if he wants some relief from the canoe's weight while traversing a portage. The most common way to find rest now is to keep one's eyes open for two trees growing closely together along the trail, and then to gently, but assuredly, wedge the canoe's bow between the trees. In a landscape dense with thick forests of pine and birch, such a sighting would seem easy, but rarely is ease the experience of the canoe carrier. Somewhere around one hundred rods, I find that the weight of the canoe, regardless of size, becomes a nagging issue in my head. I begin to wonder about the end of the portage, and then, soon thereafter, to question whether or not I will be able to make it without stumbling and being crumpled beneath the canoe. Dull shoulder ache can begin to rise into inordinate fear and suddenly I am seeking the necessary pairing of trees. At first I might try to assuage the pain with the hope that the portage's end, surely, is just over this rise or around that bend; but when an opening fails to appear, from beneath the shadowy weight overhead, I seek the forest's assistance, two trunks between one and two feet apart, with no low or overhanging branches.

Everyday of our lives can be a bit of a BWCA wilderness experience. Our "terrain" can change quickly and often. To paddle all day over calm waters would be enough, but usually we are confronted by more challenging surfaces, and always, we need to get out and portage to and through the next challenge. And who among us doesn't need the occasional respite, a canoe rest? Creator of All Things Wild and Placid, today I venture out into my "daily wilderness," and I need your assistance. Sure, I want to be strong; I want to patiently endure the challenges of this day, but I also know that somewhere down the trail I could sure use a canoe rest. Jesus proclaimed that God's yoke was easy, and his burden light. Life rarely feels that way, but I look to his assuring words that you will, indeed, be along my trail willing to catch me before I fall, willing to lift the weight from my shoulders momentarily so that I might rest before moving on. As I travel today without specific signposts and defined rest stops, I will look to you confidently for the assistance and comfort that I will surely need.

July 14
Kateri Tekakwitha, Mohawk Holy Woman

Within the Christian religion, today is the Feast of Kateri Tekakwitha, renowned as a Mohawk Indian holy woman, a Saint. As one who honors and follows many of the old traditions of the indigenous people of North America, I must admit that I often find such "feast days" as being a bit ironic. When Europeans first came to this continent, their New World exploration was often assisted by a religious zeal, Christian missionaries longing to bring the light of their Christ to the dark, pagan world of "the savages." I have no doubt that the intentions of many of these missionaries were true and good, but for others, the general lack of respect they showed the Native peoples, the disregard they had for the Natives' own vibrant spiritual beliefs, and, ultimately, the decimation, even genocide of these people by the Europeans erases most to all of their "best intentions" in my heart. Hence, the honoring of a single Native woman who long ago espoused the European Christian tradition, embracing their missionary message, always seems a bit of a trifle to me. What caused her, amongst the thousands who likely did not, to accept the Christian message of salvation through Jesus. Did God speak to her heart in ways that other Natives could not comprehend? Did she freely choose her conversion, or was there an element of coercion or some form of bribery? And how was her new spiritual path received and lived out amongst her own people? In seeking the answers to these questions, I must confess that I would read the "historical records of the life of Kateri" as more closely related to a kind of mythology and would resolve that the "facts" of her life story went with her to the grave.

In an age where religious and spiritual pluralism are more easily acknowledged and accepted, stories of grand conversion can carry less impact. If the Christian claim that Salvation only comes through the acknowledged acceptance of the person of Jesus Christ, and only some Natives, Kateri Tekakwitha being of special note, "accept" him, does that mean all of the other Natives who had the "opportunity" for acceptance but chose to follow their people's own and ancient ways are somehow damned? We swim in murky waters and climb slippery slopes when we start designating which "one" of all of the spiritual traditions of the world most exemplifies, or even more, *is* "God's way."

I hope, indeed, that Kateri Tekakwitha and other Natives of her and this time found and find great peace and strong fervor in their conversion to Christianity; but alongside that hope, I hold a belief that God loves her ancestors and descendants who chose and choose to follow a different spiritual path with equal depth and intensity. In our creation, in our simply being born, we are called into a relationship with the Creator. I do not believe that *every* tradition develops and enhances that relationship *equally*, but I do believe that all traditions do invite and encourage us into that relationship. And while God eagerly awaits our response to the myriad of invitations, what we do with the invitation is ours, not God's.

God of Many Faces, People and Traditions, our world is so often wracked with the "competition" of spiritual traditions. When I look upon the wonders of creation, the incredible variety of all things, I cannot help but believe that you have also provided a grand variety of spiritual approaches, of ways of being in relationship with you. Today, I can honor the choices of Kateri Tekakwitha and pray that her choices brought her more closely in relationship with you; but I also pray that those who choose differently than Kateri will also find solace in you and a depth in their relationship with the one who created us all.

July 15
The unCommon Loon

Somewhere right now on a northern Minnesota lake, or some other remote lake in Canada or the northeastern United States, a loon is quietly floating like an abandoned fishing bobber, unsuspected and slung low in the water. I don't exactly believe that each of us carries some special connection to an animal spirit, but if we do, the loon is certainly mine. The character, yes, the very spirit, of these amazing aquatic birds captivated me when I first heard them as a teen, and then, after studying them shortly thereafter, I have held them as something of a model for my life.

Although they are birds with a strong and powerful wingspan and flight, the structure of their bodies makes getting airborne difficult. Likewise, with their legs set so far back on their heavy bellied bodies, land movement is even more awkward, but as they must nest on land, they have managed to adapt to their shortcoming and have survived as the descendants of one of our oldest bird ancestors. The water is where they are most comfortable, their body's shape most naturally adapted for the tremendous swimming and diving skills of these fascinating birds; but they know each of the elements of air, land and water – must know them to survive – and have struck an important balance.

Their voices are also magnificent in their expressive range of all human emotions. While most people might recognize them for their haunting wail of deep sadness that often echoes over their remote lake habitats at night, their wide vocal range seems to embrace each human emotion. On the opposite end of their wolf-like wail is their tremolo, a sometimes maniacally sounding laughter. A short, one-syllable hoot is also used to maintain contact between mated pairs and chicks, a simple term of endearment, perhaps, shared about their family. Finally, there is the male's unique yodel, a song used in defense and identification of a territory, for we all like to claim our "own space." Like their balance of communion with the elements, their voices seem to express the necessary balance of our emotions as well.

Finally, although it has been more recently disputed, loons are thought to be primarily monogamous in their mating habits, returning to their same nesting site each year after their necessary winter migration. And while their nesting habits show close and shared family ties, when they do migrate, the couple appear to go their separate ways; now, a few months is a little excessive, but I have always supported the idea that a little necessary space now and then is essential to every good relationship.

The fact that the loon is the state bird of my home state of Minnesota surely adds to the connection, but more than anything, all of their characteristics create such a wonderful model of life for me. To succeed, to endure, we must learn to adapt to all different kinds of environments. To be whole, we must know and embrace the wide range of emotions that are inevitably a part of human life. And in relationships, we must be devoted and faithful, but always open to giving each other some necessary space when needed.

Creator God, today I thank you for the special relationships that I hold with one or more of your wondrous creatures. The sound and sight of a loon can draw me into a special place of reflection and can lead me to an unsuspected insight about how I am living or ought to live. Help me to live each day with awareness, my heart open and seeking to learn from the simplest of gifts and creatures that you might have swim, fly or walk across my path this day.

July 16
Tree-Hugger

The first time I hiked into a forest of redwood trees, long before digital cameras, I only had one picture left on my last roll of film, and I knew exactly how it was going to be used. Somewhere down the trail, I snagged a fellow hiker and asked if she would mind taking a picture of me beside one of these quiet, ancient giants. With her agreement, I sidled up beside a great elder and facing the tree, stretched my arms as far as I could around the girth of its base. My solicited photographer may have thought that I was trying to show the expansiveness of the tree by putting my own body and outstretched arms in relationship to it, but what I was really doing was giving the tree a big hug. I have no shame in admitting that I am a "tree-hugger."

You best believe that I still have that photo, a more youthful semblance of me, poised and leaning into the redwood's incredible trunk. Looking closely at the picture, I can see the smile on my turned face and then remember the depth of reverential satisfaction from which it grew. My arms, stretched out in both directions as far as they could go, were still unable to even begin to encircle the ruddy base of this primeval relative. It was a sacred moment for me, a first embrace of one of the planet's most magnificent creatures.

I have hugged many other redwoods since then, as well as numerous other varieties of trees, and have even embraced the granddaddy of girth, the Giant Sequoia. These enfoldments are no trivial or frivolous gesture for me; each embrace is truly an act of respect, an opportunity to feel the pulse of creation. Although there is no actual sensation of a heartbeat, when I lean into an old and weathered tree, I feel as though I am touching history; a mythological past, whose origin is unknown, awakens in my arms, and the tendrils of my heart seek out the stories of the tree's life: what it has seen; what it has endured; and what its magnificent though mute presence might teach me.

I realize that logging is a business that fueled and still maintains economic and developmental growth in our nation's past and present, but it's a job in which I could never participate. Like humans, not all trees command equal respect, but all deserve it. From seedling to root, from trunk to limbs, from branches to leaves, a living tree is a study in determination. Wild trees know no coddling. They have sought and fought for water and light so that they could grow; they have suffered and endured the extremes of heat and cold and wind so that they would live; who am I to take their life before its time?

To be a tree-hugger, to honor any and all of God's wondrous creations, is to change the way we see the "order of creation." If the entire universe is created just for "us," humanity, then, I suppose, "have at it" as you will. But if we recognize the sacredness of *all* creation, even if it can be utilized in some part for our own sustenance and maintenance, then we must realize and recognize the reverential respect that all things deserve. If Life is sacred, then all living things are sacred.

Living God, Creator of All Things Great and Small, your presence permeates the universe. The pulse of creation ripples through the earth, rolls through the waters and waves through the swaying movements of trees. The life that you have breathed into me you have given to all creation. As I can be a source of the life and the support that you offer to all humanity, so too are the creations a sign and a source of your life giving existence. In embracing a tree, in embracing all of your grand creation, I embrace the One who created them all.

July 17
Trees: Models of Faith

If honoring the sacred nature of trees seems too much for you, perhaps seeing them as a simple model of prayerful living will suffice. Indeed, the natural world abounds with living sculptures of the challenges and joys of the spiritual life, but none so embody it as do trees.

Every faith life needs a solid, rooted foundation, and clearly, as with trees, not all are given the same nutritive grounding. People of faith try to provide their own children with good soil, for we recognize that a firm foundation stimulates growth, but we also marvel at those people of faith, who like the seed that finds a crevice in the rock, manage to take root where there appears to be no soil at all. No matter where the seed of a tree takes root, and no matter what its substantive needs are, all trees and people of faith will lean and reach for the source of life. Roots run deep or spread out wide seeking water while branches and leaves extend their limbs to absorb the sun; so too, a life of faith must run deeply, seek widely, and extend upwardly through prayer, meditation and ritual.

Even when firmly established and with growth apparent, the life of faith is not all buds and blossoms. Again, as with trees, seasons of change will unquestionably challenge the development of our faith. Growth inevitably comes in cycles. At times the conditions of our lives seem perfect and the fruits of our growth abound; but drought and heavy weather can test our best intentions, snapping branches and leaving the very taproot parched. Refreshed and energized by life's kindnesses, we spring to life and our faith flourishes, but growth also comes through challenges, and at these times we must learn the often painful truth of letting go; and nothing quite exhibits this difficult dynamic of release like the changing leaf clinging to its branch.

Standing beneath the limbs and canopy of a broad and majestic old oak tree is like sitting before a most holy model of faith; even though it may be impossible to know all that this "giant" has endured to reach this state, one cannot help but be awed by his expansive and sturdy framework.

God of My Grounding, all your creation provides me with figures of faith, but none so completely, perhaps, as the trees. In them I see faith's determination and the willingness to embrace even the most difficult conditions. Through the seasonal cycle of their lives, I can recognize the growing pains of faith: budding, blossoming, changing, and letting go, only to be enriched and nourished for greater growth. As if the breath of the Creator, the wind blows around and through their branches and leaves and their gentle rustling becomes a soft prayer of praise in response. May your welcomed presence in my life move me to such growth and such spontaneous whispers of praise.

July 18
The Beartooth Pass

Hanging in the dining room of our home is a poster-size photograph taken by my father-in-law sometime back in the early 1970s of Dewey Lake, an incredible pocket of water nestled high in the rugged peaks of the Beartooth Mountains in Montana. The picture was taken on one of his hikes over the Beartooth Pass, a trail of which I have heard numerous stories from many in my wife's family. It is a place of stunning beauty, and as an avid backpacker myself, I dreamed that one day I too would course that trail and feast my eyes on its chain of lakes and spectacular vistas.

After making preliminary plans one spring with a special hiking partner to finally grasp my dream hike, my hopes seemed dashed when an important conflict in his schedule arose preventing him from joining me that summer. But with my heart's designs already engaged, I proceeded forward with the intention to go it alone. Unhappy with my resolve and concerned about safety issues, my wife and her family encouraged me to seek out a partner, and I soon found one, a coaching colleague who, although he had never done such a hike, seemed most eager and willing to join me. I instructed him on needs, informed him about the course, and a month or so later, we met up in Montana excited about the dream unfolding.

On the first day of our hike, we got a rather late start, but like a racehorse stuck in the gate, I was ready to make the charge up the first steep and rugged climb. Although my partner was an active bicyclist, I was soon to find that he was not quite as eager or prepared for the task as I had initially assumed. Arriving at the first lake of our opening day charge, we found all campsites already occupied, and so I urged my partner to join me in a push to the next elevation. With no knowledge of what was truly ahead, he agreed, but as the light of the day began to fade and the space between us lengthened, I shouted back to him that I would rush ahead and try to locate a campsite at the next lake in the mountain's elevated tables. By the time he arrived at my chosen site, he was exhausted, at least, and seemed a bit out of sorts with our opening day push. After setting up camp, I began to fix a full coursed dinner as a reward for our efforts, while he chose to catch a quick nap. Once the dinner was ready, however, my partner admitted to feeling rather sick, thinking that he was perhaps dehydrated. He drank Tang while I shoveled down two meals so as not to feed the bears.

The next day's hike was better, but when we arrived at the picturesque Dewey Lake still another day from the pass, mosquitoes descended like a veil while rain initiated in a storm that was quickly roiling in the north. My partner's appetite was no better this night, and his pounding headache now brought forth stories of his altitude sickness while skiing years before. After taking in some soup and fluids, he retired to the tent quickly, as the lightning and thunder began to crash all around us. The rain pelted us through the night, and while I drifted between sleep and sheer enjoyment of the light and sound show that engulfed us, my partner tossed and turned in a private agony. Just before dawn, in an ironically hushed tone, the lightning bolt of his words rocked me awake fully. "You know when I had that altitude sickness skiing, they had to carry me down the mountain." My dream hike came to an abrupt halt. I told him to pack his things and get ready while I would break camp and prepare to head back down the mountain.

Sometimes despite all of our dreamy plans, we are forced to reevaluate our intentions and actions, and occasionally, even trash them for a greater and more immediate need. That morning, camped in the clouds and mist and mosquitoes beside Dewey Lake, I had to let go of my desire and embrace the needs of another. Don't get me wrong, as I trudged back down that trail, there was more in my backpack than just our food supplies and my gear; I carried a load of disappointment as well. But having invited someone else into my dream, I had a responsibility to see to it that my dream did not become his nightmare.

Companion God, I am not in this world alone, and no matter how grand my dreams and ideals may be, I must be willing to let them go sometimes for the sake of a greater need. My own selfish desires can be as difficult to overcome as climbing the Beartooth Pass; help me in my times of weakness, when my selfish desire is my greatest strength. Lift from me this pack of desire, and let me carry more faithfully a craving to serve others selflessly in their times of need.

July 19
The Little Things that Kill

Before marrying, my wife and I used to amuse ourselves a bit over what we might argue about in our marriage. Arguments, *they* say, are a natural part of any relationship, and I guess that I find this view generally true. But the easy going nature of both of our personalities and the independence and freedom that we grew to love about and from each other made the idea of "arguing," even broaching a significant disagreement or major annoyance, seem nearly impossible. And then we married.

Honestly, over the life of our marriage, we have never truly "argued," but I think that we both have stumbled upon aspects of the other's personality or behavior that each find, at least, gratingly annoying. Raised in the home of a pharmacist with a conscientious attention to germs and then having lived on her own for much of her adult life, my wife had developed a highly sensitive aversion to the sharing of food and/or plates or utensils. Conversely, I had grown up in a highly "communal home" and had raised my own children in a very similar atmosphere. We not only shared each other's space, but thought nothing of finishing another's leftovers or digging freely into the ice cream box with our personal spoon. Needless to say, these habits of mine were discovered with horror, and a compromise of our background training and history seemed impossible. Furthermore, I do not simply seek to waste not, but when I am enjoying anything delicious, I do not want to miss even one morsel of the tasty goodness and will, subsequently, scoop and scrap and swipe at every last savory tidbit. This cleaning up of my plate, however, can create something of a clatter that obviously touches a nerve in my wife that goes far beyond a simple scraping of nails on the chalkboard. But ask me to stop and to relinquish those last morsels - oh, *please!* And so we find that we are not *perfect* for one another.

Now, each of these unnerving habits or views are, to be sure, quite trivial. Yet, often times the trivialities of our lives are the very things upon which we can become unhinged in any given situation. A stressful day at work after a restless night of sleep mulling over potentially expensive home repairs is met with one more scrape across the plate and - *kaboom!* And then "Must you do that?" collides with a firmly planted "Yes!" bringing a delicious mealtime to an indigestible end.

It is no news that no two people are exactly alike, and yet, ironically, we all tend to expect our loved ones to embrace, or at least, forgivingly accept, all of our many and various habits, foibles and imperfections. Conversely, we might expect the other to at least modify, even change her behavior so that it more suitably adheres to my way of seeing things. The key to acceptance, of course, is always within ourselves. Surely, some behaviors can be changed, but just as surely can my way of seeing things be altered as well; and while I cannot control another, I can control myself.

Loving God, you created a universe with a night and a day, with hot and cold, with strengths and weaknesses, with happiness and sadness. The created order is decorated with the concepts of yin-yang; there is no *one* way of doing, perhaps even of being. So often I too firmly plant my feet in *my way* and fail to honor and respect the way of another, even and especially those whom I most love. If I should feel myself becoming unhinged by the differing views or actions of another this day, help me to remove myself, either literally or figuratively, and to learn anew of the variety of styles in which we live.

July 20
Biting the Habit

All of my children, and their mother, were nail biters at one time; my son still struggles with the habit during nervously intense times. At the nail ravaging height of their habits, they tried everything to get themselves to stop, using tape and various nasty tasting polishes to remind themselves that this is not what they should be doing. In my effort to help them break the biting-fetish, whenever I would glance at them and see them gnawing away, I would simple say their name; embarrassedly they would momentarily drop their fingers from their mouth, and usually add, "I can't help it!"

I know this "I can't help it" excuse all too well. My past penchant for popcorn and my present one for ice cream have often received that line when I have failed to curb my appetite for them. Annoyingly scraping a plate to get the very last morsel of tasty food or caustically scraping people's nerves as I tease them about some miscue or character flaw have also received this flimsy rationalization. Curbing one's bad habits is no easy task, but I badly deceive myself when I say, "I can't help it."

A frequent piece of advice for changing our bad habits is to remove ourselves from the situation or environment which causes the outbreak of the habit. Sure, I can choose not to buy ice cream and make my late night desire for it a moot issue, but if I bite my nails whenever I am nervous, how do I avoid "nervous situations." Life happens, and it is truly difficult to disengage from our sometimes habitual responses to life events. But to say "I can't help it" is to reduce myself to some trivial and uncontrollable urge. I *can* help it; the question is more about how much do I really *want* to help it? If I can come to some understanding that I am not my body, and that there is something that more truly and more deeply defines who I am, then either the power of the habit will significantly diminish or the importance of taming it will greatly increase.

Patient God, there are so many undesirable habits that I carry around with me. Some of these things are fairly harmless, while others are not only unhealthful to me but potentially injurious or hurtful to others. Help me this day to analyze the driving force behind these habits; why do I allow them or make myself believe that they are necessary? In their grip, sometimes I do feel miserably helpless, and so I turn to you for assistance. I have been given a challenge of the will; I can rein-in my desires or I can let them run wild over me. Strengthen and encourage me to fetter my desires, to recognize that I am in control of my actions, and to tame these habits of mine.

July 21
Making Time

I spent the first part of last summer traveling to various points west, visiting dear friends and family along the way who warmly opened their doors and tables to me, welcoming me into their homes and lives. When I returned home, I put at the top of my latest "to do" list the writing of thank you cards to these many kind people. My wife and I have received written words of gratitude and even extravagant gifts from people to whom we have opened our home, and I always find these remembrances such simple but wonderful acts of kindness. I wanted to do likewise. But the list had many other tasks as well, and each day while some "to do's" got crossed off, there, at the top, still sat that line, "write thank you notes."

A couple of evenings later, after what felt like an already full day, I sat down at the table to "take care of business." Before I did, however, I took the time to do a quick peruse of the Internet, wondering about any local concert offerings. To my great discovery, a favorite band was appearing that very night - but in Cincinnati, two hours away. Quickly eyeballing the clock, I surmised that if I left right now, I could, in fact, still enjoy the show, although I might be a little late. I hadn't been to a good concert in, well, a lot of months, and certainly not to a band of this caliber and liking. With incredibly wonderful spontaneity, I grabbed "concert necessities" and hit the road. Let me tell you, the concert was outstanding, and I enjoyed myself to no end, although I regrettably missed the first four or five songs.

Oh, the thank you notes? Well, of course, they were still there when I got home very late that night and I did get to them days later.

Isn't it interesting how easily we can *make* time for things that we really *want* to do, those things that are easy and bring us immediate pleasure, but how we stumble so to *find* time for the things that really *need* or ought to be done? Dear God, you have created me with an insatiable thirst for enjoyment and pleasure, and I do well, quite often, to quench that thirst. Help me to be mindful of the enjoyment and pleasure that my selfless, though simple, acts of kindness can bring to others. I easily make time for me; help me to do likewise for others.

All of us probably have some pet peeves, those little quirks in life that just seem to get on our last nerve, no matter how small and insignificant they really are. One of mine is when someone takes up more than one parking space. In parking lots, the space hoarder is usually paranoid about getting his car dinged in some way, so he takes up two spots figuring that if everyone else occupies the space they are supposed to, his car will remain safely unscathed. I must confess, sometimes I just want to pull right up beside the hoarder's car door, really tight on the driver's side, so that he can't even get in or out. But usually, the really paranoid types also park further out in the lot for the same security reasons; so, I figure I will let them go for their sake of consistency. With street parking, the space-coveter will waste space between two driveways; where two cars could park if the car noses up or huddles back to the nearest driveway apron, the prodigal paranoid parker plants her vehicle right in the middle, and unless you have a European Smart car, no one can legally fit in front or behind. With these, I figure if I just hit them squarely from the back, maybe I could push them forward enough without causing significant damage to either of our bumpers. But with so many bumpers nowadays made only of some heavy plastic, there's a slim chance I'll get by with that, so I circle the block again for a simple piece of parker's paradise.

At the heart of this parking angst, I suppose, is my deep disdain for the thoughtless greed it represents for me. Look, some people are just poor parkers and mean nothing by their wasteful use of space. These might just be so happy to have gotten their vehicle curbside that they haven't a clue what is before or after them. But I suspect that others snatch more space than is necessary not simply because they can, but because they feel they "deserve" it. You know, "the early bird gets the worm," and, in this case, the "worm farm."

My lack of care for others and for other's needs can manifest itself in so many ways, encroaching on other's parking space is just one simple example. What is it that makes me snatch for more than I need, more than I deserve, and more than I will ever use? O God of Limitless Space, sometimes I seem to think that I am the Lord of Space, that I deserve and can have all that I want. Help me to be mindful of the needs of others, to recognize that they "deserve" time and space and help just as much, if not more, than I do. Remind me to move a little forward, or to inch back just a bit so that another can find some room to move and breath and park around me.

July 23
Empathetic Aid

Like many couples and families, I suspect, when my wife and I take an extended road trip, we usually share the driving. Amusingly, so often when it is her turn to drive, the weather seems to shift and the impending storm that lurked in the distance whilst I drove, moves right over head and pounds us as she drives. Now, I doubt that anyone likes to drive in a disturbing downpour, but my wife often seems to get particularly rattled by it. I, too, would prefer a dry and clear drive, but there is something about a good electrical storm, even in a car, that makes me "light up." The sudden flash that brightens the darkness, the persistent patter of the deluge, and the car-wash fury of neighboring traffic provide an adrenaline rush and challenge my concentration and driving skills. My wife, meanwhile, already a driver of concentration, seems absorbed by the terror of the moment.

In such stormy occasions, I try to lend a helpful hand to her tempestuous challenge, offering another set of eyes to see the road and suggestions about how to maneuver through or around some especially threatening position. For my wife, however, my unsolicited assistance probably sounds more like a drill instructor barking directions to the new recruit, and rather than helping out, I only serve to exacerbate the problem all the more. Needing calm and gentle assurance, she gets from me, albeit unintended, mercurial excitement with a taint of condescension.

Sometimes our efforts to be of help to those in need are not truly considerate of the other's real need, but are based more on our own perspective of what should be done, our personal "need." Projecting ourselves into the situation or concern, we assume that our way of dealing with the dilemma is, in fact, *the* way of addressing the challenge. More often, however, each person willingly accepts her own challenge and is not so much looking for advice, but rather simple comfort and support. Real empathy is the need, not well intended, but selfishly motivated guidance.

Comforting God, I am often eager to serve the needs of others, to step in and help rescue others from frightening and difficult situations. In my eagerness, however, I sometimes forget that the "need" I seek to address is not mine, but another's, and I fail to respect the other's able response. Help me to be more empathetic in my efforts to serve others, a consoling advocate assisting when truly needed while gently supporting in the interim.

July 24
Standing on Sacred Ground

I am not an advocate of reincarnation, although I have no particular aversion to the idea either; in many ways, its "logic" is no more or less logical than any other "after-life" belief. Ultimately, one's position on "the next life" is a "faith-based" perspective, founded primarily on what one has been taught about life after death and what one has experienced in this life. Nevertheless, although I do not adhere to the reincarnation concept, I will never forget the feeling I had when I first laid eyes on and then stepped into the expansive overhang of Ash Cave in the Hocking Hills area of Ohio: "I have been here before." This was not simply a déjà vu experience, for I remember feeling in a deeply spiritual way as though I had truly come upon something that was "home" to me. And on that first visit, I decided that someday I must wake up beneath that glorious expanse.

As the site of Ash Cave is within State Park grounds which close each night at dark, I will not venture too far into the details of my quest, but suffice it to say that presented the *Letter* of the Law and the *Spirit* of the Law, I will almost always choose the latter, and, in this case, the Spirit was calling me forth. In truth, I have spent more than one night beneath the imposing shelter of Ash Cave, communing with darkness, reveling in a full moon's arc across the overhang's lip, and celebrating a return to "sacred ground." That first day that I entered the undefined circle of the sacred grounds, I felt, almost palpably, the spirits of "ancestors" who had lived there once and had called this place home. If these walls could speak, I thought to myself, and when I would spend a night beneath them, I was nearly certain that they did.

One morning, after watching the dark, amorphous silhouettes of the forest and the cave's outline slowly shift into definition and then color in the sun's rising and early light, I showered beneath the waterfall's baptismal spill and then cleaned away any sign of my night's stay. As I sat nestled on a rock drinking in the morning glow and some freshly prepared coffee, a young family strolled back into the sacred grounds, a grandfather evidently in tow with the couple's adventurous young ones. With the grandchildren drawn playfully towards the water, their grand elder slipped up to a spot near where I was sitting, and apparently recognizing the joy of the night and its morning spilling out of me, he smiled at me and said, "Well, you look as though you've got the world by the tail!" Yes, my smile returned in affirmation, I believe I do. In truth, I did not "have the world by the tail;" rather, I had received an invitation to experience the world - life - more deeply, and in responding to it, I was given a new tale to tell.

O God of Cavernous Depths, how many times spiritual seekers have been drawn to encounter you in caves; from Elijah to Muhammad, from the desert fathers to the Greek Island mystics, people great and small have gone within, literally and spiritually, to better see and understand what is without. This place of "enlightenment" need not be a cave, but perhaps there is someplace where each of us is called to, a place where we intuitively feel "at home" though we must work to get there. Heighten my insight, Deep One, to be aware of your invitations to go within, and strengthen my resolve to respond to them so as to uncover the tale waiting to unfold.

July 25
The Truth of the Story

The stories of the gods and goddesses of Ancient Greece, and later, we are told, adopted and renamed by the Romans, are frequently studied in high schools and colleges across our nation. Interestingly, people rarely if ever question this practice as some form of religious indoctrination. These ancient stories, the students are told, are merely "mythology," and the gods and goddesses are certainly fictional characters, creative embodiments of the natural forces that the people of ancient Greece could not understand and often feared. Tacking the mythology label onto these stories, we reduce them to a simple form of entertainment, classic fables to be enjoyed. But if the Greek and the Roman people were as advanced as we historically make them out to be, I suspect that these were not simply clever mythological stories to them; more than likely, they truly were part of their religious tradition.

Religious stories from time periods and traditions other than our own are frequently labeled as "myths" and set aside as a fanciful genre. Minimizing these stories, however, not only disrespects the culture and the people who first honored them, but it also blinds us from seeing the mythology of our own time period and our own religious traditions. It is a curious habit we humans have: the stories and vision of my culture are "the truth" while the stories and perspective of another culture are folktales and falsehood.

Fundamentally, all myths are traditional or legendary stories that convey an episode in the life of some being, often a superhuman or a god or goddess of some sort. In our culture today, we tend to associate "the truth" with "fact;" and since the label of "myth" assumes that the story is fictional and not fact, it stands, therefore, that the story also cannot harbor any truth. The error in this line of thought, however, is that "truth" and "fact" are not the same, and, in fact, fiction can sometimes reveal truth. Subsequently, myths of another culture may offer us some perspective of the truth, while what we hold to be the truth in our own culture may well have been nurtured by a fictional story.

As one religious tradition clamors to reveal the truth and to be *the* beacon of truth, too often it ridicules or minimizes the vehicle by which truth might be found within another religious tradition, forgetting as well, that truth transcends the vehicle. Sometimes, the truth is not found in the facts of the story, but in the myths.

Ancient God of the Stories, you are The Truth of Life written into and between the lines of our stories. So often I read the traditional sacred texts seeking clarity of the truth of you only to be blinded by the "facts" that I misconstrue to be the truth. Help me to be moved in and by the light of your truth that transcends understanding, that is deeper than fact and more mystical than any mythology.

July 26
The God of War

One of the flaws of our mythological thinking is the way we *see* God, the way we understand the nature and personality of the Divine. Again, in the "my view versus your view" competition, another culture's perspective of God is simply "mythological," and therefore not the truth; and our view, being "the truth," can never be viewed through a mythological framework. But a more objective look at all the stories tends to reveal the mythology within them all. Such a revelation does not make the stories void of truth; rather, it diminishes the importance of the "facts" of the story while we seek the greater good, the deeper truth of the story.

For example, almost all mythology – and all sacred texts – often portray God in anthropomorphic terms; God is given a human form and God's personality knows and expresses the range of human emotions. Even God engages in the "us versus them" mentality, seeming to validate our human tendency to do so. Zeus becomes the King of the Gods by usurping the throne of his father, Cronus, who had already done so to his father, Uranus. The Hindu God, Vishnu, in many of his avatars (incarnations), takes the form of some hero (for example, Rama and Krishna) and aids one tribe against another or overcomes the challenges of a demon. The God of the Israelites, Yahweh, frequently commands and then assists "his people" in their battles against the Canaanites and the Philistines. Christians put on the "armor of Christ" who is the incarnation of God to fend against the wiles of Satan, the evil one. And today, some Muslim extremists will war against those opposed to their brand of Islam commissioned by and in the name of Allah, the Most High and One God. And yet, if God is the Creator of all things and all people, and if humans are not the first in the order of things created, is it not strange that God's beingness and God's personality would be most like humans with all their whimsical behavior, and that God would favor only some while seeking to wage war against and annihilate so much and so many of his very own creation? Is it not more likely that as human beings have sought to understand God that they would naturally think of and see God in terms that they can understand and in actions that they have known – in human terms? And if I see the limitations of one perspective, can I imagine the limitations of every perspective which attempts to define a Being, God, who transcends all definitions, who is beyond all knowing?

The truth is that we want God involved in our lives, even in the mundane and the profane, and we sometimes imagine God's presence entering into all of these situations as we would – with human emotion and activity. I don't doubt that God frequently, if not always, is involved in all aspects of our lives, but I do question that the God who transcends all understanding would respond in ways so much like ours. And so I return to the stories seeking truths deeper than the simple mythological portrayals of God.

God of Many and All Faces, I long to know you as you are, and not limit you to how I want you to be. I imagine that you, the Creator of All, embrace and love all, but, perhaps, even this view is my "too human" perspective just as I assume that the warring portrayals of you are. How can I know you best? I shall be still, first of all, and know that you are God; and I shall listen and watch and hope that in the fullness of time, mine or yours, I shall know you as you truly are.

July 27
Seeing a Good God in a Bad Situation

A more personal and, perhaps, a more deeply troubling question that is also intimately connected to the way we see and understand the Divine is the ongoing inquiry into why bad things happen to good people. No question, perhaps, challenges people's faith more than this one. Again, when we assume that God operates, at least, from a human sense of justice, and no doubt something far better, swallowing the tragic evils that have befallen good people seems an impossible task. No answer is satisfying. However, once again, maybe we need to rethink the "mythology" that surrounds the question of "why do bad things happen to good people?"

A sense of entitlement seems to lie at the very heart of the question. Whether or not one believes in and follows the Hindu concept of Karma, which can be very loosely translated as "what comes around goes around," most people seem to generally buy into the idea. If I live healthfully, honestly and justly, I have a reasonable expectation of equal returns for my efforts. Yes, an occasional undesirable event can slip into our lives (just to remind us of the difference between "good" and "bad"), but should a loved one's life be threatened by an accident or cancer, or a large group of people dies at the hands of some needless catastrophe, the big "why?" question arrives on the scene quickly. Many religions have sought to appease this question with the solace of a "heavenly reward," and while this response offers some believers consolation, for others, as it was for Karl Marx, it is "the opiate of the masses numbing their capacity for outrage." Instead of engaging in a search for "justification," however, perhaps, once again, we need to reconsider how we see the Divine - *and* how we see ourselves.

Because of our ability to reason (along with the assumption that other animals and things can't), humans generally believe that they are superior to all other things in the universe and, subsequently, think that a different set of rules somehow applies to them. But examining the "universe of things," one might observe that our human sense of justice has no natural home in the general ways of how things work. When a lightning strike ignites a forest fire wiping out the habitat of numerous plants and animals, most people don't usually ask, "Why did that bad thing happen to those good plants and animals?" Instead, we assume that such an event, tragic though it may seem, is merely part of the natural order of things. Furthermore, asserting our "superiority complex," humans create similar and worse results when, in the name of "development," we clear-cut an entire woodland or fill in a wetland for the sake of our "economic building project," often thinking very little about the lives that are taken and the habitat that is destroyed. But if we step down from our "reason-abled" sense of superiority and see that we too are players in the grand universe of things, then the more "tragic" events (lightning strikes, earthquakes and the like) might be seen in a more natural light.

Now, such a perspective seems to remove the Divine entirely from the picture, or makes God appear to be a careless creator with little to no regard for what God has created. Here again, we are challenged to see God differently. Whether we like to admit it or not, most of us have experienced the occasion of where suffering, brokenness and death have not only reaped something different, but something better. Letting go – change - is not easy, but it is absolutely in the natural order of things; it is the way God created and continues to create the universe. The earth and all things on it, move and shift, and disorder and apparent chaos are sometimes the result. But this movement and its ensuing disorder eventually create a change; life regenerates, resurrects if you will, and things get better. It is the way life is, and if I believe that a loving God created all of this, then God is still right there in the midst of the movement, the suffering, the chaos, and the change. Such a view does not make unpleasant and difficult experiences "good" or easy, but it invites, and then welcomes us to engage more deeply in the Divine "universe of things," of which we are a part.

God of Mystery, I can never *know* with certainty the ways of the universe, nor the whys and the wherefores of my own life. As I struggle to make sense of why certain things happen a certain way, of why bad things happen to good people, perhaps I am missing the point altogether, and there is no "human sense" about it at all. I am not in charge, and so I only consider these things with great humility. Help me to find my place in the universe and to better understand my role in helping to create, alongside you, good things in the world.

July 28
An Ancient Dance

While watching a travel episode set in Ecuador on a PBS program recently, I was struck by the dance style of the people. The Ecuadorian music, framed by the cultural instruments of the pan flute and the drum, provided a simple rhythm to which the people stepped on light feet, a gentle dance dynamism that softly moved in a circle. Enjoying the simple music and its solicited steps, I was captivated by the circular movement of the dancers in their heart-felt, two-step cadence, and the way that this movement was so reminiscent of others' dancing. Far north of these people, and perhaps very distant relatives to them, Native Americans also celebrate life and tell some of life's stories through dance that moves about in a circle, with steps so gentle and sure that they honor and respect the very land upon which they prance. Their music, driven more exclusively by the drum, almost seizes the listener, and its beat all but forces one to lift his feet in celebrative movement. Also very drum-driven, the music of the Aboriginal people of Australia and the Yoruba of Africa have the same effect; the heart, stirred by the passionate percussion, pounds synchronistically with the music and the body inevitably begins to move.

While modern music is transferred across international airwaves and can be marketed through an international industry, the music of aboriginal people everywhere had no such universal forum. These "ancient ones" played a beat that echoed from the one within them, and composed a rhythm that reflected the world around them, and their experience of it. Today, New Age "elevator music" often uses this ancient tribal sound as a basis, and then overlays other electronic and natural sounds to create its soothing melodies. Other musical forms of our age are constantly evolving and giving birth to various musical hybrids, but these simple ancient sounds and the rhythm that they so naturally seem to solicit from us remain. And isn't it amazing how similar they all are?

Amidst all of the cultural and racial and ethnic upheaval that we too often read about in our world today, we are often asked to examine the simple, but unifying fact of "the same blood that flows within us all." But while blood is unquestionably a physiological connection between all people, its unifying presence never seems as significant as the divisive effect that comes with differing skin color and facial features. Yet, beneath the physical separations, and even

239

deeper than the kindred blood flow, is this natural dance of the human spirit that seems to have found its way all around the globe when the universal sharing of music was impossible. Touched by sound, the lineage of our most ancient peoples reveal the connection of us all, the oneness of all people.

God of Sacred Sound and Holy Movement, your presence and the thread of our oneness is woven into the dance of our most ancient forbearers. With a sound that reflects the essential heartbeat within us all, perhaps a sound that quietly permeates the universe itself, these people step rhythmically to the beat of life. May their simple model of a joyous and shared step help me to better understand my connection with all humanity. May the beat of their sound and the rhythm of their step invite me too into the sacred dance of life.

July 29
Lord of the Dance

When I was a teen, I loved to go to rock concerts, to celebrate in the vibe of a favorite band and the ambience created by the crowd. Unlike the atmosphere of the event itself, I was usually pretty subdued, choosing to be more of a listener and an observer than a truly active participant in the concert milieu. Many years later while attending a rock concert with my then late-teen, eldest daughter, I was fascinated by her "full-bodied" experience of the music, an uninhibited emotional and physical release. Sneaking glances at her unencumbered enjoyment of the show, I was stung with the truth that I had for years been fettering my own live music experience. Apparently restrained by a fear of appearances, it slowly dawned on me that I had no doubt enjoyed the sounds of concerts-past, but I had missed out on some of the more primal rapture of the events. Although I could not yet bring myself to "cut loose" at that show, still tethered to a concern of how idiotic I might appear, attending my next concert alone, I began to let go.

Since that time, while I am unconcerned in a competitive sense with regards to my level of enjoyment in relationship to others, I do fancy the fact that by the end of a show that I attend now, there are few people who have received and have experienced the show as deeply as I have. Today, a concert attendance is for me a full body workout, an incredible release of emotion, and a spiritual transcendence of time and space. I recall at one show a group of teens annoyingly interrupting me during my mid-song frenetic dancing to offer me one of their "main floor wristbands" because, "Dude, there is no one in this arena who is jammin' harder than you are. You deserve to be down there!"

Music is an incredibly therapeutic gift. It can create an ambience for any number of needs, can soothe the worst of tension, and can help to release any manner of emotion. When I go to concerts now, I allow the music to fully enter my being. I do not simply enjoy the sounds to which I am listening, but I literally invite them into my body and as they move around within me, I then release them back, my body offering its emotional movements in harmony with the sound. My eyes closed and oblivious to the sometimes amused looks of others, I find myself

240

transported to, what feels like, another plane of existence. By the end of the concert, euphorically exhausted, I am transformed.

In Hinduism, the god Shiva is sometimes represented as Nataraja, the Lord of the Dance. In the famous iconographic representation of Nataraja, the deity expresses the marvelously unified and dynamic composition of the rhythm and harmony of life. Every limb of the four-armed, two-legged dancing deity holds an important representation of the energy of his dance of life; and from the flames arching from his hair and head symbolizing the cycle of birth and death to the lotus flower pedestal, symbolizing the creative forces of the universe, upon which he dances, Shiva's whole image exudes his cosmic Dance of Bliss, wherein inner tranquility is paradoxically united with outer exertion. When we dance, we may not intend to be reflections of Shiva, but we just might tap into some of the life force and energy that the wonderful image of this deity conveys.

O God of the Divine Dance, the bodies that house our souls, you have created with a sacred nature as well. Music, an expression of the rhythm of Life, calls me to engage, with my body, in that Sacred Song of Life. I thank you for my body's ability to move and to give expression to the emotions of my heart; help me to utilize this gift, free of the unnecessary social inhibitions which can keep me from fully enjoying the pleasurable gifts of Life that you offer me.

July 30
Just the Ticket

While attending a concert to "rock out" and dance is probably one of my favorite "hobbies" and most therapeutic forms of stress release, it is usually pretty important to me, however, that I know and like the band's music; the effect just isn't quite the same with an unfamiliar band or new music. So, when my son asked me one night if I was interested in going to the *Band of Horses* concert with him, I was a bit torn. Concert with my son? Very good. Familiarity with the headliner and knowing their music? Hmm...not so good. In truth, both of us had only recently been introduced to *Band of Horses* when they were the warm-up act for my all-time favorite concert band, *Pearl Jam.* My son had liked their sound, and had since become something of a fan of theirs, so he was ready to roll. As for me, I had been so excited about seeing *Pearl Jam* that I had not paid that much attention to their warm-up guests, and since that show, was only familiar with a couple of *Band of Horses* tunes. On top of all that, I was feeling a little financially pinched and just wasn't sure it was all worth the expense.

Two weeks later, at some social event with my son and his wife, he learned over to me and said, "Oh, about that *Band of Horses* concert next week, you're going. I'm free, my wife is good with it, and I want you along. So, I'm buying you a ticket and you're going. Enough said." Okay, then, I guess that settled that question.

On the day of the concert, I still wasn't any more informed about the headliner's music, so as I got ready for my day, I searched them on the Internet and lined up some free listening which I turned on every break I had. Helping to parry the stress of my work expectations, *Band of Horses* joined me for my morning coffee, serenaded my lunch and provided the back drop to my dinner preparations. By the end of the workday, I had a much better feel for them and what I might expect. Yielding finally to my son's compulsory concert idea, I concluded that the band would provide an evening of easy listening music, and while they probably wouldn't satisfy my usual "rock out and dance" routine, it would be an enjoyable "kick back" and listen.

Arriving at the "general standing" venue a little early, we were happily surprised to find a comfy spot just above the stage on the right side wrap around balcony, and settled in with a beverage to await the show. A rumor floated my way that *Brad*, a side-band project of one of *Pearl Jam's* guitar players was to open. Wow, I thought, that would be extra fun! But a bloke named Blake stepped out instead, and while I enjoyed his impressive guitar licks, his slow melodies seemed lost on most of the crowd. Following his short set, maneuvers about stage prepped it for what we anticipated to be *Band of Horses*, but when Stone Gossard walked out with his band *Brad*, I turned to my son immediately with a broad smile and admitted, "This keeps getting better!" Midway through their short but delightful set, my gratitude for my son's "coercion" was beginning to brim, and by the set's end, it was spilling over.

After another stage shuffle, *Band of Horses* emerged and proceeded to "rock the house," and my anticipated "kick back" gratefully stepped aside allowing me instead to dance the night away as I grooved to this "new band" with a recognizable sound slowly emerging. By the concert's end, having drunk fully from my overflowing cup of gratitude, I was entirely quenched.

There can be a fine line between being manipulated by other people's agendas and occasionally allowing the spirit of their "better judgment" to pull you along. My son invited me to step over that line that night he took me out for "his concert" experience. Who knows if he really knew what I needed just then or if it was merely his own self-interest that grabbed my hand; either way, my son seemed a divine instrument that night providing music to more than just my ears. God of Sound Advice, sometimes you nudge me towards what my spirit needs, encouraging me to open up, through the simple, kind words and actions of those around me who know me well. You know me best; I trust that sometimes you will work in concert with them – and that's a ticket I'll buy.

July 31
Chocolate Flavored Care

"Okay, we're ready to do the polishing now," the dental hygienist told me as she laid her picking tool aside. "Would you like mint flavor, or raspberry, or chocolate, or banana, or cookie dough? I think that's all we have today!" she added. Smiling at the wonder of the selections, I stabbed a choice: "You know, I don't think I've ever had the chocolate flavor; maybe I'll give that a try." Mint or orange are my most common choices of anything flavored, but after choosing orange for a nasty pre-colonoscopy cleanser, I wondered about the bad association that might develop. To be sure, I love chocolate too, but it seemed a safe choice for the tooth-polishing step of my semi-annual teeth cleaning.

Applying the polishing mash to her mechanical wand, she started the process while I gazed open-mouthed through the bright light and up to the ceiling. As my taste buds offered a positive appraisal of the chocolate-flavored polishing mash, I suddenly broke into a smile while I considered the irony of this dental indulgence. I was always taught and grew up believing that chocolate needed a kind of benign forbearance. It was never an evil, but it was a "good" of which someone could have too much, and, in doing so, one of its most feared consequences was tooth decay. And now here I was having the flavor of it, at least, smeared all over my teeth for the sake of polishing them! It just didn't seem right!

Sharing the humor of my ironic reflection with the hygienist, I got to thinking about how many other things there are that, on the one hand, we sometimes view with social repugnance, while, on the other hand, we find occasions where the use of the same product is absolutely acceptable. This ironic usage of a "bad thing" for a "good reason" ultimately got me thinking about whether or not there even is a "natural thing" that is truly or absolutely bad. "Bad" should be delegated only to something that is *always* "not good" – unhealthy, destructive, and at its worst, evil. But really, is there anything "natural" that fits such a description? (Okay, poison ivy and mosquitoes do jump to mind!)

As with nearly everything, the key is moderation. Dark chocolate, an antioxidant, is especially known to increase blood flow and reduce blood pressure. So it is "good"! But, of course, the sugar content, if taken in excessively heavy doses would probably not be so good for, well, one's teeth at least! Cigarette smoking has become one of the world's most controversial habits with no end to campaigns against its public and even private usage, and yet, in my Native tradition, tobacco is one of the four most sacred medicines. I carry tobacco with me almost everywhere I go to use as an offering, and have used it medicinally on wounds as well, but clearly, its continuous consumption through daily smoking can have some very significant, long-term negative effects.

The teachings of Siddhartha Gautama, the Buddha, are referred to as "the Middle Path," for ultimately what he discovered is that moderation in all things is the key to simple happiness. Born into a lavish and extravagant lifestyle, he later chose one of extreme deprivation and asceticism; in neither of these did he find contentment. It was the simple happiness that he found on the middle path of moderation that led to his historic enlightenment; and I am most certain that he enjoyed some chocolate now and then too.

God of Pure Contentment, perhaps you are the only one for whose excess I might argue. It seems I could never have enough or too much of you. In a world full of "good" and "bad" labels, perhaps we need to rethink and redefine what makes something "bad." All that you have created is "good" whether the goodness of it be apparent and known or not. The key that "unlocks" the "badness" is not in the creation but in me. Moderation. Can I utilize something for and toward a "good cause," or will I abuse and misuse it toward a destructive and unhealthy end? Moderation. Now there's a flavor I can sink my teeth into!

August 1
Spiritual Indigestion

Nearing the end of my long biannual solo cross country trip one year, a drive to and from Minnesota, I stopped in Indianapolis to visit a niece and her husband who had recently moved there. I had been looking forward to the visit, and welcomed the break from the steady diet of driving with which I had fed the day. We met up at a local pub and restaurant, and as we sat down I assured them that all I had been doing for hours was sitting, and that I had more hours of that ahead, so a simple light meal and drink would be best for me. But as I sipped a rewarding beverage, the menu of deep fried appetizers looked mighty fine, and we soon ordered what appeared later as "one of everything!"

I try to eat lightly when I am traveling because, truly, all one does is "sit on his food" for hours. Yes, hunger may creep in, but there is little energy being expended to justify the normal caloric intake. But it had been a long day, and I had not eaten much all day, and the combination of appetizers and a cold beer grew increasingly more favorable with each nibble and sip. The conversation was rich and fattening as well, and in between stories, I dove full-fingered into another swath of deep fried satisfaction. As the hours rolled by and my time to depart neared, I shot a glance at the scattered remains, appetizer-shrapnel flung across my battlefield of travel-diet willpower. "Waste not, want not," I figured, and swooped in for a final cleanup of the remnants. Less than an hour later, back on the road, I was much more aware of "waist-want-not," as indigestion exploded within me like roadside bombs.

Why is it that even when we know what our bodies need and don't need, we can so easily overlook our body's best interest for the sake of our desires' fleeting interest? Indeed, the struggle between what the body desires and what the body needs is an ongoing battleground where many good intentions get laid to waste, or, as I experienced, get laid *on the waist!* When I experience the "casualties" of one of these little uprisings, I am reminded anew of the battle that rages within me always, of how I must continually shore up my defense if I am to keep these revolts against the will at bay. The body's desires can mount some particularly strong offenses against my better judgment, and if the will is to be in command, as it should be, it often needs some disciplined training.

O God of Discipline, you have created me with the gift of desires, hungers to satiate the appetites of comfort, taste and ease. These inclinations are not evil of themselves; they simply need to be trained - their energies harnessed so as not to gain too much power over the will of the body. Help me to exercise my will power often, to discipline my body in knowing better the difference between what it wants and what it needs. Some celebration in life is a good thing; but when the celebration leads to discomfort, the desires have won the battle over the will. May the only hunger that I can never satiate be my desire for you.

August 2
Love in Action

Leisurely seated on the lawn of a general admission concert venue, I had the good fortune to observe romantic love in action. Have no fear – nothing inappropriate occurred, no public improprieties commenced. No, it was simply my good fortune to vicariously, if not a bit voyeuristically, watch love unfold.

From what I could tell, they were an unmarried couple of about thirty, or perhaps a few more, years old. It was certainly "a date," although not their first together, for they seemed comfortable enough with each other while their eyes and body language suggested that passive searching to discover something more of the other's inner sources. Leaning into each other now and then, I could sense the spark that would arc into an electrical surge when they moved apart again. A wordless glance, eyes locking momentarily, brought a soft smile that started first in the heart and then creased the face; I heard exactly what was not said. Occasionally the woman would stand up and move forward to snap a picture of the stage, and her partner's eyes would watch each step, not lustfully, but with an admiration that obviously stirred his emotions in a gentle blending. Returning to his side with the awareness of his gaze still lingering like a scent, she would lean down and offer a simple peck of a kiss, as if a small token of gratitude given to a street musician's soft serenade. Later, with the concert fully engaged, they stood, sometimes differently dancing, asserting independent expressions, and sometimes swaying in unison or grasping hands expressing their connection.

Perhaps you have experienced the joy of romantic love's unfolding in your life, or maybe you yet long for its blossoming; either way, it's good to be reminded now and then of "what it looks like," to see the magic of love's transformative energy. God *is* love, and we, made in the image and likeness of that love, reveal God when we reveal love. Romantic love is, perhaps, the least of love's many forms, but it imparts an almost magical aura that, when done well, is received by more than just the immediate couple.

God of Romance, the gift of who you are, the gift of Love, is so wondrous that it must take on many visages. Today, I thank you especially for romantic love and for the appropriate ways that it can be expressed and experienced. When I see romantic love in action, I see you working your magic into the very heart of our lives, transforming us through smiles, tenderness and a gentle touch. May love's unfolding in me and in all who are kissed by it also be experienced as a deepening of your presence in our lives.

August 3
The Blank Slate

Some time ago I was chatting with a young neighbor who had a certain penchant for making short conversations long. At the time of our visit, this young mother of two children was holding her oldest son in her arms as she sped from one topic to another in her usual rapid-fire delivery. Suddenly, the young boy reached up and tried to place his hand over her mouth. Initially unfazed by the boy's action, the mother then realized the intention of his efforts and pausing in her conversation, she looked at him and said with a kind of embarrassed shock, "Are you trying to get me to shut up?" It was a rather bold move on his part, I thought, the child trying to modify the parent's behavior; normally, it would be the other way around.

Honestly, I remember very little if any of the specifics of my Child and Developmental Psychology classes that I took in college toward my degree in Education. Certain names linger – Jean Piaget, B.F. Skinner and Lawrence Kohlberg jump to mind first – and some of their and others' theories – constructivism, behaviorism, and moral development; but mostly, I remember discussions about human beings arriving in this world as a "blank slate" upon which many beliefs and behaviors will be written. For the most part, it does seem as though children's development is governed by and large by what they are taught and what actions and language they see and hear consistently. I am absolutely convinced that no child is born with anger, hatred, resentment or violence; if a child takes on these characteristics and acts upon them, it is because he has been taught to do so or has seen that "that is the way it works." Arguably, one might then contend that we are no more born with love than we are with hatred, but I do think that there is a notably different drive in us for love than there is for hatred. The prejudice and discrimination that can be found in the hearts and actions of so many in the world today do not arrive with each person's birth. No one is born making distinctions between ethnicities, religions, races, and political ideologies. These are images and boundary lines that "adults" draw for us as we develop, and if it is "the way it works," it is only because adults have bought into the nonsense that they were taught when they were children.

At certain times, the rantings and ravings of many "real adults'" prejudicial diatribes could use the less than subtle reminder that my neighbor's child provided his mother. It would be rude, and a denial of the other's fundamental freedom, for us to simply put our hand over the mouths of such banter; and, though we may often feel it, even more rude to just say, "Oh, shut up!" But we do need to speak up and to act out in better ways so that the children of the world know that *this* is "the way it works" – through kindness, respect, forgiveness, and love. In this sense, we are all "parents" standing before the child-like blank slate of the world population: our words and actions reaffirming the goodness and the love to which we are all drawn or establishing the violence and the hatred that will continue to tear us apart.

Parental God, your children long ago ceased in behaving as one, happy family. Families will have disagreement and dissension, but the rancor that plagues our world today has gone way beyond the boundaries of decency. We have forgotten who we are: children of the one family of God. What is it that my actions and words would teach a child standing beside me? Help me to be a message of love on the world's messy and distorted slate, and may my actions be a hand over the mouth of hatred and violence.

August 4
Your Tree Self

Many of us, perhaps, have a "special tree" in our lives – literally, a tree that, for whatever reason, we have come to know and love. Maybe it is the sheer size of it that captured your attention, the tree's girth or height or expansive network of limbs; or maybe the tree's spring blossoms have sparked new life in you in the thawing months, or its fall colors have showered you with joy despite the obvious chilling signs of the dying season. Trees are such magnificent creatures!

It is easy to draw correlations between trees and humans. Like trees, the diversity of humanity is self-evident. Like the races of humankind, trees can quickly be grouped by immediate external features, from deciduous and flowering fruit trees to evergreens and boreal, one might see obvious differences, but within each of these categories, of course, there is a myriad of differences. Like trees, the races of humanity seem to have had specifically conducive climates and geographies in which they once thrived, but exceptions and variety can now be found nearly everywhere. From size and shape to resource and resourcefulness, we humans have many analogous connections to our tree relatives.

I used to ask each of my students each year, if you were a tree, what kind of tree do you think you are, and then what kind of tree would you like to be? Because the correlations are so simple and obvious, it is an interesting exercise to consider what characteristics or features you hold that might provide your "tree identity." You should avoid overemphasizing the size and shape aspects, and think more in terms of the qualities of the tree: how and where and why it grows, and what it produces or provides for the environment around it. Such considerations provide a simple reflection on "who I am." Unlike trees, however, we can choose to be something more or something different, and so the second question, what tree would you like to be is also an interesting consideration with which to follow the first answer. Like trees, our "colors" may change, but unlike trees, we may even change the kind of tree we might be. Would our growth be more lush and produce other fruits or largess in a different environment with diverse nutrients?

O God of the Trees, you have gifted the earth with this grand, "standing nation." Providing us with shade, cleansing our air, beautifying our environment, these humble and sometimes towering relatives also offer us some thoughtful reflection about ourselves. How and where do I stand in this world? What fruit, what gifts, do I offer the people and environment around me? Today, I take some time to reflect on my "tree self" so that I might better understand who I am and what I might like to be. Help me in this growth.

August 5
Sodden Expectations

As we donned our backpacks at the northeast trailhead entrance to the Dolly Sods wilderness in West Virginia, the skies looked threatening enough that we paused to dress our packs in their rain covers before heading down the trail. Arriving at our hiking destination late in the afternoon after hours of driving, we planned a short entry hike into our weeklong excursion, three miles and some loose change. Starting on a high mountain ridge, we stepped through open spaces that had no doubt been clear-cut decades ago, and then slipped into the veil of dense deciduous and pine forests, their canopy sealing from our view the ever-darkening sky. The first sprinkles of rain made their way through the canopy perhaps about the same time the distant rumble of thunder began, and more than one in our foursome contemplated their rain gear: now; a little later; or will we escape the worst?

Any hesitation was costly as the unseen skies above opened and spilled increasing downpours upon us while the thunder and lightning accelerated in their intensity and proximity. When we stepped off the trail and under the boughs of some tall red pines for a quick change, I deemed it too late for cover and accepted the fact that I would be rain-soaked for the extent of this first day hike. Just then, and shortly thereafter, two cracks of lightning exploded directly overhead, seeming to rattle the trees and the ground upon which we stood. Paralyzed in our pause, we waited for the worst to pass before we reconvened our hike on a trail that was quickly becoming a creek bed. The rain descended as steeply and as surely as our trail while the rocky terrain of this ancient mountain became more slippery and challenging. If there were grand views or observations to be enjoyed, we missed them entirely as each step required concentration and care. Eventually, after a nearly thousand foot cautious descent, we arrived at our intended campsite a little worse and a lot wet for the wear; by now, even my feet locked within my "waterproof" boots were squishy as the rain had soaked through my pants and socks and pooled in the inner sole. As we dropped our packs at the campsite, the rain too dissipated, but now we faced the task of finding dry, sustainable firewood to provide us with some comforting warmth as the evening reined in.

All windfall limbs and branches were just too saturated for fire use, and it seemed that even the standing dead trees, once harvested, would be a challenge for fire making. But buoyed by the pause in the rainfall, we clamored through the dense forest surrounding the campsite and foraged what would become a handsome woodpile for the approaching night and the next morning. Then, with a determination as sure as the wood was wet, we brought a fire to life, and with its light and warmth, all wet and chilly doubts about our venture dried up or melted away. Before the sun even rose the next morning like a glorious reward for our efforts, our spirits had confronted the demon doubts and had risen above them.

O God of All Sacrifices, perhaps nothing truly comes to life nor reaches fruition without there first being a necessary surrender. My willingness to let go of my doubts and fears and to step headlong into the volatile downpours allows your love to reign over me and to pool in the core of my being. In this shower of love, the skies above me open up and I either see anew the potential for warmth even in my saturated turmoil, or the challenge itself abates and I am left with a glorious dawn. To the reign of your presence hidden in the rain of my life – I give thanks.

"Have you guys had any problems with bears?" asked one of the two young women we met on the trail as we hiked out on our last day in the Dolly Sods Wilderness. "No, and we've hardly seen any sign of them," we responded collectively. "Why? Did you have some problems?" Indeed, on their one night in the woods they had heard "something large" move through their campsite, and then shortly thereafter, while huddled fearfully in their tent, they heard a bear easily tear into their inadequately hung food bag, proceeding to devour its contents.

Interestingly enough, I had bushwhacked down the mountainside with a friend just two days earlier emerging at the very site at which the two women had been camping, and on that hike we had encountered our surest signs of bear activity, some paw scratchings and a pile of scat full of the blueberries we had been enjoying for days on end. But beyond those small indicators, we had neither heard nor seen anything of real concern through our whole six-day hike. In fact, inflated by an ignorant sense of assurance that there was nothing to fear, we had, perhaps rather unwisely, taken very little precaution each night to secure our week's worth of food supplies. These two hikers had not been as fortunate, even though they had actually taken some precautionary measures.

Life is full of such inequitable experiences and challenges. Ben Franklin is credited with wisely suggesting that "an ounce of prevention is worth a pound of cure," but sometimes even the best prevention cannot adequately provide for the impending dis-ease. Many times, through no fault of our own and despite our best preventative measures, the bear strolls through our camp and snatches away our best intentions - and food supply. Meanwhile, just up the trail, others sleep away ignorantly with little to no safeguards in place, and arise morning after morning with all goods intact. The results might be "good or bad," but the law of averages suggests that they are not "right or wrong." In such cases, from this westerner's perspective, the Hindu law of karma simply doesn't apply.

Recognizing the truth of this disparity should not excuse one from taking appropriate measures of protection and safeguard, but it can help a person to better and more easily embrace the simple truth that "bad things can and do happen to good people." Heading out a day earlier than intended, we had a surplus of food to offer the misfortunate hikers, and did, but they too were already heading out and declined our offer. They did accept a map and some encouraging advice as to where to hike that day, but all in all, they seemed grateful that the worst of their troubles had been some lost food and were embracing the new day and its challenges with a smile. When an ounce of prevention doesn't work, a pound of positive attitude is a wonderful salve.

Lord of Life, the diversity and unpredictability of the wilderness ought to be a sign to us of the way life is. I believe that in your original design all the creations were harmonious, and that even today, our ultimate end should be to recover that harmony. But the balance has been deeply and broadly upset, and we must live within the challenges that such imbalance creates within our lives. When I am confronted with some unjust or inequitable experience, help me to not attach so quickly a personal reason for its occasion, or to seek blame and retaliation. Perhaps a hungry bear just happened to pass through my camp on this day, and I had the necessary goods. I sure hope he enjoys the fare.

August 7
A Line of Defense

There is family of chipmunks that have taken up residence under our home, or at least along the foundation walls of it. I'm not quite sure just how I feel about this yet. For most of my life, I always viewed chipmunks as cute little furry animals; their copper colored hides had a warm earthy appearance and the distinct parallel stripes with the black highlights running down their back gave them special character unlike other squirrels and rodents. So when we spotted the first one hanging around a couple of years ago, racing this way and that through the gardens in the front of the house and down into the gaping space where the tilted driveway has settled away from the concrete pad of the garage, he was kind of "cute." But since then, he seems to have taken on a partner, and through their "partnering" more have arrived. Now there seems a network of holes on every side of the house, and occasionally one will get inadvertently cornered in the garage snooping for birdseed, or worse yet, get caught poking around in our back porch. They just seem to be getting a little too comfortable around here, and I definitely don't want one getting into the house!

At this point, however, the alternative seems to be to kill them or catch them in a live trap and move them far away. The first of these I just *can't* do, and the latter, I don't *want* to do; but every time we surprise one another, sending me yelping and jumping and it racing toward the nearest hole or up the porch screen, I find myself thinking, "Okay, buddy, I've had about enough of you!" The problem is these chipmunks simply represent a large number of things in our lives which seem harmless and cute at first, but in time, our approach to them goes from cute to tolerable to annoying to, well, not very nice thoughts which can lead to equally not so nice actions. And it's one thing to try to eradicate bad habits and chipmunks, but we all know these same feelings can happen in some fashion with our human relationships too.

Regarding critters about the house or bad habits that we house, we can easily argue that one has every right to "protect" one's home, and so, within reason, one might do what one needs to do. But when it comes to dealing with a fellow human who has become intolerable in our lives, our procedure needs to be much more diplomatic and kind. With these, one would hope, we can reason. Of course, we all, perhaps, have encountered the less than reasonable and annoying person who really tests the best of our benevolence and compassion. At times like those, some divine intervention may be necessary.

In the spirit of "mitakuya oyasin," a Native phrase which means "all my relations," all things are my relatives, deserving respect and dignity; but life often times reveals conflicts between "relatives" and we may have some "right" to protect our own homes and our own dignity. Sometimes I honestly don't know where to draw the line between the two positions, and so I come to you, God of Tolerance and Respect, seeking some assistance, some clarity. I don't need to be boorish and bully my way through life with an aspect of "protecting my own," but I also need to be careful and sensible enough to shield those I love and myself from unnecessary harm and discomfort. I seek awareness in discovering and truly understanding the difference between what I can do and what I should do.

August 8
A Turtle's Response

In Wilfred Owen's thoughtful anti-war poem, "Arms and the Boy," the British World War One poet insightfully conveys humanity's unnatural penchant for violence, noting instead that we must be taught and trained for war. In the poem's final stanza, Owen observes that our "teeth seem for laughing round an apple" and in our supple fingers "there lurk no claws" and "God will grow no talons at his heels, nor antlers through the thickness of his curls." Indeed, there is little about our soft-tissue bodies that suggest that we should ever engage naturally in violence, either in offense or defense.

Some would argue, however, that the ingenious nature of our minds provides us with our greatest weaponry as we have learned to intellectually fashion weapons of various destruction. I prefer to consider, on the other hand, how our minds are our greatest defense mechanism. Without creating something designed for ruination, our intellect can also train us to transcend vulgar acts of violence unnatural to our physical makeup and, instead, learn to negotiate with reason and sensitivity while rising above the negative emotions which sometimes suck us into ignoble responses. Although our bodies and even skeletal structure seem unfit for violent activity, we have within our capacity a kind of affinity with the turtle.

Turtles are quiet, unpretentious animals discreetly going about their business. If one should happen upon one of these gentle creatures (snapping turtles being an exception!), its natural defense is to "go within" itself for protection. The soft tissue parts of the turtle, the head and legs, naturally retract to the safety of its protective shell. A predator might come along creating a nuisance, but the turtle receding to its safe interior, offers the intruder only a tough and tasteless outer shell. Patiently enduring the threatening interruption, the turtle emerges from its place of safekeeping once the danger has passed, no further damage or harm done.

Often enough, people ignorantly lost in their own self-importance, greed and hunger for power and control try to intimidate us into submission. Emotionally riled, we respond with knee jerk reactions, argumentative words and postures of violence. The turtle's way, however, is not retaliatory, although it is not submissive either. It truly transcends both responses. When we are confronted by aggression, we can strike back in our protection, like a venomous snake, but we will also create further harm. The turtle's way is not to avoid or ignore the confrontation, like the cartoon image of the ostrich with its "head in the sand."

The turtle is very present to the altercation, but he chooses not to respond in violence, seeking instead protection within. Once the emotions have subsided and the "danger" has passed, the turtle can reemerge from its protective cover and get back on with life. Ultimately, he is an image of "non-violence," present in and to the situation, but without lashing out with his own emotionally charged, often violent, response.

Our bodies and hearts are not meant for physical nor emotional violence, and, subsequently, the gift of our intellects would be better used in devising peaceful plans rather than violent ones. A peaceful alternative is too often thought to be "weak," while an act of violence is considered "strong." To take the turtle's approach requires a tremendous inner strength, a courage with a tough outer shell that can endure the hurtful onslaughts of others, and then get right back to work moving in a direction of intention. Protective God, be my shell of defense, safeguarding me from imprudent responses. You have created me to be a person of heart and intellect, not of hostility and brute force. Let me not be sucked into violent emotional and physical reactions, but turning instead to the deeper strength of my inner being, help me to remain calm through the chaos, so that I may move forward in creating rather than destroying.

August 9
Running for Your Life

He was certainly not the best runner I ever coached; in fact, he was "average" at best. Although he ran on the varsity squad a few times, he earned that honor as much via the shallow pool of quality runners at the time as he did through his own hard work. And yet, there are few runners who I will remember more for their tenacity, their dedication and their humor than Kevin Mullin.

Kevin joined cross-country his freshmen year of high school mainly because his older brother, entering his senior year, had discovered and fallen in love with the sport the year before. His brother was "a natural runner" with a sleek build and a talent that had helped to push the team toward new heights of success. Kevin, still wearing a little of that middle school "baby fat," had always been a baseball player by talent and a basketball player by choice; running was just some new grind that his brother said he should do too. Hardly a blip on the radar screen, he jogged through his freshmen season under the shadow of his brother's success. With his brother graduated, Kevin's sophomore season was his own, and his comic antics and one-liners, often at the expense of himself, became as familiar as our daily stretches. While his running improved incrementally, his humor became his most important asset to the spirit of the team.

Kevin lost nothing of his humor with his maturity, in fact, he probably got a little more brazen, as he also added a renewed sense of desire to his running work ethic. Figuring that this was the year his brother "came to life," Kevin started his junior season with a firm goal to be not only a varsity member, but a significant contributor as well. His preseason and first meet efforts showed promise, but then overuse injuries arrived looking for their "tax share" and he soon found himself slipping down the depth chart. After rallying for a last good "hurrah" in the season finale, Kevin became so driven for improved success that he quickly dedicated himself to some off-season training, and made plans to let go of his beloved baseball in the spring so that his running might improve through participating in track and field. Early that December, while lifting weights with a friend, he complained of some vision problems. His friend convinced him that what he was experiencing was not normal, and trips to an optometrist and then an oncologist confirmed that it was worse than "not normal."

Diagnosed with a brain tumor the size of a lemon, Kevin underwent surgery around Christmas time, and then quickly began absorbing chemotherapy and radiation treatments. Physical improvement was less incremental than his running success had been, and yet with the same spirit that he brought to his cross-country efforts he wrote, "Before I found out about this horrible tumor I was happy... and I want to remain happy! So I am going to remain happy!" In the spring, the beauty of his mother's garden blossoms were lost to his blindness, and when the teams began summer preparation for what would have been his senior season, other motor and speech faculties were fading fast as well.

Kevin died on this day in 2001, but before he completed the race of his life, I was gifted with a number of rare opportunities to witness his fortitude, to listen to his strength as well as his frustrations, to sit beside him and guide his hand as we initialed team headbands that would be worn in his honor, and to kneel at his bedside in awesome silence the day before he made it to his finish line. The "best" runners don't always win the race, but they win our hearts and teach us all about how the race should be run.

God of Loss and Sorrow, so many loved ones, and far too often good, young people, slip away from this life long before any of us are ready to let them go. From the perspective of those of us here, it is too soon, too much before "their time," and we are left with unanswerable questions. For all of those who right now are suffering from the trauma and the diseases of cancer, I offer my simple, but heartfelt prayer; strengthen them in their resolve as they fight for their lives and comfort them through the pains and fears which they face daily. And for the families and friends who stand beside them, or who already grieve their physical absence, grant them the insight that is necessary to see through the loss, and to learn from the lived example of the one whom we love, how we can be better examples of how to live.

August 10
Use Your Talents

It is hard to know if Jesus of Nazareth ever really intended the blossoming of Christianity, as we know it today and its various institutionalized expressions, in the wake of his earthly life. But whether one calls himself a Christian or not, there is much to be learned and followed in the teachings and actions of Jesus' life. Like so many great spiritual leaders before and after him, the intentions of Jesus' words and actions are not always as transparent as the observer would like. One such parable from Jesus that caused disdain in me for many years concerned a master who provided his servants with unequal "talents" (the word was also rendered as a form of money at the time) and instructed them to care for the talents in his absence. The servants, of course, yield different levels of care for the talents and upon the master's return, two servants are rewarded while one is punished. The parable ends with the teaching: "For to everyone who has, more will be given and he will grow rich; but from the one who has not, even what he has will be taken away" (Matthew 25:29). Admittedly, I never liked this passage because it always sounded unfair, like an endorsement of the worst of capitalism where the rich get richer and the poor get poorer. But one day it was suggested to me that I not look at the parable with such literal eyes. Instead of seeing the "talents" as material things, money especially, see them as more spiritual, more emotive, things. Once I made that transition, like the blind man in one of Jesus' healings, the scales fell from my eyes, and the whole passage became far more meaningful.

In my defense, the words "money" and "invest in the bank" are also included in the parable, so understanding "talents" in monetary terms is certainly not crazy. But if one simply reads the word in the sense of a "gift," any gift really, but especially a gift like love and kindness, then the teaching offers not simply a challenge to "invest well," but a simple truth of life: if you don't use it, you lose it.

Many of us have received a wealth of care throughout our lives. Born into a safe and comfortable existence, I have been provided a quality education and opportunities for experience well beyond the average citizen of the world. Being loved so well, cared for so tenderly, provided for so richly, should I not be expected to respond in kind to others in the world, all who, like me, "deserve" none of it. Additionally, is it right for me to expect the same respect and compassion that I might be expected to give from one who has been born into squalor, suffered abuse, and endured injustice all of her life. Surely the other, to whom little was given, might muster some favorable response, but it should not be expected that it match that of the person to whom much was given. The other truth of the passage is, when I do act generously with my love and kindness, frequently I do receive much more love and kindness in return; and even if those who had little to begin with share little or no love or kindness, what little they have will likely atrophy and "will be taken away."

O God of our many Talents, we are not all gifted equally. To some, much has been given while to others... not so much. Help me to live inside that truth, recognizing that we all are *not able* to respond with the same levels of respect, kindness and love. But more to the point, help me to recognize my giftedness and call me into an active and responsible use of those gifts. For if I fail to give, to be patient, to be merciful, whatever I have will likely fade away.

When I was a child, the semi-annual or annual trips to the dentist were never a source of excitement. Quite the contrary, dentist appointment days were always laden with anxiety, and, if my memory serves me correctly, with good reason! With my body slightly folded and tilted backwards, and my mouth pried and wedged open with some type of sucking apparatus, the dentist (today, the dental hygienist) would proceed to scrape, pick, and probe his way throughout my mouth, doing things that not only felt, but sounded injurious. Occasionally I would receive the fine-tipped blast of refreshing water, but this I was to swish and then spit into the swirling repository beside me, inevitably leaving a fishing line of drool between my mouth and the mini-toilet bowl. If the stars were really aligned against me, and in childhood this seemed to be so often true, then would come the drilling and filling of cavities appointment, where even the thought of the sounds and the Novocained mouth discomfort makes me sit up straight and shudder with discomfort today.

For most of my adult life, however, trips to the dentist have not been so painful, difficult or anxious. Nearly all of my hygienists and dentists now are so friendly and empathetic, and, I must admit, I rather like that feel-every-tooth-again-cleanliness that I feel when my tongue sweeps across the backside of my teeth after a semi-annual cleaning. And not of small consequence, through improved dental health care and education, rarely if ever do I have to reschedule for the dreaded cavity drilling and filling. Unfortunately, despite all of my and my dental associates best care, my teeth are just plain old – and, after all, I have essentially been using them every day of my whole life. Subsequently, I have recently redeveloped some childhood dental anxieties as my teeth seem to be cracking, chipping, or just plain falling out at an alarming rate. Add to this the fact that now *I* pay the big dental bills and not my parents, and, well, the sucking and drilling sounds are only exacerbated.

We all probably have some dental horror story, the worst of which might be that you have never gone to a dentist; in which case, the real horror stories are just ahead! For thousands of years people apparently got along just fine without dentists, and some people apparently still do, but for those of us who enjoy biting into a crisp apple or gnawing satisfactorily on a fine piece of meat or nibbling on a crunchy dessert or hors'dourves, a healthy set of teeth is more than just a convenience. And like cars, shoes, furniture, homes – an endless list of comparisons - if one wants them to last, she has to take good care of them, sometimes embracing the anxiety, the sounds, the pains, and yes, sometimes even the "humiliation" of good cleaning and care.

Surprise, surprise! Much the same can be said about the care of our spiritual lives. We would like to believe that a healthy spiritual life is as simple and easy as twice-a-day brushing of one's teeth. But sometimes, our best intentions crack, decay or fall away, and we find ourselves in need of more than just our own expert guidance. Such occasions are not easy and are laden with anxiety, but if we open wide our hearts, God can provide some master care.

God of Care and Empathy, these bodies that house our spirits are neither indestructible nor infinite in their capacity to endure the wear and tear of daily life. Sometimes we need a little preventative care to maintain proper health. Spiritually, I may need some "doctoring" from time to time as well, someone or something to come along and pick, probe and polish my best efforts. As I often agonized over trips to the dentist as a child, and even now as an adult, so too I can be excessively sensitive to the spiritual challenges that I must embrace. Help me to never cease brushing up on my spiritual practices, so as to avoid the cavities of spiritual decay.

August 12
Life Can Bite Too

When I felt its teeth clamp down just behind my right hip and sink into the fleshy part of my butt, I invoked a name for God in a less than prayerful fashion with a scream full of shock and a hint of terror. The initial trauma seemed to arise as much from the surprise of the attack as it did from the pain of the bite. Caught so unaware, my alarmed reaction seemed to frighten even the dog itself away from me and back to its owner. One moment I was enjoying a taxing run through a hilly and wooded Pennsylvania backcountry road on a beautiful late summer afternoon, and the next moment I am gripping my backside in horrified alarm.

In all my years of running – over thirty now – an enjoyable jaunt down a country road has always carried with it a certain element of concern for loose dogs all too willing to protect not just their owners' land, but *all* the space adjacent to it. I have had numerous close encounters with aggressive canines before, and have learned a few ways to appease their apparent hostility. Step one: don't be afraid – or, if you must (and when it's a large dog, how can one not be!), try your darnedest not to show your fear. Step two: stop running, turn and address the dog with authority and a sense of assurance that you are not afraid of it and intend to be in control of the situation and the dog. Step three: depending on the size and appearance of the dog, playfully "visit" with it and command it to return from whence it came (I sometimes enjoy saying all kinds of nasty things to it at this point but in a kind and playful tone assuming that it has not yet mastered the English language.). Step four: start jogging again, at first backwards, then sidestepping and finally, if the dog seems satisfied with the façade, turn and resume your run. Another, and less "confrontational" response I have adapted, is simply to keep running altogether, but again pulling the reins back a bit so as not to appear fearful. This tactic lets the dog think it has done its "protective duty" and while it yaps away nearby it lets me pass through. Unfortunately, this latter technique is the one I assumed when after passing the Pennsylvania country residence without hearing a sound or seeing any evidence of a dog, I suddenly heard a single bark from behind me and then sensed a dog coming my way.

Sometimes we get lulled into believing that we have all of our "safety bases" covered. Awareness – check. Fear under control – check. Danger thwarting tactics – check. And then, BAM – we get bit anyway! At such a moment, one more "base" must be employed, and that is, how will I respond if all of the previous bases fail? In the spiritual life, this last one is, perhaps, the most important of all because despite all of our best intentions and preparations, in life we are not in control of anything but our response to life. And if I want to live, predominantly at least, in a place of peace and contentment, then I must learn to control my responses to the bites that we inevitably run into in life far better than some back country Pennsylvanian dog owner did with his pet that rear-end-forsaken-day I went for a run past his property.

Healing God, despite my best purpose and precautionary measures, a healthful run down the road of life can still sometimes bring injury and sudden alarm. I doubt that I can ever be fully prepared for what happens to me in life, but I do seek to willingly accept and deal with the shocking attacks that will inevitably happen, in ways that do not betray who I am nor undermine the relationships I strive to build with all people, places, and things. Most physical wounds will heal; protect me from the deepest bites, and keep me infection free from a poisonous response to the gnawing challenges and the sudden attacks in life.

August 13
The Cliffs

When I was in my teens, there was a very special hangout that my friends and I would frequent, and occasionally I used to retreat there on my own as well. The place was known as "the cliffs," although the cliffs themselves were not actually rock, but a towering clay embankment; the drop off from the dangerous edge to the ox bow turn in the river below had to have been at least fifty feet. A side trail descended from the rim above and then branched off into other trails below; when the water level was low, one could ford the river and then wend his way through the woods on the opposite side. Most of the time, however, we spent our afternoons and the occasional night sitting on the rim gazing to the winding river below, dreaming of the way this might have looked centuries before.

One summer week, after a massive rainstorm had swept through the area, word got around that a portion of the cliffs had collapsed. With the news, a couple of friends and I made quick tracks to get out and survey the damages. After taking the long dirt field access road to the back portion of a farmer's field where the land gave way to our adventurous fantasy land, we parked the car and raced to the cliff's edge. Just as reported, indeed, a central portion of the clay structure had eroded, and then a massive wall had simply slid down into the river below. While this collapse was impressive, what we saw happening to the river below was equally stunning. Rather than being damned up or temporarily stymied by the new pile of earth that could have consumed the river flow, the river had forced itself into the woods and was already carving a new and crooked bed through what had been the opposite bank.

The cliffs never had quite the same appeal after this collapse and our visits there decreased along with the increased presence of encroaching real estate development. No longer the harrowing drop off, the cliffs were now more of a steep but sloping approach to the river. The course of the river too was never the same; once a meandering horseshoe at the base of the cliffs, it now carved a jagged and abrupt turn into the woods and then back out again. Homes now ride the edge where we spent endless summer days, and I wonder if anyone today, looking off their back deck, imagines what this place was like hundreds of years ago - or maybe just thirty to forty, as we once knew it.

Very few of the places of our childhood memories are what they once were. Everything changes, and sometimes we even get to see the changes before our very eyes. Nature shows us how to change. When shifts occur on the earth and things change, nature moves with the change. Clay cliffs cave in and become a steep slope; a riverbed is momentarily impeded and then carves a new course of action to continue its steady flow to wherever it is going. It does not look back and groan over what was nor live in a past dreaming of what used to be. The shift occurs, and it adjusts.

O Timeless God of the changing universe, so much of my life is often spent resisting and fighting the inevitable changes that happen around me with frequency. Help me to look to the earth and its many natural inhabitants to see how I might better receive and accept change. Like so many of the shifts in my life, I cannot stop a cliff from falling into a river, but I can learn from the cliff and the river about how to embrace and to adjust to changes. They take on a new shape and carve out a new direction and keep moving. When changes come my way, help me, God, to embrace my new shape, carve out my new direction, and to keep flowing to wherever it is you would have me go.

August 14
Sacred Responsibility

Years ago I made something of a small pilgrimage to the Traverse des Sioux Treaty site in St. Peter, Minnesota, to prayer for and with my Native ancestors. My hometown, Mankato, is just twelve miles upriver of St. Peter and holds the infamous claim of being the site of the United States' largest mass execution when thirty-eight Dakota Sioux men were hung on December 26, 1862. This execution, technically, marked the end of a decade old United States-Dakota War that had sprung from the heels of the broken treaty of Traverse des Sioux. As almost always happened with every U.S.-Indian treaty, at Traverse des Sioux the Indians gave up way more than what they were to have received in the bargain, and then, the bargain was never upheld anyway.

While visiting the historical memorial site of the Treaty, I sat down amongst the native prairie grasses to pray with my personal *chinoopa*, the sacred pipe. It was a hot, late summer afternoon, and I had shared the space with no one except the spirits of the betrayed ones who I had invoked to join me in prayer, and the many mosquitoes that I had apparently rustled up from the tall grasses. Just as I was finishing my prayer, a young couple that had recently arrived to walk the trails of the grounds spotted me, and as they walked by the young man respectfully said to me, "You have quite a responsibility there." Still absorbed in the intentions of my prayer, I looked up at him with some confusion, not sure I had heard clearly what he said nor what he meant. Repeating himself, he nodded simply to the pipe that I now cradled in my arm. Almost with embarrassment, I affirmed his observation, and then fell into the pool of his simple insight.

In the Native tradition, the sacred pipe is a living thing, and one develops a very personal relationship with his personal pipe. Proper care and handling of the pipe is as necessary and expected as the care and handling of one's child, and praying with a pipe is an act of deep and desirous devotion. I certainly knew these things that day when I purposefully made my pilgrimage to that broken Treaty site to pray, but this passing stranger called me more consciously into the truth of my presence there. Fundamentally, as a carrier of a personal pipe, I had an obvious responsibility to it; but further, sharing an unknown and yet palpable connection with these forsaken ancestors, my intention to pray for and with them was not just an isolated moment, but carried with it an ongoing responsibility. For to truly pray for someone or something means that you take whatever the need is into your heart, and like my pipe that I cradled that day, you hold it carefully and tenderly. Furthermore, you take the need of the prayer with you even after you have finished your prayer. If, for example, I pray for peace, then I must live and be peace as well; that is my responsibility.

Sometimes I allow even the sacred to become mundane. I may know in my head the specialness of a sacred object or the importance of my prayer, but I may not always carry that knowledge as honorably in my heart. Sacred God, keep me mindful of all that I do, and especially of the sacred nature of so much of what I do. The sacred is all around me, and my daily life can be a living prayer; help me to remember my responsibility to all that is around me and to all that I am.

August 15
Dandelion Bouquet

Teaching young immigrant children the English language and other essential educational needs, my wife arrived home from school one day with a special gift from one of her Somali students. As she lifted the sandwich bag from her backpack-briefcase, she revealed what appeared to be some kind of chocolate-looking cookie or cake. A bit smashed even at its offering, the edible gift was the young boy's humble offering, a cultural delicacy he had brought her especially from his home. Despite the gift's tousled appearance, the young boy was, to be sure, proud of his offering, and my wife was equally honored by its giving, even though she didn't seem to rush into tasting it. I couldn't help seeing in the simple generosity the handfuls of dandelions I received from my own children when they were growing up.

Most of us have likely been on the receiving – and the giving – end of a dandelion bouquet. Almost innately, at least as children, we are captivated every spring by the shining yellow face of the flowering weed, and learning – or also knowing intuitively – that the common gift of flowers almost always has an uncommonly warm reception, we pluck the simple blossoms and offer our bouquet proudly. It is for many, perhaps, one of the first lessons in the art of giving, the realization that *what* we give is often not half so important as *why* we give. Indeed, we all love to receive gifts, but we seem to learn quickly and heartily that giving perhaps provides an even more sublime joy.

A gift conceived and given from the heart, no matter what its pragmatic or tangible value might be, takes on a kind of divine sheen. Whenever a person truly and selflessly gives of himself and his own time, the extended gift goes beyond the recipient, touching the heart of God as well. Native people honor this truth when they exclaim to the cook of both an extravagant or a humble ceremonial meal "that this food sure has lots of good feelings in it." Practitioners of karma yoga know this too when they cheerfully and diligently offer even the most menial of tasks as an effort given of love. And Jesus reminded his followers that "whatever you do for the least of these," is done for God as well. To let go of my own needs and to pause for another – be it to hold open a door, to pick up someone's dropped item, to listen attentively to another's concerns, or simply to offer a bouquet of dandelions or a well-intentioned, even if a little rough, dessert – is an act of love that reaches beyond the receiver to the Divine One who is love.

Giving God, you have loved the universe and each one of us into life, and then you invite us to be participants in as well as receivers of your universal love. Your proffered love, shining like the sunny face of the dandelion and spreading out like the flower's dried seedlings floating in the wind, is often in our hands. Sometimes I forget that my reflection of your love does not need to mirror your infinite generosity. What matters most is what is at the heart of my giving, my sharing, and my loving. The simplest of gifts, the most meager of gestures, and the most plain words can be gift and food and love enough when they come to us from a selfless and gentle heart. Let me joyfully receive the broken but care-filled cookies that might be offered to me this day, and help me to empty my hands of my own busyness so that I might pluck a few dandelions and offer someone in need a genuine bouquet of love.

August 16
Paddling through the Lifeblood

Kayaking is a small, hobby-like outlet for me, and while central Ohio is not exactly a mecca for such activity, the numerous rivers and river-like creeks that course their way through the state have always intrigued me. So when I resigned from my teaching career, I bought myself a cheap and simple recreational kayak as a "retirement gift" and looked forward to an occasional water adventure exploring these often hidden tributaries.

On a recent paddle down Alum Creek, a key waterway through the heart of Columbus' eastside, I was rather disheartened by the amount of garbage and, perhaps, even illegal dumping I encountered. Inquisitive blue jays and perturbed blue herons graced the banks and shallow waters, while various ducks and fish life swam above and below the deeper water. Amidst the beauty of this quiet urban flow, however, were many pockets of intentionally dumped refuse along with assorted rubbish that had drifted into the creek through any number of storm sewers and smaller run-off creeks. Juxtaposing my personal interest and desire to explore these channels with the truth of what I was encountering, it suddenly struck me how all such waterways are like the circulatory system of our earth's body. The parallels are so obvious that I quickly assumed my analogy was certainly not a new discovery, but I floated the idea further, just as resolutely as the kayak itself.

Like the blood in our own bodies, water is the life source for nearly everything around us, while streams, creeks, and rivers are the essential veins and arteries of our Mother Earth's circulatory system. When we are not feeling well or something appears significantly wrong with our bodies, frequently blood is drawn and analyzed in order to see what the problem is. If the blood isn't right, then the body isn't healthy, and vice versa. The blood stream often knows and can reveal some of our less than healthful behaviors, and eating and drinking habits. And so do the arteries that move water from one place to another across our varied landscapes. Clean water and thriving wildlife in and around these waterways show a healthy relationship between our Mother and her inhabitants. Abnormally tainted water and garbage-strewn shorelines reveal a disrespectful and careless attitude for the very source of everything that gives us life. And just as when we are imprudent or reckless with our own bodies and must suffer consequences, so when we are insolent with the earth and its lifeblood, water, we will inevitably pay a severe price.

Life-Sustaining God, you have created an unavoidable link between humans and our Mother earth; we cannot survive without all that she provides, most especially clean and healthy water. Help me to recognize this bond, and to seek out ways of living more healthfully within my own body as well as the body I live upon, the Earth. Water is an essential life source for us all, and its tributaries are the essential arteries and veins through which this life flows. As I paddle down the river of life, may I work to respectfully maintain healthy channels from which life can flow.

August 17
Compassionate Forgiveness

If love were easy, the world would surely be a different and even better place, but life is full of attempts and errors that pull hard on love's grasp, and it seems that we spend a lifetime trying to get it right. Through various small failures, we often embarrass ourselves while causing thin hairline fractures in our love relationships. Other times, the infractions are more severe, and in the anguish of the fracture, love loses its grip and slips away. Indeed, a strong and lasting love takes a tremendous amount of compassionate forgiveness.

Over my lifetime, I have had ample opportunities to experience both sides of forgiveness, the giver and the receiver, and neither is an enviable position. Knowing one side, however, certainly informs the other, and in this way, real forgiveness can become compassionate. With the ardor and the zeal of passion, compassionate forgiveness meets the penitent beloved on an empathetic common ground. The pardoner stands with an open door of hope and does not talk through the screen of derision; perhaps he even dares to invite the remorseful one in.

My first wife and I divorced after seventeen years of marriage. It was not as though we had sixteen years of bliss and then misery and despair crept in one night, nor was it by any means seventeen years of hell, and finally it was over; like most marriages, we had our peaks and valleys, and neither of us could claim total innocence in the errors that would eventually lead to the end of our marriage. But after sharing my life that closely, that intimately with one person for seventeen years, and then losing it all, I was forced to do some real soul searching on the nature of my failures as well as some deep introspection on the nature of compassionate forgiveness. Through it all, I would dare to say that the partners of a dissolved marriage that once knew love, if they are truly honest with themselves, will face one of the most emotionally difficult and painful resolutions of their lives. If the love was strong enough, the marriage, perhaps, might have survived; but when it doesn't, is there love enough to offer one another the compassionate forgiveness that will allow each other the grace to move on in the happiness of real absolution? In these thoughts today, I offer a prayer for all separated and divorced couples who struggle yet to forgive one another, granting each other the happiness that we all seek.

Compassionate God, how many times have I offended a stranger, a friend, and a dear loved one and have needed to seek forgiveness; and how often have one of these caused me emotional wounds and have sought my forgiveness? We are such flawed and fragile creatures who do no end of disservice to the one who created us through our measly self-interested actions and our miserly willingness to forgive others for theirs. Through my own errors, grant me the grace to be a person of compassionate forgiveness and teach me the art of living in love: to be a better friend, a better spouse, and a better human being.

August 18
Skydiving into Faith: the Freefall

When the door to the small Cessna plane sprung open, the instructor, seated on the floor behind me, gave me a little nudge. "Look out the door!" he shouted into the blast of rushing air. It was a sea of space – clear, amorphous air with the earth as its floor, ten thousand feet below. I had been wanting to experience a skydive for decades, and here I was now, the door yawning open and inviting me to leap out into the expansive space. It was not exactly fear that gripped me then; more acutely aware than ever of the daunting nature of my endeavor, I seemed to awaken more to the apparent "craziness" of the desire. And when the instructor said, "Okay, step out onto the platform," a small ledge *outside* of the plane below the wing, I knew for sure, "This is nuts!"

It was a tandem jump, a first-time experience where a skilled jumper was clipped in and tethered very tightly to my back; although I would initiate various steps, my instructor-guide literally "had my back." Still, there was the sensation of being on my own. Although I could certainly feel the weight - even the breathing of my partner, so tightly were we attached - he was unseen, and I was the one advancing each step. Crouching, with my hands firmly gripping the doorframe, I stretched my right leg out the doorway's opening and planted my foot onto the square foot platform just above the plane's right wheel. Then, shifting my hands to the angled strut of the wing outside of the plane, I stepped fully out the door and planted myself – and the instructor I was assuming – firmly on the platform. The blast of wind on my goggled face was incredible, although I was shocked to find how steady I felt on this ledge; but when my instructor shouted from behind me - "Okay, I've got it. You can let go now!" –the rushing wind became thick and heavy with a nervous fear. Swaying to the right and to the left, he counted out "One, two, three" and then we leapt away from the plane whose sight and sound seemed to vanish within a second. All I remember then is that I forgot everything. In a sudden freefall in excess of 120 miles per hour, the force and sound of the wind is incomprehensible to the beginner; I have no idea how we were falling or in what direction or directions I was facing or spinning. I have no palpable correlation to the sensation of such a hurling through space. Perhaps twenty seconds into our free fall, I felt my instructor grab my arms, and then his legs kick at mine and it was then that I remembered more fully what I was supposed to be doing, and I quickly arched my back, extending my arms and curling my legs backwards. I could feel the flesh on my face almost flapping, being stretched into contorted visages, and I fought for breaths in between exhilarating screams and shouts. I remember wondering how long this intense freefall would continue and whether or not I could keep up with its power and force. And then, with my instructor's signal, I reached down, grabbed the ripcord's handle, and giving it a pull, all was silence and calm.

My first skydiving experience was an incredible mixture of apprehension and exhilaration, a sensory overload of stimulation. Reflecting on it days later, however, it occurred to me how this leap was not my first dive into such apparently contrasting emotions. Faith itself, and life in general quite frankly, are very often skydiving experiences. I may long for a more intense encounter with God, but when the door flies open and I am face to face with the power and energy of the Creator, my desires no longer seem unflappable. I stepped out onto a ledge with a guide knowingly strapped tightly to my back, but in faith, the assurance of that guide is not so firmly tethered to my consciousness. And falling away from safe footing, I can so quickly lose my sense of direction and forget what it is that I could and should be doing. Faith challenges me to trust in the Guide that "has my back."

God of Support and Guidance, sometimes through my choices and actions, I find myself freefalling through life unable to find direction and even gasping for the very air to keep going. Perhaps I have taken a leap of faith counting on your assistance, or maybe I find myself tumbling through an unexpected experience, questioning and grasping for the handles that faith can sometimes provide. As is necessary, take hold of my hands, give my legs a little kick, and whisper – or shout! – to me reassuringly, "Okay, I've got it. You can let go now!"

Understandably, the greatest fear for someone considering skydiving is "what if the chute doesn't open, and I fall to my death?" It is a possibility, of course, just as surely as every time one slides behind the wheel of an automobile an accident awaits him at the end of the driveway. The "chance," in both occasions is clearly there, but the percentages *are* quite low. I remember my instructor jokingly saying to me as we reviewed the skydiving procedures of stepping out of the plane and positioning ourselves, "The worst thing that could happen is that we will fall, but we are going to jump anyway, so falling is really not a problem!" It's the truth; most of the time our worst fears are grounded in concerns that, while real, have very little actual potential of occurring or, if they happen, the results are often far less catastrophic than we imagine. Still, lingering doubts shrunk the footing of the platform outside of my plane to the size of a postage stamp, while my need to grip tightly the plane's structure swelled. But letting go, and freefalling into the depths of my doubts, I was swallowed by the overwhelming sensations of the speed of the fall, the violent rush of the wind, and my absolute sense of disorientation. Immediately and wholly, there was nothing for which to grab and I discovered a new layer concerning the truth of life that we are not in control.

When my instructor's hands waving back and forth suddenly appeared before my face, however, I remembered his counsel, and I reached down to my waist, felt the ripcord's handle and gave it a tug. In an instant, all the commotion ceased, and my world drifted into an immense peace. With the winged-canopy open above us, the incredulous sensory rush was immediately swallowed by an equally powerful, though antithetical sense of quietude. Although we were still surely drifting towards the earth at a relatively fast rate, the chute of safety erased the noise and the mayhem of the freefall, and I now rested comfortably in the wonder of my airy environment; all fears were as calm as the soft float in which I was now suspended.

To be sure, not all "leaps of faith" have such extremes of hysteria and then calm, but the message of faith does assure us that in letting go, in discovering that we are not truly in control, that we will encounter in the Universe of things that we are embraced, that we are supported, that we are safe in the arms of the Creator's loving energy. With each daring step into the unknown, the amorphous expanse of a life lived in faith, there will inevitably be doubts, but like an experienced skydiver, the repetition of steps no doubt provides a reassurance that the contents on one's back – the depth of faith known in one's heart – will blossom into a supportive and bright canopy above one's head.

Supportive God, while I carry the belief of your advocacy of my life like a parachute packed on my back, and I feel your presence as assuredly as that bright orange ripcord handle, I still faithfully leap into life full of fears and doubts. As I tumble through apparent freefalls, buoy me with the confident comfort of your loving support. To pull the ripcord while standing on firm ground is a waste of the packaging; invite me, encourage me to fall into the unknown where I will more fully discover the canopy of your loving embrace.

August 20
Skydiving into Faith: the Landing

Even when the canopy opens and we realize that we are not entirely out of control nor are we alone in the midst of our freefalls in life, doubts and confusion still seem to be part of the tethering lines between ourselves and the safety chute above us. It is only when our feet are resting again on "terra firma" that we believe we are truly "safe." How ironic all of these "illusions" are.

Near the end of Tom Stoppard's play, *Rosencrantz and Guildenstern are Dead*, Ros notes that "Life is a gamble, at terrible odds – if it was a bet you wouldn't take it." In fact, the play's entirely existential theme underscores a truth about the randomness and happenchance of all of our lives. Peering out of the open plane door and then stepping onto a diminutive step outside of it while ten thousand feet in the air can provide understandable fear; letting go of the plane wing's strut and aimlessly freefalling can be fear made manifest; and feeling the supportive grasp of the parachute's blossoming above provides a realization of the sense of support that we can know through even our worst travails. But each stage of the fall always seems accompanied by some level of doubt, disbelief or trepidation. We all want the supportive assurance of "solid ground," as if all will be well and no fears will reside.

On my first skydive, somewhere between five and two thousand feet in the air, my tandem instructor and I practiced our landing. Pulling on both handles of the steering ropes and lifting our legs up and out, we swung into an upward glide, the maneuver he insisted upon for our safe landing. While the canopy overhead assured us that we would not come crashing to the ground, there was still more work to be done to soften further our reentry onto the terrain of familiarity and apparent safety. Our reckless plummet abated and our slow descent afforded by the canopy's grace-filled opening, I danced in a kind of weightless joy and gratitude as we twirled and carved arcs in the open air all around us as the reality of the landing drew closer. With aided steering toward our earthly target, I readied myself for the final crunching blow; but, just as instructed, pulling down on the ropes and lifting our legs up and out, we skidded to a harmless landing. Now back on terra firma, all would be fine, no?

O God of the Falling and the Catching and the Standing Still, it is so easy, natural even, for me to be moved to great fear in the unknown, to be enamored to reassurance by supportive intervention, and to be blindly captivated to comfort by the sense of solid ground. Some stages of my life present obvious challenges and create understandable tension, but all phases of my life are forever fraught with potential enigmas and their accompanying stress and strain. Be at my back, beside me, above and beneath me – Great God, be all around me in every movement of my life, not to prevent me from experiencing life, but to enable me

266

to more fully engage in the experience without being overwhelmed by my fears and my concerns about the falling, the catching and the crashing to the ground.

August 21
Distracted Listening

To pray and to work at my best and most focused levels, I need a very quiet and often private space; subsequently, when at home, I frequently retreat to my back porch for prayer time and seek its refuge for other reflective activities as well, such as writing or just sitting and thinking. Most of the time, with its border of flowers and bushes, I feel adequately secluded and encased in the solitude I seek. But sometimes, the bubble of my quietude gets popped when neighbors decide to mow their lawns, or daytime traffic on the side street strangely increases, or the local airport's flight patterns have planes flying overheard periodically. When these sound intrusions wreak havoc on my concentration, I often think of what the world would have been like prior to all of these unnatural noises that we have created. How much easier it must have been one hundred and more years ago for people to find privacy and a quiet space for prayer.

While the noise pollution all about me is often a significant distraction to my concentration and meditative needs, I find that my other senses too are often barraged with a variety of unhealthy distractions. "It's easier 'to sin' today," I used to tell my students sympathetically, "to make choices that are less than kind and 'good,' because we so easily *can*." Anonymously saying hurtful and denigrating comments about someone is far more easily and "effectively" done today through various social networks, from email to Facebook. Reading and viewing and participating in activities that are simply detrimental to our spiritual well-being are also far more easily accessible today through our Internet access. And while an exercise-induced walk, hike or run might have provided a person with some private time for thought, again, a set of headphones plugged into our iPod, Bluetooth or some other cell phone connection probably keeps the depths of our thoughts in shallow waters at best, and on dry, parched land at worst. "I can't help thinking," I would conclude to those same students, "that people in the past simply did less 'evil' because they had less access to it."

Through the incredible conveniences and accessibilities of our modern life, the world is "smaller." But this availability also makes our world more cluttered with various pollutions that so easily attract and distract our "sense-abilities." One can make a prayerful effort anywhere, and a person can use any space and time to pause for thoughtful reflection, but I am certain that the quality of both my prayers and my thoughts is greatly enhanced or reduced by the nature of the environment within which I pray and think. One can learn to desensitize himself from the noise and other sense-pollutions, ignoring or overlooking them, but at what cost will that be then to those things that we *should* hear and see?

We hear each other, ourselves, and our God more clearly when we have less distractions around us. Places of worship are typically designed to create a sacred space wherein I can go within and quietly sit before and with the one who lives out and inside of me. I can sort through my own thoughts, and can listen more attentively to the gentle voice of the Spirit when I provide them a quiet space within which they can be heard. God of Stillness, I believe you have words for me to hear, and longings for me to carefully consider. Mindful of my need for uninterrupted intermissions of silence to better hear my own heart and you, I ask your assistance in helping me to find and to create some space where I can more faithfully meet with you.

August 22
An Ocean of Awareness

While on a rather exotic retreat one winter in the Bahamas, I took advantage of an offer one afternoon to go snorkeling off the edge of a reef some miles out from where I was retreating. Although large bodies of water have always been something of an Achilles' heel to my personal fear factor, I had always wanted to at least have the most simple opportunity to explore the underwater world. So I quickly seized my chance, paid my fee, and boarded the boat heading out toward a distant ocean island.

The proprietor of the boat knew just where the diving might be most satisfying for his patrons, all novice snorkelers with shallow pockets to afford the best experience. Reaching our destination, he supplied us with the essential equipment although he failed to provide any explanation or example of how to use it most effectively. Given the minimal cost, however, I accepted the shortcomings of the excursion, donned the gear and excitedly dove into my longtime desire.

I have, of course, watched many nature programs and documentaries on ocean life and the world beneath the water's surface, and these exhibits were far more exotic than anything I experienced, but that doesn't mean that my experience was anything less than fascinating and marvelous. In crystal clear ocean waters no more than ten feet deep, I drifted as if suspended in outer space in a world unlike any I had ever encountered. Schools of fish bedazzled in vibrant yellow, iridescent blue, shimmering green and cosmic orange swam all about me, fearlessly welcoming me to their world with inquisitive proximity. Sea urchins, sponges and fans swayed gently back and forth in the unseen rhythm of the ocean's flow like delicate seductresses, and beneath the water, all sounds muffled and silenced, there was a quietude of deep holiness.

To dive into and to experience such an unusual and astonishing world, even as briefly as I did that day, is to taste, even if only a sip, the incredible wonder of the universe, the expansive and unknown realities of life. Land-locked in our little private worlds, we humans fool ourselves into thinking that we understand and know so much. But beneath the water that covers more than half of our planet there is an entirely different and amazing world of which we know so little. And what might be the ocean of our spiritual lives? Religions, perhaps, provide detailed maps of the landscapes of spirituality, but what of the oceans that surround them? How much more might we experience and know beyond what we have already been given? Just when I think I have God's terrain and my spirituality figured out, I stumble upon the vast ocean and discover that I know so little.

Creator God, your wonders stretch from the furthest reaches of outer space to the depths of the ocean floor, and, I am led to believe, well beyond even these nearly infinite boundaries. In awe and wonder of my own little world, experiencing it as something magnificent and vast, I fall into an ocean of otherness. Who am I to even dream that I might know and understand you, and yet, I believe that you do call me into your presence, invite me to dive into the ocean of your being. May my brief underwater excursion bring humility to what "I know," and enticement for what could be known. Today, I once again put on my meager equipment and dive in!

August 23
An Ant's Eye View

Rather than taking a dive into the coral reef waters just off some Bahaman island, a far less extravagant way to gain some perspective on our place in the universe is to sit and watch a colony of ants. Henry David Thoreau once famously recorded his fascinated and rare observation of black and red ants at war with one another in his "The Battle of the Ants," but for a more spiritual comparison, I would steer you towards their more mundane daily life. I find it interesting that no matter where I go, I almost always encounter some manner of ant activity. It is a simple testament to their adaptability, and in this way one might begin an analogous comparison between ants and the towering two-legged giants that must frequently disrupt the industrious flow of their lives.

Finding a colony, be it a small, indistinct gathering or some large mound incredulously occupying a small circle of space teeming with ant activity in a woodland or field, sit quietly by and watch. As you observe their ceaseless movements, the trekking back and forth, their descent and reemergence from the city-mound, you cannot help but be drawn to wonder what it is that they are so busy about. Whatever your answer, you will have to agree, however, that there is an apparent design to their activity; there is intention, focus and resolve here. If you try to experimentally thwart the activity of this or that one, it will respond to the sudden challenge, remove it or move around it, and then return to its previous task. Given this resolve, you can easily begin to imagine with just a little bit of creative, personified spice, that there is tremendous commerce at work every day quietly beneath our feet. Then, try to envision what the world looks like from the perspective of these amazingly assiduous and persevering six-legged creatures. While they appear to cover much ground, their sphere of reference is no more than two hundred meters from their nest, and this only in the most foraging of their species; thus, for most, the perimeters of their "universe" extend no more than a football field. And if they had the eyesight of a human being, what must we two-legged and all other creatures appear to be, and how threatening!

Now, allow yourself to imagine that the universe as we know it, is nothing more than the "universe of the ants," that the far reaches that we know and imagine are, relatively speaking, not much different than those of the ant. In other words, we know nothing, or to be sure, very little of what truly is. And yet, like the ant who fearlessly bites at me when I ignorantly set my bum in its territory, we fiercely defend all that "we know" and often attack those who might have us consider otherwise.

The intention of my analogy is not to question all that we know nor to render what we do and what we believe as inconsequential. Like ants, there is an amazing design and a valuable attentiveness about much of what we humans do. But like the "ant universe," there is, perhaps, so much more outside the sphere of our "known reality" – universes more! And it is here that I implore a deeper attentiveness to the spiritual realm. Humans can be so assuredly fixed on things temporal and on the scientifically identifiable that they fail to admit into the land of possibilities a spiritual realm that would reduce our knowledge and understanding to the size of an ant.

Cosmic Creator, I am humbled and honored to say that I belong to the universe of things. To see my life and the world from the ant's perspective does not make me meaningless, but rather, your love for us all the more magnificent. That I, but an ant in the universe of things, can be in relationship with you is more overwhelming and wondrous than even the universe itself. Allow me to ascend, ant-like, my simple mound of diligence and bow humbly before you.

August 24
An Ultimate Gift

Over a decade ago, a young, local bicycle enthusiast was riding his two-wheeler down a country road when he was unexpectedly clipped from behind by a passing van. Tossed from his bicycle into the ditch, Andy died alone, and with no witnesses to testify against the accidental crime. To this day, the hit-and-run driver has never been indentified.

One of Andy's best friends was a former student-athlete of mine. The two young men had met years before Andy's tragic death while playing Ultimate Frisbee on opposing teams in the collegiate club sport leagues throughout Ohio. From what I can tell, they not only shared a love of Ultimate Frisbee, but each also possessed a magnetic spiritual gift. Their kind, upbeat and humorous personalities floated about like a lazily tossed disc, and people naturally leapt and latched onto each of them. When Andy died, his friend, my former student, was devastated and his faith in a benign and loving God was tossed into the ditch as recklessly as the accident's victim.

A couple of years after Andy's death, his friend, in some collaboration with Andy's parents, organized an ongoing memorial fundraising event in honor of Andy. Ultimate teams from all around the state of Ohio and some beyond its borders convene on a patch of Ohio State University playing fields and playfully compete for twenty-four straight hours. Hosting this marathon of Ultimate play, Andy's friend has provided monies for a variety of nonprofit organizations working on behalf of young boys and girls for well over ten years now. Beyond the fund raising, however, the greater gift of this event is how it has kept the spirit of Andy alive.

The vast majority of those who participate in this memorial today never knew Andy, and many likely don't even know his story; in this way, the event is no longer even about Andy, but about the gift of his spirit. Through the heartfelt efforts of a friend, Andy's magnetism somehow continues to descend upon the playing fields and transcend the tragedy of his death. Whether they knew Andy or not, hundreds of Ultimate players come together each year, choosing to sacrifice time, energy, money and sleep; and, in doing so, they not only have a tremendous amount of fun but they also recreate and revitalize the spirit of a young man who brought much joy and laughter to many people years before. And as for my former student's crippled faith: could his dedicated and selfless efforts more exemplify a love for life and the spirit of faith in action?

Lord of Life, too often the lives of dear and energetic loved ones are snatched from us too soon. In the face of our losses, we are often left speechless, answerless, and even, faithless. The reasons for Andy's death are as enigmatic as the perpetrator of his crime; and yet, somehow, grace flows from his tragedy. For all of us who have suffered and who suffer the loss of a loved one, I offer a prayer of comforting peace, of resolution; but in our mourning, help us to also seize upon the gifts of our late-beloveds, to pedal their energy throughout our world and to let the grace of their lives fall softly upon us, like a hundred drifting discs descending gently to the earth.

August 25
Humidity

Where I live, humidity is frequently one of the most common weather challenges. We don't have many ninety-degree days, and even less reach one hundred or more, but our humidity often runs quite high and a humid day can absolutely zap one's energy. When I was teaching in a room with no air conditioning to lighten the weight of the humidity, everything felt damp; paperwork curled, clothes were wet and sticky with inevitable perspiration, and the students' attention seemed to slog to a mired pace. And like a bad joke, although the week or two before the school year's commencement might be filled with beautiful late summer days, just the right temperature and low humidity, on the first week of school, like clockwork - BAM! - the humidity would jump and we all would melt.

But while humidity zaps us of energy and leaves us feeling lethargic and wet, it also provides some very beautiful things. The damp night air condenses, and in the morning, the grass is softened and glistens with a thick dew. Crispy, dry lawns are afforded an early morning sip, and colorful, autumnal flower gardens linger at summer's closing door. And sunrises and sunsets...ah! With horizons curtained in the humidity's haze, skylines become a palate of deep and rich colors in the sun's new or fading light, and should thin clouds join the parade of light, the effect is positively ethereal.

So many of the events and experiences of our lives need to be seen through this yin-yang like lens. Melting under humidity's thick, oppressive blanket, I can so easily miss the beautiful colors of its fabric. Rather than concentrating only on the difficulty and the turmoil of the struggles that inevitably dampen the air of our lives, we need to look up and out and in at what graces these challenges might also provide. When the humidity of life beats us down, we need to raise our heads and see the wonder that is still around, in fact, around because of what we endure.

Loving God, I want life to be comfortable and easy, and sometimes it is! But when I grow weary of the weight of it challenges, when the air seems too thick with life's pressures, I often lose sight of the gifts of life that are ever before me. Help me to look up and to look out and to see the colorful beauty of your blessings even through the thick haze of my discontent.

August 26
The Dark Night of the Soul

Ten years after the death of one of the most highly recognized "Saints" of the modern era, Mother Teresa of Calcutta, a book that consists primarily of a series of more than forty letters written by her to her confessors and superiors over a sixty-six year period was published by one of those confidantes. Upon its release, the book created quite a stir both among the faithful as well as the faithless, for throughout the correspondences one cannot help but be shocked by her almost overwhelming "dark night of the soul." In Mother Teresa's words, this "night" lasted for some part or all of that sixty-six year period.

A "dark night of the soul," a label first used by the Christian mystic, St. John of the Cross, refers to a time when one's spiritual life is so challenged by loneliness and a sense of abandonment that one's very faith, it would seem, is put to question. Such periods of doubt are not unusual in the lives of saints and mystics, and I would dare say, they are even more common in the spiritual lives of ordinary people like you and me. In a life of consistent service and prayer as we imagine of Mother Teresa and John of the Cross, one can certainly conceive that periods of austere desolation and despair would naturally creep into the view of their work and commitments. How much more so with us who are less dedicated and less consistent with our prayerful attention? Living in the world of commerce and socialization as we do, we are constantly bumping up against experiences, attitudes, and beliefs that not only do nothing for our spiritual lives, but worse yet, call our faith into question. If we went about our economic and scientific business the way that we go about faith, in the trust and confidence in something of which we cannot prove, we would quickly be swept away and disregarded.

I have been asked many times, "Why do you believe in God? Why do you have faith in a God?" It is not an unreasonable question, but I can never offer a truly and fully "reasonable" answer. That I cannot prove *anything* in the realm of faith, sometimes, unquestionably, leads me to feel like *everything* is untrue; these are truly my "dark night" moments. And yet, so far, I always emerge from them because of what I have experienced in and through faith. As if in response to those dark nights, I remember where I have been, what I have seen, and how I have felt; and I realize that in my experience of *something, everything* is made possible. The difficulty, of course, is that I cannot "contain" faith; I cannot encapsulate it and hold it up as a specimen for all to see. Faith is, ultimately, very personal, and that fact is both its blessing and its curse.

I have experienced the ecstasy of great joy and pleasure, and I have known the depths of despair wherein I could have willingly taken my own life. Remembering both of these extremes helps me to hang onto the present moment, the goodness of now, even though I cannot offer you or myself an actual encounter with those very feelings and sensations right now. My inability to conjure them now or to make them "real" for you at *any* time does not, however, invalidate the truth of their existence. I will undoubtedly go through more "dark nights" in my lifetime, but I am confident that the "great lights" of my life will see me through to a new dawn.

In the Christian scriptures, in two of the Gospel crucifixion stories of Jesus, the writers record Jesus' "dark night" words from the cross as he essentially quotes a Hebrew Psalm: "My God, my God, why have you forsaken me?" I take great solace in knowing that Jesus, like Teresa and John, and like you and me, knew of the "dark night of the soul." God of Our Darkest Doubts, I have often felt that my faith in you is built upon a very sandy foundation. But when the waves of doubt have rolled in and crashed against the structures of my beliefs carrying away the beach sand, I have discovered beneath me the solid rock of my most mystical and grace-filled experiences. When clouds darken even my most wide open spaces, help me to remember, if not see, the Light that I have known, and bowing humbly within my fears and doubts, await the dawn.

August 27
Soulful Operations

Like many surgeries, an appendectomy, the removal of an infected or inflamed appendix, is a fairly routine operation today. Barring complications, a person can be relieved of appendicitis with little significant harm or invasion to the rest of the body – in and out in no time! When I was a child, such a procedure was not so simple, however.

At eight years old, I had an emergency appendectomy complicated by some internal infection. While today such a procedure is done through laser surgery or entry through the navel, my abdominal incision cut through muscle sheathing and the like and left a significant scar, a kind of lifelong tattoo that runs along my right side; and, instead of an overnight stay at the hospital, I took up a week long residency replete with some therapy to regain movement and encourage healing. Weeks after my release from the hospital, with the doctor's final okay to return to the activities of my childhood, I bolted from the bars of my surgical restrictions and set out to make up for lost time. Heading to a local athletic field and track, I looped around the cinder oval like an accomplished distance runner, and leaped over hurdles and fencing as if I were a storied decathlete. The next day, I was paralyzed by muscle soreness and fatigue.

Advancements in the medical world have something of a false parallel in the "upgrades" of contemporary spiritual exercises. Just as quick and easy fixes have been created in surgical maneuvers, so too have "advanced" methods been proclaimed within spiritual practices. But what works for the body does not necessarily work for the soul. While less invasive and more expeditious operations have been developed for the diseases and maladies of the body, the same is not so easily applied to the operations of the soul. When our spiritual development atrophies or becomes infected through misguided use or neglect, operative healing may only come through "old school" approaches. True, more and "improved" spiritual exercises have been recovered or discovered, but like the medical practices of the "old days," one can't just expect to leap back into the heart of things and expect no residual effect. Just as the body then needed a more gradual and methodical recovery, today, as has always been, the soul needs a careful prodding and a deliberate exercise program.

Many times people want a quick spiritual fix with modern surgical finesse, but injuries and maladies of the soul will always need an old school approach. Indeed, while valuable exercises and practices have been introduced into the "therapy of the heart," these will always need patient and consistent attention.

Healing God, when my spirit has been injuriously damaged and my soul enters into a dark night, I come seeking your therapeutic touch. My desire is for a miraculous spiritual surgery to remove the pain and fear, and for a non-invasive, scar-free approach; but the wounds of the soul run deep and their healing will take time and constancy. Gently nurture me in my times of need, and keep me from rushing head long into hasty forms of recovery. In time, my spirit will dance and play again, but let the slow rhythm of my heart be its tender guide.

August 28
Parental Love

I must have caused my parents a world of misery and concern the spring and summer of my high school graduation year. Engaging in all things athletic, musical and spiritual for most of my high school career, apparently I found it necessary to "make up for lost time" in the teenage and high school party worlds that last year. Skating through school work at a leisurely pace, I dropped out of organized athletics after the fall sports season that final year of high school and landed my first real job in replacement, arguing that I would need money for the following years of college, although there were no specific plans in place at the time as to what or when or where I was going. The truth is, the money that I earned through the job merely supplied me with a more fluid cash flow for drinking and drugs, and little of it was ever saved. The drinking age at the time was eighteen, and while I didn't reach that age until the end of my senior year, accessibility and acceptance of alcohol flowed as freely as the beer itself. My parents, lulled to sleep, perhaps, by my years of healthy involvement and spiritual pursuits, seemed blind to my downturn, or, as I was the youngest of their five children, maybe they were just too tired to worry about what they felt they had already seen before. Having to retrieve me from the police station in the early spring should have been a wake-up call.

Returning in the middle of the night from a big party in the country, I had, to my credit, thoughtfully stopped drinking hours before I drove home. But a carload of teens was probably suspicious enough and after being stopped for purportedly "crossing the center line" the police hauled me downtown. Now of legal age and ultimately "under the limit," I was never charged with any drinking infraction, but clearly something was awry. The summer nights only served to worsen the situation. Closing out bars and walking a very thin line between life and death through mixed consumption, I dangerously stumbled home countless nights rarely confronted by my parents over my new and increasingly bad habits. It was perhaps their loves' "blind spot." Meanwhile, with the college issue hanging in indecision still, I unwisely chose a school in North Carolina, unvisited and nearly fifteen hundred miles from home.

By the end of the summer, our parent-child relationship was antagonistic at best, and I can't help but think that while I must have worried them sick with my exploits, they may given into the college decision just to appease the uneasiness in the home – and perhaps, to have me out of it!

My parents, however, were tremendously supportive and loving to all of their children for all of our shared lives, although in my case, perhaps to a fault. For years I had been a reasonably cooperative son, admirable in my extra-curricular involvements and successes, laudable in my uncharacteristically deep spiritual pursuits. So when I shifted and started to make some bad decisions, they too easily overlooked them, giving me the space and room that I wanted, but not the limitations and corrections that I needed. It seems an odd twist on this greatest of gifts, but love can err sometimes in being given too extravagantly with little to no boundaries.

God of Love, you are the most extravagant giver of love and compassion that I know. You lovingly give and support our lives even though you often receive nothing in return. Love does not seek recompense, I know, but it ought not be disrespected and neglected either. As I am a friend to others, a lover to my spouse, and a parent to my children, help me to establish fair and reasonable boundaries of respect in my loving relationships, offering words and actions that support my beloveds without blindly and unwisely enabling them.

August 29
Bless One Another

When my tumultuous post-high school summer drew to a close, my parents helped me gather the pieces of my disarrayed life, packed them in their car along with other practical, first year of college items and headed out on a three day journey to North Carolina and my "mystery school." Despite all of my self-destructive choices and antics that summer, I was still actually venturing off in search of a potential religious vocation. That yearning had everything to do with my choice of a distant college, and probably had much to do with my parents' ability to swallow the choice. Even with my best intentions, however, my youthfulness and its summer larks did not endow me with my finest spiritual focus as I arrived on the campus; I knew it and my parents likely did too.

After a couple of days of orientation and my settling in, my parents prepared to cut the home tethers of their youngest child and head back to Minnesota. Standing beside their car in the parking lot, we all shuffled through the uneasiness of our good-byes; unspoken questions and concerns must have weighed in heavily on each of our shoulders. Suddenly, feeling like the Prodigal Son of Jesus' famous parable, but in this case leaving home instead of returning to it, I turned to my Father and said, "Dad, I want your blessing," and then I dropped to my knees before him. Honestly, I have no idea what he said, and I can only imagine the wild mixture of emotion that he must have been juggling within; all I remember is that he put his hands on my head and then my shoulders, and he cried. It was more than enough blessing for me.

Over thirty-three years later, I returned to Minnesota for my final visit home to help ease my Mother's final steps in her journey toward death. Dad had died a little over a year before, and now his beloved of nearly seventy years was preparing for her reunion with him, her aging body failing quickly from Leukemia. For ten days the parent and child roles were reversed, and Mother allowed me to care for her with the tenderness that she had given me all of my life, and most especially as a child. But when a brother came to relieve me of my "parental role," and knowing almost certainly that I would never see her alive again, I once again reclaimed my child status. Up early to see me off now on my own long southern trip home, she sat weakly at the kitchen table when I entered the room and once again, as the child kneeling before the parent, I asked for her blessing. As my Father had done years before, she placed her frail hands on my head and then wrapped her accepting arms around my shoulders, affirming my whole life with her affectionate blessing.

Too often, blessings are delegated only to priests and ministers and other religious leaders. But as we are all children of God imbued with the Divine Spark, we have not only the ability, but more importantly, perhaps, the responsibility to bless one another. Unfortunately, because most of us have relinquished this responsibility, we also need to call it out of one another, to honor the holy ones in our lives by asking for their blessing.

God of All Blessings, you have cared for me throughout my life through the tenderness and devotion of my parents, through the sustenance and beauty of the creations, and through the loving support of spouse, children and countless friends. And still I need your blessing given to me through the hands of my most dearly beloveds. Through them, I have so often seen and known you. Encourage me to turn to them more often and to ask of them their blessing so that I may receive once again, the grace-filled embrace of your loving care, and honor them by recognizing their ability to provide it.

When I was schooling in my teens, corporal punishment, or more directly, "paddling," was still legal and practiced. By the time I entered the teaching profession, it was not yet "outlawed," but it was certainly not commonly practiced anywhere; in fact, touching or grabbing a student as part of a reprimand was discouraged. Over the years with growing improprieties between teachers and students escalating, the level of "contact" that a teacher might have with a student, regardless the cause, grew more and more thin. Finally, one year in our opening meetings prior to the start of a new academic calendar, the administration issued a directive that said we would do well to avoid any physical contact with our students, not simply regarding punishments, but more specifically now, even regarding "positive strokes" that might be misinterpreted as "inappropriate physical contact." Furthermore, we were instructed to never meet with a student alone behind a closed classroom door. I remember shaking my head that day, and privately refusing to accept this new edict. To forbid me to touch a student or an athlete was to remove the humanity from both us.

Obviously, there is "inappropriate touching," but a hand on the shoulder or a gentle grasp of the arm had long been part of my teaching and coaching demeanor, part of my "human engineering." The human touch is essential; we all need it. As a teacher and a coach, I came to realize that my asking a student or an athlete how s/he was doing was greatly enhanced when that same question was accompanied by a hand on the shoulder or a touch of the arm; these simple actions said, "no, *really,* I mean it - how are *you* doing?" I know the truth of this experience as both the giver and the receiver; there is a kind of "current of connection" that happens when human beings touch. And while I knew that the administration was merely trying to protect its staff and institution from any potential allegations, I felt that if someone wanted to misconstrue the intentions of my actions, my touch, he could do that, but I was confident that the history of my sincerity and concern for those under my care would win out. The valuable impact of human touch was far greater than the fear of erroneous reprisal.

One of the most famous images in Michelangelo's Sistine Chapel ceiling painting is of God the Father reaching out to touch fingers with Adam, the Creator's "first human." Leisurely prone, Adam appears to reach out in a kind of relaxed oblivion to receive the electrical charge that will truly give him life – the touch from his Creator. Whatever the physiological facts of touch actually are, I know not, but I am convinced that we, like the image of Michelangelo's Creator, have an enlivening potential within our most simple yet very tender grasp.

Tender and Touching God, what grace-filled touch of yours sprung me – and the universe! – into life? I do not know the mysteries of Creation, but I have experienced the power of the creation in the mystery of the human touch. Surely, I can misuse that power and use the gift of touch in inappropriate ways; steer me clear of such thoughts and abuses. May my gentle touch of another provide life and be a message of true concern and care for the needs of those who receive it.

You're probably familiar with the cliché concerning one's movement through life of "don't forget to stop and smell the roses." It's an important reminder for us to not get too caught up in life's movements and thereby miss the simple joys along the way. Enjoy the successes of your labor, the cliché implies, and appreciate the, often, many unearned gifts. Sometimes, however, we also need the reminder to be mindful of the path along which these roses grow.

When I coached cross-country running, I always encouraged my runners before the competition began to jog through the course they were about to race, and to be very mindful of the terrain as they did so. In a time of drought, the earth was often as hard as a rock, and a simple rift in the landscape could become an imposing and potential stumbling block. Frequently races coursed through woodlands where roots criss-crossed trails and emerging rocks created easy trips. At what point in the race might there be a hill, and how might its placement, early or late in the race, govern one's preparedness for it? Sharp turns or confusing confluences, water hazards and fallen trees or overhanging branches - all of these and more were reason enough to be mindful of the terrain of the race course. And in a race, there was no time for "stopping to smell the roses."

Our daily lives are much like these cross-country race courses. After the race, during one's warm-down, a person can take the time to smell the roses, but before and during the race, one might do well to be very attentive to the course itself. Dear God, today I seek your training advice. Help me as I move through the course of this day to be mindful of the terrain. Let this time now be a thoughtful walk-through of how I might approach the challenges of this day, and once inside the "day's race," help me to be more attentive to my course. Sometimes I need to stop and smell the roses; sometimes I need to run for the roses.

September 1
Pick Your Punishment

Most teams in interscholastic high school sports often develop a motivational theme for each year, and then this theme gets worked into a team t-shirt for the given season. Other teams might opt away from the chummier, more personal, motivational theme and simply go with one of the many standard slogans unique to each sport that eventually become a bit cliché. When I was coaching cross-country, one of my favorite of these latter slogans was "Our sport is your sport's punishment!" I always loved reading that boast across some runner's chest because, although it is a rather odd, seemingly masochistic claim, ultimately, it was true. Against the bravado and chest pumping of the main sports, cross-country was often viewed as not simply a lesser sport, but certainly not one that required much "athletic chutzpah." Ironically, however, in all of those other sports, when an athlete messes up, shows up late or does some other "punishable act," the threat is often to "run laps." And in cross country, that is all one does – and not simply run laps, but run mile upon mile, and often up hills!

For those who like running, of course, there is nothing punishment-like about it. One former runner of mine, after taking some years away from it, returned to it with a passion, admitting that "running is what I do; it's what I get up for every day." Still others that I coached admitted to never liking running; they just loved cross-country. For these individuals, the camaraderie of the team and the sense of self-improvement and esteem that they experienced in the sport were worth the "punishment."

Many people find that the discipline necessary for a truly lived spiritual life is also something of a "punishment." They don't mean that it is a "punishment for" some wrong-doing, although some acts of penitence can certainly carry this connotation, but that like any form of exercise, there is likely a commitment of time and an acceptance of some "discomfort," be it physical, mental or emotional. In the sport of cross-country, for most, such punishment was ultimately worth the inconvenience of time and discomfort. What each runner gained individually and experienced collectively made all the effort worth it. As we journey across the countryside of our lives, I am convinced that spiritual disciplines reap similar and far greater rewards.

God of Commitment, I want the course of my life to run towards you. There are numerous training programs out there that all claim to draw us closer to you, but no training regimen will ever work without my first stepping forward and embracing the discipline necessary to improve. Such an effort often feels like a "punishment," a drudgery; but help me to be mindful that I inflict upon myself a greater punishment when I fail to fully engage in the life that you have given me. That "punishment" may be void of pain, but it may also be void of life.

September 2
Hill Work

When I was coaching the sport of cross-country, each year I would seek to establish a theme for the new season, a unifying focus upon which the runners might rally. As I simultaneously matured into my own coaching skills and spirituality, these two aspects became more united in my choice of a theme; hence, the seasonal focus was often just as much a call to prayer as it was a call to the dedication to team and to individual goals. One year, after the teams had fared miserably on hilly courses the previous season, I sought to remedy that weakness with the aid of our new theme, a kind of exasperated, playfully facetious, prayerful statement: "God, I love hills! Hill, yes!"

Not all parts of the country have access to varied terrain, but every really good cross-country course will offer the challenge of hills somewhere in the race. Few people *like* to run hills, but most cross-country runners realize that hills are a natural part of the sport, and, many times are the obstacle or challenge that separates the true cross-country athlete from the simply, naturally talented distance runner. Subsequently, if one wants to excel in the sport, then she has to be willing to train hard and frequently on hills, and usually hills that are far worse in intensity than anything she will encounter in a race.

Indeed, there is nothing quite as taxing in running as "hill work." Ascending a fairly steep half- mile long hill will truly test the mettle and question the quality of one's physical condition very quickly. The legs become heavy and leaden while the heart, pounding out a bass drum rhythm as it tries to adequately supply energy to the oxygen-depleted muscles, feels as though it might explode within the runner's chest. Half way up the hill, a runner's breathing becomes more like gulping for air, a fish out of water gasping with its mouth and eyes wide open. But it is the conditioning, the endurance of just such training, that will one day push the runner up the hill and to the top of his race. Through such training, one also learns about patience and steadiness. Like a driver trying to maintain her speed up a hill, the runner has to push the accelerator down a little bit more, but if she punches it, there will be an inefficient waste of energy. A controlled "attack" of the hill is what is needed, learning to run within the limits of what the body can actually provide.

The spiritual life too is replete with "hill work," trials that challenge our meditation and prayers right down to the very core of our faith. Life is full of peaks and valleys, and like the true cross-country runner, if one is to rise above the "norm" of living, to live more fully and deeply, then he will have to put some dedicated time and effort – even discomfort – into his training regimen of meditation and prayer. But adequately conditioned in this strength training, when faith challenges arise like a demanding hill in a cross-country race, the faithful embrace the affront and ascend with confidence.

God of All Terrains, my life and the world in which I live are full of challenges, not so much personal attacks, but simple and natural hills that test the depths of my commitment to living the gift of life fully and healthfully. Help me to see these demanding rises as opportunities to improve the quality of all of my relationships, with myself, with others, and with you. Rather than succumbing to the challenge, may I raise my breathless voice to you and with my heart pounding out the rhythm proclaim, "God, I love hills!"

September 3
Labor Day

When I left my teaching job of twenty-eight years, our nation's economy had floated into its shallowest and rockiest waters since the Great Depression, and every day the newspapers reported more alarming numbers of unemployment and new threats of job loss. I read stories almost daily of people who had been looking unsuccessfully for a new job for months, some for over a year. And here I was about to walk away from a job I liked, with good pay, good benefits, and a community that seemed to like and support me. As I wrestled with my decision, my new emerging mantra was "Are you nuts?" But everything in my heart said, "You've got to do it. You've thought about this for a few years now; it's time for you to move on." And so I did, and I've never looked back with doubt ever since.

A job is essential on so many different levels. Pragmatically, of course, it pays the bills. If one chooses to live in this society, she needs to work to afford, at least, food and shelter. Beyond the skin and bones, however, it opens up other social and personal possibilities to explore and to discover people, places, emotions, experiences – the list is as extensive as one's income might allow. But if a person works "full time," we'll say forty hours five days a week, that's a third of every work day donated to a single place and task; one had better enjoy whatever it is that she does, or for that time and for much of the "down time," she will be miserably unhappy. Liking one's job, however, is really not enough. I can like my job because the working conditions are agreeable, or my colleagues are essentially good and fun people to be around, or the job itself is more than "tolerable"; but the deeper issue of job compatibility is whether a person finds her work fulfilling.

A fulfilling job is arguably a "relative label." If one's goals are to be wealthy and powerful, and one's job achieves such goals, I can't argue that such a person has not found a fulfilling job. But the fulfillment of which I speak is based on something far more intangible; it is about how the work makes one *feel* as a human being. Does my work "matter"? Does it chisel away at me and help sculpt me into a better person? Does it give me an opportunity to bring hope, or happiness or just general good cheer to others? If I am exhausted at the end of my workday, are my work and efforts worth the exhaustion? If I can answer "yes" to most or all of these, and the job at least covers the pragmatic fundamentals, then my work is likely to be fulfilling.

A career, a daily job, can feel like "a life time." Ironically, in the end, one's life is pretty short. No one wants her "short life" to be made tediously long by an unfulfilling job. Many people frequently talk about and look forward to retirement from their job as if it is the end of some prison sentence. Such a view suggests that many people are quite unfulfilled in their jobs - and *that* hole in their lives is very unfortunate. On a day when our nation stops working to honor the fact that we work – Labor Day - it is good for us to also consider why we work and whether we find our work fulfilling. I used to tell my students, "You will soon be working for nearly the rest of your lives; you had better choose a career or work that you enjoy for you will be doing it for a very long time." During tough economic times, one may not always have the luxury of such a choice, but without the choice, one's work time will likely always be tough no matter the economy.

God of Labor and Rest, our nation pauses every year to honor the value of work on Labor Day. May we as a nation, and may each of us individually take some time to consider the value of our work beyond its pragmatic necessities. Work helps us to discover and to define who we are. Help me to find employment that not only allows me to contribute to an economy, but also provides me opportunities to truly give of myself and to receive fulfillment in who I am.

September 4
Under Pressure

During my twenty-eight years of teaching high school, I also coached the sport of cross-country every fall; subsequently, "school" always began by the first week of August. While I grew to love coaching this sport, it always put me "behind the eight-ball" right away every fall. The school day ended at 3:00 PM, but then the coaching part of my job consumed the next two to three hours. Once home and fed, the call of grading essays and other paperwork had to be answered each night. Of course, every Saturday in the fall was drowned by nearly a full day of coaching, and when I would come up for air, it was to organize either the annual cross-country overnight meet and/or the Invitational attended by 1200 runners from thirty schools which our team hosted. By the end of September, I suspect that internally and externally, I looked something like the Beetle Bailey character just after Sarge has given him a tussle.

I loved coaching, but I also loved teaching, and I wanted to be a "good teacher." This meant not simply knowing the material and presenting it well, but staying on top of the paper work so that students could receive their assignments in a timely fashion with adequate response, encouragement, and direction for improvement. But with so many demands before me, the stress of the jobs and the feeling of inadequacy that rolled in as I slipped further behind in my grading was a dense morning fog. I knew that the light of the day was out there, above me somewhere, and that the sun would burn away this cloud eventually, but for the indefinite moment, I floundered pathetically knowing that it would be the end of November before I would truly be on top of my "teaching game."

Whether you are a teacher, or a secretary, or a doctor, or a garbage collector facing your route after a holiday, we all know the ugly, awful stress of being behind. I go to bed each night covered by the heavy blankets of what didn't get done, and awake to the fog of where do I go now, which tasks most need to be addressed today and what new ones might I bump into along the way. Unfortunately, we fail to realize that the weight we carry and the darkness within which we move are often due to our own choices. Is this stress, are these pressures, what God wants for us?

O God of Air and Light, too often I am consumed by the responsibilities that come with my choices. The weight of deadlines seems to crush me, and the pull of expectations, personal and otherwise, is a chain about my neck constricting my breathing. Help me to pause this day, everyday, and to exhale the unnecessary guilt and fears that I suck in, and to inhale the goodness that was once at the heart of my well-intentioned choices. And, perhaps, it is time for me to reevaluate those choices. Is this how you want me to live? How might I serve you, those around me and myself better? Guide me through this fog and lift me from this oppressive darkness into your vibrant light and fresh air.

September 5
The Local Farmer's Market

A simple community pleasure that seems to be experiencing a bit of resurgence in recent years is the local farmer's market. From mid-summer to early autumn, makeshift malls are erected for a few hours once a week in various neighborhood parks and locales; small tents, canopies or awnings popped up in front of a parked truck or trailer or even an old station wagon serve as the storefront with the proprietors wares spread out on tables beneath these coverings. Lately, I have taken to indulging periodically in a stroll through these simple market places, usually purchasing a few staple items.

The most simple farmer's markets are the best, those void of any commercial businesses, but sometimes these larger businesses can more easily afford a little outlay of samples, and I excuse their intrusion when they do so. The initial joy of a stroll through these temporary outposts of locally grown or baked items is the color. Tomatoes and peppers of numerous hues invite the customer to linger and peruse the tables; vibrant reds, sun-splashed yellows, and luscious greens dominate the eyescape, but streaked and mottled vegetable varieties add flair alongside the deep-toned purple eggplants. Sweet corn, from silver queen to yellow to bicolored offerings spill from baskets and crates, and while it doesn't sell for the dollar a dozen price tag I grew up on, I am easily enticed to buy four to six ears. Baked goods of breads, muffins and pies weigh in on the higher cost market, but their lure is also worth a stop and frequently includes a teasing sample slice.

The other significant pleasure I find at these farmer's markets are the people themselves. The sellers literally and figuratively stand behind their displayed food. Their hard work and love of the soil and growing things spreads out before them like an artist's canvas. These are not trinkets that they offer, but real sustenance plied and nurtured with their own hands, and there is unquestionable and reasonable pride in their artistry. Admittedly, my first stroll through the arbor is to take in the sights - and to check the price offerings – but part of my surveillance includes the integrity and the honest friendliness of the vendors. Most of us buyers are looking for a good deal, but we also know that food like this, that comes from the hand and the heart, is additionally spiced with a love that cannot be found in your average supermarket. When one works the soil and the seed with his own sweat, and harvests the produce and then spreads it across a simple table to be sold with his own hand, from soil to sale, there is a kind of love that is infused in the offering that inevitably enhances the flavor as well.

Bountiful God, a simple wonder of creation is that you invite us to be co-creators in the provisions of our own sustenance. You are the one who truly makes things grow, but you have made it so that we might nurture and increase this growth. When our hoes and hands dig affectionately into the soil of your creation, we join hands with you in providing food and life to others. Today I offer a prayer of blessing upon all of those who toil with the soil to provide fresh and wholesome goodness for others. May the work of their hands be connected to their hearts, and may we, the benefactors of their efforts, be nourished not only by their flavorful produce, but also by goodness of their intentions.

September 6
Prayerful Rest

I don't know why it is, but every fall it seems I go through a transition in my sleeping habits. Perhaps it is the summer's ease that allows sleep to come so easily to me then, and in the fall, with a tradition of a teaching and a coaching schedule, I get all uptight and have a hard time falling asleep. I've gotten a little better at not just getting upset right away, but the constant tossing and turning of both the body and the mind can really get me "up-fizzled," and oftentimes I now accept defeat and just get up and read for an hour or two.

When this restlessness goes on for over a couple of days and now is spilling into a week long or more battle, I start to get more nervous about how my health might be compromised by the lack of sleep. Along with trying to read myself into drowsiness in bed, one of the most effective sleeping tools that I have discovered is prayer. Of course, I have been to some rather lackluster prayer or liturgical or meditative services before, but I don't advocate those as your remedy. Rather, I find that when I am struggling to get to sleep, a simple mantra or mantra-like prayer can often serve as the best comfort. First of all, when I am struggling to get to sleep, and I look over to see the clock slip by midnight, then one AM, and now inching towards two, I inevitably start to exacerbate the problem as I calculate how short it will be before the alarm rings and how few hours of actual sleep I will have had when it does. RELAX!! - I tell myself, but then must change the tone to "relax," as I rummage a bit for a "mantra." Years ago, the rosary was often a good source of comfort for me; the repetition of the "hail Marys" and the "Our Fathers" usually never got much further than a decade or two, and I was adrift in slumber land. These days, with my own more personal mantra, I fall back on it, and sure enough, before long, the frustration of my sleeplessness is over for another night.

Besides the gift of the facts that this simple, repetitive prayer can relax me, take my mind off the pressures of the previous or upcoming day, and then pack me off towards slumber, perhaps one of the best parts of it is the thought of how I am entering that sacred world of sleep - through prayer. It is extra comfort to me to think that my last words of the day are, specifically, prayerful ones; as I cross the bridge of sleep that carries me from one day into another, I like knowing that the suspension across is a spirited one of prayer. I don't know if or how often God speaks to us through our sleep and in our dreams, but it does seem that our prayerful entrance into them can also serve as an invitation to our God to join us there.

Restful God, St. Augustine once noted that our hearts are always weary and "restless until they rest in you." Indeed, too often my heart and mind restlessly fight against my body's need for sleep. When I struggle with such sleepless aggravation, help me to recognize that time as another opportunity to lay down my cares and body beside you. Prayer is a source of comfort to me throughout my day; make it a source of rest for me throughout my night as well. As my day is charged with opportunities to pray, may my night be blanketed by the soft grace of prayer.

September 7
Balance of the Seasons

More than any of the other seasons, autumn seems to be the season of balance. Winter and summer, of course, are something of opposites. The former challenges us with a stretch of continuous cold, sometimes threatening to fall to temperatures beyond our bodies' natural ability to sustain its necessary warmth, while the latter reverses the equation and challenges our bodies' cooling system. Snow and ice exacerbate people's tolerance of winter as these precipitations make all forms of traversing the most difficult; in the height of the summer, the lack of precipitation in droughts threatens crop production and often leaves the earth hard, crusty and unforgiving. Spring, meanwhile, has more variety to offer as it slowly sloughs off winter's cold. As the frozen waters and snow thaw, the earth drinks in the nourishment and readies herself for the renewal of life all around. Yes, there is some balance here too, but once the winter corner has been turned, the rush of spring rains and emerging buds, and the energetic morning songs of birds play out a passionate song of a sensual union that cannot be slowed down. Autumn's movement is much more measured.

Temperature changes are, perhaps, the first small sign of the imminent and new seasonal phase, and here too is the first model of balance. While the nights may toss more than subtle hints about the impending winter, the days often unfold their feathers like a peacock, puffing out their warm and expansive chest as our bodies and the earth soak up the last and the best of summer's dying heat. With the cold and sporadic rains come the soft whispers of change in the trees. The first yellowing trees spark the fury of color that will transcend across the land in the weeks to come, but in each phase the balance of summer's green and autumn's fanfare offers a varying crescendo of color. Even the great lights, the sun and the moon, display a deepening balance as their sky path becomes more aligned and the equilibrium of darkness and light is sometimes punctuated by a rising sun opposite the setting moon.

Our own lives are much like these seasons, an ebb and flow of balance. Would that I could be more like the autumn season, a lovely blend of the extremes all dressed in a festive hue, but I know the extremes well, spiritually and emotionally. Too often my relationships have been born in a tone of spring and then have taken only a summer and winter rhythm. Prayer life can dance with a summer's passionate intensity and, despite clarity, can then grow icy like a winter's stream. As I age, however, I find my life gravitating more and more to the autumn balance, realizing more clearly what matters most in life, and separating the needs from the wants.

God of Balance, the world that you created reveals a message of balance, and calls me into that sacred harmony as well. I too easily oscillate between extremes, losing my place in the holy rhythm of this creation. Move me today towards balance, and help me to take my appropriate place in each season of my life.

September 8
Showing up for Practice

During my years of coaching the sport of cross-country, I would usually head off on long runs with some group of runners, enjoying the connection of conversation or even just the shared rhythm of our quiet breathing. Occasionally, however, I might delay my start or feign running at all so that I could "drop-in" unsuspectingly on the various groups of runners just to see how they were doing, or, perhaps more truthfully, "to keep them honest." Often times on these drop-bys, I would encounter a group of student-athletes who had decided that rather than engaging in the daily workout, they would take a more leisurely stroll, cut a few corners and then jog back in at the appropriate and anticipated time. Now, some of the kids simply hadn't built up their stamina adequately for a true "long run," but most of the time their ambulation was just a case of laziness. As I would suddenly "appear" behind them or just around a corner they were approaching, caught in the laughter and visiting of their social walk, they would suddenly spring back into a run or sometimes a more honest jog.

At the beginning of each season before long training runs, I would frequently encourage the young athletes to fight through the desire to walk. Every time you stop, I would tell them, you add another brick to the wall that sooner or later you will have to run through. When you feel the urge to walk, I would add, look up ahead and challenge yourself to make it to the end of the next block or some other natural marker. It was always a little extra disconcerting when I would find upperclassmen in the midst of these walking groups knowing that their unclaimed influence was not establishing a very positive role model.

Like long distance running, the spiritual life demands some discipline and a significant dose of will power. Religions, by their nature, usually offer a healthy sense of community, just as a cross-country team does. But being a member of a team or a religion doesn't necessarily mean that one is fully engaged in the life of that community. One can show up for services and "practice" one's faith, and attend all of the fun social gatherings, but unless one commits oneself personally to spiritual exercise, these other associations may have little effect on one's healthy development. What kind of heart do I bring to my spiritual practices, and what kind of disciplines do I assert beyond the social gatherings? What restraints and discretion do I personally employ that will enhance my involvement in the community efforts? It is just as easy to walk when no one is watching as it is to simply show up when the expectation of one's presence is anticipated. How we manage our spiritual practices when we are on our own will make all the difference in how well we ultimately run the race.

God of Discipline and Constancy, I long to increase the depth of my relationship with you, to go the distance in establishing a healthy rhythm. Admittedly, sometimes the spirit is willing, but the flesh is weak. Coach me, challenge me to remain true to my commitment to you; stay just before me, an encouraging source of energy stretching my effort out beyond my latest feeble attempt. You are my end, my finish line; keep me running towards you always.

September 9
Seeds of Life

As I sliced through the crisp, green membrane and let the halves fall apart like an empty shell, the seeds from the sweet pepper spilled onto the cutting board. The small, white flecks, breaking from the layered rows that formed a clump beneath the stem core, were unsuspecting, tiny chips of life. Next, delicately slicing thin layers, I pushed to the side the amoeba-like inner membrane that fell away from the inside of the tomato, the seedling-eyes a dumb gaze in the goo. These eyes, and the tiny, green pepper seedlings were destined for the garbage, an ironic twist, I thought, as I prepared the two for the dinner salad. But it's true; consider nearly any vegetable or fruit. We slice, bite, cut or tear it open, dispose of the seeds and then eat the "flesh" or "meat" inside.

Seeds seem disposable, but, of course, they are the source of the fruit or vegetable itself. Interestingly, in nearly all things that propagate themselves, the seeds are usually quite plentiful, a sort of survival instinct it might seem, knowing that it often takes many just to get one to survive. But each seed, amazingly, holds the potential for so much; each seed is a small miracle.

Take an apple, for example. We enjoy a wide variety of apples, varying in color, size, texture and, most importantly, flavor. Wrapped inside the core of each one of these apples are those small, brown, tear-shaped seeds. There is nothing about the seed itself that identifies it as an apple seed, and that "identity issue" is true of all fruit and vegetable seeds. You may recognize them because you have seen them before, but you would not know the power they pack otherwise. And this small brown seed does not become an apple, it becomes a tree; and then this tree born of a small brown seed, in time, might bear many apples!

It's hard to ignore the fact that we humans, too, start out as a kind of "seed," and that our original shape looks nothing like what we become even though, like the fruit and vegetable, all "the genetic stuff" is already there inside that simple seed. While each of us holds this miraculous power and source of life within us, we so easily take life for granted. Like the many seeds spilling out on my cutting board, so many human lives seem expendable.

I am not advocating a "propagation festival," for the seeds I speak of go well beyond mere procreative analogies. Each of us has a kind of "life energy" within us that we can use for creative, life-giving purposes, or that we can thoughtlessly push aside like so much garbage. We often willingly give to others from the bounty of our gardens and fruit trees; what of ourselves can we give that will also nourish?

Miraculous God, you have placed seeds of life within each of us, but too often we neglect or ignore or fail to even realize the potential of these seeds. Open me up this day, and let me hold, and give away, and plant the seeds of life that you have given me. Help me to nurture the seeds with which I have been blest, and then to give of them freely as I contribute to the big banquet of life.

September 10
Learning Much?

During my first fifteen years or so of teaching, I felt adamantly attached to the curriculum I was given to teach and to the lesson plans that I fashioned to accomplish this curriculum. If the course was British Literature, I wanted to cover the Anglo-Saxons right through James Joyce and into the Post Modern Period. If it was Judeo-Christian Scriptures, then I set my sights on Genesis through Revelations. Never was there time enough to cover all that my heart desired for my students, nor did I fulfill every goal and objective in the curriculum's Graded Course of Study. Interruptions to the daily and weekly schedule only exacerbated my angst; confounded already, I would worry about how I was failing my students by not availing them to all of this important and essential information and instruction.

I don't know if there was a specific moment or school year where I finally turned the corner on these concerns, but somewhere in the ripening of my teaching career I realized that "how much" I covered, and how far I got through the curriculum's agenda really didn't matter that much. This change in perspective, however, was by no means a complacency or laziness on my part; there were no "study halls" in my courses, and my daily classes continued to be mostly "bell to bell." The shift grew out of a variety of alterations in my perspective.

Of least importance, but not unimportant, was my realization that, for the most part, the students could care less how far we got. Most young people live very much "in the now." History and historically significant pieces of literature, art, theology and philosophy are interesting, but they are still "the past" after all, and from the young person's limited scope of life, these things don't matter "*that* much." Secondly, whatever "past material" I was able to cover was still "new" material to them, and without really knowing what wasn't covered, what was covered always seemed plenty adequate. How well we covered and understood material became far more important to me than how much we covered. Finally, the most important reason for the changes in my personal curriculum was an internal transformation in me about why and what we teach. For so long, it seemed, covering expansive stretches of material was essential for the student's academic future. The more they read and the more they knew, the better prepared they would be for future academic pursuits. What I realized more acutely, however, was that "what they knew" was often very "temporary." Students read and study for a test, and many times then, just let that information go. So, what and how much a student knows is not half so important as how and why a student "knows." Critical thinking and discussion skills emerged as more important "abilities" for me to teach and to encourage rather than how much I taught. If we learn to think well, then whenever and whatever we read and study will be understood and appreciated more deeply than just chalking up "another book" and memorizing its specific statistics, characters and views.

Spiritually, our approach should be much the same. Doing and knowing much are not immaterial, but the how and why are more important. Reading sacred texts with a critical eye and a thoughtful heart are essential for personal spiritual growth. And what of my accompanying prayer life – the introspective practice that stimulates and gives deeper meaning to my learning? Reading the entire bible may seem a landmark accomplishment, but to what end? What evaluative measure do I bring to my reading and how do I allow the readings to move within me?

God of All Knowledge and Understanding, in my desire to be in relationship with you, I can be easily led by a wealth of information while remaining spiritually poor. I realize that I can know much, but still understand so very little. Help me to not be overly concerned with how much I know about you, but to be driven instead by how and why I come to understand and to love you. Teach me to be a critical thinker and a spiritual seeker.

September 11
9/11

I was sitting alone proctoring a writing lab when the school psychologist poked his head in the door and said with his usual expressionless face, "A plane just crashed into one of the Twin Towers." Always a bit confused by his dry, deadpan sense of humor, I initially thought that he was just joking; an odd joke, to be sure, but how could a pilot have been so errant I thought? "No, I'm serious," he added, and I swung around to turn on the television monitor just above my head. As the screen came to life, there it was, my first image of the burning tower: white smoke pouring out the side of the wounded tower like a malfunctioning chimney. Again I thought to myself, what had happened to that plane, assuming that the whole incident was a horrible accident? As I watched in dreadful awe, suddenly another plane, entering from the left of the screen, came blasting into the second tower. In abject confusion, I realized then that this was no accident.

The rest of my school workday was a blur. As news reports began to piece together the string of bizarre hijackings deciphering the nature and intention of the attacks, a wave of pandemonium rippled across the nation. In my own school, as was happening everywhere in the country, parents began pulling their children out of school, fearfully expecting some kind of full force frontal attack on the entire nation. For those of us who remained, a heavy pall of shock and disbelief hung over every class; how could one teach on such a day? Prayer seemed to be the only appropriate response.

With all after-school practices, games and matches cancelled, I peeled away from school sometime after the day's final bells and headed home still trying to soak in the numbing reality of the morning's grotesque events that were now being replayed on television as if in a continuous loop. By this time, the word was out that the hijackings had all been part of a single masterminded terrorist attack, and more sordid details about who was behind it and what their intentions had been continued to leak into the churning murky waters of despair, anger, disbelief, heartache and outrage. Many questions rose, but the largest one that lingered was, as the world's most powerful nation, how was the United States going to respond to this attack on its own soil?

The outpouring of care, concern and sympathy from the world community was almost overwhelming. As a nation that rushes to other countries' aid so many times, it was our nation that was now receiving the curative attention of others. Most impressively, while retaliatory anger seethed, many Americans began to ask a most important introspective question of "why would someone want to do this to us?" It was not simply an incredulous question, but one that wondered, almost as if for the first time, "What have we done in the world to make someone so hateful and resentful towards us?" Unfortunately, within months the apparent answer to the questions must have been, "Nothing!" and as our nation geared up for retaliatory war, angry nationalism surged ahead of thoughtful patriotism.

September 11th was hardly the United States' first encounter with terrorism, but it did mark the day that the doors of terrorist activity were blown wide open, and because of it, our world will never be the same again. *No* act of terrorism is *ever* justifiable, but whether we like it or not, agree with them or not, there are "reasons" that terrorists do what they do. No one is born a terrorist. People are led and conditioned to think and believe what they do. The plot of that horrible and infamous day was not born on one morning or in one year or even over several years. September 11th was a horrendous response to a history of resentment toward Western oppression and domination; and, again, whether the perpetrators' perception was accurately conceived or not, we would do much better if we openly tried to understand that perception rather than denying it and warring against it through what will only be perceived as the very thing that caused the attack in the first place: further domination and oppression.

God of Peace and Understanding, I want to say that the horrible attacks on the United States on this day in the year 2001 are unforgivable, but I do not believe that "unforgivable" is even in your vocabulary. I believe that your love for us *all* transcends all actions, however horrendous they may be. Those attacks will always be *unacceptable* and always *evil*, but whether I like it or not, I believe you call *all* of us toward forgiveness, understanding and reconciliation. I pray today, first of all, for the families of all of the victims of 9/11 who suffered such deep and, no doubt, lasting sorrow. There is no "good reason" for the horrible hole left in their lives. Then, I pray for all terrorists, that they might look into their hearts, reevaluate their hatred, and see the senselessness and horror of their actions. Finally, to these prayers I add another: that we, as citizens of the world, might work to understand the *causes* of terrorism. I might never be able to agree with the causes, but I cannot truly defend the world or myself against terrorism until I better understand why anyone would willingly do what the terrorist does.

September 12
Never Forget. Always Remember. Never Surrender

Today is the day after my wife's birthday, and my sister-in-law's, and my wife's cousin, and one of her aunt's as well. That's right; they were all born on the same date: September 11. That's right; September 11, that day of infamy and terror blazoned on our nation's memory. I believe that it has been speculated, at least, that the terrorists chose that date in a kind of sick mockery of our national emergency code: 9-1-1. But the horrible attacks of that day could have been on any date, and the notorious memories would be the same. That they happened on my wife's birthday, however, has forever given the date a slightly different spin for me.

My wife's day started like every other birthday of hers, with that special excitement that this was "her day," a special day of honor and recognition. I snuck a humorous birthday card into the lunch I fix and pack for her, and stowed a more serious one away for the evening's celebration. A friend of ours whose birthday was the day before was in town that day on business, and we had made earlier plans to gather for dinner at a favorite restaurant. When he arrived at our home late in the afternoon, he was operating on only hearsay of the day's events and tuned in immediately to get caught up on the tragic news. When my wife arrived home, we proceeded with our plans, and headed out to celebrate their birthdays despite the awful pall that had fallen across the entire day. Travelling to the restaurant, we were appalled by the growing lines at the gas stations as concern had turned to worry and now to panic. By the time we finished dinner and stopped for ice cream, the panic lines of automobiles getting gasoline were now nearly a block long, and as we sat outside the ice cream shop trying to celebrate their lives in the face of destruction and now fear, we watched local gas stations elevate their prices by almost a dollar. Without really understanding what exactly the fear was, we soon succumbed to the alarming response flooding in all around us, and decided that we too, perhaps, ought to go top off our gas tanks; just in case of what, we were not sure.

Years later on the anniversary of the attacks, I see signs that read: "Never Forget. Always Remember. Never Surrender." And I am left wondering what part of that day should we never forget and always remember; and what is it exactly that we will never surrender? Every year since September 11, 2001, my wife and I, and also those kin who share her birthday, have been faced with a somewhat awkward dance. While our nation pauses – as do we - to remember one of its most historically tragic days and the thousands of victims of the horrific crimes of that day, we also want to celebrate the lives of some very dear and special ones whose birthday it is as well. We cannot forget the chaos, the fear, and the sorrow that is now associated with the date of September 11; and we will always remember the images of horror when humanity so turned on itself that day causing so much heartache and bloodshed while initiating a whole new generation to the dreadfulness of war. And yet, we also choose to always remember that life is a great gift and it deserves to be celebrated. We choose not to cower in fear or to respond in angry retaliation to the hatred and misconceptions of others. We will never surrender our belief that Life transcends even death, that goodness, chosen and lived honestly, is greater than any evil.

God of Life, all creation reveals that from the ashes of destruction and death, new life can emerge, stronger and healthier than ever. As members of that creation, humanity has the unique opportunity to choose that truth or to reject it. While it is good for us to never forget the evils that we are capable of, help us to not dwell on them in such a way as to rekindle anger and to remember resentment. May we choose life and never surrender to the insidious nature of evil.

September 13
Seasonal Change

For weeks it had been oppressively hot. Day after day, the temperature rose into the nineties or hovered just below it with a humidity stirred into the heat of the day that then hung in the air like a heavy blanket well into the night. The predawn hours and the first hour or two of light would offer a temporary reprieve, but once the next morning's sun rose above the trees, the thermometer rose steadily with it pushing the heat back down like a weight on the day. And then, rather suddenly even, one evening I could feel a shift in the air. The infrequent wind that had felt like a blow dryer for weeks, swirled in with a kiss of coolness to it, and as it picked up momentum, the heat, perhaps even weary of itself, seemed to get pushed around. Before night had fallen, I had turned off the air conditioning, thrown open all the windows and was welcoming real air back into the house. By morning, my wife and I were grabbing for the covers that had been nightly kicked to the floor for weeks as the cool air rolled in like waves engulfing us. Almost overnight, it seemed, autumn had arrived.

Dramatic changes in the weather are not uncommon, but they are infrequent enough that when they do happen, we take notice. The same can be said for many other shifts in our lives as well. Miscommunication leading to no communication in a relationship can leave us wandering in dense, humid air. And then one day, someone figures, "enough," and offers a word that slices through the heavy atmosphere. The storm clouds begin to lift and the goodness of friendship is lapping along the shoreline once again. Or a move, or a new job can bring apprehensive fears and discomfort to one's daily routine when the awkwardness of the new environment becomes like stumbling over rocky terrain in the dark; and then, suddenly, one grasps that she knows her way around here now, or he realizes that people are reaching out to him; and the unwieldy surroundings are then familiar and friendly as the sense of home swallows up the foreign feel.

Most of the time change happens so subtly that we never recognize nor appreciate the shift that has occurred. But occasionally, the swing comes sudden and dramatically and we cannot ignore that something significant has been moved, and life is different and better. A change in the weather, I can't control, but I can help initiate and stimulate other changes in my life. We all have, perhaps, felt at some time or another, trapped in a relationship or an environment or a spiritual quagmire, and everything around us feels like weeks of oppressively hot and humid late summer days. But just as surely as the seasons will shift, necessary transformation can and will occur in our lives; the air lifts, we feel light again and we throw open the windows to our best selves.

God of All Changing Seasons, today I pause to consider the atmosphere in which I live. If all is light and fresh around me, I give you thanks. But if storm clouds of misunderstanding linger above me or on my horizon, if the humidity of tension and uneasiness are draped over me, or if the landscape of my spiritual life is arid and thirstfully without water, I seek help from you in initiating and creating change. What words or actions can I offer to awaken the air and to stir the waters of my discontent so as to bring the revitalizing freshness of change back into my life?

September 14
A Wake-up Call

I woke up early this week with a horrible nagging ache all across the back of my shoulders. I had been backpacking over the weekend, but this pain did not feel like a soreness from the load I was carrying. In fact, it has been a growing pain that seemed to start in my forearm, a response to the excessive typing I have been doing, and has since stretched all the way up my arm and is now curling around my neck and across my shoulders. My gut tells me what it is immediately, but my mind wants to counter the advice and find some other source of the problem, like, say backpacking. But no, the real culprit is stress, and I just don't want to believe it. How can it be, I think to myself; my life couldn't be any less stressful right now. Obviously, I have been kidding myself.

Generally, I am a "high bar" person. I don't do much of anything if I am not going to give it one hundred or more percent effort. When I choose to do something, I choose to do it well and with as much gusto as I can give it to help it

293

succeed; and, of course, my sense of its "success" is not simply completing the task – "to finish" – but to arrive at a respectful, even honorable, place. So while I have recently abandoned the normal work-a-day routine easing my stress level, I have obviously acquired a new source of stress as I privately, and perhaps sometimes subconsciously, set standards and routines at which I feel I should be working. To this new life-approach of mine, add emerging opportunities for which I am both eager and forlorn; on the one hand, I am excited about a new possibility, while on the other hand, I do not want to seize it just yet and lose the joy of my most recent, youthful changes. Thus, when I awake with stress curling itself around my back and neck like a heavy python moving stealthfully in for the kill, my body and my guts know the truth though my "I'm-in-control-here" mind wants to say otherwise.

In the heat of our passions and obsessions, we are so often blind to the residual effects. Altruistically, we are certain that what we are doing is not only the right thing at the right time, but that it also feels good and true too. In such cases, if our compulsion isn't disease enough, we add denial to the mixture. I believe I woke up in a pool of both of them this week. Now I must fight to reclaim my life, the physical and the spiritual, by reevaluating not simply my choices, but more importantly, how I am responding to my choices.

Today, God of my aches and pains, you come with an uneasy message for me: slow down. In my desire to live this gift of life that you have given me, I sometimes become compulsive and obsessive in my behavior, fixing more attention on how I do a job and what its results are rather than on embracing the job itself and enjoying the challenges for growth that it offers. If I am living ignorantly, bring my ignorance to light, Great One, so that I might emerge from its darkness and more healthfully enjoy the gift of living that you offer to me this day.

September 15
The Birth of My Son

In 1981, at 6:36 PM on this date, my one and only son was born. I don't think that I favor him in any way over my two daughters, but as I am a man, and he is my only son, there is certainly something unique about our relationship. In some respects, I probably have less in common with him than I do with my daughters, but I think that men, as it is for women too, have some special connections that are naturally shaped by our shared genders, and that he is my son only accentuates that connection all the more.

It may seem too personal for print, but I know that my son was conceived just after I finished my last course work for my teaching degree. With only student-teaching ahead of me, his conception was part of a celebratory exhale for both his mother and me after years of a shared struggle to complete my schooling. We were young and poor, but our determination had pushed us up the mountain, and now, as if above the tree line, we could see the hope of our future in a valley below. Appropriately, my son was born in the second or third week of my new teaching career. In a new city and state and with a young, dedicated, and wonderfully caring new obstetrician seeing us through the last two months of pregnancy, his mother and I were climbing a different mountain when he entered our lives.

On my son's birth day, I left for work as usual in the morning, but with that persistent awareness that today could be "the day." In the middle of my first period class, the school secretary appeared at my door with a phone message, and my students - aware of the impending birth - and I knew immediately what it meant. Exiting quickly, I raced home to retrieve the laboring mother and our first born, who we delivered to new friends on the city's north side on our way to the west side hospital. Once there, labor grew intermittent, but because the pregnancy was already late in its term, the doctor insisted that we stay, and by late afternoon she increased "a drip" that would help induce the labor. He finally arrived on the scene hours later. My son's reluctance to enter the world could perhaps be the symbolic *modus operandi* for his life.

So many years ago today, a son entered my life, and I have never been the same since. His birth was not the crucial shift of my life, but his life has created numerous pivotal moments throughout my life. As with every relationship, and most especially with one's child, once lives become intertwined in any fashion, we are never the same people that we once were. With each of my children, but today especially thinking of my son, I so often wonder at how different my life has been because of that one life. Every day, there may be a person or an experience that I will encounter that will change my life forever. Knowing that, I need to keep my heart and mind and eyes wide open to receive the possibility of a new gift of change.

God of Birth and New Life, my son's birthday today provides me with not only a wonderful memory but also a reminder that changes can be around any corner or atop any mountainous climb. I thank you for his healthy birth and life, and for the lives of each of my children, all of whom have birthed something new and different and better within me. In honoring them, may I also honor and welcome the possibilities for even further and deeper changes in my life ahead.

September 16
Family Nesting

During a recent visit to my home state of Minnesota, I had the opportunity to spend some time with a niece and her husband and their rambunctious family of two very energetic toddler boys and their newly arrived sister. Additionally, just after a nephew and his wife doubled their parenting duties with the birth of their first son, joining their toddler daughter, I was able to witness the newborn's first bath and watch his big sister's initial excitement over the arrival. Both of the visits brought back some very fond memories of the births of my own three children, although most of the details seem a distant blur.

I recently told my married son, and I have shared this known truth with so many of my former students in years past, that the addition of a child/children in a relationship, in a marriage, changes everything. It is not simply the addition of another body in the house or another mouth to feed; it is more about how the human dynamics of our relationships change and how "time enough" seems to vanish. The spreading out of affection and attention is as inevitable as the need to stretch the size of the nest. Like newly hatched birds in the nest, the mouths of the young chirp wildly and are open wide, anxiously awaiting the parents' next morsel of fulfillment. With each year, the needs change and expand, and while the incessant chirping becomes its own, more personal song, the clamor for needed attention never seems to cease.

When my youngest child left home for college years ago, she was already spreading her own new wings and learning to fly independently. Returning for a visit a year after her graduation, she came home to a familiar spot in the now quiet nest, but during her absence that space had become an overflow for other stuff. Before her arrival, we found a temporary closet or corner for the stuff, and welcomed her home. Time was filled with visits, special meals and day trips, and when she left again, the space around our lives looked for an old, new rhythm. The ebb and flow of family life - the creation of a new nest, its fulfillment, and then its emptying - is such an important opportunity to learn about life, both in general and more personally. Nothing in life is truly constant. Each day brings something new, and with each new arrival, be it big or small, things change! We are strong and we are weak; we are hungry and we are satiated; we are refreshed and we are exhausted. And these movements of change happen throughout our lives. Not just once, and then are done, but over and over again, and each time, the movement is slightly or entirely different.

At this moment, the nest is entirely bare in this quiet morning light. Tonight the table at which I now sit alone will be filled with the conversations and laughter and food that celebrate two birthdays in the family. God, you know fullness and emptiness, yearning and dread, receiving and letting go. Families give us the opportunity to experience all of these, and so much more. Today, help me to see how the ebb and flow of my family has shaped me, and how my receiving and letting go of my family has and will help to shape them. May I better understand how the clamorous joy of fullness and the quiet joy of emptiness are both gifts of the nest.

September 17
Burning Resentment

Our interests seemed similar enough, so I felt comfortable in inviting this new friend of mine to camp out in what I considered one of my most sacred campsites, a deep cove nestled under an enormous outcropping of rock over one hundred feet above. In planning for the outing, he offered to drive from our city to the trailhead, while I would provide the necessary details of the excursion, but when he arrived to begin our trek, I realized that he had another important detail that he wished to include in the night out. In the backseat of his car was a completely dried and frail old Christmas tree. As we drove to our destination, his story of the tree would unfold.

Within the past year, he had been enduring a painfully difficult divorce. His wife had left him and their young child, presumably for another relationship, although it was uncertain if that was the central reason. While he had maintained primary care for their child, arrangements had been made and were continually evolving for some shared care and visitation time, a reality he resented in light of her initial abandonment. Shortly after the Christmas season, he had removed his small Christmas tree from his home, but not wanting to dispose of it immediately, he planted it in a snow bank just outside of his front entrance to enjoy it for a short time more. Naturally, despite its cold and snowy basis, the long since dead tree continued to dry, its short, bunched needles turning a deep, rusty hue. One day when his estranged wife stopped by his home to pick up their daughter, she commented disparagingly about the dead tree, suggesting that it was an embarrassment to the house and that it was time enough for it to be taken to the garbage. Hearing her disdain, my friend discovered that the dry, prickly needles of the tree were a kind of affliction to his former spouse. In his anger and resentment towards her, he vowed to leave the tree there as long as he could, knowing that each time she dropped by, its very presence would inflict a little discomfort. It stayed there outside his door until the following fall, when he put it into the back of his car and brought it along on our camping excursion.

As we travelled, my new friend explained to me that he had recently realized that he needed to move beyond his anger and resentment. Although he took some sick joy in the tree's ongoing annoyance to his former spouse, he knew that the spite in which it was now firmly grounded was an unhealthy growth outside of his door. He needed to uproot it all. And so, there was this old parched and spindly Christmas tree, once decorated and brightly lit, as his marriage had no doubt once been, travelling towards its final letting go. Arriving at the trailhead, he hoisted the puny and prickly burden over his shoulder and carried it through the woods, full of strong and towering living trees, to our campsite. Settling in, the fire started, he broke off bough after bough of the wretched little tree, each limb now a growth of resentment, pain, and anger. As he tossed each dried branch into the fire, our cove glowed with new warmth.

Forgiving God, so many of us carry the brittle, dead weights of anger and resentment throughout our lives. Like the eyesore of a lifeless, dried tree outside our door, we either ignore their effect or spitefully stand firm within them. But there is no growth here; nothing healthful is produced. Help me to recognize how the pain and anguish of my life might be distorting my views, and with that insight, let me cut away and purge the malignant animosity that prevents me from burning most brightly, more ardently.

The main pool of the parking lot was filled as I arrived, so I swung my car into the wave of arrivals that spilled towards the outer reaches of the lot's checkered boundaries. Although it was a beautiful, autumn Sunday afternoon, the loaded lot was not at a local park, nor for a late-scheduled church service. No, the congregating stream was moving toward a local "watering-hole," *Buffalo Wild Wings,* just before the nationally scheduled kick-off time for another week of NFL football. Nearly every patron that passed through the restaurant-bar's portal was sporting the jersey or colors of some favored team, and I was no different dressed in my Minnesota Viking purple t-shirt and hat. I couldn't help but laugh a bit at myself and certainly the whole situation as I entered the subdued narthex of the establishment before passing into the raucous nave. Innumerable television screens, strategically placed, dotted the interior perimeter like stations of the cross in a Catholic church. With eight different games being simultaneously broadcast and received at this one site – like so many other sites just like it across the nation - each team's faithful followers found their monitor of homage telecasting the specific game they sought while always within easy eyeshot of every other ongoing game.

As football games get underway each fall weekend, it truly is an amusing, if not utterly amazing tradition of how loyal diasporas of each team's fan base congregate at local bars and restaurants, find each other through their shared display of team colors, and lift their voices – and glasses - in communal support of their team and in aggressive denial of their opposition's success. If there were ever a need for an argument confirming humanity's desire to experience and be community, these weekend rallies would have to be a powerful example. Although competition and an identifiable common enemy are the driving forces of these unions, there still is something uniquely special about the way total strangers can come together and so boisterously support one another and their teams each week. At its best and most detached level, I find myself even mingling with the opposition's faithful, aware that, as with interreligious gatherings, despite all of our grand fervor, we all come sporting colors and allegiances to what was likely "given to us."

Spiritually, such rallies of the faithful are played out weekly as well, although appropriately without the same kind of frolic. We do need such gatherings in support of our faith just as we do for our favorite sporting teams; of course, the intentions ought to be significantly different! Unfortunately, some religious gatherings can become competitively driven and enemy-focused as well, but ideally, our gatherings should emphasize support of one another in responding to our call to faith. There should be pride in our commitments and rituals, traditions that help give additional meaning to the spoken beliefs of the community and, perhaps, the more personal understandings that individuals bring privately to the table. But such pride should not spill over into aggressive, antagonistic and competitive behavior toward the spirited traditions of others. Such antics rarely work well at the local watering hole; and they have no place at a eucharistic table.

We may wear different colors at our gatherings, but in our spiritual communing, everyone can emerge a winner - something we should all be cheering about.

Creator of All Colors and Congregations, you have been called Victorious God by many generations of people. But your victories are over despair, hatred, injustice and death, not denominational teams and theological ideologies. While we wear the colors of different traditions and follow varying spiritual game plans, you are the shared victory that we all seek, a banner under which all colors and people become one voice. My prayers today are for the success of not only my own team's colors, but of all those who faithfully seek you in so many colorful ways.

September 19
Slowing the Pace

The runners that I used to coach always thought that I was some great distance runner in my prime. The truth is, I never even ran distance mileage until I began coaching it. I was an above average sprinter in my high school years, and anything over a quarter of a mile was "distance" to me then. At the "height" of my own distance career while coaching, I stroked around a 28:30 five-mile race once, about a 5:45 mile average, but any 5K under 18:00 and any five miler near 30:00 I counted as coups. Once I found the groove of distance running though, I preferred not to race, enjoying the release and fitness of it more than anything. When I ran consistently, my daily runs were anywhere from four to seven miles on average at about a 6:45 to 7:00 minute per mile pace. Recently, however, after taking some time off from running, I found it very difficult to get inside that groove again.

Working my way back into some consistent running, I became disenchanted by the physical labor that I fought through every time I went out for a run. At three miles, I would be ready to quit as my legs felt heavy and my breathing was desperate. I had never suffered from any kind of asthma or allergy, but gasping for air after so short of a run, I was convinced that I must be developing some new ailment. Stopping in the middle of a run or walking briefly were never even options in my past, but now I found myself easily giving into the fatigue, certain that something must be wrong. Five miles would be my top distance, at a pace no faster than 7:15 to 7:25, and the final two miles done with a kind of "bite the bullet" mentality. I thought of going at a slower pace, but since I already was, the idea only made me feel more weak and pathetic. Finally, after talking with a friend about how I was feeling, one day I purposely set out to "go slow."

I dropped in at a local running park one morning hoping that a former runner of mine might be there for her morning run; I knew that if I had a partner that forced me to slow down my pace I would feel less feeble, and visiting when I run always makes the miles fall away more quickly as well. Providentially, she was there that morning, and catching her just as she was about to begin, I carved a pleasant four miles alongside her, feeling so good at the trail's end that I added another half mile. Of course, our pace had been about 8:45.

Too often we want to hurry everything that we do, expecting strides of grand improvement almost immediately. Occasionally such success does come to some, but more often than not, we need to be more patient with ourselves and with the process that leads to our progress. Just as I experienced physically, spiritually one also needs to be patient with the process. If I have not had a regular routine of prayer, should not expect to suddenly start one and contentedly stay with it. Like running, one needs to build into it, develop a kind of prayerful stamina. Meditation looks easy, but when I try to empty myself and be still for more than ten minutes at a time, I quickly realize that meditation is a long distance challenge. And like all exercise forms, one needs to be consistent; once or twice a week is better than nothing, but I won't likely find the contentment that I am looking for in that pithy of an effort.

I am continuing to fight my way back into a more satisfying running condition, but I have had to first face the truth about the shape I am in and to alter my training accordingly. Resilient God, I want my spiritual condition to be equally as fit as my physical. Help me to recognize that in things spiritual I also must be consistent in my efforts and respectful of the stages of my development. Let me not grow frustrated with the slowness of my pace and the labor of my efforts, but work diligently – faithfully – toward a steadfast, spiritual stride.

September 20
Autumn Air

Every year around this time in central Ohio, there is an almost overnight shift in the daily temperature and in the feel of the air. After weeks of late summer humidity and heat spilling into the early fall calendar, it is almost as if one night the summer decides to pack up its baggage and quietly move out without announcement. In the wake of the summer's exit, the air becomes cool and fresh. The windows of the house, locked and sealed up for months to keep the humidity's dampness at bay, are celebratively thrown open again and the new unsullied air comes rushing in. The autumn parade is coming to town!

Some people, of course, will rue the loss of the summer's heat and view the autumnal changes as a short walkway to the door of winter's dreadful chills. But while I enjoy the shirtless warmth of summer days, I always welcome this seasonal shift and the purification it seems to bring. For while the daytime temperatures shift to a more easy and moderate level, the nights' chill cleanses the air and each morning is the dawning of freshness. The labored breathing of my daily humid runs is resuscitated, and my strides feel light and new again.

We often take our air for granted and fail to recognize the intimate life connection that we have to it. Thoughtlessly breathing throughout our days and nights, we expect the air around us to be as constant and as natural to us as the blood that flows through our veins. Occasionally we read stories or see images of Los Angeles smog or Chinese air pollution, or perhaps we know someone who individually suffers from any variety of allergies; in these instances, we know that the air can be infected, but generally, most people breath in and breath out with little thought or concern about it.

Our connection to the air is much like our relationship with God. For those of us who believe in God's loving existence, God is forever present to us whether we choose to acknowledge the presence or not. As with the air, we cannot live without God's presence ever surrounding us and the gifts with which God sustains us – the air and water being, perhaps, our two most important lifelines. Failure to respect these gifts, however, like abandoning our relationship with the Creator, can jeopardize the quality of our living, polluting the air and causing spiritual allergies. Like miners trapped in a collapsed mine, a neglected spiritual life and an irresponsible use of God's gifts can place us deeply in harm's way.

Revitalizing God, I thank you for the change in the air that comes with each autumn season, a refreshing inhale that also reminds me of my intimate connection to you. As the air, you sustain me whether I acknowledge you or not; but as with our air quality indicators, when I am more mindful of my relationship with you, and when I live with thoughtful recognition of your presence and gifts all around me, then I breathe in more respectfully and more cleanly the life that you give me and breathe out my shared and cooperative role in this life.

September 21
Bait and Switch

On a recent weekend of camping with my wife, she asked me not long after the sun had gone down on our warm, sunny, and lazy autumn day of hanging out, "Do you think it's late enough to go to bed yet?" It was only 9:15, but I acknowledged that one of the joys of camping was that time didn't matter. "When it gets dark, if you're tired, you go to bed," I replied. It is true; there's not much to do when you're camping once it's dark, so shortly thereafter, she headed off to bed down in the tent while I stayed up a while longer shifting time between the fire's warm glow and gazing at the bright night sky. The next morning, I got up early and stoked the fire, prayed, wrote a bit, and then fixed some breakfast. Almost two hours after my rising, I thought that maybe I should awaken her. My wife's approach to camping is significantly different than mine, but I was just happy to have her out there with me, for her camping presence is not very common.

When my wife and I first started dating, she willingly joined me a number of times in some backcountry experiences, and I thought how wonderful it was to have a romantic partner join me camping. But once we got married, she never went with me again. For years I kiddingly chided her for what I called her "bait and switch" routine: bait me with a belief that she shared my love of backpacking and camping; then, once married, switch and abandon it altogether. In truth, however, her early willingness to join me, and her later readiness to let me go off on my own are signs of her true love for me.

Early in a relationship, one needs, even desires to explore "the world" of the other; it is how we get to truly know what makes the other tick. But once one has made

301

enough small "discoveries" *about* the other and the larger discovery of love *for* the other emerges, the explorations are not as necessary, especially if they are not truly of interest to the explorer. True love for another does not need to engage in all of the other's interests. Sharing in the experience of another's interest and finding it "acceptable" is enough; then, one can choose to love the other for who he is, and not for one's ability to hold every interest in common. For my part, to have my wife return to some camping with me is fun and exciting, but I also know that as she has accepted and encouraged this interest of mine through the years, with or without her, my love for her needs to allow her to experience "my interest" at her own pace and comfort level. So, if she likes to go to bed early and then sleep in as well, that's what I'm going to let her do!

God of Loving Flexibility, you may not "enjoy" all of my interests and actions, but I believe that you love and accept me completely for who I am, and that you call me to love others with that same unconditional nature. The ideal of romantic love seems to be that one finds a partner with whom he can share all of his life's interests and goals; perhaps that does happen for some, but I tend to believe that a greater love is born out of our ability to love another fully despite our differences. To share in my beloved's interest without it being my own, and to have her share in mine, this is a love that makes my fire glow and my stars shine – and she can sleep on that all that she wants!

September 22
Sikh and You Shall Find

Many North Americans mistakenly assume that a man they see wearing a turban is a Muslim. In fact, Muslim men have no dress code at all concerning the covering of their heads, although regionally, such as in Afghanistan, head coverings for Muslim men are quite common. But a man wearing a true, neatly wrapped turban anywhere in the world, and especially here in North America, is most likely an adherent of the Sikh religion. As with the confusion of turban wearing itself, Sikhs are a much-misunderstood religious tradition.

Sikhism is one of the "newer" religious traditions of the world with its foundation dating back to only the late Fifteenth century. Its founder, Guru Nanak Dev, was an extraordinary holy man whose story should serve as a model for us all today. Born and raised in the Punjab region of what is now eastern Pakistan and northwestern India, Guru Nanak's spiritual origins are planted within Hinduism; but equally influenced by his lifelong contact with Islam, early in his life, Nanak rejected the strict codes of Hinduism and sought a more common ground between the two religious traditions of his homeland. At the age of thirty, historically a very common age of spiritual enlightenment in many religious traditions, Nanak suddenly disappeared one day when he plunged into the River Bain, in honor of his Hindu roots, for his daily bathing. While those dear to him feared that he had drowned, Nanak reemerged after three days of communing with the Creator; he was a changed man with a brilliant glow about his eyes and face, and when he broke his silence he simply uttered: "There is no Hindu, no Muslim." Seeking to cut through the rituals, the sacred texts, and the authority that had created such division and animosity between the two religions, Nanak proclaimed, in a very Muslim fashion: "There is but One God, His name is Truth, He is the Creator." And then he continued in a much more Hindu-like tone: "He fears none, He is without hate, He never dies, He is beyond the cycle of births and death, He is self illuminated, He is realized by the kindness of the True Guru. He was True in the beginning, He was True when the ages commenced and has ever been True, He is also True now" (Japji).

For the next forty years, Guru Nanak would preach a simple message of daily devotion to God, but without blind rituals; a rejection of all caste, creed, racial and gender distinctions; and a dedication to family life, honest labor, and social responsibility. He died on this day in 1539, and even in his death, he exemplified his commitment to the reconciliation of the two opposing religions. With followers from both religions wishing to honor him in their own traditional fashions, Nanak told them as he sensed his impending death: "You place flowers on either side, Hindus on my right, Muslims on my left. Those whose flowers remain fresh tomorrow will have their way." The next morning, when his followers lifted the sheet that had covered him in his passing, they discovered nothing except the flowers – all of which were fresh.

The word "Sikh," in the Punjabi language, means "disciple." As a mark of dedication to their discipleship to God - the True Guru - and to the Sikh community, Sikhs today do not cut their hair; it also serves as a reminder to live as the Gurus and many other spiritual prophets have done. The turban, known as a "dastar," which covers their unshorn hair is a symbol of the royalty and dignity of one who is a disciple of the True Guru, the Creator.

For Sikhs, Guru Nanak Dev did not self-orchestrate an attempt at wedding two religious traditions; he received a vision that directed him to do what God wanted for all people. I cannot say that Sikhism is the way for all people, but I am certain that the God of Sikhism, the God of Islam, the God of Hinduism, the God of Christianity, the God of Judaism – the God of every theistic Tradition – is the God of All.

Creator, God of All, your servant, Guru Nanak, recognized the divisiveness that too often grows amongst and between religions creating a gash that wounds the very heart of their message of love and devotion to you, and respect and care for one another. In whatever tradition I follow, may I never forget that you are the Creator of us all and that my greatest witness to that truth, as shown through the actions of Guru Nanak, is the way that I love and serve everyone.

September 23
Cold Crickets

Autumn temperatures in Ohio, as I am sure they do in other parts of the Midwest, usually deliver a wide and varied range that is surpassed only by the array of colors offered by the accompanying changing leaves. When the sun sinks away on the day, temperatures tend to drop fairly quickly, and by nightfall, words like "cool" and "chilly" are commonly used in neighborly weather talk. If the summer's humidity is lingering or rebounding, the brisk morning air is downright damp, but it will also get things brewing more once the sun cracks open the new day. By noon, the color palate is on display and baking in the rising temps that remind one that summer is not so distant of a memory.

Weeks ago, while the day's heat loitered longer into the evening and night, the crickets and katydids began their late summer/early fall mating charge, the males seductively attempting to draw the females in with their rhythmic chirping. Now, as the temperature diminishes in the evening and throughout the night, their chirping slows with it, and by morning when I step out to greet the day, they sound tired and chilled. Even like us warm-blooded creatures, the movements and sounds of these nocturnal cold-blooded insects are affected by the changing climate. With us, however, it is not just the colder temperatures that slow us down and trim our voices; a chilly atmosphere can slow and silence us as well.

We have all likely had the warmth of our goodness quickly refrigerated by the cold looks and the cold shoulders that we sometimes receive from others. The causes can be as ranging as the autumn temperatures, but the chilling effect is usually the same. Like a bedroom window open to the autumn air, sometimes we can even inherit the air around us; the cold air is not ours, but it blows into our space and chills everyone inside. In the fall, the morning sun begins to soften the night's chill and by afternoon, warmth is restored. In uncomfortable situations iced by cold hearts, each of us can be like that morning sun providing warmth to the new day. It is not about "fixing a problem," for like the autumn temperatures, oftentimes we are not responsible for the chill nor can we control it. But like the sun, we arrive with warmth and the cold edges begin to melt; we shine, and the darkness abates and the color of life is restored.

In this changing season of the year, we can hear and see and feel all around us reflective examples of how we live. While there is so much glorious life around us to be enjoyed, we sometimes are greeted by cold looks, shoulders and air that can silence us and suck out the glory of the day. But we can respond to these temperatures with the warmth and glow of the sun, just as you, Invigorating Creator, do for us on our brilliant and colorfully unfolding autumn days. Will I take the Creator's lead on this day, or will I shrink away quietly like the katydids and crickets?

September 24
Ahimsa: True Nonviolence

Ever since the Vietnam war, when guerilla warfare became especially common, many "war crimes" seem to me a strange contradiction. After luring our youth (they generally don't recruit people beyond their early twenties - the older a person is the less he will believe and buy into the system) into the ranks of the "elect" with financial aid for schooling, protective benefits, job training and just general, good "oo-rah" fun and excitement, our military branches must teach these recruits how to kill, for killing does not come naturally to most human beings. By demonizing the enemy, who are really comprised of people just like our recruits fighting for a cause that they have also been led to believe is right, just and true, we make them less than, or certainly "other than" human, and, therefore, more "easy" to kill. Properly and fully trained, the recruits are then shipped off to remote places, quite foreign to the upbringing of most, and are placed in dangerously volatile situations of life and death where they will now have to react and respond within the confines of their training. Ultimately, what they have been taught and the environment in which they now must live and fight look nothing like the society from which they entered; and yet, given all of these extraordinarily high levels of tension and stress, the soldiers are expected to act within the boundaries of the law and of human decency. If they don't, they may be arrested and tried before a military tribunal court and possibly sentenced to imprisonment. For me, the logic of such "preparation" and then the demands that succeed it run so counter to what I believe about human nature and the spiritual dimension of our lives that I have no option but to be a pacifist.

Martin Luther King, Jr., a Christian, was famous for his "gospel of nonviolence," but his philosophy was especially influenced by Mohandas K. Gandhi, who was often labeled as a Hindu, although I suspect that he would not have claimed any singular religious tradition. The blossom of Gandhi's nonviolence more truly emerged from his Jain influence, another though smaller indigenous tradition within India. The central guiding principle of life for Jainism is *ahimsa*. An unchangeable, eternal law, the Sanskrit word "ahimsa" is most loosely translated as "nonviolence" or "not desiring to harm." But ahimsa is so much more than simply practicing nonviolence towards other human beings. For Jains, ahimsa encompasses all life forms and it goes well beyond the fundamental prevention of physical harm, enjoining the intentions of all actions, words and thoughts. True or complete ahimsa is only realized when one eradicates all passionate desires from one's heart and mind, and lives with an active compassion for all living things.

Ahimsa, nonviolence and pacifism are not a "death sentence" to passivity; self-defense and a desire to survive seem to be very natural, innate, human qualities. But these three approaches to life do pose deeper inquiries into the intentions of our thoughts, words and actions, and challenge us to consider why violence is our response and if there are not other alternatives. The pinnacle of Jain ahimsa may seem extreme, but it seems less unnatural than training young men and women to go out and kill others in support or in defiance of a political, economic, or religious ideology.

God of True Peace, if you are the creator of all things, and if all that you have created is essentially good, then the harm or destruction of any part of your creation seems an act of less than complete and true goodness. It is absolutely improbable that I can go through this or any day without causing some kind of harm or damage to something, but I can learn to live more mindfully and more respectfully toward all that is around me. Life is a most precious gift for which I am deeply grateful; help me to more faithfully honor the life of every other living thing as well.

The United States has built an incredible industry of professional sports. I cannot believe that there is anywhere else in the world where a country and its people put so much time and energy and emotion into so many professional sports. Oh yes, the Europeans and Central and South Americans are obsessively supportive of their futbol, or as we Americans call it, soccer teams, but no nation can possibly rival our "industry" of so many sports, each with their incredible stadiums, courses, salaries, advertising and fan bases. To be sure, I am part of this "amazing" network.

Like many people, I suspect, as I have aged, I find that my affections and interest in sports has shifted considerably. When I watch our favorite football team with my son, I sometimes get concerned about his excessive emotional tantrums, highly charged, and sometimes vicious outbursts cast at "our team" or its opponents. But then I remember, when I was his age, sitting with my wife on a Sunday afternoon, "enjoying" another fix in my addiction to the American vicarious sports experience; "my team" had just suffered another setback in "our pursuit" of victory, and frustrated and disgusted, I hurled the pen with which I had been simultaneously grading papers at the television. I had finally "crossed the line" and my wife, disgusted with my reaction, rose and walked out of the room. Some weeks later, or maybe it was in another season altogether – they are all such a blur in my memory any more – I had suffered through yet another "slipped through our hands" Monday night football game loss, and going to bed late with work early the next morning, realized all of my insides were tied up in aggravated knots. Lying in bed too tightly wound up to fall asleep, I tripped right over the obvious and huge truth that prevents so many others from ever caring for or viewing competitive, especially professional, sports at all. I had just spent over three hours of my very crowded time watching grown men play a game of honed natural ability and physical skill, cheering and anguishing privately in my home where my emotions did nothing for the participants, and the end result for me was frustration and sleeplessness. Tomorrow morning, hung over with the ill-effects of another loss, I would go back to work with less accomplished than might have been had I not watched the game, and "my team," absolutely ignorant and probably indifferent of the ill-effects of last night's game on this wretched soul's life, would go about their sporting business. In the darkness, a light emerged within me that if I was to continue "to enjoy" professional sports then something had to change in my approach to them.

Vicarious experiences, of many kinds, are very valuable. Transfixed in the physical and emotional efforts of others, we do garner some necessary satisfaction in the thrill of their victory as well as the agony of their defeat. Ideally, while we titillate ourselves in our desire for a shared success, in the celebration of "our victory" and in the anguish of "our loss," we learn to be better winners and losers. But when our identity with a given team becomes excessively personal, and we are unable to separate ourselves and our emotional state of being from "their game," something needs to change – and it isn't "our team's" game plan.

Supportive God, my vicarious involvements can be valuable opportunities for emotional release as well as mental empowerment, but I do need a sense of perspective. Help me to develop a strong line between my enjoyable support of another and my excessive emotional devotion to another. All of my cheering won't likely change "my team's" world anymore than their victories will change mine. May my voice of positive energy buoy their efforts, and may their efforts provide me with encouraging results. As for the wins and losses, somebody somewhere will always be happy while someone else will be disappointed; knowing this truth, may I stand firmly in who I am while the balls, pucks, javelins, darts - whatever! - fall where they will.

September 26
Giving Your Whole Self

Over my many of years of coaching cross-country, I was blessed with a tremendous corps of supportive parents. When one group would exit with their graduating children, I would wonder how are we going to do without them? Who will pick up the slack and cover the needs now? And every year a new group would show up almost seeming to up the ante of service and support and outdo the previous year's efforts. In my private "Hall of Fame of Parents," one mother in particular will always have her own special nook.

Suzanne, and even her daughter who joined our team in her freshmen year, knew nothing about the sport of cross-country when we first met, but, like most parents, she arrived on the scene ready to support her child's new interest and efforts. It didn't take her long to get involved and to become one of the team's most vocal supporters during the races; to this day, I have only to close my eyes and listen carefully to hear her raspy, excited voice shouting out, "Let's go, Hawks!"

Over the years, a tradition developed of parents bringing the runners snacks and drinks for after the races. In the early years, the selections were too often rather unhealthy choices, cookies and the like. Suzanne always brought bagels, but not just any dry, hard old bagel; she started bringing boxes of *Panera* bagels, at the time a new chain of "coffee-shop-bagels" that were to die for. I always made sure to slide by the team's tent and campsite between races to snap up one of those tasty treats before the kids devoured them post-race. Another team tradition was our annual preseason camping trip where I took "these city kids" out into the woods for a few days to train, to play and to pray. It was always an important team-building time as well as an early training session, and it always needed much parental support. I don't remember if Suzanne made it down to help out on her daughter's freshmen season, but I am pretty sure she was there for each of the next three seasons. And, once the season started, *if* she did miss a meet/race, it was only because she was at her other daughter's field hockey game that conflicted with our schedule.

As her daughter's final season drew to a close, Suzanne would often lament about what she would do now without her cross-country family, for, according to her, we had become as important to her as she was to us. Announcing one day that

"I'll just have to come back next year, anyway!" she was chided by a special parent-friend that surely she would find something more important to do. But Suzanne insisted, and a friendly one hundred dollar bet ensued that she would not be around next year. At the following year's banquet, the fall after her daughter's graduation, she received a one hundred dollar bill from her friend, for not only was Suzanne, once again, at camp that season, but she never missed one meet, and we never failed to hear her beloved cry, "Let's go, Hawks!"

The following year, she did finally back away, but two weeks before her planned attendance at one of her favorite race venues, she passed away suddenly due to a brain aneurysm. I had the opportunity to visit and pray with her one last time in the hospital where she was hooked up to machines keeping her body alive while her family made preparations, per her request, to donate all of her organs so that, in the end, sixteen other lives could be enhanced or saved. Today, on the anniversary of her death, both literally and figuratively, she lives on in and through the lives of so many.

Generous God, thank you so much for the many wonderful people who have moved though my life, touching me and those I care about with an indelible mark. Made in your image of generosity, we are all called to provide love and caring service to one another; and sometimes, we are reminded of this vocation through the incredible munificence of an other. In thanking you for and in honoring these wonderful lives, may I also prayerfully consider how I am living out my vocation of service. What kind of model am I to the world today?

September 27
Passing Trains in the Night

Carved into the base of the mountain, a railroad track runs along the east-northeast bank of the New River in West Virginia transferring people and coal up and down the stretch of the river's groove every day. In the more northerly reaches of the river, small towns dot the banks like a steady Morse code, but down along the stretch of the gorge region and the National River designation more to the south, the train is one of the only vestiges of humanity. On the opposite bank of this section, in national forest land, a series of very accessible, but limited campsites have been established right along the river. Night comes early in these parts nestled deep in the canyon and surrounded on all sides by dense forests; when the sun slips behind the mountain tops, the canopy of trees drops a dark blanket over all and the night sky lights are only visible through the holes in the fabric. On weekends and especially during the height of the river-rafting season, these campgrounds are crawling with campers who keep the dark stillness of the night at bay deeper into the night with their campfires and lanterns and flashlights. But on an off-season night, the silence is as thick as the darkness – until a train comes.

It was a lonely early fall night the first time I camped in this region. My wife and I had settled down amongst the rocks on the southwestern bank of the river to watch the sun drift through the clouds and down the backside of the mountain as the river slipped by us just as lazily. Suddenly we heard a distant rumble coming through the trees, and while we were aware of the train track bed sliced into the opposite river bank and camouflaged by the foliage, this was our first sound and sight of the locomotive barging through the forest's interior. Soon it rumbled by directly across from us, a hundred or so cars passing between the tree trunks and undergrowth, a low, steady thunder with periodic shrieks of metallic lightning. When the last train car slipped by, the wake of sound slowly dissipated until all around us was empty silence again. We wondered then what the frequency of this colossal intruder might be through the night, figuring that, whatever its cargo, it was probably more of a daytime episode.

Bedtime came early in the density of the darkness, and sleep arrived quickly in the quietude, but sometime in the middle of that night and then again later, we were awakened by the slow, steady rumbling of the train charging through the trees along the riverbank. Had we not experienced it once by daylight, the approaching grumble may have been more shocking, for it starts like a low grade earthquake and builds into a bellowing yawn, a monstrous presence crashing through the woods. What must the Native people and the indigenous animals have thought upon their first encounter of it, seen or unseen?

Tumultuous intrusions occasionally break into our lives in forms known and unknown. From unexpected familial guests to a new workload expectation to something truly wild and dangerous, these impositions, catching us unaware, can arrive with an uncertain terror. Even if we recognize who and what they are, and know that there is nothing for which to be afraid, the sheer unexpectedness of the intrusion can leave us feeling unsettled. And if the intrusion is truly unknown, how much more disturbed we can be by the burden of it! At such times, we need to rally our best defenses, not in retaliation, but against the unwarranted fears that can exacerbate a situation. I am reminded here of the old adage, "expect the unexpected." Knowing that change or simple intrusions can come at any time, we need not fight back, but rather step back, perceive the situation more accurately and then respond appropriately.

God of Steadiness, sometimes the quiet calm of my life can be suddenly upset by an unexpected intrusion. Snug in the comfort of my routines, my personal space and my contentment, any number of intrusions can disrupt the flow and ease of my life and send me running in fear or striking out blindly. When the thundering trains of interruptions upset the quiet ease of my life, help me to not respond with alarm and worry, but gaining some perspective, to embrace them with acceptance, perhaps even amusement and wonder, knowing that soon they will pass by and the quietude will return.

September 28
Building Bridges

Crossing over the New River Gorge Bridge in West Virginia, one would never realize the expanse that opens below him nor see the amazing architectural feat that supports his vehicular traverse of the span. With four lanes and a wide berm set between the high-walled barriers on either side, one would have to be in a high bus or a semi-tractor trailer to get a glimpse of what is below while crossing the over half mile expansion. But if one pulls into the Visitor Center on the southeast side of the bridge, he will see the 876 foot drop that falls away beneath the bridge to the popular whitewater rafting river below and she can read extensively of how this amazing structure was designed and built. Completed in 1977, the New River Gorge Bridge, built on a single steel-arch structure, was once boasted as the longest and highest bridge of its type. While it continues its claim as the highest vehicular bridge in the Americas, other such structures in China and France have now surpassed it; nevertheless, descending the wooden walkway from the visitor's center and viewing the bridge from the wooden platform below, one cannot help but marvel at the engineering and craftsmanship that went into its creation. Although the bridge weighed in at a final cost of $37 million dollars, it has provided a far safer mode of traversing the gorge and at a substantially faster rate. One piece of literature speaking of the bridge's value notes that the "completion of the bridge cut the travel time from one side of the gorge to the other from 45 minutes to 45 seconds."

There are bridges all across North America, let alone the world, that are phenomenal expressions of human ingenuity and unbelievable feats of construction. I have watched the construction of a number of local bridges spanning less than three hundred feet in width over rivers no more than fifty feet below, and have still marveled at the process. The engineering and construction involved in joining two pieces of land separated by a river or a valley or a river gorge is a monument to the initiative, the will, the inventiveness and the skills of humanity. Roads carved into and through mountainsides are phenomenal enough, but when they leap through the air joining separated lands as bridges do, they almost defy limits.

Despite all of our architectural and engineering feats, however, human beings seem incapable of bridging their differences. From political and economic issues, to cultural and religious traditions, wherever we encounter significant differences of opinion, we humans tend to build walls and barriers rather than bridges and overpasses. The annual percentage of our nation's annual budget that is given to things military and defense has always been a staggering sign of our unwillingness to seek true accord and peace. How many dollars have been spent, how many great minds have been employed for the sake of war and control in comparison to real efforts of peace and mutual respect. Oh, the latter is not neglected entirely, but all too frequently, such efforts also have economic and political advantages attached. And while nearly every religious tradition in the world today preaches a message of love, why is it that so many people go neglected and so many more continue to die in the defense – or even offense! – of their religious beliefs. Where are the bridges of hope, kindness, and service that would defy these differences? As with actual bridge building, the intentions of such efforts need not be to make two pieces of land one, but rather to link two separate pieces, making one side conveniently and neighborly accessible to the other.

Creator God, Architect of the Universe, we human beings masterfully engineer passageways into remote interiors and erect bridges over expansive separations of land. And yet, amongst ourselves we often create deep crevices and churn raging waters of differences that not only separate us, but do so with hostility as well. You have gifted us with the ability to ingeniously create connections and to traverse differences through bridge building. As we have achieved such feats so well in the physical realm, help us to seek the engineering necessary to peacefully and humanely bridge our political, economic, cultural and religious differences with equal wonder.

September 29
Illimitable Love

Even during my most competitively driven years of coaching, I never believed for a minute that God cared one iota as to which team or athlete won. What I did "coach," however, was a belief that God was well pleased by great efforts, that God was honored when people chose to reach for and realize their potential. If an athlete sought a little extra "umph" from God, then his "try" had to first exceed his own imagined limits before there would be any chance of a "divine triumph" – and even then, I'm not really sure God cared one way or the other. Competition is a human thing; it can suck the best out of any of us or reduce us to pathetic ruin, but it is not likely that God is tallying championships. Competition too often breeds conflict, disdain, envy, arrogance, and even violence; these are not the trophies and medallions of love that God would award. In Buddhism's "Brahmaviharas," a series of high bar moral codes of conduct, we receive what I believe best mirrors God's approach to our competitions. "The Four Illimitables," each a deeply challenging aspect of love, are four qualities of which we can never have enough.

The first two of these, "loving kindness" and "compassion," appear to be nothing more than the art of love itself. But "metta," the Pali word used by the Buddha to label the first "illimitable," and "karuna" the second, require universal love. The nature of both of these two illimitables is exemplified beautifully in a story of Jesus when his understanding of Jewish law and moral code is challenged by one of the "experts" of his time. A dubious Jew in the eyes of the Jewish authorities because of his willingness to question regulations, Jesus is asked by a "scholar of the Law" whose intention was to test him, "Teacher, what must I do to inherit eternal life?" Always quick on his feet, Jesus turns the question back on the scholar, "What is written in the Law? How do you read it?" Without hesitation, the scholar responds with "the Great Commandment": "You shall love the Lord your God with all your heart, with all your being, with all your strength and with all your mind, and your neighbor as yourself." Agreeing with the scholar's response, Jesus simply adds, "Do this and you will live." But then comes the enlightening turn when the scholar, wanting to push Jesus further, asks, "And who is my neighbor?" Again, ever the ready sparring partner, Jesus does not answer directly but offers one of his most famous parables, a teaching story, "The Good Samaritan" (Lk. 10:25-37).

In this parable, a man is beaten and robbed and left to die along a road. Two Jewish officials, a priest and a Levite, pass by the dying man, but busy with their own affairs fail to stop and help him. A Samaritan, a man of mixed race who would have likely been highly disrespected by the scholar, then approaches, and after stopping, sees to it that all of the victim's needs are cared for. As Jesus ends the story, he returns to a question: "Which of these three, in your opinion, was neighbor to the robber's victim?" Of course, the scholar could only answer, "The one who treated him with mercy." To which Jesus stamps his answer, "Go and do likewise." Notice that Jesus does not really answer the question of "Who is my neighbor?" but offers instead and much more importantly, "what a 'neighbor' looks like." There is no "who" because *all* are included; everyone is your neighbor, he is saying. Ironically, while Jesus certainly jabs his point home by citing a Samaritan as the caregiver, the important issue is still not so much "who" provides the care, but that care was provided. The Samaritan stops not to show that Samaritans are better than Jews, but to show one human being who feels compassion for another. The law is to love illimitably, and that love should flow out of me in illimitable directions guided by an empathetic awareness that everyone around me, regardless of labels and appearances, is just like me.

Jesus' parable had some bite to it because of the "competition" in his time between Jews and Samaritans; but Jesus and the Buddha's challenge transcends competition. We are simply to act with a boundary-less loving kindness that is driven by a compassion of affinity, where everyone lives within our borders. Illimitable God, your love for all of your creations knows no boundaries, and is not limited to certain teams or people. Each of us, made in your image and likeness, are challenged to see God in one another and to be the hands of God for one another. My greatest competition is with myself; help me to overcome my own self-interests and to follow the Buddha's lesson of illimitable love, and Jesus' words to "go and do likewise."

September 30
Illimitable Joy and Equanimity

Prior to tournament races, I would always gather my runners together for what I intended to be a motivational "chalk talk." Having spent countless hours scouting the results of other teams and highlighting their strengths and weaknesses, I would present my analysis of what our team's and some individuals' potential finishes might be trying to be as honest as possible, but always willing to reach a little for the stars. All of our training from preseason and through the season, and all of our meets and invitationals along the way would come down to this race, I would remind them. This is when we want to put it all together, when we want to attain our peak performance and to achieve our season-long sought-after success. Of course, privately I was aware that just about every other coach who had a respectably talented team was saying and thinking and preparing in a very similar fashion. And at the end of the tournament race day, some of us would be disappointed at not having reached our imagined potential, and others of us would go home elated by our success and start thinking about the next week's challenge.

In my early years of coaching, I had some very disheartening tournament weekends where my athletes just didn't seem adequately prepared either physically or mentally or both, but in my last years, I weathered the ups and downs much better. Although I didn't really think about it consciously then, I now realize that my slightly less stressful later tournaments were due in large part to my more Buddhist-like approach, embracing more of the spirit of the final two of the Four Illimitables of Buddhism. The third Illimitable, "mutta," is "sympathetic or appreciative joy," while the fourth, "upekkha," is "equanimity."

At the Regional Championship of my last State qualifying team, as I spurred my runners on to the finish line, I was convinced that our efforts had come up short of our desire. The girls had emotionally given their all to the race, but it was not their best collective effort, and as I watched the stream of runners cross the line and tried to gather at least a general estimation of the scores, I felt so certain that our endeavor would come up short that I freely began consoling our runners about our season's end. Not long after this, however, heartache rose to incredible elation when it was announced that we had in fact qualified, and the original tears of sadness now flowed with a far different flavor – for my girls. But there were lots of tears of sadness streaming from the faces of other teams' runners. This is competition: some win and are happy; others lose and are sad. The third illimitable of sympathetic joy, however, pushes aside the duality that is ever-present in competition. This joy appreciates the success and the good fortune of all, no matter if they are related or not. From this perspective, there is happiness no matter what the personal end result, because if I lose, someone else has won; others have succeeded in realizing their goal, and for their success, I am joyful. Of course, such an approach tends to fly in the face of "true competition," and subsequently, the fourth illimitable of equanimity is so important, and, so very difficult.

On a beautiful autumn day, spread across an open field, over one hundred cross-country runners will line up for the start of a race. With the sun shining brightly overhead, its warming rays spill across the entire space and over every single runner. Everyone receives the gift of the sun equally; it is not impartial to those who have trained best or to those who have the kindest heart or to those who, after years of losing, finally deserve to win. The sun simply shines indiscriminately, and that is the spirit of equanimity. I wish well for all, and I wish well for all always. I do not support some because they deserve or have earned it, or because they have been so kind and supportive of me; nor do I wish ill for some because they have succeeded unfairly or excessively, or because they have always been our greatest arch-rival. Equanimity. All receive my loving kindness, my compassion and my sympathetic joy equally.

As one can imagine, it would be very difficult to be a good, American coach and to truly live within the spirit of The Four Illimitables at the same time. As I noted yesterday's entry, there is not much about God that suggests a favorable approach to competition, with the exception of "competing against oneself" and trying to grasp for one's full potential; and that approach would be its own reward. Victorious God, success by your standards might be better measured by how we all get along, by how we manage to overcome our differences and by how we succeed in living happily together. I live in a world driven by competition, that pits me against individuals, groups, and even countries. For the sake of my human spirit, perhaps, I can compete playfully, but keep me free from all malicious thoughts and actions. Help me to find joy in all people's joy, avoiding the duality that always separates us, and to offer my love and care for others just as your sun shines equally and freely on all.

October 1
Pizza, Beer and Desserts

After a steady week of work that had ridden on the rails of an emotional rollercoaster, I was eager to meet up with my wife, son and daughter-in-law for some pizza and beer at a favorite local pub, and collectively glide into our weekend. A bright and brilliant fall Friday was gliding to its finish as well as I slipped through the doorway of the tavern and paused momentarily to allow my eyes a quick adjustment to the darkened space before tossing explorative glances in search of my family. Accustomed to always being late, I smiled smugly at my being the first to arrive, and not immediately spying an open table, I sidled up to the bar and perched myself on a stool to watch for the others' entrance.

I had no more than ordered up my first beer of recompense for the week when a middle-aged man stepped before my half-turned roost and looking me in the eyes, smiled wryly and asked without words, "Do you remember me?" Having taught for nearly thirty years, I figure former students of mine must number in the thousands, and I have grown somewhat used to such random encounters; but as my eyes threw back a blank response, he broke the wordless Q and A: "Mr. Ryan? I'm sorry I don't remember your first name..." His voice cracked open my memory shell, and his name leapt from me immediately. Twenty-five years ago he had been a snarly youth daily crumpled in one of my classroom desks enduring the educational process. A state-qualifying wrestler as a teen, he had grappled his way through life since then and now stood proudly content with who and how he was, freely offering stories of the "take-downs" and "reversals" of his life that had now brought him to this place. As my family arrived and we moved towards a table, he managed to slip in beside us and take our match into overtime. "You probably didn't know this," he continued, "but you were one of the few teachers I respected. You got on 'our level' and treated us with respect."

With the pitcher emptied and the pizza devoured, I stepped back toward the bar to retrieve my tab and pay the bill. As I crossed through the tavern's tight quarters, my eyes tripped over a set of familiar faces just entering, five more former students, a group of former high school "girlfriends" out for the evening, a respite from their families and jobs. Through the noise of the cluttered space, one of the women's wandering glances bumped into my awareness of their entrance, and we volleyed simultaneous "Oh my gosh! It's you!" smiles toward each other. She quickly moved my way and helped me release the twenty-years-ago-names for which I was blindly grasping in the shadows of my memories. "You guys!" she exclaimed as she steered me towards her once "girl" now "women friends." No introductions were necessary as everyone quickly offered cups of memories from our own private pitchers. The visit was brief, but as fulfilling as the pizza had been filling. Just before I turned to leave, one of the women stopped me, and with a kind of shy embarrassment said, "Mr. Ryan." "Kevin," I responded emphatically. She smiled again, "I just want you to know that *you* are the reason I became a teacher. Your classes were just so interesting. I always looked forward to your class." Pubs don't usually offer desserts, but I had just been served a platter full of them.

When I taught that man and those women, I was much younger than they all are now. Teaching was my freshly chosen and slowly cooking career then, a beloved profession to make family ends meet. I did the best I could, always flavored with how-I-thought-I-should, and taking it from the oven twenty and more years later, I guess it all tasted pretty good. I didn't realize back then the impact I was having on each of them; I wonder if they realized the impact their words had on me so many years later.

We all touch and are touched by one another's lives in countless unknown ways. If we knew the impact we might have, we would probably fail to serve the meal-of-delight with as much satisfaction as we do. Nevertheless, it is good once in a while, to be reminded that what we do and what we say really does matter – so we had better do and say it well! Quiet and Unassuming God, somebody might need me to notice them today, a simple word or an ordinary gesture. What I do and what I say matter, whether I am aware of it or not. Help me to be faithful and true to whatever service I might offer.

October 2
Squirrel Ready

The squirrels in my backyard have been so busy lately. I suppose they have done this every year, but having never been home and able to observe them in this way, I never knew. It was the same outside my school room all those years though. Every fall throughout the day, the front yard of the school would be a bustle of activity as squirrels would race across the lawn collecting the falling acorns, burying some for an apparent safe-keeping – a winter safe-deposit box – and scurrying up the towering oak trees to misshapen bundles of leaf-nests wedged into the cruxes of the trees. I always wondered if they really remembered where they buried those nuts, or did they return to them through a sense of smell or some other marker.

Today, in my backyard, there is even a more rambunctious vitality about the step of the squirrels. Their bodies seem younger, more lithe, and they do not simply do their usual hop and sprint movement, but have added a ground spring, a literal leap into the air from all fours, as well as a playful tumble, a lissome rolling from branch to branch in the tangle of bushes and trees that form a yet green wall along the back edge. At school, the aged ones seemed voraciously determined to gather all that they could, not always working together, however, as they chased after one another when they sensed their space being violated. But here, these younger ones, while busy, seem ready for play and a bit of amorous courtship amidst the daily work routine. Their chase is playful, not malicious, and occasionally ends in a hurried and tender mounting.

These squirrels know that something is coming; in the air, they can feel the change that is building all around them, and they are preparing for it. The old ones, much more aware of the harshness of the winter ahead, more dutifully attend to the chores of preparation; the youth, not ignorant of the task, but with a little less discretion, seem equally interested in stocking the winter shelves as they do in propagating themselves. But there is much movement here, a distinct attention to necessary preparation.

We human beings sense change too. We see the signs of autumn all about is in the shifting colors of grass and leaves, and feel it in the variance of temperature each morning and evening. But not only with weather and seasonal shifts, we also often have an awareness of something changing within us or even in the intangibles around us. Unfortunately, despite these apparent awarenesses, we often don't seem to thoughtfully prepare for changes in quite the same way that the squirrels do. Obviously, we don't need to gather nuts nor hurriedly procreate, but we do need to more mindfully observe what is happening within and around us, and prepare our minds, bodies and hearts for the movement ahead.

O God of Eternal Motion, the energy of your spirit moves about us at all times altering the course of our lives. I can see in the creations the cyclical movement of the seasons, and can observe many preparing to embrace these changes. I too need to do some mindful preparation for the changes that naturally occur in my life, both seasonal and otherwise. Help me to be attentive to the signs of change around me, and reading these signs, to make the necessary adjustments in my life so that I can comfortably and lovingly embrace the challenges that change often brings.

October 3
Meeting My Children

While watching a football game recently, my son commented that maybe we should find a common weekend soon, before it is too cold, to get out for a quick weekend backpack trip. Excited that he would not only be interested, but then even initiate such an excursion got me jumping right away and looking for a compatible date. Although my son and I are both outdoorsmen, given a beautiful sunny day, I would choose the woods, mountains or canyons to hike, while he would likely choose a golf course to play. On the other hand, he will arise early not only for a tee time, but for hunting as well; whereas, I will get up early for a run, or another hike! We are certainly a good bit different, but we seek to share in each other's interests as well. Two of my own brothers are avid golfers like my son, and I always enjoy watching him engage with them. They can talk bunkers, greens and clubs with language and experience of which I am nearly empty. My son will endure pictures of my latest backpacking trip, and seek to make relative his hunting experiences of what might be seen and heard in the quiet morning hours of the waiting and watching in the woods. Essentially, we appreciate each other's passion although we may not be able to share in it deeply.

With sports, in general, and Columbus hockey and Minnesota football in particular, we connect very easily and frequently. We have spent numerous hours enjoying games together, either in a stadium seat, or a comfy chair at home or on a stool at the local sports pub. During these hours, we let go of work, family and other real life concerns, and just vicariously lock into the match-up of the day cheering on our teams, thoroughly enjoying our shared enthusiasm. Occasionally, with some irony, my son will seize these opportunities to share or to ask about some of his ongoing life concerns. While I would characterize myself as the one more interested in discussing serious issues, I would rarely, if ever, introduce them into my "game day" environment; he, on the other hand, must find this environment more easy and open for such talk. Subsequently, he might bring up a topic of which I have great interest, and there I am, fighting my urge to say, "Look, can we talk about this later; there's a game going on here right now." Most of the time, however, we are "wearing our colors" and fully engaged in the athletic battle that unfolds before and within us.

Most parents, if not all, want to have a good relationship with their children. We are often taught, however, like teachers with their students, that our children are not supposed to be "our buddies" or friends; we are to be a parent. But once they grow older, early adulthood, at least, I feel a little "buddying" is just fine; in fact, I seek it and want to increase it with each year. My children, physically and naturally related to me, obviously share some very significant connections with me. But my child is not me, and so, we have much to learn and to give each other as we grow older. Finding time to share with each of my children is essential in my getting to know who they are, and for letting them know who I am, not allowing our *observations* of each other to be the core of our understanding. We don't have to be exactly alike, perhaps it is even best that we are not, for in our differences we help each other grow and widen perspectives. I actually watch the final round of some golf tournaments now, and my son has called me numerous times to alert me to a particular episode of "Man Versus Wild" that my be in a place he knows that I have hiked. Meeting people where they are and how they are is how we all grow.

Wondrously Diverse God, you are not just "one thing" but all things. In you, all things wonderful and amazing, and common and simple, are to be discovered. You have created all life as a gift to all life; we have only to open the grand array of packages that come to our doorstep. My children are wondrous gifts to me; help me to be more present to the people that they are and, perhaps, will become. May I be encouraging and supportive of their lives, and may we meet as our lives unfold, as parent and child, human to human, friend to friend, and in any other way that you deem necessary. As you have guided me, may I be a source of guidance to them, and, in time, willingly receive their guidance as well.

October 4
Fire Keeping

On the rare camping excursion with my son, I quickly noticed his interest in taking care of the fire, so I turned that pursuit over to him, quietly letting go of the task I often find most comforting and rewarding when I am camping. Some might call the tending of a fire a job or a task, but I always see it more in the realm of an art, and then a relationship. Watching my son work with the fire throughout the night, I realized I had taught him nothing about fire keeping, and that he had, from my perspective, some things to learn.

In many of my communal prayer experiences, fire is often one of the central symbols and foci of the ceremony. I hesitate to even refer to it as a symbol, for I really view the fire as a living thing, not some object that we humans believe we can manipulate for our own purposes. Fire is a powerful energy and deserves a tremendous amount of respect. While it must be one of humanity's greatest "discoveries" – or perhaps, received gift – providing light, warmth and protection to name just a few of its blessings, we all know well enough how deadly and devastating fire can also be. Like its brother/sister, water, fire is a gift essential to our livelihood, and yet, disrespected and left unattended, it too can match its nurturing power with a moribund force.

When starting a campfire, I try to keep things as natural as I can, avoiding matches and lighter if possible. Beginning with the tiniest of twigs set atop my dried nest of starter material, I seek to nurture the heart of the fire, that deep, inner glow that is both the memory of the fire's origin as well as its hottest spot. Gradually, larger kindling is added and the girth and the height of the fire increase accordingly until small logs assist in the evolving life and force of the fire. Throughout this growth, I look to the fire as a respected companion, a desired and necessary one many times, and an emerging friend. Like all relationships, time and care are essential if a valuable friendship is to alight, and gentle prodding, along with a little discomfort, are to be expected if not necessitated.

That night watching my son work the fire, I saw how many people approach fire, almost like an adversary, thinking that they must master and control the fire. Although almost everyone enjoys building and maintaining the fire, too often unnecessary wood is piled on before it is needed, and wood, wet and unripened for the fire, is the fuel. When the smoke of a smoldering fire wafts about and irritates the keeper's eyes, he curses it and bellows about his bad luck as a "smoke magnet." But if one turns this scenario to the art of friendship, how differently the work and response to the fire will be.

God of Light and Warmth, the fire keeper of all life, today I thank you for the gift of fire, for all the comforts it affords me as well as the art of friendship it teaches me. On a cold night of camping, there is nothing more welcomed and desired than a fire; in the cold loneliness of our lives, there is nothing more welcomed and desired than a friendship. Both of these gifts need to be nurtured, and so I look to you, the Creator and Nurturer of all things bright and comforting, for the guidance and the patience that are necessary to cultivate a fire as warm as friendship, and friendship as comforting and lively as fire.

October 5
The Aches of Age

Coming off a recent backpacking trip, I found my hips a bit sore for the next couple of days, and my feet equally as tender. The pack was a little more heavy than usual at the start of the hike, and its weight on my hips was certainly reason enough for the inflammation; and the jarring movement of my up and down hill strides is to blame for the feet, but I remember a time when my resiliency was much better. Since I've started to spend more time "writing" - which really means typing - I've also developed a nagging ache that runs from my right hand all the way up my arm and into my shoulder. Obviously, the ergonomics of my typing posture are in need of correction, but also, this question of resiliency nags at me again. As my Father used to say, "Getting old is not for sissies!" No matter how much I work out, run and try to stay fit, the fact of the matter is, my body just does not respond in quite the same way anymore.

Trying to stave off these inevitable aches and pains of aging through some healthful choices is one of my first responses to realizing my aging process, but the other, more difficult one, is learning to accept and embrace the changes as well. For those of us who have lived fairly active, athletic - physical - lives, facing the deterioration of one's own body, its lessening resiliency, and its narrowing ability is no simple step. It is, in fact, consciously stepping inside one's mortality.

Call it rationalization if you will, but I do wonder if part of this slowing down of the body is not simply an effort on the part of the mind asking the body to step with it a little more harmoniously. When I was younger, more supple and more buoyant, I dashed off to and into all kinds of things, but a bit mindlessly. Doing things, and many things, was most important; thinking about what I was doing could come later. But with age, I find that *being in* things is now more important, thinking more about what and why I do things, not just doing them. However, I have a long history of doing, and so my inclination could easily be to just keep doing, except that my body needs me now to just take it a little more easily, and so, well, welcome aches and pains. Through this slowing down though, I now find myself spending more time being in a moment, reflecting more upon the simple and the sublime features of an experience.

O Ageless One, while my soul is a part of the infinite life, this body of mine is quite limited. Each year I may find the flexibility and the mobility of my physical life a little more reined in, and I rue these losses. But you have made me so much more than just the body; you invite me into a deeper spiritual awareness where I can enjoy endless expansiveness and elasticity. Soothe my physical aches and pains this day with the salve of awareness, a deeper understanding of my beingness and a thirsting desire for a stronger spiritual fitness.

October 6
The Mirror of Self-Pity

It has been pretty quiet around the house lately, an unhealthy hush for which, I know deep down, I am responsible. My wife and I are not talking much. We are not angry with each other; we are just not communicating very well. This uneasy quietude happens now and then, although it shouldn't, when one or the other or both of us get too wrapped up in our busy lives. Today, in my mind, it's her. My pace right now is pretty easy as I have some comfort time while I work on some personal writing; meanwhile, my wife is in the throes of a new school year: weekly preparations, daily grading and the constant reconfiguring of plans and meetings. I look forward to our evening time together, try to have a nice meal ready and try to be present to her stories of the day. But deep down, I am wanting more response, more attention, more affection; and while she juggles all of the tasks before and around her, she doesn't recognize my "needs." So I grow quiet and feel myself unhealthily turning within to meet myself at my self-pity party.

When we do talk about the day's events, I hear my voice responding, not avoiding conversation nor rudely snapping back, but it lacks an honest tone of kindness and care. When we crawl into bed at night weary from the day's efforts, I notice my body shuffle ever so slightly away from hers, not willing to give her full access to its warming comfort because I feel like I haven't received it from her today. And she should recognize and realize all of this subtle body language, my mind tells me, and do something about it! If not, I will slip away just a little farther.

Self-pity is an awful sinkhole. We know that good relationships develop through good communication, but sometimes we expect our partner or our friend to be the great mind-reader, the great provider, and the great communicator without our having to say a thing. They should know us and our needs by now, we reason! But a solid relationship is built on more than just good communication; it also involves a recognition of who the other is and what the other carries. When I selfishly get locked into what I want or what (I think) I need, very little recognition of the other happens, and, along with it, very little good communication. Yes, ideally, we want our loved ones to read us like a book, but sometimes the print of our book is way too small, pages are missing, and perhaps it is not even in a language they can read. Self-pity and self-interest make very bad printers.

Selfless and loving God, sometimes I find myself in a room full of mirrors, seeing only what I want and what I need. When I speak, even out loud, it is only to my own reflection. If I am lonely today, perhaps it is because I have not truly invited anyone else into my room of mirrors, nor cared enough to enter theirs. If I truly desire to seek your divine self, I will not find it by focusing on my selfish concerns. When I look away from my own reflection and stare into the heart of another's life, there I will see your face, and in that visage, my emptiness will be filled.

October 7
A Portrait of Myself

On one side of the main hallway of my wife's and my home, there is a series of old photographs capturing moments and images in the lives of some of our families' ancestors. On the opposite wall are the typical high school graduation pictures of the three children. Centered just above these three portraits, with a certain intentional inconspicuousness is a small, dark painting given to me years ago. The painting, mounted well above eye level, is a rather curious addition to the lively, smiling faces below it and the history reflected in the photos across from it. People rarely notice it, and even fewer ask about it, but I know that it is there, and have allowed it to remain despite its apparent incongruity amongst the other hallway adornments.

The painting was presented to me many years ago by a former student-athlete of mine who was an exceptional artist and who has continued to foster her gift. About a year before she gave me her simple painting, we had met at a reunion fun run which I hosted each year for parents and alumni runners of our school's cross-country program. At the time I was deeply wedged in the throes of divorce; my world had been rocked like never before, and without my truly realizing it, the exuberance of life that I had shared with my students and athletes for years was now a desert landscape. To cope with my emotional instability, I ran constantly, and with my appetite waning as well, my body gave up twenty pounds. When I look at pictures of myself at that time, I see a gaunt and fragile human being. And that is precisely what this dear artist friend of mine saw at this alumni reunion event.

A year later, the former student-runner-artist returned to the annual alumni fun run, but this time with a small gift she intended to give me afterwards. Having pulled myself from the precipice of my own demise, I probably looked a little more healthful and spirited this time around, but she cornered me all the same to share with me her insight. "I did this little painting a long time ago," she began, "and never really knew what to do with it. When I saw you here last year," she continued, her eyes capturing and holding me in dead earnestness, "I knew that this picture should go to you. You look happy again, well... better, at least, but I want you to know what I saw last year. It might serve as a reminder of where you were." The still-life painting, all in dark tones, shows only a small vial in a shadowy corner, with a mere drop of water in the corner of its base. "This is what I saw when I looked at you last year," she finished, handing me the painting, "a nearly empty jar."

For many years now, I have been so far removed from that nearly empty, dark jar existence, my life buoyed by refreshing spring waters, that its placement in my hallway may seem terribly inappropriate. But oddly enough, I like the reminder. Whenever I glance up and see it, I not only remember the depths of despair to which I descended, but am made ever more appreciative of the inspirational heights to which I have ascended. I do not dwell on where I have been, but rejoice in where I have come from.

Rejuvenating God, to dwell on our past mistakes and to live in our former failures is nothing but self-defeating. What has been has been, and all of my concern and anguish over it will not change what has been. Today I am grateful for what is, but my joy in this gratitude is increased by remembering what has been. Once, in despair, I nearly emptied myself of my entire life. Were it not for you, and the grace of your love that embraced me in that darkness, I might not be here today. Now, so happily alive, I honor and respect the fragility of our lives, and offer my prayers and the model of my own existence to others who are in need of the spring waters that will refill to overflowing their lonely, dark and nearly empty vials.

October 8
Orion

On a crisp, early fall morning when the dewy wetness of the grass is desperately resisting the bite of first frost and the droplets seem to reflect the sparkle of a wide open predawn sky, I thrill to step outside, and looking to the southeast, see the constellation Orion on the rise. This massive astral hunter who leaps from the darkness of the morning has long been a favorite sky attraction for me. With his bold belt about his waist and his protective warrior arms upraised with bow in hand, his grand posture always captivates my eyes, my imagination, and then my expectations.

During my semester of student-teaching, a thousand years ago, one of the courses I taught was a semantics and vocabulary class. As I presented the students with a new set of words each week, covering the etymology, pronunciation, and context for each word, I simultaneously expanded my own word awareness as well. One word from that course that has never left me is *harbinger*, "a forerunner that gives notice of the coming of another." The foreshadowing of a harbinger is neither good nor bad; its news will be interpreted as the receiver deems it, and for me, the constellation of Orion is a wonderful harbinger of the oncoming winter season. Sneaking in night's backdoor, it shows up each year in the fall just before the dawn in the southeast sky. But as the winter moves in, it arrives on the scene earlier and earlier, until it is a magnificent and imposing image across the southern sky throughout the night. Then, by early spring, it creeps out the front door, dropping away into the southwest sky not long after sundown, eventually vanishing until the next fall. So, as I am a lover of the winter, he is a welcome autumnal guest at my sky-gazing door, a harbinger of the season of dazzling white and enlivening cold.

Not many people look forward to winter, so that is not my point here, but we do all have something to which we look with spirited expectation, and a harbinger to that arrival stirs our excitement and quickens our awareness. Some of life's best gifts show up totally unannounced and unanticipated, but there are also those whose advent provides a certain hope and joy in our lives long before their full realization. A surprise visit from an old friend or a grown child is always a special blessing, but the anticipated visitation is added pleasure, like enjoying the wonderful savory scents of a cooking meal hours before I take in its succulent flavors. And so Orion is for me a harbinger of the star dust of freshly fallen snow, of the profound quiet of a frigid night, of the gentle shush of cross country skis, of glistening hoarfrost on brittle branches, of the snuggling warmth of the fireplace hearth and so much more.

God of the Present and the Future, of the Eternal Now, sometimes we need a little scent of what's ahead to stimulate the juices of today. I am grateful for the gift of life that I receive this day, but I am sometimes humbly consoled by the possibilities of what lies ahead of me. As I arise today like Orion in the early fall sky, bold and brilliantly hopeful, may I live in gratitude for what already is, while mindful of the harbingers around me stimulating my appreciation for what is to come.

October 9
The Autumnal Concert

The leaves have begun their autumnal fanfare. It is such a magnificent time of year to be living in or near woodlands. The question each fall is never *will* the fall colors be beautiful this year, but rather, *how beautiful* will the fall colors be? Soon, the hillsides will be dripping with color and a country drive on a sunny afternoon will be a dangerous exercise of the neck, with little attention to the road and a constant cranking of the head, the mouth slack-jawed, as I try to take in the panorama of color.

Away from their important water source, young, inland sycamores, like yellow candlelight against the backdrop of green, seem to give way first. Sumacs and ivies wrapped like garlands around trees provide the first dashes of red, and when the maples join the chorus, I simply have to stop and listen. Neon oranges, exuberant reds and dazzling yellows are the maples' stunning visual crescendo, with the soft yellows of birch and poplar providing soft harmony. Finally, the denouement of the ash and oak families provide the cadence of "Taps" to the joyful funeral dirge that is autumn. It is "the season of dying," and yet the colors display Dylan Thomas's command to his dying father, "Do not go gentle into that good night."

Like spring buds on trees, we are all born innocent and unaware. Maturing, we tend to accept our spot in the masses, a similar attire and role as everyone else. But aging, we do realize that there must be something more, and seeking it out, we discover that, in fact, there is! Do we seize it now and flower, or bide our time for just the right moment to unfold? However we come to know and to embrace what is most important in our lives, the autumn trees tell us to celebrate it. In the downward turn of their cyclical, seasonal lives, their display is not a mournful submission, but a festive celebration, one so dazzling that all who are near must feel invited to join in and enjoy the visual concert.

O God of Splendor, although it may take us a lifetime to understand, you invite us into deep living and encourage us to celebrate all of life's experiences. The leaves of the trees, now in their old age, take up the poet's song and "burn and rave at close of day," their colors singing an exuberant "Yes!" to the life that has been and is. Let me not fail to observe this grand concert to which I am invited each year, and as a witness to it, may I step forward and participate more fully in the ongoing song of life.

October 10
Miles of Smiles

It has been twenty years since I ran my last marathon, and nearly a dozen years since I last raced through a half marathon. In the first ones I ran, the primary goal was simply to finish, and then to finish "respectably." But once those were achieved, and then some time goals as well, I just lost interest in maintaining that kind of training mileage. I have continued to run regularly over the years since then, in many ways more steadily than I ever did back in those days, but the time required and the leg-pounding endured on ten to twenty mile runs just lost its flavor and interest. I felt something shift on me this morning, however, when I jumped into a half marathon race to help out a couple of friends who were participating.

I figured out my race-help strategy the night before, plotting where my friends would be at a certain time based on their projected pace. One was a former student-athlete friend, more of a nephew to me now, who would be running just around seven minute miles, and the other was a friend near my age who was shooting for just under nine minute miles. I parked my car just beyond the eight mile point of the 13.1 mile race enough ahead of "my nephew's" estimated arrival so that I could stand along the road side and cheer on the runners ahead of him while I waited. While there were few spectators where I was standing, the few who were there stood quietly by, maybe not quite awake yet or maybe just fascinated by the desire of these waves of runners to get out and do what they were doing. Vaguely remembering its value, I kept up a continuous applause, and tossed out periodic shouts of encouragement. I was quickly struck by how uplifting my simple clapping and words were to so many runners. Aroused by my attention to them, their eyes would shift toward me, and we would lock in on each other momentarily. "Great job!" I'd lob their way. "You're looking great!" Some would answer with an appreciate smile and flash a "thumbs up," while others would literally pitch a "thank you" back at me. Thank *me*, I thought to myself? You're the ones who have put in all the prerace work and are out here running now!

"Coach!" I heard my nephew shout as he came cruising by on the opposite side of a pack of runners. Almost missing him, I bolted out from my supportive perch and joined the fray beside him. His pace was much quicker than I had anticipated, so I made a fast adjustment and fell into step with him. We visited briefly about his race, how he was feeling and what pace he had settled into, and always the coach, I guess, I offered encouragement and "strategy" for his last miles. Caught up in the flow of the race beside him, I received ample support myself from various spectators who recognized their old coach or teacher, and shouted their confirmation of what they figured was my race effort. I sheepishly nodded, caught in my little, private lie. After a few quick miles, I gave my nephew a final push of supportive words, and then dropped off to circle back to pick up the next friend coming through. Arriving at my planned spot, I was soon greeted with another shout of excitement as my next partner caught sight of me as he approached. Just beyond the ten-mile mark, he was beginning to grow a little weary, and my presence gave him the boost that he needed. I settled into his goal-and-better-pace for a couple of miles, and when we hit the twelve-mile mark, I told him, "The last 1.1 is all you! Go for it!" and I peeled off again and started jogging back toward my car. Running back against the grain of the race's flow, I picked up my applause and encouraging shouts again, and quickly saw doubtful eyes flash new life, slouching shoulders lift again, and fatigued hearts slough off the sweat with a reinvigorated stride. When I returned to my "starting line," I realized that I had been so uplifted by the people who thought I was uplifting them, that I started to think for the first time in many years, maybe next year I'll run a half marathon again.

Sometimes a person's most simple words or one's simple presence can bring so much life that as one feeds another, so he is fed. Long distance running is a pretty lonely "hobby," and with so many road races these days, the efforts of so many go unnoticed. The range of runners I saw in that race, people of all ages and shapes and sizes, were an inspiration to me, far more than my meager applause and kind words could ever have provided them. If I ever get back out there again, I'll be sure to look those on the sidelines right in the eyes, and thank them, as the runners did me, and know that there will be some mutual feeding going on once again.

Supportive God, too often I forget the many subtle ways that you offer me your soft hands of support. I am reminded today how each of us is called to be the eyes, the hands, the feet – the body of the Divine – for one another. Giving is so wonderfully reciprocal. I offered a small token of my time, a little solo-ovation to those runners for their hours of dedicated training, and it all bounced back to me making me feel like I had won the race. Be my running partner today, Great One, and we'll bring smiles to others' miles.

October 11
The Law of Love

A former student commented to me the other day that she really wasn't enjoying any of her new college courses this semester. When I asked her what she was taking, she answered with a list of math and science courses, to which I replied with a smile, "No wonder you're not enjoying your classes!" My study and degrees were in English and Theology; the Humanities are what move me. I was never horrible at math and science, but I never enjoyed them. The well-defined structures and steps of the latter disciplines, I suppose, just didn't quite appeal to my more loose-fitting, more malleable and arguable areas of study. While I don't think of it consciously, I seem to like that the views I might hold may run counter to the norm, that somehow the norm is a concession that I prefer not to accept so quickly and easily.

For example, the great law of physics says "that for every action there is an equal and opposite reaction." Now, I certainly won't dispute all of the empirical evidence that supports that "law," but I have observed that the world of love in which I prefer to live operates on an entirely different premise. The Law of Love would be that for every action there is (perhaps) a greater and similar reaction. According to the law of physics, if one loves (the first action), then what will come back is an equal amount of hate (the opposite reaction), assuming hate to be the opposite of love. But in my experience, love begets love.

In the Native tradition, at the end of a special ceremony there is often a "giveaway," a presentation of gifts from one person or family to others, even the larger community. Ironically, those presenting the give-away have probably already made some other sacrifice, but because they are grateful for the people's support in that sacrifice, they give even more. One year at the end of a long ceremony, some dear friends of mine were offering their giveaway, and in a most traditional way, by giving from what they had. Essentially, they gave away everything but the house it seemed. Fine cookware, blankets, tools – much of what they had, they gave to the people who they felt needed these things even more. As the giveaway unfolded, it became apparent that my friend only then began to realize what he was doing; he was not sharing his excess, but he was truly giving from his own needs. It was a very emotionally charged experience. This giveaway, however, was done through the law of love, so, accordingly, you can believe that in less than a month "the return" on their action of giving from the heart was incredible. As is so often true with the law of love, though they had given lavishly, they found that in return they had received even greater.

God, the Lawmaker of Love, your ways so often defy mathematical equations and empirical laws. Having created the natural world with its many calculable facets, you appear to have set out to show that not all of what seems to be necessarily is. Love, that is you, seems to defy almost all hypotheses and natural laws. But lacking the surety of the scientific and mathematical realm, I also find that my acceptance of love's ways is not always such an easy course either. Write the constitution of love in my heart, and let me live and die by that, for I am sure, that if I act in love, I shall receive an equal and greater response.

October 12
The Daily News of Life

For many years, one part of my morning routine has been the perusal of the daily newspaper. During my teaching years, it was always important for me to leaf through the national, international and local news to see if there was anything happening that could be immediately connected to my classroom studies. I wanted my students to live with their eyes wide open, informed and actively engaged; and I tried to model that desire by being so myself. Of course, because I needed to head off to work each day, I was very limited in how much of the paper I was able to address each morning. Since I have been writing, however, I have been able to read the entire newspaper more thoroughly each morning, but I am not sure that this has necessarily been a good thing. Quite frankly, the news of our world is usually not very good. Many people complain that all newspapers do is report the "bad news" because it sensationally sells, and avoid the mundane "good news." It doesn't matter if I agree with that or not, the fact of the matter is there is a tremendous amount of awful news out there; and if that sells better than charming and happy news, that fact only says something worse about us human beings. From international wars and genocides to national politics mired in partisan stalemates to local crimes and murders, I find that there is much for which to pray but not much by which to be uplifted.

One morning during a recent campaign season, which seems to be nearly a constant these days, the newspaper was typically littered with stories and editorial letters offering yet another wheelbarrow full of the constant mudslinging which has become so commonplace in the political process. Subconsciously, I must have hit my limit of the political negativity in which I had apparently been engaging for weeks, and after getting through the first section of the paper, I found myself so depressed and frustrated with the ugliness of the news and the political process of which I had been reading that as I turned to share my feelings with my spouse, I suddenly found myself fighting back tears and forcing words around the lump in my throat. More than a bit embarrassed by my overflow of emotion, I set the paper down, deciding that I had had enough of it for this day to be sure.

A few hours later, I found myself out on my friend's farm engaging in the planned task of cutting, hauling and stacking firewood. It was an overcast day that had flirted with rain, but the cool temperature invited such hearty labor and the surrounding woodlands provided a welcoming backdrop for it. After loading the truck with a healthy cache of dead, windfall wood, I nestled satisfactorily into the passenger seat absorbing the beauty of the surroundings as my friend slowly drove across a wide open field of tall fall grasses teeming with autumnal wild flowers and groves of small saplings reclaiming a once plowed field. Passing a certain corner, I observed to my friend how earlier in the summer on another hunt for wood we had stopped at this very spot and had gorged ourselves on blackberries and wild raspberries. Now the brambles were thinning with the changing leaves, and the greens were giving way to golds and browns, a wild assortment of color. As in the news of the daily paper, things here too were dying, but this was a life-giving story unfolding before us, not like the life-absorbing stories of death in the news. With the morning's lingering sadness beginning to lift from my heart and to be blown away like dusty pollen, I turned to my friend and said, "I need to come out here and read the news of nature more often than I read the daily paper."

It is important to stay abreast of what is happening in the world, but it is equally, if not more important that we provide our hearts the necessary balance with which we can receive the daily news. If my days are consumed with work and my private down time is filled with news of a world in turmoil, I will live and breathe an unhealthy air. I need to get outside regularly and just be with the creations, observing and working with their rhythms. There is a cold reality out there too, but at the heart of it is the give-and-take of life, not the taking of life that the daily news gives.

Wondrous God, as a social being, I should stay informed of the life and death that happens around me daily; but as a human being, I need to form the stays of my inner life so that I can brace myself against the difficult, challenging and deadly news and experiences of my outer life. You give me a deep source of life through the beautiful and significant changes that occur right outside my door in your grand creations. As I step out my door to pick up the daily news, may I also look out to read the news of life written daily in your creations.

October 13
The Homecoming Season

After being involved in high school and college education as either a student or a teacher for nearly forty years now, when the crisp air of fall cracks open, I can't help but catch a scent of "the homecoming season." With a month or a little more of the new school year unfolded, and administrative plans and faculty routines finally finding their comfortable groove, most schools seize this mid-fall opportunity to regroup and to celebrate their school's identity as a "home." As a teacher, every year homecoming rolled around, I got to thinking not only of some of my former students and athletes returning to the school for a visit, but perhaps even more, of my own nostalgic considerations of the very idea of "homecoming" itself.

As the youngest of five children, I developed a unique view of "homecoming" throughout my "home-growing" years. My oldest sister and brother both left home when I was just beginning my school years, while my other two brothers matriculated during my teen years. For a handful of years, I was the only child left at home, and so, along with my parents, I was the "welcoming committee" of annual family homecomings. Christmas was the most common homecoming season, but whenever an arrival was imminent, there was always much excitement and anticipation. Frequently, Dad or I would fashion some sort of handmade "Welcome!" sign that would be posted on the garage door or an entryway to the house. Like a greeting card, it showed the honored "returnee" that her arrival had been lovingly awaited. As the youngest and only child at home, I especially remember my own personal enthusiasm as I impatiently awaited the arrival of a sibling. Calculating an arrival time, I would frequently slip into the dining room and peak through the sheer curtains that looked onto the driveway, out to the cul-de-sac's end and down the long street leading to our home, just waiting to see car lights approaching in hopes of being the first to shout, "They're here!" I never experienced the other side of the return so much, being the last one to leave home, but I received a special perspective on what home and "homecoming" meant. Years later, with my own family, the welcome mat of signs and eager hugs became part of our tradition as well, with greeting signs posted for any extended stay away from home of either child or parent.

Homecoming – coming home – should be a very good thing, for all parties involved! Home should not be seen as simply a place of refuge, for where a person comes from now may also be a kind of "home" for him. Home is a place to which I desire to return because in "this place" I feel comfortable, I feel loved, and I know that I will be welcomed. A place of homecoming holds valuable memories, and not so that I will return and try to relive the past, but in revisiting these memories, I am reminded of how the goodness of my past has helped to shape the goodness of my present. Not all, of course, enjoy homecomings, and this fact has always been a source of discomfort for me. Certainly, some people choose to reject the good will of others and set up impossible walls preventing the warm welcome extended them. But in the past when a graduating student would boldly proclaim, "I am never coming back here!" I always took his statement personally as a bit of a failure on my part. How did I not make him feel welcome in my classroom? Why does she not feel accepted and validated here?

Although I may not be closely involved with "school homecoming festivities" any longer, I am still reminded of them and celebrate the spirit of them whenever any of my own children now return home, or when I return to places of comforting welcome myself. For me, such places have gone beyond walls and roofs, and now include wild places where I feel I belong and where the Universe holds me in a tight embrace. Where are the places that you call "home"? And when was the last time that you returned there and allowed yourself to receive that warm welcome that reminds you of who you are and where you came from?

Welcoming God, union with you is my ultimate home, but in this earthly existence I am given simple opportunities to experience the loving comfort of "home," places where I have grown through the acceptance and support of others. Today, pausing to remember these places, I offer a prayer of gratitude for them, and send out a supportive prayer in return to them. May the warmth of their desired welcome pull me back towards them soon so that I may receive their loving embrace once again, and offer one in kind.

October 14
A Homecoming Welcome

When I was but a wee grade schooler, the large concession stand and equipment pavilion of my future high school's stadium was reshingled with a message blocked into the new roof. "Welcome Alumni" it proclaimed. "Alumni?" I recall thinking back then; what is that? "Welcome," of course, I understood, but that second word was a source of confusing interest to me for years, and it was not until my own high school years that I even began to grasp the "homecoming welcome" that was extended to the school's former students the year round.

Most high schools and colleges host a Homecoming Week sometime every fall, and while, by definition, it is a special time to welcome alumni back to their old school stomping grounds, most often it is just a celebrative time for those who are still at "home." On the upside, during homecoming, the present student body honors the heritage of the school and commemorates the traditions through special spirited activities. Through these animated activities, however, the literal intention of "homecoming" is often lost. For most high school and collegiate students, "homecoming" is about wacky dress-down days, float building, king-queen-and-class-competitions, floats and parade, the football game, and, of course, the Homecoming Dance. But all of these events are about the "present students" who are still "at home," whereas the title of Homecoming itself is directed toward the Alumni, those who have left "home" and who are now invited to return.

This skewing of the intention's focus is not unique to "homecoming weeks," however. We humans have a way of making many things "about me" or "about us," instead of steering the attention toward some appropriate "other." Just as I failed to even understand the welcomed subject matter printed across a pavilion's rooftop years ago, from players on teams to employees in jobs, people frequently don't see or understand, or soon forget the bigger picture of the larger family to which they belong. So easy is it for us to get caught up in our own self-interested ideas, goals, and events. It is not that we don't care about others, but rather that we tend to care more about ourselves. And so, while homecoming is intended to be a celebrative welcome for "returning family," it often becomes a spirited festival for those who don't quite understand what "alumni" even means just yet.

Almost inevitably, whenever we return "home," we find things have changed, and that things look a little different. Frequently, of course, we are the ones who have changed and so the "old place" just doesn't feel the same to the "new self." But this sense of change is why it is so important that we do remember, honor and respect those returning. Today's framework is set upon yesterday's foundation, and tomorrow's roof will be stretched over the entire structure. The steps of each new class are given guidance and direction by the efforts of the preceding classes. What we do today is important, and should be honored in its own way and time, but it is equally important that we also periodically show appreciation, offer thanks and extend welcome to those who have built and supported the traditions to which we too can return and find a comforting and welcoming place called "home."

God of Past, Present and Future, while the experiences of my schooling and my life are uniquely my own, they do not happen within a vacuum, void of the influence and efforts of others. I need places in my life to call "home," places where I have a sense of rootedness, where I feel welcomed and embraced. Help me to also establish and nurture such places for others as well, to greet them when they return to "our home" and find that, while things have changed, here the welcome will always remain the same.

October 15
Cyclical Checkpoints

Upon my resignation from teaching high school, I found that my daily routine was altered considerably when the new school year began in the fall. I used to get up each morning at 5:45, and after taking care of the common "first-things-first-needs," I would step outside and greet the day. Even in the school year's beginning and ending, at such a time, the sky was always yet dark, and all of the world was still in that quiet, predawn slumber. But now, I wait until my wife gets up before I start my day, and that isn't until nearly seven; by then, in the beginning of the school year, the sky is already beginning to throw back the covers of the night, and the eyes of the day are straining in the first glints of sunlight. When I step outside to greet the day at this time, amidst the early-to-work neighborhood traffic, the new day seems to be wearing a wry smile and asking me, "Where have you been?"

Humbled by the question, I forced myself to get up earlier; something within me yearned to feel, smell, hear and see that predawn darkness again. It was already mid-October, a good seven weeks off my old annual early morning starting date, and the cold and the darkness were gaining that late surge which stymies the dawn into a slower start. Stepping outside, my eyes immediately swung to the sky, the dazzling display of stars an immediate seduction. And there he was, my faithful friend, Orion, already planted in the south with the seven sisters, the Pleiades, definitively dipping toward the west. With my feet planted firmly in the frost-covered grass and my head tilted back, mouth agape in the wonder of the sky, I felt the emotion of the morning ripple through me like a light pebble dropped into the open pond as a tear fought its way to the surface, emotion manifested. In that moment of delirious joy, I couldn't help but wonder what was it that was so magnificent to my soul in the simple and still darkness of my backyard.

Here was a homecoming, a cyclical rejuvenation. I realized at that moment how powerful and necessary is our circle of life. There was nothing especially important about that particular morning, except that I was greeting familiar faces once again. The darkness, the chill, and the dazzling sky were all old friends that welcomed my return just as surely as I embraced them in that new day about to dawn. It was a reunion at one of the many cyclical checkpoints in my yearly pilgrimage.

Many of us spend much of our lives developing big dreams and pursuing colossal adventures with a subconscious sense that wherever we are now is not good enough. The call of the wild, the Sirens beckoning Odysseus, are loud and strong and alluring, but I suspect that we also have a great inner need for some common markers as well. We need that sense of surety that some things don't change, that some things can always be counted on, that no matter where I go, I can always look to a sky and know that I am always home, even if everything around me is vastly different.

O God of Constancy, is it any wonder that people of all times have placed your reign in the heavens above? My life, always strained by the curse and the blessing of change, longs for a sense of faithfulness, requires the security that some thing always is. And that is you. Thank you for manifesting your fidelity of presence in the wonders of the universe; help me to recognize your aspect in these magnificent and simple gifts, and may I draw from them the comfort I need as I step into and through the inevitable changes of each day ahead.

October 16
The Good Race

When I was coaching cross-country, and even now when I return to watch a race periodically, I am always so impressed by the effortless rhythm of the best runners and marvel at the way in which they finish their race. For most runners, myself included, a race is truly hard, painstaking, cruel work. Although we may run five and more miles regularly, the pace of the five kilometer (3.1 miles) cross-country race can turn our legs to lead while our lungs gasp desperately for more air and our hearts seem ready to explode out of our chests. Not so the great runners. Their race stride appears more smooth and rhythmic than the gait of my easy daily training run, and rarely do I see the tension and fight-for-life in their face and body that I definitely feel in mine when I am racing. And most amazing of all, when the top runners finish, they frequently walk directly through the finish line chute, yes, perhaps momentarily panting heavily, but after consuming a quick cup or more of water, immediately appear ready for their warm down jog. The rest of us? Exhausted, we stop, crumple over with our hands on our knees and profusely suck air as our hearts seek to stabilize. Some literally fall immediately to the ground like a limp, forsaken doll cast aside, while a few others, having swallowed back the urge to vomit for the last half mile, finally release the acidic, watery refuse.

Like anyone who achieves greatness in whatever field, the best cross-country runners are truly and naturally gifted; they simply can run long distances faster and more easily than the average runner. But it is not all gift that makes what they do look so effortless. These great runners have logged numerous miles and have trained at speeds and with repetitions that have taxed their bodies like a race does mine. They are dedicated and they are determined; their minds and their bodies have made a pact, and their whole system has agreed to work this out together. And as they receive the rewards of success, the satisfaction and enjoyment of a race well run, their dedication and determination are recommitted and deepened.

The spiritual life is really no different. As beings made in the image and likeness of the Creator, our hearts are naturally drawn to the Source of all life, but if there is to be a healthy and rhythmic synchronicity with our God, then we must take hold of the natural gift and train diligently. To run with a divine-like stride in our spiritual life, we need to practice with dedication and determination. Once a week, or even three times a week won't do; we'll get through the race, but it won't be easy and it won't look pretty. Daily prayer and/or meditation must be part of my training regimen, and the heart and mind must invite the body to participate as well through good works, fasting and a little conscientious sacrifice now and then. All of these will open our hearts, minds and bodies to more deeply receive the Divine and to run more swiftly and rhythmically with our God.

Dedicated God, my desire to run my life in stride with your design is merely a starting line. If I am to truly run a "good race," I need to devote time and energy to the cause, to resolve my heart, my mind, and my body to your guidance. I do not seek such training just to "look good," for that focus is only of the ego; but I desire the spiritual conditioning that allows me the confidence to know that no matter what the race conditions or the distance, I am well prepared to finish the race feeling good.

October 17
Sleeping In or Getting Up

Sleeping takes up such a large chunk of our daily lives, and in the long run, our life, that I've never been much of an advocate for sleeping in. Granted, some days and nights get so long, that a little additional sleep time is necessary for one's health. But normally, I would just as soon get up reasonably early and get the day started. Except that there are some days when I really just don't want to get up.

A rainy, late fall morning would be an excellent "exhibit A" for the "just let me sleep in syndrome." With my body still in transition with the weather change, not quite ready to embrace the new chill of the season, I know that the air outside the bed and its warm covers will definitely be cold: reason number one for just staying in bed. To get my most restful sleep, I have, unfortunately, developed a need for a dark environment; I don't sleep well with lights on, and once the sun is pouring in, it is hard for me to ignore the call of the day. However, before daylight saving time rolls back the clock an hour, fall mornings are inevitably dark; add to this natural darkness a rainy morning, and I could almost open my shade and keep sleeping: reason number two. And, of course, besides the sound of clothes gently tumbling in a warm dryer, is there anything quite so appealing and sleep-inducing as the soft patter of rain on the roof overhead: reason number three. As you can see, for me, a certain ambiance is necessary to lure me into my stay in bed, but I know for many people, no reasons are necessary; they simply want to stay in bed and sleep some more. So what does get us up and going in the morning? How are we able to shake the drowsy drug of sleep from our warmed and comfortable bodies, to step out into the cold air of the room, squinting into the day's first light, and say "Yes!" to whatever will dawn. Since not all do, it is worth some consideration.

The motivation to get out of bed for most people is probably a job. Jobs help us pay our bills, and make our home and sustenance possible, and hopefully provide us the wherewithal for a little entertainment and fun as well. But if my job is only a means to an end – paying for my expenses – then, even more than sleep, we invest a lot of time for what must seem a disproportionate return. Thus, I may *have* to get up for a job, but do I *want* to get up is the more important question. When someone tells me that she doesn't want to get up in the morning, a fairly common malady, then I think that she must not have anything worth getting up for, a fairly common tragedy.

Some mornings, when all around me is cold and dark and wet, I just want to stay in bed and sleep some more. But most of the time, I am eager to embrace what the day has to offer, and am satisfied, even happy, that the work I must do is not just a job, a means to an end, but feels fulfilling and valuable in itself. If I am not eager to get up most days, then I know that something is awry in my life, and for my best health, I had better do some soul-searching as to why.

O God of Restful and Refreshing Sleep, I am grateful for the night's rest, and I pray that it will adequately revitalize my new day. Some days the comfort of the bed seduces me to stay, but you have made me to live and to experience life fully. My embrace of each new day should be a resounding "Yes!" to the gift you have given me; a disinterested and lackadaisical approach to each day should be a warning to me. Help me to seek a path of employment or chosen tasks that provide fulfillment, satisfaction and happiness, that make getting up each day as welcome as my occasional rainy-fall-morning-need to just stay in bed.

October 18
A Hangover

An old high school buddy of mine drove in from a neighboring city last weekend to join my son and me for an evening of football as our favorite, home state team played a nationally televised game. Besides the fact that our team played the worst game of its season and lost, I drank too much beer and ate too much fattening food, and the next morning I felt like I had not simply watched a losing effort but had physically been a part of the debacle. It was a miserable day and, quite frankly, it had very little, if anything, to do with the football game. An involuntary mantra rose from every part of me throughout the day: "Why do you do this to yourself?"

When we are young, it seems "natural," I suppose, that mind and mood altering drinks and substances have a certain allurement about them. We humans are curious beings with strong oral fixations; witness infants and toddlers constantly grasping for whatever is within their reach and pulling it toward their mouths. As we get older, the appearance and scent of something can be a deterrent, but early on the parental "no" seems the only fencing to our desirous and eyeful wandering. Most often we believe, in our maturity, that our experiences should be our best teachers. If something we try doesn't work or fit or feel good, next time we will know better to avoid it. Unless, of course, we willfully accept the rather ignorant lesson from and of experience that I reencountered last weekend: We can quickly forget or ignore the lessons of our past mistakes.

I love my body and, usually, fully appreciate all that it has allowed me to do. In honor of this appreciation, I live quite healthfully, eating wisely and exercising regularly. Additionally, I see a significant connection between my spiritual and physical "lives" and try to embody my spiritual vision in my physical practices; but when I wake up feeling like I did after my night of overindulgence, I can only shake my head and wonder, "What was I thinking? Have I not learned anything?" And then I realize how much more I have to learn, and how much more practice and discipline I need.

God of the Body and the Soul, forgive me for being so ignorant so often. Have pity and be merciful to this slow learner. You have gifted me with a wonderful life, equipped with spiritual vision and an able body. When I fail to use that vision and abuse that body, appropriately I am sometimes given more than a sign of my ignorance; I know it – experience it – palpably. I am not so ignorant as to think that I shall *never* pass "that way" again, but do help me to be more mindful of these "learning opportunities." May I remember these thoughts and feelings of self-dissatisfaction when I think to once again dismember the best of my spiritual and physical self.

October 19
The Sky is Falling!

During our childhood years, most of us were introduced to the entertaining and subtly teachable stories known as fables. Animal characters with catchy names would get themselves into all kinds of fixes, and despite the apparent danger of their situation, they would usually humorously emerge from their quandary, their narrow escape – or demise – providing a lesson for the listener. Around this time of year, I am often reminded of the famous tale of "Chicken Little" and his frightful doomsday report that "the sky is falling!" Bonked on the head by an acorn, Chicken Little assumes that since something "from above" fell on his head, it must have been the sky, so he runs off in alarm readily announcing to all that the end is near. Now, you might assume that I am reminded of this story because it is that time of year when oak trees are giving up their fruit and acorns are dropping all around us; I just wish that it were that simple and trite.

Weeks away from the first Tuesday in November, the traditional "Election Day" in the United States, I always find myself so exasperated by the barrage of political advertising as well as the countless news stories of candidates jockeying for top position in whatever their political race is. These are the acorns I hear and see and feel. If all of the noise and print were truly informative, I would not find these weeks leading up to the elections so maddening, but because so little of the information carries anything of merit or value, I find myself counting the days until it is all over. The whole process has become so negative. Much of the advertising says little about what its favored candidate stands for or believes; instead, it hammers away at the opposition, pounding the public with the perceived, and rarely real, failures of the opposition. Even more importantly and more directly connected to Chicken Little is the "fear factor" that is so often inserted into modern politics.

To Chicken Little's stupid favor, he actually believed that the sky was falling, and so when he ran around announcing it, the other equally dim-witted barnyard animals had "good" reason to believe him. But politicians and political analysts today seem to be the fox in the henhouse dressed up in Chicken Little costumes announcing all kinds of doomsday scenarios if this and that person are elected or if these and those policies are enacted; and they count on us to be the dull barnyard animals, rising to hysteria and campaigning for them, fed fat on their feed of fear. Unfortunately, when elected, too often these politicians continue their fear mongering tactics.

In contrast, I am also reminded of Franklin D. Roosevelt's famous first inaugural address given in the spring of 1933 as he and the nation that he was elected to lead truly faced some incredibly daunting economic crises. In difference to the banter we hear today, he announced that "the only thing we have to fear is fear itself." Driven by fear, we run and hide, failing to see the truth or, in seeing it, fail to act now frozen by the fear. Fear stirs us to make rash decisions, and like the ending of one version of the Chicken Little story, we follow Foxy Loxy into his den but "never, never come out again."

Later in that same first address, Roosevelt seemed to name the malaise of our own times: "Small wonder that confidence languishes, for it thrives only on honesty, on honor, on the sacredness of obligations, on faithful protection, on unselfish performance; without them it cannot live." God of Truth, as this great country of ours heads toward another election, let us not follow the hysterics of the Chicken Little's and be led into a panic. Help us, instead, to lay aside the weapons of fear and to put on the armor of confidence, trusting that if we live and work with honesty, honor, sacredness, faithfulness and unselfishness that not only will the sky not fall, but it will be bright and beautiful once again.

Perhaps in fall migration, hummingbirds have been dropping by my wife's flower gardens more than ever this fall, drawn in by the spectacular colors that adorn the beds. Unfortunately, their visits are usually quite brief, as the nectar they come in search of is unsatisfactorily found in these blossoms. One flower in particular, beautiful red salvia, seems to catch their attention more than others. A tall, resplendent plant, its blossoms rise in a ladder of red cups, little open mouths, pursed and ready to kiss. But the hummingbirds' long, thin, sword-like beak seems generally disinterested in stabbing into the salvia's blossom, hovering briefly, backing away in consideration, and then zipping off for a better, proffered kiss.

It can't be as though the salvia are void of nectar, however, for I have noticed that the bees have also been dropping by and they seem quite content to bury their whole faces into the porcelain interior of the scarlet cup. Appearing more dutiful and thoughtful in their approach, the bees dance into the flowerbed skipping from one plant to another, and then settle into the delicate blossoms of the salvia.

Even where they are common, hummingbirds carry a fascination on their quick wings and luminous bodies. So tiny in size and so speedy in flight, the hummingbird's unparalleled ability to hover in place and to fly backwards gives it an honored place amongst the winged-ones. Bees, on the other hand, often conjure fear. Their buzzing hum, quieter but not unlike that of the hummingbird, can send people into a panic, fearing a strike from their stinger. Although bees may provide us with deliciously sweet honey, their presence is deemed a nuisance while the productionless hummingbird is welcomed, even fed with artificial nectar bouquets. Our different responses to the two, however, have an interesting parallel to the way we accept different human beings as well.

The elegant and rarified human gets our "special observance" attention. Although these hummingbird humans can probably get all that they need, we still supply them with our own adulation, hoping that they will take notice of our offerings and grace our space with their presence. The bees of humanity, on the other hand, are out working for what they can find, and their efforts are not merely for sustenance but also for production. Despite that they create what we enjoy, we often fear them, keeping them at a distance and sometimes even trying to eradicate them. Interestingly, the bumbling bee beings can find useful sustenance and resource where the haughty hummingbird humans might find only discontent. What is an insufficient offering to one becomes the substance of sweetness to the other. While real hummingbirds and bees naturally deserve a different appreciation, perhaps we might better appreciate the natural differences between hummingbird humans and bee-like beings.

God of All Things Great and Small, I marvel at the wondrous gifts of even your tiniest creatures. Sometimes, however, I fail to see the gifts of these little ones, even in their usefulness, and many more times, I fail to see the giftedness and the usefulness of all human beings, giving unwarranted honor to some and unnecessary alarm to others. Help me to see into my superfluous adulations of some and beyond my petty fears of others. There is a beauty and a resourcefulness in all; may I honor and respect each accordingly.

October 21
Meteoric Faith

The newspaper was aglow yesterday with a report on the Orionid meteor shower that was making its annual pass through earth's orbit. A cosmic dust remnant from the 1986 Halley's comet, the meteor shower was purported to be at its height of viewing pleasure last night between 12:30 and 5:30 AM. I have delighted to such shows in the past, although always with a little disappointment as well, as the flurry of the shower has never measured up to what they say it will be. Nevertheless, I thought that I would get out last night and take in the free show, as I always delight in such cosmic spectacle.

Originally, I made plans to head far out into the country away from all city lights, but after my wife encouraged me to check out a nearby field from which she had just returned from a walk, I thought, well, I could save some time and gas by forgoing the drive. So at 12:30 I dressed warmly, grabbed my camp chair and a blanket and headed for the field. Orion had just arrived on the scene before me and was hanging out low in the southeast sky. In some ways, sharing some time under his shape was joy enough, but I had come for a dazzling display that because of its proximity to the constellation had received its name from it, the Orionid meteor shower. After a little more than a half hour, and still awaiting sign of my first blaze of the night, I decided that while the reported expectation of twenty to twenty-five meteors an hour was probably a little exaggerated, perhaps it really was just a little too early yet. So, I went home and to bed setting the alarm for 4:45 a.m.

I momentarily questioned my alarm setting when it went off, but then figured, unlike most people, today, I could afford to lose some sleep now and sleep in a little later. Dressing again, I headed back out to the field and reconvened my sky gaze, with Orion now standing tall in the due south direction. At least ten minutes went by before I contemplated the possibility of being shut out again, and just then, a rather spectacular meteor shot from right over my head diving toward Orion's, followed by a softer streak from south to east. Ah, I thought, let the show begin! In the next half hour, I saw but three more, one almost as beautiful as the first one I had viewed; the other two were short, simple glints. Feeling a little disappointed again, I reflected that I was glad that I had only "bought" a "lawn seat" and had not paid for a front row chair. Before I gave up on the viewing and headed back home to bed, I began to see an interesting correlation between these star gazings and faith.

In the core of my being is a deep desire to engage with the Creator, and I suspect that I am not alone in that desire; however, our spiritual lives and pursuits, ultimately, must ride on faith. Now, faith is not some flimsy, ignorant give-yourself-over-to-a-crazy-idea concept; faith is built, first of all, on some deeper yearning that seems embedded in the human soul, and then is fostered further through deeply felt experiences that, while they sometimes transcend reason are not always altogether unreasonable. But the truth of our faith lives is that most of us could really use some "tangible evidence" now and then to assure us that this spiritual path that we walk is not simply a phantasm of our mind. And so we go star gazing, searching the sky for the purported truth of a meteor shower. Like faith in a God, we are told the meteors are there; but like our experience of that God, we often come away from the viewing slightly disillusioned, a little disappointed in not having seen the grand display that shouts, "See, here I am!" And yet, we do see just enough, and maybe more, that make our hearts hunger for more. Maybe I just wasn't looking in the right place at the right time; maybe I closed my eyes at just the wrong time. And we find ourselves lingering for a while longer, or gazing skyward even as we walk away. For myself, I can say, I'll be back out there tonight, but maybe I'll head further out into the country.

O God of the Infinite and Dazzling Stars, I so long to walk the spiritual path that leads directly into you, the heart of all things. But your beingness is so beyond my grasp, so far beyond comprehension, that I often find myself sitting in the darkness gazing out and up hoping for some small sign. I don't want my faith in you to be hinged to a sign, but I must confess that the eyes of my heart still often gaze the skies of my life looking for that dazzling meteor that says, "Yes!" Calm the fears of my faith, and light the path of my faith walk. Help me to be ever faithful in my search for a deeper and brighter understanding of you. And if you want to streak a meteor across my sky tonight as well, I'd be okay with that too!

October 22
Raining on the Show

Most of the time, I try to accept and embrace rain realizing that it is an essential source of nourishment to the land, and ultimately to all life. When a rainy cold front moves into our area and hovers for days, however, I can get a little testy, longing for the other necessary and restorative energy, the sun. In the middle and late autumn season, I can also get a little apprehensive about rain, as a strong or steady wind and rainstorm can quickly wash out or end the colorful possibilities of this glorious season. Just last week, after a series of days when the trees were a splendid promenade wearing their autumn colors, brilliant and inspiring in the warm sun, I awoke to a light rain and the chilling thought that the best of the season may be coming to a close.

For weeks I had been enjoying the slow transition that is the nature of the autumn season. While the temperatures are shifting, the leaves of trees and bushes of all ages begin their magnificent grand exit from the yearly stage. With hues and contrasts that visually arrest one's attention, the trees are adorned in subtle earthen tones as well as vibrant neons; like photographic memoirs, some leaves present themselves in a matte finish while others show up in glossy prints; and, having won acclaim for their beauty in previous exhibitions, specific trees garner special attention from the appreciative audience who stand dropped jaw in awe that this majestic presence can be so chameleon as well. But then the rains arrive, and like an outdoor concert suddenly stung by an electrical storm, the performers and the audience thin out, a dripping exodus of color.

Yet, all of this transitioning seems absolutely ordered, if a bit disorganized and unpredictable, by the grand artist of the seasons of life. While we often, sometimes impatiently, await what must necessarily be the passing of difficult times in our lives, just as surely we should know that "all good things must pass" too. This virtually free visual concert that is autumn, with its priceless, gratis ticket, must expire because all things do, whether we hold them to be good or bad. Such is the cycle of the natural world and such is the cycle of our own lives as well; and so, autumn not only provides a dazzling display for us each year, but an opportunity for us to reflect on the inevitable and beautiful movement of all life. Like the leaves battered by the autumn rain, clinging to their branches, we too can often find ourselves holding on to what is no longer truly in our grasp; but if we look to the leaves, we might also notice that as they loosen their grip and slip away from their branches, they dance and swirl in their free fall to the ground. Here, after thrilling us with their magnificent display, they offer us a final gift, a lesson in letting go.

Dazzling God of wondrous displays, once again you teach me how to live by observing the wonders of your creation. I am so grateful for the simple, yet profound beauty of the autumn season, but like so many glorious occasions in my life, I find myself wrongfully clinging to the fading glory. Help me to hold my inspired appreciation close to my heart without grasping it tightly in my hand. I so often receive your gifts freely; may I learn to share and to release them just as freely, celebrating your generosity in a swirling, free-fall dance.

October 23
The Scent of Memory

As I slipped my shirt on today and buttoned it up, I caught the slightest scent of its previous owner and wearer and suddenly a flood of fond memories washed over me. The shirt was originally part of the attire of my dear, old, French neighbor. When he passed away, his own sons had shown no particular interest in his clothing, but not wanting to just "get rid of them," his wife offered if I might want any of his old clothing and accessories. My neighbors, Andre and his wife, Yvonne, had been like surrogate parents to me ever since I had moved in next door to them during my separation and eventual divorce. A first generation French-American, Andre had built a life and a business in the states after escaping the German invasion of World War II. Along with his French-Canadian bride (who just happens to share the birth date and the same, very different middle name as my youngest daughter!), they settled in Ohio and raised their family after early years in my home state of Minnesota – an important connection that was never lost on us. When I remarried five years later, still living beside them, they received my new bride with an equal if not greater embrace than they had received me. Although he had an ornery sense of humor, in his retirement, Andre frequently offered or freely gave his help to any number of project needs that I had around the house. His response to my gratitude, always given in his thick, French accent, was, "That's what neighbors are for!"

Our sense of smell, studies have shown, has a very close link to our memories. From foods to house scents to clothing and beyond, our brains make associations between the smell of something and the experience or people that we associate with it. Later, if we sniff that scent again, we are often naturally drawn back to the association we have with it. And so, today Andre stepped back into my life through the scented-memory of one of his old shirts. When I visit my daughters, they will often pull away from an embrace and exclaim to me, "Oh, Dad, the smell of your clothing so reminds me of home!" I like that connection and find that it is just one more way that God has provided us with the gift of keeping people and memories alive.

As with my shirt this morning, when I catch the odor of something that links me to my past, a special person or an event, I seize the opportunity to remember the connection and relish the chance to keep the best of that person's spirit alive or to honor the gift of that experience one more time. In doing so, that spirit not only remains alive within me but also is given the possibility of living anew through my own generous response or action born of the good memory.

God of My Senses, the gifts of people and experiences are often reborn in me through the simple wonder of my sense of smell. You have touched my life so often through the generosity of others and in the serendipitous experiences of my life. When these blessings of people and experience are brought to me again, a spiritual connection wafting in on a simple aroma, may I not only seize the memory, but also give the goodness of the person or event new life through grateful remembering and consequential acts of kindness.

October 24
A Competition to be Heard

Sometimes when I sit quietly out on my back porch in the predawn of an autumn morning, I am amazed at the volume of the crickets and other nocturnal insects making their voices known. But then, as I hunker down into my swinging chair and quiet myself for prayer, I am also suddenly struck by the volume of the interstate highway some two miles or so away, semis roaring to their destinations and rush hour traffic already building. And shifting my auditory attention from one noise to the other, I begin to hear them as almost in contest to each other, the chirping voices rising in a crescendo only to be pounded back by the incessant drone of the roadways, one trying to drown out the other.

In the nearly fifteen years that I have lived in my present home, the landscape around me has been changed significantly. Not only in my area, but in nearly all sprawling metropolises, so many trees have been cut down and so much farmland has been paved over in the names of "progress" and "development." On quiet nights and in still morning darkness, the natural world seems to repetitiously chant a sorrowful message of the injustice done to it, while the highway sounds seem to roar in reply, "We must move on, and let me lead the way!" But if the highways would be still for a while, as nature often is, the natural world would creep back into its old habitat and reclaim what has been taken.

It's an awkward and delicate balance. Socially, we need the commerce we have created, represented by our paved environment, to survive economically; and yet, we need the land that we maim and the trees that we destroy to survive biologically and spiritually. Without our even asking, the trees filter and cleanse the very air that we breath and that keeps us alive; and without quiet, open and preserved natural landscapes, spiritually, we would likely become as desolate as an empty parking lot in the middle of the city. But, as our capitalistic system will likely forever grasp at further progress and prosperity, it is highly unlikely that our nation's people will ever return to an agrarian lifestyle again. And so the unnoticed, noisy debate seems to spin endlessly around me.

Great God of Creation and Creativity, help us to be mindful of this delicate balance between the created world which breathes life into us, and the world we create as we blow our creative energies into the commerce of our socio-economic lives. Help us to make decisions that respect the needs of as well as the lives within our developing societies while not being blind to how these decisions affect the sustainable growth of the natural world that, ultimately, sustains our lives. You have created us and this world, and we are now co-creators in the evolutionary process. May we remain in communion with the Creator as we move forward in creation.

October 25
Social Nirvana

I have always passionately cared for issues of social justice. Subsequently, I have found it necessary throughout my adult life to stay abreast of political issues and tides, for a nation's politics consistently affect, if not govern, the various issues of social justice. The older I get, however, the less able I find myself to stomach the politics of our time. On nearly every issue, it seems, the political parties, their constituents and supporters, are polarized. Disagreeing with whatever "the other side" has to say seems far more normative than finding common ground or sitting down in civilized discussions to better understand the other's position or perspective. A microcosm of the macrocosmic international world of politics, each side seems far more concerned with proclaiming itself as *the* holder of *the truth*, of what is good and right, rather than assuming that, perhaps, each side bears some part of that truth, and seeking that truth through shared insights. Worse yet, so much of the disagreement seems, ultimately, based on a selfish view: what best serves me and my supporters, not necessarily the common and the global good.

Within Buddhism, the truth or true enlightenment is obtained through a state of "nirvana." Loosely, nirvana means "to blow out or to extinguish," but while the definition uses an active verb, nirvana is not so much about an action as it is about a state of being. Nirvana is realized, becomes one's state of being, when one blows out or extinguishes one's selfish desires. It is not about extinguishing life – dying - but rather, snuffing out the selfish influences and demands that too often govern our lives. When we empty ourselves of ourselves - our selfish desires - then, we open ourselves to being filled with love and concern for all things.

It seems to me that if our government is of the people, by the people, and for the people, then we could use a little "social nirvana." If our elected officials are to "represent us," and truly do so, then we all could use some snuffing out of selfish desires, of self-interest that does not truly seek the good of *all* the people. O God of the people and for the people, I pray today for the good of all of the people of this world. Help the leaders of this great earth that you have created to better understand that they are to represent and work for the good of all people; and help each of us to better understand that if we truly want what is best for all of the people, that we will likely need to blow out the selfish interests that stand in the way of that goal. When I blow out the flame of my selfish desire, I brighten the path toward the light of social justice.

October 26
Coaching Success

Over the last decade or more of my secondary education career, coaching always felt like such a natural extension of my teaching that the consideration to leave one and not the other never seemed plausible. In my first years of coaching, I was more driven to be a successful coach in terms of wins and losses, but in the later years, I found that when I put on my "coaching hat," little changed in me from the one I wore during my teaching day. During those last ten to fifteen years of that dual career, I was more interested in "coaching *and* teaching" young adults to live fully, faithfully, and happily with passion and wonder, and I became far less concerned with measuring success by the win column. Oh sure, I always loved the emotion of a victory and the thrill of an achievement, but these pursuits became more like the whip cream on an already delicious sundae.

In the United States, competition, and the need to succeed in it, has become the engine that drives our machinery. From small retail businesses to large corporations, from local politics to national platforms, from pee wee football leagues to war-time patriotic fervor, so many Americans surf through their lives on the waves of competition: shirts against skins; us against them; me against you. And while there is great value in it, the value is so often misplaced as being in the prize of winning. If one wins, then all of the hard work and preparation was worth it; but if one doesn't, then what? So much of the true value of competition is in the self-discovery that accompanies the efforts that go into the drive to succeed; however, if success is measured only by the ultimate achievement of "winning," then our world is clearly full of "losers."

Choosing to participate in something – anything – is important because the choice marks a certain personal investment. When I am expected or forced into joining something, I will probably lack the heart to work towards my best. It is essential that I *want* to be involved if there is any hope of my ever achieving something special. And winning is not the only achievement; in fact, in many ways *the process* is the achievement. From the choice to participate, one can learn about commitment. From the sweat, pain and exhaustion of the practices, he can realize the binding nature of real and imagined personal limitations, and can seek to stretch those. From the heat of game day competition, she can understand that body preparation is but one part of the sacrifice for success, and that mental and emotional preparation are almost as important. And from the results of such competition, we learn that sometimes all of our commitment, limitation stretching and preparation can achieve great rewards, but most of the time, they reap smaller, less glittering, but more long-lasting successes and realizations. Our best, more often than not, is not *the best*, but we are still better because of it.

As a coach, my teams won a few championships along the way, but I count every year of coaching a success if I got a handful or more of young student-athletes to think better of themselves, to realize that they were better athletes, better students, and better human beings than they had originally thought. To challenge one's self, to put aside one's ego, and to learn to work together with others and not always against them – these were successes I witnessed every year, and if the young student-athlete took these with him throughout life, than I was truly victorious.

It is a lie to say that "we all are created equal" with regard to our abilities and even our opportunities. But whatever our gifts and deficiencies are, we all have chances to expand the gift and to explode the deficiency. Limitless God, help me to redefine "success," and to rewrite a broader definition into the hearts and minds of those around me. May I not limit myself to the idolatry of a "win column," but pursue the greater, more lasting victories of the human spirit.

October 27
Daring to Commit

During my years of coaching cross-country, I had a number of parents who had a child running for our team while another child of theirs was simultaneously participating in some other sport. Occasionally, one of these parents would privately confide with me that his cross-country child's experience was just so enlivening, so positive and affirming, while the other child's athletic experience left the young athlete feeling stressed out and brow-beaten. "And I often hear the same adversity from parents with kids in other sports as well," he might add, concluding, "I think that you should host a coaching clinic and teach other coaches about how you can be positive and still be successful." Such conversations always made me very uncomfortable.

While the sport of cross-country, by its very nature, lends itself to a more encouraging family-like environment, I knew that there was some truth to the parent's compliment, that my coaching approach was in fact more than a little different than most. To that end, I certainly appreciated the intention of the parent's admiration, and understood that perhaps I might have a little insight to offer other coaches, but that "invitation" was not what made me feel uneasy.

Years before I had known great success as a track and field coach, and after numerous seasons I found myself more worn out by the pressure of "what will it be this year" than I was enlivened by the triumphs and achievements of another season. But the tremble I felt at this parent's request represented an unspoken challenge that ran even deeper, because his appeal confronted my character, my very being.

I would guess that everyone enjoys, even needs, a nice compliment every now and then; but compliments do have a kind of "dark side" to them. A compliment, especially when it is true, is a spoken recognition of what we are capable. And once our capabilities are brought to the light, once people acknowledge them, with the compliment comes a certain expectation. When a runner of mine would have a break-through race and achieve a new standard, a personal record or better, I would often add to my congratulatory compliment, "Now that you have achieved that, there's no turning back." I did not mean that I expected the runner to run that time or faster every race from this point forward, but I was recognizing that she was capable of far more than she once knew, and that new awareness should be reflected in every new effort. To that end, I do believe that some students and athletes never truly give their best for fear of what will be expected of them once they do. In my case, what the parent was observing was not a physical achievement, but an ethical, moral, even a spiritual one, and that was a flame to which I was not sure I wanted to be held. Oh yes, I want to be ethical, moral and spiritual, but on my own terms, not on another's expectations; and yet, at least in some part, isn't that what the spiritual life is about: pursuing the truth of ourselves in God's eyes?

Becoming a truly spiritual person takes commitment, and most of us do not want to commit ourselves to the rigors of the spiritual life. Like marriage, it is a vow that, once taken, should be lived 24/7/365; and, if possible, this lived vow moves toward an even deeper level than our marriages because it goes to the core of our very being. The spiritual life is a relationship with God, which is then a relationship with everything; there is never a separation. God of Commitment, I do long to be in a deep and loving relationship with you and with all through and by which you are known and reveal yourself. I fear that I am often not up to the task, but do not let my fears get in the way of my promise, my dedication to you. Complement my commitment with your loving assistance.

October 28
God's Wink

While the presence of the constellation Orion allows me to measure the seasons, particularly early fall to late spring, encountering the whereabouts of the Morning and the Evening Star is not so predictable. Interestingly, these two wonderful stars are not stars at all, nor are they two; what we call the Morning Star and the Evening Star is actually the planet Venus caught in different phases of its orbit around the sun. But like so many people do unknowingly, I prefer to do wittingly, observing this shining planet as the sometime Morning Star and the sometime

Evening Star. Even more so, I like to think of their unsuspecting appearance as "God's wink."

I used to believe that this celestial body had a regular seasonal orbit, such as Morning Star in the spring, and Evening Star in the fall. But its movement is much more erratic than that, and knowing that now I realize how much more fitting it is for me as God's wink. A wink, of course, is a simple facial gesture, an eyeful acknowledgment that can make the receiver pause and his heart momentarily skip. It is a secret glance done publically, a simple but intimate connection fired softly across a room between the giver and the receiver; in fact, to catch the wink between two people always feels a little voyeuristic.

On countless unanticipated mornings, I have slid from my bed in morning darkness and sneaking a glance out my east facing window have been greeted by God's wink, the Morning Star extending love into the very heart of my awakening. Similarly, I have had numerous occasions when I have looked longingly to the west, sipping the sunset's last flares, and there have received the graceful wink of God in the Evening Star. Although it is a small speck in a vast sky, its brightness turns my head every time and I realize that I, a small speck in a vast universe, am recognized and loved.

Celestial God, thank you for loving me into life this day, for greeting me with a morning wink, or tickling me with an evening twinkle. It is said about humans that "the eyes are the windows to the soul." When I catch the gaze of your heavenly bodies, I feel as though I am given a glance, a window, into the presence of the Divine. I count on your love as surely as I look for the sun each day, and sometimes, when I least expect it, I receive "God's wink" as an assurance.

October 29
Scheduling Conflicts

My life in the teaching profession, probably not unlike most other professions, was constantly governed by goals and objectives, all of which were encased in padded time frames. The school year with its predetermined breaks was the master schedule, but within that larger structure there were programmed meeting and conference dates which brushed up against the daily teaching framework. The pedagogical arrangement within each curriculum was then fashioned by goals and objectives, sometimes mutually fashioned by department members, but often prescribed from the top of the district down. For the sake of "accomplishment" and the facilitation of charting "success," I understand the "need" for all of these structural mechanisms, but when I step back from these institutional occupations, and even more, step *out* of them, I am quickly struck by the manufactured nature of so much of our lives.

Time schedules, and devised goals and objectives certainly give us a framework within which we might expend our lives most efficiently, but that, of course, assumes that "efficient accomplishment" is a fundamental pursuit in life. The downside of all of this structure is that it leaves little if any room for spontaneity and the growth that is inherent in change. Goals provide focus, yes, but what if the movement and interests of our lives and of those with whom we work and teach need to go otherwise? The need for structured uniformity in our society is so great that each of the first twenty or more years of our lives has built in expectations, bars of successful accomplishment. But imagine if all people learned what they wanted and at whatever pace they wanted? I know, it sounds a bit like anarchy, but in many ways that is only because it doesn't fit our "structure," and it certainly wouldn't support the socio-economic targets of our society.

I acknowledge that it is more than a bit impractical to truly consider such "social deviation" on a large scale, but if we would at least loosen some of the grip of our "directed lives," and allow for a little more creative spontaneity, I suspect that the "learning curve" on happiness would greatly improve. Imagine living in an "enlightened" state of consciousness, not one driven by selfish desires and prescribed needs, but one where a person truly listened and acted upon the spiritual inner workings of one's heart or soul, and the goal was simply to remain true to that pursuit. In this "curriculum," a person's end or goal would be unlimited as the new possibilities of change would periodically redirect it. Even our sense of time would be revised as "on time" would no longer include a specific time frame in which we might be early or late, for, potentially, wherever we are and whenever we are there is when we should be there.

Again, I offer these hypothetical considerations fully realizing their impractical and impossible nature in a structured society such as our own, but I tender their consideration because on an individual basis, we can make subtle alterations in our personal lives which will not only provide us with a new perspective, but far more importantly, with increased contentment. God of my Goals, so often the fixed ambition and aim of my life can become a pseudo-god, where all else falls in homage to the objectives of the targeted end. With you as my true goal, help me to steer clear of such idolatry, and of such slavery to prescribed notions that may have little to nothing to do with the goodness of my soul. May the scaffolding of my work not be larger than the construction of my life.

October 30
Changing Leaves

With the exception of the oak trees, most of the leaves are down now, and the woodland floor is blanketed in a thick ruffle of leaves. Gazing upward in my neighborhood, the sky yawns more openly, the tangle of empty branches a sieve for the blue grandeur. The sounds of mowers and blowers echoing down the streets are a dirge to the fall's last remnants, as all is finally raked together and piled at the curbside. It is the funeral procession of the seasons although the tone of it is far from a lamentation.

On a run through a nearby forest, I am struck by how covered all of the trails are by the new layer of dried and browning leaves. The verdant canopy of months before gave way to the bright but brief display of autumn's fanfare, and now all is but crunchy leaf-meal beneath my rhythmic strides. Casting a glance into the deeper pockets of the forest, I notice the mounds of dead leaves and consider where they will go, realizing, of course, that beneath this new mound are the stratum of decades of leaves, and I think, as if for the first time, "This is truly life!"

Every year of our lives we go through a variety of changes, most of which we resist like the brittle oak leaves that refuse to let go, choosing to face the wintry winds in the high, wide open rather than huddling with the others in the rotting humus below. During difficult times when the green vibrancy of our lives seems to drain and we feel fragile, weakly clinging to what we thought was the best of ourselves, we forget all that this autumnal season proclaims: there is beauty in our transition; there is nourishment in our letting go; and there is richer life in our dying. The leaves cannot stop the cessation of chlorophyll from their veins any more than we can prevent change from happening in our lives. But as the leaves lose what surely they must feel is the best of themselves, they flourish in a new and exotic way. Falling from their nutritive source, indeed they must feel that all is lost and forsaken, and yet their landing will provide regeneration as they become a source of nourishment. And from their dying, new life will spring forth as they grow to be part of a far grander network of life than the solitary one they once knew and clung to. Truly, this is life.

When I look back over all of the most painful as well as the most easily embraced changes of my life, I see in their aftermath, a stronger, more vibrant, more real me. The creations tell us of that truth each autumn, but most of us somehow manage to ignore it. We prefer to think of ourselves the strong and sturdy oak tree, not realizing that we are, more simply, the obstinate dead refuse clinging to its branches until new buds of life come along and finally slough us off. How much better it would be for us to just let go and to offer our experiences as nourishment for the growth that is as inevitable as our change?

Lord of Life, only you are truly constant. Everything around me, especially in this season, speaks the truth of my "becoming." The wholeness of myself is within me, but the layers must be peeled away a changing season at a time until one day, perhaps, I may find my completeness in you. As I look to the signs of this season, help me to not cling so tightly and so resist the changes that are a necessary part of my growth. Would that I could be the leaf-meal nourishment of my ever-evolving life.

October 31
Halloween

Tonight is the traditional night for "trick-or-treaters," a rather unusual "holiday" that we honor in our nation. There are many theories about its origin and evolution, and my own understanding and belief about it is probably some kind of conglomeration of many of these. As with a couple of Christian holidays, the progression of Halloween with its euphemistic labels and activities seems a rather interesting sociological tale.

Halloween, as its name originally implied, "All Hallow's Eve," is the nigh
the Christian celebration of All Saints Day. "Hallow" is to make sacred o₁
and so Halloween was the eve of the day of the sacred and holy, the sain.
Although most secular tales of this day's history avoid it, the origins of "dressing
up" in costumes on Halloween is more than likely rooted in European villages
celebrating the eve of All Saints Day, when the townspeople would perhaps dress
up in the guise of their personal or patron saint. As some more prurient versions
of Christianity evolved and frowned upon such festivities, and then later, as
societies took on a more accepted secular approach, hallow became more hollow,
and saints were more simply "the dead." Despite the influence of Christianity's
belief in the resurrection, traditionally, Western Europeans feared death and
consistently conjured all sorts of ghoulish imagery of the dead, not least of which
can be seen in the horrifying aspect of a decaying human body. Thus, expanding
"all saints" to the more generic "the dead," people then began dressing up in more
frightening outfits, from simple skeletons and ghosts to the more exotic monsters
that are "beyond the living." Saintliness was cast aside and the night of the living
dead stepped forward. Today, college students and other "adults" have taken
Halloween to a whole new level, not necessarily a higher one, and use it as an
opportunity for debauchery, dressing up in all sorts of trampy sexual outfits;
perhaps a new emphasis on "trick"? The night of the spiritually-dead living?

Commonly known now as "Beggar's Night," another interesting euphemism to
consider, children and many teens will converge on their own and many other
neighborhoods, knocking on doors and shouting, "Trick or Treat!" For this effort,
the little "beggars" will receive a piece or two of candy, or at more healthful
residences, a piece of fruit which won't be eaten anyway for fear that it is loaded
with razor blades or narcotics. At its most simple, secular premise, however,
Halloween truly is a wonderful evening where children do get to roam the streets
for a couple of hours dressed up in some creepy, amazing, or silly costume
demanding candy – and they get it all for free by the bag full or some other
pumpkin head container!

Whichever way you choose to celebrate this very interesting "holiday," a word
itself that comes from "holy day," take some time today or tomorrow to remember
the exemplary lives of those who have gone before us. Generous God, while
children will celebrate our more self-centered design of receiving candy, let us
also be mindful of our more saintly, selfless design of giving. Tonight or this
weekend, perhaps I will *dress up* as some other person or thing, but may I never
cease *to be* a saint, a model of a faith life well-lived.

My Father was one of the most kind and generous men that I have ever known. Nearly always a gentle man, he was a truly a gentleman who had great control over what he said and when he said it. Like everyone, he harbored some prejudices, but I always saw him working to better understand, if not overcome, those prejudgments of his, and rarely, if ever, did he consciously act on them. He donated more time, money, and personal energy to more causes than I could list here, and while he received numerous honors for his charity, such honors would never be found on a list of why he did what he did. He gave from a grateful heart, and because he always felt that giving was the good and the right thing to do.

While Dad gave lavishly to all sorts of councils, organizations and charities, his own children were frequent benefactors as well. I am certain that all five of his children received countless "starters" as their needs arose. From life insurance policies as children to home mortgages and car loans as young adults, he never hesitated to step forward and volunteer his financial help so that we could "get started." These gifts did not create irresponsibility either; they were not simply lump sums of money given freely. Encouraging a repayment plan, he taught us to fish rather than just giving us the fish, but after years of "fishing" and giving "our catch" in repayment, it was not unlike him to say, "Okay, I think we're even now," long before we ever were. And forgiveness, my, did that man know how to forgive! Who knows how many times I must have wounded his heart, and I am pretty sure I was not alone in doing so, and yet right up to the end, each one of us knew that we were deeply loved and respected, and if necessary, forgiven. On the night before the day he died, his whole family gathered around his hospital bed, and we sang songs for hours, show tunes and children's melodies, campfire songs and popular hits, a shared love of music that he had taught us all and that he shared with all. Slipping in and out of wakefulness throughout the sing-along, at one point with full awareness, he looked up and around at each of us, and wearing a simple but proud smile, he said, "I just gotta say, this is one wonderful family!" It was, essentially, his final blessing on us all.

My Father died on this day – All Saints Day - in 2008; there could not have been a more appropriate date or a more beautiful death. He truly lived a life of faith, beginning and ending each day in prayer, and modeling the faith of those prayers through his actions. At Dad's funeral, my next oldest brother appropriately proclaimed Dad's birthday as a new feast day: St. Francis the Irish. I hope that everyone has a saint in their lives to which they can look for guidance, support, and a model by which to live.

God of the Saints, nearly all traditions honor people whose lives of great faith, generosity, and peace provide an ideal example for how one ought to live. From the Gurus of Hinduism and Sikhism to the Patriarchs of Judaism, from the Tirthankaras of Jainism to the Bodhisattvas of Buddhism, from the Saints of Christianity to the Prophets of Islam – all of these heroic men and women of their individual traditions offer us guideposts by which we may fashion the steps of our own walk through life. May people everywhere today be afforded the wondrous gift of a living example, a saintly mentor into whom they can lean whenever it is necessary.

November 2
Cancer Sucks

Some years ago, a growing furrow of concern was carving its way across my wife's face as she lay on her back in bed and could feel rather large growths in her abdominal region. Wanting to vanquish her worry, I could only confirm her fears when I too felt the growths' prominence as I gently pushed on her stomach. After various trips to the doctor and eventual surgery, to her good fortune, she was much relieved to discover that the growths were benign uterine fibroids and cysts. A harrowing month of apprehension and a slow year of surgical recovery was a far better fate than the reality of our worst worries. Within months, however, one of my dearest colleague friends followed a path very similar to my wife's, but the end of her surgical trail had none of the exhaled relief that we enjoyed.

With signs of malignancy in the growths removed from my friend, she immediately responded to the vile cancerous attack with further surgery and chemotherapy treatment. Always a ray of sunshine cutting through even the most cloudy day, my colleague wore a face of confidence buoyed by her deep faith. She embraced her loss of hair with humor, accepted her changing appetite tastefully, and cuddled her tired body with plenty of rest. On my rare visits and periodic phone calls, I marveled at her wit and was awed by her strength, and I privately wondered if, given the same circumstances, I could be so poised. Within a year, tight, beautiful salt and pepper curls were growing from her scalp again, "my chia pet" she called it, and her vibrant smile was no longer fighting through clouds but was filling a bright and healthy sky. Still, I can't help thinking that she awakes everyday with the memory of what was and a fear always of what could be.

More recently, I received word that the husband of another dear acquaintance, the "matchmaker" of my wife and me, was facing a renewed attack from the contemptible cancerous enemy. Separated by miles and years, I read of his battle through a "Caring Bridge" blog, and helplessly sigh, again wondering if I could possibly be so buoyant and optimistic. Boorish and uninvited, cancer arrives in the lives of so many and in so many places and ways. I have feebly stood by and watched a sister-in-law, cousins, dear friends and total strangers in their courageous crusades against this most despicable foe. Ultimately, theirs is a solitary fight, but I will do all I can to send in my armaments of prayer and loving support.

God of Strength and Courage, I offer up these many loved and unknown ones who must daily face the challenging clash with cancer. Doubtful that I could possess their grace and fortitude, I send out my certain support, prayers of potent love armored with vigorous stamina. There is no good reason for this war that they must wage, so I seek no answers for their unwanted foe's presence, but grant these warriors the soft support of family and friends, the strength of a confident army, and the divine armament of hope.

November 3
The Right and Responsibility to Vote

Twenty-four hours away from the close of the voter registration deadline during an election year, a local news station stopped by at The Ohio State University campus to interview a few students about both registering and voting. One of the young men being interviewed sheepishly admitted that he had not yet registered, but didn't plan on voting anyway this time because, "I don't feel like I know what the issues are or enough about the candidates to vote." As I listened to the student's response during the brief report, I appreciated his honesty and thought him "noble" to not want to cast an ignorant vote, but I couldn't help thinking that as a citizen of this nation, he was still shirking his new and important responsibility. Many Americans have no idea what a privilege and an honor it is to be a part of the democratic voting process of our nation. In many parts of the world where democracy is a struggling governmental form, a façade of freedom at best, people are literally dying in their attempts to have a voice in their country's government and its "elected" officials. Worse yet, our nation has jumped into military conflicts and arguably engaged in wars on behalf of establishing the freedom of democracy in another country; in which case, American soldiers are dying so that another country's people will have a voice in their country's governing body through their right to vote. And yet, in awful irony, fifty percent voter turnout is considered "good" during an election year in our country where, since at least sometime after the Civil Rights Act of 1964, coercion or threat of life for voting have been essentially nonexistent. It is free and easy; we kill and die for it; and yet, often nearly half of American citizens don't exercise their right to vote.

Near the end of every October, I always took a break from the usual agenda of my year long Theology course, "Faith, Beliefs and World Religions," and dedicated a two-week portion of the class to the informational instruction and encouragement of thoughtful political involvement. Some might have questioned my intentions and the appropriateness of such considerations in a Theology course; but so many, if not every, political issue is a *life issue* affecting the very lives of some or all of our nation's citizens, and people of faith, spiritual people, *must* act on behalf of the good of all. Essentially, I urged my students to be responsible members of society. Politically, that means, on a fundamental basis, to be informed about the wide range of issues and the broader implications of candidates' platforms, and to vote accordingly. Rarely, if ever, will I find a candidate who postures him or herself in exactly the same way as I do, but, in recognizing that, I should also be careful not to align myself with a candidate or a party based solely on one issue.

I have to acknowledge that in recent decades the partisanship of campaigns and the governing that follows elections seems to have gotten worse and worse. The vitriol and mudslinging that goes on during elections and even throughout the governing process has lessened my support of our country's political leadership and government in general. But almost because of that as well as in spite of it, we citizens of these United States must stand firm in our commitment to our country, a large part of which is being an informed and active participant in the voting process.

God of Freedom, Equality and Justice, as a member of a democratic society, I have been given a great right to participate in the life of my government through the election of its officials and by voting for or against certain laws and amendments. Enliven the hearts of the people of this and other nations who have gained such an awesome responsibility so that they may seize the opportunity that so many others can only long for. And for the process of our country's elections, I offer this prayer as well: The people need leaders who truly serve the good of the country, not their own or a small group's special interests. Bless those who seek office and may they do so only with the very best of intentions and with their most honest actions and efforts.

November 4
The Kingdom of God is at Hand

I have long felt that one of the most significant oversights of the early Christian Church and of one of its most heroic and prolific spokespersons, St. Paul, was the overemphasis on Jesus' divinity and its movement away from Jesus' message. I have no interest in issuing blasphemous statements or in engaging in theological diatribe; I merely believe that the emphasis on the salvific act of Jesus, his death and resurrection for the sins of humanity, which so defines Christianity today, shortchanges the message of Jesus, which so defined his salvific act.

If one focuses on the synoptic gospels of Matthew, Mark and Luke, as opposed to the more Gnostic tone of John's gospel, one of the most central messages of Jesus' teaching career is "the Kingdom of God/Heaven is at hand!" This was, and still is, an incredibly bold statement. People in Jesus' time, as well as our own, were looking for a release from political oppression, and prayerfully hoped for the restoration of a world that would truly reflect the Creator. Thinking that Jesus might be the political leader who would lead them to a revolution of government and spirit, many were very likely disappointed when they discovered that his intentions were not about the political policies of this world. He came teaching a message of love, a love so radical that it alone could change the world – could bring the Kingdom of God right here on earth. It was so simple, but we have made it impossibly difficult.

Nearly everything he did cut through and across the standards of all politics and all religions of his time. "Love one another," he said, and that is really all there is to it. Imagine, if everybody everywhere got over themselves and all of their political and religious ideologies, and simply, but truly, loved one another, what would we have: the Kingdom of God at hand. God, who is the very essence of love, creates the universe out of the creative energy that is love, and then this God asks us to do and to be the same. "Love one another," Jesus said, and then showed how much and how far we must love one another by willingly dying for the sake of the message. He didn't go out and start a war on behalf of his message, nor did he establish a political platform from which to announce it, nor did he promulgate religious regulations whereby one could receive it. Instead, he challenged the leadership of politics and religions to rethink their policies, and then he met with and embraced all of those who were most often neglected by those very leaders.

When Paul and others right up to today only point towards Jesus as the incarnation of God, and his death and resurrection as the salvation of all humanity, they too often seem to forget what Jesus preached. "The Kingdom of God is at hand," he proclaimed, if we simply go out and "love one another." God of Love, Jesus came into this world showing people that the spirit of faith and of love is known first in the heart and then it is shown in actions. Rituals, regulations and laws are not wrong, as long as our hearts are first of all in the right place. It seems that our world needs to be reminded of that message again today. Why must we wait for some "kingdom come," for some eternal "afterlife" when what we seek could be right here, right now? Help us all to truly love one another, and so make your Kingdom of love right here at hand.

November 5
Step Aside, the Kingdom Comes

Sometimes I try so hard to orchestrate the "perfect evening" with my wife or even with a small group of friends, but it rarely turns out in quite the way I had intended. It may not be a bust, but usually it doesn't have half the magic I was imagining. Conversely, there have been many other times when I had no plans or expectations at all, and things just came together. It reminds me of how a student one time shared with me a wonderful night that she had with one of her friends.

Tired of the "so what do *you* wanna do?" routine that so often marks a teenager's weekend (and can often continue right on through adulthood!), the young gal had decided to just stay home and make something of her own evening. Not far into the night, however, another girlfriend of hers called her feeling much the same way, but "just checking in" all the same. Agreeing that the two of them should just get together and watch a movie or two, they picked up some fun munchies as they met up and decided on a couple of movies at the local video store. I don't recall specifically what the movies were, no doubt a couple of good "chick flicks" with just the right balance of laughter and romance, but with the movies spent and only crumbs left at the bottom of the munchy-bags, they sprawled out and started visiting "about things," perhaps spurred a bit by the content of the movies. One topic led to another, she told me, and they soon found themselves rolling on the floor with laughter, and then, shortly thereafter, brushing aside tears that would only be followed by another round of therapeutic laughter. "It went on for hours," she told me, her eyes lighting up as if she were describing a grand mystery, "and when we finally paused, exhausted from the emotional roller-coaster, we discovered that it was 4:30 in the morning! We couldn't believe where the time had gone, and we promised each other that we have to get together and do this more often!"

Her story finished, she stared at me as if waiting for a response, some affirmation that her experience had been magical and rare. And it was, although I wasn't quite sure how to tell her just how special it had been. "You experienced the Kingdom of God that night," I started, "a 'transcendent now' moment when we get to experience what the Creator really had and has in store for us. Jesus said 'it is at hand,' and he wasn't kidding," I continued. "But we don't believe it; we think that such an existence is only when we die. Yet every once in a while, we unknowingly open ourselves to it, and there it is!" Figuring I had already long lost her, I pushed on anyway. "You're not likely to recreate it, however, because it just 'is.' What you can do though, is open yourself to it; believe in it and in the power of love, and you will find the Kingdom manifesting itself many times and in many places."

I suspect that we have all had such an experience, when everything just seems to come together perfectly even when there wasn't a plan. It is the way God intends it to be, but we have to get out of the way, let go of our egos and expectations and just let our love for life and one another be the guiding force of God. God of Love and Tender Moments, you give us samples of how wonderful our existence can be if we would only step aside and let your energy move us through this life. Yes, there is work in this world to be done, but your Kingdom, the active presence of love, also longs to come into this world. Help me to more mindfully engage in this love as I work and when I play.

November 6
What's Cooking in the Kitchen?

It was a simple conversation in the kitchen between my youngest daughter and me as we tried to reconfigure an ever-changing schedule during my annual trip to Arizona to visit my two daughters and their families. "Perhaps you could take me out to the trailhead and pick me up a couple of days later," I said to her just before noticing what appeared to be a delicate crack in her china-like features. "I just don't want to create any further stress for her," I added, referring to my eldest daughter's overflowing cup of responsibilities, and the youngest seized the suggested favor like a lifeguard's grasp of a sinking child. "Yes!" she affirmed, "I can do whatever is needed," but again I thought that I detected the glint of a tear she seemed to be withholding from the scene. Months before the trip, a full slate of plans had begun to form, and within a week of my leave taking, each day of the two week visit appeared organized. But when I arrived, the health of my eldest daughter's mother-in-law had slipped considerably, and all previous preparations were necessarily shelved. Already juggling her full time job, continuing education and significant health concerns of her own, my oldest daughter, in full "eldest child mode" of being the great organizer, had been trying to maintain a calm sense of levity as she daily coordinated our ever-shifting plans. Her younger sister, her dear companion, was seeing right through the façade of control and strength, and now with me was privately leaping in to quietly rescue the sinking schedule. Tentatively agreeing to her "taxi service," I hesitantly pressed her about my own suspicion of her emotional fissure.

My question was the simple key to the doorway of release, and my youngest eased into my awaiting hands her concerns for her sister. "I just don't like to see her crying, hurting so," she admitted. "She is carrying so much right now, and I just want to help her, to lift some of her burden, but I don't know how, or, it's like, she won't let me." We quietly shared our concerns for our beloved daughter and sister, and I offered my apologetic observation of their very different but very shared burdens of responsibility: the eldest child and the quintessential child of divorce. And then, into this communal sharing of tears and love, stepped the eldest: "What's going on in here?" she asked delicately reentering the kitchen where our emotions were being trimmed of their protective fat. So we told her, tearfully, of our concern and love for her, of the desires that each of us have to save one another from the inevitable harsh difficulties of life, and of our own sense of helplessness in adequately doing so. And then we encircled one another in a group hug agreeing to share our needs a little more freely, a little less selfishly.

Such raw experiences of loving support reveal the true essence of what it means to be human. Yes, we can plan our lives around all kinds of self-interested recipes and schedules, but when the pots are boiling over in the kitchens of our loved ones, we feel the immediate need to rush in, open the windows and offer ventilation to the heat of the moment. In this kitchen of love, I don't think that there can be too many cooks.

Loving and Supportive God, so often we want to show our strength and courage in independently enduring and overcoming the challenges and obstacles in our lives. But we were not conceived, nor do we enter this world alone. You have given me family and loved ones who wish to support me in my struggles just as surely as I wish to lift the burdens of their lives from them. Help each of us to recognize that we are not in this – all of the "this's" of our lives – alone. May I not be afraid to ask for help when I truly need it, and may I too have the compassion to step forward and offer my assistance to those in need.

November 7
Haste Makes – Something

I had counted on a three day hike into and through the desert, but given the circumstances of my trip, I had to scale it back to two days. One night was all I had, and then, delayed further, I was finally stepping onto the trail at 5:09 PM; I checked my watch as I passed the trailhead marker and made a disgruntled note to myself that the sun was already slipping behind the southwest mountain ridge line. Getting into the desert and then nestling under its grand canopy of stars were my simple goals, but as I headed up the trail of Boulder Creek Canyon, my haste took the driver's wheel and my better judgment fell asleep in the back seat.

Less than a quarter of a mile down the trail, the path split, almost imperceptibly, one course ramping up the steep hillside which would lead to the ridgeline crest, the other dropping off slowly, then without distinction, sliding away into the canyon wash of over-sized boulders – hence, the canyon's name. The former path would have been the obvious choice to achieve my simple goal, but its carve was faint while the latter path grabbed hold of my hasty hand and the next thing I knew, I was boulder jumping down the canyon's dried river bed, my backpack's weight now scolding me for my hasty, thoughtless start. Fifteen minutes later, the sunlight still caressing the upper regions of the eastern ridge high above me, shadows had given to dark shade in the canyon and I knew for sure that my window of light was closing fast. There were no invitations nor welcome mats – nor trails – heading up either side of the rugged desert canyon as I kept shooting speculative glances to both sides looking for an escape route and a place to lie down that night and enjoy a full spread of stars. Up ahead to the right, there seemed an interesting window rock and pillar formation high above teasing me to join them for the night, but when I spotted a lower cliff edge jutting out on the left side, I opted for the shorter climb and began scrambling up through the loose volcanic scree and perilous desert flora. Once at my spied goal, I convinced myself that it would be a fine place to spend the night, and donned my headlamp in the settling darkness to search for some desert firewood along the narrow hillside ledge. Scavenging some dead Palo Verde branches and other decaying cacti remnant, I readied my fire supply and then set to moving the jagged, loose rock away from the one place that looked big enough for me to lay down that night, a bit of a downward angle, but it would do.

Three days and two nights of desert revelry had been reduced to a hasty, ill-fitted one-nighter it seemed as I settled into my Crazy Creek chair and thought about fixing some dinner. But as I savored my simple dish of hot rice and tuna, and leaned back watching the stars slowly ascend and skate delicately overhead, I realized that all would be – was – just fine! In Robert Frost's famous poem, "The Road Not Taken," much emphasis is given to his classic closing lines: "Two roads diverged in a yellow wood, and I, I took the one less traveled by, and that has made all the difference." In these words the challenging choice of his road "less traveled by" seem to be the poem's issue, but I think a careful inspection of the poem renders a deeper point, that whatever his choice had been, how he "lived with it" is truly what makes all the difference.

Sometimes through our haste and misdirection, we lose our way on our "life paths," trails that can include relationships, jobs, education, spirituality and more. Frequently, these trails are not as well marked as we would like, and often, in our haste to "achieve," we make less than perfect decisions. O God of Life, more than anything, I want my trail to lead into the oneness of you. I want to pitch my camp under the canopy of your starry grace each night. If I should lose that trail, help me to not lose my hope and my intention to regaining that course. Help me to live with where I am and not lose sleep over where I think I should be.

November 8
Wandering God's Trail

The morning after my night on the Boulder Creek Canyon ledge was a brilliantly fresh and cool desert spread. Carefully eyeing the contour lines of my map, I cast a judgment on my whereabouts, and made directional plans for the day's hike ahead. I was sure that the trail I had intended to hike was somewhere on the inaccessible ridgeline high above me, and if I was to rejoin it, a confident trek through the canyon would provide its meeting point. Scattering the traces of my ledge-night, I gingerly made my way back down the steep and loose terrain pausing frequently to reconsider my path's proximity to a dangerous step. Once in the canyon, I quickly delighted, with a much lighter heart than the evening before, to the bouldering effort of the hike, awe-fully gaping at the narrow rising walls on either side and wondering at the white sandbar beds and high water marks along the way. Three different times, in the narrowest slots, the vegetation grew thick and wild, and there I would inevitably find an oasis pool, frogs leaping in with my intruding noisy steps and small fish wondrously surviving in this austere environment.

Eventually the canyon widened, and with it my hope for finding the trail for which I was looking. An hour later, however, as the desert day continued to heat up, this hope seemed to be evaporating as quickly as my sweat and water supply. I had hiked the desert before, and knew that on infrequently travelled trails such as the one I sought, evident footpaths were not always so easy to find. Cairns, simple piles of rocks assembled graciously by previous hikers, often were the best indicators of a trail, and I watched carefully for any signs of these along the way. Occasionally, when the boulders would give way to a sandy bar, I would spot a human footprint and knew, at least, that I was not the first to pass this way. The map clearly indicated that a trail would cross this wash, but if I missed it, the dry riverbed appeared to sweep into the middle of desert nothingness, and I knew I did not want to go there.

As I so often do, I soon broke into sacred songs, honoring the creations around me and acknowledging my vulnerability in the shadow of their magnificence. I stayed mindful of the hopeful trail ahead, but knew that with each mile, the balance of enjoyment and worry was shifting. Not long thereafter, I spotted evident signs of a former campsite, and then another, and, finally, with them, a very obvious trail. With a quick look at my compass and map, I knew I was where I wanted to be, and began my hike back to the trailhead.

Ascending the canyon switchbacks and drinking in the incredible vistas that encircled me, I got to thinking about how haphazardly this whole adventure had started. I mused about my nagging concerns over the past twenty-four hours now from the secure vantage point of a well-worn trail, and while I was certainly happy to be on it, I couldn't help being grateful for all that I had inadvertently stumbled upon and taken in. Had I come in "the right way," chances are I would never have enjoyed "God's way." Too often in our daily lives when we make poor decisions and appear to be stumbling directionless, we focus only on our errors and the fears that can encircle them like vultures hovering in the sky above. But these off trail paths often lead to some extraordinary adventures and learning possibilities; a little hope-filled "what might be" can sometimes assuage a more fear-filled "what is."

O God of Surprises, sometimes my erroneous judgments and decisions can steer me off the course to what I think leads to you, and I find myself living with a disheartening fear; but, perhaps, you want it that way, knowing that another path will provide deeper awareness and more salient knowledge. Help me to not lose hope, wherever I am, but to trust that my faith in you will someday, someway, lead me back to more solid ground, with a new wealth of wisdom in my pack.

November 9
Spontaneous Planning

My oldest daughter used to laugh at me on our road trips together as we waited for our camp food to cook when I would pull out the map and consider the nightly question of "tomorrow's course." "You are so much like Uncle Tom," with whom she had traveled France and Switzerland as a teen, she would tell me and, of course, just like her Grandpa too who was well known for loving to plot his, or his children's, journey across AAA maps or a Road Atlas. Not surprisingly, she too is now a great planner and lover of maps; she's been well-influenced. But in the spirit of sage spiritual advice, even with maps and plans, sometimes one needs to let go.

When I left for Phoenix recently to visit my daughters and son-in-law, I left a fairly well organized itinerary with my wife concerning my anticipated whereabouts. By the time I arrived in Arizona, however, my son-in-law's mother's health was increasingly diminishing, and all maps and schedules become fairly meaningless in the face of her impending death. So we let go of all of the preplanning, and pretty much lived out my visit on a day-to-day basis. And sometimes, that turns out to be the best way to do it.

Over the next week and a half, while daily monitoring and caring for his mother, my daughter's husband occasionally joined us and at other times encouraged us to venture off and play. In true spontaneous form, in twos, threes or fours, we cheered on a football victory via TV at a local bar; drove north and west into the desert for two days of hiking and a night under the full moon; later, I stole away for a two day solo; took in a battle of the bands concert with my youngest, and a lively trio of musicians with the other two at a favorite pub; ran daily in mid-80 to low-90 degree weather; hiked "A" mountain on the edge of the ASU campus; shared a yoga session with my oldest and then was treated to my first professional pedicure; and for sustenance, we ate out at special Greek, Mexican and Italian restaurants, capping my visit with morning breakfast at the ever-popular IHOP.

And in the middle of all of this "unplanned" journey, in the midst of all of this movement, was the sacred pause, the precious gift of sharing in my son-in-law's mother's walk into the next life.

Just one week after the first anniversary of my own Father's passing, I could not imagine receiving a greater gift than to be present with and for my loved ones as they too were witness to this amazing part of our lives, gently singing songs and holding our loved one's hands as she slipped away from this life.

Who among us wouldn't like to map out the plans for his/her life and ideally follow them through? But sometimes the best-laid plans aren't half as good as the serendipitous kind. I love to scour maps and make plans, but occasionally, I too can let them go and just live the given moment. My Arizona trip in November was a moment I'll be savoring for a long time.

O God of Spontaneity and of Planning, most of the time, we organize our lives around tight, inflexible schedules, believing that we are making the best use of our time. Perhaps there is "a plan" for our lives, but, perhaps, sometimes that plan is for us to live more spontaneously. Help me sometimes to let go of my maps and schedules, and to simply let my heart and the immediate needs around me shape the course of the day. For in these moments of serendipity, I am likely to encounter you along the way.

November 10
Constellation Perspective

One night as I sought some solitude in the desert, eagerly lying back beneath the expansive blanket of stars and its swaddling Milky Way band, I discovered something about an old dear friend, the constellation Orion.

The sun had slid beneath the covers of the western ridge and then pulled up the dark mantle of the night; I snuggled into the black quietude that spread across the desert, leaned back in my camp chair and gazed skyward into the deep, infinite pool above. Venus was an eye-magnet in the southern sky, the bright jewel that glistens first in the sun's afterglow each night that it is in our night-sky range, but soon I was drawn to a large cluster of stars rising directly in the east. Hovering just above the ridgeline, their compact brightness captivated my attention and I reached for my binoculars to pull them in a little closer. In the field of my magnified glasses, there appeared a football-shaped assembly of vivid stars with a swirl of lighter stars in a tail beneath them. As a city dweller, I don't often get such rich views of the night sky, but I still wondered how this grouping had escaped my observation in my numerous years of wilderness nights. Returning to them frequently as they ascended their dark ladder overhead, I soon noted a bright nugget of almost reddish hue following their path an hour later, and with its emergence, I began to wonder if perhaps the cluster was the Pleiades, the Seven Sisters that Orion pursued, and that this budding red nugget was Aldebaran or Alpha Tauri, what I always referred to, in "my own mythology," as the eye of the dog guarding the sisters from Orion's pursuit. But despite the obvious appearance of these stars, their sky proximity didn't make sense to me. Orion, who chased the Pleiades and who had not yet risen that night, I knew advanced across the southeastern sky, and these celestial lights were clearly due east. Perhaps, I thought, my geographic location in the desert southwest as opposed to my usual eastern United States home was the cause for the shift; but I loosely waved this idea figuring even my continental shift of place could not fully account for the visual shift of the stellar pathway. I would await the entrance of my friend Orion to solve my simple mystery.

Sure enough, a couple of hours later, my bold hunter friend appeared as he always does for me, rising in the southeast sky; but by this time, the beautiful star cluster that I had observed much earlier, and its red-eyed follower had risen high enough in the sky that they appeared to be on the same path as Orion's southeastern course. And as they continued to track overhead throughout the night, Orion appeared to be in hot pursuit, though directionally he was actually far south of them. What I had always assumed as a relationally shared pathway was, in fact, something of an optical illusion.

I have watched Orion and his desired consorts' late fall rise to early spring descent for decades; his and their presence have become something of a faithful friendship to me. I thought that I understood and knew their movements. I was wrong. Many times we think we know our family members and friends quite well, even more, often believe that we've got mere acquaintances pretty well figured out. But many times, we are likely wrong. Each of us is so complex; beyond our DNA, so many experiences have shaped and scarred who we are that is it possible for any one to fully know another? Sure, I can hold "understandings" of others, but my whole night desert view of Orion taught me that there is likely always something that can and will change my perspective of someone I thought that I have known so well.

Mysterious God, so many of us in this world believe that we have "figured out" even you. So many religions seem to have "God in a box," a tidy theology that explains the what, why and wherefores of the Great Mystery. Sometimes I hardly know myself, and surely I am not as clear about my loved ones as I believe I am. Help me to live my life with an openness to different perspectives. Even in my closest relationships, including my desire for knowing and understanding you, I no doubt have much more to experience and to appreciate. May I never reduce the constellations of my comprehension of you, or anyone, or anything to an unchangeable and predictable perspective.

November 11
Veterans Day

World War I, sometimes referred to as "The Great War," officially ended with the signing of the Treaty of Versailles on June 28, 1919. But over seven months prior to that official treaty signing, a cessation of the fighting occurred on November 11 - on the eleventh hour of the eleventh day of the eleventh month – when the warring parties agreed to a temporary ceasefire. Believing that World War I would be "the war to end all wars," a year after that November ceasefire, President Woodrow Wilson sought to commemorate the "beginning of the end" by officially proclaiming November 11 as "Armistice Day," the day the fighting stopped. Unfortunately, World War I was not the war to end all wars as twenty years later the world would begin its engagement in a Second World War with more battlefronts and subsequent carnage than ever before, nearly quadrupling the casualty count of WWI. Today, our nation honors the original date of Armistice Day, but has altered the title, Veterans Day, so as to revere the efforts of all

American war veterans who dared to sacrifice their lives in patriotic duty and service to the common good.

From my perspective, no war's origin is ever based on truly moral or "good" grounds, and subsequently, nothing truly good can ever come from war. As a citizen of a nation that prides itself in being a "defender," yes, I can understand the necessity of engaging in wars against those whose hearts have sincerely been darkened by visions of power, greed and all forms of discrimination; and World War II was nothing if it wasn't that. Who will turn back that vile wave when, as it has before and continues now, to pound against the shores of so many countries' boundaries? Nevertheless, I have been unable to conclude that war is simply a "necessary evil." It is an evil, of that I am sure, but necessary? The history of humankind would certainly suggest so, but as a person of faith, a faith that believes that all have been created in God's image and likeness, I believe that in some cosmic way, we destroy ourselves even when we kill our "enemy." Furthermore, my faith proclaims that this earthly existence is not all that there is, and, even more, that what is to come is a far better, more *peaceful* if you will, state of being than what we know here. Upholding that belief, I find the justification of my killing someone else for the sake of my earthly existence and ideological perspective over that of another's rather contradictory. Negotiating with terrorists and the enemy are often portrayed as signs of weakness, but, generally, nobody dies during negotiations, and further, how do we justify the killing of thousands just so we don't "look weak"? I realize all too well that scriptures of any tradition can be easily manipulated to fit whatever one's end may be, but as I look to Jesus of Nazareth as the Master Teacher of all time, I hear his counter-cultural challenge "to love your enemies" and "to turn the other cheek" loudly, and his perceptive observation that "those who live by the sword, die by the sword" clearly.

Armistice, which refers to the cessation of hostilities for the sake of a truce, etymologically means "to stop or to stand still the tools and weapons of war." As with Memorial Day, which honors those who died in war, I deeply respect the intended efforts of soldiers everywhere, but I feel that my greatest support for them comes though my sincere prayers for peace, for true and constant armistice. When we "stand" for the stoppage of the tools and weapons of war, for Armistice, then the ever-growing lists of Veterans that we honor on Memorial Day will stand still as well.

God of Peace, on this Veterans Day, I stand to offer my thankful prayer for the service that so many have given on behalf of our country's freedom and for the sake of justice in the world. But killing one another is not what you created us for nor do I believe that it comes to us naturally; and so for those who have returned from the fight, alive, but forever wounded by what they have seen and done, I offer a prayer of healing and comfort. Allow them to live healthfully and happily again. And finally, on this day that remembers Armistice Day, I pray for peace. As truces and treaties have been brokered to end wars, help our world leaders today to seek a lasting armistice so that the fears, the anguish, the guilt, and the terrors of war will forever stand still.

November 12
Grocery Store Samples

During an especially tough economic time in my life, my son and I used to make a point of going grocery shopping on Saturdays. On this day at some of the local grocery store chains in our city, there would always be "grocery store samples." Now, we didn't really go expecting to garner a meal out of it, but recognizing our tight means, it seemed an opportunity in frugality to do what needed to be done – shopping – and to pick up some "freebies" along the way. Whether one needs the grocery store sample for real sustenance or not, I always find the idea of the handout kind of fun.

Of course, grocery store samples never satisfy; their proportion and quantity are always less than a hors d'voures, and the quality usually hovers somewhere around "average." But most of us are willing to forgo a little quality for something that is easy and free, and so we willingly accept the proffered paper cup of cheese and a pretzel or cracker, or a spoonful of yogurt or a bite-size cookie, and then maybe even take the coupon as we listen to the vendor's brief "on sale" pitch thinking that we've helped her feel as though she has succeeded at her promotional job. And then we move on, only teased by the morsel, but hardly satisfied.

Oftentimes, we approach our spiritual lives with a similar grocery store sample mentality. When I read about the many different religious traditions of the world, I am often captivated by the tremendous insights of each and can be drawn to a desire to dabble in a little bit of each of them. But this "sampling" often prevents me from truly living and walking one path consistently, faithfully, fully. Like the grocery vendors' offerings, these morsels that we pick up about one tradition or another are fine, but like a Saturday afternoon walk through the store, we will not leave truly nourished or satisfied. We need to sit down and enjoy the full meal.

Once at meal, choosing from only one menu, or one religious tradition, may seem too limiting, but for the sake of our spiritual nutrition, a steady diet of one tradition is probably better for our spiritual development. Having perhaps sampled the menus of different traditions and choosing one, we orient our spiritual bodies on a more consistent diet and can thus better reap the benefits of it. The shared samplings then might be better seen as "desserts," enhancements to our regular meals, but not the meal itself.

God of Nourishment, many samples of spiritual delight have been afforded us. Your presence has been made manifest in so many wonderful traditions that I often simply go about sampling them without ever really sitting down and taking in true nourishment. Help me to commit myself to a more singular path where I might better enjoy the full benefits of a consistent diet. I gratefully receive the desserts offered by others, but may I find a welcome place setting and meal at a table that I can call home.

November 13
Constantly Inconsistent

Sometimes I really have to laugh at myself when I catch myself driving around a parking lot looking for a closer parking spot, and I feel *really* ridiculous when I realize that earlier in the day I went for a five or more mile run. I have run long distances for well over half of my life, and yet, sometimes I lazily seek out a more convenient parking spot just so I won't have to walk "so far!" It's a silly incongruity in my life, but it makes me wonder with what other incongruities do I muddy my life.

I run because I enjoy running, and it makes me feel healthful. I also enjoy doing healthful things for the environment, so I try to drive less if possible. But when I drive around a parking lot looking for a "better" spot, I violate both of the previous intentions. This is a small matter, but surely there are much greater incongruities in my life as well. Some form of the "the Golden Rule," that we should not do to others that which we would not want done to ourselves, is a central maxim found in every spiritual tradition in the world. On the simple, public actions of my life, I probably manage this directive quite well, but in the nitty-gritty issues, in the more private prejudices that we all surely hold, how am I doing?

Most religious traditions today have moved away from outward, aggressive forms of proselytizing. Mission work today is not so much about recruiting people into a religious tradition, but "converting others through our actions." In John's gospel, Jesus instructs his disciples "to love one another. As I have loved you, so you also should love one another. This is how all will know that you are my disciples, if you have love for one another" (13:34b-35). It's a simple directive, and one that every religious tradition would place as fundamental to its practices. But how consistent are we in truly living up to this "simple" commandment? Mohandas K. Gandhi, primarily identified as a Hindu, studied and knew well the scriptures and the teachings of many different religions. I have read that he once was asked why, after studying the teachings of Jesus of Nazareth, he never chose to become a Christian. He responded by saying that "I like your Christ, I do not like your Christians. Your Christians are so unlike your Christ." It may seem a broad indictment, perhaps, but I can't help thinking that, too often, he is absolutely correct.

One of the great challenges of nurturing a spiritual life is learning to live it in a consistent fashion. From the doctrines and dogmas of the Roman Catholic Church to the jewels and vehicles of the Buddhist sangha, each religious tradition provides its devotees with directions that will hopefully move them forward on their spiritual journey. But all of these guidelines and directives are meaningless unless each individual first chooses to embrace, nurture and cultivate them into his or her personal life. Choosing to live life from a consistently spiritual perspective – to see the presence of God potentially alive and active in any given moment – can change just about everything we do as well as *how* we do everything.

Constant and Loving God, to seek union with you is to become love, constantly. Living out my spiritual commitment is no easy task, and so I seek your help and the aid of others in the community of faith in which I am surrounded. Help me to be a consistent, living sign of love, a sign of your presence among us always.

November 14
An Autoimmune Disease

My oldest daughter suffers from multiple sclerosis, an inflammatory disease that affects the ability of nerve cells in the brain and spinal cord to communicate properly with each other. The disorder, which in most cases begins episodically, is believed to be an "autoimmune disease" where the body misinterprets certain agents as pathogens, infectious germs, within its own system, and subsequently attacks itself. In effect, the body's immune system kicks into high gear thinking that it is protecting itself from an intruder when ultimately it is harming itself and causing some permanent damage to the central nervous system. At present, there is no "cure," but certain medications seem to soften side effects and symptoms as well as stimulate a better negotiation between the brain and the body's defensive immune system.

It seems to me that the body of our world suffers from a kind of multiple sclerosis as well when all across our globe every day, human beings are attacking and destroying one another. Some days I can hardly stand to pick up a daily newspaper, so ill at ease am I at what new human impropriety I will read of. How is it that we human beings can be so ruthless and destructive of one another; surely, we must be diseased?

One of the most simple but amazing "gifts" of the space program is the image that it has provided us of the earth. Here on earth, we have divided the landscapes into nations and have separated people by ethnic and racial lines. But seen from space, there truly is but one earth, one home, one body upon which we all live. If we see the earth as a single body, and all of the creations as functioning organisms within that one body, then we human beings truly suffer from a kind of "autoimmune disease." Driven by the fear of pathogen people, we send messages out into our world claiming protective purposes. But while we claim to be warring against infectious infidels and "germinators," like an autoimmune response, we are ultimately destroying ourselves and our single bodied planet.

As with MS, there seems to be no cure available to stop the madness of our self-ruination. Negotiations and treaties between nations and peoples serve as the drugs that medicate symptoms and side effects, but daily somewhere a war is raging and others seem near the boiling point. In response to this dismal situation, many point to human history and suggest that war and violence are natural to human beings, and that we will never change that. Gratefully, as the father of a child with MS, such resignation has not been our response to that disease, and I refuse to let it be my response to the "autoimmune disease" that seems to plague the body of our planet.

Healing God, I am but one cell in and on this magnificent earth, and I am all too aware that I cannot solely find the cure for the ills that affect the health of our globe. But I offer this prayer today as a member of and on behalf of the one body, that all humanity might continuously seek to find real solutions to the evil diseases of misunderstanding, fear, greed, and power that plague our planet. Love and understanding are the true antidotes to achieve the healthful existence of peace. Let me be a living aspect of that cure.

November 15
Hunting for My Son

With the exception of pesky mosquitoes and various biting flies, I have never hunted nor intentionally killed anything. Well, okay, I have spent numerous hours fishing, and considerably fewer hours cleaning fish, so let me revise that opening and say, I have never hunted or killed anything that does not live in the water. As one who sees *all* things infused with the presence of God, to take the life of *anything*, for me, would be most difficult.

Ironically, somewhere in his early adult years, my son took to hunting. Annually he sets out tracking a deer with which to load his freezer - and usually succeeds, and once he proudly bagged a wild turkey with his father-in-law. For my part, I have obviously never encouraged his hunting, but neither have I discouraged it; hunting is a pleasure he pursues, and I do my best to listen to his stories of the ones that got away as well as the ones who have fallen. One year, while he was recovering from a hernia surgery, my son asked me to go with him to the woods where he hunts and to help him take down his tree stand. Knowing that his physical capabilities were temporarily restrained, I agreed and headed out with him late one afternoon.

Now, I spend lots of time in the woods, and my son would know that the wilderness is where I best "go to church," but I was still more than a bit struck when, as we drew nearer to the woods in which he hunts, he reached over and flipped off the music we had blaring in the car. "I always like to approach this space in quiet," he said. Reverential, I wondered? Yes, clearly, I soon realized, we were entering what was for him "sacred ground." Parking the car, we strolled into *his* woods, space he had often entered in morning darkness and solitude, landscape he had watched come alive in the soft and sometimes foggy glow of first light. He shared stories not only of this and that hunt, but also of his clandestine observations of unknowing animals and of experiences of the forest slowly arising from its night slumber. When we got to his tree stand, he began to disassemble it, while I feebly tried to help. Although his recent surgery seemed to demand my assistance in this task, his swift efforts left me feeling unnecessary. And then I suddenly realized that I really had not so much been asked to help retrieve a deer stand, as I had been invited into the sacred space that is my son's world of hunting. He simply wanted me to know something about him of which my own past and present had no context.

We often need the affirmation and support of significant others in our lives. We seek them out and share our story not looking for advice or direction, but a simple kind of communion. Great God of Communion, help me this day to recognize the quiet, subtle requests from those around me who seek my loving support. Too often, I am too quick to lend my advice or my opinion, when all that is really needed is my listening and simple affirmation. Can I willingly accept the offer to enter another's woods, to stand within them quietly, and to embrace the shared sounds and stories that drift to the ground like autumn leaves?

November 16
Work and Rest

I took an unsolicited two week break from my writing projects while I tried to fully embrace a long-planned-for trip. It was the first time that I was to visit my Arizonan daughters without school work and other outside responsibilities hanging over my head, and I decided that I wanted to just be fully present to each moment, and to not allow even my newest and most flexible agendas to get in the way. During occasional down times, I furtively snuck in some necessary reading, and on solo hikes and rare mornings, talked my thoughts into a small tape recorder for later retrieval. The trip seemed a valuable hiatus from my daily writing regimen, but I quietly worried all the same about the effects of wandering off of the not yet fully established trail of my new routine. As each day unfolded, however, I began to think all the more that my recess from writing and my full engagement in living might provide some new fertile soil when I reconvened with my work.

The day after I returned, although I felt eager to resume my work regimen, was my least productive day ever, and I felt a nervous fear creep into me that somehow I might have lost "my groove" and my desire to write. Ideas log-jammed within me, but the words to pry them apart and to float them down the river of reflection seemed desperately absent. After a couple of hours of futile attempts, I simply gave into the apparent aridity and set the work aside to read instead. The next morning, I found myself purposely "oversleeping," resisting my previous discipline of early rising, afraid that I might face the same parched effort. Once up and nourished, indeed, the words did come slowly, but suddenly a fissure in the wall of my resistance seemed to give way, and the ideas and the words came streaming together again; I jumped aboard my keyboard raft and let their united flow carry me.

All work and creative efforts can easily lose their luster when we fail to give them some restful suspension or a rejuvenating break. The cessation of work, however, can also lull us into a complacent lethargy. Sucked into the ease of laxity, we can lose the rhythm of our motivation and the precision of our vision. Finding the proper balance in our work and rest is part of the job itself. Too much work and we become tiredly ineffective; too much rest and we become defectively unproductive.

O God of Work and Rest, I come to you seeking balance in what I do and in what I am. I am not my work, although my work surely can enliven and help to define me. Help me to find meaning and value in the tasks before me, but let them not consume me so that I forget the simple joy of being alive. Rest, too, is good, but do not let my times of leisure abate my desire to utilize and fulfill the gifts that you have given me, often expressed and realized through my work. Bring me to that place of balance, with a heart fully ready to serve buoyed by a soul that fully knows how to rest.

November 17
Let Your Hair Down

For almost as long as I can remember, I have personally favored long hair. When I was a small child in the early sixties, a close-cut hairstyle - we called them a "heiney" - was quite vogue. I hated the buzz cut even then but I had no say in the matter; Dad said get it cut, and it got cut. Then the Beatles came along, and the "four mop tops" stretched the boundaries of style considerably, although if you look at early Beatles' pictures, their hair was not particularly long. In high school, I had a little more say about my hair length, but my football coach demanded a very short style, almost a crew cut, and so every late summer, whatever had grown through the year would get whacked off. My first true act of "hair rebellion" was not until I went away to college.

I distinctly remember my parents all but pleading with me to "go in and get it trimmed up before you leave," but by then I had had it with the designs of others, and I obstinately refused. They were not happy with me. Two years later, while working construction, a crusty old plumber who frequently offered his opinions without request, looked me over one day and then asked me during lunch, "Criminy sakes! If you wanted to be a girl, why the hell wasn't you born one?" Well, I'm not really sure what my motivation or desire for long hair was, but it certainly was not a desire to be a female. I just liked it, I guess, and, perhaps, I saw it as being a little counter-cultural and I tended to swing that way, at least.

After finishing college and beginning my teaching career, I succumbed to what I felt were the "pressures of societal convention." I didn't wear my hair short, but it certainly wasn't long by my standards; it was "socially acceptable." When the mullet gained popularity, I jumped on that style for a while for it met my two needs: respect for social convention ("business up front") and my personal desire ("and party in the back"). But for most of my early adult life and teaching career, I was so concerned about "what others thought" that I consistently relinquished what I felt and wanted. And then I got divorced.

Divorce was never a part of my vocabulary; I never dreamed that such a thing could happen to me. Not only was it against my religious beliefs at the time, but in my mind, it flew in the face of what I thought was "socially acceptable." Married for seventeen years, with three children, and involved in all kinds of church and social organizations and councils, my first wife and I were the picture of the "good, Christian, American family." But all was obviously not well. When trouble started simmering, I tried to "change" what I could to satisfy my wife's expectations and needs, but whatever change I made, the need for another one cropped up like a weed. We tried counseling, individually and together, but still I couldn't seem to be the man she needed, and when the relationship finally ended, I was left with what felt like the greatest failure of my life. All of my years of conformity and effort came rushing to the graveside of that great death. Failing at what seemed to be the most important relationship of my life, I was overwhelmed by a sense that little else that I had ever done mattered; but as I sifted through the pieces for the next year, I began to see that truly one of my biggest failures – throughout my life – had been my inability to be true to my own needs and feelings. Not just selfish desires and designs that need to be curbed, but those that truly define who we are. And in that realization, the cutting of my hair over all those years became a symbol of my sure defeat. For all of my adult life, I conceded to what "the social norm" dictated, a willing accomplice in the scheme because I believed that for the collective good, the sacrifice was worth it. But sitting amidst the ruin and the rubble, I discovered that the concessions had guaranteed me nothing, and that through the process of yielding to the conventions, I had lost myself. And with that discovery, I said, "Enough" – not with belligerence, but with the resolve to be true to who I am; and from that day forward, I stopped cutting my hair to meet the expectations of others.

I still certainly believe that there is a time and a place for most everything, and we all need to compromise our own designs and views now and then for the sake of the collective good; but each of us has been created as an individual with our own unique gifts. We are not meant to be "one thing" or to follow "one way." Inimitable God, it is not a rebellious spirit that I seek, nor an iconoclastic visage, but only the true reflection of my own face. Help me to recognize and to strike the balance between making necessary concessions and being true to myself. You have created this unique individual; allow me to let my hair down and not cut away the person that I am.

November 18
Keep Moving

I have had a few opportunities to join a large group of high school seniors as a chaperone on a multi-day trip and experience of our nation's capitol, Washington D.C. Visiting this city can be more than a little overwhelming, as its offering are enormous, and each sight-seeing opportunity seems to deserve more time than one could possible have to give. For example, the first time I went through the Holocaust Museum on one of those trips, I remember wanting to take in everything. The museum itself has four floors. A visiting group, such as we were, is first given a brief introduction to the museum in the lower level of the building, and then is brought to the entrance of the exhibits via an elevator to the top. At this top level, there is nearly a small library of information, provided in stunning photos, historical documents and displays, and thorough explanations, covering the twentieth century history of Germany, the rise of the Third Reich and then their ensuing philosophical and ideological movements. Like Dante's Inferno, one will then descend in a spiral movement to the depths of the horrors of the Holocaust. Although we had two or more hours to make our way through this stunning museum, I discovered that just as I was about to finish the first of the four floors, I had only fifteen minutes before our group was set to reconvene.

As always happens to me in such interesting, informative and fascinating places, my initial movement is to take in everything, moving slowly, reading all the explanations, and examining all of the pictures and artifacts. But somewhere along the line, I realize that my pace is too slow and I will never fully make it through the exhibit unless I move more swiftly and be a little more discriminating in my study of what is offered.

In walking through the labyrinth of our spiritual lives, we often move rather slowly too. At times, this slow pace is necessary and good as we carefully reflect on our direction while studying the signs and readings provided along the path. But, sometimes I have to wonder if the reasons for the slowness of my pace are under the false pretense that I am trying to take it all in and to make sure that I am getting it all right, when maybe, I am just being spiritually lazy. For different reasons, perhaps, but with the same conclusion as when I walk through museums and informative exhibits, I find that I need to get moving with my spiritual life.

We need to be vigilant students of our spiritual lives, careful observers and readers of all that is sacred around us; and we also need to encouragingly move forward. It is certainly unwise to traverse our spiritual journey blindly and ignorantly, but it is also important for us to be actively engaged in our journey: students and practitioners. God of Reflection and Action, to grow in my faith, to nurture my spiritual development, I need to carefully observe, read and study the many guideposts that have been provided me. Absorbing these guides, however, I also need to keep moving, to keep pursuing active expressions of my faith. In my journey towards you, help me to be a good observer and a good practitioner.

November 19
Naked Acres

One of my dearest couple friends lives on a forty-acre piece of farmland in north-central Ohio. It has long been their dream to create a self-sufficient lifestyle, growing and raising as much of their own food as they can, from vegetables and fruit to poultry and goats. In the variety of names with which they have labeled their land is one that always brings a smile: Naked Acres. Along with the self-sufficient dream was a desire to live in a place remote enough that if they chose to walk about their land naked, no one would know or see or be offended. Quite frankly, I really don't know if they do this "naked walk" about their land, but they could, for their driveway is at least a quarter of a mile stretch off an already quiet country road, and the land itself is surrounded by others' fields and their own woodlands.

Farming is a tough way of life. While one might enjoy the flexibility of setting one's own work schedule and not having to punch a time clock, the other side of this flexibility is that, especially if one is raising animals, it truly is a seven day a week, every week of the year job. Subsequently, once or twice a year, my wife and I try to give our friends at least a weekend break. Either by their request, or our volunteer, we "farm sit." Now, while we might bask in the belief that we are providing a wonderful reprieve from the daily grind of our friends' farm life, the truth of the matter is, as so often happens when one "serves," we get far more out of our stay than they, perhaps, get from their time away.

My wife and I live in a suburban village, surrounded by numerous other suburbs which all join together with the hub of the city to form a sprawling mass of concrete and steel and other forms of fabrication. Nestled in our "quiet, little neighborhood," we can lay in bed at night and hear the incessant drone of the interstate freeway more than a mile away, or hear the wail of fear or tragedy in every emergency siren that might suddenly burst from its waiting place. But just forty-five minutes from our home is Naked Acres, a place of quiet solitude; and when I am there, I am reminded of many other far-off places to which I have traveled and explored.

In addition to the remoteness of its setting, Naked Acres is also void of the distraction of television and the internet. Subsequently, one is inevitably "drawn out" to the land more easily, and captivated by sunrises and sunsets, and the sounds and the movements of all the inhabitants of the land. Surely farm life must have a schedule, but it is not an exacting schedule; feeding time is "around this time" and chores get done as necessity demands.

We all need a "Naked Acres," a place where we can go and just strip away the demands of our modern world, take off the heavy overcoat of schedules right down to the underwear of expectations that we step into each day. Whether we live in the city or not, we are all too easily caught up in the stresses and turmoil of life, forgetting or, perhaps, not even realizing the quiet reality of life.

God of Quiet Spaces, I need to take some time today to ask myself, "where is my Naked Acres?" In asking that question, I offer an additional prayer in thanksgiving for my place of refuge, or for the awareness of my need to discover one. Having said and prayed these things, help me to make some plans to get there soon, that quiet place where I know you will always be found awaiting me.

November 20
Looking at Death

I have sat bedside stroking my father's hand as he inched his way across the threshold of this life, and have quietly chanted songs of release beside my daughter's mother-in-law as she too slipped into the great sleep, but I felt oddly ill-prepared to witness the slow death of a mere squirrel. Perhaps, somehow, despite the unsurety of it all, we think we know something about human death and can envision welcoming spirits receiving our loved ones as they cross into the next life, whatever that may be, bathed in a warm and glowing light. But animals, wild animals, what of their leave-taking?

I had been busy about my work that day, sitting as I usually do while writing in our simple dining room, with its wide window inviting the activity and beauty of the backyard into my sphere of presence. Glancing up with frequency, a kind of subconscious searching for a sip of inspiration, I noticed a large bundle of gray nestled atop the strong arm of a tree's limb directly in my window view. Through the few remaining fall leaves and the tangle of other brush, I could not make out clearly just what the bundle was, but I assumed it was a gray squirrel nestled into the crux enjoying a late morning snack. The lack of movement, however, piqued my curiosity, and each time I glanced up, my eyes were immediately drawn to the same spot, looking for a change. After a short while, out of the corner of my eye, I detected the slow movement of a squirrel down the trunk of the tree, and looking over found it so, except that I also noticed another squirrel still hunched over on that strong ledge of the tree's limb. Wow, I thought to myself, that must have been some intense "love-making," as I assumed that the idle one was still recovering from her ecstasy. Her lover, as I imagined the scenario, quietly stole away embarrassingly satisfied with their union, slipping to the ground and then vanishing into the mat of groundcover below. Still, there was no movement above.

I had seen squirrels mate before, and thought that their rhythm was intense and quick: a speedy mount, a quiver of muscles, and with the job done, a carrying on as if nothing had happened. This scene was strangely very different, and captivated now, I sprung to the back room for binoculars so that I might have a more detailed perspective. Zeroing in on the resting squirrel, I was shocked to see what appeared to be blood about its mouth and chest. Suddenly, the image of affection that I thought I had voyeuristically encountered morphed into more sordid thoughts. Had there been a fight? Had the larger, motionless bundle I had first observed been a death bite and grip of one over the other? Soon there was slow movement from the perched squirrel, and with my magnified vision I could see that one of her front paws was maimed, and perhaps there was a wound on her underside, just below her neck. All of the leaping and excitable movement that so marks my impression of the squirrel-life outside my window was gone. I stared into its eyes through my binoculars and wondered what thoughts coursed through its little head at a time like this. Was it aware of its impending death? Did it feel the pain of its wounds as it gently preened? The back of the squirrel arched carefully, and it tucked its head into its chest, curling into a kind of fetal position. Interestingly, all other squirrel activity appeared to move away, as if they all sensed the shift in their companion, and stepped away to give it privacy. But here I was, now truly the voyeur, watching what appeared to be a labored rise and fall in its breathing.

After some time, the squirrel rose up again, and then I could see a little more clearly the extent of its injury, particularly to the paw. Gingerly, it three-stepped down the trunk of the tree and, reaching the ground, seemed to pause with each step, considering if and where to go next. I carefully tracked its movements to the fence line of the yard, and when it disappeared around the corner of the house, I slid out the front door to see its next course. For a moment it paused and I swear it looked me straight in the eye; if I could read a squirrel's mind I would say that it simply asked for some privacy: "Leave me alone and let me die in peace." And then with its three good limbs, it scampered off through the leaves and undergrowth and was gone. Rushing back inside to the back windows again, I saw only the resumption of the wild and busy scampering of the rest of the squirrel clan preparing for winter. I watched all of their movements carefully, looking for the wounded gait and the blood stained fur, but there was the fullness of life in these; perhaps my subject had quietly gone off to die.

The cycle of life and death is always all around us, but how infrequently we have the chance or make the effort to observe it. Lying sick in bed one day, the seventeenth century poet turned preacher, John Donne, observed the peal of a funeral bell and offered the profound observation: "Do not ask for whom the bell tolls; it tolls for thee." The death of a loved one is always a sure and certain reminder to us all of our own mortality, but no less than that was this squirrel for me that day. In truth, the assumed unknowns of its demise called me even more deeply into the dark questions of our own existence. Does welcoming light call it forth to the other side as we assume it does for us?

God of Life and Death, of Warmth and Welcome, I place the wonder of life in your hands. Religions offer answers and visions of what awaits us, but as I have watched all kinds of life slip away, I cannot say with absolute certainty, this or that is what I shall see and become. Faith in you provides me comfort, and in this interim life, I choose to live as hopefully and as happily as my faith will permit. Comfort me in my observations of death and sooth me in my own aging with the gentle assurance of your universal and welcoming peace.

November 21
My First Hunt

During an interfaith retreat at a Hindu ashram, I met a Yaqui medicine man who was one of the presenters. His "theology" resonated most closely with my own, and I quickly found myself drawn to him, hoping that we might have a chance to visit during some free time. Pursuing this design, I managed to seize an hour or more of his time one afternoon as we found a quiet space beneath swaying palm trees and rustling magnolia bushes. At some point in our conversation, while I was sharing with him some thoughts about my children, I spoke, perhaps with a little embarrassment, about my hunter son – embarrassed because I consider myself a pacifist and would avoid the killing of all life forms. Ignoring my posture, he asked me if I had ever gone with my son on a hunt, or if I had ever validated that part of him. "He is a hunter-warrior," he said, "and he needs your blessing." Then, with a thoughtful pause he added, "Wait a minute; I've got something for you; wait right here." Returning from his temporary housing, he offered me two small coins, very specific in nature, and instructed me to make a medicine pouch both for my son and for myself. When they are completed, he noted, go on a hunt with your son, and call the prey in with a prayer. "Be there with him," he concluded, "and bless what he is, a hunter. He needs that from his father."

Almost a year later, having already presented the medicine pouch to my son ceremoniously at another time, the two of us went on our first hunt together; I, of course, carried no weapon. Entering the forest in moon-glow darkness on a cold late fall morning, I simply followed my son's lead, having never ventured into woods with an intent to kill before, stepping as quietly as possible through the crisp air and crackling leaves and twigs. Finding his desired spot, we sat down amidst the bare trees on a bed of fallen leaves as the morning sky soon waxed into a steel grey and a gentle breeze blew light into the eastern horizon like breath to an ember. If we spoke, words were brief and in hushed whispers, our fullest attention given to any sight or sound of movement around us. After over an hour, the sun now fully engaging the daylight, my son leaned into me, nodded, and pointed to the ridge just ahead of us and to our right. There, through the open maze of trees and brush, four deer softly crowned a hill. In stillness, we awaited their advancement into the shallow ravine between them and our sentinel post, but after a few nearly soundless minutes, the deer turned and quietly slid out of sight and sound back down the opposite hillside from whence they had no doubt emerged. They were our only sighting that day.

Arriving back at our vehicle hours later, my son was mildly disappointed with the inactivity of our hunt; I, on the other hand, found myself fully satisfied that on this first outing we had captured a quiet sunrise, the soft footfalls of woodland creatures, and the morning movements and songs of birds in the netting of our togetherness. There will, no doubt, be another chapter to this story where the calling in of the deer and an offering over its sacrificed life will be performed, but on this day, our shared time was blessing enough.

Creator God of All Things, my life has been spent hunting for a deeper and more meaningful connection with you. Throughout this search, however, I have often pursued you only in the lands that I found accessible, following trails that I deemed valuable. Help me to be a more attentive watcher and a more thoughtful listener, for your footfalls may be encountered at any time in the most unsuspecting setting and with a most innocent companion.

November 22
Recognizing the Signals

I was told once that there is about a twenty-minute delay between the body's registering satiation and our brain's awareness of it. The point was, when a person is engaged in a feast of which he is unwilling to let go just yet, and is questioning whether that next round of helpings is "necessary," he should wait twenty minutes and see what his body "tells" him before digging in for more. Certain animals, again I have been told, don't seem to have that little built in "alarm system" that tells them, "I'm good; I have had enough to eat for now," and they just keep right on eating into sickness and even death. Gratefully, humans aren't equipped that way. Our bodies do send signals to us that they have been satiated after consuming a healthy – even an unhealthy – meal. Of course, sometimes we don't heed this signal and plow right into a third helping, only to pay a very uncomfortable price of indigestion for hours after.

Actually, our bodies are very good at alerting us about many excesses in our lives, not just eating or drinking, but physical activities and, I would dare to say, emotional ones as well. Physically stressed and pushed to the limits, our muscular structure will simply fail us when its demand for oxygenation exceeds the heart's ability to produce the requested amount. Like the eating signal, this one comes with considerable certainty, and is more quickly apparent than the twenty-minute satiation-signal delay. The emotional signal, however, is more subtle than either of these physical "too-much-alarms"; but while it demands a more sensitive read, attention to the warning signs is no less important, perhaps more important, than the physical alarms.

The range of emotions with which we humans have been equipped is wonderful, and all must have their place at some time in our lives, but I tend to think that God intended for us to be, more than anything else, "happy." Exuberance and ecstasy are the high ends of our happiness, and are not to be daily, common fare, but the happiness of contentment and simplicity ought to be part of our daily diet. When melancholy and lethargy occupy a large portion of our meal plate, something is not right in our lives. Sadness sometimes creeps into our lives like a bad habit taken on slowly; like an extra helping of potatoes or a second dessert, it appears as a harmless need, and then sticks around as a lump of empty calories. And just like when we overeat, sadness slows down our bodies' activities; we become bored, disinterested, unengaged, and, certainly, *not happy*. We know the physical signals of overindulgence, and when they happen we ought to know well enough that the excess must stop; but we need to be mindful too of the signals of emotional over-indulgence, and when we sense these, we must pursue the root cause of our sadness, our discontentment, and seek ways to once again get us back on the diet of happiness.

God of Subtle Signs, as a physical being, I am often very much aware of the excesses of my life with regards to eating, drinking and physical activity; but as a spiritual being, perhaps less informed, less intuitive, and less sensible, I am not always as aware of my emotional excesses. Align my body and spirit so that I might be more sensitive to my emotional needs, just as I am to my physical ones. Help me to recognize when my spirit is emotionally imbalanced, and to respond to that deficiency in healthful, therapeutic measures that will lead me to true happiness.

November 23
A Thankful Pilgrim

With so few of our extended families living anywhere near us, my wife and I don't often host or create much of a traditional Thanksgiving Day dinner, but the holiday we celebrate this week has long been one of my favorite holidays of the year. Perhaps it is because there are no especially significant religious traditions associated with it, no births or deaths, no miracles or salvific acts, just a plain and simple, but bountiful thanksgiving for all that is. As a child, of course, like most American children, the hors d'oeuvres of Thanksgiving that I fed upon were the wonderful mythological stories of the Plymouth Rock pilgrims. Images of the

Indians coming to the rescue of the early pilgrims, helping them through a brutal first winter, and then teaching them some New World planting and harvesting techniques were balanced by the reciprocity of gratefulness, the Pilgrims' inviting the Indians to a grand picnic, a spread of epic proportions, tables, no doubt, lined with turkeys, corn, squash, stuffing, cranberries, and plenty of pumpkin pie. A little less highlighted in the story telling was that, apparently, some years later, the welcome mat of both parties would get more than a little worn, and the death and scalp of the other would become the preferred victual. But never mind that; it's Thanksgiving, a time to truly be grateful for our excess.

For almost two decades now, my own Thanksgiving Day ritual is to first honor that part of the mythology that has been lost, along with the people that have been forsaken in the wake of our Thanksgivings, the Native Americans. The story of the first Europeans' survival here in the "New World" is truly an incredible narrative of courage and determination. That Native peoples helped these daring early settlers in those first years is a credit to the inherent goodness of their hearts, if not a discredit to their lack of foresight of what was to come. But each Thanksgiving Day morning, after offering my own prayers of gratitude for all of the gifts that I have received from the land, by hand or through demand, I dance on the bountiful earth to honor the spirits of the people who knew and honored this land first, long before there ever was a first Thanksgiving Day. Only with that first simple act of contrition can I then move into the traditional bounty of this special holiday.

We here in the United States are so richly blessed. Other countries have landscapes as beautiful, if not more, than ours, but the expansive diversity of our country is truly astonishing. And while other countries may provide an incredible wealth of a certain resource, again, few, if any, can rival the diversity of resources that this continent offers. Additionally, in this modern world, very few countries could boast of the standard of living that is so common place here; yes, there are certainly impoverished U.S. citizens, but the vast majority of our citizens take for granted certain amenities that would only be luxuries of the rich in other lands. And if one should be especially in need, there is perhaps no better time throughout the year than Thanksgiving to find a welcoming table and the free offering of necessary groceries. Yes, we have very much for which to be thankful!

Before sitting down to the grand spread of a familial Thanksgiving Day dinner, many families make it a tradition to prayerfully remember and share something for which each person present is thankful. It may seem a simple and contrived gesture, but I believe that it is a valuable tradition to carve into the hearts and hands of all present a collective portrait of our gratitude, and then to dish up a second helping of prayers for those most in need and for those sacrificed and forgotten.

Gracious God, my heart is full, as my stomach so often is. Sometimes I cling to the memories of what I have lost and linger on the desire for what I have not yet obtained, forgetting all the while the cornucopia of blessings that I ungratefully enjoy every day. During this week of Thanksgiving, help me to be especially mindful of the tremendous abundance with which I have been blessed, not simply with food, but with family, friends, comforts, safety, freedom, beauty and all. And as I celebrate my profusion, may I also remember the lives of those who in the past were plowed under through the harvest of our bounty, and may I serve the needs of those who today truly hunger for more food and justice.

November 24
Desert Firewood

A simple, and quite frankly, very practical rule of thumb regarding the collection of firewood when camping is that one should only collect fallen limbs and branches, loose and dry material. One might suspect that camping in the desert would make firewood collection a bit difficult, as we don't normally associate trees with the desert. To the contrary, however, depending upon the type of desert environment in which one is encamped, there often is a fairly good stock of firewood to be found in the desert, much more than just cactus. Palo Verde, mesquite and a variety of scrub brush can all yield some small firewood, and with an especially careful eye, some parts of old, dead cacti can also be salvaged. Not surprisingly, desert firewood tends to be very dry, and what one can collect is usually quite small in size as well; in fact, my biggest pieces of firewood in the desert would be seen as nothing more than kindling in a woodland environment. Subsequently, even a small fire on a cold desert night will consume a firewood supply rather quickly.

Given the brittle, dry nature of desert firewood, starting a fire is usually not a problem; keeping the fire going, however, takes pretty constant attention. The grey finger-like bones of wood promptly catch and provide a flash of heat as the flame leaps to life, but this arid kindling is quickly consumed, leaving an airy pile of embers that, lacking density, swiftly fade to a soft pile of ash. In the desert, an attentive fire keeper must constantly coax the fire with more of the dry diet as the fire consumes the offering hungrily.

Just as a desert fire requires attention and care, so too do the needs of others lap like a hungry fire for our consideration. With the variety of social safety-net programs apparently available, it is often as easy for us to overlook the needs of the poor and the homeless as it is for us to consider the need for a fire in the typically oppressively hot desert. At this time of year, with temperatures dropping and the holidays rising, we are more prone to remember the needs of those less fortunate than ourselves, but those needs are not seasonal. Many times we feel that our service efforts, our acts of comfort and assistance on behalf of others really are not all that necessary. Subsequently, our "offering" might be rather infrequent and often, like desert firewood, pretty "small and dry." Not that these efforts are inconsequential, however, for they do provide a burst of warmth and comfort, but again like the desert fire, our efforts can be rather short-lived, a quick flash of temporary comfort, and then a small pile of ash. We may have a large cache of dense and sizable firewood at home, but when we show up to volunteer our services, we often only bring the desert kindling that starts fast and ends quickly. The homeless, in particular, tend to get more attention in these approaching cold months, but let us be mindful that a meager pile of "desert firewood" will not serve their needs for very long; as with a desert fire, we need to be vigilant and consistent.

O God of All Things Warm and Bright, so much of our world is in need of the soothing comfort that a fire provides. So often, I fail to recognize the needs of others, and the world's need for my attentive assistance and care. Help me to bring an adequate supply of wood to the fire of true needs, and to faithfully sit beside the flame and feed it with attentive care. I may not always be able to bring the largest and most dense offering, but may I always be willing to bring the best that I have to give in armfuls of devoted care.

November 25
Giving Can Hurt

I have been donating my blood regularly for at least twenty years. That's not a boast, for many people have no doubt donated for many more years than I have and they have likely been far more regular as well. But I offer my timeline partly to just encourage giving – blood, or many other things or in many other ways – and partly to provide some context for my experience of giving. The thing is, I don't exactly *like* donating blood, and, I think, for a number of "good reasons."

My children love watching television shows about surgery where they go right inside the operating room. Not me. I am absolutely amazed by the wondrous inner workings of the human body, but I don't really need to *see* them, and that includes blood. Donating blood, however, pretty much puts it right out there. With bags of blood being processed, and people laid out on chaise lounges with small tubes of blood flowing from their arms, it is pretty hard to avoid "the sight" of blood when I show up to donate. Secondly, I have decided that I don't have to worry about ever becoming a heroin addict, because I don't think I could ever shove a needle in my arm; and I don't much like it when someone else does it either. But, it would be pretty much impossible to donate blood without somebody poking a needle into the pumped up blood vessel coursing down my left arm. The third reason perhaps could be anticipated in the second: it kind of hurts. I mean, I really don't like that little prick they give my middle finger just to "test" my blood and see if it's good enough, let alone the larger poke ten minutes later! Most of the time, the "blood-letters" do a very fine job of slipping that needle into my arm with little pain (and I always let them know of my gratitude when they do), but I never watch them and I always wince just before they do it. I admit it, I am not a masochist, although some might think that of me given many of my other "enjoyable" hobbies and interests. Once the needle is in and the blood is flowing smoothly from me to the cute little pouch, it is really not so bad, and I even glance up once in awhile from the book that I am reading or the papers that I used to grade and take a quick peek at how the process is going; but I am always well aware when I squeeze that little stress ball to keep the blood pumping that I am not exactly *relieving* stress with each compression. Next, I have seen people pass out after giving blood, and I remember the first handful of times that I donated, I too felt rather light-headed when I got up from the recliner; so, naturally, I always know that it *could* happen again, and that is not something that

I would choose, given the choice. Finally, some people might say they donate blood because of all the good treats they offer in the canteen afterwards. Don't kid yourself; the snacks are very high in calories and fat content; the fruit punch or lemonade are usually way too sweet or just plain bland; and the coffee has probably been in that container all day long – yum.

Okay, so I'm probably not doing a very good job of selling someone on the idea of donating blood; so why do I? Because like all giving, it may be a little inconvenient and it might even hurt a little bit and the immediate rewards really *aren't*, but, way more important than any of those "discomforts," it is the good and the right thing to do. If you have ever had a loved one in the hospital or read some story of a stranger's tragic malady, and you have said to yourself, "Wow, I would do just about anything to help them out," then donating your time, your energy, your blood or your organs is doing just that. Giving of ourselves in whatever way we can for the good and the health of others is one of the best gifts we can offer. Giving may not always *feel* good, but it will always *be good.*

God of Life, we have within our hands noninvasive ways to enhance the quality of some people's lives who often so desperately need it. Through the gifts of time, energy and money we can lend a helping hand; through the donation of blood, organs and other tissues, we perhaps extend the life of those in need. The temporary pain or discomfort that I might experience in my simple offerings is nothing compared to the ongoing needs of others whom I might help. May the blood I donate, or the time and talents I give be a lifeline to those most in need.

November 26
Obituaries

I read obituaries in the daily newspaper every day now. It's not some morbid curiosity that draws me to those pages; I am sincerely interested for a number of reasons. My most practical motive is that, after thirty years of teaching and coaching in the same city, I know a lot of people. From former students and athletes to their parents and sometimes other relatives, and on to former colleagues and old coaching friends, my field of friends and acquaintances stretches out like wide-open grasslands. I sometimes browse through the obituaries like someone walking through a suspicious prairie of snakes, cautiously stepping from one name to the next, hoping I don't read of someone I know. On a more personal level, like all of the people that I know, I am getting older too, and with my own aging I find myself more openly curious about death. So, I must admit that as I peruse the obituaries of the daily edition, I am also drawn to pictures and dates of people who are around my age or younger. Rarely is the cause of death included, but all the same, it gives me pause to consider why I get to be alive today while these names I read of do not.

Death comes to us all, and some, through the unfortunate circumstances of their lives, go out looking for it. If we live in a safe and healthy environment when we are young, we don't think much about death. So far away in years, it seems death is not part of our youthful landscape. But as we grow older and ascend various rises in the contoured landscape, we can see evidence of death more readily on the horizon, and eventually we get close enough to it that we have glimpses of its face. I remember when my parents, who both nearly reached ninety years old before their deaths, spoke of going to funerals as if it was their social life. Standing graveside of so many friends, relatives and acquaintances, they reached an understanding of death's nearness, and accepted the limits of their own lives.

Through my own aging, and having experienced the deaths of some family and friends, I have also come to a different understanding of the need and value of comfort that should surround a death, and it is this understanding that also helps me open the obituary page each morning. Even when we anticipate a death, the final goodbye is never easy. Although I embrace the belief that this earthly life is not our "end," death definitely changes the dynamics of my relationship with another. The loss of a loved one's voice and physical presence inevitably creates a void that takes time for each person remaining in this life to reconcile. And when death comes sudden and unexpectedly without giving us a chance to even have a last good bye, the void can feel especially lonely and all-consuming. Into this new emptiness, I try to throw a simple line of support. I cannot change the feelings of loss that another might experience, but I can offer my simple prayers and my heartfelt words as some small measure of support to a friend in need. Through a card, a phone call, or a visit, I tell my companion that she is not alone, and while I cannot restore what has been lost, I willingly stand beside her in her grief offering a shoulder for or a story of the one who has passed.

God of the Living and the Dead, for you, perhaps, our eternal lives don't change all that much. But for us here in this earthly existence, death changes everything. I know that death is as natural to my existence as was my birth, but the passing of loved ones ends my fond and tangible connection with them, and creates a void that I am not sure how or even if I want to fill. As I know these feelings, so too do I recognize them in others. Help me to be a source of comfort for my friends and acquaintances, however simple it might be, whenever they must stand before the grey landscape of their loss and seek ways to move ahead.

November 27
A Feathered Chorus

It is believed that one of the final senses to slip from our consciousness as we die is sound, or our sense of hearing. While music has always been an important part of my life, when I go, (as if I have any say in the matter!) I would like to be surrounded by the songs of birds. To me, the sounds of birds provide us with one of the most simple but most wonderful gifts of the natural world. Additionally, one of the wonderful gifts of the senses is that they provide us with connections to our past, and so, the coupling of the two, bird songs and their connections to my world of memories seem a wonderful way to transition into the next life. While I'm at it, maybe I'll even specify what birds I would especially like to hear.

Top of the list would be the loon, and I would appreciate a full range concert – its laughter, hoot, tremolo, and the haunting wail as an extended encore. The songs of the loon always take me back to my roots, Minnesota, and especially the deep serenity, like nowhere else on earth, of the north woods and Boundary Waters Wilderness. Robins are more memorably present in my childhood than any other bird, and I like their commonness throughout my life and everywhere. As one of the loudest spring morning songsters, robins' tune always seems an ode to joy. Cardinals too are rather common birds in many parts of North America, but they held a special place in the hearts of my mother and father and I can't help seeing a cardinal without thinking of mom and dad. The bird of choice of a number of states, they are also the State Bird of Ohio, and as an Ohio resident for over thirty years, I have lighted to their beautiful melodies in every season of the year. Once distinguished, the cardinals' song variety is as beautiful and as striking as the males' flashy red plumage and black highlights. For a little frivolity, I would have to invite the great-tailed grackles of the Southwest to drop by for a song or two. Along with reminding me of visits to my Arizonan daughters, these regional birds, with their long magpie-like tails, always make me smile; sometimes, in response to their showy songs, I literally give way to giggling. Connecting me to my wife's North Dakotan roots and to my life of questioning, the western meadowlark would have to make an inquisitive entrance. Its warm warbling always sounds like a query to me, from a slightly annoyed, "What are *you* doing here?" to a more thoughtful and gentle, "It sure is a beautiful day, isn't it?" Finally, I would send out a special invitation to the woodland thrush permitting him to hide out as he always does in some dense background if he would just agree to pleasure me with his songs. When I first started hanblechia, days of prayer and fasting, in the woodlands of eastern Ohio, this very shy bird would provide the last and most beautiful songs of the evening, and then return to "sing the sun up" in the morning. Every time that I hear its voice I am immediately transported to a state of prayerful awareness.

Of course, there are many other birds I might like to include: owls and mourning doves for their haunting tones; hawks and eagles for their majesty; pileated woodpeckers and whippoorwills for their delightful range. But I should think that the previous list will provide memorial songs and memories enough.

God of Sound and Song and Memories, sometimes the joys and sorrows of my life come back to me in simple music, often in the most simple tones and notes of creation. Many times, I have been lifted to a spiritual exhilaration or transfixed in a mystical melancholy through the songs of birds. Perhaps, at times, they are your voice, gently urging me into a more thoughtful and prayerful space, but that they stir so much of my past and present, while hinting at the beauty of the future, is enough. Like their songs, I give you thanks and praise.

November 28
Of Beds and Sleep

A good friend called me recently to tell me that he and his wife had bought a new bed and wondered if my wife and I might want their old one. I suppose many people would balk at accepting someone else's old bed, but the funny things is, the one we were sleeping on quite contentedly was their previous old one before this latest new purchase. So I figured, why not? I liked what we had, their old one, and this "new old one" would be an upgrade, so I said yes!

Since setting up their "new old one" in our room, I do think that my sleep has been even better. I was content with the previous set, but over the past year or so, I did wonder sometimes if we weren't due for a new bed, and even did some preliminary searching. Like so much else, the bed market is a pretty big industry too. With so many brands, both local and national names, styles and sizes, and then the potential "bells and whistles," it is obvious that we take our sleep pretty seriously. It stands to reason, of course, for if eight hours is the recommended sleep time, that means one third of every day is spent lying on a bed!

Now, I like sleep, but I often feel like it is kind of a waste of time. I mean, if I live until ninety, one could conjecture that I will have slept for thirty years. Think of all that I might miss during that time! The older I get, however, the more I do realize how much I need sleep. For many years, five hours seemed an adequate amount of sleep time for me, but not anymore, at least not on a regular basis. When I really lack sleep or short-change it for a series of days, I realize its absolute necessity. Severe lack of sleep actually makes me feel sick, nauseous and lethargic. No wonder that sleep deprivation is sometimes used as a form of torture. Like food and water, we need it. Even in the first creation story of the Hebrew Scriptures, after six days of creating, God rested on the seventh day; the message always seemed to say to me, "look, you've worked hard, now take a rest – even God had to!"

It's easy for me to take sleep for granted and to only think about what I might be missing while I am sleeping. But many religious traditions have extravagant stories of the visions and visitations and dreams that have come to spiritual people during their sleep. I don't go to sleep now because of those stories, but it does seem worth considering that there is potentially something to be missed if I don't sleep as well. Yes, beyond the pragmatic needs for sleep, there may be some deeper spiritual insights awaiting my slumber too; and if I should only get a restful sleep that rejuvenates my energy, what could be wrong with that?

Restful God, thank you for the gift of sleep. There is no other gift that we can receive for which we work so little and, essentially, pay nothing. Yet, this simple act of lying down and being still, of giving my mind, body and soul to the soothing ointment of sleep is an absolute necessity for the quality of my waking hours. I desire to live life fully, awake and aware of the bounteous gifts and opportunities of each day; tonight and every night, grant me a restful and peaceful sleep.

November 29
A Dreamy Reality

Who among us has not slowly awakened from a dream, still wrapped in morning sleep like the warm blanket that covers us, trying to disseminate "the truth" of what we have just experienced? Did that event really happen just now, or even yesterday, or some other time in my past, - or was that all only a dream, a fantastical illusion at which I now grasp and find only empty hands?

Occasionally in my dreams I fly. The sensation is truly incredible, so real that when I wake up, despite the obvious impossibility of the event, I scour the experience searching for evidence that might prove it otherwise true. In these dreams, I soar at about telephone line height, and slightly higher; I know this measurement because in the dream I not only observe these obstructions but am careful not to fly into them. My arms do not sprout into feathery wings, but their strong and rapid flapping create the same flight effect. The sensation of the wind in my face, through my hair and over my body is truly palpable as I catch currents that help to lift me higher, and, then losing them, feel myself descending and in need of renewed arm flapping. Traffic moves unsuspectingly below me, and even if I am spotted, I sense that the onlooker would be only bemused not shocked, like catching a glimpse of an owl in the city or at midday. The truth is, I would love to be able to fly under my own capacity, and in these dreams, I surely come as close to the actual sensation as is possible.

Surely, we all have dreams that seem to blur the lines of what is reality and what is fantasy. For me, this thin line tweaks another question which delves into the nature of reality and life itself. Buddhist teaching proposes that all life is an illusion. On one level, this statement may simply refer to our mottled understanding or interpretation of a given reality; but, in some circles, it does in fact mean that the world, as we think we know it, truly is an illusion - a dream. Like Plato's analogy of The Cave, imagine, if you will, that the life in which we live right now is no more real than those dreams we sometimes encounter, emotionally leaning toward their actuality, but rationally convinced of their impossibility. And yet, nearly all of the great mystics and spiritual leaders throughout history suggest, if not proclaim, something quite similar - that this world is not the end and that our true destiny is an existence far greater than anything we know in this earthly existence.

Whether all life is truly an illusion, or, at the very least, the importance that we place on so many things in this life is an illusion, our dreams do seem as if a door to the greater possibilities of our existence, either here or in another life. Great God of my dreams and of my reality, it is difficult for me to *truly know* anything. Often times, my life is guided by dreams I have conceived and choose to pursue. Help me to carefully perceive what is at the heart of my dreams, both those of my sleep and those of my awakening - to what end, and to whose benefit are these dreams I pursue? Although I cannot fully perceive you, I believe that you truly are the one reality; may my dreams fly into the heart of your reality.

November 30
Life Flight

Returning home on a late autumn afternoon, I was absolutely captivated by an enormous flock of European starlings that were apparently regrouping on their annual southward migration. For at least a half mile stretch along the road, wing to wing on every line of a five wire power-line system, they gathered, some yet jockeying for an open spot, while others still circling in the air overhead apparently unwilling to act as bookends at the far reaches of either end. Each fall, I thrill to such amazing displays of camaraderie amongst the birds when I see thick banks of them rise, cut, dive and then ascend again in a kind of synchronized pandemonium of flight. When I see so many gathered in one place or in flight, however, I am also drawn to consider not only where they are all going, but where do they all go when they die. It has long been a curiosity of mine that with all of the amazing array of animals that roam freely in the "wild," and with my fairly regular visits into their domain, how infrequent it is that I encounter any one of them dead. Where is it that they all go to die, and why is it that when I do stumble upon one of their fallen, it seems so shocking? The carcasses of road kill I "understand," but what about the rest: do they tire of the daily grazing, the running and the hiding, the copulating and the raising of young, and one day decide that today is a good day to die, and so just wander off or bed down and never get up?

Wandering through woods, I am constantly confronted by limbs that have snapped and trees that have buckled beneath their own outstretched reaches. When was it that their lives became too brittle and could no longer withstand the forces of wind and gravity? And what was the sound of their dying: was it a crashing tragedy or a subtle giving way with a soft but awkward tumble to the ground? While spending an afternoon on the forested land of a friend, I chanced to get caught up in a wild storm that was churning throughout the day. High winds rolled over the countryside, and like an invisible flock of birds, rose over the cresting hillsides of woodlands and then came diving down the other side, the tops of the trees pitching to and fro, each warily teetering beside its neighbors' unsteadiness. Lodge pole pines swayed back and forth and in circles on their skinny leg, their brush tops leaning together and against one another. In the near distance, I heard the rumble of a falling tree roll up a hillside toward me, and moments later, watched a series of lifeless, fragile ones snap and the earth receive their brokenness, a consoling clinch of their imminent but slow decay. So this is the sound and the appearance of their dying, I thought, but did they "know" it?

And what of my own death, how will it come and what of it will I know. Yes, for some death comes in the untimely flash of an accident, while others linger outside death's door almost forsaken by the apparent denial of its opening. But when it does come, suddenly or slowly, is there a moment when the façade of time will finally slough off and, suspended there, I will be able to look about and say, "Ah, so *this* is death!" We think of life as being so active and so hopefully long, while death is simply a finality, a dead end of a long, active life. But perhaps there is an extensive seam that both separates and joins these two fabrics, not just one cloth with a cuffed end. Or maybe there is no seam at all, but a change only in the design of the material. Schemes of life, and reflections and evidence of death are all around us, but the mystery of each is still within the experience of each. As I have wandered woods, considering the lives and the deaths within their confines, so too have I been bedside watching attentively for a loved one's last breath, wondering at her awareness. Every moment, every day, every year of living into life is an equal part movement into death. Perhaps they truly are but one thing, a steady migration with power-line rests along the way; a powerful wind shears through the thick growth of my existence and I fall to a new perspective, a different role.

Lord of Life and Death - or are they but one thing, an ongoing flight in which I rise and fall, circle and bend – I come to you today in the prayerful wonder of it all. From all that I have observed and considered, I know that I will never truly know before the actual experience of each step itself, and so to know more deeply, I must experience more fully. Knowing that, I seek comfort in camaraderie, support in fearful sways, and the calming reassurance that you are always in the air beneath my wings, the wind into which I lean, and the breath that will carry me from my experience of life into my experience of the other.

December 1
Excessive Overindulgence

There is an old Bill Cosby stand-up routine that I have remembered quite well at certain times in my life when I failed to make the best decisions with regards to drinking. In the act, Cosby describes the choices, the actions, and the results of many people who "work for the weekend." Overindulging in drink, the character he portrays rests his head against the porcelain toilet stool, thanking it for being so cool as he both desires and fights the urge to purge his excess of drink; he adds in reflection, "And now, you will put your head where no head is supposed to be!" With all of the excesses we inflict upon our bodies, it is a wonder that they do not reject or give out on us sooner than they do.

One of the central understandings that must be reached in Buddhism is that "I am not my body." The famous guru, the last tirthankara in the Jain religion, Mahavira, grew to understand this point so deeply that he is revered for his extreme rejection of the body, ultimately starving himself to death. Most of us cannot begin to imagine Mahavira's awareness and view of the separation between body and soul. In western culture, influenced as it is by Christian theology, the body and the soul are wedded in the belief of a physical resurrection. But however it is that we ultimately perceive this duality, for most of us, the fact of the matter is that we have this one body to get us through this earthly life (the one or many, depending upon one's belief again), and, subsequently, we would do well to care for it appropriately.

With all of the great beauty of the creations that surround us, and the ingenious ways that we have created to get out and enjoy them, and with all of the wonderful food and drink that either God has naturally provided us or we have creatively modified in some way, it seems to me that we are intended to "enjoy life." But, again, the Middle Path of Buddhism offers an important insight here: "In all things, moderation." Extreme forms of deprivation, as with Mahavira, will inevitably take their toll on our physical well-being, but in some equal fashion, so will our more common penchant for over-indulging in the luxuries and delights of the body's insatiable desires.

Mysterious God of the body and the soul, help me to care for this body that you have given me. I am so much more than the body, and I so frequently forget that it is my one and only housing in this life for the soul, my truest self. To abuse my body in any way is a certain desecration of the gift of life that you have given me. Keep me ever mindful of my responsibility to honor and to care for the sacred gift of life that I hold within my hands each day.

December 2
A Sick Perspective

When I am miserably sick with a stomach flu, I prefer to be left alone. Feverishly shifting between sweats and chills, I sense that my body odor ought to be signal enough for anyone approaching to just stay away; or, perhaps, my pale, emaciated appearance, the result of the virus having its way with my digestive system, might cast a spotlight on the "I'd turn back if I were you" sign that seems hung around my neck. Pitiful and pathetic, I prefer to curl into a fetal position and hope that this ugly bug will pass through and away from me soon enough. In the meantime, please leave me alone.

Early in my first marriage, I made a curious discovery, however: not everyone feels like I do when they are ill. I remember the first time my wife was stricken with the flu bug. All of her physical symptoms were very familiar to me; like me, she was reduced to the most pathetic version of herself. So, recognizing those physical indices, I quickly surmised that she would want, as surely as I would have wanted from her, for me to just go away for a spell, to leave her alone in her misery until this ugliness should pass. And so I did.

Now, I don't remember exactly if it was after the illness had passed, or if it was somewhere in the midst of its awful churning that she brought to my attention that the virus she fought was rivaled by my very inconsiderate lack of care and empathy. Why had I not sought ways to relieve her of her misery, asking of her needs and nursing her to health, and, if nothing else, sitting beside her quietly with the assurance that she was not alone? You mean, I thought, you wanted me in there with you, privy to your apparent dehumanization!? To shift a familiar saying a bit: What's good for the gander isn't necessarily good for the goose. And so I came to realize, in a sick sort of way, that my needs are not always the same as the needs of those I love.

Of course, it is not just in how we respond to illness that we will find differences in our pools of needs and wants. As unique human beings, we obviously have unique sets of needs and expectations for how people should meet and relate to us. How self-centered it is of me to expect that the way I experience something will be, or worse yet, *should be* the same for everyone! And yet, too often, this view is my standard operating procedure.

God of Comfort, oftentimes you must wish to send out your tendrils of love through those you have created in and through love; you ask us to be your presence, to be love for one another, and at the heart of that love is selflessness. Help me to step outside my way of seeing things and to get inside another's perspective; to cast off my needs and to slip inside another's needs. Help me to recognize that while in my illness, I may need to be alone, to leave another alone in her need is an illness to us all.

December 3
The Disease of Dis-Ease

At this writing, the latest illness fear that is sweeping the world is H1N1, or better known as "Swine Flu." It is not at epidemic proportions yet, nor is it likely to reach them, but because its symptoms are so much like the more "common influenza," while its results can, literally, be deadly, there is reasonable concern and much warning. Already decades ago, the disease of AIDS slowly spread around the globe, and with it came waves of fear that it might reach epidemic proportions. Indeed, it is now referred to as the AIDS epidemic, even though people in general seem less afraid of it today than they once were. Unlike AIDS, which most often requires certain physical action, albeit healthfully or unhealthfully intended, to be transmitted, a disease like H1N1 can simply be "inhaled," transferred unknowingly without my doing anything. No matter their cause, their symptoms or their results, diseases seem to endlessly float about our world bringing illness and untimely death to too many.

As these awful diseases bring fear to many, I am often captivated by the simple etymology of the word, "disease." The prefix "dis-" is an active negation of something; it separates and prevents the joining of things. "Ease," of course suggests physical comfort, but even more, the lack of difficulty provides a kind of mental or emotional tranquility. Thus "disease" negates comfort and tranquility; where once people felt safe and secure, now they reside in a place of fear, alarm, and even panic. Given this definition, "dis-ease" itself is epidemic in our world today.

The causes and symptoms of dis-ease are a bit interchangeable, it seems. War, hatred and poverty can all be associated with the disease of dis-ease, but are they the cause or are they symptoms; does war cause hatred and poverty, or do hatred and poverty spawn war? The answer appears to be "yes!" - to both questions. The more important issue, however, is that because of all of these dis-eases, we human beings often fail to live up to our best potential. When our economy or politics or religion fails us, we contract a dis-ease that disengages us from being actively and consistently involved in the world around us. Afraid that we might lose more money, unable to trust the words of a politician, or embarrassed by the hypocritical actions of a faith community's leadership, we sometimes pull back and apprehensively wait inside for a new assurance before we dare to go back out into the infected air. Like infectious diseases, dis-ease sucks life right out of us as we toss and turn in restless sleep, and think and speak in cynical tones.

O God of Health and Healing, our world is ill, too full of diseases and dis-ease. Today, I begin my prayer by turning outside of myself to pray for comfort and healing for all those who suffer under the grip of the many diseases that ravage our healthful experience of life. But I also need to look within for the dis-ease that mars my existence as well. Help me to not be paralyzed by fear, resentment and ignorance. Provide me with the antidote of hope and with the elixir of love; then, with the healthful spirit of comfort and tranquility may I go into the world and bring healing to others.

December 4
The Scales of Judgment

Interviewing for a job or showing up for the first day of a new job, most people are frighteningly aware of how first impressions can often be lasting ones. Even if we profess to understand that our body is not who we are, it is difficult to ignore the fact that most, if not all, of us engage in a bit of first impression judgment of others. This fact was no more self-evident to me than when I accepted my civic duty to serve as a juror. As one in a pool of twenty-four potential jurors for a murder trial, I had the opportunity to see "judgment" from a perspective that I had truly never known before. Although I was not one of the selected final twelve jurors, as I spent well over two hours engaging in the lawyers' examination of the jury pool, I couldn't help sneaking periodic glances and even, I'll admit it, lingering looks at the defendant in the case. He was pleading innocent, and in light of the trial process that was unfolding, one might assume that there was good reason for his plea; and in the United States judicial process, one is innocent until proven guilty. But I couldn't help wondering what it felt like to be over there: dressed in a government issued t-shirt and a "I-am-being-held-as-a-prisoner-for-now" band around his wrist, the accused sat quietly beside his attorney who was wearing a fine suit, matched only by the attire of the prosecuting attorneys; even the albeit simple, but respectful courtroom attire of the jury pool notably separates him from all others in the courtroom. Despite what the language of the law says, the visual seemed to suggest that this man before the court system really was guilty until proven innocent.

My intention is not to criticize the U.S. court system, for I believe it to be, much more often than not, incredibly fair and just; in fact, the system itself enabled me to make this quiet reflection about the life of another human being who, like me, had a mother and a father, hopes and dreams, joys and sorrows – and was now waiting to see if the world that was falling to pieces all around him would fully crash down on him. I don't know what the end of his trial will be, nor do I have any clue as to his innocence or guilt; I only know that he and I hold our humanity in common, and on that single day, for those meager hours, I could only wonder at all that must have been coursing through this fellow human being's mind and heart, as well as those around me in the jury pool. Obviously, this young man had, at least, the misfortune of being in the wrong place at the wrong time, or of knowing those who were, and now the scope of his immediate life was hanging in a balance adjudicated by the words, impressions, perspectives, and, finally, the decision of others.

We all seek control of our lives, and are able, through certain façade-like financial and other structures, to give ourselves the appearance and feel that we are in control. The fact of the matter is, of course, that we have far less control of our lives than we think we do. But this defendant, as normal looking as any human being I had ever seen, must have felt that now he truly had lost control of his life. How did his simple appearance affect the way people thought about him that day; what was our "first impression"? And even after the trial, guilty or innocent, could any of us ever see him "fairly" again? Would he not always be the "suspect" in "that trial"?

Jesus once taught the important lesson: "Judge not lest you be judged." But in a court of law, judgments necessarily happen, and often, in our simple daily lives, for better or worse, the balance of people's lives can hang on our judgment, a judgment sometimes based solely on a first impression. O God of Just Judgment, help me today to see the innocence of people's lives. Perhaps their innocence has been smattered by the ugly twists of life, and today they need "the benefit of a doubt," the opportunity to have their innocence restored. It is so easy for me to see only the appearance of another and to cast judgment rather than to see beyond the outward appearance of words and looks and to see someone for whom s/he truly is. From a soliciting stranger at my door, to a potential employee, to an accused person on trial, my judgment might make or break someone's day today, even his or her life; may the scales of my judgment be accurate and true.

December 5
Mending a Broken Heart

I have never had a broken bone in my body, although I have endured a number of overuse injuries and muscle pulls. Suffering through an injury always makes me rather miserable, as I not only have to deal with the specific local pain of the wound, but also the way it incapacitates my normal routine in life. Being around actively involved young people for most of my life, I witnessed some horrible injuries in athletics over the years, and often cringed at the extensive "repair work" that the athlete endured followed by months of physical therapy. We all do our best to avoid the injuries of accidents, but if they happen, we have no choice but to face the slow road to recovery.

While I have avoided the worst physical breakdowns, I have not been so lucky with emotional injuries. The end of a significant relationship can be like a compound fracture of the heart, and although such a wound does not necessarily incapacitate us, when we are hurt deeply enough, a broken and bleeding heart can manifest itself in many physical ways as well. Both injuries, physical and emotional, need "doctoring" and demand some time for healing, but the source of the curative for these two wounds can be significantly different. A broken bone needs special medical attention, and after I receive it, I will have to deal with a cast or a splint or worse while I wait for the healing to take place. However, when I am hurt by harsh words, inconsiderate actions or the deliberate neglect of others, I can take immediate action to alleviate an extended period of healing. Sometimes, of course, the emotional injury is so deep that medical attention is necessary, but most often, we are capable of being our own best "doctors."

With emotional wounds, healing begins with forgiveness, and forgiveness comes in a variety of "bandages." Even if the person who caused me heartache does not seek forgiveness, for the sake of my own healing, I will need to forgive. To neglect or ignore this fundamental step will inevitably create resentment, and resentment is not dissimilar to taking a hammer to my broken bone each day, or continuously tearing the scab off of a wound and watching it bleed. Not much healing will take place when I allow resentment to be part of my "doctoring." Instead, I forgive, which literally means "to give completely," and in this giving I begin to receive healing. Like any physical injury, I can acknowledge that I have been hurt and can feel the bruise of rejection, but I do not need to hold onto that hurt and push and scrape and bang on it. Forgiveness allows me to give it up, to release it, and thereby, to mend.

When a hockey player blows out a knee, if he wants to ever play the game again, there will come a time when he will need to step back out on the ice and face the possibility of another injury. Emotionally, it is no different, but if we do not let go of our anger and resentment from a previous injury, then like the hockey player who skips the physical therapy, we run a great risk not only of reinjury but also of ever playing or living at full capacity again.

Forgiving God, I have known great anguish from the pain of a broken heart and the hurt of unkind behavior. But I believe that the one who treated me disrespectfully was not acting on behalf of his best self, and "forgot" who he was – like me, a child of God. I cannot change what has been done, but I can bring healing to the offender and myself by forgiving him, and moving away from the injury. Release me from the residual restraints of resentment so that I can rise to real and full emotional health.

December 6
Holistic Health

One year when my oldest brother was struggling with some nagging back issues, he decided that he would add the opinions of an experienced chiropractor and reflexologist to the medical investigative diagnosis of his ailment. I remember him telling me after his visit to this practitioner that with my brother laid out on his stomach, and with no particular foreknowledge of my brother's history, the practitioner began to indicate some of my brother's habits and eating preferences simply by looking at and touching his feet in specific places and ways. Each of the practitioner's insights was, essentially, right on. At the very least, like my brother, I was intrigued.

For many years and for many people yet today, chiropractors have been considered little more than "quack doctors" whose diagnosis and treatment of neuromusculoskeletal disorders were to be taken with a grain of salt or ignored and disregarded altogether. The work of acupuncturists was also highly suspect, although these practitioners seem to have gained more respectable footing in the past decade or more. Today, other holistic practitioners often receive the kind of scant acceptance that chiropractors did in the past; from the "palm healing" of the Reiki specialist to the scents issued by the aroma therapist, all modes of healing that do not involve a specifically scientific method are frequently viewed as "placebo practices" at best.

Throughout history, there have certainly been some highly questionable avenues on the road to good health, but I find our modern "addiction" to the scientific method alone an unfortunate one way street. We are so much more than just physical beings, and an attention to just the body ignores the inherent interconnections of body, mind *and* spirit. Holistic medicine, which has been gaining some significant ground of acceptance in recent years, tries to foster a cooperative relationship between these three facets of our being, including the emotional, and sometimes the social, as well. Holistic medicine recognizes that when I am not well emotionally, it is very likely that my "illness" will take on a physical manifestation. Additionally, each of my senses can be links to both my physical and mental well-being; a touch, a scent, and a sound can each have an important impact on other emotional and physical "energies" housed within the human body. As a person of prayer and of the spirit, I find the possibilities of such interconnections not simply fascinating, but highly probable.

People often scoff at the measurable, observable and improved effects that sometimes come to people through means void of any real "medical" value. Known as the "placebo effect," skeptics at once dismiss the improvement as being only in the person's mind, failing to acknowledge instead that perhaps the improvement has arrived *because of* the person's mind and spirit. I often find myself thinking if the placebo works, who cares why? A placebo merely suggests that indeed, our minds, our spirits, our emotions and our bodies are all very interconnected, and if we want to live fully and wholly healthfully, then we ought to approach our lives and our health holistically.

God of Body, Mind and Spirit, you have created the human body with such amazing interconnections, not just between one physical part and another, but also between all aspects of our lives. In a world so certain of its scientific and intellectual prowess, I can easily forget the depths by which you know me and touch my life. Let me not be afraid to live more effectively by embracing a more holistic lifestyle which honors more fully the wonders of your creation of the human body. I have known you in things beyond the physical; why should you not reach out to my good health in ways beyond the physical as well?

December 7
Spiritual Reading

For many years, I have had a daily routine of grazing through the morning newspaper as I eat breakfast and before the work part of my day begins to unfold. I have always felt as though it was a good way to stay abreast of significant local, national and world events. When I was teaching, "being informed" helped me to make connections between what I was teaching and what was happening in the world around us. Frequently my students may have been unaware of a current event, and it gave me the additional incentive to encourage a more observant and thoughtful view of their world.

While allowing time for my typical American fixation of checking out the latest sports developments, I usually would only have time enough for the "A Section," in my main morning news fare, that section of my local newspaper which covered national and world events and sported the editorial opinions in the closing pages. I must confess that in recent years I have begun to question my practice of reading the morning news, for while I have been gaining information, too often I have found myself entering the rest of the day angry or upset about the latest human atrocity or someone's shared opinion that, from my perspective, screamed ignorance, bred fear or displayed selfishness.

As the rest of the day unfolded, I would be consumed by more reading, but now the grading of student's essays and the keeping abreast of their (and subsequently, my) assigned reading. This reading caused me far less duress, but often created far more stress as one stack of completed papers only uncovered the next stack, and an enjoyable novel now slipped into the category of "work."

Overall, informative, thoughtful and creative writing are great gifts stimulating their readers to see the world and life in broader perspectives. We do and should make time for such reading if we truly want to be, not only more informed human beings, but more thoughtful and entertained. But while the aforementioned readings speak to our minds, what about our hearts, our souls, our spiritual selves? Indeed, we find, even make time for newspapers, magazines, and other pleasure reading, but what about some spiritual reading and reflection time as well. Being informed does not help me to solve the world's problems although it does help me better comprehend them. God of All Understanding, help me to write into the schedule of my life, some time for spiritual reading and reflection wherein my informed understanding might be blessed by a deeper ability to "accept the things I cannot change; courage to change the things I can; and wisdom to know the difference."

December 8
The Sacred OM

Sit very still and listen deeply to the quiet. Inevitably, you will hear some sounds, either faintly or annoyingly loud, coming from known and undeterminable places. If you wish, think about the nature of these sounds and what is creating them? In every case, no matter what the sound, there will be at least two "elements" involved, for all sounds that are within our range of hearing are created by things either striking each other or vibrating together. These strikes or vibrations generate pulsating waves of air molecules which reach our ears and then get transferred to our brain's interpretive center as sounds. While it is probably much more fun to just enjoy the sounds than to think about everything that is going on when we hear them, this fascinating consideration can also lead us to the conclusive question of, if all sounds are made up of at least two elements, what was the first sound, and how was it created?

"Anahata Nada" in the Hindu Sanskrit tradition means "the unstruck sound," and is a thoughtful consideration of this question of the first sound. The ancient writings suggest that the audible sound which most resembles the "Anahata Nada" is the syllable we refer to today as the "sacred OM," the sound of primal energy, the sound of the universe itself. Westerners, understanding little if anything about this sacred sound, too often reduce it to a stereotypical picture of some Hindu mystic lost in a meditative trance or a group of Buddhist monks collectively suspended in nirvanic chant of the sacred OM. This misunderstanding is our loss.

Like St. Thomas Aquinas' "unmoved mover" and "uncaused cause," the unstruck sound of the universe acknowledges an energy source that goes beyond and deeper than "origins," an energy or an existence that simply is, and into which we

393

are called either knowingly or unknowingly. While the sacred OM appears as a single two-letter syllable, the ancient tradition of this sacred mantra-like word and sound suggests four different sounds or elements. The first three "elements" of OM are vocal sounds captured by *A, U,* and *M,* while the fourth brings one back to the Anahata Nada, the sound of silence that begins and ends and surrounds every audible sound. There are many variations of meaning about the three-letter sounds, based on tones and how and where in the mouth the sound emanates, but one simple symbolic model that resonates best within me is a kind of meditation that invites the cosmic energy of the Divine that is all around us to enter and resound within us. With the first letter, *A* (a short "a" sound as in "ah"), one considers the energy of God's love, infinitely expanding from the beginning of time throughout our universal existence. Then, without breath, the sound seamlessly shifts to the *U* (a soft "oo" or "ou" sound as in "you") which is the manifestation of the divine energy, the invisible becoming more tangible. And, finally, as the lips gently close to a soft hum of the third sound, *M,* one absorbs this divine energy, invites the love of God to be integrated into one's very being, and feels it resonate within through the buzz of the hum. As the breath given to this simple mantra expires, one is left with the grand silence of gratitude, the quiet thanksgiving that courses between lovers who have no need for words when the radiance of one another's presence is word and sound enough. Softly repeated, it is the waves of divine love ceaselessly rolling to our shore.

Sound is truly sacred. The way drums can move a person to dance, the way soft melodies can move one to tears, the way energized rhythms can invigorate passion, and so many more responses reveal the deep connections between the body and the soul and sound. And like the love of God that the person of faith professes, Anahata Nada - the sacred OM – echoes that we are surrounded always by the divine essence whether we can see and hear it or not. God of the Deepest and most Triumphant Silence, in the whispers of quiet times I am drawn more thoughtfully into your presence. But surrounded by sound or immersed in quietude, I am always enveloped by your sacred energy. Today, let me more mindfully listen for your holy existence all around me and invite it more wholly into my very being.

December 9
Decorative Rituals

Occasionally when I am invited over to the home of friends for a leisurely dinner party, I find myself caught in a curious conundrum of etiquette that I suspect nearly everyone has encountered at one time or another. Excusing myself to use the restroom, I take care of what needs to be done there and then turn to wash my hands. In the most challenging of these puzzles, I am faced with two questions, but one or the other would suffice. As I rinse my hands, my eyes begin to reach for the soap, but I quickly notice that the soap in the dish has not yet been used because it is those cute, little flowery balls of soap. From shell formations to cupcakes to even parfaits, decorative soap has always been a curiosity to me; am I supposed to use it or not? When there is other soap available, the answer is clearly, no; admire it, but leave it alone. But when it is the only offering, I am very confused, and often resort to just a good hot water washing – which leads to the next problem: decorative towels. Most of us own them, but we rarely use them unless we intend to make our bathrooms a little bit of a museum piece, in which case, we assume people will know, "ah, look, but don't touch!" But it's a bathroom for heaven's sake, I think to myself, and if I had just dropped in on these people, I could understand that they might not have been planning on me to use the museum-bathroom, and so they didn't set out anything else. At a dinner party, however, I figure, well, surely they knew people would use their bathroom and, being a dinner party and all, people would be especially inclined to wash their hands; in fact, they would *want* me to, wouldn't they? Now, when they are *really* good friends, I actually stick my neck out and ask, "Hey! Can I use this soap and towel in here?" but sometimes even with family I can be a bit reticent.

There are many other somewhat awkward situations that we find ourselves in from time to time when we venture into places where we are not familiar or entirely comfortable with the "local procedures." At times, we just flounder through them and do the best we can with what little we know, but sometimes these situations can be important "educational moments." In the religious world, for example, especially within the context of rituals and community prayers, there are often so many different steps, words, or gyrations with which everyone else seems quite familiar, but I might find myself looking around for help. In such situations, assuming that one's presence there in the first place is not prohibited, it is always best to ask. Most people are proud of what they do and will enjoy the opportunity to share the movements of their ritual and the reasons for them with me. Instruction like this also often leads to further questions, and through these inquiries, misunderstandings and misconceptions are more easily avoided or cleared up altogether. Life is full of opportunities to learn, and many of them come right up to us without our ever even having to seek them out. Don't wash away your chance to learn something new today.

God of All Understanding, there is so much in life for me to experience and to know, but many times I find myself washed up by the mystery of it all, confused as to what to grab for. Some things come to me in deep mystery, while others appearing trivial, may carry significant meaning. Give me a heart of inquiry and don't let me drop like slippery soap the opportunity for clearer awareness; and teach me the sensitivity to respectfully pursue understanding even if sometimes I have to stick my neck out and ask.

December 10
The Theater of Life

My wife and I don't go to movies very often, in fact, hardly at all, but when we do go I find myself drifting back to "the old days" when I joined neighborhood friends for the Saturday afternoon matinee at one of the two local theaters downtown. The cinematography of movies today is far superior, of course, and most often the screenplays are vastly improved as well. But when I think about "the old days," it is the experience of the theater itself that I am remembering.

In the old days, upon entering the theater – especially on a sunny afternoon – one was immediately thrust into an extraordinary darkness. There was almost a feeling of being sucked into some sort of "black hole" where, though there was a floor beneath me, the darkness left me with a dense feeling of uneasiness, not knowing if the next step would send me hurtling into an endless abyss or drifting into an eternal space. Once the door to the auditorium slammed shut behind the movie patron, all light was absorbed by the intense darkness, and the best one could do was to just stand still, hold the position, and wait for the eyes to adjust. And eventually, no matter how impenetrable the darkness initially seemed, the eyes would adapt and one could carefully move forward or survey the space for the best open seat. Movie theaters today are much more lighted, safer I could propose, but sometimes I do miss that temporary limbo of unsurety that I knew as a child.

Perhaps those darkened, childhood theater days have helped me in my adulthood when I have had to face some deep unknowns in my life. Oftentimes, faced with a decision of significance, one can feel like I did as a child entering the movie theater engulfed in an imposing darkness. Arriving at a new employment environment or stepping into new spiritual terrain, a person can feel a bit overwhelmed by the unknowns of the situation, threatened by the darker questions that seem to close out the light of potential. But if I stand strong "where I am," if I can live in and with the questions that are more fearfully portrayed in my mind than in reality, I find that the eyes of my heart and spirit begin to adjust, and I see things once again with clarity and can then move forward.

God of Light and Darkness, sometimes the houselights of my life go dark, and I find myself stumbling about a dark theater of fear and obscurity. Although I have encountered you in both the darkness and the light, in the tenebrous moments of my life, I often feel very alone. Be by my side in those times when I am lost and wavering; provide me just enough light so that I may be assured that this darkness is only temporary, and that soon enough, the lights of life's show will resume and I can more fully reenter the story.

December 11
Cloud Cover

I got up early this morning feeling like something was churning inside of me wanting to get out. Yesterday had dawned with a brilliant wide open sky, a rich blue canvas ready to receive the sun's oozing golden light; but this morning, a cold, grey stillness hangs over the awakening world, and though the sun is somewhere out there in the east pushing away the darkness, the shroud of the night lingers. Staring out the window, sipping the day's first light, I realized that I was looking into a mirror of my emotions.

When I first met my wife, we were late and mid-thirties with matured, youthful spirits. For our ages, we had both known our share of the peaks and valleys that seem common on the topography of most human, and especially, romantic relationships. Ours had been a very long distance courtship, over fifteen hundred miles separating our daily lives. Emails and phone calls kept us in touch and nurtured our evolving interest and then desire for each other with their simple daily morsels, while every holiday and summer for three years, we would host one another at love's table, embracing family, friends and each other. Ever aware of the next impending separation, during these reunions, "the other" was all that we needed, and we savored every moment of time together. Returning to my home or sending her off, I would imagine how wonderful a lifetime of such sharing would be; so, finally bridging the distance that separated us, we married.

I will never forget our first trip as a married couple back to her homeland. Premarriage, I was her everything in this environment, but now that she had "her everything" on a daily basis, the family that she had sacrificed in getting married and moving away would now receive the attention once delegated to me on my visits. Viewing our visit as something of a "honeymoon vacation," I was devastated by her lack of attention to me and her desire to spend each day just being with family. After all, her internal argument must have gone, we had every day together now, and this was a time for catching up with her other dear ones. But in married life, "every day" was a workday, and while I certainly enjoyed the fact that each day began and ended beside her, I often resented that constantly on the other side of each other were our piles of work gnawing at our time and attention to one another. Eventually I was able to make peace with the truth of this new shared reality, but every once in awhile – like right now – I melancholically long for the vibrancy of our love's youth. I went to sleep under that blanket last night, and like static cling, it followed me out to my morning time view of a very grey dawn.

Most people know well that love is not to be reduced to the infatuations and excitement of a relationship's origin, but isn't it just so easy to "go there" anyway? The simplest activities, sometimes even doing nothing, pulsated with love's energy then, while the touch of the hand and a thoughtful glance might be all the eroticism needed. It seems an awful sleight of hand that these emotional hormones pull on us.

I can't change the grey reflective pool of the sky that I look into this morning, but I can alter the way I let it reflect me. Behind that cover of clouds, the sun is shining brightly, as warm and vibrant as love itself. Too often, I allow my selfish desires to overcast the truth of my love for my wife and many of my other beloveds. Worse yet, sometimes storm clouds drift in and rain down self-pity; then things can get really messy.

O God of the Embracing Sky, your love for all of your creation shines as surely as this morning's sun though its bright face be shielded by a gray cover, and energizes me as thoroughly and indisputably as the air I breathe. I too want to be that kind of love in the world, bright and fresh and constant. Burn away the cloud cover of my selfish needs and let the true light of my love be a source of energy for my wife, and for the world, this day.

Having family in the mountainous Northwest and in the desert Southwest has naturally enhanced my love of travel and exploration. Both of these environments, while apparent opposites, have become favorite terrains of mine, each offering very different and almost magical experiences. Mountain vistas, achieved through rigorous hiking, often unveil thunderous streams and jeweled lakes tucked secretly in the folds of the mountain forests and valleys, and their sheer height receives and holds its snow cover like a festive garment. No less challenging in their traverse, the high and low deserts conceal incredible plant and animal life waiting to be discovered, and while their nights often descend with surprising coolness, their days provide the revitalizing heat of the sun.

One year in the early winter, I visited family in Montana eager to also enjoy a nearby ski resort. To my disappointment, no snow had fallen in the valley where I stayed, nor had it descended upon the peaks as well. Expecting cold and snow, I found only mild temperatures and a need to search for a different outdoor outlet. Months later with spring dawning, I visited my children in Arizona eager to slough off the winter frost at home and absorb the evolving year's new warmth. Hiking into the desert, however, I needed a light jacket to hold my own warmth, and when the sun descended over the lunarscape, additional layers were essential. Expecting arid heat, I encountered only desert chill in a reluctant unfolding of the spring.

We often approach people, vacations, environments – life – with preconceived notions of what we will find and experience. We use expectations almost like a headlamp guiding what we see and where we will step. But much to our surprise, and often displeasure, *what is* is not always what we expected. Snow may be desired in the mountains, and heat may be anticipated in the desert, but the expectation of one may in fact be the reality of the other. I may desire the expectation, but I need to always anticipate the adjustment. While I can, in some part, control where I go, I cannot, for the most part, control what will happen there. If I carry expectations in one hand, I would do well to hold adjustments in the other.

Infinite God, my desire to be in control of my life often has me fettered to my expectations. Grateful that I have choices in where and how I go, help me to realize and to accept that my choices are not intimately connected to my expectations. I can choose, but I cannot control. What I can control is my receptivity and ability to adjust to whatever I encounter. When I choose to seek you in the mountains and in the deserts, may I be willing to find you on your terms and not on mine.

December 13
Short-Term Memory

The short-term memory, "they" say, is the first thing to go. I've never been quite sure who "they" are, but on this one, I do believe that "they" are right. I often marvel at what I can remember years ago, as in decades, but for all my marveling, I am equally worrisome about what I can't remember from last year, last week, and worst of all, a minute or three ago! At a grocery store or a restaurant or wherever, I might run into a former student or athlete from twenty-five years ago; "Hi Terry! How are you doing?" correctly leaps from my mouth before I even have the chance to think, did I have this person as a student, and if so, what is the person's name? However, a short time later, I may happen upon a student from last semester, and while I certainly recognize him or her, I will draw an absolute blank searching for the person's name. Brushing my teeth in the morning before leaving for work, I think to myself, when you get done here, be sure to pack that one item in your brief case that you left out last night. Arriving at work shortly thereafter, undoubtedly I will realize that in between that "remember moment" and the completion of brushing my teeth, I forgot all about packing that item, and never thought of it again until it is now too late. I go to the grocery store with a list of things to buy, but while I am there, I think of something else I need aisles away, and, of course, by the time I get to that aisle, if I ever even go down it, the item is forgotten.

The key, I tell myself, is writing it down. If I write it down, I claim, my mind is like a steel trap. Indeed, writing something down does seem to help me process the information, besides the fact that I have a written record of what I was supposed to do or to buy. Regarding former students, sometimes I wonder if my brain is like a computer's hard drive, and I have simply run out of memory space in the most recent years. I'm not sure which students and athletes are more shocked: those from long ago whose names I recall with ease, or those from last year who look at me a bit traumatized and hurt that I have so soon forgotten their name. I sometimes wonder if these most recent names and faces that slip through my short term memory net so easily will be quickly brought to mind years from now when they become part of my "long term memory."

I have found that as I grow older, by design and desire I more easily let go of past failures and am less driven by future expectations. I am simply happy for each new day that arrives at my doorstep like the morning newspaper, and that I am able to retrieve it. My main and daily goal is to simply live more in the present, appreciatively aware of what each day holds as it unfolds. So when I fail to remember something so recently thought or someone so recently encountered, it concerns me with regards to how well I am living in each present moment. Ironically, each occasion of forgetfulness becomes a reminder to me of how well I am or am not living in the present. Then again, as noted, maybe "they" are right, and I am just getting old and losing my ability to properly remember.

Our memory is a great gift. While we should not dwell on the past, for better or worse, our present is built in large part upon decisions and actions that we have made, or have failed to make, and by our experiences of people and events in our past. The past holds joys just as surely as it can retain traumas. God of the Short and of the Infinite Past, I am grateful for the memories that keep me connected to my healthful and necessary past. As new memories are shaped in my present reality, help me to retain what is healthful and necessary in the here and now as well. I don't want to forget how wonderful a memory is!

December 14
A Memorable Presence

Some nights when I step into my backyard to offer a closing prayer for the goodness of the day or the gift of just being alive at this moment, I am drawn to places well beyond the boundaries of my little grassy plot. Gazing up at the mysterious pool of darkness overhead mottled with soft and brilliant stars, or tripping over the wonder of my moonshadow underfoot, a dark silhouette born of a reflective shine millions of miles away, I smile as the memories of the many places where I have also stood in awe under the night lights whisper their names to me. I remember high desert mountaintops where these same stars seemed almost close enough to touch and Dakota plains where the dark blanket of the night stretched to corners I could never see anywhere else. I recall dense Appalachian forests where the canopy could not refuse the moon's glow entirely as its light spilled through leafy keyholes, and northern lakes which echo the night's glowing orb with their own shimmering reflection.

And there are times of quiet aloneness when almost lonely, I invite the memories of friends into my space, and they become a blanket beneath and over me, a soft and comfortable embrace. I hear the cheerful laughter of this one, and the comfortable silence of that one; I remember her kind words of support when I was sure all in my life was lost, and his playful provocation to just stay put and enjoy what is rather than pushing on to what might be.

Memory is not only important for remembering the names of people and the things that need to be purchased or collected, but it also seems to be a way for us to stay in touch with the Creator. When I am still and empty, and memories seep through the fissures of quiet and fill the hollows of my heart, I know that the Divine One is dropping in on me and whispering sweet nothings into my ears. One might disagree with me and say that these are "just memories," and are of "only people and places," but that person is wrong. God, the creator of all, is infinitely one with all people and all places, and when I deeply commune with any and all them, I encounter the Infinite One as well. And when I remember these communions or they serendipitously revisit me, I momentarily touch the eternal now where what is past is made present again in all of its warmth and glow.

Timeless One, let me take this quiet time, right here and now, to remember a place and a person through whom you have touched my life in the past. I invite them and you to be here in this eternal moment where the shell of the past falls away and the kernel of the infinite now is present. Thank you for memories and remembering me, and for the way I remember you through the memories of them.

December 15
A Contemplative Life

Vowed contemplatives, monks and nuns who commit themselves to a life of prayer and reflective meditation, can be easily misunderstood in a world that places so much value on doing things for the sake of attainment and achievement. Choosing to be "a spiritual person," however, ultimately means being a contemplative, although one need not enter a monastic community to do so. In fact, while "doing contemplation" may involve prayer and meditation, the real challenge is "to *be* contemplative." This means that contemplation is not "an action," but a "state of being."

Ultimately, a contemplative person must empty the ego, let go of the self, and recognize the communion of things. Ironically, we might think of the contemplative monk or nun as doing just the opposite. Seeking a mystical union with God, he selfishly removes himself from the mainstream society and devotes his life to both private and communal prayer and meditation. But this stepping away from society is often necessary when we realize that social conventions do, in fact, stir us toward more selfish views and desires. *Being* a contemplative *in* the world is difficult, for our society tempts us constantly to fulfill our own wishes and dreams and is constantly drawing lines of division between "us and them." In answer to these temptations, a monastic way of life more patently provides a way to avoid these pitfalls, removing our senses from the allurement. So how can I live in society and still be contemplative?

Interestingly, the final stage of Hinduism's four stages of life is the "sannyasin" or wandering ascetic. After schooling and learning about life in stage one, the Hindu practitioner engages fully in the commerce of life in stage two while raising and supporting a family. Later in life, loosely referred to as "retirement," the devotee lets go of his previous responsibilities and sets off to rediscover the meaning and purpose of life through contemplation. If and when this third stage is achieved, he returns to the society, living in it without becoming a part of it – meaning, he is now a living sign to all that see him that the things of this world, including the self, are nonessential. He is now *being* contemplation. In a similar fashion, the Buddhist bodhisattva while seeking the bliss of nirvana and at once glimpsing its radiance, chooses not to selfishly slip into it, but to return again and again so that others may see her path and obtain the joy as well. She is now *being* a contemplative. And the story of Jesus climaxes when his teaching "to love your neighbor (who is everyone) as yourself" becomes enfleshed in his willingness to selflessly die for the sake of all. His death was a living contemplation.

To be a contemplative means that my life is not governed by my own self-interests, but is driven instead by the wonder of the oneness of all things. To be a contemplative is *to be* kindness and *to be* peace. For some, this contemplation will be realized best through a physical rejection of erroneous societal values and a selfless life of prayer; for others, its witness may be in choosing to live within a society but to not become engaged with the erroneous values of the society.

God of All Contemplation, my heart yearns to more fully embrace the Oneness of All Things that is You. Living in this world, it is so easy for me to be distracted by the glitter of sensuous things as well as the stench of disturbing things. So often I wish to rush toward one and run away from the other, forgetting that none of us will ever be satisfied by the one extreme nor safe from the other. *Being* at the heart of all things and living in you is where I will find true satisfaction and security. Let this be my contemplation every day.

December 16
Back and Not Forgotten

Before a dear teacher colleague of mine left our school system and moved to another school, I remember her saying to me one time that "people are easily forgotten. You think that someone might 'have your back,' but once a person moves on, she is quickly forgotten." Interestingly, the first year of her departure, her home was tragically burned to the ground near the Christmas holidays, when an open flame accidently started some drapery on fire. As if in unconscious defiance of her earlier private remarks, her former colleagues and many of her former students from our school swooped to her aid and wanted "to have her back." I even remember thinking, "you see, you have not been forgotten." Years later, however, and now almost fully out of touch with her life, I wonder again about what she said and reconsider the truth of it. If the tragedy were to occur this year, how well would we respond now? Would we do as much for her now as we did then, or would we only think, "gee, how sad; I knew her once," and then not really do much of anything about it?

The point of my friend's initial comment years ago was that a person really has to look out for herself, because others, ultimately, won't. The tone of that sentiment seems so awfully negative to me and so necessarily self-centered, but I am no longer so sure that it is untrue. After leaving a job that I held for twenty-eight years, I was surprised by how quickly "out-of-the-loop" I felt. I did not feel neglected or avoided, but I realized that other people's lives, just as mine had been, are so busy and all of our "stuff" seems so important that it is hard for us to let go of our needs and responsibilities and see into the needs of others' lives. And so, people quickly *appear* to be forgotten. We still do care, but with their presence out of our immediate picture, so too go their cares, concerns and needs.

If what my former colleague once said is true, and if what I have experienced in my new time away from the decades' long array of familiar and friendly faces validates her belief in some part, I still feel a resistance within me to accept it carte blanche. Perhaps we humans do lose track of one another too quickly and too easily, but I hope that we don't forget that such a loss is not a good thing. Yes, the bright lights of our busyness can sometimes blind us from the concerns of others, and even good memories and relationships grow shadows, but we need each other – always.

God of Friends and Relationships, part of the wonder of your creation is that we experience you through the healthy and loving relationships that we have with one another. I am certain that my friend has found new support and love in her new colleagues and I see new relationships forming in my life as well, but I have been blessed and I have known you through the lives of many other dear ones whom I should never forget nor entirely neglect. They have been beside me for so many years; keep them before me even as our lives change and may I always be ready to have their back.

December 17
Collective Backs

Another area of our lives where we sometimes fail "to have each other's back," exposing our too often forgetful behavior, concerns our social behaviors. In general, when significant needs arise in our communities, in our nation and even across the globe, we humans quickly rally our support and open hearts, hands and wallets. But give whatever the tragedy is a little time to sink below the horizon of our immediate view, and it can soon become little more than a blip on the radar screen of our hearts.

We all have seen, perhaps have even been a part of the massive rush of aid that floods towards the victims of various natural disasters and many humanly created ones. These are people we don't even know, and yet, the whole world, it seems, responds to their needs. The international community's outreach at these times is a stunning example of the power and the goodness of human solidarity. A horrific tsunami unexpectedly slams into Southeast Asian countries, and as its devastating surge flows back to the sea claiming the lives and livelihoods of thousands, people from all over the globe provide a new wave of medical and food aid. An earthquake rips open the already hungry and aching belly of a deeply impoverished Haiti, and once again, the world community arrives to help mend the terrible gash. These, and certainly many other examples suggest that given the need, we will have each other's collective back. But, a year and more after the initial tragedy, how well do we serve each other then? How soon do we believe that our immediate efforts have covered the loss and restored good health to the land and its people?

Corruption within national governments and ill-intentioned purveyors of the international aid too often taint the immediate effort and stymie some of the desired long-term effects of the assistance. And yet, in time, most of us do lose interest, if not heart, in the depths of the tragedy.
Find and look through a list of the most devastating natural disasters in the last twenty-five years; you'll be amazed at how many you will remember, but have "emotionally forgotten." Why is that? We are not callous and careless people, but we do seem to move on fairly soon after the all the cataclysmic dust settles. Perhaps the immediate needs of any given victim are met with the initial and subsequent massive global aid, although a little investigative work will usually suggest differently, and now those caught in the center of the tragedy must piece

together their own lives. But I am certain that a wealth of prayerful help will always be necessary if not appreciated.

God of the Lonely, the Neglected and the Forgotten, I pause today to recognize and to remember the many human beings who are in need of more assistance than I could ever give. I can never understand why things happen as they do, but in many places throughout the world, people are suffering through innumerable wars, acts of inhumanity and natural disasters, and they feel absolutely forsaken. Perhaps all I have this day and at this time is my simple prayer, but let it rise up from the ashes of their lonely and destructive environments and rain down upon them with the grace of a first drought-ending rain. We are not alone; no one should feel forgotten.

December 18
Storage Units

During a daughter's recent visit home, I emerged one morning wearing an old favorite shirt of mine. When I asked my daughter if she remembered the shirt, she quickly raised her eyebrows and said, "Oh yeah, that's the shirt you were wearing in our family Christmas letter photo taken in Jeffrey Park about twenty years ago!" I do have a hard time letting go of "comfortable and practical things." As a teacher, I always enjoyed the fact that each year I got a completely new roster of students who had never been to my classroom before; subsequently, whatever outfit I wore - the first time around, of course - was "new" to them. No need to renew the wardrobe, unless something literally fell apart or would hopelessly never fit again. Yes, new things might be added from time to time, but even these were often welcomed "hand-me-overs."

Indeed, our entire house might appear a veritable museum to many people. *Anything* of nostalgic nature relating to family and significant past events, my wife proudly displays in the "living space" downstairs. On the main floor of our home, all walls and surfaces are gladly festooned with "his and hers" memorabilia, mementos, photos, paintings - a few of which are, specifically, "ours." My wife and I, with playful thoughtfulness, often muse over what we would grab if our house were on fire. So much stuff in so little space!

All American cities now have numerous "holding pens of stuff"; storage units with round the clock surveillance can be found in every suburban development. Ah, but we love our stuff, and treasure the meaning that we place within the beheld object. Such stuff, of course, and the holding on to it, are not bad or evil or sinful - to a point. The real question is always about, in the translated word of the Buddha, "attachment." Having stuff is okay, so long as I am able to let it go, without remorse, if I must; and the problem is, the longer I do hold onto something attaching significance to it, the more difficult it will be to let it go. Even Jesus did not exactly condemn wealth and possessions, but his quip about "the camel passing through the eye of a needle" certainly seems an acknowledgment of the difficulty there is in letting go of our attachments.

Wondrous God, you have given me many things with which I prop up my comfortable life. As I use and enjoy these things, help me to remember that many are just *things* of enjoyment, but not of need. Help me to enjoy their usefulness or their beauty, but to not become so attached to them that I should suffer at their loss. If my home should burn down, and all things are lost, may my relationship with you go unscathed.

December 19
Sacred Snowfall

There is something absolutely sacred about watching snow fall. Caught in an unsafe environment lacking necessary sustenance and cover, one's experience of a snowstorm would likely be a far cry from holy, but nestled comfortably in the quietude of one's own home or stepping gently through the snow's quiet descent in an open prairie or woodland is wholly sacred.

Unlike rain, snowfall, generally, has no sound, and yet, the aura of silence that engulfs a deep snowfall seems to exhale a sacred Om. The whisper of a snowfall draws me into the quiet center of myself where I am mesmerized, immobilized by a vision sublime. The ethereal air around me becomes three dimensional, and I view the present moment in layers, seeing *through* the air and giving distance a series of boundaries. While a snowfall does not shout for attention, I find its soft murmur irresistible and willingly let it captivate me.

Although I have never *seen* grace, only its effects, I suspect that grace descends much like a soft, big-flaked snowfall. Snuggling into the crooks of trees and brush, blanketing the sores and wounds of the earth's weary and sprawling body, a gentle snowfall provides a comfort that embraces all. Like a rambunctious child that needs settling, the whole world seems drawn to a calming suspension of activity as the blanket of tenderness is wrapped around its shoulders. In this descending moment, my soul bows naturally in meditation.

So many people bristle and fuss over snow, viewing its arrival as another challenge to be endured and another task to interrupt their already busy lives; and it can be those things if we choose to see it only that way. But it can also be seen as an invitation to experience the grace-filled love of God, the gentle presence of the divine, as palpable and as invisible as the air itself.

God of Grace, when the snows of the winter season slide into my town like an unexpected guest, help me to pause, welcome them and invite them into the home and hearth of my heart. May the gentle snowfall give me cessation to recognize your gentle blessing encompassing the earth and all of its inhabitants everyday. Lead me into the meditation of your grace descending, a sacred moment in a sacred place.

Today is or nears the winter solstice, the shortest day of light, the darkest day of the year. At this writing, in the monthly lunar cycle, last night was a "new moon." That term has always amused me some because a new moon, in the phase of its cycle, is one that we cannot see. Of course, just as the sun is always illuminating the earth even on thick, cloudy days, so too is the moon always orbiting our planet, but each month we only see it from various perspectives as the moon glides through it phases, from new to full and back again. I always count it as a special blessing when I get to see a full moon rise and set, and even more special are the rare occasions when I can watch the moon setting just as the sun is rising.

There is something extra special about a full moon night, and it is no wonder that people of many cultures have even named the full moon of different seasons. The brightness of a clear sky, full moon night is incredible, and one often feels drawn outside no matter what the temperature to just stand beneath and gaze at the moon. I am always so fascinated by the roundness of the moon, pregnant in the fullness of its monthly rotation, and of the connection between its twenty-eight day cycle and a woman's "healthy and regular" menstruating cycle; the cosmic link seems undeniable. So too is the wonder of the moon's gravitational effect on the ocean tides; even the vast waters which cover so much of our planet are attracted to and affected by the influential moon!

On a birthday card that I once gave my wife, there was a colorful drawing of the sun and the inside caption read: "Welcome to another cycle of the sun!" Indeed, life is full of cycles, and one need only look to all of the creations around us to realize that *all* life is very cyclical. Because we humans like to place things on "time lines," we often lose the cyclical nature of our own lives. It is not just the seasons and the moon and the sun that are in a cycle around us; we too are part of the cycle. Yes, things change in our lives, but they always come back around again. If things are not going well for you right now, I can assure you they will get better; they may get a little worse first, but they will improve. And the opposite is also true. It is simply the cycle of our lives: we meet an "experience," and we resist or embrace it; the experience changes us in some way and in that change, a part of us "dies," only to be reborn with new eyes and a new perspective to another experience.

Seeing ourselves as somehow superior to everything, we fail to see how we truly are not only like everything else, but linked to it as well. In the creation stories of the Hebrew Scriptures, God tells Adam, "For you are dust, and to dust you shall return" (Gn. 3:19), acknowledging our connection to the earth and our relative, cyclical nature. The moon reminds me of this connection every month, and, especially if I feel caught in a life-struggle, in its reminder I hear God's whisper of patience and assurance: Be patient with what is, I assure you, things will come back around.

God of the Cycles and the Seasons, although you are eternal, existing beyond time and space, you invite us to experience and reexperience the mystery of life through the web of cycles all around and within us. Through these cycles, you give me the opportunity to see what I once missed, to improve upon what I failed before, and to live on even through my dying. May I live in the patient assurance of the cycles that in the fullness of my time, I will know and experience you more perfectly.

December 21
No Horizon

Driving across the wide-open plains of South Dakota one winter, en route to a holiday in Montana with family, my wife and I found ourselves on the front edge of a penetrating snowstorm. Aware of the impending threat, we had left early in the morning from Minnesota and had made good time racing across the wide open space, but by midday, the sky and the landscape became one. Dressed in the first snows of the season, the Dakota grasslands were an undulating sea of white stretching to the horizon in every direction and dissolving into the white of the sky. Gazing into that endless expanse of white, I was reminded of the Norwegian settlers in O.E. Rölvaag's book, *Giants in the Earth,* who were driven to madness in their "new world" by this unrelenting view that my wife and I now encountered. Venturing into what they dreamed was a world of hope, some of these pioneers encountered a boundaryless void where all of their hopes were swallowed, consumed by a bitter cold, white nothingness. Unlike those earlier residents of this land, maddeningly isolated in their frozen sod huts, we drove on until a rare city poked its head upon the horizon, encouraging us that our destination, though miles of cold and lonely roadway ahead, would provide the reprieve of warmth and fellowship for which we sought.

Human struggle and the endurance of difficult and dangerous times have a very long history, and it is likely that all of us carry our own stories of travail. At times, the horizon of hope vanishes from our view, and all that we can see is the continuation of a bleak existence. But just as so many pioneers prevailed through persistence, and as my wife and I determinedly drove to our desired destination, we must know that the union of the land and the sky is an illusion, that the horizon does hold hope.

O God of the Endless Horizon of Hope, perhaps my journey today begins without a proper sense of hope, without a clear view of what's ahead; or, perhaps, many around me this day are isolated in a frozen stupor of loneliness and despair. Help us all to see and to understand the illusions of our journeys, to know that the landscape ahead does not melt into nothingness nor dissolve into the infinite sky. Comfort awaits us just as surely as we are invited to be sources of comfort to others, inviting them to come in from the hopeless cold.

December 22
Intermission: A Scheduled Break

The finish line of any race, the completion of any project, and the end of any academic calendar are, most always, sought after goals. Any well-planned, well-intentioned endeavor also seeks closure, a time when the participants can once again, momentarily at least, relax and recover before preparing for the next onslaught ahead. Perhaps the activity leaves us physically exhausted, and our bodies thirst for recovery time. Maybe the effort is merely one in a series of steps, and this intermission provides invaluable time to reflect on the work that has been done so as to help us reconfigure our next course of action. School systems usually build a couple of significant breaks into every school year. As an educator, I have always appreciated these vacations as a time to rejuvenate "the system;" a break from paperwork and preparations is a necessary relief so that I have the mental stamina to make it through the next quarter or semester of the school year. Sometimes these endings or pauses, however, can be slightly dangerous to the momentum of our lives.

In my recent sabbatical from teaching, I sometimes worried about what the extended respite might do to my motivation and my dedication to whatever it was that I did next. Yes, we can become such slaves to alarm clocks and schedules, but without them, too many people can slip into a kind of lethargy about life and its daily challenges. While I grow weary of a 5:45 AM arousal, the flexibility of summertime or weekend sleep hours can wreak havoc on some other valuable routines that I more easily incorporate into my more scheduled life. A significant example would be daily prayer. Similarly, when I take a break from an exercise regimen, and quickly discover my body losing its more healthful physical condition, I also find it more difficult to return to the routine, not only because I am enjoying the time off, but because the exercise literally feels more demanding and positive results come less easily.

Establishing good, healthy habits in our lives, it seems, is an effort in itself. Unfortunately, bad habits seem to develop quite naturally. We don't *try* for bad habits; they just seem to arrive when, well, we are *not trying* at all! It is certainly good and necessary for us to periodically slow down our busy lives, and to take some time to reflect on the direction and purpose of our movement; but we need to also be careful that our intermissions do not spill over into the start of the next act.

In the first version of the Judeo-Christian creation stories, the writers wisely wove into the fabric of the story that on the seventh day, God rested from all of the work of creation. The message is clear: rest and reflection are important, even God needed it! What is not said, but can certainly be inferred by what follows, is that on the eighth day - or the new week - God got back to work. O Wondrous God of all creation, help me to recognize the value of taking a break, to truly rest and revitalize my mind, my body and my spirit. But help me also to avoid the maladies of complacency and bad habits. May I learn to master my schedule without being mastered by it or lazily escaping from it altogether.

December 23
Filling the Feeder

I sometimes get rather neglectful of the bird feeder outside our dining room window; it can go for weeks of empty attention before I find reason enough to attend to it. After a deep snowfall recently, the birds stared at me from the bushes just beyond the forsaken feeder as I worked away cozily inside. Three sets of cardinals, the males' vibrant red, electric against the snowy backdrop, two plump robins looking as if they had missed the train south, a couple of blue jays parading about as if unaffected by any seasonal change, and myriads of wrens and sparrows congregated in the starkly stripped bushes. Rustling through the lower branches scavenging for any dry, old berries – anything edible – they would swoop back to higher platforms and with their lean and hungry looks shoot guilt-inducing glances my way. Recognizing their famished travail, I finally donned some boots and stepped out to refill the feeder's empty, gaping mouth. Returning inside, I wondered how long it would take for them to respond to their apparent fulfilled request.

Within five minutes, the parade to the feeder began. As always, the sparrows, wearing their impoverished looking drab colors, sidled in without fear or pride, eager only to seize the free and easy spread. Their rapacious persistence seemed to keep others at bay, but I noted that along with the logistical problem of size, there was a certain social structure to the feeding as well. The cardinals, all regal in their charming scarlet fanfare, hung back a bit, suspicious of the gift, and wondering if all of this ease wasn't just a little bit below their stature. But after observing the sparrows' voracious frenzy, they figured, in times of great need, a little humility is not such a bad thing; thus, despite their size and shy disposition, the haughty were soon nestled beside the humble enjoying the gratis feast. The robins, meanwhile, with their plump, rust breasts just seemed too fat to comfortably find a spot at the feeder and maneuver around their own excess; but the chatter of a new food source must have spread fast, for soon there was a half of a flock of them gathering together in the low branches discussing the possibility of a group raid on the feeder. The blue jays too, who were in fact just a little too big for the feeder, made their fearless dive anyway, scaring away all other takers momentarily. Soon frustrated, they gave up and the sparrows swooped in again immediately for more of the simple banquet. Apparently some starlings heard the robins' chatter, and soon an entire flock, as they are a very communal group, arrived in their motley and disproportionate wear, their short-tailed, stocky bodies hungrily musing if there was room enough for them. They scoured what was left of the bushes' berries, then took their chance at the feeder; but finding their size and long beaks too awkward in the cramped quarters, they retreated and only dreamed of what others were obviously enjoying.

Finally, somewhere out there I had to assume, my harrier neighbor, the Cooper's hawk, must have been plotting his attack from some far away limb, measuring the space and time when he would swoop in and snatch one of the greedy attendants in midair, now a well-fed victim.

Like the birds outside my window ensconced in the wintery scene, we too are all hungry for things that seem beyond our reach. Need can sometimes make us ravenous in our grasping, but pride often trips us in first step and we slink back reconsidering the need and the value of our desire. Jesus once instructed his followers to observe "the birds in the sky" who "do not sow or reap, yet your heavenly Father feeds them" - sometimes, perhaps, through our birdfeeder assistance. The point is, we aught not fret and fear so about what we have or don't have, about what we wear or how we look. What we most need is freely given, or within our workable reach; and what we have to give should be freely offered, our plenty shared and spread to those in need. Many of us have known or witnessed the frigid, wintry lack of care for those most in need. The birds of exigency hover outside our windows, and sometimes nest within our empty hearts; can I step out into the cold today and fill the feeder?

God of Nourishment, in subtle and sometimes miraculous ways, you care for the needs of the world. But it seems apparent that part of your design is for us to be part of that caring and nurturing offer. Open my eyes this day to the needs of others, and move me to respond to those needs with a selfless and humble spirit. May the warmth and fullness that I enjoy bring sustenance to the cold emptiness of others.

December 24
Jealousy

While love is perhaps our most sought after jewel, like most precious stones, there can be many facsimiles and artificially forged versions of this most prized affection. So rare and priceless is love that I dare say that no one can adequately describe it or define its parameters. Subsequently, while it seems that most all humans desire and pursue love, our understanding of it is as varied as the people who desire it.

Because of love's amorphous brilliance, people often confuse and misconstrue the qualities and nature of love. Enraptured by what one imagines love to be, a person can too easily overlook the flaws in the false gemstone and be hoodwinked into believing that what he possesses is truly genuine. One very common defect is jealousy. While the attributes of jealousy – fear, suspicion and envy – look nothing like love, its subtle link is in its *desire to preserve* that which is imagined to be love. Ironically, the very presence of jealousy ought to be a signal that love is not at the heart of the relationship, or if it was, an insidious imperfection is now tainting the jewel. With love being so prized, like all things precious, no one wants to lose it. But unlike prized, precious jewels, love cannot be possessed. If one seeks to "possess" another, as with jealousy, than love is immediately invalidated. While I may enjoy and even desire the give *and take* of love, true love, ultimately, is only about giving, and true giving lets go of all fears, suspicions and envy – of jealousy

An axiom made famous in songs, poems and romantic literature says that "if you love someone, set him free!" This is not an invitation to leave or a desire to end the relationship, but it does suggest an open door, a freedom for the beloved to be who and what and how he truly is. In love, of course, I desire for my beloved to stay, and given her freedom, I hope that she does. And if she chooses to stay, and perhaps even freely modifies some part of who and what and how she is for *our* sake, not because of the chains of my jealousy, then indeed I may embrace the precious jewel of love.

God of My Desires, you are Love, and as Love, you have given me the freedom to be who and what and how I want to be. Surely, you long for me to be "a certain way," but if I fail in that, you continue to love me into and through life. Such unconditional love seems almost impossible for me, and yet, created in your image, I believe that you challenge me to be that very source of love for others as well. As I have known and know your love, help me to let go of all of the petty jealousies and misconceptions of love that prevent me from truly experiencing and being love.

December 25
God in the Flesh

One of the central reasons why many people struggle with the issue of faith, of embracing the reality – the "truth" for believers – of a Divine Being is what they perceive as God's inaccessibility, or their inability to "see God." Conversely, I find God very accessible, as near to me as my own heart and as obvious to me as the beauty and wonder of the creations right outside my door. One might argue that these are simply my perceptions, but for a person of faith, what may appear as a perception to one person is a deeply rooted experience for the other. In some religious traditions, however, the Divine One takes the ultimate step in accessibility and becomes a human being.

Christianity, of course, seems most unique in its claim of Jesus the Christ's divinity. For Christians, Jesus was not simply a human being who rose or ascended to divinity; he is the incarnation of the Divine One. He is God "in the flesh," a human being whose "beingness" is divine. On this day, Christians throughout the world celebrate the day Jesus of Nazareth was born, into the flesh. Although he never forsook his religion of birth, Judaism, he clearly challenged many of its laws, regulations and authorities. Many Gentiles (non-Jews) of his time and some Jews as well, recognized him as "the Anointed One," the Christ, and these followers essentially spawned Christianity by preaching about Jesus as the Christ. In this way, Christianity's fundamental origin is based on the belief in the Incarnation of Jesus. But Jesus of Nazareth is not the only example in the religious world of God becoming enfleshed.

Hinduism, too, most especially honors a variety of avatars, a Sanskrit word which means "descent" and "crosses over," referring to the Divine descending from the heavens and crossing over into our human condition. Unlike Christian theology, Hinduism does not seem to argue for the avatar's complete humanity, but rather simply recognizes that the Divine chooses to dwell among us in the appearance of a human being or sometimes, some other creature of the earth. Like Jesus,

411

however, the presence of the Divine is always marked by extraordinary teaching and often significant intercession on behalf of the people in need. Krishna, an avatar of the god Vishnu, would be the finest example within this Hindu tradition. While Buddhism does not claim divinity for Siddhartha, the Awakened One, bodhisattvas within Buddhism are somewhat like incarnations. Although human in origin, the continuous manifestations of Avalokiteshvara, the Buddha of Infinite Compassion who comes to guide people toward enlightenment, certainly draws avatar-like parallels. The Native American Sioux tribes also have something of an avatar as well in the person of the White Buffalo Calf Woman who came to the people long ago giving them the sacred pipe and teaching them how to pray.

Central, of course, to each of these stories of an incarnation or an avatar is the fact that God brings God's self into humanity, and is made entirely accessible, becoming tangible for each of us. Additionally, whether one chooses to honor the fullness of the incarnation's meaning or not, the avatar or the incarnate one comes to teach us how to spiritually live better. These avatars are truly not concerned with the politics and the economics of their time, but in fact, challenge the people, through the model of their own lives and teachings, to transcend all worldly concerns in embracing truly spiritual lives. God makes God's self very accessible, and if one should follow in the footsteps of a tradition that honors an incarnation or an avatar, then God has been as near and dear to us as a brother and sister. But even if one chooses not to believe completely in God's entering fully into our human condition, he is foolish to ignore the teachings and role model that these "sacred ones" have brought to us all.

Infinite One, you are so "other than" we are, and yet as the Creator of us all, your love for us runs so deeply that you have chosen to come into our world to convey your love for us and to show us how we might commune with you more completely. How you reveal yourself to me through all that is around me is enough for me, but still you give me more in these enfleshed revelations of yourself. I thank you for your living love and ask for your continued guidance in following the examples that you have given all people.

December 26
The Warmth of Frostbite

Perhaps it is a result of early frostbite from my years of outdoor hockey as a youngster growing up in Minnesota, or maybe it is just because I'm aging and my circulation is deteriorating, the blood flow struggling to reach the tips of my extremities; but I go through some horrible fits of numbness in my fingers these days, especially during the winter season. If I go out for a hike or a ski on a cold winter day, I can pretty much count on some "digital discomfort." At first my fingertips will simply be "a little cold," but even with the constant flexing of my hands and fingers around the handle of the ski pole with the dig of each stride, inevitably my digits will become increasingly more cold until they are essentially numb. Usually, as the mild frostbite sets in, the body will then respond, it seems, working extra hard to pump blood to those suffering zones. Periodically, I will slap my hand against my thighs or chest thinking that those blows will help to

412

stimulate the flow, but usually it is simply a matter of slow time, and then the feeling will begin to return. Even the increased blood flow and restoration of feeling is a bit of a mixed blessing. Eventually, when all is recovered, my fingers will be cozily warm, even sweaty in some cases, but the transition is, quite frankly, very painful. The dull but nagging ache of frozen fingers thawing creates a subtle nausea in my gut, and if I didn't know that the end result would be satisfyingly warm, I would probably become more anxious about the "healing" than I am about the numbness that precedes it. Interestingly, I have come to "enjoy" the suffering of the thaw knowing now how fine things will be fairly soon, and usually for the remainder of my time outdoors that day; even so, when the numbness reaches really deep, I will feel a tender ache in the very tips of my fingers, sometimes for days afterward.

One might rightfully ask why I would be so foolish as to go out, sometimes day after day, and endure such pain when I could just as well stay inside where the temperature is regulated and safe, and avoid this ridiculous movement from cold to "frozen" to thaw to warmth. But my choice to go out into the cold and to risk these episodes of frostbite is no different than my daily choice to "live life fully." A life well and fully lived is inevitably wrought with risks, challenges that can cause both physical and emotional pain. To stay "inside," safe from the elements and their sometimes harsh treatment may be a wise preventative measure, but it also guarantees that one will not have the opportunity to experience the unknown and many joys that can emerge from such risk-taking when one chooses to step outside. It is not an issue of "no pain, no gain," nor is it some kind of masochistic desire to toughen up and endure suffering; the choice to step outside is a choice to engage in life fully, knowing that while I might get burned, either by heat or frost, I may also encounter some extraordinary sights, people and experiences. Indeed, I may even carry the ache of the journey within me for days, or for the rest of my life, but the wellspring that flows from a fully engaged life will provide healing and joy long beyond the pain that might come from the process. To stay "within" may free me from "physical discomfort," yet in the long run, perhaps a different numbness will set in and my life will become frozen, lacking the heat of a life lived fully.

God of Extremes, you do not ask me daily to risk my life, but you do call me daily into taking the risk *of* life. Help me to not live numbly, frozen by fears and indecision. The world can provide some cold and harsh challenges, but to step into these challenges, to move through them with the confidence that a thaw will occur, is to embrace the heat of the Extreme One and to live fully in your sure and loving warmth. Life-Blood, comfort my fears and heal the dull aches and pains that will inevitably come when I step out and into the fullness of life.

December 27
Snow Day

A phone call at five in the morning will most often be cause for concern, but if you are a school teacher in a snowy part of the nation during winter, a 5:00 a.m. wake up call just might be reason to rejoice. A Snow Day! An unexpected, unscheduled free day that drops into your lap courtesy of Mother Nature. During my years of teaching, I spent countless nights stretching hope over the day's conclusion, my gaze shifting between a TV weather report and the snow's progress outside my window, lusting for the assurance that tomorrow would dawn with a Snow Day report; and I've curled up on the couch in the dark and cold morning stillness of the house, the blue glare of the television my only light and warmth, apprehensively scanning the cancellation scroll bar pining for my school's name to show, only to have my wish dashed like a kid brother pushed into the snowdrift. It took me years to understand that if a Snow Day is to happen, I would do well to not think, pray and certainly not count on one dawning no matter how grim the weather report was. Most often, when a Snow Day arrives, it comes as quietly as the snow itself, sneaking in overnight on a back road with headlights off, dumping its load across the city streets and walks, a clogging of arteries that brings teachers and students their unique euphoria.

Except with the most extreme snowstorms, most other jobs, like the old U.S. Postal Service motto, will go on "despite rain, sleet or snow." Indeed, Snow Days are a special "perk" of the education system, and, believe me, teachers long for them just as much, if not more, than their students. Everyone looks forward to a vacation, but the unexpected joy of a sudden free day is a winning lottery ticket. Of course, the next challenge is to not squander the monies of your unexpected windfall. After seizing some extra sleep and slowly nestling into the joy of the day off, half the day can slip by with little to show for it. And, maybe, that's the way it should be, sipping slowly the simple pleasure of an unexpected gift, no more demands than to savor its taste fully.

We often put so much time, energy and stock in our own plans than when a simple gift is freely offered to us, we fail to receive it with adequate appreciation. Snow Days, by their very nature, clog the wheels of our incessant rush of life and allow us to just slow down for a day, to regroup and to rejuvenate the energy cells within. Snow Days invite us to get outside and enjoy the gift: exercise the body with some shoveling; revisit childhood joy in sledding; spread some care by assisting an elderly neighbor; and then fall into the soft cushions of relaxation while sipping the hot chocolate of rest.

God of Repose, I thank you for the unexpected gifts in my life, like the simple joy of a Snow Day. Often I fail to create the space and time that my body and spirit need to function at my best, and so, sometimes, you seem to provide it for me. May I not greedily expect such gifts and cheat on the work that must be done; but may I also fully embrace the simple pleasures and treasures that an unanticipated gift can hold. Let it snow!

December 28
Mindful Miles

Running is one of my meditative and physiological "hobbies. As a new teacher and coach fresh out of college years ago, I decided that if I was going to be out there coaching and encouraging youth to run, then perhaps I should get running myself. And so I did. Eventually, after building up my stamina, I challenged myself with the simple goal of logging one thousand miles each year. Now, for serious runners who train with a passion, this mileage could be consumed in four months or less, but for the little more than average "hoofer" like myself, running a thousand miles a year meant being a consistent runner, putting in an average of twenty miles a week. Given that the earth's circumference is just under 25,000 miles, I figure I have easily run all the way around the world by now.

At the end of one calendar year, in the midst of some significant personal upheaval, I went on retreat at a Hindu ashram on Paradise Island, Bahamas, preparing ahead of time that while there, I would cross my thousand mile goal for the year. Two arching bridges, one for coming and one for going, separate Paradise Island from the capital city of Nassau on New Providence Island, and it was on one of those bridges that, hitting my mark, I stopped to offer my traditional offering and prayer of thanksgiving for another year of fitness, for having a body that is *able* to run. But while standing there with a tributary of the ocean, the connective waters of the entire earth, passing beneath the arches of the bridge and my feet, I realized that it had been a very long time since I had taken a break from running. So, as I closed my prayer, I vowed that I would not run again until "I felt like it." It took me two and a half months before I truly felt like running again, and when I did, it came in very sporadic spurts. I had put away the mileage calendar and its sometimes nagging voice that would tell me "You had better get some more miles in this week or you'll get behind your pace!" and had replaced it with a simple monitor of need and desire.

Having a regimen for our physical training is often necessary if we truly want to stay fit, and the same is true in developing fitness in our spiritual lives. But both of these exercise forms can become a bit mundane, and after years of the regimen, we may need to reevaluate why we do what we do and what the goals of our efforts are. A consistent prayer and/or meditative routine is valuable, but if we find that we have lost or forgotten the reason for what we do, or what we do no longer seems to satisfy the need, then we would do well to reconsider our actions, focus and plan. As with physical training, any workout or prayer is better than no workout or prayer at all; but if we really want to enjoy and reap the benefits of our efforts, then sometimes a little break from the routine and some thoughtful and prayerful reevaluation might be in order.

God of Order, the created universe projects a kind of divine design, a dependable plan; and yet, there are clearly times of upheaval, when the even flow is disrupted and we must reconsider our place in the "universe of things." Encourage me to occasionally let go of the routines of my life, even the spiritual ones, so as to reevaluate and to remember why I do what I do. Prayer itself is good, but truly mindful prayer will be even better.

December 29
Carpe Diem

In the Cavalier poetry of seventeenth century England, as well as in some of John Donne's metaphysical poems, the theme of "carpe diem" was made popular. It was not a new concept with which they toyed, but they certainly blew new life into a term that the great Roman poet, Horace, first used in the first century B.C.E. Simply put, the Latin phrase translates as "seize the day," but Horace, perhaps, fine tuned his intentions by adding, "trusting as little as possible in the future." The British poets 1700 years later, used the concept of carpe diem thematically; while they too encouraged leaning into the present rather than toward the future, their argument was focused a bit more on seizing and celebrating youthfulness and beauty while it is here, rather than simply mistrusting the future. Either way, the embraced conclusion of its usage today seems to be more along the lines of "eat, drink and be merry, for tomorrow you may die."

A more spiritual approach to carpe diem might be "live for today," but this line too can be easily misconstrued into a more hedonistic view. The truth is, we *will* die in some unknown "tomorrow;" however, knowing this, we need not assume that we need to fulfill all of our desires today. For the poets, our inevitable future deaths seemed a rallying point for the seizure of pleasure now, assuming that if we have a life up ahead, surely it will lack the luster that comes with the present attractive energy. But for the person of prayer, carpe diem and living for today are not pleasure seeking cries; rather, they encourage the practitioner to live more thoughtfully, not seizing the day with some reckless abandon, but living each moment fully and well.

Living the present moment more fully means living with awareness, not looking over my shoulder at the past or too far up ahead at my future. When I live in the present moment, I prayerfully and carefully observe and experience the present. The gift of this day arrived at my bedside this morning. Lost in the errors of the past and worrying over the concerns of my future, I can easily overlook the gift and miss the simple and, perhaps, wondrous joys that this day might offer. Driving to work anguishing over the full schedule ahead, do I miss the lovely sunrise breaking over my shoulder right now or the energizing gift of song playing in the background?

Sacred Presence, life itself is sheer gift. Yes, I cannot irresponsibly neglect the tasks that come with my daily life, nor should I ignore the lessons of my past that might help to shape some part of my decisions for the future. But right now, I have been given this day, this moment - gifts that are to be embraced and discovered as well. Help me to seize this day, a newly ripened fruit, and biting into it, to enjoy all of its juicy potential.

December 30
The Eternal Now

Engaging in discussions about earthly life and eternal life, I would often ask my students when they felt "eternal life" or "eternity" began. Because of their strong Christian influence which tends to emphasize "Jesus' act of salvation on behalf of their eternal lives," they would almost always answer the question with "when I/we die." I find that answer to be so typical of the more self-centered aspects of Western religions, even Western theology; the unspoken assumption is that everything revolves around me. When does *eternity* begin? When *I* die! Now, if eternity is time without end - and beginning - then it is already happening; we are already within eternity right now. And if by "eternal life" I mean, more specifically, *my own*, even then, here I am; I am already in it! From this perspective, I might ask further, "how are you living your eternal life - now?"

We all spend so much of our time fretting over past decisions and actions, and worrying about the future ones. With embarrassment or regret, we sometimes drag the ill-made choices of our past into our present, often failing to act on current needs weighted down by the close memories of past miscues. In fear and anxiety, we darken the potential of the future by using only the flashlight of past mistakes and failures. And like an abuse of our resources, we sometimes waste the light of the present day with a false assurance that we will always have tomorrow's sunlight to guide our way.

I once read that "eternal life is not life for all time, but life outside of time." Living in eternal life is living in the *eternal now* - a state of being that transcends time. From this perspective, we can let go of our concerns for the past and the future, and live more freely now. The past and the future are not immaterial; I can still learn from my past and I can still dream about my future, but I must also embrace more fully this present moment. "This is the day the Lord has made," the psalmist wrote, "let us rejoice and be glad in it." I would add: "And *live* it fully." How often have I missed the joy of an eternal now moment while I was working for and dreaming of some hoped for future eternity? And I do not mean here some hedonistic joy, but a true gift, freely given, right now in my life.

Eternal God, made in your image and likeness, you have called me into your eternal life already, right now! Too often, locked in my finite sense of time, I limit myself to thinking only of this earthly existence, constricting my decisions and actions with past failures and future fears. But you call me to step outside of time, to think beyond this worldly realm, and to live the present and eternal now more fully. Lift me above the constraints of my excessive concerns for time, and let me soar in the joy of the gift of eternal life expanding in all directions around me right now.

December 31
Every Day is a New Year

Although not all cultures observe the same calendar as we do in the West, New Year's Eve and its celebrative shift into the New Year is still a fairly common gala throughout the world. For most of my adult life, the festive spectacle of New Year's Eve and Day have always been a bit of a conundrum, a curiously overrated holiday. At best, the two day New Year event seems a sort of birthday celebration for *our* measurement of the planet's life; at worst, it seems a silly convention that simply stimulates the local economy by encouraging a lavish night of partying. And yet, like celebrating birthdays, it does seem natural to festively mark the turn of a calendar year in some fashion or other.

The New Year is celebrated on different dates in different parts of the world, based on the cultures' chosen calendar or on how the culture interprets the cyclical current in which our planet turns. For much of the world, apparently, the dead of winter seems a perfect time to put one year to rest and to introduce another, renewing the calendar at the darkest period of the earth and sun's relationship and looking forward to the burgeoning light. Native peoples, however, might argue that spring, even into June, is the more appropriate "new year time," because "new life" in the cycle of things is just being born. Why honor a time when all the natural world turns within and appears dead in its dormancy? Given these different symbolic perspectives, the date of a "new year" is, obviously, rather arbitrary. What seems more important then is *how* we celebrate this turning of the page; what are our thoughts and intentions when we close out one year and welcome the next?

I don't believe that we need to be constantly psychoanalyzing ourselves, but like signs along a highway and trail markers on a hike, times and places that give us a periodic pause to scrutinize our place on the map of life can be valuable checkpoints, especially with regard to our spiritual journey. To that end, New Years seems as good or better time than most to consider "who I am" and just "where am I going." And such questions do not have to have any connection to "resolutions" or "turning over a new leaf." More like with the use of a compass, one checks his "position" and direction, and in doing so either validates or questions the bearing of his present course.

While I sleep each night, the world continues its slow spin just as surely as it does during my waking hours. Whether I am asleep or awake, Life is alive, and the presence of the Creator continues to permeate all. To understand that the Divine can be experienced everywhere and at all times means that even when I sleep, I am awake. Every day is its own new year, pregnant with the possibilities of deeper discoveries and engaging encounters with the one who has set the universe in motion and graciously blows life into it as steadily as the rise and fall of my very own breaths. Am I aware of this amazing rhythm in the new year of each day?

Tonight, some people will drift off towards bed long before the much celebrated new year arrives at the strike of midnight; others may very purposefully gather or seek quiet space alone to contemplate the old year's experiences and dream of the new year's possibilities; and others still will party their way into oblivion with little concern for the past, present or future, perhaps tomorrow wondering only about what surpassed last night and why they feel so lousy today. There's not a right or a wrong way to celebrate New Year's, but perhaps there is a good and better ways to do so. Seeing God everywhere, and choosing to live my life as a prayer is a daily commitment. It does not require a resolution, only honest and awakened living.

Creator God, on this New Year's Eve, like every day of my life, I pause to rededicate my life – my seeing, my hearing, my speaking, my smelling, my feeling – my very being, to you. Another day within a new year is dawning, and in "this every day" you invite me once again to participate in the experience of you, revealed in all that is around me. Help me to live wide awake in this celebration of Life.

Made in the USA
Charleston, SC
08 June 2012